Brief Contents

FIFTH EDITION

BUSINESS ETHICS

Ethical Decision Making and Cases

O.C. FERRELL
Colorado State University

JOHN FRAEDRICH
Southern Illinois University at Carbondale

LINDA FERRELL
University of Northern Colorado

Houghton Mifflin Company   *Boston*   *New York*

Executive Editor: George T. Hoffman
Senior Development Editor: Susan M. Kahn
Project Editor: Patricia English
Associate Project Editor: Claudine Bellanton
Editorial Assistant: Mollie Young
Senior Production/Design Coordinator: Sarah L. Ambrose
Senior Manufacturing Coordinator: Marie Barnes
Marketing Manager: Steve W. Mikels

Cover Illustration: © Vadim Vahrameen/Stock Illustration Source

Printed in the U.S.A.

Library of Congress Catalog Card Number: 2001131492

ISBN: 0-618-12414-4

123456789-EB-05 04 03 02 01

Contents

PART TWO   Cases   259

This book is dedicated to:

My mother: Kathlene Ferrell

O. C. FERRELL

My wife and children: Debbie, Anna, Jacob, Joseph, Joshua, and Lael

JOHN FRAEDRICH

My parents: Norlan and Phyllis Nafziger

LINDA FERRELL

Preface

We have revised the Fifth Edition of *Business Ethics* to be the most practical and applied business ethics text available. Using a managerial framework, we explain how ethics can be integrated into strategic business decisions. This framework provides *an overview of the concepts, processes, and best practices* associated with successful business ethics programs. Some approaches to business ethics are excellent for exercises in intellectual reasoning but do not deal with the actual ethical decision-making situations that people in business organizations face. Our approach prepares students for ethical dilemmas they will face in their business careers.

We have been careful in this revision to provide the most up-to-date knowledge while retaining the strengths that have made this text one of the most widely adopted business ethics texts available today. This book has been successful because *it addresses the complex environment of ethical decision-making in organizations and real-life issues.* Every individual has unique personal values, and every organization has its own set of values and ethical policies. Business ethics must consider the organizational culture and interdependent relationships between the individual and other significant persons involved in organizational decision making. Without effective guidance, a businessperson cannot make ethical decisions while facing organizational pressures and day-to-day challenges in the competitive environment.

By focusing on the issues and organizational environments, students are provided the opportunity to see the role and responsibilities they will be facing as they advance in the workplace. Our primary goal — as always — is to enhance the awareness and the decision-making skills students will need to make business ethics decisions that contribute to responsible business conduct. By focusing on the concerns and issues of today's challenging business environment, we demonstrate that studying business ethics provides vital knowledge that contributes to overall business success.

Philosophy of This Text

Business ethics in organizations requires values-based leadership from top management, purposeful actions that include planning and implementation of standards of appropriate conduct, as well as openness and continuous effort to improve the organization's ethical performance. Although personal values are important in ethical decision making, they are only one of the components that guide the decisions, actions, and policies of organizations. The burden of ethical behavior relates to the organization's values and traditions, not just to the individuals who make the decisions and carry them out. A firm's ability to plan and implement ethical business standards depends in part on structuring resources and activities to achieve ethical objectives in an effective and efficient manner.

The purpose of this book is to help students improve their ability to make ethical decisions in business by providing them with a framework that they can use to identify, analyze, and resolve ethical issues in business decision making. Individual values and ethics are important in this process. By studying business ethics, students begin to understand how to cope with conflicts between their personal values and those of the organization.

Many ethical decisions in business are close calls. It often takes years of experience in a particular industry to know what is acceptable. We do not, in this book, provide ethical answers but instead attempt to prepare students to make informed ethical decisions. First, we do not moralize by indicating what to do in a specific situation. Second, although we provide an overview of moral philosophies and decision-making processes, we do not prescribe any one philosophy or process as best or most ethical. Third, by itself, this book will not make students more ethical nor will it tell them how to judge the ethical behavior of others. Rather, its goal is to help students understand and use their current values and convictions in making business decisions and to encourage everyone to think about the effects of their decisions on business and society.

Many people believe that business ethics cannot be taught. Although we do not claim to teach ethics, we suggest that by studying business ethics a person can improve ethical decision making by identifying ethical issues and recognizing the approaches available to resolve them. An organization's reward system can reinforce appropriate behavior and help shape attitudes and beliefs about important issues. For example, the success of some campaigns to end racial or gender discrimination in the workplace provides evidence that attitudes and behavior can be changed with new information, awareness, and shared values.

It is important to recognize the relationship between personal morals and ethical business decisions. While business ethics reflects acceptable conduct based on the social, cultural, political, and legal environment at a point in time, personal morals reflect deeper and more enduring philosophies about life. Whereas virtues linked to the high moral ground of truthfulness, honesty, fairness, and openness are often assumed to be self-evident and easy to apply, business decisions involve complex managerial and social considerations. Some business ethics perspectives assume that ethics training is for people who have unacceptable personal moral development, but that is not necessarily the case. Since organizations are culturally diverse and personal values must be respected, a collective agreement on organizational ethics is as vital as other managerial decisions.

Complete Content Coverage

In writing *Business Ethics,* Fifth Edition, we have strived to be as informative, complete, accessible, and up-to-date as possible. Instead of focusing on one area of ethics, such as moral philosophy or codes of ethics, we provide balanced coverage of all areas relevant to the current development and practice of ethical decision making. In short, we have tried to keep pace with new developments and current thinking in teaching and practices. General issues such as conflict of interest, honesty, truthful communication, and legal compliance are addressed to provide an understanding of appropriate conduct. Specific ethical issues including Internet privacy, discrimination, falsification of information, and other issues that may cause social or environmental damage are covered through dilemmas, examples, and cases.

Organization of the Text

Part One, "Understanding Ethical Decision Making," consists of 10 chapters. The purpose of these chapters is to provide a framework to identify, analyze, and understand how businesspeople make ethical decisions and deal with ethical issues. Several enhancements have been made to chapter content for this edition. Some of the most important are listed here.

Chapter 1, "An Overview of Business Ethics," has been revised with many new examples and recent results of surveys to describe issues and concerns important to business ethics. The Ethics Resource Center's 2000 National Business Ethics Survey has been used in this and other chapters to provide the most recent information about the current state of business ethics practices. The section on the development of business ethics has been updated. Chapter 2, "Ethical Issues in Business," has been updated with new examples and issues. A number of new tables provide statistics on ethical concerns in business organizations. Issues related to various functional areas of business have been revised. A new section on technology ethical issues, including monitoring of employee use of technology, consumer privacy, web site development and online marketing, and legal protection of intellectual property, has been added. New examples have been added to Chapter 3, "Applying Moral Philosophies to Business Ethics." Chapter 4, "Social Responsibility," has been revised with new examples that provide understanding of legal, ethical, economic, and philanthropic issues.

Chapter 5, "A Framework for Understanding Ethical Decision Making in Business," has been revised and updated to reflect current research and understanding of ethical decision making. Chapter 6, "Organizational Culture and Ethical Decision Making," discusses the impact of organizations on ethical decision making. A new section on the relationship of styles of ethical decision making has been added. Chapter 7, "Organizational Relationships and Conflicts in Ethical Decision Making" has been updated with new examples and data that illustrate the interdependent relationships in organizational ethical decision making. Chapter 8, "Development of an Effective Ethics Program," has been refined and updated with corporate best practices for developing effective ethics programs. Chapter 9, "Business Ethics in a Global Economy," contains new examples of international business ethics issues, conflicts, and cooperative efforts to establish universal standards of conduct.

Chapter 10, "Business Ethics and Organizational Performance," provides updated evidence that good ethics is good business. An improved ethical climate in an organization is associated with the pursuit of quality, customer satisfaction, and employee commitment. A good company reputation is associated with creating financial value.

Part Two consists of fifteen cases that bring reality into the learning process. All of the cases have been written or revised specifically for the Fifth Edition. The companies and situations are real, names and other facts are not disguised, and all cases include developments up to 2001. By reading and analyzing these cases, students can gain insight into ethical decisions and decision making.

Two appendixes provide further real-world examples and practice in identifying and weighing ethical issues. These appendixes include association, industry, and company codes of ethics. We have added several codes of ethics that provide good examples of comprehensive codes that are being implemented today.

The Fifth Edition provides three new behavioral simulation role-play cases developed for use in the business ethics course. The role-play cases and implementation methods can be found in the *Instructor's Resource Manual with Test Bank* and on the web site. Role-play cases may be used as a culminating experience to help students integrate concepts covered in the text. Alternatively, the cases may be used as an ongoing exercise to provide students with extensive opportunities for interacting and making ethical decisions.

Role-play cases simulate a complex, realistic, and timely business ethics situation. Students form teams and make decisions based on an assigned role. The role-play case complements and enhances traditional approaches to business learning experiences because it (1) gives students the opportunity to practice making decisions that have business ethics consequences; (2) re-creates the power, pressures, and information that affect decision making at various levels of management; (3) provides students with a team-based experience that enriches their skills and understanding of group processes and dynamics; and (4) uses a feedback period to allow for the exploration of complex and controversial issues in business ethics decision making. The role-play can be used with classes of any size.

Business Ethics Learning Center Web Site

The web site developed for the Fifth Edition provides up-to-date examples, issues, and interactive learning devices to assist students in improving their decision-making skills. "The Business Ethics Learning Center" has been created to take advantage of information available on the Internet while providing new interactive skill-building exercises that can help students practice ethical decision making. The site contains links to the e-ethics sites highlighted in each chapter; Internet exercises; ACE (A Cyber Evaluation) interactive quizzes, which help students master chapter content through multiple-choice questions; links to association, industry, and company codes of conduct; case web site linkages; company and organizational examples; and academic resources, including links to business ethics centers throughout the world. Four Ethical Leadership Challenge scenarios are available for each chapter. Training devices, including Lockheed Martin's Gray Matters ethics game, are also available on-line. In addition, students have access to their own set of PowerPoint slides to help them review and master the text material.

To access the text's web site

- Go to *http://college.hmco.com*
- Select "Instructors" or "Students"
- Select "Go to Your Discipline" and then "Business"
- Select Ferrell/Fraedrich/Ferrell, *Business Ethics* from the Textbook Sites menus

Effective Tools for Teaching and Learning

Many tools are available in this text to help both students and instructors in the quest to improve students' ability to make ethical business decisions. Each chapter opens with an outline and a list of learning objectives. Immediately following is an "Ethical Dilemma" that should provoke discussion about ethical issues related to the chapter. The short vignette describes a hypothetical incident involving an ethical conflict. Questions at the end of the "Ethical Dilemma" section focus discussion on how the dilemma could be resolved. Each chapter now contains one or more e-ethics links to Internet sites that may provide additional information on related topics or specific organizations. Whenever the e-ethics icon ℯ.ethics appears in the text, you will find a corresponding link on the text web site. At the end of each chapter there is a chapter summary and an important terms list, both of which are handy tools for review. Also included at the end of each chapter is a "Real-Life Situation" section. The vignette describes a realistic drama that helps students experience the process of ethical decision making. The "Real-Life Situation" minicases presented in this text are hypothetical; any resemblance to real persons, companies, or situations is coincidental. Keep in mind that there are no right or wrong solutions to the minicases. The ethical dilemmas and real-life situations provide an opportunity for students to use concepts in the chapter to resolve ethical issues. Each chapter concludes with a series of questions that allow students to test their E.Q. (Ethics Quotient).

In Part Two, following each real-world case are questions to guide students in recognizing and resolving ethical issues. For some cases, students can conduct additional research to determine recent developments, since many ethical issues in companies take years to resolve. Students can also study the codes of ethics in Appendixes A and B to determine ethical issues that companies attempt to resolve.

The *Instructor's Resource Manual with Test Bank* contains a wealth of information. Teaching notes for every chapter include a brief chapter summary, detailed lecture outline, and notes for using the "Ethical Dilemma" and "Real-Life Situation" Sections. Detailed case notes point out the key issues involved and offer suggested answers to the questions. A separate section provides guidelines for using case analysis in teaching business ethics. Detailed notes are provided to guide the instructor in analyzing or grading the cases. Simulation role-play cases, as well as implementation suggestions, are included. A test bank provides multiple-choice and essay questions for every chapter in the text. A computerized version of the test bank is also available. Instructor-only PowerPoint slides are available on the password-protected portion of the web site. Finally, a selection of video segments is available to help bring real-world examples and skill-building scenarios into the classroom.

Acknowledgments

A number of individuals provided reviews and suggestions that helped to improve this text. We sincerely appreciate their time and effort.

Carolyn Ashe
University of Houston–Downtown

Russell Bedard
Eastern Nazarene College

Greg Buntz
University of the Pacific

Peggy Cunningham
Queen's University

Carla Dando
Idaho State University

James E. Donovan
Detroit College of Business

A. Charles Drubel
Muskingum College

Philip F. Esler
University of St. Andrews

Joseph M. Foster
Indiana Vocational Technical College–Evansville

Terry Gable
California State University–Northridge

Robert Giacalone
University of Richmond

Suresh Gopalan
West Texas A&M University

Charles E. Harris, Jr.
Texas A&M University

Kenneth A. Heischmidt
Southeast Missouri State University

Neil Herndon
Hofstra University

Walter Hill
Green River Community College

Jack Hires
Valparaiso University

David Jacobs
American University

R.J. Johansen
Montana State University–Bozeman

Edward Kimman
Vrije Universiteit

Nick Lockard
Texas Lutheran College

Terry Loe
Baylor University

Nick Maddox
Stetson University

Isabelle Maignan
University of Groningen

Phylis Mansfield
Andrews University

Randy McLeod
Harding University

Patrick E. Murphy
University of Notre Dame

Carol Nielsen
Bemidji State University

Wanda V. Turner
Ferris State College

Cynthia A. M. Simerly
Lakeland Community College

Jim Weber
Marquette University

Filiz Tabak
Towson University

Ed Weiss
National-Louis University

Debbie Thorne
Southwest Texas State University

Jan Zahrly
University of North Dakota

The authors wish to acknowledge the many people who assisted us in writing this book. We are deeply grateful to Barbara Gilmer for helping us organize and manage the revision process and for preparing the *Instructor's Resource Manual with Test Bank*. Debbie Thorne, Southwest Texas State University, provided advice and guidance on the text and cases. Dana Schubert, Robyn Smith, and Jane Swoboda assisted in preparing and updating the cases in this edition. Finally, we express appreciation to the administration and to our colleagues at Colorado State University, Southern Illinois University at Carbondale, and the University of Northern Colorado for their support.

We invite your comments, questions, or criticisms. We want to do our best to provide teaching materials that enhance the study of business ethics. Your suggestions will be sincerely appreciated.

O. C. FERRELL
JOHN FRAEDRICH
LINDA FERRELL

PART ONE

Understanding Ethical Decision Making

An Overview of Business Ethics

CHAPTER 1

Chapter Objectives

- To explore the conceptualizations of business ethics from an organizational perspective
- To understand the linkages and differences between business ethics and social responsibility
- To examine the historical foundations and evolution of business ethics
- To gain insight into the extent of ethical misconduct in the workplace and the pressures for unethical behavior
- To understand why business ethics initiatives are needed in both small and large organizations

Chapter Outline

Business Ethics Defined

Social Responsibility and Business Ethics

The Development of Business Ethics
Before 1960: Ethics in Business
The 1960s: The Rise of Social Issues in Business
The 1970s: Business Ethics as an Emerging Field
The 1980s: Consolidation
The 1990s: Institutionalization of Business Ethics
2000 and Beyond

Why Study Business Ethics?
The Problem
The Solution

Framework for Studying Business Ethics
Ethical Issues in Business
Applying Moral Philosophies to Business Ethics
Social Responsibility
A Framework for Understanding Ethical Decision Making
    in Business
Organizational Culture and Ethical Decision Making
Organizational Relationships and Conflicts in Ethical Decision
    Making
Development of an Effective Ethics Program
Business Ethics in a Global Economy
Business Ethics and Organizational Performance

An Ethical Dilemma*

John Peters had just arrived at the main offices of Dryer & Sons (D&S) from Midwest State University. A medium-size company, D&S manufactured components for several of the major defense contractors in the United States. Recently, D&S had started a specialized software division and had hired John as a salesperson for both the company's hardware and software.

A diligent student at Midwest State, John had earned degrees in engineering and management information systems (MIS). His minor was in marketing — specifically, sales. Because of his education as well as other activities, John was not only comfortable discussing numbers with engineers, but also had the people skills to convey complex solutions in understandable terms. This was one of the main reasons Al Dryer had hired him. "You've got charisma, John, and you know your way around computers," Dryer explained.

D&S was established during World War II and had manufactured parts for military aircraft. During the Korean War and then the Vietnam War, D&S had become a stable subcontractor for specialized parts for aircraft and missiles. When Al Dryer and his father started the business, Al was the salesperson for the company. In time, D&S had grown to employ several hundred workers and five salespeople; John was the sixth salesperson.

During his first few months at the company, John got his bearings in the defense industry. For example, when Ed, his trainer, would take procurement people out to lunch, everyone would put money into a snifter at the table. The money collected was usually much less than the bill, and Ed would make up the difference. Golf was a skill that Ed required John to learn because often "that's where deals are really transacted." Again, Ed would indirectly pick up the golfing bill, which sometimes totaled several hundred dollars.

Another of Ed's requirements was that John read the Procurement Integrity Section of the Office of Federal Procurement Policy Act and the Federal Acquisition Regulation, which implements the act. In addition, John had to read the Certificate of Procurement Integrity, which procurement agents had to sign. As John read the documents, he noted the statement in Section 27(a)(2), forbidding agents to "offer, give, or promise to offer or give, directly or indirectly, any money, gratuity, or other thing of value to any procurement official of such agency; or (3) solicit or obtain, directly or indirectly, from any officer or employee of such agency, prior to the award of a contract any proprietary or source selection information regarding such procurement."

"Doesn't this relate to what we're doing, Ed?" John asked.

"Yes and no, my boy, yes and no," was Ed's only answer.

One Monday, when Ed and John had returned from sales calls in St. Louis and Washington, D.C., Ed called John into his office and said: "John, you don't have the right numbers down for our expenses. You're 10 percent short because you forgot all of your tips." As John looked at his list of expenses, he realized that Ed was right, yet there was no item on his expense report for such things. "Ed, where do I put the extra expenses? There's no line on the forms for this." "Just add it into the cost of things as I've done," replied Ed, showing John his expense report. As John looked at Ed's report, he noticed some numbers that seemed quite large. "Why don't we mention this problem to Mr. Dryer so that accounting can put the extra lines on the reports?" John suggested. "Because this is the way we do things around here, and they don't like changes to the system. We have a saying in the company that a blind eye goes a long way to getting business done," Ed lectured John. John didn't quite grasp the problem, and did as he was told.

On another trip John learned the differences between working directly with the federal government procurement people and the companies with which D&S subcontracted. For example, certain conversations of the large defense contractors were relayed to D&S, and then Ed and John would visit certain governmental agencies and relay such information. In one case Ed and John were told to relay a very large offer to an official who was entering the private sector the next year. In addition, Ed and John were used to obtaining information on requests for proposals, as well as other competitive information, from procurement agents. When John asked Ed about this, Ed said: "John, in order to excel in this business you need to be an expert on knowing exactly where things become legal and illegal. Trust me, I've been doing this for fifteen years, and I've never had a problem. Why do you think I'm your trainer?"

John started reviewing more government documents and asking the other salespeople about Ed. Two replied that Ed was a smart operator and knew the ropes better than anyone at the company. The other two salespeople had a different story to tell. One asked, "Has he tried to explain away his padding of the expense reports to you yet?" "But I thought that's what everyone does!" John exclaimed. "Ed has been doing business with the Feds and the large defense companies for so long that he sometimes doesn't realize that the rules have changed. He's been lucky that he hasn't been caught. Watch your step, John, or you'll find yourself with dirty hands and nowhere to clean them," the second salesperson said.

At the end of another trip to Washington, D.C., Ed called John into his office. "John, your numbers don't add up," he pointed out. "Didn't I tell you to add at least 10 percent to your totals for tips and miscellaneous items? Let's get with it. Do you want to be in training forever? You know that I have to sign off before you can go it alone, and I want to make sure you understand the ropes. Just between you and me, I think Dryer is finally going to make a vice president slot, which should go to me because of my seniority. So hurry up and learn this stuff because you're my last trainee. Now just sign the document with these revised numbers on them."

What should John do?

Questions ■ Exercises

1. What is Ed's ethical dilemma?
2. What are the ethical and legal considerations for John at D&S?
3. Identify the ethical conflict in this situation.
4. Discuss the implications of each decision John has made and will make.

* This case is strictly hypothetical; any resemblance to real persons, companies, or situations is coincidental.

Business ethics is one of the most important, yet perhaps most misunderstood, concerns in the world of business today. The field of business ethics deals with questions about whether specific business practices are acceptable. For example, should a salesperson omit facts about a product's poor safety record in a sales presentation to a client? Should an accountant report inaccuracies discovered in an audit of a client, knowing that the company will probably be fired by the client for doing so? Should an automobile tire manufacturer intentionally conceal safety concerns to avoid a massive, and costly, tire recall? Should pharmaceutical companies widely advertise improved lifestyle "wonder drugs" that should be prescribed only to a small percentage of the population? Additionally, at what cost do these lifestyle improvements come? Regardless of their legality, the actions taken in such situations will surely be judged by others as right or wrong, ethical or unethical. By its very nature, the field of business ethics is controversial, and there is no universally accepted approach for resolving its issues.

On the other hand, government is encouraging organizational accountability for ethical and legal conduct. Organizations are being asked to prevent and control misconduct by implementing ethics programs. Many businesses are communicating core values to their employees to develop an ethical climate in the organization.

Before we get started, it is important to state what this book is and what it is not. First, it does not moralize by telling you what is right or wrong in a specific situation. Second, although it provides an overview of group and individual decision-making processes, it does not prescribe any one philosophy or process as best or most ethical. Third, by itself, this book will not make you more ethical, nor will it tell you how to judge the ethical behavior of others. Rather, its goal is to help you understand and use your current values and convictions in making business decisions, to encourage you to think about the effects of your decisions on business and society, and to better understand how organizations manage very diverse employees. To this end, we aim to help you learn to recognize and resolve ethical issues within business organizations. The framework developed in this book therefore focuses on how organizational ethical decisions are made and on ways the organization can improve ethical conduct.

In this chapter, we first develop a definition of business ethics and link and compare it with the concept of social responsibility. Next, we examine the evolution of business ethics in North America. Finally, we provide an overview of our framework for examining business ethics in this text.

Business Ethics Defined

The term *ethics* has many nuances. Ethics has been defined as "inquiry into the nature and grounds of morality where the term morality is taken to mean moral judgments, standards and rules of conduct."[1] It has also been called the study and philosophy of human conduct, with an emphasis on the determination of right and wrong. *The American Heritage Dictionary* offers these definitions of ethics: "The study of the general nature of morals and of specific moral choices; moral philosophy; and the rules or standards governing the conduct of the members of a profession."[2] One difference between an ordinary decision and an ethical one lies in "the point where the accepted rules no longer serve, and the decision maker is faced with the responsibility for weighing values and reaching a judgment in a situation which is not quite the same as any he or she has faced before."[3] The other difference relates to the amount of emphasis placed on the person's values when the decision is being made. Consequently, values and judgments play a critical role in the making of ethical decisions.

Building on these definitions, we can begin to develop a concept of business ethics. Most people would agree that high ethical standards require both businesses and individuals to conform to sound moral principles. However, some special aspects must be considered when applying ethics to business. First, to survive, businesses must make a profit. If profits are realized by misconduct, this often means that the life of the organization will be short. Second, businesses must balance their desires for profits against the needs and desires of society. Maintaining this balance often requires compromises or tradeoffs. To address these unique aspects of the business world, society has developed rules — both legal and implicit — to guide businesses in their efforts to earn profits in ways that do not harm individuals or society as a whole.

Most definitions of business ethics relate to rules, standards, and moral principles as to what is right or wrong in specific situations. For our purposes and in simple terms, **business ethics** *comprises principles and standards that guide behavior in the world of business.* Whether a specific required behavior is right or wrong, ethical or unethical, is often determined by stakeholders, such as investors, customers, interest groups, employees, the legal system, and the community. Although these groups are not necessarily "right," their judgments influence society's acceptance or rejection of a business and its activities.

SOCIAL RESPONSIBILITY AND BUSINESS ETHICS

The concepts of ethics and social responsibility are often used interchangeably, although each has a distinct meaning. **Social responsibility** is the obligation a business assumes toward society. To be socially responsible is to maximize positive effects and minimize negative effects on society. *Fortune*'s annual list of America's most admired companies is based on eight key attributes of reputation, including social responsibility. McDonald's, Du Pont, and Herman Miller were rated the highest for social responsibility on a ten-point scale, while Fruit of the Loom, Caremark Rx, and Amerco were rated the lowest.[4] An important question to consider is why some companies are rated high while others are rated low. High ratings usually reflect a company's reputation for doing things that embrace the welfare of society. Low ratings are often related to negative publicity for ethical and legal misconduct and are often linked with poor economic performance. Social responsibility includes economic, legal, ethical, and philanthropic responsibilities.[5]

The **economic responsibilities** of a business are to produce goods and services that society needs and wants at a price that can perpetuate the business and satisfy its obligations to investors. The **legal responsibilities** of businesses are the laws that they must obey. At a minimum, companies are expected to be responsible for their employees obeying local, state, and federal laws.

Ethical responsibilities are defined as behaviors or activities that are expected of business by society but are not codified in law. Many businesspeople refer to this set of responsibilities as the spirit of the law. Consider, for example, the responsibility issues for many riverboat casinos that serve their patrons as many free drinks as they want. The result is that drunken patrons may attempt to drive and then cause accidents, sometimes fatal ones. For example, one patron at the Players Casino in Lake Charles, Louisiana, had twelve drinks in two hours, got into his pickup, and then crashed into a van carrying five people. Three of them died, including an 18-month-old child.[6] Although the casino operators fulfill their legal responsibility to provide alcoholic beverages to adults only, they sometimes fail to address the ethical issues presented by the spirit of the law. Casino operators, as well as operators of other drinking establishments, have an obligation not to contribute to situations in which customers may drive while drunk. Responsible operators monitor consumer consumption and refuse to serve patrons who appear drunk. Debates over ethical issues or responsibilities are often resolved through civil legal actions. For example, American Airlines passengers instituted a class-action lawsuit against the Allied Pilots' Association. The lawsuit seeks to recover damages suffered by thousands of American Airlines passengers because of poor service, including delays and canceled flights, related to a dispute the pilots were having with the company.[7] Another example involves Priceline.com, Inc., the on-line retailer that allows consumers to name their own price on airline tickets, gasoline, and long-distance telephone calls. The Connecticut attorney general opened a consumer protection investigation into "whether there had been full and accurate disclosure of product terms, prices and conditions." The previous month, the Better Business Bureau had revoked Priceline's membership for "failure to eliminate underlying causes of complaints" made by numerous customers. The complaints included misrepresenting products, failure to provide promised refunds, and failure to correct billing problems.[8] Some complaints involved multiple connections, long layovers, added fees, and higher prices than those available directly from the airlines.

The final obligation a business assumes toward society is its **philanthropic responsibilities.** Philanthropic responsibilities are those behaviors and activities that society desires and business values dictate. Philanthropic responsibilities represent the company's desire to give back to society. For example, Ben & Jerry's donates 7.5 percent of pretax profits to charity. Giving to charitable organizations, supporting community projects, and volunteering employee time are forms of philanthropy or volunteerism for a company. A survey of ninety-seven of the one hundred fifty largest companies in the United States found that corporate contributions increased by an average of 12 percent last year. Merck, Johnson & Johnson, and Pfizer topped the list as the largest contributors when counting both cash and product donations (see Table 1–1).[9]

The idea of social responsibility became prominent during the 1960s in response to changing social values. Many businesses have tried to determine what relationships, obligations, and duties are appropriate between the business organization and society. For example, the Internet involves many ethical issues related to individual rights of privacy and property, as well as questions of community standards. (This topic is examined more closely in Chapter 2.) Social responsibility, then, can be viewed as a contract with society, whereas business ethics involves carefully thought-out rules of business organizational conduct that guide decision making. Business ethics relates to rules and principles that guide individual and work-group decisions; social responsibility concerns the effect of organizational decisions on society.

TABLE 1–1 Corporate Giving	
Company	Annual Monetary and Product Donations (in millions)
1. Merck	$221.0
2. Johnson & Johnson	176.2
3. Pfizer	123.9
4. Eli Lilly	121.4
5. IBM	116.1
6. Microsoft	104.7
7. Intel	101.0
8. Bank of America	91.5
9. Procter & Gamble	73.2
10. General Motors	71.1

Source: Reprinted from Business Week, *January 24, 2000 by special permission. Copyright © 2000 by The McGraw-Hill Companies, Inc.*

THE DEVELOPMENT OF BUSINESS ETHICS

The study of business ethics in North America has evolved through five distinct stages — (1) before 1960, (2) the 1960s, (3) the 1970s, (4) the 1980s, and (5) the 1990s — and continues to evolve in the twenty-first century. Business ethics continues to change rapidly as most organizations recognize the advantages of improved ethical conduct in business, and there is an increased understanding of the link between business ethics and financial performance.

Before 1960: Ethics in Business

Before 1960 the United States went through several agonizing phases of questioning the concept of capitalism. In the 1920s the nation experienced what was called the Progressive Movement, which attempted to provide citizens with a "living wage," defined as income sufficient for education, recreation, health, and retirement. Businesses were asked to check unwarranted price increases and any other practices that would hurt a family's "living wage." In the 1930s came the New Deal, which specifically blamed business for the country's troubles. Business was asked to work more closely with the government to raise family income. By the 1950s the New Deal had been repackaged into the Fair Deal by President Harry S Truman; this program defined such matters as civil rights and environmental responsibility as ethical issues for businesses to address.

Until 1960 ethical issues related to business were often discussed theologically. Through churches, synagogues, and mosques, individual moral issues related to business ethics were addressed. Religious leaders raised questions about fair wages, labor practices, and the morality of capitalism. Catholic social ethics, expressed in a series of papal encyclicals, included concern for morality in business, workers' rights, and living wages; for humanistic values rather than materialistic ones; and for improving the conditions of the poor. Some Catholic colleges and universities began to offer courses in social ethics. Protestants also developed ethics courses in their seminaries and schools of theology, and addressed issues concerning morality and ethics in business. The Protestant work ethic encouraged individuals to be frugal, work hard, and attain success in the capitalistic system. Such religious traditions provided a foundation for the future field of business ethics. Each religion applied its moral concepts not only to business but also to government, politics, family, personal life, and all other aspects of life.

The 1960s: The Rise of Social Issues in Business

During the 1960s American society turned to causes. An antibusiness attitude developed as many critics attacked the vested interests that controlled the economic and political sides of society — the so-called military-industrial establishment. The 1960s saw the decay of inner cities and the growth of ecological problems, such as pollution and the disposal of toxic and nuclear wastes. This period also witnessed the rise of consumerism — activities undertaken by independent individuals, groups, and organizations to protect their rights as consumers. In 1962 President John F. Kennedy delivered a "Special Message on Protecting the Consumer Interest," in which he spelled out four basic consumer rights: the right to safety, the right to be informed, the right to choose, and the right to be heard. These came to be known as the **Consumers' Bill of Rights.**

The modern consumer movement is generally considered to have begun in 1965 with the publication of Ralph Nader's *Unsafe at Any Speed,* which criticized the auto industry as a whole, and General Motors Corporation (GM) in particular, for putting profit and style ahead of lives and safety. GM's Corvair was the main target of Nader's criticism. His consumer protection organization, popularly known as Nader's Raiders, fought successfully for legislation that required automobile makers to equip cars with safety belts, padded dashboards, stronger door latches, head restraints, shatterproof windshields, and collapsible steering columns. Consumer activists also helped secure passage of several consumer protection laws, such as the Wholesome Meat Act of 1967, the Radiation Control for Health and Safety Act of 1968, the Clean Water Act of 1972, and the Toxic Substance Act of 1976.[10]

After Kennedy came President Lyndon B. Johnson and the Great Society, which extended national capitalism and told the business community that the U.S. government's responsibility was to provide the citizen with some degree of economic stability. Activities that could destabilize the economy began to be viewed as unethical and unlawful.

The 1970s: Business Ethics as an Emerging Field

Business ethics began to develop as a field of study in the 1970s. Theologians and religious thinkers had laid the groundwork by suggesting that certain religious principles could be applied to business activities. Using this groundwork, business professors began to teach and write about corporate social responsibility. Philosophers entered the arena, applying ethical theory and philosophical analysis to structure the discipline of business ethics. Businesses became more concerned with their public images, and, as social demands grew, many businesses realized that they had to address ethical issues more directly. The Nixon administration's Watergate scandal focused public interest on the importance of ethics in government. Conferences were held to discuss the social responsibilities and moral and ethical issues in business. Centers dealing with issues of business ethics were established. Interdisciplinary meetings brought business professors, theologians, philosophers, and businesspeople together. President Jimmy Carter attempted to focus on personal and administrative efforts to uphold ethical principles in government. The Foreign Corrupt Practices Act was passed during his administration, making it illegal for U.S. businesses to bribe government officials of other countries.

By the end of the 1970s a number of major ethical issues had emerged, such as bribery, deceptive advertising, price collusion, product safety, and the environment. *Business ethics* became a common expression and was no longer considered an oxymoron. Academic researchers sought to identify ethical issues and describe how businesspeople might choose to act in particular situations. However, only limited efforts were made to describe how the ethical decision-making process worked and to identify the many variables that influence the ethical decision-making process in organizations.

The 1980s: Consolidation

In the 1980s business academics and practitioners acknowledged business ethics as a field of study. A growing and varied group of institutions with diverse interests promoted the study of business ethics. Business ethics organizations grew to include thousands of members. Five hundred courses in business ethics were offered at colleges across the country, with more than forty thousand students enrolled. Centers of business ethics provided publications, courses, conferences, and seminars. Business ethics was also a prominent concern within leading companies, such as General Electric Co., The Chase Manhattan Corporation, General Motors, Atlantic Richfield Co., Caterpillar, Inc., and S. C. Johnson & Son, Inc. Many of these firms established ethics committees and social policy committees to address ethical issues.

In the 1980s the **Defense Industry Initiative on Business Ethics and Conduct** (DII) was developed to guide corporate support for ethical conduct. In 1986 eighteen defense contractors drafted principles for guiding business ethics and conduct.[11] In 2000 there were forty-seven members.[12] This effort established a method for discussing best practices and working tactics to link organizational practice and policy to successful ethical compliance. DII's web site provides more information.

First, DII supported codes of conduct and their widespread distribution. The codes of conduct had to be understandable, with details provided on more sub-

stantive areas. Second, member companies were expected to provide ethics training and to develop communication tools to support the periods between training.
Third, defense contractors were to create an open atmosphere where employees
felt comfortable reporting violations without fear of retribution Fourth, companies needed to perform extensive internal audits and develop effective internal
reporting and voluntary disclosure plans. Fifth, DII insisted that member companies preserve the integrity of the defense industry. Sixth, member companies had
to take on a philosophy of public accountability. These six principles became the
foundation for the United States Sentencing Commission's sentencing guidelines
for organizations (discussed in the next section).[13]

The 1980s ushered in the Reagan/Bush eras, with the accompanying belief that
self-regulation, rather than regulation by government, was in the public's interest.
Many tariffs and trade barriers were lifted, and businesses merged and divested
within an increasingly global atmosphere. Thus, while business schools were offering courses in business ethics, the rules of business were changing at a phe-
nomenal rate because of less regulation. Corporations that once were nationally
based began operating internationally and found themselves mired in value
structures where accepted rules of business behavior no longer applied. While
corporations had more freedom to make decisions, the government was developing new mandatory federal sentencing guidelines to control firms that were involved in misconduct.

The 1990s: Institutionalization of Business Ethics

The Clinton administration supported self-regulation and free trade. However, it
had also taken unprecedented government action to deal with health-related
social issues, such as teenage smoking. Its proposals included restricting cigarette
advertising, banning vending machine sales, and ending the use of cigarette logos
in connection with sports events.[14] The Clinton administration supported the
concept of organizational accountability for misconduct and damages.

The **Federal Sentencing Guidelines for Organizations,** approved by Congress
in November 1991, set the tone for organizational ethical compliance programs in
the 1990s. The guidelines broke new ground by codifying into law incentives for
organizations to take action to prevent misconduct, such as developing effective
internal ethical compliance programs.[15] Provisions in the guidelines mitigate
penalties for businesses that strive to root out misconduct and establish high ethical and legal standards.[16] The guidelines focus on firms taking action to prevent
and detect business misconduct in cooperation with government regulation.

The federal government created the United States Sentencing Commission to in-
stitutionalize ethical compliance programs and thus help prevent misconduct.
Organizations are being held responsible for the misconduct of their employees.
If a company lacks an effective ethical compliance program and its employees
violate the law, it can incur severe penalties. Table 1–2 shows the number of organizations fined or required to make restitution for the top five organizational offenses. At the heart of the Federal Sentencing Guidelines for Organizations is the

TABLE 1–2   Top Five Primary Offenses of Organizational Defendants

Offense	Total Number of Organizations
1. Fraud	86
2. Environmental — hazardous/toxic pollutants	37
3. Environmental — other pollutants	23
4. Antitrust	18
5. National defense	14

Source: U.S. Sentencing Commission, "Sentencing Practices," Table 51, http://www.ussc.gov/ANRPT/1999/table51.pdf *(accessed November 20, 2000).*

carrot-and-stick approach: by taking preventive action against misconduct, a company may avoid onerous penalties should a violation occur. A mechanical approach using legalistic logic will not suffice to avert serious penalties. The company must develop corporate values, enforce its own code of ethics, and strive to prevent misconduct (a "good citizen" corporation).

The United States Sentencing Commission evaluates the effectiveness of an organization's ethical compliance program according to these seven criteria: (1) development of standards and procedures capable of detecting and preventing misconduct (a code of conduct), (2) appointment of high-level personnel responsible for the ethical compliance program (for example, vice president of human resources, ethics officer, general counsel), (3) care in delegation of substantial discretionary authority to individuals with a propensity for misconduct, (4) effective communication of standards and procedures via training programs and publications (ethics training), (5) establishment of systems to monitor, audit, and report misconduct (for instance, hot lines and web sites with anonymous links to the ethics division), (6) consistent enforcement of standards and punishments in the organization, and (7) reasonable steps taken in response to an offense as well as continuous improvement of the ethical compliance program.

2000 and Beyond

Business ethics today is an evolving field of study, concentrating on ethical issues in business activities. Business ethical issues can be approached from the perspective of law, philosophy, theology, or social sciences; or they can be dealt with in a pragmatic spirit, seeking solutions for specific managerial problems. The study of business ethics does not mean simply moralizing about what should or should not be done in a particular situation. Rather, it systematically links the concepts of ethical responsibility and decision making within the organization. Business managers, academics, and the government are attempting to develop systematic guidelines that can help individuals and organizations make ethical decisions.

The current trend is away from legally based ethical initiatives in organizations to cultural or integrity-based initiatives that make ethics a part of core organizational values. Organizations recognize that effective business ethics programs are good for business performance. Firms that develop higher levels of trust function more efficiently and effectively.[17] An ethical organizational climate and intrafirm trust have been linked. An organizational ethics program that stresses values and compliance activities as suggested by the Federal Sentencing Guidelines for Organizations will be the most effective. One study found that the most desirable employee behavior is achieved when both values and compliance approaches are applied together.[18] President George W. Bush is emphasizing the role of responsible individuals and organizational accountability. Bush will appoint or reappoint four out of five Federal Trade Commissioners before 2005. As a believer in limited government, he plans to appoint commissioners who will provide more opportunity for businesses to play a key role in regulatory decisions. President Bush is committed to making it easier for religious organizations to obtain federal funds to provide some social services that have been provided traditionally by government. Bush has a "personal moral values" perspective on some societal issues. For example, he opposes the use of fetal tissue in federally funded research. The Bush administration appears to focus more on individual values than on organizational initiatives for business ethics.

As you continue through this book, it will be clear how business misconduct can damage company reputations and product images. However, we will also show how proactive culturally based organizational ethics initiatives have helped support many positive and diverse organizational objectives, such as profitability, hiring, employee satisfaction, customer loyalty, and supply-chain relationships.

Globally, businesses will work more closely together to establish standards of acceptable behavior. As a result of the European Union, MERCOSUR (Argentina, Brazil, Paraguay, Uruguay, Bolivia, and Chile), the World Trade Organization, the North American Free Trade Agreement, and, more recently, the Council on Economic Priorities' Social Accountability 8000, the Ethical Trading Initiative, and the U.S. Apparel Industry Partnership, we are already seeing collaborative efforts to establish goals and mandate minimum levels of ethical behavior. Signatories to the agreements indicate acceptance and support of these goals. Some companies will not do business with organizations that do not support and abide by these standards. The development of global codes of ethics, such as the Caux Round Table, highlights common ethical concerns for global firms. The Caux Round Table is a group of businesses, political leaders, and concerned interest groups that desire responsible behavior in the global community. It will be covered in more detail in Chapter 9.

e.ethics 2

WHY STUDY BUSINESS ETHICS?

The Problem

Ethical wrongdoing is increasingly a concern today. The Ethics Resource Center conducted the National Business Ethics Survey (NBES) of fifteen hundred U.S. employees to gather reliable data on key ethics and compliance outcomes and to help identify and better understand ethics issues that are important to employees. The NBES found that observed misconduct is higher in large organizations — those with more than five hundred employees — than in smaller ones (Figure 1–1) and that there are differences in observed misconduct across employment sectors — for-profit, government, and nonprofit (Figure 1–2).[19] More results from the NBES are presented in this and later chapters.

Insider trading of stocks and bonds, bribery, falsifying documents, deceptive advertising, defective products, employee theft, and questionable activities associated with on-line companies are all problems cited as evidence of declining ethical standards. For example, MCI WorldCom, Inc., agreed to pay a $100,000 fine to the government because of deceptive advertising about its 10-10-321 and 10-10-220 long-distance phone service.[20] Time, Inc., agreed to pay $4.9 million into a consumer fund as part of a settlement concerning the company's use of sweepstakes promotions that were viewed as misleading to consumers.[21] Wal-Mart filed suit against a former senior computer programmer, alleging that the employee set

FIGURE 1–1   Observed Misconduct by Organizational Size

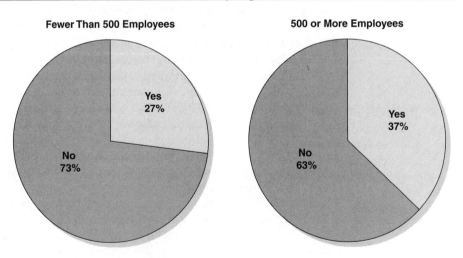

Have you observed misconduct in the workplace?

Source: Ethics Resource Center, 2000 National Business Ethics Survey: How Employees Perceive Ethics at Work, p. 29.

FIGURE 1–2   Observed Misconduct by Employment Sector

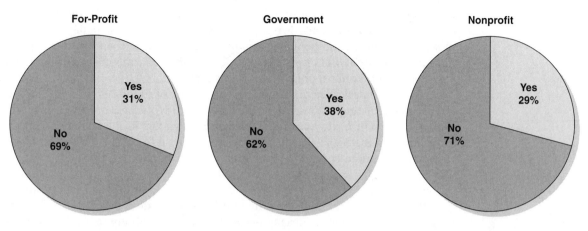

For-Profit   **Government**   **Nonprofit**

Yes 31%   No 69%

Yes 38%   No 62%

Yes 29%   No 71%

Have you observed misconduct in the workplace?

Source: Ethics Resource Center, 2000 National Business Ethics Survey: How Employees Perceive Ethics at Work, *p. 28.*

up an external e-mail account and sent details about Wal-Mart's highly confidential "Click n' Pull" package for its Sam's Club Internet site to himself and his new employer.[22] Medicineonline.com, a California-based health care site, launched www.bidforsurgery.com, which attempts to match prospects for cosmetic surgery with a network of thirty-five surgeons who bid for the job.[23] Such highly publicized cases strengthen the perception that ethical standards in business need to be raised.

Colleges and universities have been put on probation and in some cases given the "death penalty" — complete suspension of their athletic programs — for illegally recruiting or paying players. In government, various politicians and some high-ranking officials have had to resign in disgrace over ethical indiscretions, including scandals concerning the House of Representatives' bank and post office. And several scientists have been accused of falsifying research data, which could invalidate later research based on those data and jeopardize trust in all scientific research.

Whether made in science, politics, or business, most decisions are judged as right or wrong, ethical or unethical. Regardless of what an individual or a business organization believes about a particular behavior, if society judges it to be unethical or wrong, whether correctly or not, that judgment directly affects the organization's ability to achieve its business goals. For this reason alone, it is important to understand business ethics and recognize ethical issues.

The Solution

Studying business ethics is valuable for several reasons. The field is not merely an extension of an individual's own personal ethics. Many people believe that if an organization hires good people with strong ethical values, then it will be a good citizen organization. But as we show throughout this text, an individual's personal values and moral philosophies are only one factor in the ethical decision-making process. True, moral rules can be related to a variety of situations in life, and some people do not distinguish everyday ethical issues from business ones. Our concern, however, is with the application of rules and principles in the business context. Many important ethical issues do not arise very often in the business context, although they remain complex moral dilemmas in one's own personal life. For example, although abortion and the possibility of human cloning are moral issues in many people's lives, they are usually not an issue in a business organization.

Professionals in any field, including business, must deal with individuals' personal moral dilemmas as these issues affect a person's ability to function on the job. Normally, a business does not establish rules or policies on personal ethical issues such as sex or the use of alcohol outside the workplace; indeed, in some cases, such policies would be illegal. Only when a person's preferences or values influence his or her performance on the job do an individual's ethics play a major role in the evaluation of business decisions.

Although a person's racial and sexual prejudices are also a concern of individual ethics, racial and sexual discrimination in the workplace create an ethical problem within the business world. Indeed, race, gender, and age discrimination are a major source of ethical and legal debate in the workplace. Between seventy-five thousand and eighty thousand charges of discrimination are filed annually with the Equal Employment Opportunity Commission (EEOC).[24] Sexual harrassment filings with the EEOC average about sixteen thousand per year.[25] (The EEOC's web site provides more information and guidance to both employees and employers who need assistance in addressing discrimination concerns.) Mitsubishi Motors paid $34 million to several hundred women to settle a sexual harassment case that revealed widespread harassment, upper-management knowledge of the situation, and no systematic program in the organization to prevent the behavior.[26] Two years later, the EEOC indicated that monitors overseeing Mitsubishi's efforts to combat sexual harassment reported that the company had "sexual harassment in the plant firmly under control."[27]

Just being a good person and, in your own view, having sound personal ethics may not be sufficient to handle the ethical issues that arise in a business organization. It is important to recognize the relationship between legal and ethical decisions. While abstract virtues linked to the high moral ground of truthfulness, honesty, fairness, and openness are often assumed to be self-evident and accepted by all employees, business strategy decisions involve complex and detailed discussions. There is considerable debate over what constitutes antitrust, deceptive advertising, and violations of the Foreign Corrupt Practices Act. A high level of personal moral development may not prevent an individual from violating the law in an organizational context, where even experienced lawyers debate the exact meaning of the law. Some business ethics perspectives assume that ethics training is for people who have unacceptable personal moral development, but that is not necessarily the case. Since organizations are culturally diverse and personal values must be respected, a collective agreement on organizational ethics (that is, codes reasonably capable of preventing misconduct) is as vital as other managerial decisions.

Many people who have limited business experience suddenly find themselves making decisions about product quality, advertising, pricing, sales techniques, hiring practices, and pollution control. The values they learned from family, religion, and school may not provide specific guidelines for these complex business decisions. In other words, a person's experiences and decisions at home, in school, and in the community may be quite different from the experiences and the decisions he or she has to make at work. Many business ethics decisions are close calls. Years of experience in a particular industry may be required to know what is acceptable. For example, the Securities and Exchange Commission (SEC) alleged that Jonathan Lebed, a 15-year-old New Jersey youth, used the Internet to manipulate small-company stocks, resulting in gains of $272,826. The SEC charged that the teenager had purchased a block of thinly traded stock and then, within hours, sent "numerous false and/or misleading unsolicited e-mail messages touting the stock he just purchased." He then sold his shares at a profit. When first approached by SEC officials, Lebed claimed he had done nothing illegal. However, the SEC says he broke securities laws because, using fictitious names, he posted baseless predictions about stock-price increases and other false information about company prospects. Without admitting wrongdoing, Lebed agreed to abide by securities laws and turn over profits and interest totaling $285,000.[28] Lebed's personal experiences and decisions at home did not prepare him for the intricacies of SEC regulations and what is right and wrong in stock trading.

Studying business ethics will help you begin to identify ethical issues and recognize the approaches available to resolve them. You will also learn more about the ethical decision-making process and about ways to promote ethical behavior within the organization. By studying business ethics you may begin to understand how to cope with conflicts between your own personal values and those of the organization in which you work.

FRAMEWORK FOR STUDYING BUSINESS ETHICS

We have developed a framework for this text to help you understand how people make ethical decisions and deal with ethical issues. This framework includes an introduction to the concept of business ethics, an overview of major ethical issues that businesses face today, and a discussion of moral philosophy. We also examine a framework that describes how people make ethical or unethical decisions. We then explore in some detail each of the factors that influence ethical decision making. Finally, we discuss ways of sensitizing business to ethical standards and of applying business ethics on an international scale. Figure 1–3 illustrates how each element in the framework relates to the others and to the decision maker and where each topic is discussed in this book.

FIGURE 1–3   An Overview of This Book

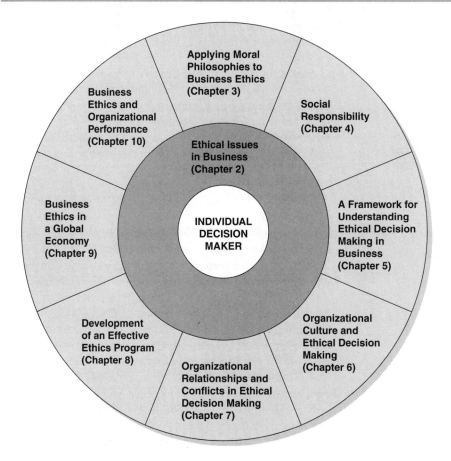

Ethical Issues in Business

Ethical issues, discussed in Chapter 2, are problems, situations, or opportunities that require a person or organization to choose among several actions that must be evaluated as right or wrong. To some extent, the business firm and interested parties define what constitutes an ethical issue. Most ethical issues relate to conflicts of interest, fairness and honesty, communications, or technology.

In general, businesses seem to be more concerned with ethical issues that could hurt the firm through negative publicity, such as bribery, and issues related to consumers and the general public, such as environmental impact. Scandals related to bribes, deceptive communications, and ecological disasters have severely damaged public trust in business institutions and have helped focus attention on activities that could do further harm. Studying ethical issues should help prepare you to identify potential problems in an organization and to understand alternatives and ethical solutions to the problem.

Applying Moral Philosophies to Business Ethics

In Chapter 3 we explore moral philosophies, which are principles or rules that people use to decide what is right or wrong. People learn these principles through socialization by family members, social groups, and formal education. Each moral philosophy has its own concept of rightness or ethicalness and rules for behavior. These rules and concepts of rightness form the basis on which a person decides how to act in a particular situation. We do not make judgments as to which moral philosophy is best to use in business. Instead we present a number of different moral philosophies so you can compare and contrast the usefulness of each in the business environment. These moral philosophies can provide rules for making ethical decisions.

Social Responsibility

Chapter 4 examines major factors that shape social responsibility in business. The concept of social responsibility for business covers four types of responsibilities: *philanthropic,* which society desires from business; *ethical,* which society expects from business; and *legal* and *economic,* which society requires of business. The discussion of social responsibility in Chapter 4 also includes environmental factors, such as fluctuations in the economy, laws and regulations, competition among businesses, technological advances, and the attitudes and desires of society. For example, Safeway, Inc., the nation's third-largest supermarket chain, responded to societal attitudes and voluntarily recalled its brand of taco shells after consumer concerns were raised that some of the shells might contain a type of genetically modified corn not yet approved for human consumption.[29] Examining how social responsibility and the environment create ethical issues and influence ethical decisions will enrich your understanding of business ethics.

A Framework for Understanding Ethical Decision Making in Business

In order to establish policies and rules that encourage employees to behave ethically and in accordance with organizational objectives, business managers must understand how and why people make ethical decisions. Philosophers and social scientists have developed models explaining how factors such as personal moral philosophies, opportunity, organizational culture, and the influence of other individuals contribute to individual ethical decision making. A general framework is discussed in Chapter 5. Although a descriptive framework may not explain how to make ethical decisions in specific situations, it will help you understand the major factors that influence ethical decision making in business.

Organizational Culture and Ethical Decision Making

How an employee responds to a moral or ethical issue depends in part on the structure and culture of the organization, which are discussed in Chapter 6. A person may learn ethical or unethical behavior while mastering other aspects of the job. Business ethics is a matter not only of understanding moral philosophies but also of recognizing how these moral philosophies are altered or blocked by organizational influence. An organization that actively fosters an ethical climate provides an example of how its employees should behave. Organizations must take responsibility for employee conduct and establish an organizational culture that provides a supportive value system encouraging ethical conduct.

Organizational Relationships and Conflicts in Ethical Decision Making

Individuals learn ethical or unethical behavior not only from society in general but also from superiors, peers, and subordinates with whom they associate in the work environment. Chapter 7 discusses the role of these significant others in the decision-making process. The more a person is exposed to unethical decisions by others in the work environment, the more likely he or she is to behave unethically. There may be a conflict between what the organization appears to expect of its workers and managers and what employees' personal ethical standards lead them to expect of themselves. Powerful superiors can directly influence an employee's behavior by putting into practice the company's standard of ethics. The status and power of significant others are closely related to the amount of pressure they can exert on an employee to conform to their expectations. In organizations where ethical standards are vague and supervision by superiors is limited, peers may provide the most guidance in an ethical decision.

Both opportunity and conflict influence ethical decision making. An individual who is rewarded or is not punished for unethical behavior is likely to continue to behave unethically, whereas a person who receives no reward or is punished for behaving unethically is less likely to repeat the action. Thus opportunity is an important consideration in understanding ethical decision making, and so is an understanding of ethical conflicts.

Development of an Effective Ethics Program

To encourage ethical behavior, organizations must be responsible for developing an ethics program. As discussed in Chapter 8, a reasonable ethical compliance program for preventing misconduct should include a code of ethics, oversight of the program, employee training, methods for employees to report misconduct, and provisions for monitoring and enforcing the program. (Figure 1–4 shows the percentage of organizations in the National Business Ethics Survey that have a written ethics standard.) Organizations need to analyze potential areas of ethical risk and design a program that addresses problem situations or internal conditions. In addition, they should revise their program on a regular basis in response to misconduct and overall ethical improvement. Finally, organizations have to understand and abide by industry standards of conduct and comply with all legal requirements.

FIGURE 1–4   Organizations with Written Standards of Ethical Business Conduct

1994

2000

No
40%

Yes
60%

No
21%

Yes
79%

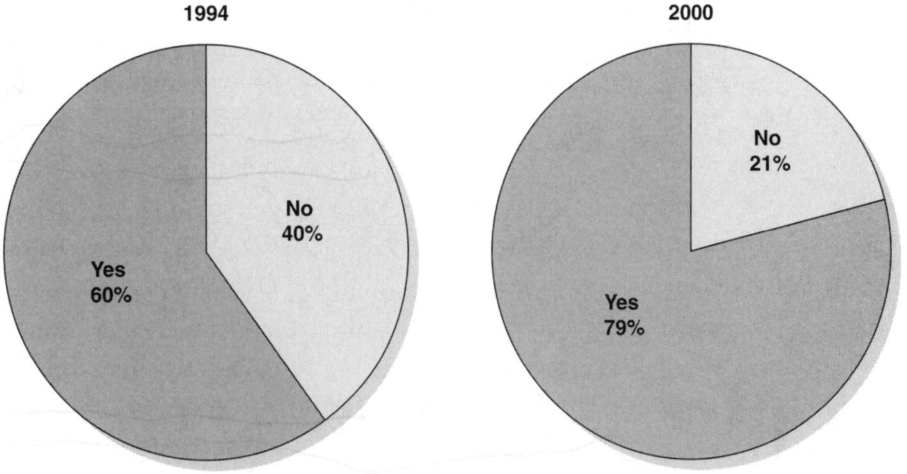

Does your organization have any written standards of ethical business conduct—for example, a code of ethics, a policy statement on ethics, or a guideline on proper business conduct—that provides guidance for your job?

Source: Ethics Resource Center, 2000 National Business Ethics Survey: How Employees Perceive Ethics at Work, *p. 16.*

Business Ethics in a Global Economy

Increasingly, businesses are operating across national boundaries and even globally, often in cultures where different moral standards and business ethics prevail. Chapter 9 addresses business ethics on an international scale. Certain international business ethical issues derive from differences in cultures; others relate to discrimination, bribery, pricing, and the impact of multinational corporations. For example, although the U.S. Foreign Corrupt Practices Act prohibits U.S. companies from using bribery in international business dealings, companies from other countries may not be limited by such laws. Some Americans have protested that this law unfairly limits their ability to compete with firms from Japan, Korea, and elsewhere on an international scale.

Business Ethics and Organizational Performance

As discussed in Chapter 10, there is increasing evidence that resources used to improve corporate ethical value systems improve business performance. An improved ethical climate is associated with a keener pursuit of quality, customer satisfaction, and employee commitment. Overall good corporate citizenship contributes to financial performance. In the case of countries, social institutions that support ethical systems generating trust promote the economic well-being of society. Finally, a good reputation is important to creating the value of a business.

We hope that this framework will help you develop a balanced understanding of the various perspectives and alternatives in making ethical business decisions. Regardless of your own personal values, the more you know about how individuals make decisions, the better prepared you will be to cope with difficult ethical decisions. Such knowledge will help you improve and control the ethical decision-making environment in which you work.

It is your job to make the final decision in an ethical situation that affects you. Sometimes that decision may be right; sometimes it may be wrong. It is always easy to look back with hindsight and know what one should have done in a particular situation. At the time, the choices may not be so clear. To give you practice in making ethical decisions, a number of cases are provided in Part Two of this book. In addition, each chapter begins with a vignette and ends with a minicase involving ethical problems. We hope they will give you a better sense of the difficulties of making ethical decisions in the real business world.

SUMMARY

This chapter provides an overview of the field of business ethics and introduces the framework through which it will be discussed in this text. Business ethics is a set of moral principles and standards that guide behavior in the world of business. Social responsibility is the obligation a business assumes to maximize its positive effect and minimize its negative effect on society. It can be viewed as a social contract, whereas business ethics relates to moral principles and rules that guide decision makers.

The study of business ethics evolved through five distinct stages. Before 1960, business ethical issues were discussed primarily from a religious perspective. The 1960s saw the rise of many social issues in business and the emergence of a social conscience. Business ethics began to develop as an independent field of study in the 1970s. The field of business ethics developed as a recognized discipline, with academics and practitioners exploring ethical issues and attempting to understand how individuals and organizations make ethical decisions. In the 1980s centers of business ethics provided publications, courses, conferences, and seminars. Many companies established ethics committees and social policy committees. The Defense Industry Initiative on Business Ethics and Conduct was developed to guide corporate support for ethical conduct; its principles had a major impact on corporate ethics in the United States. However, less government regulation and an increase in international operations raised new ethical issues. In the 1990s government continued to support self-regulation. The Federal Sentencing Guidelines for Organizations set the tone for organizational ethics programs. These guidelines provided incentives for organizations to take action to prevent organizational misconduct. Companies were encouraged to develop ethics programs and strive to be good citizen corporations.

In the twenty-first century, organizations seem less bound by legal issues and more concerned with maintaining ethical organizational cultures. A new emphasis on integrity-based initiatives that make ethics a part of core organizational values will be seen. Good ethics will be associated with good business.

Studying business ethics is important for many reasons. Recent incidents of unethical activity in business underscore the need for a better understanding of the ethical decision-making process and of the factors that contribute to ethical and unethical decisions. Individuals' personal moral philosophies and decision-making experience may not be sufficient to guide them in the business world.

Finally, the text introduces a framework for studying business ethics. Each chapter of this book addresses some aspect of business ethics and decision making within a business context. The major concerns are ethical issues in business; moral philosophies; social responsibility; ethical decision-making frameworks; organizational culture and ethical decision making; organizational relationships and conflicts in ethical decision making; development of an effective ethics program; global business ethics; and business ethics related to organizational performance.

Important Terms for Review	business ethics
	social responsibility
	economic responsibilities
	legal responsibilities
	ethical responsibilities
	philanthropic responsibilities
		Consumers' Bill of Rights
		Defense Industry Initiative on Business
		  Ethics and Conduct
		Federal Sentencing Guidelines
		  for Organizations

A Real-Life Situation*

Frank Garcia was just starting out as a salesman with Acme Corporation. Acme's corporate culture was top-down, or hierarchical. Because of the competitive nature of the industry, few mistakes were tolerated. Otis Hillman was a buyer for Thermocare, a national hospital chain. Frank's first meeting with Otis was a success, resulting in a $500,000 contract. This sale represented a significant increase for Acme and an additional $1,000 bonus for Frank.

Some months later Frank called on Thermocare, seeking to increase the contract by $250,000. "Otis, I think you'll need the additional inventory. It looks as if you didn't have enough at the end of last quarter," said Frank. "You may be right. Business has picked up. Maybe it's because of your product, but then again, maybe not. It's still not clear to me whether Acme is the best for us. Speaking of which, I heard that you have season tickets to the Cubs!" replied Otis.

Frank thought for a moment and said, "Otis, I know that part of your increases are due to our quality products. How about we discuss this over a ball game?" "Well, OK," Otis agreed. By the seventh-inning stretch, Frank had convinced Otis that the additional inventory was needed and offered to give Thermocare a pair of season tickets. When Frank's boss, Amber, heard of the sale, she was very pleased. "Frank, this is great. We've been trying to get Thermocare's business for a long time. You seem to have connected with their buyer." As a result of the Thermocare account, Frank received another large bonus check and a letter of achievement from the vice president of marketing.

Two quarters later Frank had become one of the top producers in the division. At the beginning of the quarter Frank had run the numbers on Thermocare's account and found that business was booming. The numbers showed that Otis's business could probably handle an additional $200,000 worth of goods without hurting return on assets. As Frank went over the figures with Otis, Otis's response was, "You know, Frank, I've really enjoyed the season tickets, but this is a big increase." As the conversation meandered, Frank soon found out that Otis and his wife had never been to Cancun, Mexico. Frank had never been in a situation like this before, so he excused himself to another room and called Amber about what he was thinking of doing. "Are you kidding!" responded Amber. "Why are you even calling me on this? I'll find the money somewhere to pay for it." "Is this OK with Acme?" asked Frank. "You let me worry about that," Amber told him. When Frank suggested that Otis and his wife be his guests in Cancun, the conversation seemed to go smoothly. In Cancun, Otis decided to purchase the additional goods, for which Frank received another bonus increase and another positive letter from headquarters.

Some time later Amber announced to her division that they would be taking all of their best clients to Las Vegas for a thank-you party. One of those invited was Thermocare. When they arrived, Amber gave each person $400 and said, "I want you to know that Acme is very grateful for the business that you have provided us. As a result of your understanding the qualitative differences of our products, we have doubled our production facilities. This trip and everything that goes with it for the next few days is our small way of saying thank-you. Every one of you has your salesperson here. If there is anything that you need, please let them know and we'll try to accommodate you. Have a good time!"

That night Otis had seen Frank at dinner and suggested to him that he was interested in attending an "adult entertainment" club. When Frank came to Amber about this, she said, "Is he asking you to go with him?" "No, Amber, not me!" "Well, then, if he's not asking you to go, I don't understand why you're talking to me. Didn't I say we'd take care of their needs?" "But what will Acme say if this gets out?" asked Frank. "Don't worry; it won't," said Amber.

Questions ■ Exercises

1. What are the potential ethical issues faced by the Acme Corporation?
2. What should Acme do if there is a desire to make ethics a part of its core organizational values?
3. Identify the ethical issues of which Frank needs to be aware.
4. Discuss the advantages and disadvantages of each decision Frank could make.

* This case is strictly hypothetical; any resemblance to real persons, companies, or situations is coincidental.

CHECK YOUR E.Q.

Check your E.Q., or Ethics Quotient, by completing the following. Assess your performance to evaluate your overall understanding of the chapter material.

1. Business ethics focuses mostly on personal ethical issues.   Yes   No

2. Business ethics deals with right or wrong behavior within a particular organization.   Yes   No

3. The four key responsibilities of business are economic, legal, ethical, and governmental.   Yes   No

4. The 1990s could be characterized as the period when ethics programs were greatly influenced by government legislation.   Yes   No

5. Business ethics problems are so pervasive in organizations because of individual greed.   Yes   No

ANSWERS 1. No. Business ethics focuses on organizational concerns (legal and ethical — employees, customers, suppliers, society). **2. Yes.** That stems from the basic definition. **3. No.** The four key responsibilities are economic, legal, ethical, and philanthropic. **4. Yes.** The impact of the Federal Sentencing Guidelines for Organizations means the 1990s are perceived as the period of institutional-izing business ethics. **5. No.** The impact of organizational culture and significant others is more of a force than individual greed.

Ethical Issues in Business

CHAPTER 2

Chapter Objectives

- To gain insight into the diverse causes and pressures of unethical behavior
- To explore the diversity of ethical issues
- To understand the role of organizational culture and relationships in ethical behavior
- To relate key organizational stakeholders to ethical issues in the organization
- To examine the orientations of the functional areas of business and their ethical concerns

Chapter Outline

Foundations of Ethical Conflict

Classification of Ethical Issues
Conflict of Interest
Honesty and Fairness
Communications
Technology

Ethical Issues Related to Participants and Functional Areas of Business
Owners
Finance
Employees
Management
Consumers
Marketing
Accounting

Recognizing an Ethical Issue

An Ethical Dilemma*

Carla knew something was wrong when Jack got back to his desk. He had been with Aker & Aker Accounting for seventeen years, starting there right after graduation and progressing through the ranks. Jack was a strong supporter of the company, and that was why Carla had been assigned to him. Carla had been with Aker & Aker (A&A) for two years. She had graduated in the top 10 percent of her class and passed the CPA exam on the first try. She had chosen A&A over one of the Big Five firms because A&A was the biggest and best firm in Smallville, Ohio, where her husband, Frank, managed a locally owned machine tools company. She and Frank had just purchased a new home when things started to turn strange with Jack, her boss.

"What's the matter, Jack?" Carla asked.

"Well, you'll hear about it sooner or later. I've been denied a partner's position. Can you imagine that? I have been working sixty- and seventy-hour weeks for the last ten years, and all that management can say to me is 'not at this time,'" complained Jack.

Carla asked, "So what else did they say?"

Jack turned red and blurted out, "They said maybe in a few more years. I've done all that they've asked me to do. I've sacrificed a lot, and now they say a few more years. It's not fair."

"What are you going to do?" Carla asked.

"I don't know," Jack said. "I just don't know."

Six months later, Carla noticed that Jack was behaving oddly. He came in late and left early. One Sunday Carla went into the office for some files and found Jack copying some of the software A&A used in auditing and consulting. A couple of weeks later, at a dinner party, Carla overheard a conversation about Jack doing consulting work for some small firms. Monday morning, she asked him if what she had heard was true.

Jack responded, "Yes, Carla, it's true. I have a few clients that I do work for on occasion."

"Don't you think there's a conflict of interest between you and A&A?" asked Carla.

"No," said Jack. "You see, these clients are not technically within the market area of A&A. Besides, I was counting on that promotion to help pay some extra bills. My oldest son decided to go to a private university, which is an extra $50,000 each year. Plus our medical plan at A&A doesn't cover some of my medical problems. And you don't want to know the cost. The only way I can afford to pay for these things is to do some extra work on the side."

"But what if A&A finds out?" Carla asked. "Won't they terminate you?"

"I don't want to think about that. Besides, if they don't find out for another six months, I may be able to start my own company."

"How?" asked Carla.

"Don't be naive, Carla. You came in that Sunday. You know." Carla realized that Jack had been using A&A software for his own gain. "That's stealing!" she said.

"Stealing?" Jack's voice grew calm. "Like when you use the office phones for personal long-distance calls? Like when you decided to volunteer to help out your church and copied all those things for them on the company machine? If I'm stealing, you're a thief as well. But let's not get into this discussion. I'm not hurting A&A and, who knows, maybe within the next year I'll become a partner and can quit my night job."

Carla backed off from the discussion and said nothing more. She couldn't afford to antagonize her boss and risk bad performance ratings. She and Frank had bills, too. She also knew that she wouldn't be able to get another job at the same pay if she quit. Moving to another town was not an option because of Frank's business. She had no physical evidence to take to the partners, which meant that it would be her word against Jack's, and he had seventeen years of experience with the company.

Questions ■ Exercises

1. What are the ethical issues in this case?
2. Assume you are Carla. Discuss your options and what the consequences of each option might be.

3. Assume you are Jack. Discuss your options.
4. Discuss any additional information you feel you need before making your decision.

* This case is strictly hypothetical; any resemblance to real persons, companies, or situations is coincidental.

People make ethical decisions only when they recognize that a particular issue or situation has an ethical component. Thus a first step toward understanding business ethics is to develop ethical-issue awareness. An **ethical issue** is a problem, situation, or opportunity requiring an individual or organization to choose among several actions that must be evaluated as right or wrong, ethical or unethical.

Ethical issues typically arise because of conflicts among individuals' personal moral philosophies and values, the values and attitudes of the organizations in which they work, and those of the society in which they live. The business environment presents many ethical conflicts. A company's efforts to attain its organizational objectives may collide with its employees' endeavors to achieve their own personal objectives. Similarly, consumers' desire for safe and quality products may conflict with manufacturers' desire to earn adequate profits. A manager's wish to hire specific employees that he or she likes may be at odds with the organization's intent to hire the best-qualified candidates and with society's aim to offer equal opportunity to minority-group members and women. Characteristics of the work or job and the culture of the organization and society in which one does business can also create ethical issues. Once ethical issues of any sort have been identified, individuals and organizations must decide how to resolve them. Many ethical issues are resolved through class-action lawsuits. Familiarity with the ethical issues that frequently arise in the business world will help you identify and resolve them when they occur.

In this chapter we consider some of the ethical issues that may occur in the business world. We focus first on situations and relationships that may generate ethical conflict. Then we discuss four classifications of ethical issues: conflict of interest, honesty and fairness, communications, and technology. Specific ethical issues related to the participants and functional areas of business are examined next. Finally, we assess the importance of recognizing ethical issues.

FOUNDATIONS OF ETHICAL CONFLICT

Because ethical issues often emerge from conflict, it is useful to examine the causes of ethical conflict. Business managers and employees often experience some tension between their own ethical beliefs and their obligations to the organizations in which they work.

Many employees utilize different ethical standards at work than they do at home. This conflict becomes exacerbated when employees feel that their company is encouraging unethical conduct or exerting pressure on them to engage in it. Figure 2–1 shows that 13 percent of business employees believe that this pressure is real and that they compromise themselves to meet schedules and business objectives and to help the company survive. The benefits manager at Varity Corp. felt this type of pressure when she was asked to "be inventive in coming up with a solution" to the company's problem of how to reduce its retiree health care benefits. Her memo to management detailed two "not necessarily legal" possibilities. She suggested establishing an "offshore company responsible for the retirees but not accountable under United States law and have it go bankrupt and thus terminate the health-care benefits plans." She also suggested terminating the health-care benefits plans, which would have meant "an almost certain class-action suit" and negotiating a settlement pact.[1] The National Business Ethics Survey (NBES) concluded that of those employees who feel pressure to compromise their ethical standards, 28 percent feel pressure from coworkers, 39 percent from supervisors, and 36 percent from top management.[2]

Employees observe many different types of misconduct at work. Table 2–1 lists the most common as lying, withholding information, and intimidation. Reasons for failing to report misconduct and ethics concerns include (1) belief that nothing will be done, (2) fear of retaliation, (3) fear of being viewed as a troublemaker, and (4) fear of being seen as a snitch.[3]

FIGURE 2–1   Pressure to Compromise Ethical Standards

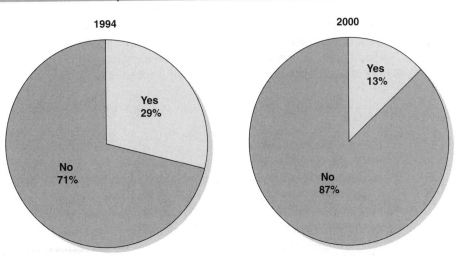

1994

Yes
29%

No
71%

2000

Yes
13%

No
87%

Do you ever feel pressured by other employees or management to compromise your company's standards of ethical business conduct in order to achieve business objectives?

Source: The Ethics Resource Center, 2000 National Business Ethics Survey: How Employees Perceive Ethics at Work, p. 34.

TABLE 2-1   Types of Misconduct

Type of Conduct Observed	Employees Observing It (%)
Lying to employees, customers, vendors, or the public	26
Withholding needed information from employees, customers, vendors, or the public	25
Abusive or intimidating behavior toward employees	24
Misreporting actual time or hours worked	21
Discrimination on the basis of race, color, gender, age, or similar categories	17
Sexual harassment	13
Stealing, theft, or related fraud	12
Breaking environmental and safety laws or regulations	12
Falsifying records and reports	12
Abusing drugs or alcohol on the job	10
Giving or accepting bribes, kickbacks, or inappropriate gifts	5

Source: The Ethics Resource Center, 2000 National Business Ethics Survey: How Employees Perceive Ethics at Work. *Reprinted with permission.*

CLASSIFICATION OF ETHICAL ISSUES

Surveys can render a useful overview of the many unsettled ethical issues in business. A constructive next step toward identifying and resolving ethical issues is to classify the issues relevant to most business organizations. In this section we classify ethical issues in relation to conflict of interest, honesty and fairness, communications, and technology. Although not all-inclusive or mutually exclusive, these classifications do provide an overview of some major ethical issues that business decision makers face.

Conflict of Interest

A **conflict of interest** exists when an individual must choose whether to advance his or her own interests, those of the organization, or those of some other group. To avoid conflicts of interest, employees must be able to separate their private interests from their business dealings. Organizations, too, must avoid potential conflicts of interest in providing goods or services. For example, Arthur Andersen LLP served as outside auditor for Waste Management, Inc., while also providing consulting services to the firm. The Securities and Exchange Commission investigated whether the consulting fees received by Arthur Andersen may have compromised the independence of auditing work provided to Waste Management.[4]

In many developed countries, it is generally recognized that employees should not accept bribes, personal payments, gifts, or special favors from people who hope to influence the outcome of a decision. However, as discussed later in this text, bribery is an accepted way of doing business in many countries. Bribes have been associated with the downfall of many managers, legislators, and government officials. One source estimates that some $80 billion is paid out worldwide in the form of bribes or some other payoff every year.[5]

When a government official accepts a bribe, it is usually from a business that seeks some favor, perhaps a chance to influence legislation that affects it. Giving bribes to legislators or public officials, then, is a business ethics issue. Fuji Heavy Industries Ltd. was investigated for bribing a government official in a situation that allegedly involved payments of ¥5 million to a House of Representatives member to allow Fuji to work on a project developing the successor to the US-IA, a search and rescue amphibian craft.[6]

The problem of kickbacks exists in private industry as well. New York Life Insurance Co. fired a bond trader, accusing him of participating in a year-long kickback scheme with help from other bond traders at as many as six brokerage firms, including PaineWebber Group and Greenwich Capital Markets. New York Life suspected that the trader sometimes shared in commissions paid to salespeople at the brokerage firms and received gifts, including lavish dinners, sporting events tickets, and trips. The cost of the scheme to New York Life was estimated at $8 million to $15 million. Two supervisors at the company were also fired for failing to adequately supervise the trader's activities.[7] Examples like these demonstrate that the problem of conflict of interest is widespread. Unethical conflicts of interest are of particular concern when they stifle fair competition among businesses.

Honesty and Fairness

Honesty refers to truthfulness, integrity, and trustworthiness; **fairness** is the quality of being just, equitable, and impartial. Honesty and fairness relate to the general moral attributes of decision makers. At a minimum, businesspeople are expected to follow all applicable laws and regulations. In addition, they should not knowingly harm customers, clients, or employees through deception, misrepresentation, or coercion. Nor should they harm competitors. German antitrust authorities accused Wal-Mart of exploiting its size and market share to sell basic food items, such as milk, sugar, and flour, below cost on a continuing basis, which violates German trade laws. According to the claim, the practice would hurt small and medium-size rivals unable to match the lower prices.[8] Although people in business often act in their own economic self-interest, ethical business relations should be grounded on fairness, justice, and trust. Buyers should be able to trust sellers; lenders should be able to trust borrowers. Failure to live up to these expectations or to abide by laws and standards destroys trust and makes it difficult, if not impossible, to continue business exchanges.[9]

Ideas of fairness are sometimes shaped by vested interests. One or both parties in the relationship may view an action as unfair or unethical because the outcome was less beneficial than expected. For example, more and more pharmaceutical companies are advertising their prescription drugs on television. Spending on consumer advertising for medications rose 40 percent in just one year (see Figure 2–2).[10] A key concern of physicians is that patients will have a false or inflated perception of what the drug will do. And a key concern for patients, many of whom are senior citizens on fixed incomes, is the rising costs of drugs due, in part, to increased advertising expenditures.

Issues related to fairness and honesty also arise because business is sometimes regarded as a "game" governed by its own rules rather than those of society. Eric Beversluis suggests that unfairness is a problem because people often reason along these lines:

1. Business relationships are a subset of human relationships that are governed by their own rules, which, in a market society, involve competition, profit maximization, and personal advancement within the organization.

2. Business can therefore be considered a game people play, comparable in certain respects to competitive sports such as basketball or boxing.

3. Ordinary rules and morality do not hold in games like basketball or boxing. (What if a basketball player did unto others as he would have them do unto him? What if a boxer decided it was wrong to try to injure another person?)

FIGURE 2–2   TV, Print, and Other Advertising Expenditures by Drug Companies

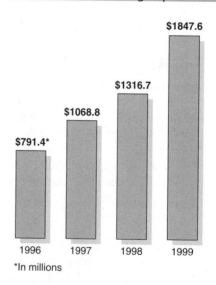

$1847.6

$1316.7

$1068.8

$791.4*

1996   1997   1998   1999

*In millions

Source: Shailagh Murray and Lucette Lagnado, "Drug Companies Face Assault on Prices," The Wall Street Journal, May 11, 2000, p. B1. Wall Street Journal. Central Edition (Staff produced copy only) by Wall Street Journal. Copyright 2000 by Dow Jones & Co., Inc. Reproduced with permission of Dow Jones & Co., Inc., in the format Textbook via Copyright Clearance Center.

4. Logically, then, if business is a game like basketball or boxing, ordinary ethical rules do not apply.[11]

This type of reasoning leads many people to conclude that anything is fair in sports, war, and business. Indeed, several books have compared business to warfare — for example, Harvey Mackay's *Swim with the Sharks* and Jay Conrad Levinson's *Guerrilla Marketing*. The common theme is that surprise attacks, guerrilla warfare, and other warlike tactics are necessary to win the battle for consumers' dollars. This business-as-war mentality may foster the idea that fairness and honesty are not necessary in business.

Many argue, however, that business is not a game like basketball or boxing. Because people are not economically self-sufficient, they cannot withdraw from the game of business. Therefore, business ethics must not only make clear what rules apply in the game of business but must also develop rules appropriate to the nonvoluntary character of participation in the game.[12]

Lack of rules and poor enforcement of the rules that do exist create opportunities for unethical behavior and even encourage it. Figure 2–3 shows that nearly half of all employees in the NBES who said they reported misconduct were dissatisfied with their organization's response.[13] Consequently, many feel that there is no reward for "doing the right thing."

FIGURE 2–3   Satisfaction with Response to Reported Misconduct

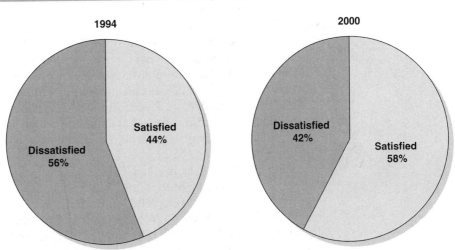

How satisfied were you with your organization's response to your report of misconduct?

Source: The Ethics Resource Center, 2000 National Business Ethics Survey: How Employees Perceive Ethics at Work, *p. 45.*

Communications

Communication refers to the transmission of information and the sharing of meaning. Ethical issues in communications relate to advertising messages and information about product safety, pollution, and employee work conditions, as well as other situations. Communications that are false or misleading can destroy customers' trust in an organization. Lying, a major ethical issue within communications, may be a significant problem. It causes ethical predicaments in both external and internal communications because it destroys trust. Results of a recent survey published in the *Journal of the American Medical Association* showed that more than one-third of doctors surveyed admitted deceiving insurance companies by exaggerating the severity of a patient's illness, listing an inaccurate diagnosis on bills, and reporting nonexistent symptoms.[14]

False and deceptive advertising is a key issue in communications. Abuses in advertising can range from exaggerated claims and concealed facts to outright lying. Exaggerated claims are those that cannot be substantiated, as when a commercial states that a certain product is superior to any other on the market. For example, Papa John's International, Inc., invested millions of dollars over the years in its "Better Ingredients, Better Pizza" advertising campaign to promote its pizza quality and taste. However, a Texas jury found that the slogan constituted deceptive advertising, and the judge stopped the company from using this claim in future advertising.[15]

The Federal Trade Commission and other agencies are monitoring more closely the advertisements for work-at-home business ventures. Consumers are losing millions of dollars each year responding to ads for phony business opportunities, such as those promising $50,000 a year for doing medical billing from a home computer.[16] Sometimes differing interpretations of advertising messages create ethical issues that must be resolved in court. For example, the television ads for HMO Kaiser Permanente state that Kaiser is a place where "no one but you and your doctor decides what's right for you" and "there are no financial pressures to prevent your physician from giving you the medical care you need." According to a lawsuit filed by a California consumer group, however, Kaiser drastically reduced its medical budget as it added hundreds of thousands of new members. The consumer group also alleges that Kaiser set quotas for doctors to reduce the number of patients hospitalized, while tying a significant portion of physician pay to meeting the quotas.[17]

Labeling issues are even murkier. For example, Mott's, Inc., the nation's leading producer of branded applesauce and apple juice, agreed to revise the labels of some of its fruit products (grape juice and cherry juice) after New York's attorney general claimed consumers were being misled. The products are often made by blending apple juice with enough grape juice or cherry juice to make the designated flavor. The labels, however, show the words "100% Juice" with a picture of grapes or cherries and the fruits' names in large lettering underneath. The attorney general felt that the presentation of the names under "100% Juice" could lead consumers to falsely assume the product is 100 percent grape juice or cherry juice. Mott's admitted no wrongdoing but agreed to pay $177,500 to cover the investigation costs and to institute a minor change to the labels in question.[18]

Advertising and direct sales communication can also mislead by concealing facts within a message. For instance, a salesperson anxious to sell a medical insurance policy might list a large number of illnesses covered by the policy but fail to mention that it does not cover some commonly covered illnesses.

In the telephone industry, AT&T sued Business Discount Plan (BDP), accusing it of using fraud and deception to routinely slam customers to its telecommunication service. Slamming refers to changing a customer's phone service without authorization. AT&T charged that BDP gave the impression that it was affiliated with AT&T. As part of the settlement, BDP had to send letters to consumers telling them that BDP was not affiliated with AT&T.[19] Such misleading behavior creates ethical issues because the communicated messages do not include all the information consumers need to make good purchasing decisions. They frustrate and anger customers, who feel that they have been deceived. In addition, they damage the seller's credibility and reputation.

Another form of advertising abuse involves making ambiguous statements, whose words are so weak that the viewer, reader, or listener must infer the advertiser's intended message. These "weasel" words are inherently vague and enable the advertiser to deny any intent to deceive. The verb help is a good example (as in expressions such as "helps prevent," "helps fight," "helps make you feel").[20] Consumers may view such advertisements as unethical because they fail to communicate all the information needed to make a good purchasing decision or because they deceive the consumer outright.

Technology

The final category of ethical issues relates to **technology** and the numerous advances made in the Internet and other forms of electronic communications in the last few years. As the number of people who use the Internet increases, the areas of concern related to its use increase as well. Some issues that must be addressed by businesses include monitoring of employee use of available technology, consumer privacy, site development and on-line marketing, and legal protection of intellectual properties, such as music, books, and movies.

A challenge for companies today is meeting business needs while protecting employees' desires for privacy. There are few legal protections of an employee's right to privacy, and businesses therefore have much flexibility in establishing policies related to employee privacy while on company property and in use of company equipment. The increased use of electronic communications in the workplace (the U.S. Census Bureau reports that 39 million employees nationally have access to the Internet at work[21]) and technological advances that permit employee monitoring and surveillance provide companies with new opportunities to obtain data about employees. According to Michael Hoffman, executive director of the Center for Business Ethics, "fifty percent, and probably more, of America's companies conduct random e-mail surveillance, and most don't warn employees they are going to do it."[22] One survey of employees found that most assume their use of technology at work will be monitored, and a large majority approved of most monitoring methods (see Figure 2–4).[23]

FIGURE 2–4   Percentage of Employees Who Approve of Certain
Monitoring Methods

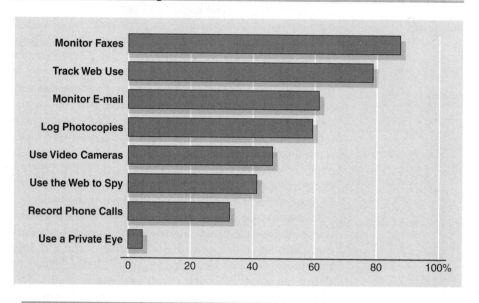

How companies address the issue of employee privacy will have both direct and indirect links to financial outcomes. Evidence suggests that positive outcomes are associated with having a clear, well-communicated, and uniformly implemented policy on employee privacy and implementation of information-gathering practices that support business needs while intruding on employee privacy as little as possible. If these practices are followed, companies should experience certain benefits. Several web sites provide model policies and detailed guidelines for conducting electronic monitoring, including the Model Electronic Privacy Act on the American Civil Liberties Union site.

@,ethics 1

A clearly conveyed policy on workplace privacy should reduce the opportunity for employee lawsuits and the resulting costs of such actions. However, if a company fails to monitor employees' use of e-mail and the Internet, the costs can be huge. For example, Chevron Corp. agreed to pay $2.2 million to employees who claimed that unmonitored, sexually harassing e-mail created a threatening environment for them.[24] Instituting practices that show respect for employee privacy but do not abdicate employer responsibility should help create a climate of trust in which opportunities for resolving employee–employer disputes without lawsuits increase.

Workplace monitoring conducted in a nonthreatening manner may contribute to increased employee performance and productivity. There is ample evidence that people use company technology for personal business while at work. A survey of 1,200 employees by Vault.com found that 37.1 percent of employees surf non-work-related sites constantly during work hours.[25] Electronic monitoring allows a company to determine whether productivity is being reduced because employees are spending too much time on personal Web activities and then take steps to remedy the situation. Internet filtering companies, such as Cyber Patrol, Surfcontrol, Surfwatch, and WebSense, provide products that block employee access to Web sites that are deemed distracting or objectionable. WebSense recently launched AfterWork.com, a personal home page for each employee at a company that allows employees to visit non-work-related Web sites during breaks and lunch as well as before and after work hours.[26] One survey of Internet-related employee behaviors found that 58 percent of employees rated using company resources for personal Web surfing as an "extremely serious" or "very serious" business ethics violation.[27] Table 2–2 provides more of the survey results.

The second ethical issue created by advances in technology relates to consumer privacy. The two dimensions of this issue involve consumer awareness of information collection and a growing lack of consumer control over how personal information that has been collected is used. For example, Sprint Corp.'s wireless unit announced plans to put global-positioning chips in its cell phones to help locate users. Privacy advocates warn that there are risks because phone users will leave "electronic footprints" and the collected data could be misused.[28]

On-line purchases and even random Web surfing can be tracked without a consumer's knowledge. A U.S. Department of Commerce study on e-commerce and privacy found that 81 percent of Internet users and 79 percent of consumers who buy products and services over the Web were concerned about on-line threats to privacy.[29] Comet Systems' popular software, which is installed on more than 16 million computers, provides for the collection of customers' unique serial numbers when they visit any of some 60,000 Web sites. Critics say the information is being collected without consumers' knowledge and that today's technology makes it possible for the company to correlate the serial numbers with consumers' identities.[30] One survey found that 38 percent of respondents felt that it is never ethical to track customers' Web activities, and 64 percent said they don't trust Web sites that do.[31]

TABLE 2–2   **Employee Internet-Related Behavior Rated as "Extremely Serious" or "Very Serious" Business Ethics Violations**

Behavior	Employee Opinion	Employer Opinion
E-mail harassment of another employee	91%	94%
Circulating pornography through company e-mail	85%	93%
Using company resources for personal Web surfing	58%	56%
Using company resources and time for personal e-mail	45%	50%

Source: "Ethical Issues in the Employer–Employee Relationship," http://www.financialpro.org/sfsp/Press/ethics/ es2000/Ethics_Survey_2000_Report_FINAL.html (accessed October 11, 2000). Reprinted with permission from the Society of Financial Service Professionals ethics survey "Ethical Issues in the Employer–Employee Relationship" (www.financialpro.org). Copyright © 2000 by the Society of Financial Service Professionals, 270 S. Bryn Mawr Avenue, Byrn Mawr, PA 19010. Distribution prohibited without publisher's written permission.

*e.*ethics 2

BBBOnline offers an on-line seal for companies that subscribe to certain standards. TRUSTe is a nonprofit global initiative offering a certification seal to Web sites that adhere to its principles. Visit e-businessethics.com for more on Internet privacy.

The third ethical issue relates to site development and on-line marketing. Marketers are increasingly being questioned on these concerns. For example, www.edu.com is a site through which registered college students can make on-line purchases with a student discount. The site collects personal information on all its users and even contacts the colleges to verify that users are actually enrolled. The company then passes collected information to its partners — computer makers (such as Apple Computer, Inc.) and credit card issuers (such as AT&T and Citibank) — in exchange for the right to sell those companies' products at a discount. The firm says it does not sell names or specific individual information but rather data on kinds of products students would like to see, hobbies in which they are involved and features they would like to see on particular sites.[32] Some on-line companies change the information provided based on the requestor. For example, a person from the government's antitrust division might get a page of information showing that a particular company is complying with the law, while someone from a competing firm might be shown a page filled with untrue marketing and product information. Customizing a site depending on the visitor may make sense from a marketing standpoint, but 46 percent of those in a recent survey said that it is unethical to alter a site so that different corporate information appears for certain visitors.[33]

The final ethical issue related to technology that we will discuss involves the legal protection of intellectual properties, such as music, books, and movies. Laws such as the Copyright Act of 1976, the Digital Millennium Copyright Act, and the Digital Theft Deterrence and Copyright Damages Improvement Act of 1999 were designed to protect the creators of intellectual property. However, with the advent of increasing technological abilities, ethical issues abound for Web sites, such as Napster.com, that allow individuals to download copyrighted music for personal use without providing compensation to the artists and for such endeavors as Project Gutenberg, a nonprofit group that wants to display books over the Internet for free.

A recent decision by the federal Copyright Office helped lay the groundwork for intellectual property rules in a digital world. The office decided to allow just two exemptions to the federal law that makes it illegal for Web users to hack through barriers that copyright holders erect around material released on-line, such as books, films, and music. The first exemption involves software that blocks users from finding obscene or controversial material on the Web, and the second involves giving people the right to bypass malfunctioning security features of software or other copyrighted goods they have purchased. This decision reflects the fact that copyright owners are being favored in digital copyright issues.[34] There have been many lawsuits related to this issue, and some have had costly results. MP3.com paid Universal Music Group $53.4 million to end its dispute with major record labels over copyright infringement.[35]

ETHICAL ISSUES RELATED TO PARTICIPANTS AND FUNCTIONAL AREAS OF BUSINESS

To help you understand and recognize ethical issues, let us examine the major participants and functions of business from which ethical concerns may arise. Figure 2–5 is a representation of the key organizational stakeholders and functions. The participants are owners, employees, and consumers; management, marketing, accounting, and finance are four major functions of any business. In this section we attempt to provide insight into some ethical issues characteristic of each participant type and function.

Owners

Most businesses, large and small, start with the vision of a person or group of people who pool their resources to provide some good or service. The business owners (or stockholders in a corporation), shown at the top of the inner circle in Figure 2–5, generally supply or obtain the resources — usually money or credit — to start and develop the business. The owners may manage the organization themselves, or they may hire professional managers to run the company.

Owners have an obligation to society. Weyerhaeuser won the American Forest & Paper Association's Environment and Energy Achievement Award for pollution prevention. Weyerhaeuser's Georgia pulp mill reduced solid waste pollution 41 percent, wastewater emissions 32 percent, and air emissions 13 percent. In contrast, Louisiana-Pacific, the largest U.S. manufacturer of oriented strand board (a plywood substitute) was fined $5.5 million under the Clean Air Act for higher than allowable emissions at a Colorado plant. The company incurred an additional $31 million in fines as a result of lying, falsifying documents, and tampering with pollution-monitoring equipment.[36] Many owners are concerned about the environment, but some either do not see its relevance in business or choose to ignore or bypass environmental laws because they are perceived as too expensive to follow.

Owners who do not understand the ethical issues that their customers, or society in general, consider important may pay for their lack of understanding in lost sales. Even practices that are considered standard within their industry may be perceived as unethical by outsiders. For example, Internet and long-distance service providers have been accused of taking advantage of customers by rounding up calls or Internet access of less than one minute to the next minute. Outsiders view this practice as overcharging consumers; insiders consider it bulk pricing.[37] Another example of alleged overbilling centers around PacBell's advertised flat-rate service fee for voicemail. Although the judge in the case found that the company had not violated the law, the company was told to take "'remedial steps" to alleviate customer confusion over its voicemail pricing. PacBell had advertised its business voicemail service at a flat rate of "only $21.95 per box, per month — just 73 cents a day" but failed to adequately disclose that separate charges applied each time the product was used.[38]

These and other practices, such as accepting gifts, giving money to foreign buyers, or accepting trips, are being judged as unethical by consumers as gauged by complaints to government. When such events occur, increased legislation is usually the response.

Finance

Because the owners of a business are responsible for providing financial resources for its operation, owners and finance are in the same segment of Figure 2–5. Owners sometimes have to borrow money from friends or financial institutions to start their business, or they may take on additional owners — partners or stockholders — to obtain money. How financial resources are acquired and deployed can create ethical and even legal issues.

Pricing is a key issue that is partially determined by financial managers. Price-fixing charges have been levied against both manufacturers and suppliers. The Justice Department's investigation of vitamin makers found that every major maker of bulk vitamins in the world was involved in fixing prices on nearly every vitamin sold in the United States. Three of the largest companies and six executives pleaded guilty and agreed to pay $750 million in fines.[39] In another example, Nine West Group Inc., one of the largest suppliers of women's shoes in the United States, settled a price-fixing case by agreeing to pay states $34 million and stop dictating the prices that stores could charge for its footwear. It was alleged that the company had stipulated when retailers could offer shoes at reduced prices and

FIGURE 2–5   **Key Organizational Stakeholders and Functions**

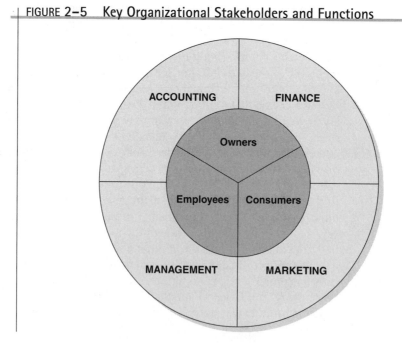

had distributed lists of shoes that could not be discounted. It was alleged that retailers who did not follow the policies were threatened with cancellations, were denied orders, or were not given discounts.[40]

Other financial issues relate to how companies' financial positions are reported to current and potential investors, government agencies, and other interested parties. Financial documents provide important information on which investors and others base decisions that may involve millions of dollars. If those documents contain inaccurate information, whether intentionally or not, lawsuits and criminal penalties may result. After an investigation at Waste Management, Inc. showed years of questionable accounting, the company and its outside auditor, Arthur Andersen LLP, agreed to pay $220 million to settle shareholder litigation in the matter.[41]

The European Union and the United States are cooperating to minimize antitrust activities by multinational companies. As a result, vendor countries can ask for raids to be carried out on companies headquartered in their country that are suspected of antitrust acts.

Organizations and individuals continue to be interested in socially responsible investing. In fact, according to a report from the Social Investment Forum, a trade group of investment funds, $2 trillion, or one out of every eight investment dollars, is now part of some kind of "socially responsible portfolio" in the United States.[42] Many socially responsible funds are performing very well. For example, the Domini Social Equity Fund, composed of approximately four hundred companies that have passed multiple social and environmental screens, posted a three-year return of 25.16 percent, beating the three-year performance of the S&P 500 of 23.7 percent.[43] The trend of conscientious investing is growing and changing. Many investors feel that it is not enough to invest in "good citizen" corporations or funds. Instead many are looking for social activist companies that go beyond legal and ethical responsibilities and consider key stakeholder and community and social concerns. Economic pressure from outside investors to improve ethical and socially responsible behavior is a strong incentive for business reform.

Another financial issue relates to whether banks should be held responsible for knowing whether large cash deposits are being "laundered" to hide the depositor's involvement in drug trafficking. Society's need to enforce drug-related laws may conflict with banks' desires to maintain the confidentiality of their customers. The Bank of New York agreed with banking regulators to strengthen compliance and anti–money laundering procedures after deficiencies were uncovered in the course of an investigation.

Employees

Employees, shown in the inner circle in Figure 2–5, carry out the work of the organization. Employees may have to make decisions about assignments that they perceive as unethical. For example, Jeffrey Wigand, a former cigarette executive at Brown & Williamson Tobacco Corporation, who has a doctorate in endocrinology and biochemistry, suggested that a safer cigarette could be made. But he alleged that Brown & Williamson disagreed with his research and canceled support. He believed that the company was hiding from the public the fact that cigarettes endanger health. The company fired him. As a result of Wigand's allegations, tobacco companies have settled with every state for hundreds of billions of dollars. The actions of one person have changed an entire industry.

Bosses may also not want employees to tell them the truth, especially if it would be detrimental to their superior or the company. Albert J. Meyer, an accounting professor who did accounting work for his small college, first became suspicious when he found a $294,000 bank transfer from Spring Arbor College to the Heritage of Values Foundation, Inc. His superior told him that the Heritage of Values Foundation was connected to a consultant who had introduced the college to the Foundation for New Era Philanthropy and that the money was earmarked for New Era.

New Era was the brainchild of John G. Bennett, Jr., who took advantage of churches and philanthropists in a giant **Ponzi scheme**. In a Ponzi scheme, investors are paid with other investors' monies, with nothing tangible being produced or supported. Bennett would tell churches that he had other, anonymous donors that would match their contributions, thus giving the churches a 100 percent return on their investments. But there were no anonymous donors, and Bennett was not investing the money in the traditional way. Even though he reported to the Internal Revenue Service that he drew no salary, the Securities and Exchange Commission charged that he diverted $4.2 million into personal items, such as a new $620,000 home, which he paid for with cash.[44]

Albert J. Meyer started probing New Era's activities by amassing financial documents and calling people who had invested. He soon recognized New Era as a Ponzi scheme. Meyer tried repeatedly to warn Spring Arbor College, but to no avail. Even though he had no permanent job with the college, Meyer persisted until the IRS and SEC took notice of him and began an investigation, which uncovered hundreds of millions of dollars worth of fraud.[45] As a result of the efforts of Meyer and others, Bennett turned over about $1.2 million in property, cash, and securities. This amount included his $620,000 home, his daughter's $249,000 house, and his Lexus, all of which were purchased with New Era funds. He was sentenced to twelve years in federal prison without parole on eighty-two counts of fraud, money laundering, and tax evasion. The judge described the harm Bennett caused the charities as "incalculable."[46]

Theft, sabotage, and use of company resources for personal business are other employee issues that companies must deal with occasionally. According to a recent survey, the Internet is the top company resource used for personal business by employees. Figure 2–6 shows the percentages of employees who utilize various other office resources for personal use. More than half of those surveyed indicated that such use is wrong.[47] Employee sabotage is usually a one-time occurrence and the work of an individual who believes that a promotion or raise was unfairly denied.

Unlike sabotage, employee theft may be an ongoing, routine occurrence. United States stores' total losses from employee theft increased 34 percent over the past three years to an estimated $12.85 billion a year. Shoplifting costs store owners an average $158.86 per incident, whereas the typical cost of employee theft per incident is $1,004.35.[48] Faced with this kind of loss, many stores have focused security

FIGURE 2–6   Company Resources Used for Personal Business

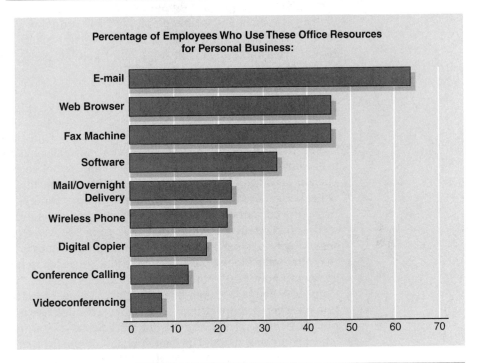

Percentage of Employees Who Use These Office Resources for Personal Business:

Source: Ziff Davis Smart Business Reader Survey in John Galvin, "The New Business Ethics," SmartBusinessMag.com, June 2000, p. 90. Reprinted from Ziff Davis Smart Business, June 2000, with permission. Copyright © 2001 Ziff Davis Media, Inc. All Rights Reserved.

cameras on backrooms and cash registers. Increasingly, insider thieves are being criminally prosecuted or sued in civil court for restitution. Several independent tracking services recently combined to form a national database of about 750,000 retail workers who have been fired by store owners for thievery. In order to add an employee's name to the list, a retailer must obtain a signed admission of theft or signatures from two witnesses to a verbal confession; the employee must be age 17 or older but does not have to have a criminal conviction. For a fee of $2 to $4, a retail member can have a job prospect screened against the database, which stores names, Social Security numbers, and theft descriptions for seven years.[49]

There may also be situations in which an employee is aware that the boss has been sexually harassing another employee but has no way of proving the offense. Will speaking out make things worse for the employee? And what will it do to the coworker, the victim? Such situations create ethical issues that employees must resolve. The difficulties are often compounded by employees' fear of losing their jobs if they protest or speak out.

There are other situations in which companies understand the importance of ethics and attempt to solve the problem with elaborate systems. However, if such systems are not based on company integrity, they usually become part of the problem. Merrill Lynch, recognized by *Fortune, Business Week,* and *Working Mother* for its progressive employee programs, settled a discrimination lawsuit with eight current and former employees. The company is establishing a program for resolving future employee claims that utilizes arbitration and litigation options. Caring about the quality of its employees' work life, Merrill Lynch strives to be sensitive to employee concerns.[50]

Management

Managers of a business have both an ethical and a legal responsibility to manage the business in the interest of the owners. Several ethical issues relate to managers' obligations to owners, especially in the area of corporate takeovers, mergers, and leveraged buyouts. For example, when a business faces the prospect of being bought or taken over by another company or individual, the managers' duties to the current owners may conflict with their own personal interests and objectives (job security, income, and power). Their loyalty to the organization and to the owners and stockholders may be brought into question. A management team may attempt to block a takeover that would benefit shareholders but reduce management's power and perhaps jeopardize their jobs. For example, Hilton Hotels Corp. was sued by a shareholder who felt the hotel chain's defense against corporate takeovers trampled investors' rights. This defense made takeovers prohibitively expensive by allowing existing shareholders to buy discounted shares when a hostile bid was made. The shareholder suit alleged that these actions taken by Hilton officials "restrict the transfer of Hilton common stock by providing that the shares cannot be transferred without also transferring the associated rights." This was not the first time Hilton's anti-takeover strategy met with resistance from shareholders who wanted the opportunity to consider a hostile suitor's offers for their stock.[51] Managers also have to face decisions about paying "greenmail" to raiders that have acquired a large stake in the firm and will not sell back their shares except at a premium price. If greenmail is not paid, the raider may acquire the company and sell off its assets piece by piece, possibly resulting in the loss of jobs for many employees.

The primary goal of management is to achieve a company's objectives by organizing, directing, planning, and controlling the activities of its employees. Management and employees are in the same segment of Figure 2–5 because managers organize and motivate workers to achieve organizational objectives. Since they guide employees and direct activities, managers influence the ethical issues that evolve within an organization.

Management should also be concerned about ethical issues that relate to employee discipline, dismissal, discrimination, health and safety, privacy, technology, employee benefits, drug and alcohol abuse in the workplace, the environmental impact of the organization, codes of ethics and self-governance, relations with local communities, plant closings, and layoffs. For example, as we said earlier, employee monitoring through both on-line and off-line surveillance is increasing. In 2000, it was projected that 80 percent of Fortune 1000 companies would be using monitoring software by 2001.[52] Xerox Corp. fired forty employees for using company computers inappropriately for Internet and e-mail messages, and, as mentioned earlier, Chevron Corp. settled a $2.2 million sexual harassment lawsuit brought because inappropriate jokes were sent over the company network.[53] When such issues are not addressed, employees and communities usually react adversely.

Managers must carefully balance their duties both to the owners or stockholders, who hired them to achieve the organization's objectives, and to the employees, who look to them for guidance and direction. In addition, managers must comply with society's wishes to have safe working conditions and safe products, to protect the environment, and to promote minorities. For example, amendments to the Civil Rights Act extend punitive damages to the plaintiff for discrimination on the basis of sex, disability, religion, or race. These amendments may encourage the promotion of more women and minorities.

Another area of potential ethical problems for managers is that of the public's concern over privacy issues and data access. Because more data are being stored in computers and the information is being sold, many consumer rights groups worry about the violation of privacy rights. More and more companies are buying, selling, and manipulating such lists to better target consumers for specific products or services. Some consumers would find it an invasion of privacy to have multiple companies know what items they had purchased at a store, the state of their mental or physical health, or what medications they are taking. Many of the leading Internet health care sites, including PlanetRx.com, have created Hi-Ethics, or Health Internet Ethics, to address privacy, advertising, and content-quality issues for Internet health consumers. The companies are committed to maintaining the highest levels of safety, security, reliability, and quality of information for their customers.[54] In addition, most Web sites now post privacy policies for users

ℰ.ethics 3   to read before registering at the site or making a purchase. The Online Privacy Alliance is a coalition of more than fifty global corporations and associations that require Web site operators to tell users what information is being collected and what choices they have regarding its use.[55] Striking an ethical balance among the needs of owners, employees, and society is a difficult task for today's managers.

Consumers

No organization will survive unless consumers purchase its products. Thus the major role of any company is to satisfy its customers. To do so, businesses must find out what consumers want and need, and then create products that will satisfy those wants and needs.

In attempting to satisfy customers, businesses must consider not only consumers' immediate needs but also their long-term desires. For example, although people want efficient, low-cost energy to power their homes and automobiles, they do not want energy generation to pollute the air and water, kill wildlife, or cause disease and birth defects in children. Consumers also expect nutritious food in large quantities at low prices and in convenient form, but they do not want food producers to injure or kill valued wildlife in the process. Thus, because dolphins were often killed in the process used to catch tuna, many consumers boycotted tuna products. Similarly, in response to public protest, several large cosmetics companies have stopped cosmetics testing that involves animals. Consumer protection organizations, like the one led by activist Ralph Nader, have been highly successful in getting businesses to halt activities deemed unethical or harmful to people and the environment. Recalls are often initiated when product safety becomes an issue. The Consumer Product Safety Commission (CPSC) has jurisdiction over 15,000 types of consumer products. The CPSC Web site lists recalls by company and product and chronologically, and allows consumers to report safety concerns. Businesses in general want to satisfy their customers and are usually willing to make requested changes in order to appease concerned consumers and avoid losses from boycotts and negative publicity. However, some companies are not willing to do this. Japan's Mitsubishi Electric knew of problems with two of its large-screen color television models for eight years before initiating a recall. The models, marketed only in Japan, could overheat and catch fire.[56] Such negative publicity can hurt not only short-term sales but also long-term customer loyalty.

@.ethics 4

In the last several years, however, some environmental dilemmas have demonstrated the tenuous nature of ethics in business. For example, should acres of forest land be preserved to save the rare spotted owl from extinction? If so, then families in such small towns as Port Angeles and Forks, Washington, would lose their jobs and whole communities might disappear. Suicides, alcohol abuse, and spouse and child abuse might increase. As one picture drawn by a 7-year-old sums up the issue, "An owl needs 2,000 acres to live, why can't I have room to live?"[57] Similar problems exist in relation to other endangered species, such as the sea lion, elk, grizzly bear, and mountain goat.

Marketing

Marketing and consumers are in the same segment of Figure 2–5 because all marketing activities focus on consumer satisfaction. Marketing refers to activities designed to provide consumers with satisfying goods and services. Marketers first gather information and conduct marketing research to find out what consumers want. Then they develop products, price the products, promote them, and distribute them where and when consumers want to buy them. Ethical issues may arise in relation to the safety of products, the advertising and selling of products, pricing, or distribution channels that direct the flow of products from the manufacturer to the consumer. For example, the Coca-Cola Company began talks with Mexican antitrust officials to try to avoid a legal battle over its sales and marketing practices in its biggest market outside the United States. Mexican authorities had been investigating allegations that Coke had abused its position in the carbonated soft drink market to shut out or reduce the presence of competitors.[58]

Some companies take the supply–demand concept to extremes. For example, the pharmaceutical industry is increasingly under attack for rising drug costs. A study by Families USA, a health care advocacy group, found that the average cost of the fifty drugs most used by the elderly rose almost 4 percent in one year, although the inflation rate was only 2.2 percent. Prices of some of the medications had jumped as much as 10 percent. Drug companies are also being criticized outside the United States for the high cost of drugs to treat AIDS and other deadly diseases in developing countries.[59]

Accounting

The field of accounting has changed dramatically over the last decade. The profession used to have a club-type mentality: those who became certified public accountants (CPAs) were not concerned about competition. Now CPAs advertise their skills or short-term results in an environment in which competition has increased and overall billable hours have significantly decreased because of technological innovations. Pressures on accountants include the following: time, reduced fees, client requests for altered opinions concerning financial conditions or for lower tax payments, and increased competition. Because of such pressures, and the ethical predicaments they spawn, some accounting firms have had financial problems.

Other issues that accountants face daily involve complex rules and regulations that must be followed, data overload, contingent fees, and commissions. An accountant's life is filled with rules and data that have to be interpreted correctly. As a result, accountants must abide by a strict code of ethics, which defines their responsibilities to their clients and the public interest. The code also discusses the concepts of integrity, objectivity, independence, and due care. Finally, the code delineates an accountant's scope and the nature of services that ethically should be provided. In this last portion of the code, contingent fees and commissions are indirectly addressed. Since the code provides them with standards, it would be reasonable to assume that accountants have a fairly clear understanding of ethical and unethical practices, but apparently that is not the case. Five former officers of publicly traded companies were indicted for alleged fraud involving accounting practices that distorted inventory figures. The defendants were accused of making their corporations appear more profitable than they were. The indictment charged the executives with conspiracy, loan fraud, wire fraud, falsifying corporate books, and lying to the auditors of a publicly traded company.[60] Different types of ethical issues exist for different types of accountants, such as auditing, tax, and management accountants.

RECOGNIZING AN ETHICAL ISSUE

Although we have described a number of relationships and situations that may generate ethical issues, it can be difficult to recognize specific ethical issues in practice. Failure to acknowledge ethical issues is a great danger in any organization, particularly if business is treated as a game in which ordinary rules of fairness do not apply. Sometimes people who take this view do things that are not only unethical but also illegal in order to maximize their own position or boost the profits or goals of the organization.

One way to determine whether a specific behavior or situation has an ethical component is to ask other individuals in the business how they feel about it and whether they approve. Another way is to determine whether the organization has adopted specific policies on the activity. An activity approved of by most members of an organization, if it is also customary in the industry, is probably ethical. An issue, activity, or situation that can withstand open discussion between many groups, both in and outside the organization, and survive untarnished probably does not pose ethical problems. For instance, when engineers and designers at Ford Motor Co. discussed what type of gas-tank protection should be used in its Pinto automobile, they reached consensus within the organization, but they did not take into account the public's desire for maximum safety. Consequently, even though they might have believed the issue had no ethical dimension, Ford erred in not opening up the issue to public scrutiny. (As it turned out, the type of gas-tank protection in the Pinto resulted in several fires and deaths when the cars were involved in rear-end collisions.)

Once an individual recognizes that an ethical issue exists and can openly discuss it with others, he or she has begun the ethical decision-making process, which is discussed in Chapter 5. When people believe that they cannot discuss what they are doing with peers or superiors, there is a good chance that an ethical issue exists.

In this chapter we have attempted to heighten your awareness of some ethical issues that may develop in a business organization. We have not tried to define whether certain actions are ethical or unethical, but only to show that they are issues worthy of moral discussion and evaluation. Just because an unsettled situation or activity is an ethical issue, the behavior is not necessarily unethical. An ethical issue is simply a situation, a problem, or even an opportunity that requires thought, discussion, or investigation to determine the moral impact of the decision. Because the business world is dynamic, new ethical issues are emerging all the time. In the next chapter, we define and explore various moral philosophies that individuals use to evaluate activities as ethical or unethical and to resolve ethical dilemmas.

SUMMARY

An ethical issue is a problem, situation, or opportunity requiring an individual or organization to choose among several actions that must be evaluated as right or wrong, ethical or unethical. Ethical issues typically arise because of conflicts between individuals' personal moral philosophies and values and the values and attitudes of the organizations in which they work and the society in which they live.

Researchers have found that ethical conflicts arise most often in business relationships with customers, suppliers, employees, and others, and as a result of certain business practices, such as the giving of gifts and kickbacks and pricing discrimination. Business executives and academics acknowledge that these are ethical issues and that they would like to eliminate many unethical practices.

Ethical issues can be classified into four categories: issues of conflict of interest, issues of fairness and honesty, issues of communications, and issues related to technology. A conflict of interest exists when an individual must choose between advancing his or her own personal interests and those of the organization or some other group. Honesty refers to truthfulness, integrity, and trustworthiness; fairness is the quality of being just, equitable, and impartial. Issues related to fairness and honesty often arise in business because many participants believe that business is a game governed by its own rules rather than those of society. Communication refers to the transmission of information and the sharing of meaning. False and misleading communications can destroy customers' trust in an organization. Ethical issues related to technology have increased as advances in technology have been made.

Ethical issues can also be explored in terms of the major participants and functions of business. Ethical issues related to ownership include conflicts between managers' duties to the owners and their own interests, and the separation of ownership and control of the business. Financial ethical issues include questions of socially responsible investment and the accuracy of reported financial documents. Employees face ethical issues when they are asked to carry out assignments they consider unethical. Managers directly influence the ethical issues that evolve within an organization because they guide and motivate employees. Ethical issues related to consumers and marketing include providing a selection of safe, reliable, high-quality products at reasonable prices without harming the customers or the environment. Accountants are also within the realm of business ethics and face such pressures as competition, advertising, and a shrinking environment. Issues such as data overload, contingent fees, and commissions all place the accounting profession in situations of ethical risk.

A good rule of thumb is that an activity approved of by most members of an organization and customary in the industry is probably ethical. An issue, activity, or situation that can withstand open discussion and survive untarnished probably poses no ethical problem. Once an individual recognizes that an ethical issue exists and can openly discuss it and ask for guidance and the opinions of others, he or she enters the ethical decision-making process.

Important Terms for Review	ethical issue conflict of interest honesty fairness	communication technology Ponzi scheme

A Real-Life Situation*

Joseph Freberg had been with Alcon for eighteen months. He had begun his career right out of college with a firm in the Southeast called Cala Industrial, which specialized in air compressors. Because of his work with Cala, he had been lured away to Alcon, in Omaha, as a sales manager. Joseph's first six months had been hard. Working with salespeople older than he, trying to get a handle on his people's sales territories, and settling into the corporate culture of a new firm took sixteen-hour days, six days a week. During those six months he also bought a house, and his fiancée furnished it. Ellen had stepped right in and decided almost everything, from the color of the rugs to the style of the curtains.

Ellen had taken a brokerage job with Trout Brothers and seemed to be working even more hours than Joseph. But the long days were paying off. Ellen was now starting to handle some large accounts and was being noticed by the "right" crowd in the wealthier Omaha areas.

Costs for the new home had exceeded their anticipated spending limit, and the plans for their wedding seemed to be getting larger and larger. In addition, Ellen was commuting from her apartment to the new home and then to her job, and the commute killed her car. As a result, she decided to lease something that exuded success. "Ellen, don't you think a Mercedes is a little out of our range? What are the payments?" inquired Joseph. "Don't worry. When my clients see me in this — as well as when we start entertaining at the new house once we're married — the payments on the car will seem small compared with the money I'll be making," Ellen mused as she ran her fingers through Joseph's hair and gave him a peck on the cheek. By the time of the wedding and honeymoon, Joseph and Ellen's bank statement looked like a bull-fighter's cape — red. "Don't worry, Joseph, everything will turn out okay. You've got a good job. I've got a good job. We're young and have drive. Things will straighten out after a while," said Ellen as she eyed a Rolex in a store window.

After the wedding, things did settle down — to a hectic pace, given their two careers and their two sets of parents two thousand miles in either direction. Joseph had realized that Alcon was a paternal type of organization, with good benefits and tremendous growth potential. He had identified who to be friends with and who to stay away from in the company. His salespeople seemed to tolerate him, sometimes calling him "Little Joe" or "Joey" because of his age, and his salespeople were producing — slowly climbing up the sales ladder to the number-one spot in the company.

While doing some regular checkup work on sales personnel, Joseph found out that Carl had been giving kickbacks to some of his buyers. Carl's sales volume accounted for a substantial amount of the company's existing clientele sales, and he had been a trainer for the company for several years. Carl also happened to be the vice president's son-in-law. Joseph started to check on the other reps more closely and discovered that, although Carl seemed to be the biggest offender, three of his ten people were doing the same thing. The next day Joseph looked up Alcon's policy handbook and found this statement: "Our company stands for doing the right thing at all times and giving our customers the best product for the best prices." There was no specific mention of kickbacks, but everyone knew that kickbacks ultimately reduce fair competition, which eventually leads to reduced quality and increased prices for customers. By talking to a few of the old-timers at Alcon, Joseph learned that there had been sporadic enforcement of the "no kickback" policy. It seemed that when times were good it became unacceptable and when times were bad it slipped into the acceptable range. And then there was his boss, Kathryn, the vice president. Joseph knew that Kathryn had a tendency to shoot the bearer of bad news. He remembered a story he had heard about a sales manager coming in to see Kathryn to explain an error in a bid that one of his salespeople had made. Kathryn called in the entire sales staff and fired the salesman on the spot. Then, smiling, she told the sales manager: "This was your second mistake, so I hope that you can get a good recommendation from personnel. You have two weeks to find employment elsewhere." From then on, the office staff had a nickname for Kathryn — Jaws.

Trying to solve the problem he was facing, Joseph, at his monthly meeting with Carl, broached the subject of kickbacks. Carl responded, "You've been in this business long enough to know that this happens all the time. I see nothing wrong with this practice if it increases sales. Besides, I take the money out of my commission. You know that right now I'm trying to pay off some big medical bills. I've also gotten tacit clearance from above, but I wouldn't mention that if I were you." Joseph knew that the chain-of-command structure in the company made it very dangerous to go directly to a vice president with this type of information.

As Joseph was pondering whether to do nothing, bring the matter into the open and state that it was wrong and that such practices were against policy, or talk to Kathryn about the situation, his cell phone rang. It was Ellen. "Honey, guess what just happened. Kathryn, your boss, has decided to use me as her new broker. Isn't that fantastic!"

What should Joseph do?

Questions ■ Exercises

1. What are Joseph's ethical problems?
2. Assume you are Joseph and discuss your options.
3. What other information do you feel you need before making your decision?
4. Discuss which business areas the ethical problems are in.

* This case is strictly hypothetical; any resemblance to real persons, companies, or situations is coincidental.

CHECK YOUR E*Q*

Check your E.Q., or Ethics Quotient, by completing the following. Assess your performance to evaluate your overall understanding of the chapter material.

1. The principal causes of unethical behavior in an organization are individuals striving to advance their own personal goals.   Yes   No

2. Key ethical issues in an organization relate to conflicts of interest, honesty and fairness, communications, and technology.   Yes   No

3. The three key organizational stakeholders are owners, suppliers, and employees.   Yes   No

4. Investing in socially responsible companies and funds has grown in recent years.   Yes   No

5. If an activity is approved by most members of an organization and it's also customary in the industry, it is probably ethical.   Yes   No

---

ANSWERS   1. No. The principal causes of unethical behavior in an organization are organizational pressures, directives, and objectives.   **2. Yes.** See pages 30–38 regarding these key ethical issues and their implications for the organization.   **3. No.** The three key stakeholders are owners, employees, and customers.   **4. Yes.** Socially responsible investing has increased in recent years, and society has increased its expectations of ethical conduct on the part of businesses, as well as its scrutiny of business practices.   **5. Yes.** An activity that is generally regarded as ethical and survives open discussion inside and outside the organization is usually acceptable.

Applying Moral Philosophies to Business Ethics

CHAPTER 3

Chapter Objectives

- To understand how the concept of moral philosophies applies to individual and group ethical decision making in business
- To compare and contrast moral philosophies used in business
- To examine teleology, deontology, and the relativist perspectives
- To consider virtue ethics as a philosophy for understanding business ethics
- To discuss the impact of philosophies of justice on business ethics

Chapter Outline

An Ethical Dilemma*

One of the problems Lael Matthews has had to deal with in trying to climb the corporate ladder is the glass ceiling issue for minorities and women. In her current position, she must decide which of three managers to promote. Her superior has informed her that making the wrong decision would not be good, either internally or externally. These are the candidates:

Liz (African-American, 34, divorced, one child) graduated in the lower half of her college class (Northwest State). She has been with the company for four years and in the industry for eight years, with mediocre performance ratings but a high energy level. She has had some difficulties in managing her staff. Her child has had medical problems, and so higher pay would be helpful. If promoted, Liz would be the first African-American female manager at this level. Lael has known Liz only a short time, but they seem to have hit it off. In fact, Lael once baby-sat Liz's daughter, Janeen, in an emergency. The downside to promoting Liz, though, might be a perception Lael is playing favorites.

Roy (white, 57, married, three children) graduated from a private university in the top half of his class. Roy has been with the company for twenty years and in the industry for thirty. He has always been a steady performer, with mostly average ratings. The reason Roy has been passed over before was his refusal to relocate, but that is no longer a problem. Roy's energy level is average to low; however, he has produced many of the company's top sales performers in the past. This promotion would be his last before retirement, and many in the company feel he has earned it. In fact, one senior manager stopped Lael in the hall and said, "You know, Lael, Roy has been with us for a long time. He has done many good things for the company, sacrificing not only himself but also his family. I really hope that you can see your way to promoting him. It would be a favor to me that I wouldn't forget."

Quang Yeh (female, Asian, 27, single) graduated from State University in the top 3 percent of her class and has been with the company for three years. She is known for putting in sixty-hour weeks and for her very meticulous management style, which has generated some criticism from her sales staff. The last area she had managed showed record increases, despite the loss of some older accounts that for some reason did not like dealing with Quang. One fact about Quang is that at her previous place of work she sued the company for discrimination and won. A comment that Lael had heard from that company was that Quang was intense and that nothing would stop her from reaching her goals. As Lael was going over some of her notes, another upper-management individual came to her office and said, "You know, Lael, Quang is engaged to my son. I've looked over her personnel files and she looks very good. She looks like a rising star, which would indicate that she should be promoted as quickly as possible. I realize that you're not in my division, but the way people get transferred, you never know. I would really like to see Quang get this promotion."

Finally, Lael's immediate supervisor came to her to talk about Liz. "You know, Lael, Liz is one of a very few people at the company who is an African-American female who is qualified for this position. I've been going over the company's hiring and promotion figures, and it would be very advantageous for me personally and for the company to promote her. I've also spoken to public relations, and they believe that this would be a tremendous boost for the company."

As Lael pondered her decision, she mentally went through each candidate's records and found that each had advantages and disadvantages. While she was considering her problem, the phone rang. "Lael, I'm sorry to disturb you at this late hour but I need you to come to the hospital. Janeen [Liz's daughter] has been in an accident, and I don't know who to turn to. Can you come?" was Liz's frantic question. "Yes, I'm on my way," Lael responded. When Lael got to the hospital, she found that Janeen's injuries were fairly serious and that Liz would have to miss some work to help with the recuperation process. Lael also realized that this accident would create a financial problem for Liz, which a promotion could help solve.

The next day seemed very long and was punctuated by the announcement that Roy's son was getting married to the vice president's daughter. The wedding would be in June, and it sounded as though it would be a company affair. By 4:30 that afternoon Lael had gone through four aspirins and two antacids. Her decision was due in two days.

What should she do?

Questions ■ Exercises

1. Discuss the advantages and disadvantages of each candidate.
2. What are the ethical and legal considerations for Lael?
3. Identify the pressures that have caused this to be an ethical and legal issue.
4. Discuss the implications of each decision Lael could make.

This case is strictly hypothetical; any resemblance to real persons, companies, or situations is coincidental.

oral philosophies have to do with ideas of right and wrong. They help explain why a person believes that one action is right whereas another is wrong; they are often cited to justify decisions or explain actions. Therefore, to understand how people make ethical decisions, it is useful to have a grasp of the major types of moral philosophies.

In this chapter we explore several aspects of moral philosophy. First we define moral philosophy and discuss how it applies to business. Next we describe two broad classifications of moral philosophy: teleology and deontology. Then we consider the relativist perspective from which many ethical or unethical decisions are made in everyday life. We discuss what is called virtue ethics and how it can be applied to today's multinational business environment. And the final section relates to evaluations of justice.

MORAL PHILOSOPHY DEFINED

When people talk about philosophy, they usually mean the system of values by which they live. **Moral philosophy** refers in particular to the principles or rules that people use to decide what is right or wrong. For example, a production manager may be guided by a general philosophy of management that emphasizes encouraging workers to know as much as possible about the product they are manufacturing. Moral philosophy comes into play when the manager must make decisions such as whether to notify employees in advance of upcoming layoffs. Although workers would prefer advance warning, its side effects might adversely affect production quality and quantity. Such decisions require a person to evaluate the "rightness," or morality, of choices in terms of his or her own principles and values.

Moral philosophies present guidelines for "determining how conflicts in human interests are to be settled and for optimizing mutual benefit of people living together in groups."[1] Moral philosophies guide businesspersons as they formulate business strategies and resolve specific ethical issues. However, there is no single moral philosophy that everyone accepts. Some managers view profit as the ultimate goal of an enterprise and therefore may not be concerned about their firm's impact on society. The emergence of capitalism as the dominant and most widely accepted economic system has created a commercial society. There is evidence that economic systems not only bring about arrangements for the allocation of goods and resources, but also affect relationships in the work force. Consequently, the success of an economic system depends both on its philosophical framework and on the presence of individuals who maintain moral philosophies that bring people together in a cooperative, efficient, and productive marketplace. There is a long Western tradition, going back to Aristotle, of questioning whether a market economy and individual moral behavior are compatible. In reality, individuals in today's society exist within the framework of social, political, and economic institutions.

Moral philosophies are ideal moral perspectives that provide abstract principles to guide an individual's social existence. For example, decisions to recycle waste or purchase or sell recycled or recyclable products are influenced by moral philosophies and attitudes toward recycling.[2] Thus the attempt to implement an individual moral philosophy within the complex environment of a business organization is often difficult. On the other hand, the functioning of our economic system depends on individuals coming together and sharing philosophies that create moral values, trust, and expectations that allow the system to work. Most employees within a business organization do not think about what particular moral philosophy they are using when confronted with an ethical issue. Individuals learn decision-making approaches or philosophies through cultural and social development. There is strong evidence that individuals switch moral philosophies depending on whether they are making a personal decision outside the work environment or making a decision on the job.[3] In examining moral philosophies, we must remember that each philosophy states an ideal perspective and that most individuals seem to adapt a number of moral philosophies as they interpret ethical dilemmas. In other words, implementing moral philosophies from an individual perspective is not an exact science. It requires individuals to take their own accepted value system and attempt to apply their philosophy in a real-world situation. Individuals make judgments about what they believe to be right or wrong. From a business perspective, though, individuals make decisions related to actions that may be based on producing the greatest benefits with the least harm. Such decisions should respect fundamental moral rights, as well as perspectives about fairness, justice, and the common good.

The virtue approach to business ethics, as discussed in this chapter, assumes that there are certain ideals and values that everyone should strive to attain in order to achieve the maximum welfare and happiness for society.[4] Various aspects of these values are expressed through specific moral philosophies. Every day in the workplace, individuals must decide what is right or wrong and act accordingly. However, they cannot be part of a large organization and yet enforce their own personal perspective, especially if they hold a very narrow view of a single acceptable moral philosophy. Individuals are not free to make their own choices in a work environment. While they are always responsible for their own actions, they rarely have the power to impose their own personal moral perspective on others. Sometimes an established company makes decisions that could be questionable according to customers' and employees' values and moral philosophies. For example, AT&T Corp. now carries a hard-core adult movie channel through its cable unit. The significant profits that AT&T can make from sexually explicit movies may satisfy some stakeholders, but others may reject or question the company's actions.[5] A company's core values will determine how decisions that bring moral philosophies into conflict are made. Most business organizations have developed a mission statement, a corporate culture, and a set of core values linked to how the organization wants to relate to its stakeholders, including customers, employees, the legal system, and society.

Problems arise when employees encounter ethical situations they cannot resolve. Sometimes a better understanding of the basic premise of their decision rationale can help them choose the "right" solution. For instance, to decide whether they should offer bribes to customers in the hope of securing a large contract, salespeople need to understand their own personal moral philosophy as well as their firm's core values. If compliance with company policy or legal requirements is an important motivation, they are less likely to offer a bribe. On the other hand, if the salesperson's ultimate goal is a successful career and if offering a bribe seems likely to result in a promotion, then bribery might not be inconsistent with that person's moral philosophy of acceptable business behavior.

MORAL PHILOSOPHY PERSPECTIVES

There are many moral philosophies, and each one is complex. Because a detailed study of all moral philosophies would be beyond the scope of this book, we will limit our discussion to those that are most applicable to the study of business ethics. Our approach will focus on the most basic concepts needed to help you understand the ethical decision-making process in business. We will not prescribe the use of any particular moral philosophy, for there is no one "correct" way to resolve ethical issues in business.

To help you understand how the moral philosophies discussed in this chapter may be applied in decision making, we will use a hypothetical problem situation as an illustration. Suppose that Sam Colt, a sales representative, is preparing a sales presentation for his firm, Midwest Hardware, which manufactures nuts and bolts. Colt hopes to obtain a large sale from a construction firm that is building a bridge across the Mississippi River near St. Louis. The bolts manufactured by Midwest Hardware have a 3 percent defect rate, which, although acceptable in the in-

miliar. Although the company's actions benefit society in general, in the long run they also benefit IBM.

We now return to the hypothetical case of the salesperson who must decide whether to warn the bridge contractor that 3 percent of Midwest Hardware's bolts are likely to be defective. If Sam Colt is an egoist, he will probably choose the alternative that maximizes his own self-interest. If he defines self-interest as personal wealth, his personal moral philosophy may lead him to value a $25,000 commission more than a chance to reduce the risk of a bridge collapse. An egoist Colt, therefore, might well resolve his ethical dilemma by keeping quiet about the bolts' defect rate, hoping to win the sale and a $25,000 commission. He would rationalize that there is a slim chance of an earthquake and that bolts would not be a factor in a major earthquake. Besides, no one would know that defective bolts could cause the bridge to collapse.

Utilitarianism Like egoism, **utilitarianism** is concerned with consequences, but the utilitarian seeks the greatest good for the greatest number of people. Utilitarians believe they should make decisions that result in the greatest total *utility*, that is, achieve the greatest benefit for all those affected by a decision.

Utilitarian decision making relies on a systematic comparison of the costs and benefits to all affected parties. Using such a cost-benefit analysis, a utilitarian decision maker calculates the utility of the consequences of all possible alternatives and then selects the one that results in the greatest utility. For example, the Supreme Court has said that employers are responsible for the sexual misconduct of supervisors, even if the employers knew nothing about the behavior. Thus it has established a strict standard for harassment on the job.[7] Apparently, the Court has decided that the greatest utility and benefits to society will result from forcing businesses to prevent harassment. One of the Supreme Court justices indicated in the ruling that the employer's burden to prevent harassment is "one of the costs of doing business."[8]

In evaluating an action's consequences, many utilitarians consider the effects on animals as well as on human beings. This perspective is significant in the controversy surrounding animal research by cosmetics and pharmaceutical companies. Animal rights groups have protested that such testing is unethical because it harms and even kills the animals and deprives them of their rights. Researchers for pharmaceutical and cosmetics manufacturers, however, defend animal testing on utilitarian grounds. The consequences of the research (new or improved drugs to treat disease, safer cosmetics) create more benefit for society, they argue, than would be achieved by halting the research to preserve the animals' rights. Nonetheless, many cosmetics firms have responded to the controversy by agreeing to stop animal research.

Now suppose that Sam Colt, the bolt salesperson, is a utilitarian. Before making his decision, he would conduct a cost-benefit analysis to determine which alternative would create the most utility. On the one hand, building the bridge would improve roadways and allow more people to cross the Mississippi River to reach jobs in St. Louis. The project would create hundreds of jobs, enhance the local economy, and unite communities on both sides of the river. Additionally, it would increase the revenues of Midwest Hardware, allowing the firm to invest more in research to lower the defect rate of bolts produced in the future. On the other hand, a bridge collapse could kill or injure as many as one hundred people. But the bolts have only a 3 percent defect rate, and there is only a 50 percent probability of an earthquake *somewhere* along the fault line; there might be only a few cars on the bridge at the time of a disaster.

After analyzing the costs and benefits of the situation, Colt might conclude that building the bridge with his company's bolts would create more utility (jobs, unity, economic growth, company growth) than would result from telling the bridge contractor that the bolts might fail in an earthquake. If so, the utilitarian Colt would probably not call the bridge contractor's attention to the defect rate.

Utilitarians use various criteria to determine the morality of an action. Some utilitarian philosophers have argued that general rules should be followed to decide which action is best.[9] These "rule utilitarians" determine behavior on the basis of principles, or rules, designed to promote the greatest utility, rather than on an examination of each particular situation.

One such rule might be "bribery is wrong." If people felt free to offer bribes whenever they might be useful, the world would become chaotic; therefore, a rule prohibiting bribery would increase utility. A rule utilitarian would not bribe an official, even to preserve workers' jobs, but would adhere strictly to the rule. Rule utilitarians do not automatically accept conventional moral rules, however. If an alternative rule would promote greater utility, they would advocate changing the convention.

Other utilitarian philosophers have argued that the rightness of each individual action must be evaluated to determine whether it produces the greatest utility for the greatest number of people.[10] These "act utilitarians" examine the action itself, rather than the rules governing the action, to determine whether it will result in the greatest utility. Rules, such as "bribery is wrong," serve only as general guidelines to act utilitarians. They would agree that bribery is generally wrong, not because there is anything inherently wrong with bribery, but because the total amount of utility decreases when one person's interests are placed ahead of those of society.[11] In a particular case, however, an act utilitarian might argue that bribery is acceptable. For example, a sales manager might believe that her firm will not win a construction contract unless a local government official gets a bribe; moreover, if the firm does not obtain the contract, it will have to lay off one hundred workers. The manager might therefore argue that bribery is justified because saving a hundred jobs creates more utility than obeying a law.

Deontology

Deontology refers to moral philosophies that focus on the rights of individuals and on the intentions associated with a particular behavior rather than on its consequences. Fundamental to deontological theory is the idea that equal respect must be given to all persons. Unlike utilitarians, deontologists argue that there are some things that we should *not* do, even to maximize utility. For example, deontologists would consider it wrong to kill an innocent person or commit a serious injustice against a person, no matter how much utility might result from doing so, because such an action would infringe on that person's rights as an individual. The utilitarian, however, might consider as acceptable an action that resulted in a person's death if that action created some greater utility.

Deontological philosophies regard certain behaviors as inherently right, and the determination of rightness focuses on the individual actor, not society. Thus these perspectives are sometimes referred to as **nonconsequentialism, ethical formalism,** and the ethics of *respect for persons.*

Contemporary deontology has been greatly influenced by the German philosopher Immanuel Kant, who developed the so-called categorical imperative: "Act as if the maxim of thy action were to become by thy will a universal law of nature."[12] Simply put, if you feel comfortable allowing everyone in the world to see you commit an act and if your rationale for acting in a particular manner is suitable to become a universal principle guiding behavior, then committing that act is ethical. For example, if a person borrows money, promising to return it but with no intention of keeping that promise, he or she cannot "universalize" borrowing money without any intention of returning it. If everyone were to borrow money without the intention of returning it, no one would take such promises seriously.[13] Therefore, the rationale for the action would not be a suitable universal principle, and the act cannot be considered ethical.

The term *nature* is crucial for deontologists. In general, deontologists regard the nature of moral principles as permanent and stable, and they believe that compliance with these principles defines ethicalness. Deontologists believe that individuals have certain absolute rights:

- Freedom of conscience
- Freedom of consent
- Freedom of privacy
- Freedom of speech
- Due process[14]

To determine whether a behavior is ethical, deontologists look for conformity to moral principles. For example, if a manufacturing worker becomes ill or dies as a result of conditions in the workplace, a deontologist might say that the methods of production must be corrected, no matter what the cost — even if it means bankrupting the company and thus causing all workers to lose their jobs. In contrast, a utilitarian would analyze all the costs and benefits of changing production processes and decide on that basis. This example is greatly oversimplified, of course, but it helps clarify the difference between teleology and deontology. In short, teleological philosophies consider the *ends* associated with an action whereas deontological philosophies consider the *means.*

Returning again to the bolt salesman, let us consider a deontological Sam Colt. He would probably feel obliged to tell the bridge contractor about the defect rate because of the potential loss of life resulting from an earthquake-caused bridge collapse. Even though constructing the bridge would benefit residents and earn the salesman a substantial commission, the failure of the bolts in an earthquake would infringe on the rights of any person crossing the bridge at the time of the collapse. Thus the deontological Colt would probably inform the bridge contractor of the defect rate and point out the earthquake risk, even though doing so could mean the probable loss of the sale.

As with utilitarianism, deontologists may be divided into those who focus on moral rules and those who focus on the nature of the acts themselves.

So-called rule deontologists believe that conformity to general moral principles determines ethicalness. Deontological philosophies use reason and logic to formulate rules for behavior. Examples include Kant's categorical imperative and the Golden Rule of Judeo-Christian tradition: Do unto others as you would have them do unto you. Such rules, or principles, guiding ethical behavior override the imperatives emerging from a specific context. The basic rights of the individual, coupled with rules of conduct, constitute rule deontology. For example, a video store owner accused of distributing obscene materials could argue from a rule deontological perspective that the basic right to freedom of speech overrides other aspects of the situation. Indeed, the free speech argument has held up in many courts.

"Act deontologists," in contrast, hold that actions are the proper basis on which to judge morality or ethicalness. Act deontology requires that a person use equity, fairness, and impartiality in making and enforcing decisions.[15] For act deontologists, as for act utilitarians, rules serve only as guidelines, with past experiences being weighted more heavily than rules within the decision-making process. In effect, act deontologists suggest that people simply *know* that certain acts are right or wrong, regardless of the consequences or any appeal to deontological rules. In addition, act deontologists regard the particular act or moment in time as taking precedence over any rule. For example, many people view data collection by Internet sites as a violation of personal privacy. Regardless of stated rules or policies, many Internet users want to be left alone unless they provide permission to be tracked while on-line.[16]

As we have seen, ethical issues can be evaluated from many different perspectives. Each type of philosophy discussed here would have a distinct basis for deciding whether a particular action is right or wrong. Adherents of different personal moral philosophies may disagree in their evaluations of a given action, yet all are behaving ethically, *by their own standards*. All would agree that there is no one "right" way to make ethical decisions and no best moral philosophy except their own. The relativist perspective may be helpful in understanding how people make such decisions in practice.

The Relativist Perspective

From the **relativist perspective,** definitions of ethical behavior are derived subjectively from the experiences of individuals and groups. Relativists use themselves or the people around them as their basis for defining ethical standards.

The relativist observes the actions of members of some relevant group and attempts to determine the group consensus on a given behavior. A positive consensus signifies that the action is considered right or ethical. Such judgments may not remain valid forever. As circumstances evolve or the makeup of the group changes, a formerly accepted behavior may come to be viewed as wrong or unethical. Within the accounting profession, for example, it was traditionally considered unethical to advertise. However, as discussed in Chapter 2, advertising has been gaining acceptance among accountants. This shift in ethical views may have come about by the steady increase in the number of accountants, which has resulted in greater competition. In addition, the federal government has investigated the restrictions accounting groups have placed on their members and has concluded that the restrictions inhibited free competition. Consequently, an informal consensus has emerged in the accounting industry that advertising is now acceptable.

In the case of the Midwest Hardware salesperson, a relativist would attempt to determine the group consensus before deciding whether to tell his prospective customer about the bolts' defect rate. To do so, Sam Colt would look at both his own company's policy and general industry practice. He might also informally survey his colleagues and his superiors and consult industry trade journals and codes of ethics. Such investigations would help him determine the group consensus, which should reflect a variety of moral philosophies. If Colt learns that general company policy, as well as industry practice, is to discuss defect rates with those customers for whom faulty bolts may cause serious problems, Colt may infer that there is a consensus on the matter. As a relativist, he would probably then inform the bridge contractor that some of the bolts may fail, perhaps leading to a bridge collapse in the event of an earthquake. Conversely, if Colt determines that the normal practice in his company and the industry is to not inform customers about defect rates, he would probably not raise the subject with the bridge contractor.

Relativism acknowledges that we live in a society in which people have many different views and many different bases from which to justify decisions as right or wrong. The relativist looks to the interacting group and tries to determine probable solutions based on group consensus. When formulating business strategies and plans, for example, a relativist would try to anticipate the conflicts that will arise between the different philosophies held by members of the organization, its suppliers, its customers, and the community at large.

Virtue Ethics

A moral virtue represents an acquired disposition that is valued as a part of an individual's character. As an individual develops socially, he or she may become disposed to behave habitually in the same way and with reasons, feelings, and desires that are characteristic of what may be considered a morally concerned person.[17] A person who has a character trait of being honest will be disposed to tell the truth because it is considered to be right and comfortable. This individual will try to always tell the truth because of its importance in human communication.

A virtue is considered praiseworthy because it is an achievement that an individual develops through practice and commitment.[18]

This philosophy, termed **virtue ethics,** posits that what is moral in a given situation is not only what conventional morality or moral rules (current societal definitions), however justified, require, but also what the mature person with a "good" moral character would deem appropriate. Virtue ethics assumes that what current societal moral rules require may indeed be the moral minimum for the beginning of virtue. Many who believe in virtue ethics assume a series of transcendental constants that permeate the moral equation. These constants are defined as timeless, without cultural specificity. Furthermore, virtue can be enhanced by belief, knowledge, and subsequent behavior.

The viability of our political, social, and economic systems depends on the presence of certain virtues among the citizenry that are vital for the proper functioning of a market economy.[19] Indeed, virtue theory could be thought of as a dynamic theory of how to conduct business activities. Which virtues to pursue would depend on the employee's position in the organization as well as the type of organization. Specific virtues, such as truthfulness, provide sensitivity to circumstances and opportunities as well as clarity of purpose.[20]

There is a belief that to have a successful market economy, society must be capable of carving out sanctuaries, such as family, school, church, and community, where virtues can be nurtured. These virtues can play a role in the functioning of an individualistic, contractual economy. Virtues such as truth, trust, tolerance, and restraint create obligations that make social cooperation possible. The operation of a market economy based on virtues provides a traditional existence where individuals in the economic system have powerful inducements to conform to prevailing standards of behavior. While some philosophers think that virtues may be weakened by the operation of the market, it is felt that institutions and society must maintain a balance and constantly add to its stock of virtues.[21] Some of the virtues that could lubricate a market economy are listed in Table 3–2. The list is not comprehensive, but it provides examples of the types of virtues that support the business environment.

The elements of virtue important to business transactions have been defined as trust, self-control, empathy, fairness, and truthfulness. Attributes in contrast to virtue would include lying, cheating, fraud, and corruption. In their broadest sense, these terms appear to be accepted within all cultures. The problem of virtue ethics comes in its implementation within and between cultures. Those who practice virtue ethics go beyond societal norms. For example, if an organization tacitly approves of corruption, the employee who adheres to the virtues of trust and truthfulness would consider it wrong to sell unneeded repair parts despite the organization's approval of doing so. Some may call such people highly ethical and, in order to rationalize their own behavior, judge such ethics as going beyond what is required by their job or society. They may argue that virtue is an unattainable goal and thus one should not be obliged to live up to its standards. To those who espouse virtue ethics, this argument is meaningless, for they believe in the universal reality of the elements of virtue.

TABLE 3–2 Virtues That Support Business Transactions	
Trust	The predisposition to place confidence in the behavior of others while taking the risk that the expected behavior will not be performed. Trust prevents activities that monitor compliance with agreements, contracts, and reciprocal agreements and saves costs associated with them. There is the expectation that a promise or agreement can be relied on.
Self-control	The disposition to pass up an immediate advantage or gratification. It indicates the ability to avoid exploiting a known opportunity for self-interest. The tradeoff is between short-term self-interest and long-term benefits.
Empathy	The ability to share the feelings or emotions of others. It promotes civility because success in the market depends on the courteous treatment of people who have the option of other competitors. The ability to anticipate needs and satisfy customers and employees contributes to a firm's economic success.
Fairness	The disposition based on a desire to deal with the perceived injustices of others. Fairness often relates to doing the right thing with respect to small matters to cultivate a long-term business relationship.
Truthfulness	The disposition to provide the facts or correct information as known to the individual. Telling the truth involves avoiding deception and contributes to trust in business relationships.

Source: Adapted from Ian Maitland, "Virtuous Markets: The Market as School of the Virtues," Business Ethics Quarterly, *January 1997, p. 97.*

In the case of Sam Colt, he would probably consider the elements of virtue and tell the prospective customer about the defect rate and about his concerns regarding the bridge and the risk of injury, death, and destruction. He would use no puffery in explaining the product or its risks and, indeed, might suggest alternative products or companies that would lower the probability of the bridge collapsing.

Justice

Justice evaluations in business ethics relate to evaluations of fairness, or the disposition to deal with perceived injustices of others. Justice is fair treatment and due reward in accordance with ethical or legal standards. In business this means that the decision rules used by an individual to determine justice could be based on the perceived rights of individuals and on the intentions associated with a business interaction. Therefore, justice is more likely to be based on deontological moral philosophies than on teleology or utilitarianism. Justice deals more with the issue of what individuals feel they are due based on their rights and performance in the workplace. For example, the U.S. Equal Employment Opportunity Commission exists to help employees who suspect the injustice of discrimination in the workplace. Employees who feel they are suffering injustices can find the correct governmental agency for information about their rights at the National Labor Review Board web site.

Three types of justice provide a framework for evaluating fairness in different situations (see Table 3–3). **Distributive justice** is based on the evaluation of outcomes or results of the business relationship. If some employees feel that they are paid less than their coworkers for the same work, they have concerns about distributive justice. **Procedural justice** is based on the processes and activities that produce the outcome or results. Procedural justice concerns about compensation would relate to the perception that the processes were inconsistent. Evaluations of performance that are not consistently developed and applied can lead to problems with procedural justice. Procedural justice examined from an organizational perspective has been associated with helping behaviors. A procedural justice climate is expected to positively influence workplace attitudes and behaviors related to work-group cohesion.[22] **Interactional justice** is based on an evaluation of the communication processes used in the business relationship.

Distributive justice is difficult to develop when one member of the business exchange intends to take advantage of the relationship. For example, General Electric Capital Corporation and its wholly owned subsidiary, Montgomery Ward Credit Corporation, agreed to make $60 million in restitution payments to customers for inducing them to pay debts they did not legally owe.[23] In this case the outcome resulted from the manipulation of customers in the companies' debt collection activities. This example demonstrates that business often has to make restitution when society determines that the outcome involved an inequity in rewards or benefits.

Procedural justice results from an evaluation of the processes or activities used in the operations to obtain the outcomes. Supervisor visibility and work-group perceptions of cohesion are associated with procedural justice.[24] General Electric Capital Corporation used collection tactics that did not provide openness and ac-

TABLE 3–3   Types of Justice

Justice Type	Evaluations of Fairness
Distributive justice: based on the evaluation of outcomes or results of the business relationship	Benefits derived Equity in rewards
Procedural justice: based on the processes and activities that produce the outcome or results	Decision-making process Level of access, openness, and participation
Interactional justice: based on an evaluation of the communication process used in the business relationship	Accuracy of information Truthfulness, respect, and courtesy in the in process

cess to participation in decision making.[25] On the other hand, Wainwright Bank and Trust Corporation in Boston has made a commitment to promote justice to "all its stakeholders" with a "sense of inclusion and diversity that extends from the boardroom to the mail room."[26] This example illustrates that procedural justice seeks to establish relationships by providing understanding and inclusion in the decision-making process.

Interactional justice is linked to fairness in communication and often entails the individual's relationship with the business organization based on the accuracy of information. In the General Electric Capital Corporation case, consumers were told that the company had filed agreements with bankruptcy courts when in fact it had not done so. Thus consumers received false information about the debt collection process.[27] Employees can also be guilty in interactional justice disputes. For example, workplace absenteeism costs businesses millions of dollars each year. Many employees admit that they stay home when they are not really sick if they feel they can "get away with it." Being untruthful about the reasons for missing work is an example of an interactional justice issue.

As the example of General Electric Capital Corporation shows, all three types of justice could be used to evaluate a single business situation and the fairness of the organization involved. In the example of Sam Colt, Colt's response to implementing a justice perspective would be identical to using a deontological moral philosophy. He would feel obligated to tell all affected parties about the bolt defect rate and the possible consequences. In general, justice evaluations result in restitution seeking, relationship building, and the gauging of fairness in the business relationship.

SUMMARY

Moral philosophy refers to the set of principles or rules that people use to decide what is right or wrong. In a business context, managers often must evaluate the "rightness," or morality, of alternative actions in terms of their own principles and values. Moral philosophies present guidelines for resolving conflicts and for optimizing the mutual benefit of people living in groups. Businesspeople are guided by moral philosophies as they formulate business strategies and resolve specific ethical issues, but they do not all use the same moral philosophy.

Teleological philosophies stipulate that acts are morally right or acceptable if they produce some desired consequence, such as realization of self-interest or utility. Egoism defines right or acceptable behavior in terms of the consequences for the individual. In an ethical decision-making situation, an egoist will choose the alternative whose consequences contribute most to his or her own self-interest. Utilitarianism is concerned with maximizing total utility, or providing the greatest benefit for the greatest number of people. In making ethical decisions, utilitarians often conduct a cost-benefit analysis, which considers the costs and benefits to all affected parties. Rule utilitarians determine behavior on the basis of rules designed to promote the greatest utility rather than by examining particular situations. Act utilitarians examine the action itself, rather than the rules governing the action, to determine whether it will result in the greatest utility.

Deontological philosophies focus on the rights of individuals and on the intentions associated with a particular behavior rather than on its consequences. In general, deontologists regard the nature of moral principles as permanent and stable, and they believe that compliance with these principles defines ethicalness. Deontologists believe that individuals have certain absolute rights, which must be respected. Rule deontologists believe that conformity to general moral principles determines ethicalness. Act deontologists hold that actions are the proper basis on which to judge morality or ethicalness and that rules serve only as guidelines.

According to the relativist perspective, definitions of ethical behavior are derived subjectively from the experiences of individuals and groups. Consequently, relativists define ethical standards using themselves or the people around them as their base. The relativist observes behavior within a relevant group and attempts to determine what consensus has been reached on the issue in question.

Virtue ethics views every situation and defines alternatives according to a set of constants that do not change in response to dynamic cultural norms, rules, or other people. Those who profess virtue ethics do not believe that the end justifies the means in any situation. Although they may consider cultural norms or rules to be the beginning of virtue, they are convinced that virtue can grow beyond these limits. Virtue comprises such elements as trust, self-control, empathy, fairness, and truthfulness as opposed to lying, cheating, fraud, and corruption.

Justice evaluations in business relate to evaluations of fairness. Justice is fair treatment and due reward in accordance with ethical or legal standards. Distributive justice is based on the evaluation of the outcome or results of a business relationship. Procedural justice is based on the processes and activities that produce the outcomes or results. Interactional justice is based on an evaluation of the communication process in business.

Important Terms for Review

moral philosophy	nonconsequentialism
teleology	ethical formalism
consequentialism	relativist perspective
egoism	virtue ethics
enlightened egoists	distributive justice
utilitarianism	procedural justice
deontology	interactional justice

A Real–Life Situation*

Twenty-eight-year-old Elaine Hunt, who is married and has one child, has been with United Banc Corp. (UBC) for several years. During that time she has seen it grow from a relatively small to a medium-size company with domestic and international customers. Elaine's husband, Dennis, has been involved in the import-export business.

The situation that precipitated the current problem began six months ago. Elaine had just been promoted to senior financial manager, which put her in charge of ten branch-office loan managers, each of whom had five loan officers who reported to him or her. For the most part, the branch loan officers would go through the numbers of their loan people, as well as sign off on loans under $250,000. But recently this limit had been increased to $500,000. Any loan over this amount and up to $40 million had to be signed off by Elaine. For larger loans, a vice president would have to be involved.

Recently, Graphco, Inc. had requested a $10 million loan, which Elaine had been hesitant to approve. Graphco was a subsidiary of a tobacco firm embroiled in litigation concerning the promotion of its products to children. When reviewing the numbers, Elaine could not find any glaring problems, yet she had decided against the loan even when Graphco had offered to pay an additional interest point. Some at UBC applauded her moral stance while others did not, arguing that it was not a good "financial business decision." The next prospective loan was for a Canadian company that was doing business in Cuba, exporting cigars. Elaine cited the U.S. policy against Cuba as the reason for not approving that loan. "The Helms-Burton Amendment gives us clear guidance as to what we shouldn't be doing with Cuba," she said to others in the company, even though the loan was to a Canadian firm. The third loan application she was unwilling to approve had come from Electrode International, which sought $50 million. The numbers had been marginal, but the sticking point for Elaine was Electrode's unusually high profits during the last two years. During dinner with Dennis, she had learned about a meeting in Zurich during which Electrode and others had allegedly fixed the prices on their products. Because only a handful of companies manufactured these particular products, the price increases were very successful. When Elaine suggested denying the loan on the basis of this information, she was overruled. At the same time, a company in Brazil was asking for an agricultural loan to harvest parts of the rain forest. The Brazilian company was willing to pay almost two points over the going rate for a $40 million loan. Because of her stand on environmental issues, Elaine rejected this application as well. The company obtained the loan from one of UBC's competitors.

Recently, Elaine's husband's decision making had fallen short of his superior's expectations. First, there was the problem of an American firm wanting to export nicotine and caffeine patches to Southeast Asia. With new research showing both these drugs to be more problematic than previously thought, the manufacturing firm had decided to attempt a rapid-penetration marketing strategy — that is, to price the products very low or at cost in order to gain market share and then over time slightly increase the margin. With 2 billion potential customers, a 1 cent markup could result in millions of dollars in profits. Dennis had rejected the deal, and the firm had gone to another company. One person in Dennis's division had said, "Do you realize that you had the perfect product — one that was low cost and both physically and psychologically addictive? You could have serviced that one account for years and would have had enough for early retirement. Are you nuts for turning it down?!"

Soon afterward an area financial bank manager wanted Elaine to sign off on a revolving loan for ABCO. ABCO's debt/equity ratio had increased significantly and did not conform to company regulations; however, Elaine was the one who had written the standards for UBC. Some in the company felt that Elaine was not quite up with the times. For example, several very good bank staff had left in the past year because they found her regulations too provincial for the global marketplace that was emerging for UBC. As Elaine reviewed ABCO's credit report, she found many danger signals; however, the loan was relatively large, $30 million, and the company had been in a credit sales slump. As she questioned ABCO, Elaine learned that the loan was to develop a new business venture within the People's Republic of China, which rumor had it was also working with the Democratic People's Republic of Korea. The biotech venture was for fetal tissue research and harvesting. Recently, attention had focused on the economic benefits of such tissue in helping a host of ailments. Anticipated global market sales for such products were being estimated at $10 billion for the next decade. ABCO was also willing to go almost two points above the standard interest equation for such a revolving loan. Elaine realized that if she signed off on this sale, it would signal an end to her standards. If she did not and ABCO went to another company for the loan and paid off the debt, she would have made a gross error and everyone in the company would know it.

As she was wrestling with this problem, Dennis's commissions began to slip, putting a crimp in their cash-flow projections. If things did not turn around quickly for Dennis, they could lose their new home, get behind in other payments, and reduce the number of educational options for their child. Elaine had also had a frank discussion with senior management about her loan standards as well as her stand on tobacco, which had lost UBC precious income. The response was, "Elaine, we applaud your moral outrage about such products, but your morals are negatively impacting the bottom line. We can't have that all the time."

Questions ■ Exercises

1. Discuss the advantages and disadvantages of each decision Elaine has made.
2. What are the ethical and legal considerations facing Elaine, Dennis, and UBC?
3. Discuss possible moral philosophies used in this situation.
4. Discuss the implications of each decision Elaine could make.

This case is strictly hypothetical; any resemblance to real persons, companies, or situations is coincidental.

CHECK YOUR E*Q*

Check your E.Q., or Ethics Quotient, by completing the following. Assess your performance to evaluate your overall understanding of the chapter material.

1. Teleology refers to right or acceptable behavior in terms of consequences for the individual.	Yes	No
2. A relativist looks at an ethical situation and considers the individuals and groups involved.	Yes	No
3. A utilitarian is most concerned with the bottom-line benefits.	Yes	No
4. Act deontology requires that a person use equity, fairness, and impartiality in making decisions and evaluating actions.	Yes	No
5. Virtues supporting business transactions include trust, fairness, truthfulness, competitiveness, and focus.	Yes	No

ANSWERS **1. No.** That's egoism.   **2. Yes.** Relativists look at themselves and those around them to determine ethical standards.   **3. Yes.** Utilitarians look for the greatest good for the greatest number of people and use a cost-benefit approach.   **4. Yes.** The rules serve only as guidelines, and past experience weighs more heavily than the rules.   **5. No.** The characteristics include trust, self-control, empathy, fairness, and truthfulness — not competitiveness and focus.

dustry, makes them unsuitable for use in certain types of projects, such as those that may be subject to sudden, severe stress. The new bridge will be located near the New Madrid Fault line, the source of the United States' greatest earthquake, in 1811. The epicenter of that earthquake, which caused extensive damage and altered the flow of the Mississippi, is less than two hundred miles from the new bridge site. Earthquake experts believe there is a 50 percent chance that an earthquake with a magnitude greater than 7 on the Richter scale will occur somewhere along the New Madrid Fault by the year 2010. Bridge construction in the area is not regulated by earthquake codes, however. If Colt wins the sale, he will earn a commission of $25,000 on top of his regular salary. But if he tells the contractor about the defect rate, Midwest may lose the sale to a competitor whose bolts are more reliable. Thus Colt's ethical issue is whether to point out to the bridge contractor that, in the event of an earthquake, Midwest bolts could fail, possibly resulting in the collapse of the bridge and the death of anyone driving across it at the time.

We will come back to this illustration as we discuss particular moral philosophies, asking how Colt might use each philosophy to resolve his ethical issue. We will not judge the quality of Colt's decision, and we will not advocate any one moral philosophy as best. In fact, this illustration and Colt's decision rationales are necessarily simplistic as well as hypothetical. In reality, the decision maker would probably have many more factors to consider in making his or her choice, and thus might reach a different decision. With that note of caution, we will introduce several types of moral philosophy: teleology (as represented by egoism and utilitarianism), deontology, the relativist perspective, virtue ethics, and justice (see Table 3–1).

TABLE 3–1 A Comparison of the Philosophies Used in Business Decisions	
Teleology	Stipulates that acts are morally right or acceptable if they produce some desired result, such as realization of self-interest or utility
Egoism	Defines right or acceptable actions as those that maximize a particular person's self-interest as defined by the individual
Utilitarianism	Defines right or acceptable actions as those that maximize total utility, or the greatest good for the greatest number of people
Deontology	Focuses on the preservation of individual rights and on the intentions associated with a particular behavior rather than on its consequences
Relativist	Evaluates ethicalness subjectively on the basis of individual and group experiences
Virtue ethics	Assumes that what is moral in a given situation is not only what conventional morality requires, but also what the mature person with a "good" moral character would deem appropriate
Justice	Evaluates ethicalness on the basis of fairness: distributive, procedural, and interactional

Teleology

Teleology refers to moral philosophies in which an act is considered morally right or acceptable if it produces some desired result: for example, pleasure, knowledge, career growth, the realization of self-interest, or utility. In other words, teleological philosophies assess the moral worth of a behavior by looking at its consequences. Moral philosophers today often refer to these theories as **consequentialism.** Two important teleological philosophies that often guide decision making in individual business decisions are egoism and utilitarianism.

Egoism   **Egoism** defines right or acceptable behavior in terms of the consequences for the individual. Egoists believe that they should make decisions that maximize their own self-interest, which is defined differently by each individual. Depending on the egoist, self-interest may be construed as physical well-being, power, pleasure, fame, a satisfying career, a good family life, wealth, or something else. In an ethical decision-making situation, an egoist will probably choose the alternative that contributes most to his or her self-interest. The egoist's creed can be generally stated as "Do the act that promotes the greatest good for oneself." Many believe that egoists are inherently unethical, that such people and companies are short-term oriented and will take advantage of any opportunity or consumer. For example, some telemarketers demonstrate this negative egoistic tendency when they prey on elderly consumers who may be vulnerable because of frequent loneliness or the fear of losing financial independence. Thousands of senior citizens fall victim to fraudulent telemarketers every year. In many cases, they lose all of their savings and sometimes their homes.

However, there is also enlightened egoism. **Enlightened egoists** take a long-range perspective and allow for the well-being of others, although their own self-interest remains paramount. Enlightened egoists may abide by professional codes of ethics, control pollution, avoid cheating on taxes, help create jobs, and support community projects. Yet they do so not because these actions benefit others, but because they help achieve some ultimate goal for the egoist, such as advancement within the firm. An enlightened egoist might call management's attention to a coworker who is cheating customers, but only to safeguard the company's reputation and thus the egoist's own job security. For example, Philip Morris pulled cigarette advertising from forty to fifty magazines with substantial numbers of young readers, such as *Rolling Stone* and *Sports Illustrated.* The company hopes that this action will help prevent further legal action to restrict tobacco advertising.[6]

When businesses donate money, resources, or time to specific causes and institutions, their motives may not be purely altruistic either. For example, International Business Machines (IBM) has a policy of donating or reducing the cost of computers to educational institutions. The company receives tax breaks for donations of equipment, which reduce the costs of this policy. In addition, IBM hopes to build future sales by placing its products on campus. When students enter the work force, they may request the IBM products with which they have become fa-in, in North and South America or the Middle East. The packaging will have to change by country as well as branding. Pricing strategies will need to be developed relative to our branding decisions, and of course quantity usages will have to be calculated. For example, single, multiple, supervalue sizes, etc., need to be explored. The same can be done for khat." David added, "Because of your research and your business background, I'm putting you on the marketing team for both. Of course, this means that you're going to have to be promoted and at least for a while live in Hong Kong. I know Quan will be excited. In fact, I told her the news this morning that she would be working on the same project in Hong Kong. Producto International tries to be sensitive to the dual-career family problems that can occur. Plus you'll be closer to relatives. I told Quan that with living allowances and all of the other things that go with international placement, you two should almost triple your salaries! You don't have to thank me, Myron. You've worked hard on these projects and now you deserve to have some of the benefits."

Myron went back to his office to think about his and Quan's future. He had heard of someone rejecting such an offer, and that person's career had languished at PI. Eventually, that individual left the industry, never to be heard from again.

Questions ■ Exercises

1. Identify the social responsibility issues.
2. Discuss the advantages and disadvantages of each decision Myron could make.
3. Discuss the issue of marketing products that are legal but have addictive properties associated with them.

This case is strictly hypothetical; any resemblance to real persons, companies, or situations is coincidental

The concepts of business ethics and social responsibility are often used interchangeably, but as we pointed out in Chapter 1, each of these two terms has a distinct meaning. *Business ethics,* as defined in this text, comprises principles and standards that guide behavior in the world of business. Specific behavior is usually evaluated in terms of individual and group decisions. A specific action is judged right or wrong, ethical or unethical, by the individual and by others inside and outside the organization. Although evaluations of ethical behavior are not necessarily accurate, these judgments influence society's acceptance or rejection of individual and group activities within the business environment. *Social responsibility* in business refers to an organization's obligation to maximize its positive impact on stakeholders (customers, owners, employers, community, suppliers, and the government) and to minimize its negative impact. There are four kinds of social responsibility: legal, ethical, economic, and philanthropic.[1] Ethics, then, is one dimension of social responsibility. Ethics in the context of social responsibility focuses on issues that influence a firm's positive impact on society and minimize its negative impact.

Business ethics and social responsibility are thus closely linked. Many of the cases, exercises, and vignettes used in this text have both social responsibility and ethical implications. The more you know about social responsibility and its relation to business ethics, the better informed you will be in discussing ethical and social responsibility issues (see Figure 4–1).

Corporate citizenship is the extent to which businesses meet the legal, ethical, economic, and philanthropic responsibilities placed on them by their various

FIGURE 4–1   Steps of Social Responsibility

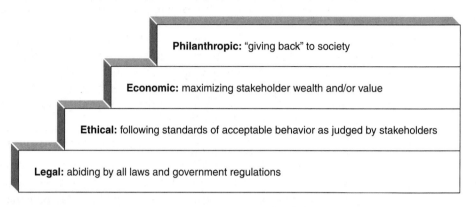

Philanthropic: "giving back" to society

Economic: maximizing stakeholder wealth and/or value

Ethical: following standards of acceptable behavior as judged by stakeholders

Legal: abiding by all laws and government regulations

Source: Adapted from Archie B. Carroll, "The Pyramid of Corporate Social Responsibility: Toward the Moral Management of Organizational Stakeholders," Business Horizons (July–August 1991): 42, Fig. 3.

stakeholders.[2] It involves the activities and organizational processes adopted by businesses to meet their social responsibilities. A commitment to corporate citizenship by a firm indicates a strategic focus on fulfilling the social responsibilities expected of it by its stakeholders. Corporate citizenship involves action and measurement of the extent to which a firm embraces the corporate citizenship philosophy and then follows through by implementing citizenship initiatives. For example, Herman Miller, Inc., a multinational provider of office, residential, and health care furniture and services, has crafted a statement it calls the *Blueprint for Corporate Community* (see Figure 4–2). This statement sets forth Herman Miller's corporate citizenship philosophy — its commitment to be a different kind of company in the way it fulfills its responsibilities to customers, shareholders, employees, the community, and the natural environment. Because this statement affects all Herman Miller's constituents and applies directly to all operations, products, markets, and business relationships, it demonstrates the company's strategic focus on corporate citizenship. In addition to a company's verbal and written commitment, corporate citizenship requires action and results.

We examine the four components of social responsibility beginning with the foundation for all business activities — legal responsibilities. Through the legal system, society enforces acceptable behavior. Organizations cannot survive in the long term if they do not respond to their legal responsibilities. The next dimension organizations should consider is their ethical responsibilities. At this level, firms decide what they consider to be right, just, and fair beyond society's strictly legal requirements. Many view the law as codified ethics. What is an option at one point in time (voluntary ethics initiatives) may emerge as a law in the future to improve overall corporate citizenship. In managing their ethical and legal responsibilities, organizations should be aware of the economic concerns of stakeholders, the third dimension of social responsibility. As will be discussed later in the

FIGURE 4–2   Herman Miller, Inc.'s Blueprint for Corporate Community

— HERMAN MILLER, INC. —

Herman Miller, Inc., is more than just a legal entity. It combines the talents, hopes, and dreams of thousands of people. At its best, it is a high-performance, values-driven community of people tied together by a common purpose. *Herman Miller* has always stood apart from the crowd because of what we believed, and we have always believed that what we stand for matters. Our strategies will change as the needs of our business change. Our core values will not. We build our business on them. How well we live up to these values will determine whether we are to be trusted by others.

What we believe in:

Making a meaningful contribution to our customers

Cultivating community, participation, and people development

Creating economic value for shareholders and employee-owners

Responding to change through design and innovation

Living with integrity and respecting the environment

Source: http://www.hermanmiller.com/us/index.bbk/US/en/AU/c2 *(accessed November 29, 2000).* Reprinted with permission from Herman Miller, Inc.'s Blueprint for Corporate Community.

text, good citizenship, through ethical and legal initiatives, supports long-term profitability. The last dimension of social responsibility is the philanthropic aspect. By fulfilling their philanthropic responsibilities, firms contribute financial and human resources to the community and society to improve the quality of life. The philanthropic and economic dimensions of social responsibility are closely linked because the more profitable the organization, the more able it is to invest in philanthropic activities. Each of these four components of social responsibility defines an area in which firms make decisions that result in specific behaviors, which society evaluates.

THE LEGAL DIMENSION

The **legal dimension** of social responsibility refers to obeying laws and regulations established by governments to set minimum standards for responsible behavior — society's codification of what is right and wrong. Laws regulating business conduct are passed because society — including consumers, interest groups, competitors, and legislators — believes that business cannot be trusted to do what is right in certain areas, such as consumer safety and environmental protection. This lack of trust is the focal point of the legal dimension. Many ethical and economic issues result in lawsuits and legislative debate.

Because public policy is dynamic and often changes in response to business abuses and consumer demands for safety and equality, many laws have been passed to resolve specific problems and issues. But the opinions of society, as expressed in legislation, can change over time, and different courts, or different state legislatures, may take different views. For example, the thrust of most business legislation can be summed up as permitting any practice that does not substantially lessen or reduce competition or harm consumers or society. Courts differ, however, in their interpretations of what constitutes a "substantial" reduction of competition. Laws can help businesspeople determine what society believes at a certain point in time, but what is legally wrong today may be perceived as acceptable tomorrow, and vice versa. Still, personal views on legal issues may vary tremendously.

Laws are categorized as either civil or criminal. **Civil law** defines the rights and duties of individuals and organizations (including businesses). **Criminal law** not only prohibits specific actions — such as fraud, theft, or securities trading violations — but also imposes fines or imprisonment as punishment for breaking the law. The primary difference between criminal and civil law is that criminal laws are enforced by the state or nation, whereas civil laws are enforced by individuals (generally, in court).

Criminal and civil laws are derived from four sources: the Constitution (constitutional law), precedents established by judges (common law), federal and state laws or statutes (statutory law), and federal and state administrative agencies (administrative law). Federal administrative agencies established by Congress control and influence business by enforcing laws and regulations to encourage competition and to protect consumers, workers, and the environment.

The primary method of resolving conflicts and serious business ethics disputes is through lawsuits, in which one individual or organization takes another to court, using civil laws. For example, Ford Motor Co. reached a $17.5 million agreement with the federal government to settle sexual harassment allegations at two factories. The company agreed to set aside $7.5 million to compensate victims of harassment and $10 million more to train managers and male workers to stop what women alleged to be a years-long pattern of groping, name calling, and parties with strippers and prostitutes.[3]

The legal system thus provides a forum for businesspeople to resolve ethical disputes as well as legal ones. The courts may decide when harm or damage results from the actions of others. For instance, the investors of Lloyd's of London sued the company because it allegedly misrepresented the risks associated with some of its insured asbestos clients. Investors argued that they were not informed of the magnitude of risk. So far, more than $4 billion has been paid out.[4] This is an example of ethical conflict resolution through a civil proceeding within the legal system. Lawsuits like this are usually the way that collective disputes over deception and wrongdoing can be resolved.

The role of laws is not so much to distinguish what is ethical or unethical as to determine the appropriateness of specific activities or situations. In other words, laws establish the basic ground rules for responsible business activities. All businesses must obey these laws.

Most of the laws and regulations governing business activities fall into one of five groups: (1) regulation of competition, (2) protection of consumers, (3) protection of the environment, (4) promotion of equity and safety, and (5) incentives to encourage organizational compliance programs to deter misconduct.

Laws Regulating Competition

Laws have been passed to prevent the establishment of monopolies, inequitable pricing practices, and other practices that reduce or restrict competition among businesses. These laws are sometimes called **procompetitive legislation** because they were enacted to encourage competition and prevent activities that restrain trade (see Table 4–1). The Sherman Antitrust Act of 1890, for example, prohibits organizations from holding monopolies in their industry, and the Robinson-Patman Act of 1936 bans price discrimination between retailers and wholesalers.

In law, however, there are always exceptions. Under the McCarran-Ferguson Act of 1944, for example, Congress exempted the insurance industry from the Sherman Antitrust Act and other antitrust laws. Insurance companies were allowed to join together and set insurance premiums at specific industrywide levels. However, a behavior may be viewed as irresponsible if it neutralizes competition and if prices no longer reflect the true costs of insurance protection. This illustrates the point that what is legal is not always considered ethical by some interest groups.

Laws Protecting Consumers

Laws protecting consumers require businesses to provide accurate information about products and services and to follow safety standards (see Table 4–2). The first **consumer protection law** was passed in 1906, partly in response to a novel by Upton Sinclair. *The Jungle* describes, among other things, the atrocities and unsanitary conditions of the meat-packing industry in turn-of-the-century Chicago. The outraged public response to this book and other exposés of the industry resulted in the passage of the Pure Food and Drug Act. Ralph Nader had a tremendous impact on consumer protection laws with his book *Unsafe at Any Speed*. His critique and attack of General Motors's Corvair had far-reaching effects on autos and other consumer products. Other consumer protection laws emerged from similar processes.

In recent years, large groups of people with specific vulnerabilities have been granted special levels of legal protection relative to the general population. For example, the legal status of children and the elderly, defined according to age-related criteria, has received greater attention. American society has responded to research and documentation showing that young consumers and senior citizens encounter

TABLE 4-1   Laws Regulating Competition

Sherman Antitrust Act, 1890	Prohibits monopolies
Clayton Act, 1914	Prohibits price discrimination, exclusive dealing, and other efforts to restrict competition
Federal Trade Commission Act, 1914	Created the Federal Trade Commission (FTC) to help enforce antitrust laws
Robinson-Patman Act, 1936	Bans price discrimination between retailers and wholesalers
Wheeler-Lea Act, 1938	Prohibits unfair and deceptive acts regardless of whether competition is injured
McCarran-Ferguson Act, 1944	Exempts the insurance industry from antitrust laws
Lanham Act, 1946	Protects and regulates brand names, brand marks, trade names, and trademarks
Celler-Kefauver Act, 1950	Prohibits one corporation from controlling another where the effect is to lessen competition
Consumer Goods Pricing Act, 1975	Prohibits price maintenance agreements among manufacturers and resellers in interstate commerce
FTC Improvement Act, 1975	Gives the FTC more power to prohibit unfair industry practices
Antitrust Improvements Act, 1976	Strengthens earlier antitrust laws — Justice Department has more investigative authority
Trademark Counterfeiting Act, 1980	Provides penalties for individuals dealing in counterfeit goods
Trademark Law Revision Act, 1988	Amends the Lanham Act to allow brands not yet introduced to be protected through patent and trademark registration
Federal Trademark Dilution Act, 1995	Trademark owners are given the right to protect trademarks and relinquish those that match or parallel existing trademarks

difficulties in the acquisition, consumption, and disposition of products. Special legal protection provided to vulnerable consumers is considered to be in the public interest.[5] For example, the Children's Online Privacy Protection Act (COPPA) requires commercial Internet sites to carry privacy policy statements, obtain "verifiable parental consent" before soliciting information from children under the age of 13, and provide an opportunity to remove any information provided by children. Zeeks.com, a site aimed at children, discontinued its chat area, free e-mail system, and other features because of the cost of obtaining and verifying a parent's permission.[6] Critics of COPPA argue that children age 13 and older should not

TABLE 4–2   Laws Protecting Consumers

Pure Food and Drug Act, 1906	Prohibits adulteration and mislabeling of foods and drugs sold in interstate commerce
Wool Products Labeling Act, 1939	Prohibits mislabeling of wool products
Fur Products Labeling Act, 1951	Requires proper identification of the fur content of all products
Federal Hazardous Substances Labeling Act, 1960	Controls the labeling of hazardous substances for household use
Truth in Lending Act, 1968	Requires full disclosure of credit terms to purchasers
Consumer Product Safety Act, 1972	Created the Consumer Product Safety Commission to establish safety standards and regulations for consumer products
Fair Credit Billing Act, 1974	Requires accurate, up-to-date consumer credit records
Magnuson-Moss Warranty Act, 1975	Established standards for consumer product warranties
Energy Policy and Conservation Act, 1975	Requires auto dealers to have "gas mileage guides" in their showrooms
Consumer Goods Pricing Act, 1975	Prohibits price maintenance agreements
Consumer Leasing Act, 1976	Requires accurate disclosure of leasing terms to consumers
Fair Debt Collection Practices Act, 1978	Defines permissible debt collection practices
Toy Safety Act, 1984	Gives the government the power to recall dangerous toys quickly
Nutritional Labeling and Education Act, 1990	Prohibits exaggerated health claims and requires all processed foods to have labels with nutritional information
Telephone Consumer Protection Act, 1991	Establishes procedures for avoiding unwanted telephone solicitations
Children's Online Privacy Protection Act, 1998	Requires the FTC to formulate rules for collecting on-line information from children under age 13

be treated as adults on the Web. In a recent study of children ages 10 to 17, nearly half indicated that they would give their name, address, and other demographic information in exchange for a gift worth $100 or more. In addition, about half of the teens surveyed would provide information on family cars and their parents' favorite stores in exchange for a "great free gift." More than 20 percent would reveal parents' number of sick days, alcohol consumption, weekend hobbies, church attendance — and whether they speed when driving.[7] The study's authors suggest federal regulation that would prohibit Web sites from using free gifts and sweepstakes to collect information from teens.

Although COPPA does not apply to government sites, the Office of Management and Budget ordered federal agencies to comply with the statute. However, major government sites are not adhering to the law. Sites operated by the Environmental Protection Agency (EPA) and the National Aeronautics and Space Administration (NASA) collect personal information from children who submit artwork to be posted on the sites. Both agencies show the child's name, age, and hometown with the published artwork.[8]

The vast number of news-format investigative programs has increased consumer awareness of organizational wrongdoing. In addition, the multitude of cable channels and Internet resources has improved awareness of problems. Such information may make consumers stronger advocates of legal regulations to support health and safety as well as free competition.

ⓔ.ethics 1   The role of the Federal Trade Commission's Bureau of Consumer Protection is to protect consumers against unfair, deceptive, or fraudulent practices. The bureau, which enforces a variety of consumer protection laws, is divided into five divisions. The Division of Enforcement monitors compliance with and investigates violations of laws, including unfulfilled holiday delivery promises by on-line shopping sites, employment opportunities fraud, scholarship scams, misleading advertising for health care products, and more.

Laws Protecting the Environment

Environmental protection laws have been enacted largely in response to concerns that began to emerge during the 1960s. Many people have questioned the cost-benefit analyses often used in making business decisions. Such analyses try to take into account all factors in a situation, represent them with dollar figures, calculate the costs and benefits of the proposed action, and determine whether the action's benefits outweigh its costs. It is difficult, however, to arrive at an accurate monetary valuation of physical pain and injury or environmental damage. In addition, people outside the business world often perceive such analyses as inhumane. From a utilitarian perspective, a company may make decisions that are best for itself or for its consumers, but according to this philosophy, it should make decisions that benefit society as well. One such example of socially beneficial decisions is provided by the pharmaceutical company Bristol-Myers Squibb, which was given the Green Star Award by the Environmental Action Coalition (EAC). The EAC cited these factors in presenting the award: the company's worldwide electricity usage decreased by 31 percent; its greenhouse gas emissions decreased by 21 percent; its emissions of ozone-depleting substances were reduced by 73 percent; its toxic releases into the air decreased by 42 percent; and its toxic releases into sewers decreased by 93 percent.[9]

Increases in toxic waste in the air and water, as well as noise pollution, have prompted the passage of a number of laws (Table 4–3). Many environmental protection laws have resulted in the elimination or modification of goods and ser-

TABLE 4–3 Laws Protecting the Environment	
Clean Air Act, 1970	Established air-quality standards; requires approved state plans for implementation of the standards
National Environmental Policy Act, 1970	Established broad policy goals for all federal agencies; created the Council on Environmental Quality as a monitoring agency
Coastal Zone Management Act, 1972	Provides financial resources to the states to protect coastal zones from overpopulation
Federal Water Pollution Control Act, 1972	Designed to prevent, reduce, or eliminate water pollution
Noise Pollution Control Act, 1972	Designed to control the noise emission of certain manufactured items
Toxic Substances Control Act, 1976	Requires testing and restricts use of certain chemical substances, to protect human health and the environment

vices. For instance, leaded gasoline was phased out during the 1990s by the EPA because catalytic converters, which reduce pollution caused by automobile emissions and are required by law on most vehicles, do not work properly with leaded gasolines. Currently, fuel cells are being investigated to power automobiles. Fuel cells produce electricity without combustion or emissions. General Motors has conceived, developed, and built the EV_1, its environmentally friendly electric car. Currently available through thirty-four Saturn retailers in California and Arizona, the EV_1 is a zero-emission vehicle that requires no tune-ups, no gasoline, and no oil changes. Its aluminum structure is designed to be strong, lightweight, and 100 percent recyclable.[10] Environmental initiatives can differentiate companies and increase their profitability and consumer acceptance.

In response to a wave of new laws, companies are also changing the way they package their products. Most states now have recycling programs in order to stem the nation's garbage crisis. Plastic containers are a particular problem. Because they do not degrade, they are taking up more and more of the limited landfill space. Nearly 50 percent of all garbage is plastic packaging, including Styrofoam containers from fast-food restaurants, plastic soft drink bottles, plastic carry-out bags, and plastic produce bags.[11] McDonald's was one of the first restaurants to drop Styrofoam clamshells for its sandwiches and wrap them in paper instead. As cities and states regulate the use of plastic and even glass containers more strictly, businesses will be forced to change their packaging to comply with the law and the environmental concerns of society. The recycling of paper has been under way for several years now. We are recycling about half of our paper today, with the marginal cost for extracting more paper from trash increasing substantially. Figure 4–3 shows steel can recycling over a ten-year period.

FIGURE 4–3   Steel Can Recycling

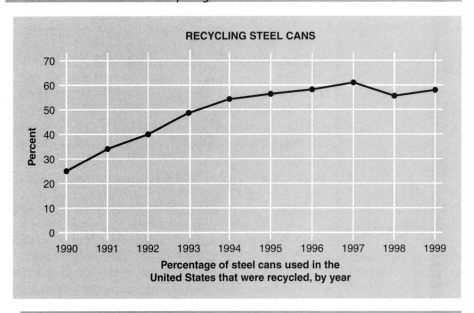

Source: "Steel Recycling Institute," USA Today Snapshots, April 18, 2000, p. A1. Copyright 2000 USA Today. Reprinted with permission.

The harmful effects of toxic waste on water life and on leisure industries such as resorts and fishing have raised concerns about proper disposal of these wastes. Disposal sites meeting EPA standards are limited in number; thus, businesses must decide what to do with their waste until disposal sites become available. Some firms have solved this problem by illegal or unethical measures: dumping toxic wastes along highways, improperly burying drums containing toxic chemicals, and discarding hazardous waste at sea. Royal Caribbean Cruises Ltd. is one such company. A five-year investigation showed that Royal Caribbean ships used "secret bypass pipes" to dump waste oil and hazardous materials overboard, often at night. Justice Department officials said the company engaged in the dumping to save the cost of properly disposing of its waste. During this time, the company was promoting itself as environmentally friendly. Royal Caribbean paid $27 million in fines and pled guilty to twenty-one felony counts. The company also spent up to $90,000 per ship to install new oily water treatment systems and placed an environmental officer onboard each vessel.[12] Congress constantly evaluates legislation to increase the penalties for disposing of toxic wastes in this manner. Disposal issues remain controversial because, although everyone acknowledges that the wastes must go somewhere, no community wants them dumped in its own backyard.

One specific solid waste problem is being created by rapid innovations in computer hardware that make many computers obsolete after just eighteen months. Just two years ago, more than 20 million computers reached obsolescence, but only 11 percent were recycled. By 2005, 350 million machines will have reached obsolescence, with at least 55 million expected to end up in landfills.[13] Computers contain such toxic substances as lead, cadmium mercury, and chromium, which can leach into the soil and contaminate groundwater. Most computers are reusable, and up to 97 percent of the parts can be recycled — either to be used in other computers or to be melted down as scrap. Companies routinely donate old computers to schools and charities. Computers to be disposed of must be handled in accordance with the U.S. Code's Resource Conservation and Recovery Act. However, the EPA does not regulate residential computer disposal. Some states are taking action. Massachusetts was the first state to forbid the disposal of computer monitors in landfills, and California's environmental agencies encourage consumers to donate or recycle computers.

Laws Promoting Equity and Safety

Laws promoting equity in the workplace were passed during the 1960s and 1970s to protect the rights of older persons, minorities, women, and persons with disabilities; other legislation has sought to protect the safety of all workers (see Table 4–4). Of these laws, probably the most important to business is Title VII of the Civil Rights Act, originally passed in 1964 and amended in later years. Title VII specifically prohibits discrimination in employment on the basis of race, sex, religion, color, or national origin. It also created the Equal Employment Opportunity Commission (EEOC) to help enforce the provisions of Title VII. Among other things, the EEOC helps businesses design affirmative action programs. These programs aim to increase job opportunities for women and minorities by analyzing the present pool of employees, identifying areas where women and minorities are underrepresented, and establishing specific hiring and promotion goals, along with target dates for meeting those goals.

Other legislation addresses more specific employment practices. The Age Discrimination in Employment Act of 1967 prohibits discrimination based on age and outlaws policies that force employees to retire before age 70. The Equal Pay Act of 1963 mandates that women and men who do equal work must receive equal pay for such work. Wage differences are allowed only if they can be attributed to seniority, performance, or qualifications. The Americans with Disabilities Act of 1990 prohibits discrimination against people with disabilities. Despite these laws, inequities in the workplace still exist. According to a report on hourly wages from the Bureau of Labor Statistics, women earn, on average, 76.5 cents for every dollar earned by men.[14] Figure 4–4 shows the median weekly income of full-time males and females by age group.

Congress has also passed laws that seek to improve safety in the workplace. By far the most significant of these is the Occupational Safety and Health Act of 1970, which mandates that employers provide safe and healthy working conditions for all workers. The Occupational Safety and Health Administration (OSHA), which enforces the act, makes regular surprise inspections to ensure that businesses maintain safe working environments.

TABLE 4–4   Laws Promoting Equity and Safety

Equal Pay Act of 1963	Prohibits discrimination in pay on the basis of sex
Equal Pay Act of 1963 (amended)	Prohibits sex-based discrimination in the rate of pay to men and women working in the same or similar jobs
Title VII of the Civil Rights Act of 1964 (amended in 1972)	Prohibits discrimination in employment on the basis of race, color, sex, religion, or national origin
Age Discrimination in Employment Act, 1967	Prohibits discrimination in employment against persons between the ages of 40 and 70
Occupational Safety and Health Act, 1970	Designed to ensure healthful and safe working conditions for all employees
Vocational Rehabilitation Act, 1973	Prohibits discrimination in employment because of physical or mental handicaps
Vietnam Era Veterans Readjustment Act, 1974	Prohibits discrimination against disabled veterans and Vietnam War veterans
Pension Reform Act, 1974	Designed to prevent abuses in employee retirement, profit-sharing, thrift, and savings plans
Equal Credit Opportunity Act, 1974	Prohibits discrimination in credit on the basis of sex or marital status
Pregnancy Discrimination Act, 1978	Prohibits discrimination on the basis of pregnancy, childbirth, or related medical conditions
Immigration Reform and Control Act, 1986	Prohibits employers from knowingly hiring a person who is an unauthorized alien
Americans with Disabilities Act, 1990	Prohibits discrimination against people with disabilities and requires that they be given the same opportunities as people without disabilities

Even with the passage and enforcement of safety laws, many employees still work in unhealthy or dangerous environments. Safety experts suspect that companies underreport industrial accidents to avoid state and federal inspection and regulation. The current emphasis on increased productivity has been cited as the main reason for the growing number of such accidents. Competitive pressures are also believed to lie behind the increases in manufacturing injuries. Greater turnover in organizations due to downsizing means that employees may have more responsibilities and less experience in their current positions, thus increasing the potential for accidents.

Despite legislation, then, businesses continue to face legal issues related to competition, protection of consumers and the environment, and safety and equity in the workplace. Society expects businesspeople to take steps to ensure that they compete fairly; to develop, promote, price, and distribute products that are

FIGURE 4–4   Median Weekly Income of Full-Time Male and Female Workers

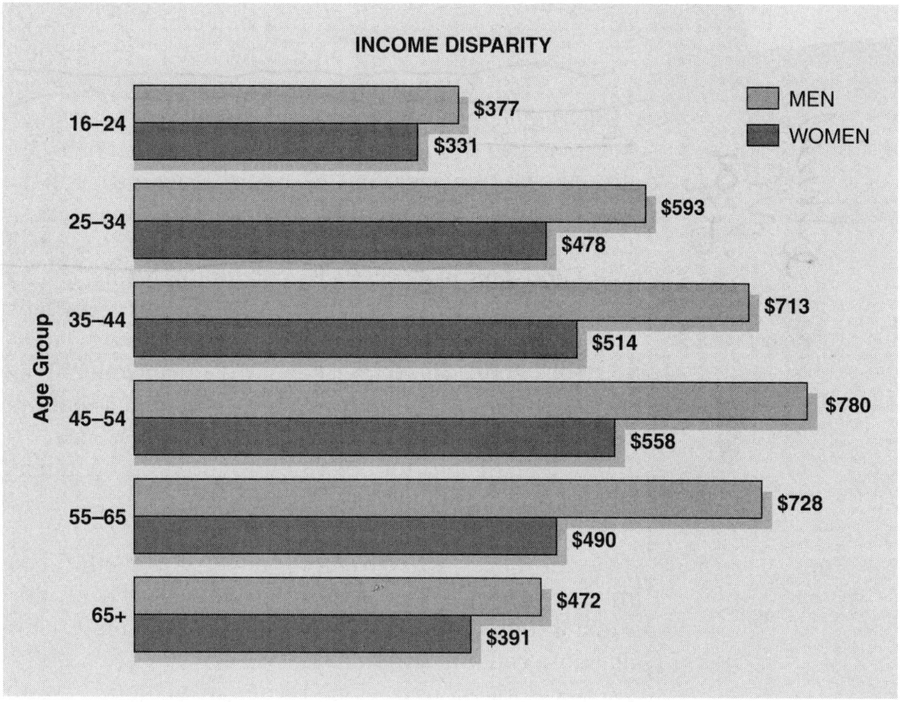

INCOME DISPARITY

Legend: ▢ MEN ■ WOMEN

Age Group:

16–24: Men $377, Women $331

25–34: Men $593, Women $478

35–44: Men $713, Women $514

45–54: Men $780, Women $558

55–65: Men $728, Women $490

65+: Men $472, Women $391

Source: "Bureau of Labor Statistics," USA Today Snapshots, March 10, 2000, p. A1. Copyright 2000 USA Today. Reprinted with permission.

safe for both consumers and the environment; to provide safe working conditions; and to develop programs to hire and promote the most qualified employees, regardless of race, color, sex, religion, and physical ability. Ethical businesses acknowledge obligations that go beyond what is required by law and consider the needs and well-being of their employees.

Incentives for Compliance: Federal Sentencing Guidelines for Organizations

Legal violations usually begin with businesspersons stretching the limits of ethical standards, as defined by company or industry codes of conduct, and then developing identifiable schemes to knowingly or unwittingly violate the law. In 1991 Congress passed a law to create an incentive for organizations to conscientiously develop and implement ethical compliance programs. The **Federal Sentencing Guidelines for Organizations** apply to all felonies and Class A misdemeanors that employees commit in association with their work. In general, business activities at the forefront of misconduct in the federal court system are fraud and price fixing/market allocation (antitrust violations).

While many people separate ethical and legal issues, the boundary between these issues is often ambiguous to the business manager, who is not ordinarily trained as a lawyer. The manager is trained to make functional business decisions and yet has a responsibility for the management of legal and ethical affairs. When it is suggested that legal and ethical decisions are independent, there is an assumption that the good executive "instinctively" recognizes differences in legal and ethical issues. While there are some legal issues that are obvious, many borderline ethics decisions result in civil litigation. In reality, civil complaints and litigation are a formal procedure for resolving ethical disputes between two parties.

e.ethics 2

With this in mind, three fundamental principles guided the United States Sentencing Commission in designing the organizational guidelines. First, the commission sought to develop a structure or model that organizations could use to define and refine ethical compliance initiatives. Second, the model was designed to provide guidance for determining corporate sentencing and fines when violations occur. Finally, the commission wanted to create an inherent incentive for organizations to comply with the guidelines. As an incentive, organizations that show due diligence in developing an "effective" ethical compliance program minimize their risk for organizational penalties.[15] Overall, the government philosophy is that through organizational values and a commitment to ethical conduct, legal violations can be prevented.

The commission developed seven mandatory steps that companies must implement to show due diligence. The steps are based on the commission's determination to emphasize compliance programs and to provide guidance for both organizations and courts regarding program effectiveness. Organizations have flexibility as to the type of program they develop; the seven steps are not a checklist requiring legal procedures for certification of an effective program. The program must be capable of reducing the opportunity that employees have to engage in misconduct.

As a first step, a code of conduct that communicates required standards and identifies key risk areas for the organization must be developed. Second, the program must have oversight by high-ranking personnel in the organization (such as the ethics officer, vice president of human resources, general counsel, and so forth) who are known to abide by the legal and ethical standards of the industry. Third, no one with a known propensity to engage in misconduct should be put in a position of authority. Fourth, a communications system (ethics training) for disseminating standards and procedures must also be put into place. Fifth, organizational communications should include a way for employees to report misconduct without fearing retaliation, such as an anonymous toll-free hot line or an ombudsman. Monitoring and auditing systems designed to detect misconduct are also required. Sixth, if misconduct is detected, then the firm must take appropriate and fair disciplinary action. Individuals both directly and indirectly responsible for the offense should be disciplined. In addition, the sanctions should be appropriate for the offense. Finally — seventh — after misconduct has been discovered, the organization must take steps to prevent similar offenses in the future. This usually involves modifications to the ethical compliance program, additional employee training, and communications about specific types of conduct. The government expects continuous improvement and refinement of these seven steps for compliance programs.[16]

Managers who define ethics as strictly legal compliance may be endorsing ethical mediocrity for their organizations. An effective ethical compliance program must feature ethics and organizational values as the driving forces of the enterprise. While legal compliance is based on avoiding legal sanctions, organizational ethical integrity is based on guiding values and principles.[17] A strong ethics program acts as a buffer to keep employees from engaging in illegal behavior. Most employees are unable to accurately interpret and assess all laws and regulations and to translate their intent into acceptable organizational behavior. Making ethical principles an important part of a compliance program is more demanding and requires broader and deeper commitment to appropriate conduct.

THE ETHICAL DIMENSION

Although the legal component of social responsibility is generally accepted, ethical and philanthropic concerns have been receiving more attention recently. The **ethical dimension** of social responsibility refers to behaviors and activities that are expected or prohibited by organizational members, the community, and society, even though these behaviors and activities are not codified into law. Ethical responsibilities from a social responsibility perspective embody standards, norms, or expectations that reflect a concern of major stakeholders, including consumers, employees, suppliers, shareholders, and the community. In other words, these major stakeholders have a concern about what is fair, just, or in keeping with respect for or protection of stakeholders' rights. Companies have a responsibility to fulfill their ethical obligations to various stakeholder groups. *Business Ethics* magazine studied corporate service to four key stakeholder groups: stockholders, employees, customers, and the community. No company excelled in serving all four groups, but the top twenty-five were at least average in serving all stakeholders.[18] Ranking was based on a scale of 1 (major concern) to 5 (major strength). Results for the top ten companies are shown in Table 4–5.

Ethics as a Force in Social Responsibility

Organizational integrity and ethics go beyond compliance with laws and regulations. Good corporate citizens develop values and principles that become a part of the business culture and operations.

Many businesspeople and scholars have questioned the role of ethics and social responsibility in business. The legal and economic dimensions are generally

TABLE 4–5   The Top Ten Best Corporate Citizens

Rank	Overall Rating	Company	Community Relations	Employee Relations	Customer Relations
1	4.15167	IBM	4.50	4.33	3.33
2	4.11000	Hewlett Packard	4.33	5.00	4.00
3	4.04500	Intel	3.67	4.50	4.00
4	4.04167	Procter & Gamble	3.83	4.67	4.00
5	4.02167	Herman Miller	4.00	4.83	3.33
6	4.01833	Xerox	4.17	5.00	3.00
7	3.96000	Tellabs	3.00	3.67	5.00
8	3.93667	Charles Schwab	3.00	4.33	3.67
9	3.87667	Fannie Mae	4.00	3.67	4.00
10	3.87000	Times Mirror Company	4.00	3.67	4.00

Source: "Business Ethics' 100 Best Corporate Citizens," Business Ethics, March/April 2000, p. 15. Reprinted with permission from Business Ethics, P.O. Box 8439, Minneapolis, MN, 55408, (612) 879-0695.

accepted as the most important determinants of performance: "If this is well done," say classical theorists, "profits are maximized more or less continuously and firms carry out their major responsibilities to society."[19] Some economists believe that if firms take care of economic and legal issues, they are satisfying the demands of society and that trying to anticipate and meet ethical and philanthropic needs would be almost impossible. Milton Friedman has been quoted as saying that "the basic mission of business [is] thus to produce goods and services at a profit, and in doing this, business [is] making its maximum contribution to society and, in fact, being socially responsible."[20] On the other hand, there is much evidence that social responsibility, including business ethics, is associated with increased profits. For example, one survey indicates that three out of four consumers refuse to buy from certain businesses, and business conduct was considered an important reason to avoid a business.[21] An important academic study found that there is a direct relationship between social responsibility and profitability.[22] The study also found that social responsibility contributes to employee commitment and customer loyalty — vital concerns of any firm trying to increase profits.[23]

Social responsiveness is the act of responding to stakeholders and concerned others in society by considering more than just the firm's own wants and needs. Systematic appraisal of the needs of stakeholders can position the firm to be socially responsive. However, if being socially responsive means just responding to ethical issues identified by others, the firm has embraced a form of relativism that may direct managers to take the path of least resistance. It is possible that, by being responsive, managers could keep things quiet, appear to be ethical, and focus on maximizing profits.[24]

It should be obvious from this discussion that ethics and social responsibility cannot be just a reactive approach to issues as they arise. Only if firms include ethical concerns in their foundation and incorporate ethics in their business strategy can social responsibility as a concept be embedded in daily decision making. A description of corporate ethical responsibility should include rights and duties, consequences and values, all of which refer to specific strategic decisions.[25] The ethical component of business strategy should be capable of providing an assessment of top-management, work-group, and individual behavior as it relates to ethical decisions.

Organizational Direction for Ethics and Social Responsibility

An ethical and socially responsible company depends on the values and moral principles held by the individuals and groups in the organization. From a social responsibility perspective, of course, the values and moral beliefs of organizational members are important, but so are those of key stakeholders — including the owners, investors, employees, and customers. The values and principles of all these participants are important in understanding a social and economic pattern of interaction. The corporate or overall business strategy determines how the organization will use human and financial resources to achieve its objectives. The value systems of the corporation and stakeholders have a profound effect on the implementation of corporate strategy. Consider these statements.

1. Business strategy must reflect an understanding of the values of organizational members and stakeholders.
2. Business strategy must reflect an understanding of the ethical nature of strategic choice.
3. Business strategy must consider the implications of its efforts on key organizational stakeholders.[26]

If we accept these statements, then ethics becomes a core concern in business strategy.[27] A common criticism of business has been that the role of ethics in business strategy has been systematically ignored; therefore, we must respond by attempting to place ethics at the very center of discussions about business strategy.

If business strategies create ethical issues, then top management, along with stakeholders and society at large, needs to assess and address these ethical issues with meaningful debate and conflict resolution. It is hard to try to address difficult ethical issues, but simply acknowledging that ethics is a component of strategy can change the firm's behavior. Firms that view ethics as a very difficult and personal subject that should be addressed only at home may ignore the dimension of social responsibility. Individuals in such organizations are then put into the position of believing that the only way decisions can be made is in accord with their own personal moral philosophies. No coherent ethical policies will emerge unless there is an understanding of the collective morality that evolves through group decision making. This does not mean that individuals should sacrifice their own personal values and ethics, but it does mean that in the resolution of business ethics issues, attempts must be made collectively to bring ethics into the firm's strategy and daily activities.

In the relationship between ethics, economics, and social responsibility and a firm's strategy, the role of top management is crucial. Organizations tend to reflect the norms and values of top managers, and top managers are regarded as role models for socialization and development of the corporate culture, as discussed in Chapter 6. Top managers must avoid verbalizing vague generalities about ethics; instead, they must demonstrate ethical behavior to others in the organization. Whether they do indeed demonstrate ethical behavior is an important issue. As shown in Figure 4–5, the Ethics Resource Center found in the National Business Ethics Survey that perceptions that top management models ethical behavior differed across employee levels. Written codes of ethics are not by themselves evidence of a business in which executives are socially responsible and which have a corporate culture that promotes legal and ethical behavior. Written codes must include specific guidelines, and top managers must demonstrate law-abiding and ethical behavior on a constant, ongoing basis.

Successful managers achieve their companies' objectives by influencing their employees' behavior. Employees' perceptions of the ethics of their coworkers and managers are often stronger predictors of behavior than the employees' personal beliefs about right or wrong. Thus the overall ethical climate in an organization sets the standards for employee conduct. Superiors in the organization can affect employees' day-to-day activities and directly influence behavior by implementing

FIGURE 4–5   Perception That Leaders Model Ethics — by Employee Level

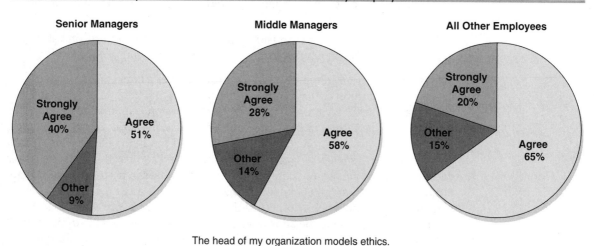

The head of my organization models ethics.

Source: Ethics Resource Center, 2000 National Business Ethics Survey: How Employees Perceive Ethics at Work, *p. 60.*

the company's standard of ethics. The role of management is extremely important in fostering ethical behavior and social responsibility in an organization.

THE ECONOMIC DIMENSION

The **economic dimension** of social responsibility relates to how resources for the production of goods and services are distributed within a social system. Chapter 10 examines the linkage between ethical and socially responsible behavior and profitability.

Investors, with their financial support, appear to have the primary impact on management's decisions. Therefore, management is faced with the balancing act of keeping customers and employees happy while staying within the boundaries of the law and satisfying investors. Two areas within the economic dimension of social responsibility are considered the foundation of social responsibility: the impact of the economy and competition.

The Economy

When people refer to the "economy," they are generally talking about such factors as inflation and employment rates and how these factors affect their ability to purchase the products they need or want. These economic factors are in continual flux, influencing decisions by both businesses and consumers.

Social responsibility, as it relates to the economy, encompasses a number of issues. How businesses relate to competition, stockholders, consumers, employees, the community, and the physical environment affects the economy. For example, the economy is influenced by the economic power of businesses as it relates to the control of resources and the supply of products. A *Business Week*/Harris poll found that 62 percent of respondents agreed strongly or somewhat that business has gained too much power over too many aspects of American life.[28] Political power often arises from the size of the business and its ability to control markets and technology and develop an employee skill base as an advantage. The *Business Week*/Harris poll found that 74 percent of the respondents felt that big companies have too much political influence.[29] Antitrust laws developed out of a fear and mistrust of big business to prohibit contracts or conspiracies that restrain trade and commerce. They specifically dealt with preventing monopolies or attempts to monopolize trade and commerce. They also prohibited price discrimination, unfair competition, and mergers that result in an anticompetitive environment.

The relationship between the natural environment and corporations also affects the economy. The EPA was created in 1970 to coordinate environmental agencies involved in enforcing the nation's environmental laws. The major area of environmental concern relates to air pollution, water pollution, and land pollution. Large corporations are being encouraged to establish pollution-control mechanisms and other policies favorable to the environment; otherwise these companies could deplete resources and damage the health and welfare of society by focusing only on their own economic interests. For example, 3M voluntarily stopped making Scotchguard, a successful product for forty years with $300 million in sales, after tests showed that it did not decompose in the environment.[30] There are many tradeoffs involved in developing both a strong economy and a safe environment.

Stockholders, consumers, and employees are important stakeholders that influence the economy. If companies do not provide a customer focus, then their profitability and ability to compete can be affected significantly. Table 4–6 shows how *Business Week*/Harris poll respondents rated specific industries in serving their consumers. Steven Covey, author of *The 7 Habits of Highly Effective People*, notes that low-trust organizations have internal conflict, higher turnover, product-quality declines, customer loss, and increases in noncompliance.[31]

The effect of business activities on the economy as it relates to employees is significant. Issues include equal job opportunity, workplace diversity, job safety and health, as well as employee privacy. In the United States, the concept of employment-at-will gives companies the right to terminate an employee without just cause and has been used to hire and determine when to terminate employees. Many companies have been involved in corporate downsizing and have ter-

TABLE 4–6   Consumers Rate Service

How would you rate these industries in serving their consumers?

	Only Poor	Pretty Fair	Good	Excellent	Don't Know/ No Answer
HMOs	43%	28%	15%	3%	11%
Tobacco companies	43%	30%	14%	5%	8%
Oil companies	39%	35%	16%	3%	7%
Insurance companies	32%	41%	21%	3%	3%
Pharmaceutical companies	27%	37%	26%	5%	5%
Airlines	22%	41%	25%	3%	9%
Telephone companies	20%	42%	31%	6%	1%
News organizations	18%	38%	33%	6%	5%
Hospitals	15%	35%	38%	9%	3%
Entertainment companies	14%	33%	38%	9%	6%
Automobile companies	12%	42%	37%	6%	3%
Financial service firms	12%	40%	34%	5%	9%
Computer companies	4%	30%	40%	10%	16%

Source: Michael Arndt, Wendy Zellner, and Peter Coy, "Too Much Corporate Power," Business Week, *September 11, 2000, p. 148. Reprinted from September 11, 2000 issue of* Business Week *by special permission. Copyright © 2000 by The McGraw-Hill Companies, Inc.*

minated millions of employees. Unemployed persons create a tremendous drain on the economy in addition to experiencing the personal hardships and suffering that come from being unemployed. The *Business Week*/Harris poll results indicate that almost two-thirds of the respondents felt that job security for employees in big companies was poor (29 percent) or only fair (36 percent).[32]

Because local governments often maintain close ties with business and even offer companies incentives to locate in their areas, citizens may believe that businesses have a social responsibility to the community. Social responsibility problems often center on differences in interpretation of this obligation. In an effort to offset hostile feelings between business and community governments and to protect workers, Congress has enacted legislation requiring a sixty-day notice for all plant closings.

Another ethical issue related to the economic dimension is that of executive compensation. Seventy-three percent of the *Business Week*/Harris poll respondents felt that pay for top executives in large U.S. companies was too high.[33] Many executives receive large compensation and bonus packages whether their organization is financially successful or not. For example, Raytheon Company CEO Daniel P. Burnham received a $900,000 bonus even though the company lost $181 million in one quarter and its stock was trading at $20, down from $76 the previous year.[34] Many large firms are paying costly prices to rid themselves of underperforming CEOs. Conseco, Inc.'s Stephen Hilbert was given a $72.4 million severance package. In the seven years prior to his departure, Hilbert made $457 million, including salary, bonuses, free shares of stock, and gains from exercising stock options.[35]

Competition

Issues of competition in social responsibility arise from the rivalry among businesses for customers and profits. When businesses compete unfairly, legal and social responsibility issues can result. Intense competition sometimes makes managers feel that their company's very survival is threatened. In this situation, managers may begin to see unacceptable alternatives as acceptable, and they may start engaging in questionable practices in an effort to ensure the survival of their organizations.

Some competitive strategies may focus on weakening or destroying a competitor. These strategies can be injurious to competition and have the potential to reduce consumer welfare. Tactics can include sustained price cuts, discriminatory pricing, and price wars. The primary objective of the antitrust laws is to distinguish competitive strategies that enhance consumer welfare from those that reduce it. The difficulty of this task lies in determining when pricing is directed toward weakening and destroying a competitor.[36]

For example, concerns of anticompetitive behavior in the software industry became evident when the Department of Justice investigated Microsoft. Ken Wasch, president of the Software Publishers Association, stated: "Justice clearly recognizes that the restoration of a level playing field in the computer software and technology industries is critical for ensuring consumer choice and ongoing innovation."[37] Microsoft's competitors were concerned because the Microsoft Network Explorer was bundled with Windows software, stifling consumers' choice as to which Internet browser they would utilize. Microsoft operating systems were used on roughly 90 percent of all computers at that time. Consumers and competitors worried that Microsoft had a virtual monopoly on this market.[38]

Intense competition may also lead companies to resort to corporate espionage. Espionage is considered an ethical and legal issue because it gives some companies an unfair advantage over competitors and because it sometimes denies the originator of a product or idea the full benefits of having developed it. Overly aggressive marketing to sell to vulnerable market segments can also create competitive pressures as well as conflicts of interest.

THE PHILANTHROPIC DIMENSION

The **philanthropic dimension** of social responsibility refers to business's contributions to the local community and to society. It provides four major benefits to society. First, the philanthropic dimension improves the quality of life. It helps make communities the type of place where customers want to do business and employees want to raise families. Improving the quality of life makes it easier to attract and retain employees and customers. Second, the philanthropic dimension reduces government involvement by providing help to people with legitimate needs. Third, the philanthropic dimension develops staff leadership skills. Many firms use the United Way campaign and other community service venues as leadership exercises. These campaigns require a marketing plan, processing plan, sales plan, and the support of the entire organization in order to succeed. Fourth, the philanthropic dimension builds staff morale. Employees who volunteer typically feel good about themselves, their company, and their community, and higher morale impacts a firm's bottom line.[39]

Quality-of-Life Issues

People want much more than just the bare necessities — shelter, clothing, and food — required to sustain life. Food must not only provide the nutrients necessary for life and good health but also be conveniently available. Consumers want their food free from toxic chemicals, and they want producers of food to avoid environmental pollution. At the same time, they do not want to see endangered wildlife needlessly injured or killed in the process of food production. For example, some environmentally minded consumers stopped buying shrimp to protest Gulf Coast shrimpers' refusal to use devices that would allow endangered sea turtles to escape drowning in their nets. Our society also expects adequate supplies of low-cost healthy grains and livestock. Thus it expects farmers to produce pest-free and disease-free products without using chemicals that are harmful to consumers or to the laborers who get agricultural products to the market.

The public wants communication systems that allow them to talk to anyone in the world and that quickly provide information from around the globe. At the same time, the public does not want the widespread availability of information to infringe on its privacy. Cisco Systems, Inc., the worldwide leader in networking for the Internet, has responded in this area. Through its philanthropic activities, it provides technological assistance to many nonprofit organizations, empowering them to use the Internet to deliver community services that focus on education and meet such basic human needs as food, shelter, and health care. Cisco technology grants have facilitated delivery of services to homeless shelters, job-training programs, mentorship and role-model programs for youth development, food banks, and national services programs.[40] The public also wants sophisticated medical services that prolong life and make it more tolerable. The pharmaceutical company Merck has responded in this realm. The company discovered that one of its products was effective against the parasite that causes river blindness in the tropical river valleys of Africa, Central and Latin America, and the Middle East, where more than 125 million people are at risk of losing their sight. Since Merck began donating the drug, 11 million people in thirty-two countries have been treated at no cost through a variety of distribution programs.[41] The public expects education to equip them to improve their standard of living. Here, IBM, which counts education as a top priority in its philanthropic efforts, has stepped in. Through its "Reinventing Education" and other strategic efforts, IBM is using advanced information technologies to pave the way for systematic reform in school systems nationwide through partnerships with school districts and states.[42] Consumers also want rapid, convenient, and efficient transportation to take them wherever they want to go, whenever they want to go. They also want clean air, but automobiles are the number-one source of air pollution. As a result, the automobile industry is facing increasing pressure to develop inexpensive, fuel-efficient automobiles that do not contribute to air pollution problems — especially since the earth's shielding ozone layer is being depleted.

People want a high quality of life. They do not want to spend all their waking hours working. They seek leisure time for recreation, entertainment, and relaxation in a pleasant environment. Quality of life is enhanced by leisure time, clean air and water, unlittered earth, conservation of wildlife and natural resources, and security from radiation and poisonous substances. Thus society expects businesses to modify their manufacturing processes to reduce pollutants and wastes.

The environmental responsibility of firms is to avoid the contamination of land, air, and water. Because business activities are a vital part of the total environment, businesspeople have a responsibility to help provide what society wants and to minimize harmful products and conditions that it does not want. Table 4–7 shows organizational support of specific environmental policies and practices.

Philanthropic Issues[43]

A final set of issues for businesses concerns their responsibilities for the general welfare of the communities in which they operate. Many businesses simply want to make their communities better places for everyone to live and work in. Although

TABLE 4–7   Organizational Support of Specific Environmental Policies
and Practices

Policies and Practices*	Yes (%)	No (%)	Don't Know (%)
Written environmental policy	83.5	7.6	9.0
Smoke-free workplace	91.8	6.2	2.1
Recycling	74.7	24.7	0.7
Influence state and federal environmental regulations	52.1	36.3	11.6
Waste-reduction investments	69.7	28.3	2.1

*Do not necessarily add to 100 percent because of rounding.

Source: Alan K. Reichert, Marion S. Webb, and Edward G. Thomas, "Corporate Support for Ethical & Environmental Policies: A Financial Management Perspective," Journal of Business Ethics, 2000, Vol. 25, p. 60. Reprinted by permission of Kluwer Academic Publishers, Dordrecht, Holland.

such efforts cover many diverse areas, some of the activities are especially noteworthy. The most common way that businesses exercise their community responsibility is through donations to local and national charitable organizations. Corporations gave $11.02 billion to charities last year, an increase of 14 percent over the previous year.[44] At Polaroid, employees make the decisions on charitable contributions through the Polaroid Foundation, which focuses on increasing self-sufficiency among the disadvantaged by building their skills.[45] Local economic development has been a part of Pitney Bowes's corporate culture for nearly thirty years. Pitney Bowes, which has revenues of $4.2 billion, has, for example, worked with organizations to improve the community by donating property for an affordable housing complex and participating in a down-payment assistance program for home ownership.[46] Philanthropic activities can support overall profitability.

Many companies have become concerned about the quality of education in the United States, after realizing that the current pool of prospective employees lack many basic work skills. Recognizing that today's students are tomorrow's employees and customers, firms such as Kroger, Campbell Soup Co., Eastman Kodak, American Express, Apple Computer, Xerox, and Coca-Cola have donated money, equipment, and employee time to help improve schools in their communities and throughout the nation. Hewlett-Packard's Diversity in Education Initiative focuses on math and science in four minority communities and works with students from elementary school to the university level. The program provides hands-on science kits to elementary and middle schools and gives forty high school students (ten from each community) annual $3,000 college scholarships. A mentor is assigned to each student, and they are given a paid summer internship at Hewlett-Packard and taught how to conduct a job search.[47]

Organizations are also interested in supporting the arts. Many aspects of the arts — museums, civic centers, and symphony orchestras — would not exist without individual and corporate help. Sara Lee Corp. donated thirty-five to forty paintings and sculptures — including works by Monet, Picasso, Matisse, and Chagall — to museums and institutes throughout the United States. Sara Lee executives felt that they had benefited from the arts and wanted to show civic and public responsibility.[48] Many U.S. businesses are giving more each year to the arts. In the 1990s, contributions reached almost $2 billion.[49] Some companies seeking to do good through philanthropy link gifts to marketing activities.

Strategic Philanthropy

Tying philanthropic giving to overall strategy and objectives is also known as **strategic philanthropy.** Strategic philanthropy is the synergistic and mutually beneficial use of organizational core competencies and resources to deal with key stakeholders in order to bring about organizational and societal benefits. For example, last year Hewlett-Packard (HP) gave $57.9 million in cash and equipment to nonprofit agencies and educational institutions worldwide. Seventy percent of the contributions went to education, the arts, health and human services, civic groups, and environmental organizations. The donations were given in areas where HP employees reside.[50] Founder's Week, McDonald's annual celebration of company founder Ray Kroc's birthday, focuses on giving back to local communities. Last year, McDonald's employees nationwide participated in twenty-five thousand hours of community service, including tutoring children, painting classrooms, planting trees and shrubs, constructing homes with Habitat for Humanity, and assisting families and children at Ronald McDonald Houses across the country.[51] Both Hewlett-Packard and McDonald's realize the benefits of supporting causes that are of interest to their target market.

SUMMARY

Although the concepts of business ethics and social responsibility are often used interchangeably, each term has a distinct meaning. Social responsibility in business refers to an organization's obligation to maximize its positive impact and minimize its negative impact on society.

This chapter described the four dimensions of social responsibility: legal, ethical, economic, and philanthropic. The legal responsibilities have been enforced by society to eliminate unacceptable behavior. Ethical responsibilities relate to what firms decide to be right, just, and fair beyond strictly legal requirements. Economic responsibilities are the foundation of all business activities. Finally, philanthropic responsibilities relate to the contribution of financial and human resources to the community and greater society to improve the quality of life.

The legal dimension of social responsibility refers to laws and regulations established by government to set minimum standards for behavior. Laws regulating business conduct are passed because society — including consumers, interest groups, competitors, and legislators — believes that business must comply with standards established by society. Such laws regulate competition, protect consumers, protect the environment, promote equity and safety, and provide incentives for preventing misconduct.

The ethical dimension of social responsibility refers to behaviors and activities that organizational members, the community, and society expect from business, even though they may not be written into law. Firms need to respond to stakeholders and concerned others in society in an ethical manner. It is important to perform in a manner consistent with social standards and ethical norms. For ethics to be a part of social responsibility, business strategy must reflect an understanding of the values of organizational members and stakeholders and an understanding of the ethical nature of strategic choice.

The economic dimension of social responsibility relates to how resources for the production of products are distributed within a social system. The economic dimension also relates to a company's focus on providing employment to sustain growth and profits and returns to investors. Ethical issues in competition arise when businesses do not compete fairly and do not use legal and socially accepted methods of gaining advantage.

The philanthropic dimension of social responsibility refers to business's contributions to the local community and to society. It provides four major benefits to society by improving the quality of life, reducing government involvement, developing staff leadership skills, and building staff morale. Companies contribute significant amounts of money to education, the arts, environmental causes, and the disadvantaged by supporting local and national charitable organizations. Strategic philanthropy involves linking core business competencies to societal and community needs.

| Important Terms for Review | corporate citizenship
legal dimension
civil law
criminal law
procompetitive legislation
consumer protection laws
environmental protection laws | Federal Sentencing Guidelines
  for Organizations
ethical dimension
economic dimension
issues of competition
philanthropic dimension
strategic philanthropy |

A Real-Life Situation*

Albert Chen was sweating profusely in his Jaguar on the expressway as he thought about his options and the fact that Christmas and the Chinese New Year were at hand. He and his wife, Mary, who were on their way to meet Albert's parents at New York's John F. Kennedy Airport, seemed to be looking up from an abyss, with no daylight to be seen. Several visits and phone calls from various people had engulfed both him and Mary.

He had graduated with honors in finance and had married Mary in his senior year. They had both obtained prestigious brokerage jobs in the New York area, and both had been working killer hours to develop their accounts. Listening to other brokers, both had learned that there were some added expenses. For example, they were told that brokers need to "look" and "act" successful. So Albert and Mary bought the appropriate clothes and cars, joined the right clubs, and ate at the right restaurants with the right people. They also took the advice of others, which was to identify the "players" of large corporations at parties and take mental notes. "You'd be surprised at what information you hear with a little alcohol in these people," said one broker. Both started using this strategy, and five months later their clients began to see significant profits in their portfolios.

Their good luck even came from strange places. For example, Albert had an uncle whose work as a janitor gave him access to many law offices that had information on a number of companies, especially those about to file for bankruptcy. Mary and Albert were able to use information provided by this uncle to benefit their clients' portfolios. The uncle even had some of his friends use Albert. To Albert's surprise, his uncle's friends often had nest eggs in excess of $200,000. Because some of these friends were quite elderly, Albert was given permission to buy and sell nonrisky stocks at will.

As both of them were earning good salaries, the Chens soon managed to invest in the market

themselves, and their investments included stock in the company for which Mary's father worked. After eighteen months, Albert decided to jump ship and start working for Jarvis, Sunni, Lamar & Morten (JSL&M). JSL&M's reputation was of a fast mover in the business. "We go up to the line and then measure how wide the line is so that we know how far we can go into it," was a common remark at the brokerage firm.

About six months ago, Mary's father, who was with a major health care company, commented that the management team was running the company into the ground. "If only someone could buy the company and put in a good management team," he mused. After the conversation, Mary investigated the company and discovered that the stock was grossly undervalued. She made a few phone calls and found a company that was interested in doing a hostile takeover. Mary also learned from her father that if a new management were acceptable to the union, the union would do everything in its power to oust the old management — by striking, if necessary — and welcome the new one. As things started to materialize, Mary told several of her best clients, who in turn did very well on the stock. This increased her status in the firm, which kept drawing bigger clients.

Albert soon became a player in initial public stock offerings (IPOs) of new companies. Occasionally, when Albert saw a very hot IPO, he would talk to some of his best venture-capital types, who then bought the IPOs and gained some very good returns. This strategy helped attract some larger players in the market. By this point in his young career, Albert had made a great many friends.

One of those friends was Barry, who worked on the stock floor. As they were talking, Barry mentioned that if Albert wanted to, he, as a favor, when placing orders to buy shares, would occasionally put Albert's or Mary's trade before the client order.

The first sign of trouble came when Mary told Albert about what was happening at her office. "I'm getting e-mail from some of the brokers with off-color jokes and even some nude photos of women and men. I just don't care for it." "So what are you doing about it?" Albert asked. "Well, I've just started not even opening my messages if they come from these people," Mary replied. "What about messages that request that you send them on? What do you do with those?" queried Albert. "I just e-mail them along without looking at them," was her response. "This isn't good, Mary. A couple of analysts were just fired for doing that at a big firm last week," said Albert. Several weeks later the people who were sending Mary the obnoxious messages were fired. Mary was also asked to see the head of her division. When she came to his office, he said, "Please shut the door, Mary. I have some bad news. I know that you weren't involved with what was happening with the e-mail scandal; however, you did forward messages that contained such material. As a result, I have no alternative but to give you your two weeks' notice. I know this is unfair, but I have my orders. Because of this mess, the SEC [Securities and Exchange Commission] wants to check all your trades for the last eight months. It seems to be a formality, but it will take time, and as you well know, the chances of going to another firm with that hanging over your head are slim. I'm sorry that it's only two months until the holidays." That night Mary fell into a depression.

To exacerbate the situation, Albert's parents were flying in from the People's Republic of China. They were not happy with Albert's marriage to a Caucasian, but they had consoled themselves that Mary had a good job. They had also said that if things should go badly for them in New York, they could always come to the parents' retirement home in Taiwan. However, the idea of leaving the United States, attempting to learn Mandarin, and raising children in an unfamiliar culture did not appeal to Mary.

Albert was also having some problems. As their income was cut in half, Albert tried to make up for the loss by trading in some high-risk markets, such as commodities and metals. However, many of these investments turned sour, and he found himself buying and selling more and more to pull his own portfolio, as well as those of his clients, into the black. He was getting worried because some of his uncle's friends' portfolios were losing significant value. Other matters, however, were causing him even more anxiety. The previous week Barry had called him, asking for some inside information on several companies that he was working with for an IPO. Albert knew that this could be construed as insider information and had said no. Today Barry called again and said, "Look, Al, I've been doing you favors for a while. I need to score big because of the holidays. You probably don't know, but what I've been doing for you could be construed as spinning, which is not looked upon favorably. I'm not asking for the IPO information — I'm demanding it. Is that clear enough for you, Al? E-mail it over by tomorrow morning." Then Barry hung up. An hour later Albert's supervisor came in and said, "Al, I need a favor from you. I want you to buy some stock for me and a few friends. When it goes to $112, I want you to sell it. We'll pay the taxes and give you a little bonus for Christmas as well. I want you to buy tomorrow as soon as the market opens. Here are the account numbers for the transaction. I must run. See you tomorrow."

Questions ■ Exercises

1. Identify the ethical and legal issues of which Albert needs to be aware.
2. Discuss the advantages and disadvantages of each decision Albert could make and has made.
3. Identify the pressures that have brought about these issues.

This case is strictly hypothetical; any resemblance to real persons, companies, or situations is coincidental.

CHECK YOUR E◗

Check your E.Q., or Ethics Quotient, by completing the following. Assess your performance to evaluate your overall understanding of the chapter material.

1. Social responsibility in business refers to maximizing the visibility of social involvement.   Yes   No

2. The primary method of resolving business ethics disputes is through the criminal court system.   Yes   No

3. The Federal Sentencing Guidelines for Organizations provide an incentive for organizations to conscientiously develop and implement ethics programs.   Yes   No

4. You can eliminate ethics problems if you abide by the laws governing your company and industry.   Yes   No

5. Strategic philanthropy represents a new direction in corporate giving that maximizes the benefit to societal or community needs and relates to business objectives.   Yes   No

ANSWERS 1. No. Social responsibility refers to an organizational obligation to maximize its positive impact on society and minimize its negative impact. 2. No. Lawsuits and civil litigation are the primary way in which business ethics disputes are resolved. 3. Yes. Well-designed ethics and compliance programs can minimize legal liability when organizational misconduct is detected. 4. No. Ethics relates to right or wrong behavior within your organization and industry, which may not relate to a particular law or regulation. 5. Yes. Strategic philanthropy helps society and the organization.

A Framework for Understanding Ethical Decision Making in Business

CHAPTER 5

Chapter Objectives

- To provide a comprehensive framework for ethical decision making in business
- To examine ethical issue intensity as an important element influencing the ethical decision-making process
- To describe the stages of cognitive moral development for individual ethical decision making in business
- To examine the impact of business ethics evaluations and intentions
- To explain how knowledge about the ethical decision-making framework can be used to improve business ethics

Chapter Outline

An Ethical Dilemma*

Bill Church was in a bind. A recent graduate of a prestigious business school, he had taken a job in the auditing division of Greenspan & Co., a fast-growing leader in the accounting industry. Greenspan relocated Bill, his wife, and their 1-year-old daughter from the Midwest to the East Coast. On arriving, they bought their first home and a second car. Bill was told that the company had big plans for him. Thus he did not worry about being financially overextended.

Several months into the job, Bill found that he was working late into the night to complete his auditing assignments. He realized that the company did not want its clients billed for excessive hours and that he needed to become more efficient if he wanted to move up in the company. He asked one of his friends, Ann, how she managed to be so efficient in auditing client records.

Ann quietly explained: "Bill, there are times when being efficient isn't enough. You need to do what is required to get ahead. The partners just want results — they don't care how you get them."

"I don't understand," said Bill.

"Look," Ann explained, "I had the same problem you have a few years ago, but Mr. Reed [the manager of the auditing department] explained that everyone eats time so that the group shows top results and looks good. And when the group looks good, everyone in it looks good. No one cares if a little time gets lost in the shuffle."

Bill realized that "eating time" meant not reporting all the hours required to complete a project. He also remembered one of Reed's classic phrases, "results, results, results." He thanked Ann for her input and went back to work. Bill thought of going over Reed's head and asking for advice from the division manager, but he had met her only once and did not know anything about her.

Questions ■ Exercises

1. What should Bill do? Describe the process through which Bill might attempt to resolve his dilemma.
2. Consider the impact of this company's approach on young accountants. Why could working long hours be an ethical problem?

This case is strictly hypothetical; any resemblance to real persons, companies, or situations is coincidental.

To improve ethical decision making within a business organization, one must first understand how individuals make ethical decisions. Some philosophers, social scientists, and other academics have attempted to explain the ethical decision-making process in business by examining ethical issue intensity, individual moral philosophy, or corporate culture, including the influence of coworkers. This chapter summarizes our current knowledge of ethical decision-making frameworks for business. While it is impossible to describe exactly how an individual or a work group might make ethical decisions, we can provide generalizations about average or typical behavior patterns within organizations. These generalizations are based on many studies and at least six ethical decision models.[1]

In this chapter we describe a framework for understanding ethical decision making in a business organization context. This framework, shown in Figure 5–1, integrates concepts from moral philosophy, psychology, sociology, and business.

FIGURE 5–1   Framework for Understanding Ethical Decision Making in Business

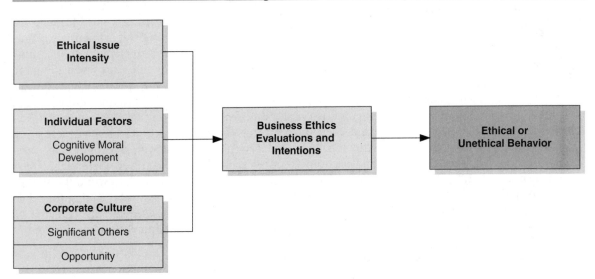

It is specific to ethical decisions made in an organization in which a work-group environment exists. Too often it has been assumed that individuals make ethical decisions within an organization in the same manner that they make ethical decisions at home, in their family or their personal lives. Within the context of an organizational work group, most individuals do not have the freedom to decide ethical issues independently of organizational pressures. The key components of the framework include perceived ethical issue intensity; individual factors, such as cognitive moral development, age and gender; and corporate culture. These factors are all interrelated, and they influence business ethics evaluations and intentions that result in ethical or unethical behavior.

ETHICAL ISSUE INTENSITY

The first step in ethical decision making is to become aware that an ethical issue requires the individual or work group to choose among several actions that must be evaluated as right or wrong. In the context of business, an ethical issue has consequences for others inside the organization and/or external to the organization. The intensity of an ethical issue relates to the perceived importance of the issue to the decision maker.[2] **Ethical issue intensity,** then, can be defined as the perceived relevance or importance of an ethical issue to the individual, work group, and/or organization. It is personal and temporal in character in order to accommodate values, beliefs, needs, perceptions, the special characteristics of the situation, and the personal pressures existing on an ongoing basis or at a particular place and time.[3] Ethical issue intensity is a cognitive state of concern about an issue, which indicates involvement in making choices.

Ethical issue intensity reflects the ethical sensitivity of the individual or work group triggering the ethical decision process. One study found that perceived moral intensity increases perceptions of ethical problems, which in turn reduce intentions to act unethically.[4] All the other factors in Figure 5–1, including cognitive moral development, corporate culture, and intentions, determine why ethical issues are perceived differently by different individuals.[5] For example, the study mentioned above found that, on average, women have more ethical intentions than men.[6] Unless individuals in an organization maintain some common concerns about ethical issues, the stage is set for ethical conflict. The perception of ethical issue intensity can be influenced by management, which can use rewards and punishments, codes of ethics, and values from the corporate culture to this end. In other words, managers can affect the perceived importance of an ethical issue through positive and/or negative incentives.[7]

Ethical issues may not reach the critical awareness level of some employees if management fails to identify and educate employees about problem areas. Employees who have diverse values and backgrounds should be trained on how the organization wants specific ethical issues handled. Identifying ethical issues that employees might encounter is a significant step in developing employees' ability to make ethical decisions. Many ethical issues are identified by industry groups or through general information available to a firm. For example, discrimination based on race, sex, or age is considered an important ethical issue by most firms. Discrimination by businesses often stems from work-group attitudes toward a particular group. For example, the minority dealership program at General Motors has had problems since it began. Through the courts and in the media, minority dealership owners accused the company of overcharging for dealerships, providing inadequate training, and giving black dealers poor economic locations. A year-long investigation of the troubles resulted in a three-inch-thick report that detailed two hundred and fifteen specific actions that General Motors needed to take. GM has adopted two hundred and thirteen of the recommendations, and results are encouraging. About 80 percent of the three hundred and twenty minority dealerships are now profitable, and one in six earned more than $1 million last year.[8] In another case, American General insurance company agreed to pay restitution of $206 million to black customers it had overcharged. The company charged blacks as much as 33 percent more than whites for burial-expense policies.[9]

In order to be in legal compliance with the Federal Sentencing Guidelines for Organizations, discussed in Chapters 1 and 4, firms must assess areas of ethical and legal risk that are, in reality, ethical issues. Issues that are communicated as high in ethical importance could trigger increases in ethical issue intensity. The perceived importance of an ethical issue has been found to have a strong impact on both ethical judgment and behavioral intention. The more likely individuals are to perceive an ethical issue as important, the less likely they are to engage in questionable or unethical behavior associated with the issue.[10] Therefore, ethical issue intensity should be considered a key factor in the ethical decision process.

INDIVIDUAL FACTORS: STAGES OF COGNITIVE MORAL DEVELOPMENT

Chapter 3 gives an overview of various moral philosophies that an individual may use as a guide to ethics evaluations. This section provides a well-accepted model that describes the cognitive moral development process — that is, the stages through which people progress in their development of moral thought. Most of the models developed to explain, predict, and control ethical behavior of individuals within a business organization propose that cognitive moral processing is a crucial element in ethical decision making. The theory of cognitive moral development is based on a body of literature in psychology that focuses on studying children and their cognitive development.[11] Psychologist Lawrence Kohlberg developed the six-stage model described in the following pages,[12] though it was not developed specifically for business. According to **Kohlberg's model of cognitive moral development,** different people make different decisions in similar ethical situations because they are in different stages of cognitive moral development. Kohlberg proposed that individuals develop through the following six stages:

1. *The stage of punishment and obedience.* An individual in Kohlberg's stage 1 defines *right* as literal obedience to rules and authority. A person in this stage will respond to rules and labels of "good" and "bad" in terms of the physical power of those who determine such rules. Right and wrong are not associated with any higher order or philosophy but rather with a person who has power. Stage 1 is usually associated with small children, but signs of stage 1 development are also evident in adult behavior. For example, some companies forbid their buyers to accept gifts from salespeople. A buyer in stage 1 might justify a refusal to accept gifts from salespeople by referring to the company's rule that defines accepting gifts as an unethical practice, or the buyer may accept the gift if he or she believes that there is no chance of being caught.

2. *The stage of individual instrumental purpose and exchange.* An individual in stage 2 defines *right* as that which serves one's own needs. In this stage, the individual no longer makes moral decisions only on the basis of specific rules or authority figures; the person now evaluates behavior on the basis of its fairness to him or her. For example, a sales representative in stage 2 doing business for the first time in a foreign country may be expected by custom to give customers "gifts." Although gift giving may be against company policy in the United States, the salesperson may decide that certain company rules designed for operating in the United States do not apply over-

seas. In the culture of some foreign countries, gifts may be considered part of a person's pay. So, in this instance, not giving a gift might represent an unfair deal for the salesperson. Some refer to stage 2 as the stage of reciprocity, where, from a practical standpoint, ethical decisions are based on an agreement that "you scratch my back and I'll scratch yours" instead of on principles of loyalty, gratitude, or justice.

3. *The stage of mutual interpersonal expectations, relationships, and conformity.* An individual in stage 3 emphasizes others rather than himself or herself. Although motivation is still derived from obedience to rules, the individual considers the well-being of others. A production manager in this stage might obey upper management's order to speed up an assembly line if he or she believed that this action would generate more profit for the company and thus maintain employee jobs. The manager not only considers his or her own well-being in terms of following the order, but also tries to put himself or herself in upper management's position as well as in the employees' situation. Thus stage 3 differs from stage 2 in terms of the individual's motives in considering fairness to others.

4. *The stage of social system and conscience maintenance.* An individual in stage 4 determines what is right by considering his or her duty to society, not just to other specific people. Duty, respect for authority, and maintaining the social order become the focal points. For example, assuring the personal privacy of employees in the workplace could be viewed by some as an employer's duty. However, potentially improper uses of internal computer networks that may result in fraud, insider trading, or espionage by a company's employees lead some organizations to use computer security software. Raytheon Systems Co.'s SilentRunner software identifies patterns of data traffic that may signal problems, and it is virtually undetectable. However, the software can also be used by a company to find out everything about electronic conversations between employees. The software's capabilities have unleashed new concerns about "Big Brother" in the workplace.[13]

5. *The stage of prior rights, social contract, or utility.* In stage 5, an individual is concerned with upholding the basic rights, values, and legal contracts of society. Individuals in this stage feel a sense of obligation or commitment, a "social contract," to other groups and recognize that in some cases legal and moral points of view may conflict. To reduce such conflict, stage 5 individuals base their decisions on a rational calculation of overall utilities. The president of a firm may decide to establish an ethics program because it will provide a buffer to prevent legal problems, and the firm will be a responsible contributor to society.

6. *The stage of universal ethical principles.* A person in this stage believes that right is determined by universal ethical principles that everyone should follow. Stage 6 individuals believe that there are inalienable rights, which are universal in nature and consequence. These rights, laws, or social agreements are valid not because of a particular society's laws or customs, but

because they rest on the premise of universality. Justice and equality are examples of principles that are deemed universal in nature. A person in this stage may be more concerned with social ethical issues and not rely on the business organization for ethical direction. For example, a businessperson at this stage might argue for discontinuing a product that has caused death and injury because the inalienable right to life makes killing wrong, regardless of the reason. Therefore, company profits would not be a justification for the continued sale of the product.[14]

Kohlberg's six stages can be reduced to three different levels of ethical concern. Initially, a person is concerned with his or her own immediate interests and with external rewards and punishments. At the second level, an individual defines *right* as conforming to the expectations of good behavior of the larger society or some significant reference group. Finally, at the third, or "principled," level, an individual sees beyond the norms, laws, and authority of groups or individuals. Employees at this level make ethical decisions regardless of negative external pressures. However, research has shown that most workers have less developed abilities to identify and resolve moral dilemmas and that their motives are often a mixture of selflessness, self-interest, and selfishness. These findings suggest that an organization's formal structure plays an important role in affecting workers' ethical behavior.[15] Kohlberg's model implies that a person's level of moral development influences his or her perception of and response to an ethical issue.

Kohlberg's model suggests that people continue to change their decision priorities beyond their formative years. According to his model, as people progress through the stages of moral development, and with time, education, and experience, they may change their values and ethical behavior. In the context of business, an individual's moral development can be influenced by corporate culture, especially ethics training. In the National Business Ethics Survey (NBES), 55 percent of employees in for-profit organizations reported that their organizations provide ethics training, while 70 percent of government employees and 65 percent of employees in nonprofit organizations indicated the presence of ethics training.[16] Eighty-four percent of the employees who reported the presence of ethics training in their organizations said that the training was mandatory.[17] Training and education in the organization commonly occur through company policies, ethics handbooks, videotapes, on-line assistance, and ethics newsletters. Fifty-four percent of the employees in the NBES indicated that ethics training was frequently useful in guiding work-related decisions and conduct.[18] However, this is not always true. One study found that the value of compulsory ethics education as a way to improve the moral reasoning of real estate salespeople was highly questionable.[19]

Experience in resolving moral conflicts accelerates progress in moral development. A manager relying on a specific set of values or rules may eventually come across a situation to which the rules do not apply. For example, suppose George is a manager who has a policy of firing any employee whose productivity declines for four consecutive months. George has an employee, Beth, whose productivity has suffered because of depression, but George firmly believes that Beth will be a top performer again within a month or two. Because of the circumstances and the perceived value of the employee, George may bend the rule. Managers in the highest stages of the moral development process seem to be more democratic than autocratic. They are likely to be more aware of the ethical views of others involved in an ethical decision-making situation.

An important question may be whether measures of individual cognitive moral development are the best predictors of ethical behavior in a business organization. A study by the authors found that only 15 percent of a sample of businesspersons maintained the same moral philosophy in both work and nonwork ethical decision-making situations.[20] One explanation may be that cognitive moral development issues that relate to a person's nonwork experiences and home and family situations are not the most significant factors in organizational ethics issues.[21] Research indicates that perceived ethicalness of the work group, rather than individual cognitive moral development, may be the most important consideration in determining ethical behavior within a business.[22] Nevertheless, most experts agree that a person's cognitive moral development plays a role in how values and actions are shaped in the workplace.

CORPORATE CULTURE

A **corporate culture** can be defined as a set of values, beliefs, goals, norms, and ways to solve problems that members (employees) of an organization share. As time passes, a company or organization comes to be seen as a living organism, with a mind and will of its own. For example, The Walt Disney Company requires all new employees to take a course in the traditions and history of Disneyland and Walt Disney, including the ethical dimensions of the organization. The corporate culture at American Express Company stresses that employees help customers out of difficult situations whenever possible. This attitude is reinforced through numerous company legends of employees who have gone above and beyond the call of duty to help customers. This strong tradition of customer loyalty might encourage an American Express employee to take unorthodox steps to help a customer who encounters a problem while traveling overseas. Employees learn that they can take some risks in helping customers. Such strong traditions and values have become a driving force in many companies, including McDonald's Corp., IBM, The Procter & Gamble Co., Southwest Airlines Co., and Hershey Foods Corp. Saturn is a division of General Motors but has developed its own corporate culture, including values related to product quality, customer service, and fairness in pricing.

The formal organizational structure determines how employees are placed into various positions, jobs, departments, and divisions. New employees learn who is important and who is not through knowing the organizational structure. More formalized organizational structures often have more procedures and written rules that are enforced. A formal organizational structure combined with a values-based corporate culture may be the best combination to promote ethical organizational conduct.[23]

Some corporate cultures provide the opportunity for unethical conduct. The following example illustrates that corporate culture can change, however. After months of legal troubles, the Coca-Cola Co. reached a tentative settlement in a class-action lawsuit that had charged the company with discriminating against blacks in promotions, evaluations, terminations, and pay. It is almost impossible for widespread discrimination and mistreatment to occur without top management, as well as supervisory management, condoning the behavior. In the case of the Coca-Cola Co., CEO Doug Ivester had demoted the company's top black executive, Carl Ware. Ware announced his retirement within days. Ware was a key link to the black community in Atlanta, and four years earlier he had written a memo on how the Coca-Cola Co. could help black employees rise through the ranks. Just months after Ware's retirement, Ivester himself was out of a job. Doug Daft, the new CEO, has tried to reinvent the corporate culture at the Coca-Cola Co. He persuaded Ware to return and has adopted some of Ware's suggestions, including tying managers' compensation to diversity goals.[24] The Coca-Cola Co. has also committed $1 billion over a five-year period to increase relationships with minority businesses and activities in ethnic communities.[25]

As shown in the example just discussed, the ethical climate of the organization is a component of the corporate culture. Whereas corporate culture involves norms that prescribe a wide range of behavior for members of the organization, the ethical climate indicates whether organizations have an ethical conscience. The **ethical climate component** of corporate culture can be thought of as the character or decision processes used to determine whether responses to issues are right or wrong.[26] Factors such as corporate codes of ethics, top-management actions on ethical issues, ethical policies, the influence of coworkers, and the opportunity for unethical behavior are all captured by the ethical climate concept. The organizational culture and the resulting ethical climate may be directly related to the recognition of ethical dimensions of decisions, the generation of alternatives, and individual cognitive moral development. In a number of studies, the perceived ethicalness of the immediate work group has been found to be a major factor influencing ethical behavior.[27] The more ethical the culture of the organization is perceived to be, the less likely it is that unethical decision making will occur. This aspect of corporate culture and ethical climate is closely associated with the idea that significant others are a key determinant of ethical decisions within an organization. The concept of ethical climate integrates collective individual cognitive moral development, significant others, and opportunity, as they relate to how the organization perceives and deals with ethics-related issues.

Significant Others

Those who have influence in a work group, including peers, managers, coworkers, and subordinates, are referred to as **significant others.** Significant others help workers on a daily basis with unfamiliar tasks and provide advice and information in both formal and informal ways. A manager may provide directives about certain types of activities to be performed on the job. Coworkers, such as peers, offer help in the form of comments in discussions over lunch or when the boss is away. Numerous studies conducted over the years confirm that significant others have more impact on a worker's decisions on a daily basis than any other factor in our framework.[28] Work groups also help determine organizational culture and opportunity, which will be discussed later in this chapter.

A worker learns ethical or unethical behavior through interactions with people who are part of his or her intimate personal groups. In other words, a decision maker who associates with others who behave unethically will be more likely to behave unethically, too. The NBES found that one in eight employees felt pressure to compromise their organizations' ethics standards.[29] Figure 5–2 shows the NBES findings on sources of that pressure.

The role that an individual plays in the organization may depend on such characteristics as age, time with the company, or expertise about the job. In the NBES, for example, employees with longer tenure (more than five years) in their organizations felt more pressure to compromise organizational ethics standards than

FIGURE 5–2   **Sources of Pressure to Compromise Ethics Standards**

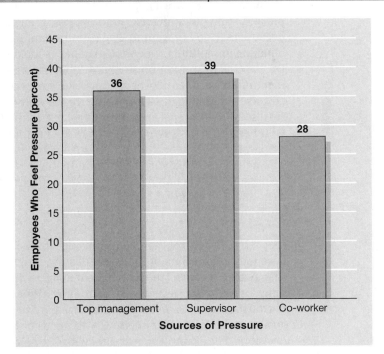

Source: *The Ethics Resource Center,* 2000 National Business Ethics Survey: How Employees Perceive Ethics at Work, *p. 38. Reprinted with permission.*

employees with shorter tenure.[30] Regardless of the assigned job, employees might ask an experienced person for advice on how to ask a superior for a raise or whether to report an incident of unethical activity by a coworker. The distance or number of layers of personnel between the person making the decision and significant others will affect ethical decisions. For example, if there are four layers of management between a decision maker and the regional vice president, the vice president may have only marginal influence on the decision maker. With fewer layers of management between them, the influence would be greater. Of course, some high-ranking managers in an organization may have so much charisma and personal visibility that their suggestions, ideas, and value system may be adopted throughout the organization.

Obedience to authority relates to another aspect of the influence of significant others. Workers usually play a particular role in performing their duties in the company, and obedience to authority can help explain why many people resolve business ethics issues by following the directives of a superior. In organizations that emphasize respect for superiors, for example, employees may feel that they are expected to carry out orders by a superior even if the orders are contrary to the employees' feelings of right and wrong. Later, if a decision is judged to have been wrong, an employee is likely to say, "I was only carrying out orders" or "My boss told me to do it this way."

Superiors can have a negative effect on ethical behavior by setting a bad example and failing to supervise subordinates. Many supervisors look the other way because they do not want to deal with the conflict and other risks associated with handling misconduct. One such instance of looking the other way occurred at the Du Pont plant in Memphis, where supervisors failed to stop the sexual harassment of a female employee by her male coworkers over a five-year period. One coworker in particular routinely referred to women in derogatory or vulgar terms. He also told other male workers not to talk to the female employee, share meals with her, or follow any of her instructions without first checking with him. The employee, who was with the company for 18 years, left with a diagnosis of posttraumatic stress disorder brought on by the years of harassment, isolation, and denigration. After charging the company with sexual harassment and winning the case, she was awarded $407,000. Additional compensation is possible because rights to loss of future pay are being considered.[31]

Workers do not have to be controlled by the company or by their coworkers if they strive to control their own decisions. Individuals who exert such efforts believe they are masters of their own destiny, and they make things happen rather than react to events. For example, a manager who consistently accepts responsibility for his or her decisions is controlling his or her own destiny. The degree of a person's self-esteem and self-confidence may contribute to the decision to either go along with ethical (or unethical) decisions or to refuse to participate in certain decisions. For example, a manager with low self-esteem and a feeling of dependence may go along with a scheme that results in an unethical action. When confronted with the unethical action, the manager may say that he or she was just doing a job. Conversely, a worker with high self-esteem and a feeling of competence may rely more on his or her values and, whether right or wrong, will take responsibility for decisions. This person will be less likely to depend on others in resolving ethical issues.

Stress on the job has been found to be a major factor influencing unethical behavior.[32] As an indication of the prevalence and seriousness of on-the-job role stress, a recent survey showed that 21 percent of the responding firms offered stress-reduction programs and 8 percent offered massage therapy to employees.[33] **Role stress** is the strain, conflict, or disruptive result of a lack of agreement on certain job-related activities. The role that an individual plays within a business, including the various tasks that have the potential to create conflict, may have a direct bearing on ethical decision-making behavior.

Some tasks require a decision maker to make many more tradeoffs and to face many more ethical dilemmas than others. Salespeople, for example, are often confronted by customers who state or imply that they will purchase a product if given extra personal incentives that may be against company policy — that is, a bribe. Accountants who are working on the audit of a company may be called aside and asked not to report information in a way that might disclose discrepancies. A personnel manager may discriminate against a minority. Marketing managers face many ethical dilemmas when making advertising decisions. For example, in an effort to increase use by business travelers, some airlines aggressively marketed coach frills and extras that were not actually available to most passengers, and in some cases, were not even available. A United Airlines' ad for Economy Plus, a roomier section in coach, failed to state that only full fare and high-mileage customers qualified. JetBlue, a New York–based airline, advertised live TV at every seat. However, TV is unavailable because the Federal Aviation Administration has not approved the necessary antenna.[34] In another case, a dramatic commercial for Nuveen Investments that was shown during the highly watched Super Bowl led some people to believe that actor Christopher Reeve could walk again. In the computer-engineered ad, Reeve, who was paralyzed in a horse-riding accident, was shown rising from a chair and walking to a stage. The executive director of the National Spinal Cord Injury Association felt the commercial might have given too much hope to paralyzed people. He said, "When you go out with an advertisement like that, you tread a very, very narrow line between trying to be creative . . . and being misleading."[35] Since there is little doubt that ethical decision making is stressful for decision makers who face conflict, the tendency is for role-stress situations to increase the likelihood of unethical behavior.

Opportunity

Opportunity is a term that describes the conditions that limit or permit ethical or unethical behavior. Opportunity results from conditions that either provide rewards, whether internal or external, or fail to erect barriers against unethical behavior. Examples of internal rewards include feelings of goodness and personal worth generated by performing altruistic activities. External rewards refer to what an individual expects to receive from others in the social environment. Rewards are external to the individual to the degree that they bring social approval, status, and esteem.

An example of a condition that fails to erect barriers against unethical behavior is a company policy that does not punish employees who accept large gifts from clients. The absence of punishment provides an opportunity for unethical behavior because it allows individuals to engage in such behavior without fear of consequences. Opportunity as an aspect of ethical decision making is explored in more detail in Chapter 8.

Opportunity relates to individuals' immediate job context — where they work, whom they work with, and the nature of the work. The **immediate job context** includes the motivational carrots and sticks that superiors use to influence employee behavior. Pay raises, bonuses, and public recognition are carrots, or positive reinforcers, whereas demotions, firings, reprimands, and pay penalties act as sticks, the negative reinforcers. For example, a salesperson who is given public recognition and a large bonus for making a valuable sale that he or she obtained through unethical tactics will probably be motivated to use unethical sales tactics in the future, even if such behavior goes against the salesperson's personal value system.

The opportunity for unethical behavior in an organization can be eliminated through formal codes, policies, and rules that are adequately enforced by management. For example, financial companies, such as banks, savings and loan associations, and securities companies, have developed elaborate sets of rules and procedures to avoid the opportunity for individuals to manipulate or take advantage of a trusted position. In banks, one such rule requires most employees to take a vacation and stay out of the bank a certain number of days every year so that they cannot be physically present in the bank to cover up embezzlement or other diversion of funds. This rule prevents the opportunity for inappropriate conduct. As another example, DoubleClick Inc., an Internet advertising company, was criticized for its plans to combine records of people's Web-surfing habits with a consumer database containing names, addresses, and other personal information — thus creating a considerable opportunity for inappropriate conduct. These plans were postponed, however, and in an effort to eliminate future opportunity for inappropriate conduct, the company appointed an independent panel that will review new products and services for their potential threats to privacy.[36]

The opportunity for unethical behavior cannot be eliminated without aggressive enforcement of codes and rules. A national jewelry store chain president explained to the authors of this text how he dealt with a jewelry buyer in one of his stores who had taken a bribe from a supplier. There was an explicit company policy against taking incentive payments for dealing with a supplier. When the president of the firm learned that one of his buyers had taken a bribe, he immediately traveled to that buyer's office and terminated his employment as a buyer. He then traveled to the supplier (manufacturer) selling jewelry to his stores and terminated his relationship with that particular supplier. The message was clear: taking a bribe is not acceptable for the store's buyers, and salespeople from supplying companies could cost their firm the loss of significant sales by offering bribes to this company. This type of policy enforcement illustrates how the opportunity to commit unethical acts can be eliminated.

BUSINESS ETHICS EVALUATIONS AND INTENTIONS

Ethical dilemmas involve problem-solving tasks in which decision rules are often vague or in conflict. The results of an ethical decision are often uncertain. There is no one who can always tell us whether we have made the right decision. There are no magic formulas, nor is there computer software that ethical dilemmas can be plugged into for a solution. Even if they mean well, most businesspeople will make ethical mistakes. There is no substitute for critical thinking and the individual's ability to take responsibility for his or her decisions.

An individual's intentions and the final decision as to what action to take are the last steps in decision making. When intentions and behavior are inconsistent with ethical judgments, the person may feel guilty. For example, an advertising account executive asked by her client to create an advertisement she perceives as misleading has two alternatives: to comply or to refuse. If she refuses, she stands to lose business from that client and possibly her job. Other factors, such as pressure from the client, the need to keep her job to pay her debts and living expenses, and the possibility of a raise if she develops the advertisement successfully, may influence her resolution of this ethical dilemma. Because of other factors, she may decide to act unethically and develop the advertisement even though she believes it to be inaccurate. Because her actions are inconsistent with her ethical judgment, she will probably feel guilty about her decision.

USING THE ETHICAL DECISION-MAKING FRAMEWORK TO IMPROVE ETHICAL DECISIONS

The ethical decision-making framework presented in this chapter cannot tell you if a business decision is ethical or unethical. We continue to stress that it is impossible to tell you what is right or wrong; instead, we are attempting to prepare you to make informed ethical decisions. Although this chapter does not moralize by telling you what to do in a specific situation, it does provide an overview of typical decision-making processes and factors that influence ethical decisions. The framework is not a guide for how to make decisions but is intended to provide insights and knowledge about typical ethical decision-making processes in business organizations. Information on decision making can be found on the web site

e.ethics 1   of the Markkula Center for Applied Ethics.

Because it is impossible to agree on normative judgments about what is ethical, business ethics scholars developing descriptive models have focused on regularities in decision making and the various phenomena that interact in a dynamic environment to produce predictable behavioral patterns. Furthermore, it is unlikely that ethical problems in an organization will be solved strictly by a thorough knowledge of how ethical decisions are made. By its very nature, business ethics involves value judgments and collective agreement about acceptable patterns of behavior.

We propose that an understanding of typical ethical decision making in a business organization will reveal several ways that decision making could be improved. Chapter 6 explores the impact of organizational culture on ethical decisions and how an understanding of culture can be used to improve the ethical climate of the organization. Chapter 7 provides more detail on organizational relationships and conflicts in ethical decision making. Chapter 8 focuses on the development of an effective ethics program. Chapter 9 examines business ethics in a global economy, and Chapter 10 considers business ethics and organizational performance.

With more knowledge about how the decision process works, you will be better prepared to critically analyze ethical dilemmas and to provide ethical leadership regardless of your role in the organization. One important conclusion that should be developed from this framework is that ethical decision making within an organization does not rely strictly on the moral philosophies of individuals. Organizations take on an ethical climate of their own, which may have a significant influence on business ethics.

SUMMARY

The key components of the ethical decision-making framework provided in this chapter include ethical issue intensity, individual cognitive moral development, corporate culture, significant others, and opportunity. These factors are interrelated and influence business ethics evaluations and intentions, which result in ethical or unethical behavior.

Ethical issue intensity is defined as the perceived relevance or importance of an ethical issue to the individual or work group. It reflects the ethical sensitivity of the individual or work group triggering the ethical decision process. All the other factors in ethical decision making, including cognitive moral development, corporate culture, and intentions, influence this sensitivity. Hence ethical issues can be perceived differently by different individuals.

According to Kohlberg's model of cognitive moral development, individuals make different decisions in similar ethical situations because they are in different stages of moral development. Kohlberg proposed that everyone is in one of six stages of moral development: (1) the stage of punishment and obedience; (2) the stage of individual instrumental purpose and exchange; (3) the stage of mutual interpersonal expectations, relationships, and conformity; (4) the stage of social system and conscience maintenance; (5) the stage of prior rights, social contract, or utility; or (6) the stage of universal ethical principles. Kohlberg's six stages can be further reduced to three levels of ethical concern. The first two correspond to immediate self-interest. Stages 3 and 4 deal with social expectations, and the last two stages focus on general ethical principles. This model may help us understand individual ethical decision making in business because it explains why some people may change their beliefs or moral values. In addition, it explains why, given the same situation, individuals may make different decisions.

A corporate culture can be defined as a set of values, beliefs, goals, norms, and ways to solve problems that members (employees) of an organization share. The ethical climate of the organization is a component of the corporate culture. Corporate culture involves norms that prescribe a wide range of behavior for organization members. The ethical climate of an organization indicates whether the organization has an ethical conscience. The organizational culture and the resulting ethical climate may be directly related to the recognition of ethical dimensions of decisions, the generation of alternatives, and individual cognitive moral development. Significant others and opportunity are two important parts of the corporate culture.

Significant others, people such as peers, managers, and subordinates who influence the work group, have been shown to have more impact on an employee's decisions on a daily basis than any other factor in the decision-making framework. Ethical or unethical behavior is learned through interactions with people who are part of a worker's intimate personal groups. Obedience to authority may explain why many business ethics issues are resolved by following the directives of a superior. The individual's own degree of self-esteem and self-confidence also contributes to decisions in some cases. Role stress, which is the strain, conflict, or disruptive result of a lack of agreement on certain job-related activities, has been found to be a major factor influencing unethical behavior.

Opportunity results from conditions that either provide rewards, whether internal or external, or limit barriers to ethical or unethical behavior. Included in opportunity is a person's immediate job context, which includes the motivational techniques superiors use to influence employee behavior. The opportunity for unethical behavior in an organization can be eliminated through formal codes, policies, and rules that are adequately enforced by management.

Ethical dilemmas involve problem-solving tasks in which decision rules are often vague or in conflict. There is no substitute for critical thinking and the individual's ability to accept responsibility for his or her decision.

The ethical decision-making framework provided in this chapter is not a guide for making decisions; it is intended to provide insights and knowledge about typical ethical decision-making processes in business organizations. Ethical decision making within an organization does not rely strictly on the moral philosophies of individuals. Organizations take on an ethical climate of their own, which may have a significant influence on business ethics.

Important Terms for Review	ethical issue intensity Kohlberg's model of cognitive moral development corporate culture ethical climate component	significant others obedience to authority role stress opportunity immediate job context

A Real-Life Situation*

Kent was getting pressure from his boss, parents, and wife about the marketing campaign for Broadway Corporation's new video game called "Lucky." He had been working for Broadway for about two years, and the Lucky game was his first big project. Kent and his wife, Amy, had graduated from the same college and had decided to go back to their home town of Las Cruces, New Mexico, near the Mexican border. Kent's father knew the president of Broadway, which enabled Kent to get a job in its marketing department. Broadway is a medium-size company with about five hundred employees, making it one of the largest employers in Las Cruces. Broadway develops, manufactures, and markets video arcade games.

Within the video arcade industry, competition is fierce. Games typically have a life cycle of only eighteen to twenty-four months. One of the key strategies in the industry is providing unique, visually stimulating games by using color graphics technology, fast action, and participant interaction. The target markets for Broadway's video products are children aged 5 to 12 and teenagers from 13 to 19. Males constitute 75 percent of the market.

When Kent first started with Broadway, his task was to conduct market research on the types of games desired. His research showed that the market wanted more action (violence), quicker graphics, multiple levels of difficulty, and sound. Further research showed that certain tones and types of sound were more pleasing than others. As part of his research, Kent also observed people in video arcades, where he found that many became hypnotized by a game and would quickly put in quarters when told to do so. Research suggested that many target consumers exhibited the same symptoms as compulsive gamblers. Kent's research results were very well received by the company, which developed several new games using the information. The new games were instant hits with the market.

In his continuing research, Kent had found that the consumer's level of intensity increased as the game's intensity level increased. Several reports later, Kent suggested that target consumers might be willing, at strategic periods in a video game, to insert multiple coins. For example, a player who wanted to move to a higher level of difficulty would have to insert two coins; to play the final level, three coins would have to be inserted. When the idea was tested, Kent found it did increase game productivity.

Kent had also noticed that video games that gave positive reinforcements to the consumer, such as audio cues, were played much more frequently than others. He reported his findings to Brad, Broadway's president, who asked Kent to apply the information to the development of new games. Kent suggested having the machines give candy to the game players when they attained specific goals. For the teen market, the company modified the idea: the machines would give back coins at certain levels during the game. Players could then use the coins at strategic levels to play a "slot-type" chance opening of the next level. By inserting an element of chance, these games generated more coin input than output, and game productivity increased dramatically. These innovations were quite successful, giving Broadway a larger share of the market and Kent a promotion to product manager.

Kent's newest assignment was the Lucky game — a fast-action scenario in which the goal was to destroy the enemy before being destroyed. Kent expanded on the slot-type game for the older market, with two additions. First, the game employed virtual reality technology, which gives the player the sensation of actually being in the game. Second, keeping in mind that most of the teenage consumers were male, Kent incorporated a female character who, at each level, removed a piece of her clothing and taunted the player. A win at the highest level left her nude. Test market results suggested that the two additions increased profitability per game dramatically.

Several weeks later, Brad asked about the Lucky project. "I think we've got a real problem, Brad," Kent told him. "Maybe the nudity is a bad idea. Some people will be really upset about it." Brad was very displeased with Kent's response.

Word got around fast that the Lucky project had stalled. During dinner with his parents, Kent mentioned the Lucky project, and his dad said something that affected Kent. "You know, son, the Lucky project will bring in a great deal of revenue for Broadway, and jobs are at stake. Some of your coworkers are upset with your stand on this project. I'm not telling you what to do, but there's more at stake here than just a video game."

The next day Kent had a meeting with Brad about Lucky. "Well," Brad asked, "what have you decided?"

Kent answered, "I don't think we should go with the nudity idea."

Brad answered, "You know, Kent, you're right. The U.S. market just isn't ready to see full nudity as well as graphic violence in arcades in their local malls. That's why I've contacted an Internet provider who will take our game and put it on the Net as an adult product. I've also checked out the foreign markets and found that we can sell the machines to the Mexican market if we tone down the violence. The Taiwanese joint venture group has okayed the version we have now, but they would like you to develop something that is more graphic in both areas. You see, they already have similar versions of this type of game now, and their market is ready to go to the next level. I see the Internet market as secondary because we can't get the virtual reality equipment and software into an Internet mode. Maybe when PCs get faster we'll be able to tap into it at that level, but not now. So, Kent, do you understand what you need to be doing on Lucky?"

Questions ■ Exercises

1. What are the ethical and legal issues?
2. What are Kent's options?
3. Discuss the acceptability and commercial use of sex, violence, and gambling in the United States.
4. Is this acceptable in other countries if it fits their culture?

This case is strictly hypothetical; any resemblance to real persons, companies, or situations is coincidental.

CHECK YOUR E.Q.

Check your E.Q., or Ethics Quotient, by completing the following. Assess your performance to evaluate your overall understanding of the chapter material.

1. The first step in ethical decision making is to understand the individual factors that influence the process.   Yes   No

2. Kohlberg's six stages of cognitive moral development can be reduced to three levels: the individual's immediate self-interest; what the individual defines as "right" related to society or reference-group expectations; and the principled level, or what the individual sees beyond norms, laws, and the influence of authority, including rights that are universal in nature.   Yes   No

3. Most people maintain the same moral philosophy in both work and nonwork ethical decision making.   Yes   No

4. The most significant influence on ethical behavior in the organization is the opportunity to engage in (un)ethical behavior.   Yes   No

5. Obedience to authority relates to the influence of organizational culture.   Yes   No

ANSWERS 1. No. The first step is to become more aware that an ethical issue exists and to consider its relevance to the individual or work group.   2. Yes. Kohlberg's six stages of cognitive moral development can be reduced to these three levels.   3. No. Roughly 85 percent of people switch between work and nonwork situations.   4. No. Significant others have more impact on ethical decisions within an organization.   5. No. Obedience to authority relates to the influence of significant others and supervisors.

Organizational Culture and Ethical Decision Making

CHAPTER 6

An Ethical Dilemma*

Dawn Prarie had been with PCA Health Care Hospitals for three years and had been promoted to marketing director in the Miami area. She had a staff of ten and a fairly healthy budget. Dawn's job was to attract more patients into the HMO while helping to keep costs down. At a meeting with Dawn, Nancy Belle, the vice president, had explained the ramifications of the Balanced Budget Act and how it was affecting all HMOs. "Being here in Miami does not help our division," she told Dawn. "Because of this Balanced Budget Act, we have been losing money on many of our elderly patients. For example, we used to receive $600 or more a month, per patient, from Medicare, but now our minimum reimbursement is just $367 a month! I need solutions, and that's where you come in. By the end of the month I want a list of things that will help us show a profit. Anything less than a positive balance sheet will be unacceptable."

It was obvious that Nancy was serious about cutting costs and increasing revenues within the elderly market. That's why Dawn had been promoted to marketing director. The first thing Dawn did after the meeting with Nancy was to fire four key people. She then gave their duties to six who were at lower salaries and put the hospital staff on notice that changes would be occurring at the hospital over the next several months. In about three weeks Dawn presented Nancy with an extensive list of ideas. It included these suggestions:

1. Trimming some prescription drug benefits

2. Reducing redundant tests for terminal patients

3. Hiring physician assistants to see patients but billing patients at the physician rate

4. Allowing physicians to buy shares in PCA, thus providing an incentive for bringing in more patients

5. Sterilizing and reusing cardiac catheters

6. Instituting a one-vendor policy on hospital products to gain quantity discounts

7. Prescreening "insurance" patients for probability of payment

Dawn's assistants felt that some of the hospital staff could be more aggressive in the marketing area. They urged using more promotional materials, offering incentives for physicians who suggested PCA or required their patients to be hospitalized, and prescreening potential clients into categories. "You see," said Ron, one of Dawn's staff, "we feel that there are four types of elderly patients. There are the healthy elderly, whose life expectancies are ten or more years. There are the fragile elderly, with life expectancies of two to seven years. Then there are the demented and dying elderly, who usually have one to three years. Finally, we have the high-cost/uninsured elderly. Patients who are designated healthy would get the most care, including mammograms, prostate-cancer screening, and cholesterol checks. Patients in the other categories would get less."

As she implemented some of the recommendations from Dawn's list, Nancy also launched an aggressive plan to destabilize the nurses' union. As a result, many nurses began a work slowdown and were filing internal petitions to upper management. Headquarters told Nancy to give the nurses and other hospital staff as much overtime as they wanted but not to hire anyone new. One floor manager suggested splitting up the staff into work teams, with built-in incentives for those who worked smarter and/or faster. Nancy approved the plan, and in three months productivity jumped 50 percent, with many of the hospital workers making more money. The downside for Nancy was an increase in worker-related accidents.

When Dawn toured the hospital around this time, she found that some of the most productive workers were using substandard procedures and poorly made products. One nurse said, "Yes, the surgical gloves are somewhat of a problem, but we were told that the quality met the minimum requirements and so we have to use them." Dawn brought this to Nancy's attention, whereupon Nancy drafted the following memo:

ATTENTION HOSPITAL STAFF

It has come to management's attention that minor injuries to staff and patients are on the rise. Please review the Occupational Safety and Health Administration guidelines, as well as the standard procedures handbook, to make sure you are in compliance. I also want to thank all those teams that have been keeping costs down. We have finally gone into the plus side as far as profitability. Hang on and we'll be able to stabilize the hospital to make it a better place to care for patients and to work.

At Nancy's latest meeting with Dawn, she told Dawn: "We've decided on your staff's segmentation strategy for the elderly market. We want you to develop a questionnaire to prescreen incoming HMO patients, as well as existing clients, into one of the four categories so we can tag their charts

and alert the HMO physicians to the new protocols. Also, since the recommendations we've put into practice have worked so well, we've decided to use the rest of your suggestions. The implementation phase will start next month. I want you, Dawn, to be the lead person in developing a long-term strategy to break the unions in the hospital. Do whatever it takes. We just need to do more with less. I'm firm on this — so you're either on board or you're not. Which is it going to be?"

Questions ■ Exercises

1. Discuss the corporate culture and its ethical implications.
2. What factors are affecting Dawn's options?
3. Discuss the issue of for-profit versus nonprofit health care facilities.
4. If you were Dawn, what information would you like to have in order to make your decisions?

This case is strictly hypothetical; any resemblance to real persons, companies, or situations is coincidental.

Organizations are much more than structures in which we work. Although they are not alive, we attribute human characteristics to them. When times are good, we say the company is "well"; when times are not so good, we may try to "save" the company. Understandably, people have feelings toward the place that provides them with income and benefits, challenge and satisfaction, self-esteem, and often lifelong friendships. In fact, excluding the time spent sleeping, we spend almost 50 percent of our lives in this second home with our second "family." It is important, then, to examine how the organizational structure and culture influence the ethical decisions made within the organization.

In the decision-making framework described in Chapter 5, we discuss how organizational factors such as corporate culture and interpersonal relationships influence the ethical decision-making process. In this chapter we describe two organizational structures and examine how they may influence ethical decisions. Next we discuss organizational, or corporate, culture and how the values and traditions of a business affect employees' ethical behavior. We also discuss the role of leadership in influencing ethical behavior within the organization. Then we consider the impact of groups within organizations. Finally, we examine the implications of organizational relationships for ethical decisions.

ORGANIZATIONAL STRUCTURE AND BUSINESS ETHICS

The structure of an organization can be described in many ways. For simplicity's sake, we discuss two broad categories of organizational structures: centralized and decentralized. Table 6–1 compares some strengths and weaknesses of the two types of structure. The structure of an organization is important to the study of business ethics because, by means of job descriptions and various roles, the structure may create opportunities to engage in unethical behavior.[1]

Centralized Organizations

In a **centralized organization,** decision-making authority is concentrated in the hands of top-level managers, and little authority is delegated to lower levels of the organization. Responsibility, both internal and external, rests with top-level managers. This structure is especially suitable for organizations that make high-risk decisions and whose lower-level managers are not highly skilled in decision making. It is also suitable for organizations in which production processes are routine and efficiency is of primary importance. Centralized organizations stress formal rules, policies, and procedures, backed up with elaborate control systems. Their codes of ethics may specify the techniques for decision making. These organizations are usually extremely bureaucratic. The division of labor is typically very well defined. Each worker knows his or her job and what is specifically expected, and each has a

TABLE 6–1   Structural Comparison of Organizational Types

Characteristic	Emphasis	
	Decentralized	Centralized
Hierarchy of authority	Decentralized	Centralized
Flexibility	High	Low
Adaptability	High	Low
Problem recognition	High	Low
Implementation	Low	High
Dealing with changes in environmental complexity	Good	Poor
Rules and procedures	Few and informal	Many and formal
Division of labor	Ambiguous	Clear-cut
Span of control	Few employees	Many employees
Use of managerial techniques	Minimal	Extensive
Coordination and control	Informal and personal	Formal and impersonal

clear understanding of how to carry out assigned tasks. General Motors, the Internal Revenue Service, and the U.S. Army are examples of centralized organizations.

Some centralized organizations are seeking to restructure to become more decentralized, flexible, and adaptive to the needs of employees and customers. For example, Coco-Cola's chairman Doug Daft announced plans to meet with top management and discuss the company's new decentralized corporate structure and more caring posture. According to a company spokesman, "we're moving away from globalization to 'multi-localization.'"[2] Decentralized decisions about ethics and social responsibility allow regional or local operators to set policy and establish conduct requirements.

Among the ethical issues that may arise in centralized organizations, where authority is concentrated at the top, is blame shifting, or "scapegoating." People may try to transfer blame for their actions to others who are not responsible. Another problem in centralized organizations results from specialization and significant division of labor. Employees may not understand how their actions can affect the overall organization because they work on one piece of a much larger puzzle. This lack of connectedness can result in employees engaging in unethical behavior because they cannot understand the overall ramifications of such behavior.

Because of the top-down approach in centralized organizations and the distance between employee and decision maker, unethical acts can occur. If the centralized organization is very bureaucratic, some employees will act according to the letter of the edict instead of the spirit. For example, a centralized organization can have a policy about bribes that does not include wording about donating to a client's favorite charity before or after a sale. Such donations, or gifts, can, in some cases, be construed as a tacit bribe because the employee could be swayed by the donation, or gift, to act in a less than favorable way, or not to act in the best interests of the firm.

Other ethical concerns in centralized structures may arise because there is very little upward communication. Top-level managers may not be aware of problems and unethical activity. Use of sweatshop labor may be one manifestation of this lack of upward communication. Sometimes using forced immigrant labor, sweatshops produce products such as garments, with laborers often working twelve- to sixteen-hour shifts for little or no pay. Many illegal immigrants in Europe become indentured slaves or earn little more than the food they eat. By outsourcing production to such sweatshops, small and mid-size suppliers are able to offer products to retailers that beat or match globally competitive prices. Many of these products end up in leading retailers' stores because of this lack of upward communication, with suppliers' top managers claiming not to be aware of how the products are made.[3]

The problem of poor communication between a company and a subcontractor in centralized organizations can also result in allegations of unethical activity. For example, automobile manufacturers utilize subcontractors who provide component parts. If the subcontractor fails to communicate data on product defects, the manufacturer will be unable to address performance quality issues because of a lack of information. Withholding such information would be unethical.

Decentralized Organizations

In a **decentralized organization,** decision-making authority is delegated as far down the chain of command as possible. Such organizations have relatively few formal rules, and coordination and control are usually informal and personal. They focus instead on increasing the flow of information. As a result, one of the main strengths of decentralized organizations is their adaptability and early recognition of external change. With greater flexibility, managers can react quickly to changes in their ethical environment. A parallel weakness of decentralized organizations is the difficulty of responding quickly to changes in policy and procedures established by top management. In addition, independent profit centers within a decentralized organization may deviate from organizational objectives. Other firms may look no further than the local community for ethical standards. If a firm that produces toxic wastes leaves decisions on disposal to lower-level operating units, those managers may feel that they have solved their problem as long as they find a way to dump wastes outside their immediate community. Table 6–2 gives examples of centralized versus decentralized organizations and describes their corporate culture.

Due to the strict formalization and implementation of ethics policies and procedures, centralized organizations tend to be more ethical in their practices than decentralized organizations. Centralized organizations may also exert more influence on their employees because they have a central core of policies and codes of ethical conduct. Decentralized organizations give employees extensive decision-making autonomy because management empowers the employees. However, it is also true that decentralized organizations may be able to avoid ethical dilemmas by tailoring their decisions to the specific situations, laws, and values of a particular community. If there are widely shared values in place in decentralized organizations, there may not be a need for excessive compliance programs. However, different units in the company may evolve with diverse value systems and approaches to ethical decision making. For example, a high-tech defense firm like

TABLE 6–2   Examples of Centralized and Decentralized Corporate Cultures

Company	Organizational Culture	Characterized by
Nike	Decentralized	Creativity, freedom, informality
Southwest Airlines	Decentralized	Fun, teamwork orientation, loyalty
General Motors	Centralized	Unions, adherence to task assignments, structured
Microsoft	Decentralized	Creative, investigative, fast-paced
Procter & Gamble	Centralized	Experienced, dependable, having a rich history and tradition of products, powerful

Lockheed Martin, employing more than 200,000 people, might end up with many different decisions on the same ethical issue if it did not have a centralized ethics program. Unethical behavior is possible in either centralized or decentralized structures, arising from specific corporate cultures that permit or encourage workers to deviate from accepted standards or cultures that fail to embrace corporate ethics and ignore legal and ethical responsibilities.

The Role of Corporate Culture in Ethical Decision Making

Another influence on ethical decision making in business, as discussed briefly in Chapter 5, is organizational, or corporate, culture. A **corporate** (or **organizational**) **culture** can be defined as "a set of values, beliefs, goals, norms, and rituals that members or employees of an organization share."[4] Corporate culture can be created by a founder and his or her attitudes and convictions, as in the case of Mc-Donald's. McDonald's support of quality, service, cleanliness, and value derives from Ray Kroc. It can also be formed by a strong leader, as in the case of Michael Dell at Dell Computer Corp. It includes the behavioral patterns, concepts, values, ceremonies, and rituals that take place in the organization.[5] Culture gives the members of the organization meaning and provides them with rules for behaving within the organization.[6] When these values, beliefs, customs, rules, and ceremonies are accepted, shared, and circulated throughout the organization, they represent its culture. All organizations, not just corporations, have some sort of culture.

Organizational culture is a broad and widely used concept. There are a multitude of definitions, none of which has achieved universal acceptance. Definitions range from highly specific to generically broad. For example, *culture* has been defined as "the way we do things around here,"[7] "the collective programming of the mind,"[8] and "the social fiber that holds the organization together."[9] Culture is also viewed as "the shared beliefs top managers in a company have about how they should manage themselves and other employees, and how they should conduct their business(es)."[10] Mutual of Omaha defines corporate culture as the "personality of the organization, the shared beliefs that determine how its people behave and solve business problems."[11] Mutual of Omaha executives believe that its corporate culture provides the foundation for the company's work and objectives, and the company has adopted a set of core values called "Values for Success" (see Table 6–3). The company believes that these values form the foundation for a corporate culture that will help the organization realize its vision and achieve its goals.

A company's history and unwritten rules are a part of its culture. Thus for many years IBM salespeople adhered to a series of unwritten standards for dealing with clients. The history or stories passed down from employee generations within an organization are like the traditions that are propagated within society. Henry Ford,

TABLE 6-3   Mutual of Omaha's "Values for Success"

Openness and Trust — We encourage an open sharing of ideas and information, displaying a fundamental respect for each other as well as our cultural diversity.

Teamwork (Win/Win) — We work together to find solutions that carry positive results for others as well as ourselves, creating an environment that brings out the best in everyone.

Accountability/Ownership — We take ownership and accept accountability for achieving end re-sults, and empower team members to do the same.

Sense of Urgency — We set priorities and handle all tasks and assignments in a timely manner.

Honesty and Integrity — We are honest and ethical with others, maintaining the highest standards of personal and professional conduct.

Customer-Focus — We never lose sight of our customers, and constantly challenge ourselves to meet their requirements even better.

Innovation and Risk — We question "the old way of doing things" and take prudent risks that can lead to innovative performance and process improvements.

Caring/Attentive (Be Here Now) — We take time to clear our minds to focus on the present mo-ment, listening to our teammates and customers, and caring enough to hear their concerns.

Leadership — We provide direction, purpose, support, encouragement, and recognition to achieve our vision, meet our objectives and our values.

Personal and Professional Growth — We challenge ourselves and look for ways to be even more effective as a team and as individuals.

Source: "Mutual of Omaha Corporate Culture," http://www.careerlink.org/emp/mut/corp.htm *(accessed November 11, 2000). Reprinted with permission.*

founder of Ford Motor Co., left a legacy emphasizing the importance of the indi-vidual employee. Just as Henry Ford pioneered the then-unheard-of high wage of $5 a day in the early years of the twentieth century, current chairman William Ford, Jr. continues to affirm that employees are the only sustainable advantage of a company. One concrete example of this high value placed on employees was his announcement that employees worldwide would be provided with a computer, printer, and Internet connection for just $5 per month.[12] However, not only good traditions are passed on. When it comes to the effect of history, centralized com-panies may have a harder time uprooting unethical activity than decentralized or-ganizations. The latter have a more fluid history, which is prone to changes that may affect only a small portion of the company. Often, when potentially unethical activity is uncovered in a company and the activity appears to be pervasive in the organization, the leadership is removed in an attempt to uproot the old unethical culture and replace it with a more ethical one. For example, Mitsubishi Motors proposed sweeping management changes after it was discovered that there had been a cover-up of auto defects going back at least twenty years.[13]

Some cultures are so strong that they come to represent the character of the entire organization to outsiders. For example, Levi Strauss, Ben & Jerry's Homemade (the ice cream company), and Hershey Foods are widely perceived as casual organizations with strong ethical cultures, whereas Lockheed Martin, Procter & Gamble, and Texas Instruments are perceived as more formal ones. The culture of an organization may be explicitly articulated or unspoken.

e,**ethics 1**

Explicit statements of values, beliefs, and customs usually come from upper management. Boeing's value statement — one example of such explicit statements — can be seen on Boeing's web site. Memos, written codes of conduct, handbooks, manuals, forms, and ceremonies are all formal expressions of an organization's culture.

Corporate culture is often expressed informally — for example, through comments, both direct and indirect, that communicate the wishes of management. In some companies, shared values are expressed through informal dress codes, working late, and participation in extracurricular activities. Corporate culture can even be expressed through gestures, looks, labels, promotions, and legends (or the lack of these). For example, some production workers have been asked to wear stickers on their hardhats to help in team building and getting along. On one offshore oil rig, workers' hardhats sport the sticker "Start to understand me," with a pattern of colored dots that supposedly tells coworkers about the personality under the hat.[14] This is a type of sensitivity training intended to help workers understand one another and to create trust, respect, and understanding among employees. Even subtle expressions of organizational values, such as the use of slogans and stickers in the workplace, indicate behavior expectations to employees.

Ethics as a Component of Corporate Culture

Top management provides the blueprint of what the corporate culture should be.[15] If the desired behaviors and goals are not expressed by upper management, a culture will evolve on its own but still reflect the goals and values of the company. If ethical behaviors are not valued by the organization, unethical behaviors may be rewarded and sanctioned. Although not rewarded or sanctioned by organizations, employee theft is growing and represents a greater loss than shoplifting in retail stores. Gift stores, as well as toy and hobby stores, lose almost 3 percent of their inventory to employee theft.[16] Perhaps the desired behaviors and goals related to this issue are not being clearly expressed by management.

An organization's ethical decisions will have a strong impact on the organization's culture. For example, in the history of college sports, university teams have often violated National Collegiate Athletic Association (NCAA) regulations by paying or otherwise compensating college athletes; as a result, many of these teams became nationally ranked. University officials were sometimes aware of the cheating but overlooked it because they wanted national recognition and alumni support. Thus the values embedded within these universities become strong indicators of an organizational culture that sanctions illegal and unethical activity in collegiate athletics. In many cases, only the deterrent of NCAA sanctions, such as the "death penalty" (not allowing the team to play), has changed the universities' orientation toward ethics.

An organization's failure to monitor or manage its culture may foster questionable behavior. Management's sense of the organization's culture may be quite different from the values and ethical beliefs that are actually guiding the firm's employees. Ethical issues may arise because of conflicts between the cultural values perceived by management and the ones actually at work in the organization. For example, management may believe that the culture encourages respect for peers and subordinates. On the basis of the rewards or sanctions associated with various behaviors, however, the firm's employees may believe that the organization encourages competition between its members. As a result, employees may intentionally or unintentionally sabotage others' work in order to win organizational rewards. Thus it is very important for top management to determine what the organization's culture is and to monitor the firm's values, traditions, and beliefs to ensure that they represent the desired culture. However, the rewards and punishments imposed by an organization need to be consistent with the actual corporate culture.

Many organizational cultures are changing as a result of years of widespread downsizing. In general, employees are less loyal to their employers and more stressed out at work. A recent survey of U.S. workers from business, government, and nonprofit organizations in the contiguous forty-eight states found that fewer than half of all employees feel strong attachment or loyalty to their employers.[17] Management must be aware of how external forces are shaping the internal culture and adjust accordingly. If employees have greater stress, less loyalty, and a need for more personal time, management must assess these concerns and related actions against the cost of turnover and of hiring and training new employees. Rewards need to be closely aligned with organizational as well as individual objectives. As R. Eric Reidenbach and Donald P. Robin state in *Ethics and Profits,* "Employees will value and use as guidelines those activities for which they will be rewarded. When a behavior that is rewarded comes into conflict with an unstated and unmonitored ethical value, usually the rewarded behavior wins out."[18]

Ethical Framework and Audit for Corporate Culture

Corporate culture has been conceptualized in many ways. N. K. Sethia and M. A. Von Glinow presented two basic dimensions to determine an organization's culture: concern for people (the organization's efforts to care for its employees' well-being) and concern for performance (the organization's efforts to focus on output and employee productivity). A two-by-two matrix represents the general organizational cultures (see Figure 6–1).[19]

As shown in Figure 6–1, the four organizational cultures can be classified as apathetic, caring, exacting, and integrative. The apathetic culture shows minimal concern for either people or performance. In this culture, individuals focus on their own self-interests. Apathetic tendencies can occur in almost any organiza-

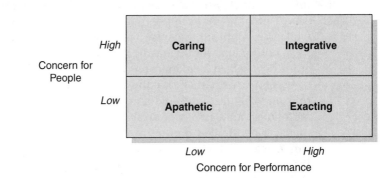

FIGURE 6–1   A Framework of Organizational Culture Typologies

Source: Gaining Control of the Corporate Culture, by N. K. Sethia and M. A. Von Glinow, copyright © 1985, Jossey-Bass, Inc. Reprinted by permission of Jossey-Bass, Inc., a subsidiary of John Wiley & Sons, Inc.

tion. For example, IBM announced a switch from defined benefits pensions to cash-balance plans, which meant pension cuts of up to 50 percent for older employees. After a massive uproar from angry employees and a letter from ten members of Congress urging the Internal Revenue Service to investigate the company, IBM officials agreed to allow thirty-five thousand employees to choose either plan. However, there were still significant losses for fifteen thousand employees. The *Wall Street Journal* reported that three hundred and twenty-five companies have adopted cash-balance plans, but more than 75 percent have allowed senior workers to keep their old plan.[20] Simple gestures of gratitude, such as anniversary watches, rings, dinners, or birthday cards for family members, are being dropped. Many companies view long-serving employees as deadwood and do not take into account past performance. This attitude demonstrates the companies' apathy.

The caring culture exhibits high concern for people but minimal concern for performance issues. From an ethical standpoint, the caring culture seems to be very appealing. Southwest Airlines, for example, has a long-standing reputation of concern for its employees. CEO Herb Kelleher is the purveyor of wit, wisdom, and continuity in Southwest's culture. Employees en masse "love the company" because they believe it cares for and is concerned about them. Employee loyalty and commitment at Southwest are very high. Kelleher has been known to go into the cargo hold of a plane attired in a dress and feather boa to assist employees with baggage. Southwest feels that if employees are well cared for, then customers will be taken care of and the competition will be surpassed. Customers must indeed feel they are being taken care of because Southwest received the fewest customer complaints for the last nine years, as reported in the Department of Transportation's *AirTravel Consumer Report.*[21]

In contrast, the exacting culture shows little concern for people but a high concern for performance; it focuses on the interests of the organization. United Parcel Service (UPS) has always been very exacting. It knows precisely how many workers it needs to deliver its 10 million packages a day. To combat the uncaring, unsympathetic attitude of many of its managers, UPS developed a community service program for its upper managers. The four-week program has the managers work with nonprofit organizations involved in building houses, mentoring young men, boxing food for the needy, or assisting adults with physical disabilities. After assisting disabled residents at a center called Orange Grove, one manager vowed to be more sympathetic to and understanding of requests from employees for time off to handle family matters. Another manager who helped build an addition on a house for a family of seven indicated the program had made him a better manager and forced him to take a harder look at the struggles of people in the workplace. UPS has invested more than $500,000 a year to send managers through the program. More than 1,200 have participated since its inception.[22]

The integrative culture combines high concern for people and for performance. An organization becomes integrative when superiors recognize that employees are more than interchangeable parts — that employees have an ineffable quality that helps in the firm's performance criteria. Many companies — among them Johnson & Johnson, Novell, and NorthWestern Mutual Life Insurance Co. — have such cultures. That does not mean, however, that they are impervious to ethical problems. For example, although Johnson & Johnson (J&J) has an excellent reputation, several years ago it shredded thousands of documents related to a federal investigation into whether the company had illegally promoted its Retin-A acne drug as a wrinkle remover. Fines and court costs totaled approximately $7.5 million, and three senior employees were fired. Did this revelation affect the culture of J&J so that this type of activity will not be repeated? Given Retin-A sales and the statement from a J&J spokesman that the company does not believe its activities violated FDA marketing rules, it is doubtful.[23]

An organization's culture — its values, norms, beliefs, and customs — can be identified by conducting a cultural audit. A cultural audit is an assessment of the organization's values. It is usually conducted by outside consultants but may be performed internally. Table 6–4 illustrates some of the issues that an ethics audit of a corporate culture should address. These issues can help identify a corporate culture that creates ethical conflict.

As indicated in the framework in Chapter 5, corporate culture is a significant factor in ethical decision making. If the culture encourages or rewards unethical behavior, employees may act unethically. Sears' automotive division in California was investigated for auto repair fraud. Employees stated that the only way they could achieve their sales objectives, as established by top management, was to unnecessarily replace certain car parts. The rewards they received were for achieving their sales goals. Sears subsequently was charged with selling used Die Hard batteries as new. If an organization's culture dictates hiring people who have specific, similar values, and if those values are perceived as unethical by society, society will view the organization and its members as unethical. Such a pattern often occurs in certain areas of marketing. For example, salespeople may be seen as unethical because they sometimes use aggressive selling tactics to get customers to buy things they do not need or want. If a company's primary objective is to make as much profit as possible, through whatever means, its culture may fos-

TABLE 6-4   Organizational Culture Ethics Audit

Answer YES or NO for each of the following questions.*

YES	NO	1. Has the founder or top management within the company left an ethical legacy to the organization?
YES	NO	2. Does the company have methods of detecting ethical concerns within the organization and in the external environment?
YES	NO	3. Is there a shared value system and understanding of what constitutes appropriate behavior within the organization?
YES	NO	4. Are there stories and myths embedded in daily conversations with others about appropriate ethical conduct when confronting ethical situations?
YES	NO	5. Are there codes of ethics or ethical policies communicated to employees?
YES	NO	6. Are there ethical rules or procedures in training manuals or other company publications?
YES	NO	7. Are there penalties that are publicly discussed for ethical transgressions?
YES	NO	8. Are there rewards for good ethical decisions even if they don't always result in a profit?
YES	NO	9. Does the company recognize the importance of creating a culture concerned about people and their self-development as members of the business?
YES	NO	10. Does the company have a value system of fair play and honesty toward customers?
YES	NO	11. Do employees treat each other with respect, honesty, and fairness?
YES	NO	12. Do people in the organization spend their time on what is valued by the organization in a cohesive manner?
YES	NO	13. Are there ethically based beliefs and values about how to succeed in the company?
YES	NO	14. Are there heroes or stars in the organization who communicate a common understanding about what is important in terms of positive ethical values?
YES	NO	15. Are there day-to-day rituals or behavior patterns that create direction and prevent confusion and mixed signals on ethics matters?
YES	NO	16. Is the firm more focused on the long run than on the short run?
YES	NO	17. Are employees satisfied or happy, with low employee turnover?
YES	NO	18. Do the dress, speech, and physical setting of work prevent an environment of fragmentation, inconsistency, and the lack of a coherent whole about what is right?
YES	NO	19. Are emotional outbursts about role conflict and role ambiguity very rare?
YES	NO	20. Has discrimination and/or sexual harassment been eliminated?
YES	NO	21. Is there an absence of open hostility and severe conflict?
YES	NO	22. Do people act in a way on the job that is consistent with what they say is ethical?
YES	NO	23. Is the firm more externally focused on customers, the environment, and the welfare of society than internally focused in terms of its own profits?
YES	NO	24. Is there open communication between superiors and subordinates to discuss ethical dilemmas?
YES	NO	25. Have there been instances in which employees have received advice on how to improve ethical behavior or were disciplined for committing unethical acts?

*Add the number of yes answers. The greater the number of yes answers, the less ethical conflict will be experienced in the organization.

ter behavior that conflicts with society's ethical values. Columbia/HCA Healthcare Corporation, the world's largest health care company, fired two top managers at its Kingsport, Tennessee, hospital for allegations of misrepresenting cost reports related to Medicare claims. With the termination of a chief executive and chief financial officer, Columbia/HCA released a statement noting that "the results of this investigation are sobering. The evidence of misconduct is substantial." Department heads of the hospital said that the chief financial officer had asked them to order equipment and supplies for their departments through a particular unit of the hospital to falsely boost yearly costs. This would allow the hospital to claim more money in future years for this unit through Medicare reimbursement.[24]

LEADERSHIP

Leadership, the ability or authority to guide and direct others toward achievement of a goal, has a significant impact on ethical decision making because leaders have power to motivate others and enforce the organization's rules and policies as well as their own viewpoints. Leaders are key in influencing the corporate culture and ethical posture of the organization. A recent survey found that less than half (47 percent) of employees in large (twenty-five hundred employees or more) organizations think their senior leadership is highly ethical.[25] Figure 6–2 shows the survey results. In this section we explore aspects of leadership that influence ethical decision making, including motivation and power.

In the long run, if group members are not reasonably satisfied with their leader, he or she will not retain a leadership position. A leader must not only have followers' respect but must also provide a standard of ethical conduct to group members. Sunbeam fired Al Dunlap from his position as CEO after an investigation of the manipulation of financial reports was initiated by the Securities and Exchange Commission (SEC). Dunlap, also known as "Chainsaw Al" for his widespread layoffs and his approach to downsizing, wrote a book entitled *Mean Business*, which took a somewhat questionable approach to achieving organizational profitability.[26]

The leadership style of an organization influences how employees act. For example, the management philosophy of Mike Armstrong, CEO of AT&T, is characterized by the observations of labs chief David Nagel: "Most bosses hate conflict. Mike is delighted when he sees us getting at each other."[27] Armstrong has been characterized as scary, demanding, a taskmaster, and a maniac — in an affectionate way. The fast-paced, intensely competitive telecommunications industry requires a "nontraditional" leadership style to achieve success. Studying the leadership styles and attitudes of an organization can also help pinpoint where future ethical issues may arise. Even concerning actions that may be against the law, employees often look to their organizational leaders to determine how to resolve the issue.

Six leadership styles that are based on emotional intelligence — the ability to manage ourselves and our relationships effectively — have been identified by

FIGURE 6–2   What Employees in Small, Medium, and Large Organizations
Think About the Ethics of Their Organizations

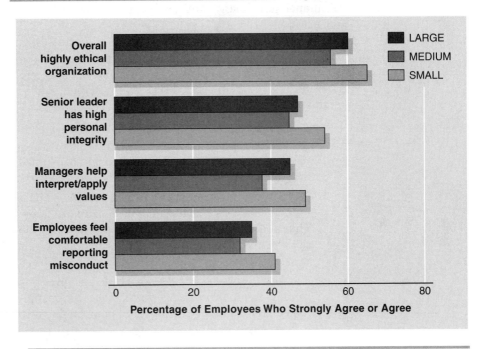

Source: "Small Virtues: Entrepreneurs Are More Ethical." Reprinted from Business Week, May 8, 2000 by special
permission. Copyright © 2000 by The McGraw-Hill Companies, Inc.

Daniel Goleman.[28] (1) The coercive leader demands instantaneous obedience and
focuses on achievement, initiative, and self-control. While this style is very effective during times of emergency, crisis, or company turnaround, it otherwise creates
a negative climate for organizational performance. (2) Considered to be one of the
most effective, the authoritative leader inspires employees to follow a vision, facilitates change, and creates a strongly positive performance climate. (3) The affiliative
leader values people, their emotions, and their needs and relies on friendship and
trust to promote flexibility, innovation, and risk taking. (4) The democratic leader
uses participation and teamwork to reach a collaborative decision. This style focuses on communication and creates a positive climate for achieving results. (5)
The pacesetting leader can create a negative climate because of the high standards he or she sets. This style works best in attaining quick results from highly
motivated individuals who value achievement and take the initiative. (6) The
coaching leader builds a positive climate by developing skills to foster long-term
success, delegates responsibility, and is skillful in issuing challenging assignments.
The most successful leaders do not rely on one style but alter their techniques
based on situational characteristics. Various styles can be effective in developing

an ethical climate based on the assessment of risks and the desire to achieve a positive climate for organizational performance. The relationship between organizational performance and an ethical organizational climate is discussed in detail in Chapter 10.

Leadership is also important because managers can use rewards or punishments to encourage employee behavior that supports organizational goals. Rewards and punishment are part of the concept of opportunity in the ethical decision-making framework discussed in Chapter 5. Researchers have identified four dimensions of leader behavior relating to reward and punishment.

1. *Performance-contingent reward behavior.* The leader gives positive reinforcements, such as recognition and praise, for subordinates' good performance. For example, a subordinate might be praised for doing the "right," or "ethical," thing even though profits were not maximized.

2. *Performance-contingent punishment behavior.* The leader uses negative reinforcements, such as reprimands, for subordinates' poor performance. Thus a sales manager may punish a salesperson who used an unethical sales technique by docking the subordinate's pay or withholding the commission.

3. *Noncontingent reward behavior.* The leader gives positive reinforcement regardless of subordinates' performance. A production manager, for instance, might ignore unethical behavior or poor-quality work and be a "nice guy" to everyone.

4. *Noncontingent punishment behavior.* The leader gives negative reinforcement regardless of subordinates' performance. For example, a finance manager might punish a worker who pointed out that some financial documents required by a government regulatory agency were inaccurate.

Performance-contingent behaviors are most productive in encouraging ethical behavior. As discussed in previous chapters, positive reinforcement for ethical behavior usually encourages that behavior. When employees who behave ethically are rewarded, they will continue to do so; when they are punished for behaving unethically, they are unlikely to repeat the unethical behaviors.

In addition, performance-contingent reward behavior is generally associated with higher levels of employee performance and satisfaction. Noncontingent punishment behavior is generally believed to have a negative effect on performance and satisfaction, with noncontingent reward behavior delivering mixed results.

Motivation

A leader's ability to motivate subordinates is a key consideration in maintaining an ethical organization. **Motivation** is a force within the individual that focuses his or her behavior to achieve a goal. To create motivation, an organization offers incentives to encourage employees to work toward organizational objectives. Understanding motivation is important in the management of others, and it helps explain their ethical behavior. For example, a person who aspires to higher positions in an organization may sabotage a coworker's project to make that person look bad. This unethical behavior is directly related to the first employee's ambition (motivation) to rise in the organization.

As businesspeople move into middle management and beyond, higher-order needs (social, esteem, and recognition) tend to become more important relative to lower-order needs (salary, safety, and job security).[29] Research has shown that career stage, age, organization size, and geographic location vary the relative importance of respect, self-esteem, and basic physiological needs.

From an ethics perspective, needs or goals may change as a person progresses through the ranks of the company. This shift may cause or help solve problems, depending on the current ethical status of the person relative to the company or society. For example, junior executives might inflate purchase or sales orders, overbill time worked on projects, or accept cash gratuities if they are worried about providing for their families' basic physical necessities. As they continue up the ladder and are able to fulfill these needs, such concerns may become less important. Consequently, these managers may go back to obeying company policy or culture and be more concerned with internal recognition and achievement.

It is possible that an individual's hierarchy of needs may influence motivation and ethical behavior. After basic needs such as food, working conditions (existence needs), and survival are satisfied, resources are available for relatedness needs and growth needs, which may become important. **Relatedness needs** are satisfied by social and interpersonal relationships, and **growth needs** are satisfied by creative or productive activities.[30] Consider what happens when a new employee, Jill Taylor, joins a company. At first Jill is concerned about working conditions, pay, and security (existence needs). After some time on the job, she feels she has satisfied these needs and begins to focus on developing good interpersonal relations with coworkers. When these relatedness needs have been satisfied, Jill wants to advance to a more challenging job. However, she learns that a higher-level job would require her to travel a lot. She greatly values her family life and feels that travel and nights away from home would not be good for her. She decides, therefore, not to work toward a promotion (need frustration) and to focus instead on furthering good interpersonal relations with coworkers (frustration-regression — focusing on an area not related to the main problem to reduce anxiety). Jill would continue to emphasize high performance in her present job. In this example, Jill's need for promotion has been modified by her values. To feel productive, Jill goes back and attempts to fill her needs. Thus Jill's frustration level may lead her to seek other employment.

Examining the role of motivation in ethics is an attempt to relate business ethics to the broader social context in which workers live and the deeper moral assumptions on which society depends. Workers are individuals, and they will be motivated by a variety of personal interests. While we keep emphasizing that managers are positioned to exert pressure and obtain compliance on ethically related issues, we also acknowledge that an individual's personal ethics and needs will significantly affect ethical decisions.

Power

A second dimension of leadership is power and influence. Power refers to the influence leaders and managers have over the behavior and decisions of subordinates. An individual has power over others when his or her presence causes them to behave differently. Exerting power is one way to influence the ethical decision-making framework described in Chapter 5 (especially significant others and opportunity).

The status and power of significant others are directly related to the amount of pressure they can exert on employees to conform to their expectations. A superior in an authority position can put strong pressure on employees to comply, even when their personal ethical values conflict with the superior's wishes. For example, a manager might say to a subordinate, "I want the confidential data about our competitor's sales on my desk by Monday morning, and I don't care how you get it." A subordinate who values his or her job or who does not realize the ethical questions involved in the task may feel pressure to do something unethical to obtain the data.

There are five power bases from which one person may influence another: (1) reward power, (2) coercive power, (3) legitimate power, (4) expert power, and (5) referent power.[31] These five bases of power can be used to motivate individuals either ethically or unethically.

Reward Power   **Reward power** refers to a person's ability to influence the behavior of others by offering them something desirable. Typical rewards might be money, status, or promotion. Consider, for example, a retail salesperson who has two watches (a Timex and a Casio) for sale. Let us assume that the Timex has a higher level of quality than the Casio but is priced about the same. Without any form of reward power, the salesperson would logically attempt to sell the Timex watch. However, if Casio gave him an extra 10 percent commission, he would probably focus his efforts on selling the Casio watch. This "carrot dangling" has been shown to be very effective in getting people to change their behavior in the long run. In the short run, however, it is not as effective as coercive power.

Coercive Power   **Coercive power** is essentially the opposite of reward power. Instead of rewarding a person for doing something, coercive power penalizes actions or behavior. As an example, suppose a valuable client asks an industrial salesperson for a bribe and insinuates that he will take his business elsewhere if his demands are not met. Although the salesperson believes bribery is unethical, she has been told by her boss that she must keep the client happy or lose her chance at promotion. The boss is imposing a negative sanction if certain actions are not performed.

Coercive power relies on fear to change behavior. For this reason, it has been found to be more effective in changing behavior in the short run than in the long run. Coercion is often employed in situations of extreme imbalance in power. However, people who are continually subjected to coercion may seek a counterbalance by aligning themselves with other, more powerful persons or simply leaving the organization. In firms that use coercive power, relationships usually break down in the long run. Power is an ethical issue not only for individuals but also for work groups that establish policy for large corporations.

Legitimate Power   **Legitimate power** stems from the belief that a certain person has the right to exert influence and that certain others have an obligation to accept it. The titles and positions of authority that organizations bestow on individuals appeal to this traditional view of power. Many people readily acquiesce to those who wield legitimate power, sometimes committing acts that are contrary to their beliefs and values.

Such staunch loyalty to authority figures can also be seen in corporations with strong charismatic leaders and centralized structures. In business, if a superior tells an employee to increase sales no matter what it takes and if that employee has a strong affiliation to legitimate power, he or she may try anything to fulfill that order.

Expert Power   **Expert power** is derived from a person's knowledge (or the perception that the person possesses knowledge). Expert power usually stems from a superior's credibility with subordinates. Credibility, and thus expert power, is positively related to the number of years a person has worked in a firm or industry, the person's education, or the honors received for performance. Expert power can also be conferred on a person by others who perceive the individual as an expert on a specific topic. A relatively low-level secretary may have expert power because he or she knows specific details about how the business operates.

Expert power may cause ethical problems when it is used to manipulate others or to gain an unfair advantage. Physicians, lawyers, or consultants can take unfair advantage of unknowing clients. Accounting firms may gain extra income by ignoring concerns about the accuracy of financial data provided in an audit.

Referent Power   **Referent power** may exist when one person perceives that his or her goals or objectives are similar to another's. The second person may attempt to influence the first to take actions that will lead both to achieve their objectives. Thus, when referent power is used, one person's attempts to influence another's decision will be seen as beneficial. For this power base to be effective, however, some sort of empathy must exist between the individuals. Identification with others helps boost the decision maker's confidence when making a decision, thus providing an increase in referent power.

Consider the following situation: Lisa Jones, a manager in the accounting department of a manufacturing firm, has asked Michael Wong, a salesperson, to speed up the delivery of sales contracts, which usually take about one month to process after a deal is reached. Michael protests that he is not to blame for the slow process. Rather than threaten to slow delivery of Michael's commission checks (coercive power), Lisa makes use of referent power. She invites Michael to lunch, and they discuss some of their work concerns, including the problem of slow-moving documentation. They agree that if document processing cannot be speeded up, both will be hurt. Lisa then suggests that Michael start faxing contracts instead of mailing them. He agrees to give it a try, and within several weeks the contracts are moving faster. Lisa's job is made easier, and Michael gets his commission checks a little faster.

The five bases of power are not independent. People typically use several power bases to effect change in others. Although power in itself is neither ethical nor unethical, its use can raise ethical issues. Sometimes power is used to manipulate a situation or a person's values in a way that provokes a conflict related to the value structure. For example, a manager who forces an employee to choose between staying home with his sick child and keeping his job is using coercive power, which creates conflict directly linked to the employee's values.

GROUP DIMENSIONS OF ORGANIZATIONAL STRUCTURE AND CULTURE

In discussing corporate culture, we focus on the organization as a whole. But corporate values, beliefs, patterns, and rules are often expressed through smaller groups within the organization. In addition, individual groups within the organization often adopt their own rules and values. Thus we look next at several types of groups, group norms, and conflicts between individual and group norms.

Types of Groups

There are two main categories of groups that affect ethical behavior in business. A **formal group** is defined as an assembly of individuals that has an organized structure accepted explicitly by the group. An **informal group** is defined as two or more individuals with a common interest but without an explicit organizational structure.

Formal Groups

Committees   A committee is a formal group of individuals assigned to a specific task. Often a single manager could not complete the task, or management may believe that a committee can represent different constituencies and improve coordination and implementation of decisions. Committees may meet regularly to review performance, develop plans, or make decisions about personnel. Most formal committees in organizations operate on an ongoing basis, but membership may change over time. A committee is an excellent example of a situation in which coworkers and significant others within the organization can influence ethical decisions. Committee decisions are to some extent legitimized because of agreement or majority rule. In this context, minority views on issues such as ethics can be pushed aside with authority. Committees bring diverse personal moral values into the ethical decision-making process, which may expand the number of alternatives considered. The main disadvantage of committees is that they typically take longer to reach a decision than an individual would. Committee decisions are generally more conservative than those made by individuals and may be based on unnecessary compromise, rather than on identification of the best alternative. Also inherent in the committee structure is a lack of responsibility. Because of the diverse composition of the group, members may not be committed or willing to assume responsibility for the "group" decision.

Although many organizations have financial, problem-solving, personnel, or social responsibility committees, only a very few organizations have committees devoted exclusively to ethics. An ethics committee might raise ethical concerns, resolve ethical dilemmas in the organization, and create or update the company's code of ethics. Motorola maintains a Business Ethics Compliance Committee, which interprets, classifies, communicates, and enforces the company's code and ethics initiatives. An ethics committee can gather information on functional areas of the business and examine manufacturing practices, personnel policies, dealings with suppliers, financial reporting, and sales techniques to find out whether the company's practices are ethical. Whereas much of the corporate culture operates on an informal basis, an ethics committee would be a highly formalized approach for dealing with ethical issues.

Ethics committees can be misused if they are established for the purpose of legitimizing management's ethical standards on some issue. In such cases, ethics committees may be quickly assembled for political purposes, to make a decision on some event that has occurred within the company. If the CEO or manager in charge selects committee members who will produce a predetermined outcome, the ethics committee may not help the organization solve its ethical problems in the long run.

It is also possible for ethics committee members to fail to understand their role or function. If members of ethics committees attempt to apply their own personal ethics to complex business issues, resolving ethical issues may be difficult. Since most people differ in their personal ethical perspectives, the committee may experience conflict. Even if the committee members reach a consensus, they may enforce their personal beliefs rather than the organization's standards on certain ethical issues.

Ethics committees should be organized around professional, business-related issues that occur within the organization. In general, the ethics committee should formulate policy, develop standards, and then assess the compliance with these requirements for ethical behavior. Ethics committees should be aware of industry codes of ethics, community standards, and the organizational culture in which they work. Although ethics committees do not always succeed, they can provide one of the best organizational approaches to fairness in resolving ethical issues within the organization. As one of many examples in the corporate world, Sunstrand Corporation, a U.S. Fortune 500 company, has established employee-managed ethics committees at each of its facilities to stimulate member ownership of ethical conduct and to distribute accountability throughout the organization.[32]

Work Groups, Teams, and Quality Circles   Work groups are used to subdivide duties within specific functional areas of a company. For example, on an automotive assembly line, one work group might install the seats and interior design elements of the vehicle while another group installs all the dashboard instruments. Production supervisors can then specialize in a specific area and provide expert advice to work groups.

Whereas work groups operate within a single functional area, teams bring together the functional expertise of employees from several different areas of the organization — for example, finance, marketing, and production — on a single project, such as developing a new product. Many manufacturing firms, including General Motors, Westinghouse, and Procter & Gamble, are using the team concept to improve participative management within their organizations. Ethical conflicts may arise because team members come from different functional areas. Each member of the team has a particular role to play and has probably had limited interaction with other members of the team. Members may have encountered different ethical issues within their own functional areas and may therefore have different viewpoints when an ethical issue arises in the team effort. For example, a production quality-control employee might believe that side impact air bags should be standard equipment on all automobiles for safety reasons. A marketing member of the team may reply that the cost of adding the air bags would force the company to raise prices beyond the reach of some consumers. The production employee might then argue that it is unethical for an automobile maker to fail to include a safety feature that could save hundreds of lives. Such conflicts often occur when members of different organizational groups must interact. However, bringing up viewpoints representative of all the functional areas helps provide more options from which to choose.

Quality circles — small groups of volunteers who meet regularly to identify, analyze, and solve problems related to their work relationships — originated in Japan but have become popular in the United States. They have been used successfully by Texas Instruments and Campbell Soup Co. Quality circles give their members, and ultimately the entire organization, an opportunity to discuss solutions to ethical problems and to improve product quality, communication, and work satisfaction. Employees usually receive no extrinsic reward for joining quality circles; they participate because they want to contribute to the organization and help improve its efficiency or the quality of its products. The Japanese have extended the concept of quality circles by creating a work environment in which everyone works together and the small groups working together constitute a large group. This approach creates a well-defined corporate culture, based on cooperation and trust between labor and management.

Work groups, teams, and quality circles provide the organizational structure for group decision making. One of the reasons individuals cannot implement their personal beliefs about what should be ethical in the organization is that so many decisions are reached collectively in the work group. Persons with legitimate power are in a position to perform ethics-related activities. The work group, team, and quality circle relationships often sanction certain activities as ethical or define unethical activities for their members.

Informal Groups

In addition to the groups organized and recognized by the business — such as committees, work groups, and teams — most organizations have a number of informal groups. These groups are usually composed of individuals, often from the same department, who have similar interests and who band together for companionship or for other purposes that may or may not be relevant to the goals of the organization. For example, four or five persons who have similar tastes in outdoor activities and music may discuss their interests while working, and they may meet outside work for dinner, concerts, sports events, or other activities. Other informal groups may evolve with the purpose of forming a union, improving working conditions or benefits, getting a manager fired, or protesting work practices they view as unfair. Informal groups may generate disagreement and conflict, or they may enhance morale and job satisfaction.

Informal groups help develop informal channels of communication, sometimes called the "grapevine," which are important in every organization. Informal communication flows up, down, diagonally, and horizontally through the organization, not necessarily following the communication lines shown on an organization chart. Information passed along the grapevine may relate to the job, the organization, or an ethical issue, or it may simply be gossip and rumors. The grapevine can act as an early warning system for employees. If employees learn informally that their company may be sold or that a particular action will be condemned as unethical by top management or the community, they have time to think about what they will do. Since gossip is not uncommon in an organization, the information passed along the grapevine is not always accurate. Managers who understand how the grapevine works can use it to spread acceptable values, beliefs, and anecdotes that reinforce those beliefs throughout the organization.

The grapevine is also an important source of information that individuals can use to assess ethical behavior within their organization. One way an employee can determine acceptable behavior is to ask friends and peers in informal groups about the consequences if certain actions are taken. Usually, informal information is passed along the grapevine about what will happen if, for example, an employee lies to a customer about a product safety issue. The corporate culture may provide a general understanding of the patterns and rules that govern the behavior of an organization, but informal groups make this culture come alive and provide direction for employees' daily activities. For example, if a new employee finds out through the grapevine that the organization does not punish ethical violations, he or she may seize the next opportunity for unethical behavior if it accomplishes the organization's objectives. The grapevine has clearly communicated that the organization rewards those who break the ethical rules to achieve desirable objectives.

Group Norms

Group norms are standards of behavior that groups expect of their members. Just as corporate culture establishes behavior guidelines for members of the entire organization, so group norms help define acceptable and unacceptable behavior within a group; in particular, group norms define the limit on deviation from group expectations.

Most work organizations, for example, develop norms governing their rate of production and communication with management, as well as a general understanding of behavior considered right or wrong, ethical or unethical, within the group. For example, an employee who reports to a supervisor that a coworker has covered up a serious production error may be punished by other group members for this breach of confidence. Other members of the group may glare at the informant, who has violated a group norm, and refuse to talk to or sit by him or her.

Norms have the power to enforce a strong degree of conformity among group members. At the same time, norms define different roles for various positions within the organization. Thus a low-ranking member of a group may be expected to carry out an unpleasant task, such as accepting responsibility for an ethical mistake of the organization.

Sometimes group norms conflict with the values and rules prescribed by the organization's culture. For example, the organization overall may value hard work done at a fast pace, and management may use rewards and punishments to encourage this culture.

In a particular informal group, however, norms may encourage doing only enough work to meet quotas and avoid drawing attention from management. Issues of equity may arise in this situation if other groups believe they are unfairly forced to work harder to make up for the underperforming group. These other employees may complain to management or to the offending group. If they believe management is not taking corrective action, they, too, may slow down and do only enough work to get by, thus hurting the whole organization's productivity. Management therefore must carefully monitor not only the corporate culture but also the norms of all the various groups within the organization. Sanctions may be necessary to bring in line a group whose norms deviate sharply from the overall culture.

IMPLICATIONS OF ORGANIZATIONAL RELATIONSHIPS FOR ETHICAL DECISIONS

Regardless of whether an organizational structure is centralized or decentralized, employees learn ethical behavior from group members and coworkers within their organizational environment. Individual decisions about how to react to daily problems are fundamentally influenced by observing other employees' behavior. As we indicated, centralized organizations stress formal rules, policies, and procedures with elaborate control systems. This type of organization makes sure that workers know how to carry out assigned tasks. Since ethical decisions are made on a daily basis in centralized organizations, ethics is learned from supervisors and coworkers.

Perceived Ethicalness of the Work Group Affects Ethical Decisions

Even though in the decentralized organization decision-making authority is delegated as far down the chain of command as possible, groups within such organizations have a strong impact on ethical behavior. In fact, research has shown that the perceived ethicalness of work groups has the greatest effect on daily ethical decisions.[33] In addition, high levels of conflict among employees may directly or indirectly influence the amount of unethical behavior within the organization.[34] The more conflict within a group, the lower its perceived ethicalness. Because coworkers are so important in accomplishing daily business activities, it is crucial for both workers and management to support ethics among coworkers.

Young businesspeople in particular indicate that they often support their superiors to demonstrate loyalty in matters related to ethical judgments. Given that in one year almost one-third of employees taking part in a national survey observed or engaged in illegal or unethical behavior in the workplace, it appears that most work groups, teams, or informal groups will have a few people who are willing to bend the rules to gain some advantage.[35] It also appears that as some people gain a supervisory role they may attempt to manipulate others or to encourage others to take actions that will cause conflict. Employees will experience conflict when what is expected of them as members of organizational groups contradicts their own personal ethical standards.

A manager in a position of authority can exert strong pressure to ensure compliance on ethically related issues. Alternatively, a manager can avoid ethical issues and be very vague, providing almost no guidance on how to handle tough ethical issues. In these cases the organization's structure may become very important in the decision-making process. Research indicates that the more a person is exposed to unethical activity by others in the organization, the more likely it is that he or she will behave unethically.[36] Many ethical issues in an organization are resolved by the group, not by the individual.

Can People Control Their Own Ethical Actions Within an Organization?

Many people find it hard to accept the fact that an organization's culture can exert such a strong influence on behavior within the organization. In our society, we want to believe that individuals control their own destiny. Therefore, a popular way of viewing business ethics is to see it as reflections of the alternative moral philosophies that individuals use to resolve their personal moral dilemmas. As this chapter has shown, however, ethical decisions within the organization are often made by committees and formal and informal groups, not by individuals.

Decisions related to advertising, product design, sales practices, and pollution-control issues are often beyond the influence of one individual. In addition, these decisions are frequently based on business rather than personal goals.

Most new employees in highly bureaucratic organizations have almost no input into how things will be done in terms of basic operating rules and procedures. Along with sales tactics and accounting procedures, employees may be taught to ignore a design flaw in a product that could be dangerous to users. Although many personal ethics issues may seem straightforward and easy to resolve, individuals entering business will usually need several years of experience within a specific industry to understand how to resolve close calls. For example, what constitutes false claims about a product? When Kellogg Co. introduced Heartwise cereal, the Federal Trade Commission insisted that the name be changed to Fiberwise because there was no conclusive evidence that the cereal benefited the heart. The branding of the cereal was a complex decision that required the judgment of many professional people in terms of the cereal's benefits. And some professional health experts do believe a high-fiber diet is related to good health, including a strong heart. There is no way to avoid ethical problems. The only thing that is certain is that one person's opinion is usually not sufficient. Group decisions are used when complex issues must be resolved.

It is not our purpose to suggest that you ought to go along with management or the group on matters of ethics within the business. Honesty and open discussion of ethical issues are important to successful ethical decision making. We believe that most companies and businesspeople try to make ethical decisions. However, because of so many individual differences, ethical conflict is inevitable.

Regardless of how a person or the organization views the acceptability of a particular activity, if society judges that activity to be wrong or unethical, then this view directly affects the organization's ability to achieve its goals. Not all activities deemed unethical by society are illegal. But if public opinion decries or consumers protest against a particular activity, the result may be legislation that restricts or bans a specific business practice. Concern about teen smoking prompted the government to regulate where advertising for cigarettes can occur. In addition, the use of characters and approaches deemed to appeal to children has been curbed. Public concern and outrage at the growth in cigarette smoking among minors spurred much of this intervention. Hoping to persuade jurors considering massive court damages in lawsuits brought by sick smokers, attorneys for Philip Morris, producer of the world's best-selling cigarette, said the company had changed its ways and now used the Internet, TV commercials, school publications, and print ads to keep teenagers from smoking. According to one attorney for Philip Morris, the company spent $74.1 million last year on producing and airing TV antismoking campaigns aimed at U.S. youths and tens of millions of dollars on other media. Arguing that tobacco companies still advertise to teenagers, the plantiffs' lawyer showed glossy cigarette ads in *Rolling Stone* and *Entertainment Weekly,* two publications popular with youths.[37]

When public opinion supports a particular viewpoint, such as opposition to state-sponsored gambling on home television sets, legislation can follow. Public reaction can also force a company to change its marketing plans. For instance, lawsuits were filed alleging that the maker of Ritalin, the drug commonly prescribed for attention-deficit/hyperactivity disorder, had conspired with a psychiatric group to "create" the disorder and later hyped the treatment's benefits. The suits contend that Novartis, Ciba-Geigy, and the American Psychiatric Association created a broad-based definition of hyperactivity disorders in the standard medical text used by physicians that had the effect of boosting sales and profits from the drug. The suits also allege that false and misleading advertising minimized the drug's side effects and overstated its benefits.[38] Based on the outcome of the lawsuit, marketing plans may have to be changed.

If a person believes that his or her personal ethics severely conflict with the ethics of the work group and of superiors within an organization, the only alternative may be to leave the organization. In the highly competitive employment market of the twenty-first century, quitting a job because of an ethical conflict requires a strong commitment and, possibly, the ability to survive without a job. Obviously, there are no easy answers to resolving ethical conflicts between the organization and the individual. Our goal is not to tell you what you should do. But we believe that the more you know about how ethical decision making within an organization occurs, the more opportunity you will have to influence decisions in a positive manner and resolve ethical conflict more effectively.

SUMMARY

In a centralized organization, decision-making authority is concentrated in the hands of top managers, and little authority is delegated to lower levels of the organization. Ethical issues associated with centralized organizations relate to scapegoating and lack of upward communication. In a decentralized organization, decision-making authority is delegated as far down the chain of command as possible. Research has shown that centralized organizations tend to be more ethical in their behavior than decentralized ones because centralized organizations enforce more rigid controls, such as codes of ethics and corporate policies on ethical practices. However, this does not hold true if the centralized organization is inherently corrupt.

Corporate culture refers to the patterns and rules that govern the behavior of an organization and its employees, particularly their shared values, beliefs, customs, concepts, ceremonies, and rituals. These shared values may be formally expressed or unspoken. A cultural ethics audit is conducted to identify an organization's corporate culture. Before the audit is conducted, it is helpful to have a framework for assessing the corporate culture. This chapter presents such a framework, delineating the organizational culture as caring, integrative, apathetic, or exacting. The corporate culture ethical audit can help identify traits that create ethical conflict. If the culture rewards unethical behavior, people within the company are more likely to act unethically.

Leadership, the ability or authority to guide others toward achievement of a goal, has a significant impact on the ethical decision-making process because leaders have power to motivate others and enforce the organization's rules and policies as well as their own viewpoints. A leader must not only gain the respect of his or her followers but also provide a standard of ethical conduct. Six leadership styles have been identified based on emotional intelligence. The six types are coercive, authoritative, affiliative, democratic, pacesetting, and coaching. In addition, leadership is important because managers have the power to reward or punish employees and to encourage behavior that supports organizational goals. Performance-contingent rewards and punishments are most productive in encouraging ethical behavior.

Motivation is an internal force that focuses an individual's behavior to achieve a goal; it can be created by incentives an organization offers employees. Motivation can be used to influence the ethical behavior of others.

Power refers to a leader's influence over the behaviors and decisions of subordinates. Reward power is exercised by providing something desirable to others so that they will conform to the wishes of the power holder. Coercive power, in contrast, penalizes actions and uses fear to change behavior. Legitimate power stems from the belief that someone has the right to exert influence, whereas others have an obligation to accept it. Expert power is derived from a person's knowledge. Referent power may exist when one person perceives that his or her goals or objectives are similar to another's goals or objectives. These five power bases can be used to motivate individuals either ethically or unethically.

In addition to the values and customs that represent the culture of an organization, individual groups within the organization often adopt their own rules and values. The main types of groups are formal groups — which include committees, work groups, teams, and quality circles — and informal groups. Informal groups often feed an informal channel of communication, called the "grapevine." Group norms are standards of behavior that groups expect of their members. They help define acceptable and unacceptable behavior within a group, especially defining the limit on deviation from group expectations. Sometimes group norms conflict with the values and rules prescribed by the organization's culture.

The perceived ethicalness of the work group has been found to be a predictor of daily ethical decisions. In addition, high levels of conflict between employees may directly or indirectly influence the amount of ethical behavior within an organization. Employees experience conflict between what is expected of them as members of an organization and its corporate culture and their own personal ethical standards — especially since organizational ethical decisions are often resolved by committees, formal groups, and informal groups, rather than by individuals. When such ethical conflict is severe, the individual may have to decide whether to stay with the organization or leave it.

A Real-Life Situation*

Gerard was worried as he sat down in his expensive new chair. What had he gotten himself into? How could things have gone so wrong so fast? It was as if he'd been walking and some truck had blind-sided him. Gerard had been with Trawlers Accounting, a medium-size firm, for several years. His wife, Vicky, had obtained a job in the pharmaceutical industry, and they were just about to have their first child. The doctor had told her that she would need to stop work early because hers was a high-risk pregnancy. So three months before her due date, she asked and received a four-month leave of absence. This was great, but the leave was without pay. Luckily, Gerard had received a promotion and now headed a department.

Some interesting activities were going on in the accounting industry. For example, Gerard's superior had decided that all CPAs would take exams to become registered investment advisers. The rationale for such a new development was simple. The client relationships that the firm had could be used to increase revenues in regard to investment opportunities. Because of the long-term relationships with many firms and individuals, as well as the implicit sense of honesty that CPAs must have

in order to do their job, clients understood that a violation of such a trust would be unlikely — or so the argument from Gerard's boss went. Many of the people in Gerard's department didn't like this; however, some who had passed the exams had increased their pay by 15 percent. During lunch, one of Gerard's financial friends engaged him in a heated discussion. "What you're doing, Gerard, is called unfair competition," the friend accused him. "For example, your CPAs have exclusive access to confidential client taxpayer information, which could give you insight into people's financial needs. Besides, you could easily direct clients to mutual funds that you already own in order to keep your own personal investments afloat. Also, if your people start chasing commissions and fees on mutual funds that go bad, your credibility will become suspect and you won't be trusted. Plus, your people will now have to keep abreast of financial, as well as tax and accounting, changes."

When Gerard got to his office, he found that some of his people had been recommending a group of mutual funds that the company had been auditing. Then someone from another of his company's accounting clients, CENA Mutual Funds, telephoned. "What's the idea of having your people suggest PPI Mutual Funds when they are in direct competition with us?" the caller yelled. "We pay you at lot, Gerard, to do our accounting procedures, and that's how you reward us? I want to know by the end of the day if you are going to continue to push our competitor's product. I don't have to tell you that this will directly affect your department and you. Also, things like this get around the business circles, if you know what I mean." With these words, the caller hung up on Gerard.

Questions ■ Exercises

1. Identify any ethical and legal issues of which Gerard needs to be aware.

2. Discuss the advantages and disadvantages of each decision Gerard has made and could make.
3. Discuss the issue of accounting firms going into the financial services market.
4. Discuss the type of groups that are influencing Gerard.

This case is strictly hypothetical; any resemblance to real persons, companies, or situations is coincidental.

CHECK YOUR E*Q*

Check your E.Q., or Ethics Quotient, by completing the following. Assess your performance to evaluate your overall understanding of the chapter material.

1. Decentralized organizations tend to put the blame for unethical behavior on lower-level personnel.   Yes   No

2. Decentralized organizations give employees extensive decision-making autonomy.   Yes   No

3. Organizational culture provides rules for behaving within the organization.   Yes   No

4. An integrative culture shows high concern for performance and little concern for people.   Yes   No

5. Coercive power works in the same manner as reward power.   Yes   No

ANSWERS **1. No.** That's more likely to occur in centralized organizations. **2. Yes.** This is known as empowerment. **3. Yes.** Values, beliefs, customs, and ceremonies represent what is acceptable and unacceptable in the organization. **4. No.** That's an exacting culture. An integrative culture combines high concern for people and production. **5. No.** Coercive power is the opposite of reward power. One offers rewards and the other punishment to encourage appropriate behavior.

Organizational Relationships and Conflicts in Ethical Decision Making

CHAPTER 7

An Ethical Dilemma*

At 26, Debbie Richardson was in her fourth year at Lamb Consulting. In that time, she had progressed from an assistant to a project manager of one of the smaller divisions within the company. Debbie had worked forty-plus hours a week for the last three years to get ahead. If no major problems arise in the next several years, top management intends to give her the nod up the ladder as senior project manager. Within the select group of twenty-five project managers, there is only one other woman, Jessica Smart.

Rumor has it that Jessica had been promoted for a variety of unknown reasons. For example, her first boss had promoted her quickly and then divorced his wife, fueling expectations that he would wed Jessica. When the rumor got to top management, Jessica's coworkers assumed that she would be fired. After all, the company's founder felt that extracurricular romances were not consistent with business and blamed women for them. Jessica's next superior fell victim to a well-orchestrated plot that showed flaws in his management style. Everyone assumed that his replacement would be someone other than Jessica; however, she received the promotion. The next step after senior project manager is director, and the directors' group has been nicknamed the "Teflon twelve."

Lamb Consulting has been in business for forty years. It started out as a one-man operation in the form of Zedikia Lamb. Over the years, the company has grown to more than a thousand employees, yet it still bears Lamb's imprint. As a result, most senior managers are high on control and low on tolerance. If something goes wrong, the general view is that the Teflon twelve will find an underling responsible and fire him or her. The company is top-down and uncaring in every sense of the word. Lamb himself hands out projects to the twelve directors, who distribute the best to their favorite senior project managers, who in turn give the best

ones to their favorites. People stay with Lamb because he pays well, and the consulting industry knows that if you can make it at his firm for two years, you are well trained to take on other opportunities.

As Debbie got back to her office, she could feel the headache start at the base of her neck and tighten all the way to her temples, accompanied by nausea. She was ill and also angry at the predicament that Susan Gatewick had handed her. Susan had come to the firm right out of college and was in her third year at the firm. She was a bright and intelligent project manager for Bob Hachet.

Susan had confided in Debbie concerning her boss:

"In the beginning, when I first came to Lamb, I didn't think anything of it. Bob would come into my office, tell me what a great job I was doing. We started going out to lunch, but the talk wasn't about work. It was about our personal lives. He would tell me how beautiful I looked and I would reciprocate. Then sometimes he'd give me neck rubs, and we'd talk about his struggles at home. We've gone out occasionally for drinks with coworkers, other times alone, but last month it just started to change. When we were having lunch he put his hand on my knee. I didn't say anything, but it just kinda unnerved me."

"Later in the week, he gave me a little kiss on the cheek and then hugged me. But last week, well let's just say he's putting his hands all over me. When I mentioned to him that I just wasn't comfortable with what was happening, he looked confused and then got angry! What am I going to do? I need this job, Debbie, and besides the pay is great, with a good future. If I stick it out, he'll probably get promoted, or better yet, I will and then the problem goes away for me. But what should I do in the meantime, Debbie?"

Debbie sighed and told Susan that, as a member of management, she was obliged to report what Susan had told her to top management. The company's code of conduct specifically states:

"Any member of management hearing in the first person of any remarks, actions, or physical activities that could be construed as sexual harassment or contributing to a hostile work environment must report such information to the proper authorities or be subject to penalties, sanctions, dismissal, and/or go without legal representation afforded by Lamb in any civil or criminal suit developed by such information."

"What are you saying, Debbie?! That you're going to make a formal report about this? I can't believe you would do such a thing. You know Bob will hold a grudge. He's like that. You remember when you two were both at the same place in the organization and he made that accounting error and you brought it to the attention of the owner. Remember how for more than a year he tried to get back at you: the backbiting, the undermining of some of your decisions, the innuendoes. And now you're going to make it public that he's been putting his hands on me? Do you realize that if he gets promoted my career is over? And what happens when I try to apply to another firm? Even though it's not true, they'll say, didn't she cry sexual harassment at her last place of employment?"

On reflection, Debbie realized that within the industry she had heard of some companies that avoided hiring women to reduce the possibility of ever having a sexual harassment problem. Others seemed afraid to hire more female employees because of the uncertainty as to what was permissible and what wasn't. As one executive told Debbie, "We [men] just don't know anymore where the line is. The courts tell us when we step over it, but it's too late then. Frankly, there are real differences between how men and women perceive things. I've got some friends who thought their behavior was OK, but then some woman cried sexual harassment and there was nothing they could do once they'd been accused. Men have become frightened of women, and so many are hiring only men."

As Debbie pondered this, she couldn't help wondering what Bob and her superior, Jessica, would do. At first she thought that Jessica might be sensitive to Susan's predicament; however, Jessica had dealt harshly with the last known similar complaint by a woman, as well as with those involved in bringing it to her attention. Debbie also didn't know whether Jessica wanted her promoted. Someone had once said to Debbie, "Jessica is a political animal. The terms *right* and *wrong* are meaningless to her."

Later that day, Debbie bumped into Bob, who hinted that someone was making waves and that he was going to talk to Jessica about the individual. "And if you want to step up to the plate for this person, know that I'll drag you down as well," he added.

What should Debbie do?

Questions ■ Exercises

1. Determine the ethical and legal issue(s), if any.
2. Discuss each individual's options.
3. What are the risks for each individual?
4. Evaluate the company's corporate culture and ethical compliance efforts.

This case is strictly hypothetical; any resemblance to real persons, companies, or situations is coincidental.

Businesspeople learn ethical or unethical behavior not only from society and culture, but also from people with whom they associate in work groups and in the business organization. The outcome of this learning process depends on the strength of individuals' personal values, opportunity, and their exposure to others who behave ethically or unethically. Organization members often make ethical decisions jointly with significant others with whom they associate in informal groups and in formal relationships within the work environment. Significant others include superiors, peers, and subordinates in the organization who influence the ethical decision-making process. Although persons outside the organization, such as family members and friends, also influence decision makers, we focus here on the influence of significant others within the organization.

In this chapter we discuss how corporate purpose in society and organizational structure and culture operate through significant others in the ethical decision-making process. We begin by examining interpersonal relationships in organizations, including the responsibility of the corporation and a view of employee conduct, role relationships, socialization, role-sets, and differential association. Then we explore the role of opportunity and conflict in organizational ethical decision making. Finally, we consider ways of improving ethical decision making in business.

INTERPERSONAL RELATIONSHIPS IN ORGANIZATIONS

Organizations consist of individuals and groups of people working together to achieve one or more objectives. If a corporation has a mission statement that indicates respect for the well-being of stakeholders and an objective of contributing to society, then management and employees should work together to their mutual advantage. The mission of Merck & Co., Inc., for example, is "to provide society with superior products and services — innovations and solutions that improve the quality of life and satisfy customer needs — to provide employees with meaningful work and advancement opportunities and investors with a superior rate of return."[1] Many organizations now publish their mission statements on the Web. Getting people to work together efficiently and ethically while coordinating the skills of diverse individuals is a major challenge for business managers. Relationships among these individuals and within groups are an important part of the proper functioning of a business organization. In fact, interpersonal relations play a key role in business ethics. To understand how interpersonal relations influence decisions about ethical issues, we first consider the corporation's responsibility as a moral agent as well as variation in employee conduct. Then we examine the role relationships within the organization, including socialization and role-sets; differential association; whistle-blowing; and organizational pressures.

e.ethics 1

Responsibility of the Corporation as a Moral Agent

The corporation can be viewed as a moral agent accountable for its ethical conduct. Another view might be that it is the sum of its employees and that ethical issues apply only to individual conduct. Since corporations are chartered as citizens of a state and nation, they have all the rights and responsibilities of individuals. Under the Federal Sentencing Guidelines for Organizations, discussed in Chapter 4, corporations can be held accountable for the conduct of their employees and for all business decisions and outcomes.

While it is obvious that the corporation is not an individual with the ability to think about ethical decisions, it is a societal moral agent that was created for specific functions in society, and it is responsible to society for its decisions.[2] Because the corporation has the characteristics of an agent, business ethics and social responsibility may be assigned to the organization as an entity rather than to individuals or work groups employed by the corporation.[3]

One major misunderstanding in studying business ethics is to assume that a coherent ethical corporate culture will evolve through individual and interpersonal relationships. Because ethics is often viewed as an individual matter, it is thought that the best way to develop an ethical culture is to provide character education to employees or hire individuals with good character and sensitize them to ethical issues. It is then assumed that ethical conduct will develop around companywide agreement and consent. However, corporations responsible for most of the economic activity in the world employ thousands of culturally diverse individuals who will never reach agreement on ethical issues. Without ethical leadership from the organization, many business ethics issues can be complex close calls, and the only way to ensure consistent decisions representing the interest of all stakeholders is to require compliance with ethical policies. The corporation has to be responsible for the correctness of the policies. This chapter provides support for the development of a centralized corporate ethics program that provides a cohesive, internally consistent set of statements and policies representing the corporation as a moral agent.

Variation in Employee Conduct

Although the corporation is required to take responsibility for ethical business conduct, a substantial amount of research and survey data indicate significant differences in values and philosophies that influence how individuals make ethical decisions.[4] When people have been asked in surveys what they would do in specific situations, their answers have supported a wide variation in employee conduct.

As Table 7–1 shows, approximately 10 percent of employees indicate that they take advantage of situations to further their own personal interests. They are more likely to manipulate, cheat, or be self-serving if the penalty is less than the benefit received from the misconduct. For example, employees may make personal long-distance telephone calls from work if the only penalty is having to pay for these calls if caught. Therefore, the lower the risk of being caught, the more likely it is that the 10 percent most likely to take advantage will be involved in unethical activities. There is limited evidence that conducting organizationwide character education can significantly reduce the number of employees who want to take advantage of situations.

Approximately 40 percent of workers go along with the work group on most matters. These employees are concerned about mutual interpersonal expectations, relationships, and conformity; they are most concerned about the social implications of their actions and want to fit into the organization. Although they

TABLE 7–1   Variation in Employee Conduct

10 Percent	40 Percent	40 Percent	10 Percent
Follow their own values and beliefs Believe that their values are superior to those of others in the company	Always try to follow company policies and rules	Go along with the work group	Take advantage of situations if — the penalty is less than the benefit — the risk of being caught is low

Source: © O. C. Ferrell 1999.

may have their own personal opinions, they are very easily influenced by what people around them are doing. Thus an individual may know that using work telephones for personal long-distance calls is improper yet view it as acceptable because others are doing it. These employees rationalize by saying that such telephone use must be one of the benefits of working at the particular business, and since the company does not enforce a policy preventing such activity, it must be acceptable. Coupled with this philosophy is the belief that by doing what everybody else is doing no one will get in trouble, for there is safety in numbers.

About 40 percent of a company's employees always try to follow company policies and rules. These workers not only have a strong grasp of the corporate culture regarding acceptable behavior, but they also attempt to comply with codes of ethics, ethics training, or other communications about appropriate conduct. The employees in this group would probably not make personal long-distance calls from work if their company had a policy prohibiting this activity. However, they would not be outspoken about the 40 percent that go along with the work group, for they prefer to focus on their jobs and stay clear of any misconduct within the organization. If the company fails to communicate standards of appropriate behavior, members of this group devise their own. Because people are culturally diverse and have different values, they interpret situations differently and vary in their ethical decisions concerning the same ethical issue.

The final 10 percent of employees try to maintain formal ethical standards that focus on rights, duties, and rules. They embrace values that assert certain inalienable rights and actions that are always ethically correct. In general, members of this group believe that their values are the right values and are superior to other values in the company, or even to the company's value system, if there is an ethical conflict. This group has a tendency to report the conduct of others or to become confrontational when it views activities within the company as unethical. Consequently, members of this group would tend to report fellow workers who make personal long-distance calls. These workers might be whistle-blowers who might expose perceived wrongdoing through internal reporting systems or to the media or government.

The significance of the variation in the ethical behavior of individuals in a company is that employees use different approaches to making ethical decisions. Since a large percentage of any work group will either take advantage of situations or go along with the work group, it is important that the organization provide communication and control mechanisms to maintain an ethical climate. Companies that fail to monitor activities and penalize for unethical behavior are guaranteeing a low-risk environment for those who want to take advantage of situations to accomplish their personal, and sometimes unethical, objectives.

Good business practice and concern for legal compliance requires the recognition that there is much variation in employees' desire to be ethical in the workplace. Although based on research, the percentages cited in this section are only estimates of the variation in ethical behavior. Each organization may vary widely in the actual percentages of the various types of employees. The important point is not the actual percentages but the fact that most evidence indicates that these variations exist in most organizations. Particular attention should be paid to managers who oversee day-to-day operations of employees within the company. Ethical compliance training is necessary to make sure that the business is operated in an ethical manner, that the company does not become the victim of fraud or theft, and that employees and customers are not abused through misconduct committed by people who have a pattern of unethical behavior. However, human resource managers must make sure that they do not violate individual privacy rights and that background checks and control activities are conducted in a legal manner.[5] Attitudes about privacy rights may vary. For example, in a study on ethical issues in the employer–employee relationship, Walker Information, Inc., found that more than 64 percent of both employees and employers believe that employer access to employees' health records constitutes a serious violation of ethical business practices. The study also indicated that 59 percent of employees and 52 percent of employers feel that conducting a personal credit check on employees is a violation of business ethics.[6]

There are many examples of employees or even top managers who have no concern for ethical conduct but are nonetheless hired and placed in positions of trust. For example, some corporations continue to support executives who ignore environmental concerns, poor working conditions, or defective products, or who engage in harmful downsizing. There is often an admiration for the executive who can get results, regardless of the consequences. Many of these executives have limited concern for ethical conduct; all decisions are based on the bottom line.

Role Relationships

Much like a part in a movie, a **role** is a part that a person plays in an organization. All the roles a person plays in an organization constitute a position and prescribe the behavior others expect because of that position. For example, in the position of supermarket cashier, the employee plays a role involving the receipt of payment for products. The cashier is expected to behave professionally and courteously while assisting customers for the benefit of the supermarket. Another role the cashier may play is as a member of a committee that deals with minimizing coupon fraud at the checkout and making certain that each product is registered at the appropriate price. Each person in an organization has a specialized task or role in helping the organization achieve its goals. Some work on the assembly line; some do clerical work; some are managers who direct the work of others. Other members, such as foremen or department heads, have broader tasks, to keep all the groups in the organization working toward the common goal. The work group has potentially the greatest effect on daily ethical decisions. High levels of role conflict between employees relating to expected behavior may directly or indirectly influence the amount of unethical behavior within the organization. For example, it is possible that an otherwise honest cashier may be informally expected to overcharge a few customers to make up for undercharging mistakes. The more conflict there is within the organization, the lower are the perceptions of ethicalness of the work group.[7] Because coworkers are so important in accomplishing daily business activities, it is vital to support the ethics of the work group. In addition to carrying out the assigned tasks, each person is expected to act according to the role he or she occupies. New employees learn through socialization how to act in their roles, including what is acceptable ethical behavior. Employees also learn accepted unethical practices, such as selling products that do not perform as represented to the customer.

Socialization   **Socialization** refers to the process through which a person learns the values and behavior patterns considered appropriate by an organization or group. Through socialization, employees are taught how to behave in accordance with their roles within the organization. For example, new employees are usually socialized to accept the principle of accountability — that they are answerable to a superior or to peers for the outcome of a project. The socialization process is a powerful influence on ethical behavior. Ethical issues such as lying, cheating, and the payment of bribes may be defined through socialization of organizational values and norms.

As an example, consider a company that provides office supplies to a university. Over the years the members of this company have developed expectations as to how salespeople will carry out their assigned tasks. The current members want new recruits to accept their standards and ethical beliefs for proper behavior and therefore try to socialize them to do so.

Ethical conflict can arise when the values and norms taught through the socialization process contradict the new employee's personal values. Suppose that an experienced salesperson tells the new recruit that the company obtained the university account because the company gave the university the lowest estimates on some specified products. However, to make up for the low prices, it was now providing lower-quality grades of paper and charging high rates on products for which no price had been negotiated. The new employee may find this practice deceitful and unethical. But the senior salesperson could explain that the company is providing a fair product for the price and that such a practice is common in the industry. These discussions may convince the newcomer to accept the company's views on this ethical issue. Similar situations, in which going along with coworkers and managers may conflict with a personal standard of morality, are not uncommon in business.

Role-Sets   A **role-set** is the total of all role relationships in which a person is involved because of his or her position in an organization. For example, an account executive in an advertising agency has relationships with immediate superiors, upper-level managers, peers (other account executives), advertising copywriters and artists, and employees and managers from other departments, as well as clients and media personnel. He or she has a different role relationship with each of these persons in connection with the account executive position. A role-set, then, explains all the role relationships with others and includes their location, authority, perceived beliefs, and behaviors. Understanding a person's role-set may help predict his or her ethical behavior.

Persons in the same department are socialized within the same immediate organizational context and often share the same specialization and knowledge base. Even when they work in different departments, members of an organization tend to be more similar to one another than to people who are not members of the organization. Boundaries between (and within) departments and organizations limit the individual's knowledge of attitudes and behaviors beyond the immediate group. Others outside the individual's group probably differ in orientation, goals, and interests. The greater the distance between the decision maker and a coworker, the less likely the other is to influence ethical behavior.

Within the organization, peers and top managers are likely to have a major influence on the ethical decisions of individuals. Top management will have more influence on the individual than peers because of its authority. This, however, does not hold when there is little interaction between top management and the individual.[8] In fact, the perceived actions of peers and top management are better predictors of unethical behavior than an individual's own personal belief system or opportunity for engaging in unethical behavior.[9] Figure 7–1 illustrates this relationship.

Because research has found that perceived actions of peers and top management are predictors of unethical behavior does not mean that individuals are not responsible for the consequences of their behavior. Sometimes the consequences of any individual's ethical actions within the group are not that easy for

FIGURE 7–1   Significant Others Are the Most Influential Factor in Ethical, Organizational Decision Making

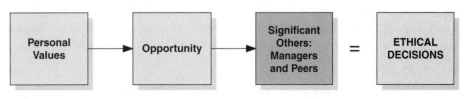

FIGURE 7–2   Values Applied in the Workplace

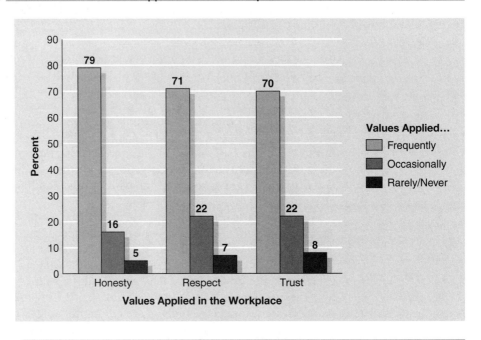

Source: The Ethics Resource Center, 2000 National Business Ethics Survey: How Employees Perceive Ethics at Work, Figure 6.1, p. 55. Reprinted by permission.

the individual to see. Ethical decisions do not just happen in the group; obviously, they are made through human choice. Personal values do play a role in the final decision, but on business matters, group decisions are often used to resolve ethical dilemmas.

When coworkers consider the rights and interests of others in making decisions that affect them, higher levels of trust should be evident. Figure 7–2 indicates that the majority of employees in the National Business Ethics Survey (NBES) felt that the values of honesty, respect, and trust are applied frequently in the workplace.[10] The relationship between ethical behavior and trust is intuitively attractive, but there is also research that supports this belief. Many studies have found a positive impact of organizational ethical climate on trust.[11] When a firm establishes a quota system that requires employees to sell a specific number of products per day or week, regardless of the needs of customers, employee trust deteriorates. It may create internal competition for customers and cause employees to engage in unethical activities to make the quota. Trust starts at the individual level with employees who are trustworthy. Then at the organizational level, employees need to trust each other, transforming the work group into a unified team with a shared vision.[12] Manipulative tactics to get workers to perform at a desired level damage the ethical climate. With a quota system that is almost impossible to meet, there could be infighting, divisive politics, and misconduct — especially misconduct directed at customers — to accomplish corporate objectives.

Employees can be influenced by significant others and the role of supervisors in supporting an ethical work environment. These findings can be alarming to individuals who feel that one's personal ethics should be a major consideration when occupying business roles. Conflicts between what you are asked to do by superiors and your personal ethics create many ethical dilemmas, as well as opportunities to improve business ethics. Because our findings show that managers often go along with peers or superiors on ethical issues does not mean that we suggest this is the way you ought to behave.

Managers who are in supervisory positions should take responsibility for the actions of their subordinates, including unethical behavior. This means developing an ethical work environment; however, a manager may be unable to influence the rogue employee who wants to take advantage of opportunities for misconduct. These employees must be dealt with or they may spoil the work environment for everyone. Managers need to get closer to their employees to develop a successful ethical environment. Openness, trust, and friendship are often cited as the key factors in building a positive interpersonal relationship. These factors seem important in communicating ethical values and encouraging responsible conduct.[13]

Differential Association

Differential association refers to the idea that people learn ethical or unethical behavior while interacting with others who are part of their role-sets or other intimate personal groups.[14] The learning process is more likely to result in unethical behavior if the individual associates primarily with persons who behave unethically. Association with others who are unethical, combined with the opportunity to act unethically, is a major influence on ethical decision making, as described in the decision-making framework in Chapter 5.[15]

For example, two cashiers work different shifts at the same supermarket. Kevin, who works in the evenings, has seen his cashier friends take money from the bag containing the soft drink machine change, which is collected every afternoon but not counted until closing time. Although Kevin personally believes that stealing is wrong, he has often heard his friends rationalize taking the money by saying that the company owes them free beverages while they work. During his break one evening, Kevin discovers that he has no money to buy something to drink. Because he has seen his friends take money from the bag and has heard them justify the practice, Kevin does not feel guilty about taking $1.00. However, Sally, who works the day shift, has never seen her friends take money from the bag. When she discovers that she does not have enough money to purchase a beverage for her break, it does not occur to her to take money from the change bag. Instead, she borrows from a friend. Although both Sally and Kevin view stealing as wrong, Kevin has associated with others who say the practice is justified. When the opportunity arose, Kevin used his friends' rationalization to justify his theft.

A variety of studies have supported the notion that differential association influences ethical decision making; in particular, superiors have a strong influence on the ethics of their subordinates. A study of marketing managers revealed that differential association with peers and opportunity are better predictors of ethical or unethical behavior than is the respondent's own ethical belief system.[16] Several research studies have found that employees, especially young managers, tend to go along with their superiors in matters related to moral judgments in order to demonstrate loyalty.[17] Hopefully, we have made it clear that *how* people typically make ethical decisions is not necessarily the way they *should* make ethical decisions. But we believe you will be able to help improve ethical decisions once you understand the potential influence of interacting with others who are part of intimate work groups.

Whistle-Blowing

When employees think they know the right course of action in a situation, yet their work group or company promotes or requires unethical decisions, interpersonal conflict will ensue and whistle-blowing may occur. Often, these employees follow their own values and beliefs and refuse to participate in corporate misconduct.

Whistle-blowing means exposing an employer's wrongdoing to outsiders, such as the media or government regulatory agencies. If employees conclude that they cannot discuss with their coworkers or superiors what they are doing or what should be done, they may go outside the organization for help. Whistle-blowers often lose their jobs. Some, however, turn to the courts and obtain substantial settlements if their grievances are determined to be valid. Tampa television reporter Jane Akre, for example, was fired after refusing to run a false report about a controversial drug used to increase milk production. In the original report, Akre and two other reporters revealed the risks of the drug, including potential links to cancer and other human and animal health effects. After threats from the company that developed the drug, the report was edited, resulting in distorted news, according to Akre. She pursued the matter in court under Florida's whistle-blower law, and the jury awarded her $425,000.[18] Whistle-blowers who exposed Medicare insurance fraud by SmithKline Beecham in the United States were awarded $52 million. However, an appeals panel later ruled that they might not be entitled to the full amount because it was unclear whether they were solely responsible for uncovering the abuses.[19]

To provide an in-house channel for reporting misconduct and voicing objections, many companies are now installing anonymous reporting services, usually toll-free numbers, for employees to express their concerns and gain internal company assistance. State employees in Florida, for example, have this option. In fact, the Federal Sentencing Guidelines for Organizations include rewards (reductions of organizational penalties) for companies that detect and address unethical or illegal activities on a systematic basis.

Organizational Pressures

Because ethics is a series of perceptions of how to act in terms of daily issues, organizational success is determined by an employee's everyday performance in achieving company goals. Middle managers may be subject to particularly intense pressure to perform and increase profits. Internal organizational pressure stemming from role-set relationships and differential association is a major predictor of unethical behavior. Although individuals can overcome this pressure, they may risk losing their jobs.

Knowing when to report a coworker who is committing seemingly unethical activities is very difficult. Organizations are setting up anonymous hot lines and encouraging employees to use them to report misconduct. But having recourse to a mechanical process such as a hot line does not solve the problem of when to report a colleague. The NBES found that only 57 percent of the employees who had observed misconduct reported it to management or another appropriate person.[20] The study showed that senior and middle managers were more likely to report observed misconduct than other employee groups and that professional and technical employees' reporting of misconduct was more than 30 percentage points below such reporting by senior managers.[21] Eighty-four percent of employees felt they could report misconduct without negative consequences.[22] The key reasons given by those employees declining to report misconduct were belief that nothing would be done and fear of retaliation.[23]

Even when an organization agrees with the employees reporting misconduct and takes action, those employees may not be satisfied with the organization's response. Nearly half of all employees in the NBES who indicated they had reported misconduct were dissatisfied with the response of their organizations.[24]

Top management and superiors play crucial roles in developing the environment that influences ethical decisions. Most experts agree that the chief executive officer and other top managers at the executive level set the ethical tone for the entire organization.[25] Lower-level managers take their cues from the top, yet their personal value systems also have an influence on the business. This interplay between corporate culture and executive leadership helps determine the ethical value system of the firm.

Now we need to take a closer look at the concepts of opportunity and conflict.

ROLE OF OPPORTUNITY AND CONFLICT

Opportunity and conflict are both important factors influencing ethical decision making in interpersonal relations. These two areas of concern are derived from the Chapter 5 framework for understanding ethical decision making. For instance, while there is an opportunity for low-cost labor in developing countries, there is a conflict in paying low wages to workers. It has been alleged that some Wal-Mart clothing is sewn at Korean-owned factories in Honduras, where the base wage of 43 cents an hour enables the factory employees to meet just 54 percent of the cost of survival. Workers there have never heard of the Wal-Mart Code of Conduct.[26] This example of allegedly taking advantage of low wages illustrates the existence of opportunity, but also conflict, at the individual, organizational, and societal levels.

Opportunity Creates Ethical Dilemmas

As discussed in Chapter 5, circumstances, which may preclude or encourage ethical or unethical behavior, constitute opportunity. Once opportunistic circumstances are discovered, an ethical dilemma often arises involving the exploitation of the opportunity. **Opportunity** is a set of conditions that limit unfavorable behavior or reward favorable behavior. It is often a situation that has the potential for a positive outcome or reward. Rewards may be internal: the feelings of goodness and self-worth one experiences after doing something beneficial without expecting anything in return. For example, if a factory worker reports to management that another employee is drinking or using drugs on the job, this brings attention to the coworker's problem and may reduce danger to others — and 10 percent of employees in the NBES reported observing the abuse of alcohol or drugs on the job.[27] Rewards may also be external — such as a raise or praise for a job well done. A salesperson who has refused a bribe, for instance, may be praised by superiors for appropriate behavior.

A person who behaves unethically and is rewarded (or not punished) for the behavior is likely to continue to act unethically, whereas a person who is punished (or not rewarded) for behaving unethically is less likely to repeat the behavior. Thus an accountant who receives a raise after knowingly preparing financial documents that are not completely accurate is being rewarded for unethical behavior and may continue to use such tactics in the future. On the other hand, both customers and society at large often punish transgressions. For example, although e-mail users complain about unwanted direct-marketing e-mail (commonly called Spam), the opportunity to use direct-marketing e-mail can bring success if the privacy of others is respected. Amazon.com personalizes e-mail to deliver information on books of specific interest to customers. Many companies refuse to use this opportunity to communicate with their customers because of rising fears about privacy issues on the Internet, which could result in restrictive legislation.[28] Information about customers' finances and buying habits can be stored without the customers ever realizing it. How this confidential personal information is used is an ethical issue. Most firms must develop an ethics policy on e-mail communication with employees and customers to control how this opportunity created by technology is managed in developing competitive advantage. If firms fail to do so, they may generate hostility. For instance, some major e-mail direct marketers have had their systems jammed by disgruntled recipients.

For many businesses, opportunity means the chance to market a product that will earn large profits and benefit customers, sometimes even saving lives. Ethical issues may arise, however, when businesses hurry those products to the marketplace without adequate testing or with dangerous flaws. Because of opportunity, some companies may knowingly either bring a product to market prematurely or modify others to existing markets.

Opportunity also comes from knowledge. The two most common types of misconduct observed in the NBES were lying to or withholding needed information from employees, customers, vendors, or the public.[29] A person who has an information base, expertise, or information about competition has the opportunity to exploit this knowledge. An individual can be a source of information because of familiarity with the organization. Individuals long employed by one organization become "gatekeepers" of its culture, unwritten traditions, and rules. They help socialize newer employees to abide by the rules and norms of doing business both inside and outside the company. They may function as mentors or supervise managers in training. Like drill sergeants in the army, these trainers mold the new recruits into what the company wants. This can contribute to either ethical or unethical conduct.

Trainers and mentors influence a new employee's decision process in two ways. First, by providing information, the trainer can determine whether the new employee will identify a certain kind of situation as posing an ethical choice. For example, 21 percent of employees in the NBES observed misreporting of actual time or hours worked and 12 percent observed falsification of records and reports.[30] Such attitudes are influenced in part by those who trained the employees. Second, by virtue of their title and its associated power, trainers can lead new employees to replace their own value systems with those of the trainer and the organization. Opportunity is lost or gained by the way trainers of new employees use their knowledge base.

Persons outside the organization can also have an impact on opportunity. Thus financial auditors, though external to the organization, encounter many ethically laden situations as a result of their profession. The primary responsibility of an auditor is to determine the financial soundness of an organization by reviewing accounting data and presenting these data in an objective manner. Opportunity for ethical conflict exists because the auditor is hired and paid by the company requesting the audit. What happens if the company screens potential auditors until it finds one that will provide a favorable statement? The auditor's credibility as an impartial reporter then comes into question because of the selection process. The auditor is under implicit pressure to give a positive judgment. The opportunity to become involved in potentially unethical situations results from the status given to the independent auditor. Recently, several accounting firms that had audited troubled financial institutions have had to face criminal charges resulting from inaccurate statements about the financial soundness of those institutions.

Conflict Resolution

Opportunity sometimes leads to or results from conflict between the values of the decision maker and those of coworkers, the organization, or society. **Conflict** occurs when it is not clear which goals or values take precedence — those of the individual, the organization, or society. When individuals must choose between two equally good goals, particularly if one may result in more positive rewards than the other, they experience conflict. A choice between two bad alternatives can also cause conflict. As noted above, conflict can occur along several dimensions: personal, organizational, and societal.

Personal–organizational conflict occurs when a person's individual values and methods for reaching a desired goal differ from those of the organization or a group within the organization. For example, suppose that a convenience store manager has strong views against the distribution of magazines such as *Playboy, Hustler,* and *Penthouse,* but the company's policy is to sell these products. In this case the organizational philosophy conflicts directly with the individual's personal philosophy. The manager has two options: to comply with the company's policy or to refuse to sell the magazines. Conceivably, refusal could mean getting fired. On the other hand, it would also bring feelings of self-esteem that come from acting in accordance with one's own values. Compliance with company policy would maintain the individual's employment and income status, but at the price of sacrificing personal values.

Employees often find themselves in such situations, especially before they have been fully socialized into the organization. Many people try so hard to land their first job in business that they fail to consider the corporate values that will govern on-the-job decisions. A person may not share the values that are characteristic of other members of his or her profession. Attitudes and values related to drinking, gambling, sex, and religion are personal moral issues. A person who believes drinking is wrong, for example, might feel uncomfortable working in an organization in which some after-hours business is conducted over drinks in a nearby bar. In such a situation, the new employee typically decides either to adjust to the work environment or to find a job in a more compatible organization. Those who choose to fight the system usually fail because they lack the power and support to change the values of the company. Also, there is a question of whose values are right. It is wrong for an individual to think that he or she has the right to force personal values on others.

Personal–societal conflict occurs when an individual's values deviate from those of society. Societal values are often stated in the form of laws and regulations established by federal and local governments. Values, such as the desire for clean air and water, can be translated into regulations on behavior. An ethics conflict may arise when different communities impose varying regulations or values. Alcohol consumption, certain types of entertainment, and Sunday business activities are other examples of behaviors treated differently by different communities.

When society believes that a particular activity is unethical although currently legal, new laws may be enacted to help define the minimum level of ethical behavior. In the realm of business, this pattern began as early as the railroad monopolies of the 1800s, which prompted passage of the Sherman Antitrust Act. In the early twentieth century, society responded to Upton Sinclair's novel *The Jungle* by raising standards for food processing. More recently, legislation was passed to restrict the use of bankruptcy laws and to regulate the use of the Internet to protect children. Because the United States is a pluralistic democracy, personal–societal conflicts will continue to evolve and be redefined.

When the norms and values of an organization contravene those of society in general, organizational–societal conflict occurs. As companies strive to develop and produce goods and services that satisfy the desires of specific markets, they share many but not all of society's values. For example, Decipher, Inc., markets a controversial trading card game called "Boy Crazy." The game has more than three hundred cards with pictures of actual young men and their "vital statistics," such as the young man's first name, his eye color, his favorite things, what he looks for in a girl, and, in some cases, his favorite pickup line. The $3.00 packs of nine cards are aimed at teenage girls and are sold on-line and in retail stores. Child advocacy groups view the game as sexist and demeaning. One parent commented, "I don't want my daughter to think that boys are a tradable commodity." Other groups are concerned that the game may breach the privacy of some of the boys who appear on the cards. Still others are worried about privacy issues for girls who register on the Boy Crazy Web site — more than fourteen thousand in the first month of operation alone. Decipher claims it takes extreme measures to protect the boys' privacy and monitors postings to its Web site. In response to critics who view the game as sexist, a Decipher spokesperson said "Lighten up!" and stated she believes the game "empowers" girls rather than stereotypes them.[31]

e.ethics 2

The marketing of new products often brings business into conflict with society, especially when the products have moral overtones for certain groups. Many groups, for example, question advertising violent entertainment products inappropriately. The Federal Trade Commission (FTC) released its findings from a year-long study of violence and entertainment. The FTC said that "the vast majority of the best-selling restricted movies, music, and video games were deliberately marketed for children as young as 12."[32] The FTC examination revealed that all fifty-five of the music recordings with labels warning of explicit content were marketed to children under 17, as were 80 percent of the R-rated movies and 70 percent of the video games containing explicit content.[33] The FTC cited internal industry memos to validate its claims. One memo about an R-rated film from a movie studio said that its promotional "goal was to find the elusive teen target audience and make sure everyone between the ages of 12 and 18 was exposed to the film." Another memo detailed how fliers and posters about an R-rated movie would be distributed to organizations such as the Campfire Boys and Girls. A memo about an M-rated (mature-rated) video game described its "primary" audience as "males 12–17."[34] Some retailers have pledged to increase enforcement of rating codes. Kmart announced it would stop selling M-rated games to anyone under 17 by using a bar-code scanner to prompt cashiers to ask for identification from youths. Wal-Mart adopted a similar policy, and some stores, including Montgomery Ward and Sears, no longer sell the M-rated games.[35]

Advertising may also produce conflict between manufacturers and retail organizations that sell their products. For example, Sears, which sells a modestly priced line of Benetton clothes in its stores, was shocked by a recent Benetton ad campaign. The ads featured photographs of and interviews with twenty-six U.S.

death-row inmates. Benetton officials said the "We on Death Row" campaign would stimulate discussion about the death penalty and draw attention to continuing executions in America. Sears received calls from angry customers, including relatives of murder victims. The calls prompted Sears to begin discussions with Benetton about the ads, but Benetton made no concessions about curtailing the campaign. Benetton has run other unconventional ads addressing such issues as AIDS, the Bosnian war, and racism.[36]

Advertising of products may also result in conflict when society believes that advertising wrongly appeals to certain groups. In recent years, many consumer groups have expressed concerns about the advertising of alcoholic beverages and cigarettes that appeals to teenagers and young college students not legally allowed to use these products.

We do not want to leave the impression that the only way to prevent unethical behavior is for the company to eliminate opportunity. Conflict is viewed as a positive event when the organization provides the opportunity for discussion and debate to resolve the dilemma. Sometimes only through recognizing conflict can an ethical decision be made. The relationships in a business are based on trust and responsible behavior. Just as the majority of people who go into retail stores do not try to shoplift at each opportunity, so most businesspeople do not try to take advantage of every opportunity for unethical behavior. Differences in personal character may have a major impact on whether an individual becomes opportunistic and attempts to take advantage of situations, regardless of the circumstances. Since there are variations in employee ethical conduct in every organization, the company must develop policies and codes to prevent improper behavior and encourage employees to support an ethical work environment.

IMPROVING ETHICAL DECISION MAKING IN BUSINESS

As we have emphasized, personal values, significant others, and opportunity all affect ethical behavior. One study concerning the values of corporate managers concluded that personal values are involved in ethical decisions but are not the central component that guides an organization's decisions, actions, and policies. This study found that personal values make up only one part of an organization's total value system.[37] Ethical behavior depends on the organization's values and traditions, opportunity and conflict resolution, and the personal values of the individuals who actually make the decisions. Some people, for instance, will not consider employment with an organization unless it maintains a certain level of ethical values. A high standard of ethics will not necessarily motivate such employees to work harder, but it may keep them from changing their own values or being swayed by peers (significant others) or money (opportunity). The corporation can be deemed a moral agent that has a responsibility to maintain core values and a set of checks and balances to encourage ethical behavior.

Consequently, ethical behavior may be a function of several different dimensions of an organization's system: the embedded organizational value system (or corporate culture), significant others, and the personal value preferences of the organization's groups and individual members. An individual member of an organization assumes some measure of ethical responsibility by agreeing in general to abide by an organization's rules and standard operating procedures. Significant others help in the socialization process that transforms the employee from an outsider to an insider. This process results in cohesiveness within the organization, with members maintaining loyalty, support, and trust.

If managers and coworkers can provide direction and encourage ethical decision making, significant others become a force to help individuals make better ethical decisions. When workers have greater participation in the design and implementation of assignments, conflict within work groups is reduced and ethical behavior may increase.

Businesses with an organizational culture that results in managers and employees acting contrary to their individual ethics need to understand the costs of unethical behavior. Some employees succumb to organizational pressures rather than follow their own values, rationalizing their decisions by maintaining that they are simply agents of the corporation. According to Gene R. Laczniak and Patrick E. Murphy, this rationalization has several weaknesses, including the following:

1. People who work in business organizations can never fully abdicate their personal, ethical responsibility in making business decisions. Claiming to be an agent of the business organization is not accepted as a legal excuse and is even less defensible from an ethical perspective.

2. It is difficult to determine what is in the best interest of the business organization. Short-term profits earned through unethical behavior may not be in the long-run interest of the company.

3. A person in a business has a responsibility to parties other than the business organization. Stakeholders, any group or individual who can be affected by the firm, and other concerned publics must be considered when making ethical decisions.[38]

Understanding the influence of interpersonal relationships within the organization provides insights into the ethical decision-making process. For business-related decisions, significant others have been found to be the most influential variable affecting ethical decisions. In extreme situations — for instance, if asked to break into a competitor's office to obtain trade secrets — employees may abide by their own personal value systems. But in most day-to-day matters perceived to be minor issues, they tend to go along with the group on decisions that appear to be defined and controlled by the work group. Hence understanding how corporate culture and coworkers influence the ethical decision-making process helps explain why unethical decisions may be made in business.

SUMMARY

Significant others include superiors, peers, and subordinates within the organization who influence the ethical decision-making process. Relationships among these individuals and within groups are an important part of the functioning of a business organization, strongly influencing ethical behavior.

The corporation can be viewed as a moral agent held accountable for ethical conduct. Because the corporation has the characteristics of an agent, business ethics and responsibility must be assigned to the organization rather than to the individual or work group. A coherent ethical corporate culture will evolve through individual and interpersonal relationships and through companywide agreement and consent.

There is a substantial amount of research and survey data indicating significant variation in how individuals make ethical decisions. Approximately 10 percent of employees may take advantage of opportunities to be unethical — that is, they may take advantage of situations to further their own personal interests. Some 40 percent of workers go along with the work group on most matters, and another 40 percent try to follow company policies and rules. The final 10 percent of employees believe their value system is superior to that of their coworkers and the organization.

A role is the part that a particular person plays in an organization; it refers to that person's position and the behavior others expect from someone holding the position. Each person in an organization has a specialized task or role in helping the organization achieve its goals. Socialization refers to the process through which a person learns the values and appropriate behavior patterns of an organization or group and the behavior expected of his or her role within the organization. Ethical issues such as lying, cheating, and the payment of bribes may be defined through socialization, which instills organizational values and norms in employees. A role-set is the total of all role relationships in which a person is involved because of his or her position in an organization. Differential association refers to the idea that people learn ethical or unethical behavior while interacting with those who are part of their role-sets or other intimate personal groups. The learning process encourages ethical or unethical behavior, depending on the behavior of the person's associates.

Pressure to perform and increase profits may be particularly intense in middle management. This organizational pressure stems from role-set relationships and differential association and is a major predictor of unethical behavior. The roles of top management and superiors are extremely important in developing the environment that influences ethical decisions. When employees think they know the right course of action in a situation but their work group or company promotes or requires unethical decisions, interpersonal conflict will ensue and whistle-blowing (or exposing wrongdoing) may occur.

Both opportunity and conflict affect the ethical content of decisions made in business. Opportunity is a set of conditions that limit unfavorable behavior or reward favorable behavior. Rewards may be internal or external. An unethical individual who is rewarded or not punished is likely to continue to act unethically, whereas a person who is punished or not rewarded for behaving unethically is less likely to repeat the behavior. An individual who has an information base, expertise, or information about competition has the opportunity to exploit this knowledge unethically. Status within an organization may also bring opportunities for unethical behavior.

Conflict occurs when there is a question as to which goals or values take precedence in a situation: those of the individual, the organization, or society. A personal–organizational conflict arises when an individual's philosophies or methods for reaching a desired goal differ from those of the organization.

Such situations occur frequently, especially for new employees who have not yet been socialized into the organization. Persons whose values do not coincide with those of others in their profession may fight or leave the organization. Before the employees leave, however, they should find out from experienced managers whether their perceptions are accurate.

Personal–societal conflict develops when an individual's values differ from those of society. When society feels that a particular activity is unethical yet at that point legal, laws may be enacted to help define the minimum level of ethical behavior.

Organizational–societal conflict occurs when the norms and values of the organization are opposed to those of society in general. The marketing of new products often brings business into conflict with society, especially when the products raise moral issues for certain groups.

Ethical behavior may be a function of several dimensions of an organization's system: the embedded organizational value system or corporate culture, significant others, and the personal value preferences of the organization's groups and individual members. Significant others have been found to be the most influential variable affecting ethical decisions in business-related matters.

If managers and coworkers provide positive role models, significant others become a force to help individuals make better ethical decisions. But when there is severe role conflict and pressure to commit unethical acts, unethical behavior in the organization may increase. Some employees may rationalize their decisions by maintaining that they are simply agents of the corporation. This is not acceptable as a legal excuse and is even less defensible from an ethical perspective. There is general agreement that a businessperson has a responsibility to parties other than just the business organization.

| **Important Terms for Review** | role
socialization
role-set
differential association | whistle-blowing
opportunity
conflict |

A Real–Life Situation*

Gordon McGinnis, assistant dean and director of student activities at Mountain State University, had vehemently banned credit card solicitations on campus for the five years he had been there. To him, it was a matter of acting in the best interests of Mountain State's thirty thousand full-time students, 95 percent of whom were between 17 and 22 years old. Over the years a number of credit card companies and banks had approached him offering deals to market their cards on campus, which would result in good money for the university. Typically, the companies and banks would propose marketing the cards at kiosks located at special school events, inserting credit card applications when purchases from the school bookstore were bagged, posting "take-one" applications around campus, and/or pitching the credit cards at sign-up tables during freshman orientation. However, Gordon had always stood his ground and turned the credit card companies and banks down.

Frequently, however, he found out through the grapevine that credit card hawkers were on campus unannounced and without permission in dormitories and high-traffic locations, trying to entice students to sign up with items such as free T-shirts, Frisbees, music CDs, chances to win airline tickets, and even promises of an easy way to pay for spring break vacations. Several times student organization members had been directly approached by the marketers, who asked them to encourage classmates to sign up for the cards in return for up to $3,000 a year. Even though the student leaders would tell Gordon that students could sign up for a card just to get the goodies and then destroy the card, Gordon always held his ground.

Gordon's rationale for reducing the prevalence of credit cards on campus was simple — students were, in effect, throwing away their credit ratings by getting into debt in exchange for a few trinkets. He had heard stories from his colleagues at other colleges where students would cut back on classes or drop out to earn money to pay off debt. And bad credit histories often hurt students seeking their first jobs, especially since many of them had both student loan and credit card debt. Gordon had even heard tales of students using their credit line to gamble on-line. He also knew from personal discussions with students that many were unprepared to manage their finances. Some did not know how to use credit or even balance a checkbook.

Gordon was not alone in his discomfort with marketing credit cards to college students. Lawmakers in several states have tried to ban card marketers from colleges altogether, and increasingly schools have been actively restricting or banning certain credit card marketers from campus. Consumer advocates who see campuses as the financial world's version of crack houses, complete with professional dealers who hook students with easy doses of credit, have blasted credit card companies. Credit-hungry students are often a card issuer's best customers, despite the fact that most have no credit history or even a job. Students are often loyal to their first credit card throughout adulthood. And once a bank secures a captive student audience, it can cross-promote other products, such as first mortgages, car loans, and — in Gordon's view, a sinister twist — even debt-consolidation loans to help students repay credit card debt.

Despite his successes to date in keeping the credit card hawkers at bay, Gordon was given a new challenge recently when he received a phone call from Elsie Lombardi, the university's treasurer and vice president for finance.

"I was just made an offer I don't think we can refuse," began Elsie. "Highland Bank Corporation's credit-card division wants us to enter into an exclusive affinity-marketing credit card program with them. They'll pay us $5 million over the next three years to allow them to be the only bank card issuer allowed to market on campus at sports events, in the student union building, and in the university bookstore, plus through student and alumni mailing lists. The card will be adorned with Mountain State's picture and logo, which will make cardholders feel more loyal to the school — for users it will be like being part of a club. They'll also give the university one-half of a percent of every transaction charge, which they estimate will amount to about $1.5 million annually. If you accept this deal, I'm prepared to turn over to your student activities division half of the revenues we make on these charges. And they'll give us $6 for each new account that's opened. What could be easier money?"

"While quite a few of our student organizations are operating in the hole and we could really use the money, I'm afraid I'll have to say 'no,' Elsie," replied Gordon. "I'm philosophically opposed to marketing credit cards on campus."

"I didn't know you were a philosopher," quipped Elsie. "What's your problem? You know the financial crisis the university is in due to dwindling state fiscal support. Plus, doing an exclusive deal with Highland will mean getting other credit card issuers off campus and give us total control. Students won't have to worry about shopping around for the best deal. They're giving our students a good one at an interest rate of prime plus 3.9 percent, where most competitors offer prime plus 6 to 8 percent. They also offer no annual fee and have no requirement for actually using the card. The credit limit will be only $2,500. It's a win–win proposition."

"No. You win, and I win, but our students lose," insisted Gordon. "Remember, very few of our students have taken a course in personal finance. The bank will tell the students that 'there's no cost to you,' but there's the hidden cost of high interest payments on unpaid balances, the possibility of high debt upon graduation, and ruined credit ratings in some cases."

"Those are the extreme cases," retorted Elsie. "Highland assures me that, although many students lack credit experience, most use credit responsibly and handle credit cards as well or better than most adults. It's a service our students want in a world where, like it or not, plastic is very important. Having a credit card helps students establish a credit history; assists them in meeting emergency needs such as a sudden trip home; makes paying for things like gas, food, rent, and books more convenient; and empowers them to become more financially responsible. Also, those who pay off their balances each month get the benefit of a short-term, interest-free loan. And Highland pointed out that almost two-thirds of the nation's parents think their children should have a credit card by age 18, mainly because it's a convenience for them since they don't need to continually send their kids money. I'll tell you what, Gordon. I'll let Student Activities have all the new-account payments of $6 as well as three-fifths of the revenue from transactions. Why don't you sleep on it and get back to me tomorrow?"

"I suppose I can do that," Gordon reluctantly agreed. He decided to seek the advice of Alan Whitehead, assistant director of student activities.

"I think we should take Ms. Lombardi up on her generous offer," opined Alan. "Even if our students graduate with average debts of around $1,000, given their likely earning power upon graduation, such levels of debt are easily recoverable, and the bank knows that. They aren't in the business of issuing credit to those who can't pay. And Highland is right — college students who qualify for credit are no different from nonstudent customers. At the end of the day, the responsibility is with the cardholder."

"Unfortunately, a lot of students, as well as adults, just aren't responsible," insisted Gordon. "Even for adults, credit cards foster bad habits. People think that because they have a $1,500 limit they can buy something that costs $1,500 and take their time paying it off, rather than saving until they have $1,500."

"Stop exaggerating," exclaimed Alan. "I think students can grasp the principle of debt. You're being nannyish. Credit card issuers will get their offer in students' faces one way or another. They won't be stopped by your righteous efforts. We tell our 18-year-olds that they're ready for the work force or college and that they can vote and even fight a war. Many work full or part time. Some are raising families. How can we tell them they can't manage their own credit card? Let's get with the program and get a piece of the action."

Gordon went back to his office, his head swimming. He thought that maybe Alan had some valid points. Maybe he was being too paternalistic. And, speaking of parents, didn't they have some responsibility for their kids' spending? Shouldn't they think twice before allowing their youngsters to have credit cards with a $2,500 spending limit? The banks are responding to demand, most students are fairly responsible, and anyway, it's the bank that is taking the risk of higher levels of default. After all, the relatively high rates of interest are justified since credit card debt is a pretty high-risk, unsecured type of loan.

Then he had an idea. Perhaps he could use some of the funds that Student Activities would get to institute a financial-education program on campus to help students understand the responsibility of owning and using a credit card. In fact, he had heard that some of the big banks and credit card companies had accepted the responsibility for providing personal finance guidance for students through media such as posters on campus, "credit awareness" brochures, interactive on-line game shows, and even seminars on financial management. Perhaps Mountain State and Highland could be partners in a program to deliver financial information and education.

Questions ■ Exercises

1. Summarize the pros and cons of marketing credit cards to college students mentioned in the real-life situation. Can you think of other reasons for and against marketing credit cards to college students?

2. Does Mountain State University have a responsibility to students in this case as a moral agent? Why or why not?

3. Discuss the organizational relationships that Gordon should consider as he makes his decision.

4. What are the decision alternatives Gordon faces? Which alternative is most ethical, will help build the most trust, and will enhance the university's reputation among Mountain State's stakeholders?

This real-life situation was prepared by Geoffrey P. Lantos, Stonehill College, and is strictly hypothetical; any resemblance to real persons, companies, or situations is coincidental. The author thanks Michael Durkin, assistant dean and director of student activities at Stonehill College, for his valuable input.

CHECK YOUR EQ

Check your E.Q., or Ethics Quotient, by completing the following. Assess your performance to evaluate your overall understanding of the chapter material.

1. Roughly 40 percent of employees will take advantage of a situation to further their personal interests.   Yes   No

2. Socialization refers to the process in which a person learns the values and behaviors considered appropriate by an organization.   Yes   No

3. Differential association means that people learn ethical behavior from their personal upbringing and socialization.   Yes   No

4. Whistle-blowers often retain their positions and continue to advance within the organization.   Yes   No

5. A person who behaves unethically and is rewarded is likely to continue to act unethically.   Yes   No

ANSWERS 1. **No.** Ten percent of employees take advantage of a situation if the penalty is less than the benefit and they are at low risk of being caught. 2. **Yes.** Socialization teaches employees how to behave with respect to their roles within the organization. 3. **No.** Differential association relates to the idea that individuals in the organization learn ethical and unethical behavior while interacting with others who are part of their role-sets. 4. **No.** Whistle-blowers often lose their jobs. 5. **Yes.** If no punishment occurs for unethical behavior or the behavior is rewarded, it is likely to continue.

Development of an
Effective Ethics Program

CHAPTER 8

Chapter Objectives

- To know and understand the seven minimum requirements for an ethical compliance program
- To understand the role of codes of ethics in identifying key risk areas for the organization
- To understand top management's role in supporting ethics programs
- To identify the keys to successful ethics training, including the types and the goals
- To examine the monitoring, auditing, and enforcement of ethical standards
- To understand the role of continuous improvement in implementing ethical compliance programs
- To be aware of the purpose and implementation of an ethical compliance audit

Chapter Outline

An Effective Ethical Compliance Program

Codes of Ethics and Compliance Standards
   Texas Instruments's Code of Ethics

High-Level Managers' Responsibility for Ethical Compliance Programs and the Delegation of Authority

Effective Communication of Ethical Standards

Establishing Systems to Monitor, Audit, and Enforce Ethical Standards

Continuous Improvement of the Ethical Compliance Program

The Influence of Personal Values in Business Ethics Programs

The Ethical Compliance Audit

An Ethical Dilemma*

Victoria started to wonder what the implications of her actions, as well as her company's strategy, would be. She had begun working for Koke after graduating from Pacific West University in both finance and marketing.

Koke International (KI) was the leader in franchised home repair outlets in the United States. In twenty-five years KI had grown from several stores in the Pacific Northwest to two hundred and fifty in much of the United States and Canada. Koke International came to dominate the markets it entered by undercutting local competitors on price and quality. The lower prices were easy to charge because KI received large quantity discounts from its vendors. The franchise concept also helped create another barrier to entry for KI's competitors. By expanding rapidly, KI was able to spread the costs of marketing to many more stores, giving the company still another differential advantage. With this active nourishment of the brand image, coupled with some technological advances such as just-in-time inventory, electronic scanners, and electronic market niching, KI's stock had soared. As a result, KI had a 50 percent share of the market. Koke International had done such an excellent job of positioning itself in its field that articles in major business newspapers were calling it the Microsoft of home improvements. The view was that "KI is going to continue to be a very profitable endeavor, with less expected direct competition in a slow-growth, high-margin market for the future."

Wendy, Victoria's boss, had brought her in on the next potential conquest of KI: the New England states of Maine, Vermont, New Hampshire, Connecticut, and Massachusetts.

"This is the last big potential market," Wendy said at a planning session with her senior staff. "I want you to realize that when we launch into these states we're going to have to be ruthless. I'd like your suggestions as to how we're going to eliminate the competition."

One person spoke up: "We first need to recognize that there are only five major players (multiple-store owners), with Home Designs being the largest."

"The top corporate people want us to attack Maine, New Hampshire, and Vermont first and then make a secondary attack on the other two states," interjected Victoria.

"Our buildings are four months from completion, and the media blitz is to start one month prior to the twenty-store grand opening. With that much exposed capital from our franchises, we need to make sure everything goes well," Wendy pointed out. "Vicky, have you completed your price analysis of all of the surrounding home repair stores?"

"Yes, and you're not going to like the news. Many of the stores are going to be extremely competitive relative to our normal pricing. In a few cases they seem to have an edge," Victoria replied.

"Ed, how much cash flow/reserves have you been able to calculate from the five players?"

"Well, Wendy, it looks like if we slash our prices for about six months to a year, we could drive all but Home Designs into near bankruptcy, providing that our promotional campaign doesn't have a misstep."

"What about personnel, Frank? Have you done the usual research to see about hiring away the five players' key personnel?"

"Yes, but many won't go unless they get a 50 percent raise, which is way out of line with our other stores."

At this point Wendy slammed her fist on the table and shouted, "I'm tired of hearing negative reports! It's our job to drive out the competition, so I want solutions!"

There was a long silence in the room. Wendy was noted for her quick temper and her quick firings when things didn't go as planned. She had been the first woman to make it this high in the company, and it wasn't the result of being overly pleasant.

"So this is what we're going to do," Wendy said softly. "Frank, you're going to hire those key people at a 50 percent increase. You're going to keep the unions away from the rest of the people. In eighteen months, when these overpriced employees have trained the others, we'll find some way of getting rid of them. Ed, you're going to lean on the players' bankers. See if we do business with them as well. See what other information you can squeeze out of them. Victoria, since you're the newest, I'm putting you in charge of breaking the pricing problem. I want you to come up with a unique pricing strategy for each of the twenty stores that will consistently undercut the competition for the next eighteen months, no matter if we have to lose money on everything in the stores. The franchisees will go with this once we explain the payout."

One of the newer staff asked, "If we're successful, doesn't that make us a monopoly in the area? Don't we have to worry about antitrust issues?"

Wendy raised her eyebrow a little and said, "We don't mention the word *monopoly* around here as if it were wrong. It took the Feds decades to break up AT&T. Microsoft was next on their list, and now it's MasterCard. We're in retail. No one has ever had problems with the Feds in this industry. By the time they deal with what we're doing, we will all be retired."

Questions ■ Exercises

1. Identify the issues of which Victoria needs to be aware.
2. Discuss the implications of each decision made by Wendy.
3. Discuss the issue of monopolies and whether they are right or wrong.

This case is strictly hypothetical; any resemblance to real persons, companies, or situations is coincidental.

Our goal in this book is to encourage you to think about the impact of your ethical decisions on business and society. Although there is no universally accepted approach for dealing with business ethics, companies should establish organizational structures and corporate cultures that foster ethical behavior and should pursue ethical business strategies. In Chapter 1, we indicated that the Federal Sentencing Guidelines for Organizations had set the tone for organizational ethics programs in the 1990s. These guidelines broke new ground by codifying into law incentives for organizations that take action by developing effective internal ethical compliance programs to prevent employee misconduct. Therefore, this chapter uses the framework established by the Federal Sentencing Guidelines to prevent misconduct. This framework for developing an effective ethics program is consistent with current research on how to improve ethical decision making and with the ethical decision-making process described in Chapter 5. Businesses and managers must assume responsibility and ensure that ethical standards are properly implemented on a daily basis. Such an approach is not without controversy. There are those who feel that ethics initiatives should arise inherently from a company's culture and that hiring good employees will limit unethical behavior within the organization. We believe, however, that in many organizations a prescribed, customized system of ethical compliance can help employees from diverse backgrounds gain a similar understanding of what is acceptable behavior within the organization.

In this chapter we provide an overview of how managers can develop an organizational ethics program. First we define an effective ethical compliance program. Then we consider the factors that are crucial for the development of such a program:

TABLE 8–1   Minimum Requirements for Ethical Compliance Programs

1. Standards and procedures, such as codes of ethics, reasonably capable of detecting and preventing misconduct

2. High-level personnel responsible for ethics compliance programs

3. No substantial discretionary authority given to individuals with a propensity for misconduct

4. Effective communication of standards and procedures via ethics training programs

5. Establishment of systems to monitor, audit, and report misconduct

6. Consistent enforcement of standards, codes, and punishment

7. Continuous improvement of the ethical compliance program

Source: Adapted from U.S. Sentencing Commission, Federal Sentencing Guidelines Manual *(St. Paul, Minn.: West Publishing, 1994), Chapter 8.*

codes of ethics and compliance standards; high-level personnel's responsibility for the ethical compliance program and the delegation of authority; effective communications and ethical training programs; systems that monitor, audit, and enforce ethical standards in the organization; and efforts needed to keep improving the ethical compliance program. (See Table 8–1 for a list of the minimum requirements for compliance with the Federal Sentencing Guidelines for Organizations.) Next we discuss the role of personal values in the organization and provide an ethical compliance audit that could be used to assess the company's effectiveness in ethical compliance.

We use the term *compliance* in this chapter from the business perspective of establishing and enforcing company policies on ethics. We do not intend to imply an objective of controlling the personal ethics and moral beliefs of individuals in the business organization. When companies attempt to assess personalities and personal beliefs that might influence ethical decisions on the job, great care must be taken to avoid infringing on employees' personal freedoms and ethical beliefs. In cases where individuals' personal beliefs and activities are inconsistent with company policies on ethics, conflict can develop. If the individual feels that ethical compliance systems in the organization are deficient or directed in an inappropriate manner, some type of open conflict resolution may be needed to deal with the differences.

AN EFFECTIVE ETHICAL COMPLIANCE PROGRAM

Throughout this book, we have emphasized that ethical issues are at the forefront of organizational concerns as managers and employees face increasingly complex decisions. Often these decisions are made in a group environment comprising different value systems, competitive pressures, and political concerns that contribute to the possibility of misconduct. In a national survey by KPMG on organizational integrity, 76 percent of the nearly twenty-four hundred workers surveyed indicated that they had observed violations of the law or of company standards in the previous twelve months.[1] While other surveys on this issue report lower percentages, all indications are that many observations of misconduct are made in most organizations. When opportunity to engage in unethical conduct abounds, companies are vulnerable not only to ethical problems but also to legal violations if those who work for them do not know how to make the right decision. Attempts to resolve gray areas or borderline ethical disputes often become legal issues.

An organizational ethics program should help reduce the possibility of penalties and negative public reaction to misconduct. The accountability and responsibility for appropriate business conduct is in the hands of top management. A company has to have an effective ethics program to ensure that all employees understand the values of the business and comply with policies and codes of conduct that create the ethical climate of the business. Because we come from diverse business, ducational, and family backgrounds, it cannot be assumed that we know the appropriate behavior when we enter a new organization or job. At the pharmaceutical company Merck, all employees are expected to uphold the organization's corporate code of conduct. Merck's sixty thousand employees participate in an interactive ethical business practices program that exposes them to real-life situations they might encounter. According to Merck's chief ethics officer, "we want employees to know how Merck's values apply to their day-to-day activities so that they can adhere to these standards and model these values whenever and wherever they conduct Merck business."[2]

If the corporate culture provides rewards or opportunity to engage in unethical conduct through lack of managerial concern or failure to comply with the minimum requirements of the Federal Sentencing Guidelines for Organizations (see Table 8–1), then the company may face penalties and loss of public confidence. The main objective of these federal guidelines is to encourage companies to assess risk, then self-monitor and aggressively work to deter unethical behavior by punishing members or stakeholders who engage in it. The guidelines encourage companies to assess their key risk areas and to tailor a compliance program that will meet key criteria of effectiveness. The guidelines also make the organization responsible for the misconduct of individual employees. The KPMG organizational integrity survey found that 61 percent of those surveyed felt their company would not discipline workers guilty of an ethical infraction, and 38 percent said that management would authorize illegal or unethical conduct to meet business goals.[3]

At the heart of the Federal Sentencing Guidelines for Organizations is the carrot-and-stick philosophy. Companies that act to prevent organizational misconduct may receive a "carrot" and avoid penalties should a violation occur. The ultimate "stick" is organizational sentencing, with fines and even organizational probation. Organizational probation involves on-site consultants observing and monitoring a company's ethical compliance efforts and reporting to the U.S. Sentencing Commission on the company's progress in avoiding misconduct. The government is viewing corporations as moral agents responsible for the conduct of their employees. In other words, the corporation is being treated as though it were a person.

Table 8–2 shows the mean and median fines imposed on sentenced organizations for the top four offense categories: fraud, two types of environmental crimes, and antitrust violations. Fraud is a purposeful act intended to deceive or manipulate in order to damage or hurt other individuals or organizations: for example, submitting false Medicare claims to the government. Fraud appears to be the most widespread type of misconduct, possibly because it is the charge used to prosecute any type of general deception. The problem of on-line fraud in connection with electronic auctions is growing as the number of people using such auctions continues to increase rapidly. The Federal Trade Commission (FTC) received ten thousand, seven hundred complaints about Internet auctions last year, compared to just one hundred and seven complaints two years earlier. Auction fraud accounts for a little more than half of all complaints about the Internet filed with the FTC.[4]

The sentencing of organizations is governed by four considerations. First, the court orders the organization to remedy any harm caused by the offense. Second, if the organization operated primarily with a criminal purpose, fines are set sufficiently high to divest the firm of all assets — in other words, to put the firm out of business. Third, fines levied against the organization are based on the seriousness of the offense and the culpability of the organization — for instance, whether top management was involved and whether the behavior was pervasive in the organization. Fourth, probation is deemed an appropriate sentence for an organizational defendant when it will ensure that the firm will take action to reduce further misconduct.[5] The Federal Sentencing Guidelines for Organizations require federal judges to increase fines for organizations that continually tolerate misconduct and to reduce or eliminate fines for firms with extensive ethics compliance programs that are making due diligence attempts to abide by legal and ethical standards. A firm cannot succeed solely through a legalistic approach to ethics and compliance with the sentencing guidelines; top management must seek to develop high ethical standards that serve as a barrier to illegal conduct.

TABLE 8–2   **Mean and Median Fine Imposed on Sentenced Organizations in Top Four Offense Categories**

		Cases with Fine Imposed		
Offense	Total Number of Cases	Number	Mean Fine	Median Fine
Fraud	86	57	$3,716,966	$96,000
Environmental — hazardous toxic pollutants	37	32	727,880	70,000
Environmental — other pollutants	23	21	427,917	50,000
Antitrust	18	18	53,152,280	725,000

Source: U.S. Sentencing Commission "Sourcebook of Federal Sentencing Statistics," 1999, Table 52.
http://www.ussc.gov/ANNRPT/1999/Sbtoc99.htm *(September 26, 2000).*

The company must want to be a good corporate citizen and recognize the importance of ethics to successful business activities. It must aspire to have an ethical corporate culture.

Until the Federal Sentencing Guidelines for Organizations were formulated, courts were inconsistent in holding corporations responsible for employee misconduct. Even with the best ethics program, there were no specific benefits for extensive compliance efforts, including effective supervision of employees. Now organizations gain credit for ethical compliance programs that meet a rigorous standard. The effectiveness of a program is determined by its design and implementation: it must deal effectively with the risk associated with a particular business and has to become part of the corporate culture.

An effective ethical compliance program can help a firm avoid civil liability, but the company bears the burden of proving that such a program exists. An ethics program developed in the absence of misconduct will be much more effective than a code of conduct imposed as a reaction to misconduct. To rule a company not guilty in civil liability cases, the court must conclude that an employee's unethical actions or behavior fell outside the scope of assigned duties and responsibilities. According to the principle of vicarious liability, an organization is responsible for the conduct of its employees in their daily execution of duties.

A legal test of a company's ethical compliance program is possible when an individual employee is charged with misconduct. Ethics officers must be aware of key ethical concerns and educate employees in company policy and procedures. The court system or the U.S. Sentencing Commission evaluates organizational responsibility for the individual's behavior in the process of an investigation. If the organization contributed to the misconduct or did not show due diligence in preventing misconduct, then organizational sentencing may occur. A compliance program is often evaluated in relation to industry standards, community standards, or the acceptance of the firm's conduct by important publics, including employees and customers.

CODES OF ETHICS AND COMPLIANCE STANDARDS

Ethical behavior can be encouraged through the establishment of organizational standards of conduct. These standards may take the form of codes of ethics or policy statements on certain questionable practices. A code of conduct should be specific enough to be reasonably capable of preventing misconduct. Very general codes that communicate at the level of "do no harm" or "be fair and honest" are not enough. The company must give enough direction for employees to avoid risks associated with their particular business. Table 8–3 shows some of the corporate trends with respect to ethical policies and practices.

Employees may have different moral philosophies and come from different cultures and backgrounds. Without uniform policies and standards, they are likely

TABLE 8-3   Corporate Trends with Respect to Ethical Policies and Practices

Policies and Practices	Yes %	No %	Don't Know %
Written code of ethics and social responsibility	90.3	4.8	4.8
Written environmental policy	83.5	7.6	9.0
Ombudsperson to handle ethical concerns	66.9	26.2	6.9
Policy on network confidentiality	48.0	34.3	17.8
Ethical behavior change over past 10 years (industry)?	27.1	41.7	31.3

Source: Alan K. Reichert, Marion S. Webb, and Edward G. Thomas, "Corporate Support for Ethical and Environmental Policies: A Financial Management Perspective," Journal of Business Ethics, 25 (May, 2000): p. 58. With kind permission from Kluwer Academic Publishers.

to have difficulty in determining what is acceptable behavior in the company. **Codes of ethics,** formal statements of what an organization expects in the way of ethical behavior, let employees know what behaviors are acceptable or improper. Lockheed Martin has such a code of ethics and business conduct, which is available on the company's web site. Also available there are "Warning Signs" (see Table 8–4) and a "Quick Quiz — When in doubt, ask yourself . . ."

@.ethics 1

Many organizations have established strong codes of ethics or policies related to ethics, as well as strategies for enforcing them. Codes of ethics will not solve every ethical dilemma, but they do provide rules and guidelines for employees to

TABLE 8-4   Lockheed Martin's "Warning Signs"

You're on thin ethical ice when you hear . . .

"Well, maybe just this once . . ."

"No one will ever know . . ."

"It doesn't matter how it gets done as long as it gets done."

"It sounds too good to be true."

"Everyone does it."

"Shred that document."

"We can hide it."

"No one will get hurt."

"What's in it for me?"

"This will destroy the competition."

"We didn't have this conversation."

Source: Lockheed Martin Web site, http://www.lmco.com/exeth/html/code/warn.html (accessed September 26, 2000). Courtesy of Lockheed Martin.

follow. These codes may address a variety of situations, from internal operations to sales presentations and financial disclosure practices.

A code of ethics has to reflect senior management's desire for organizational compliance with the values, rules, and policies that support an ethical climate. Development of a code of ethics should involve the president, board of directors, and senior managers who will be implementing the code. Legal staff should be called upon to ensure that the code has correctly assessed key areas of risk and that potential legal problems are buffered by standards in the code. A code of ethics that does not address specific high-risk activities within the scope of daily operations is inadequate for maintaining standards that can prevent misconduct. Walter W. Manley II has developed six steps for implementing a code of ethics; they are listed in Table 8–5.

e.ethics 2

In the United States, Texas Instruments (TI) has gained recognition as having one of the leading ethics programs. The company has won three major ethics awards: the David C. Lincoln Award for Ethics and Excellence in Business, the American Business Ethics Award, and the Bentley College Center for Business Ethics Award. Seventy-three percent of TI's employees feel that the company is very serious about ethics and integrity.[6] Thus it is worthwhile to take a close look at how TI implements its ethics program.

Texas Instruments's Code of Ethics

A large multinational firm, Texas Instruments manufactures computers, calculators, and other high-technology products. Its code of ethics resembles that of many other organizations. The code addresses issues relating to policies and procedures; gov-

TABLE 8–5   Code of Ethics Implementation

Six Steps to Effective Implementation of a Code of Ethics

1. Distribute the code of ethics comprehensively to employees, subsidiaries, and associated companies.

2. Assist employees in interpreting and understanding the application and intent of the code.

3. Specify management's role in the implementation of the code.

4. Inform employees of their responsibility to understand the code and provide them with the overall objectives of the code.

5. Establish grievance procedures.

6. Provide a conclusion or closing statement, such as this one from Cadbury Schweppes:

> The character of the company is collectively in our hands. Pride in what we do is important, and let us earn that pride by the way we put the beliefs set out here into action.

Source: Adapted from Walter W. Manley II, The Handbook of Good Business Practice, 1992, p. 16. Reprinted by permission of International Thomson Publishing Ltd.

ernment laws and regulations; relationships with customers, suppliers, and competitors; acceptance of gifts, travel, and entertainment; political contributions; expense reporting; business payments; conflicts of interest; investment in TI stock; handling of proprietary information and trade secrets; use of TI employees and assets to perform personal work; relationships with government officials and agencies; and enforcement of the code. TI's code emphasizes that ethical behavior is critical to maintaining long-term success and that each individual is responsible for upholding the integrity of the company.

> Our reputation at TI depends upon all of the decisions we make and all the actions we take personally each day. Our values define how we will evaluate our decisions and actions . . . and how we will conduct our business. We are working in a difficult and demanding, ever changing business environment. Together we are building a work environment on the foundation of integrity, innovation, and commitment. Together we are moving our company into a new century . . . one good decision at a time. We are prepared to make the tough decisions or take the critical actions . . . and do it right. Our high standards have rewarded us with an enviable reputation in today's marketplace . . . a reputation of integrity, honesty, and trustworthiness. That strong ethical reputation is a vital asset . . . and each of us shares a personal responsibility to protect, to preserve, and to enhance it. Our reputation is a strong but silent partner in all business relationships. By understanding and applying the values presented on the following pages, each of us can say to ourselves and to others, "TI is a good company, and one reason is that I am part of it." Know what's right. Value what's right. Do what's right.[7]

Like most codes of ethics, TI's requires employees to obey the law. In many instances, moreover, TI expects its employees to adhere to ethical standards more demanding than the law. For example, although some local laws permit companies to contribute to political candidates or elected officials, TI's code states that "no company funds may be used for making political contributions of any kind to any political candidate or holder of any office of any government — national, state or local. This is so even where permitted by local law." TI also goes beyond the federal law prohibiting discrimination against minorities and expects its employees to treat all fellow workers with dignity and respect. "The hours we spend at work are more satisfying and rewarding when we demonstrate respect for all associates regardless of gender, age, creed, racial background, religion, handicap, national origin, or status in TI's organization."

This code of ethics is not just lip service paid to societal concerns about business ethics; the company enforces the code through audits and disciplinary action where necessary. TI's corporate internal audit function measures several aspects of business ethics, including compliance with policies, procedures, and regulations; the economical and efficient use of resources; and the internal controls of management systems. In addition, the code states that "any employee who violates TI's ethical standards is subject to disciplinary action which can include oral reprimand, written reprimand, probation, suspension, or immediate termination."

Established in 1987, the TI Ethics Committee oversees all the activities of the ethics office. The committee consists of five high-level TI managers, who review and approve policy, procedures, and publications; monitor compliance initiatives; review any major ethical issues; and approve appropriate corrective actions.

To ensure that its employees understand the nature of business ethics and the ethical standards they are expected to follow, TI has three key publications: (1) *Standard Policies and Procedures,* (2) *The TI Commitment,* and (3) *The Value and Ethics of TI.* Employees are also provided with a minipamphlet containing an "ethics quick test" to help them when they have doubts about the ethics of specific situations and behaviors:

Is the action legal?

Does it comply with our values?

If you do it, will you feel bad?

How will it look in the newspaper?

If you know it's wrong, don't do it!

If you're not sure, ask.

Keep asking until you get an answer.

TI provides a toll-free number (1-800-33-ETHIC) for employees to call, anonymously, to report incidents of unethical behavior or simply to ask questions.[8]

The extent of TI's commitment to its employees is evidenced by the programs and support it offers them:

- "Open door" policy for all managers (any level)
- No retaliation, retribution, discrimination, or harassment
- Required sexual harassment training
- Required forty hours of ethics training per year
- Educational support from external sources
- Promotion from within
- Community involvement support
- Career development networks

Texas Instruments explicitly states what it expects of its employees and what behaviors are unacceptable. By enforcing the codes wholeheartedly, TI has taken logical steps to safeguard its excellent reputation for ethical and responsible behavior. When such standards of behavior are not made explicit, employees sometimes base ethical decisions on their observations of the behavior of peers and management. The use of rewards and punishments to enforce codes and policies controls the opportunity to behave unethically and increases employees' acceptance of ethical standards.

HIGH-LEVEL MANAGERS' RESPONSIBILITY FOR ETHICAL COMPLIANCE PROGRAMS AND THE DELEGATION OF AUTHORITY

An ethical compliance program can be significantly enhanced if a high-level manager or a committee is made responsible for its administration and oversight. The ethical compliance program should involve senior management or the owner of the organization, although each officer, manager, or employee has to be responsible for supporting and complying with the program. Table 8–6 shows some of the ways in which a chief executive officer can support the ethics program and its managers. The high-level manager in charge of the program is often called the compliance coordinator, ethics officer, or compliance officer. For example, at Starbucks Coffee Company, Shelley Lanza was promoted to executive vice president and general counsel–human resources, law and corporate affairs, and corporate social responsibility. Lanza was designated as Starbucks's compliance officer and heads the company's Compliance and Ethics Program, which provides the framework to support employees in following high ethical standards. Lanza also oversees environmental and community affairs, corporate contributions, and the Starbucks Foundation.[9] In large corporations, as at Starbucks, usually one or more senior managers are appointed to serve as compliance or ethics officers, but the entire senior management is required to support and be involved in the ethical compliance process. Sometimes the structure includes a special committee of senior managers and/or the board of directors to oversee the company's ethical compliance program. Many of the *Fortune* 1000 firms in the United States have

TABLE 8–6   **How a CEO Communicates Support of Ethics Initiatives**

Meeting informally with managers and employees, communicating directly with them regarding the company's ethics program

Using his or her own terms and expressions rather than a "canned" speech

Modeling ethical conduct through success stories and communicating what to avoid through stories of ethical violations or failures

Applying the same standards of behavior and discipline top down — by being decisive and firm with decisions

Acknowledging an employee who has recognized and addressed an ethical dilemma created by making a correct ethical decision but missing a financial target in doing so

Promoting ethically aware and responsible managers

Surveying employees regularly to see how they feel about policies, supervision, and so forth

Source: William T. Redgate and Michael Rion, "CEO Support Is Critical in Preventing Ethical Breaches in the Workplace," Ethikos (May-June 1998): 9–13.

established the post of ethics officer, with the vast majority of these positions created in the last ten years. Ethics officers usually have the following responsibilities:

- Coordinating the ethical compliance program with top management, the board of directors, and senior management
- Developing, revising, and disseminating a code of ethics
- Developing effective communication of ethical standards
- Establishing audit and control systems to determine the effectiveness of the program
- Developing consistent means of enforcing codes and standards
- Reviewing and modifying the ethics program to improve its effectiveness

Most Internet companies are not as advanced as other kinds of companies in developing ethics policies. Few have hired consultants or in-house ethics officers to oversee programs to comply with laws and encourage ethical standards. America Online recently hired an ethics officer, but most on-line companies are more concerned with survival than ethics. "What they may not realize," according to ethics consultant W. Michael Hoffman, "is that consumers tend to believe that companies with a commitment to ethics are more ethical — which can give companies with clear policies a distinct competitive advantage."[10] There have been few employee complaints, however, and customers have not voiced many ethical concerns. But as federal regulations increase, Internet companies grow in size, and economic slowdowns force staff cutbacks, the relaxed attitude of Internet companies about ethics probably will change.

Regardless of how the oversight of the ethics program is managed, it is important that the managers in charge of the program tailor it to the scope, size, and history of the organization. Just as important is reviewing the need for special compliance components based on the organization's legal history, industry standards, and regulatory concerns. If there is high risk due to the nature of the business, then special attention should be given to these matters and preventive measures included in the program. Furthermore, without an effective manager in charge of the ethics program, it will be impossible to develop organizational learning and records that document the company's steps in managing the program.

The high-level managers who oversee the ethics program must be responsible for avoiding delegation of substantial discretionary authority to people who are known to engage in misconduct. Information in the personnel files, the results of company audits, managers' opinions, and other available information should be used to ascertain the likelihood that managers will engage in misconduct. An adequate search must also be performed before the company hires individuals who have been convicted of offenses, if the firm knows — or should know — about these convictions. When past wrongdoing is uncovered — for instance, if the individual in question had been convicted of a felony or fired for misconduct in another organization — then the firm must take responsibility for delegating authority. Those in charge of ethical oversight within the organization have the obligation to prevent unethical people from holding positions of authority.

EFFECTIVE COMMUNICATION OF ETHICAL STANDARDS

Management expert Peter Drucker predicts that the new organization will be knowledge and communication based and composed largely of specialists who direct and temper their performance through feedback from colleagues and customers. As part of this evolution, Drucker expects employees to become connected by a common vision and set of values rather than by specific tasks and products.[11] Managers cannot motivate employees or coordinate their efforts without proper communication. Communication by top executives keeps the firm on its ethical course, and top executives must ensure that the ethical climate is consistent with the company's overall objectives. Communication is important in providing guidance for ethical standards and activities that integrate the functional areas of the business. A vice president of marketing, for example, must communicate and work with regional sales managers and other marketing employees to make sure that all agree on what constitutes certain unethical activities, such as bribery, price collusion, and deceptive sales techniques. Top corporate executives must also communicate with managers at the operations level (in production, sales, and finance, for instance) and enforce overall ethical standards within the organization. Table 8–7 lists the factors crucial to successful ethics training. It is most important to help employees identify ethical issues and give them the means to address and resolve such issues in ambiguous situations. In addition, employees must be offered direction on seeking assistance from managers or other designated personnel in resolving ethical problems. An effective ethics program can reduce criminal, civil, and administrative consequences, including fines, penalties, judgments, debarment from government contracts, and court control of the organization. An ineffective ethics program that results in

TABLE 8–7   Keys to Successful Ethics Training

1. Help employees identify the ethical dimensions of a business decision.

2. Give employees a means to address ethical issues.

3. Help employees understand the ambiguity inherent in ethical situations.

4. Make employees aware that their actions define the company's ethical posture both internally and externally.

5. Provide direction for finding managers or others who can assist in ethical conflict resolution.

6. Eliminate the belief that unethical behavior is *ever* justifiable by stressing that

   ■ stretching the ethical boundaries results in unethical behavior.

   ■ whether discovered or not, an unethical act is just that.

   ■ an unethical act is *never* in the best interests of the company.

   ■ the firm is held responsible for the misconduct of its members.

Source: Adapted from Walter W. Manley II, The Handbook of Good Business Practice, *1992, p. 87. Reprinted by permission of International Thomson Publishing Ltd.*

negative publicity regarding unethical acts in business may cause a decline of the company's stock value.[12]

Companies can implement ethical principles in their organizations through training programs. Discussions conducted in ethical training programs sometimes break down into personal opinions about what should or should not be done in particular situations. To be successful, business ethics programs need to educate employees about formal ethical frameworks and models for analyzing business ethics issues. Employees would then be able to base ethical decisions on some knowledge of choices, rather than on emotions.

Training and communication initiatives should reflect the unique characteristics of an organization: its size, culture, values, management style, and employee base. It is important for the ethics program to differentiate between personal and organizational ethics. If ethics training is to be effective, it must start with a foundation, a code of ethics, an ethical concerns procedure, line and staff involvements, and executive priorities on ethics that are communicated to employees.[13] Managers from every department must be involved in the development of an ethics training program.

Among the goals of an ethics training program might be to improve employee understanding of ethical issues and the ability to identify them; to inform employees of related procedures and rules; and to identify the contact person who could help in resolving ethical problems. In accord with these goals, the purpose of the Boeing Ethics and Business Conduct program is to:

- Communicate the Boeing values and standards of ethical business conduct to employees.

- Inform employees of company policies and procedures regarding ethical business conduct.

- Establish companywide processes to assist employees in obtaining guidance and resolving questions regarding compliance with the company's standards of conduct and the Boeing values.

- Establish companywide criteria for ethics education and awareness programs and to coordinate compliance oversight activities.[14]

e.ethics 3

To help ensure employees' continuing business ethics expertise, the company asks them to take ethics refresher training each year. On the company's "Ethics Challenge" web pages, employees (as well as the general public) can select from a variety of ethical dilemma scenarios, discuss them with their peers, and select from several potential answers. After clicking on the answer they think is most ethically correct, employees get feedback with the company's opinion and a rationale for each answer.

Ethical decision making is influenced by organizational culture, by peers and supervisors, and by the opportunity to engage in unethical behavior.[15] All three types of influence can be affected by ethics training. Full awareness of the philosophy of management, rules, and procedures can strengthen both the organizational culture and the ethical stance of peers and supervisors. Such awareness, too, arms employees against opportunities for unethical behavior and lessens the likelihood of misconduct. Thus the existence and enforcement of company rules and procedures limit unethical practices in the organization. If adequately and thoughtfully designed, ethics training can ensure that everyone in the organization (1) recognizes situations that might involve ethical decision making; (2) understands the values and culture of the organization; and (3) is able to evaluate the impact of ethical decisions on the company in the light of its value structure.[16]

ESTABLISHING SYSTEMS TO MONITOR, AUDIT, AND ENFORCE ETHICAL STANDARDS

Compliance involves comparing employee performance with the organization's ethical standards. Ethical compliance can be measured through the observation of employees and a proactive approach to dealing with ethical issues. An effective ethical compliance program uses investigatory and reporting resources. Sometimes external auditing and review of company activities is helpful in developing benchmarks of compliance.

The existence of an internal system for employees to report misconduct is especially useful in monitoring and evaluating ethical performance. A number of firms have set up ethics hot lines, often called help lines, to offer support and give employees an opportunity to register ethical concerns. Although there is always some worry that people may misreport a situation or misuse the hot line to retaliate against another employee, hot lines have become widespread, and employees do utilize them. For example, the 800 "assist" line at Sears receives fifteen thousand calls a year. The calls range from requesting coaching and counseling to ones requesting policy clarification to ones making allegations of unethical behavior.[17] The ethics line at Boeing is available not only to all Boeing employees, including those in subsidiaries, but also to concerned individuals outside the company.[18]

To determine whether a person is performing his or her job adequately and ethically, observation might focus on how the employee handles an ethically charged situation. For example, many businesses use role playing in the training of salespeople and managers. Ethical issues can be introduced into the discussion, and the results can be videotaped so that both the participant and the superior can evaluate the results of the ethical dilemma.

Questionnaires that survey employees' ethical perceptions of their company, their superiors, their coworkers, and themselves, as well as ratings of ethical or unethical practices within the firm and industry, can serve as benchmarks in an ongoing assessment of ethical performance. Then, if unethical behavior is perceived to increase, management will have a better understanding of what types of unethical practices may be occurring and why. A change in the ethics training within the company may be necessary.

Corrective action involves rewarding employees who comply with company policies and standards and punishing those who do not. When employees comply with organization standards, their efforts may be acknowledged and rewarded through public recognition, bonuses, raises, or some other means. Conversely, when employees deviate from organizational standards, they may be reprimanded, transferred, docked, suspended, or even fired.

If a company is to maintain ethical behavior, its policies, rules, and standards must be worked into its compliance system. Maintaining an ethical culture can be difficult if top management does not support such behavior. Consider, for instance, a situation that can plague high-tech companies. In an effort to keep earnings high and boost stock prices, many high-tech firms have engaged in falsifying revenue reports by recording sales that never took place, shipping products before customers agree to delivery, and recording all revenue from long-term contracts upfront instead of over the three- to five-year time span of a typical agreement. Many top executives in these firms encourage the behavior because they hold stock options — and may receive bonus packages — that are tied to the company's performance. Thus higher reported revenues mean larger executive payoffs. Of the ninety accounting fraud cases brought by the Securities and Exchange Commission (SEC) last year, more than half involved falsifying revenue records. Software maker MicroStrategy, for example, had to decrease its reported revenue by $205 million, resulting in a 62 percent drop in its stock price.[19] If top management in a corporation behaves unethically, it is probably difficult to create and enforce an ethical climate in the corporation.

Reducing unethical behavior is a business goal no different from increasing profits. If progress is not being made toward creating and maintaining an ethical culture, the company needs to determine why and take corrective action, either by enforcing current standards more strictly or by setting higher standards. If the code of ethics is aggressively enforced and becomes part of the corporate culture, it can be effective in improving ethical behavior within the organization. If a code is merely window dressing and not genuinely part of the corporate culture, it will accomplish very little.

Efforts to deter unethical behavior are important to companies' long-term relationships with their employees, customers, and community. If corrective action is not taken against behavior that is organizationally or socially defined as unethical, such behavior will continue. In the National Business Ethics Survey (NBES), two in five employees who reported misconduct were dissatisfied with their organization's response, indicating that such corrective action is often not taken.[20]

Consistent enforcement and necessary disciplinary action are essential to a functional ethical compliance program. The ethics or compliance officer is usually responsible for companywide disciplinary systems, implementing all disciplinary actions the company takes for violations of its ethical standards. Many companies are including ethical compliance in employee performance appraisals. During performance appraisals, employees may be asked to sign an acknowledgment that they have read the company's current guidelines on its ethical policies. The company must also promptly investigate any known or suspected misconduct. The appropriate company official, often the ethics officer, needs to make a recommendation to senior management on how to deal with a particular ethical infraction. In some cases, the company is required to report substantiated misconduct to a designated governmental or regulatory agent in order to receive credit under the Federal Sentencing Guidelines for Organizations for having an effective compliance program.[21]

CONTINUOUS IMPROVEMENT
OF THE ETHICAL COMPLIANCE PROGRAM

Improving the system that encourages employees to make more ethical decisions is not very different from implementing other types of business strategies. Implementation means putting strategies into action. Implementation in ethical compliance means the design of activities to achieve organizational objectives, using available resources and given existing constraints. Implementation translates a plan for action into operational terms and establishes a means by which organizational ethical performance will be monitored, controlled, and improved.

A firm's ability to plan and implement ethical business standards depends in part on the organization's structuring resources and activities to achieve its ethical objectives in an effective and efficient manner. For example, ever since its founding in 1850, apparel manufacturer Levi Strauss & Co. has communicated company values — what it stands for and what its people believe in, as well as its tradition of always treating people fairly and caring about their welfare.[22] The firm's Mission, Vision, Aspirations, and Values Statement (see Table 8–8) tells how the business should be run. People's attitudes and behavior must be guided by a shared commitment to the business instead of by obedience to traditional managerial authority. Encouraging diversity of perspectives, disagreement, and the empowerment of people within the organization helps to align the company's leadership with its employees.

If a company determines that its performance has not been satisfactory in ethical terms, that company's management may want to reorganize the way certain kinds of ethical decisions are made. For example, a decentralized organization may need to centralize key decisions, if only for a time, so that top-level managers can ensure that the decisions are ethical. Centralization may reduce the opportunity for lower-level managers and employees to make unethical decisions. Top management can then focus on improving the corporate culture and infusing more ethical values throughout the organization by providing rewards for positive behavior and sanctions for negative behavior. In other companies, decentralization of important decisions may be a better way to attack ethical problems, so that lower-level managers, familiar with the forces of the local business environment and local culture and values, can make more decisions. Whether the ethics function is centralized or decentralized, the key need is to delegate authority in such a way that the organization can achieve ethical performance.

THE INFLUENCE OF PERSONAL VALUES
IN BUSINESS ETHICS PROGRAMS

Corporate values tend to dominate most organizational cultures, particularly in the absence of individual ethical values. Although personal values are involved in ethical decisions, they are only one of the central components that guide the

TABLE 8–8   Levi Strauss & Co.'s Mission, Vision, Aspirations & Values

Mission

The mission of Levi Strauss & Co. is to achieve and sustain commercial success as a global marketer of branded apparel.

Vision

Through a relentless focus on consumers, innovation, and people, Levi Strauss & Co. will be the world's foremost authority in casual apparel.

Aspirations

All LS&Co. employees aspire to be part of a winning organization built on the strong foundation of accomplishments, traditions, and values that we have inherited and that continue to lead us to commercial success.

Values

Our values guide our success, unite us and make LS&Co. unique.

Integrity and Ethical Behavior

Honesty, promise-keeping, fairness, respect for others, compassion, and integrity guide our conduct and actions, even when we are confronted by personal, professional, and social risks or economic pressures.

Commitment to People

We want LS&Co. to be known as a great place to work — a place where satisfaction grows out of the contributions we make and that offers opportunities for professional growth.

Diversity

We value and utilize the varying backgrounds, experiences, knowledge, and talents of all of our employees. Our global workplace will reflect the ethnic, cultural, and lifestyle diversity within the communities where we do business.

Behaviors

Our behaviors will support the achievement of the company's Mission, Vision, and Aspirations.

Be Innovative

We will be innovative and embrace new and exciting ways of thinking. Innovative products, marketing programs and business practices are the keys to our success.

Take Informed Risks

We will take informed risks that enable each of us to create new opportunities and to challenge established business practices.

Be Decisive and Results-Oriented

We will act decisively to assess and act swiftly on opportunities that will contribute to our commercial success. Our decision making will be results-oriented and guided by our strategic business vision and our values.

Seek Leverage

We will work together, actively exchanging ideas and information throughout the company, in order to achieve our business goals. Successful teamwork involves using the knowledge and opportunities created by our global presense.

TABLE 8–8   Levi Strauss & Co.'s Mission, Vision, Aspirations & Values (*cont.*)

Be Accountable

We will set clear and measurable responsibilities for individuals and teams, and will hold each other and ourselves accountable for the success of the company.

Recognize Results

We will recognize and reward superior contributions to our business success. We will also acknowledge our failures and shortcomings, and respond quickly with any necessary corrective actions.

Source: Levi Strauss & Co. Reprinted by permission.

decisions, actions, and policies of organizations. An organization's values, as derived from its procedures and policies, tend to drive the company toward certain goals and along certain pathways. Thus the burden of ethical behavior relates to the organization's values and traditions, not just to the individuals who make the decisions and carry them out.[23]

The **"bad apple–bad barrel" theory** may help explain the relationship between personal values and organizational culture in business ethics. The "bad apple" argument — the notion that blame for unethical behavior rests with a few unsavory individuals — assumes that people are either ethical or unethical, depending on personal moral development, and implies that organizations can do little to influence ethical behavior. If the bad apple principle is true, then organizations should attempt to identify unethical individuals and avoid hiring them or remove them from the organization.[24]

The idea of the bad barrel is that something in the barrel poisons otherwise good apples; in other words, the corporate culture negatively influences otherwise ethical people. This view assumes that people are not inherently ethical or unethical but are swayed by the corporate culture surrounding them, including peers, superiors, and the reward system.[25] The organization can influence individual behavior by providing conditions that encourage ethical and discourage unethical behavior. This approach would support the use of codes of ethics and training programs.

People who have high cognitive moral development and are principled tend to act more ethically than others. Thus hiring people with high ethical standards can raise the ethical tone of the organization and improve daily ethical decision making. It is also true that employees with higher expectations of punishment behave more ethically. This finding implies that corporate culture has a major impact on ethical decision making. A company that wants to foster ethical behavior may pursue both approaches. It may try to hire people with socially accepted ethical standards and to develop an ethical corporate culture. In other words, the system will work best if there are both good apples and good barrels. Either bad apples or bad barrels are likely to lead to ethical problems.

THE ETHICAL COMPLIANCE AUDIT

In Chapter 5, we presented a framework that described the ethical decision-making process. Although this model does not explain exactly how ethical decision making occurs, it does provide a good overview that could be helpful in implementing an ethical compliance audit within a company. An **ethical compliance audit** is a systematic evaluation of an organization's ethics program and/or performance to determine its effectiveness. In particular, it is useful to focus on the key factors that influence how ethical decisions are made. The corporate culture, including peers, superiors, and formal systems of reward and punishment, exerts an important influence on the ethical behavior of employees. Understanding the ethical issues in an audit can help in establishing codes of ethics and other programs to control ethical behavior in business organizations.

The auditing process can highlight trends, improve organizational learning, and facilitate communication and working relationships.[26] The ethical compliance audit should provide regular, comprehensive, and comparative (current behavior vs. past behavior) verification of the views of stakeholders. Regular audits permit stakeholders to judge whether a firm is achieving the goals it has estab-

---

TABLE 8–9   Steps for Developing an Ethical Compliance Audit

1. Gain the CEO's commitment.

2. Appoint an ethics committee to guide the audit.

3. Appoint an auditing team (auditors, key managers, and organizational development experts) that will develop questions to be used in examining the firm's ethics performance.

4. Diagnose the corporate culture and investigate designated functional areas, such as employee issues, community relations, customer relationships, and environmental practices.

5. Analyze the mission statement and look for circumstances when the desired mission/goals and actual ethical performance do not coincide.

6. Determine underlying reasons that ethical performance and organizational goals are not consistent.

7. Collect relevant industry information, existing benchmark studies, and available information on competitors and industry ethical standards in each designated functional area.

8. Interview relevant stakeholders who are involved in each functional area about their perceptions of the firm's ethical and socially responsible performance.

9. Compare internal data about ethical performance and external stakeholder perceptions.

10. Write a final report for company managers and the audit committee, and, if possible, obtain an external evaluation of the report.

Source: Reprinted from "Corporate Responsibility Audits: Doing Well by Doing Good," by Sandra Waddock and Neil Smith, Sloan Management Review, Winter 2000, p. 79, by permission of publisher. Copyright 2000 by Sloan Management Review Association. All rights reserved.

TABLE 8–10   The Ethical Compliance Audit

		Organizational Issues*
YES	NO	1. Does the company have a code of ethics that is reasonably capable of preventing misconduct?
YES	NO	2. Is there a person with high managerial authority responsible for an ethical compliance program?
YES	NO	3. Are there mechanisms in place to avoid delegating authority to individuals with a propensity for misconduct?
YES	NO	4. Does the organization have effective communication of standards and procedures via ethics training programs for its employees?
YES	NO	5. Does the organization communicate its ethical standards to suppliers, customers, and significant others that have a relationship with the organization?
YES	NO	6. Do the company's manuals and written documents guiding operations contain ethics messages about appropriate behavior?
YES	NO	7. Is there formal or informal communication within the organization about procedures and activities that are considered acceptable ethical behavior?
YES	NO	8. Does top management have a mechanism to detect ethical issues relating to employees, customers, the community, and society?
YES	NO	9. Is there a system for employees to report unethical behavior?
YES	NO	10. Is there consistent enforcement of standards and punishments in the organization?
YES	NO	11. Is there an ethics committee, department, team, or group that deals with ethical issues in the organization?
YES	NO	12. Is there an attempt to provide continuous improvement of the ethical compliance program within the organization?

*A high number of yes answers indicates that ethical control mechanisms and procedures are in place within the organization.

lished and whether it abides by the ethical conduct standards it has specified.[27] Auditing also can help a company identify situations or practices that could create liabilities, thereby presenting an opportunity to resolve such problems before they result in negative publicity or expensive litigation. For example, an audit might uncover operational practices that could harm the natural environment, create deceptive business practices, or treat employees unfairly. Ethical compliance auditing is similar to financial auditing in that it employs the same procedures and processes in order to create a system of integrity with objective reporting. Whereas financial auditing focuses on all systems related to money flow and financial assessments of value for tax purposes and managerial accountability, ethical compliance auditing deals with the internal and broad external impact of the ethical performance of an organization. Table 8–9 provides steps for developing an ethical compliance audit.

Table 8–10 offers specific examples of items that could be used to assess an organization's ethical concerns and control mechanisms in an ethical compliance audit. An audit should provide a systematic and objective survey of the ethical

TABLE 8–10   The Ethical Compliance Audit (*cont'd.*)

		Examples of Specific Issues That Could Be Monitored in an Ethics Audit**
YES	NO	1. Are systems and operational procedures for individual employees to safeguard ethical behavior absent?
YES	NO	2. Is it necessary for employees to break company ethical rules in order to get the job done?
YES	NO	3. Is there an environment of deception, repression, and cover-ups concerning events that would be embarrassing to the company?
YES	NO	4. Are participatory management practices that allow the discussion of ethical issues absent?
YES	NO	5. Are compensation systems totally dependent on performance?
YES	NO	6. Is there sexual harassment?
YES	NO	7. Is there any form of discrimination — race, sex, or age — in hiring, promotion, or compensation?
YES	NO	8. Are the only concerns about environmental impact those that are legally required?
YES	NO	9. Is concern for the ethical value systems of the community with regard to the firm's activities absent?
YES	NO	10. Are there deceptive and misleading messages in promotion?
YES	NO	11. Are products described in a misleading manner, with negative impact or limitations uncommunicated to customers?
YES	NO	12. Are the documents and copyrighted materials of other companies used in unauthorized ways?
YES	NO	13. Are expense accounts inflated?
YES	NO	14. Are customers overcharged?
YES	NO	15. Is there unauthorized copying of computer software?

**The number of yes answers indicates the number of possible ethical issues to address.*

condition of the organization. Like an accounting audit, an ethical compliance audit may be more helpful if someone with expertise from outside the organization conducts it. Note that the questions under "Organizational Issues" in the audit in Table 8–10 do not prescribe specific normative ethics actions; rather, they check for mechanisms that promote an ethical organization. The specific issues to monitor in an ethical compliance audit are given as an example, and the questions contain normative evaluations of behavior. Organizations should participate in the development of their ethical compliance audit instrument to make sure that the key issues they confront are included in the audit. Top management should get involved in determining which normative issues to evaluate, based on the company's desired ethical perspective. Where ethical concerns are found, the ethical compliance audit can help management establish codes of ethics and policies as guidelines for employee actions.

SUMMARY

An effective organizational compliance program involves the following: codes of ethics and compliance standards; high-level personnel responsible for the ethical compliance program and the delegation of authority; effective communications and ethical training programs; systems that monitor, audit, and enforce ethical standards; and efforts needed to keep improving the ethical compliance program.

An organizational ethics program should help reduce the possibility of legally enforced penalties and negative public reaction to misconduct. Top management is accountable and responsible for appropriate business conduct. A company must have an effective ethics program to ensure that all employees understand the values of the business and comply with policies and codes of conduct that create the ethical climate of the organization.

The main objective of the Federal Sentencing Guidelines for Organizations is to encourage companies to assess risk, then self-monitor and aggressively work to deter unethical acts and punish organizational members or stakeholders who engage in unethical behavior. The sentencing of organizations is governed by four considerations. First, any harm caused by the organizational offense must be remedied. Second, if the firm operated primarily with a criminal purpose, fines are to be set sufficiently high to divest it of all assets. Third, organizational fines are based on the seriousness of the offense and the culpability of the organization. Fourth, probation is an appropriate sentence for an organizational defendant when it will ensure that the firm will take action to reduce further misconduct.

Ethical behavior can be encouraged by establishing organizational standards of conduct, particularly codes of ethics. Many companies have adopted codes of ethics: formal statements regarding the behavior that the organization expects of its employees. Without uniform policies and standards, employees will have difficulty determining acceptable behavior in the company. A code of ethics must be developed as part of senior management's desire for organizational compliance with values, rules, and policies that support an ethical climate.

There are six steps to the effective implementation of a code of ethics: comprehensive distribution; assisting in the interpretation and understanding of the code's application and intent; specifying management's role in the implementation; informing employees about the code's objectives and their responsibility to understand them; establishing grievance procedures; and providing a conclusion statement.

An ethical compliance program can be significantly enhanced by having a high-level manager or committee responsible for the administration and oversight of the program. Each officer, manager, and employee is responsible for supporting and complying with the ethics program. The managers who oversee the ethics program are responsible for avoiding delegation of substantial discretionary authority to people with a propensity for misconduct.

Effective communication by top executives keeps the firm on its ethical course, and top executives must ensure that the ethical climate is consistent with the company's overall objectives. Communication is important in any attempt to set ethical standards that provide integration between the functional areas of the business.

Successful ethics training is important in helping employees identify ethical issues and providing the means to address such issues and resolve them. Employees should seek help in the resolution of ethical problems from managers or other designated personnel.

Compliance involves comparing employee performance with the organization's ethical standards. Ethical compliance can be measured through the observation of employees and a proactive approach to addressing ethical issues. Corrective action involves rewarding employees who comply with company policies and standards and punishing those who do not. Consistent enforcement and disciplinary action are necessary to have a functioning ethical compliance program.

A firm's ability to plan and implement ethical business standards depends in part on the organization's structuring resources and activities to achieve its ethical objectives in an effective and efficient manner.

Although personal values are involved in ethical decision making, they are only one of the components that guide the decisions, actions, and policies of organizations. The burden of ethical behavior relates to the organization's values and traditions, not just the individuals who make the decisions and carry them out. The "bad apple–bad barrel" theory may help explain the relationship between personal values and organizational culture in business ethics.

An ethical compliance audit provides a systematic and objective survey of the ethical condition of an organization and may be more objective if conducted by someone from outside the organization.

Important Terms for Review	codes of ethics "bad apple–bad barrel" theory	ethical compliance audit

A Real-Life Situation*

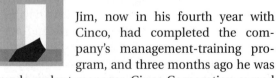

Jim, now in his fourth year with Cinco, had completed the company's management-training program, and three months ago he was made a plant manager. Cinco Corporation owned pulp-processing plants that produced various grades of paper from fast-growing, genetically altered trees. Jim's plant, the smallest and oldest of Cinco's, was located in upstate New York, near a small town. It employed between one hundred and one hundred and seventy-five workers, mostly from the nearby town. In fact, the plant boasted about employees whose fathers and grandfathers had also worked there. Every year Cinco held a Fourth of July picnic for the entire town.

Cinco's policy was to give each manager a free hand in dealing with employees, the community, and the plant itself. Its main measure of performance was the bottom line, and the employees were keenly aware of this fact.

Like all pulp-processing plants, Cinco was located near a river. Because of the plant's age, much of its equipment was outdated. Consequently, it took more time and money to produce paper at Jim's plant than at Cinco's newer plants. Cinco had a long-standing policy of starting new people at this plant to see if they could manage a work force and a mill efficiently and effectively. There was a tradition that a manager who did well with the up-state New York plant would be transferred to a larger, more modern one. As a result of this tradition, the plant's workers have had to deal with many managers and were hardened and insensitive to change. In addition, most of the workers were older and more experienced than their managers, including Jim.

In his brief tenure as plant manager, Jim had learned much from his workers about the business. Jim's secretary, Ramona, made sure that reports were prepared correctly, that bills were paid, and that Jim learned how to perform his tasks. Ramona had been with the plant for so long that she had become a permanent fixture. Jim's three foremen were all in their late forties and kept things running smoothly. Jim's wife, Elaine, was having a difficult time adjusting to upstate New York. Speaking with other managers' wives, she learned that the "prison sentence," as she called it, typically lasted no longer than two years. She had a large calendar in the kitchen and crossed off each day they were there.

One morning as Jim came into the office, Ramona didn't seem her usual stoic self. "What's up?" Jim asked her. "You need to call the EPA," she replied. "It's not real important. Ralph Hoad said he wanted you to call him." When Jim made the call, Ralph told him the mill's waste disposal into the river exceeded Environmental Protection Agency (EPA) guidelines, and he would stop by next week to discuss the situation. Jim hung up the phone and asked Ramona for the water sample results for the last six months upstream, downstream, and at the plant. After inspecting the data and comparing them with EPA standards, he found no violations of any kind. He then ordered more tests to verify the original data. The next day Jim compared the previous day's tests with the last six months' worth of data and found no significant differences and no EPA violations. As he continued

to look at the data, something stood out on the printouts that he hadn't noticed before. All the tests had been done on the first or second shifts. Jim called the foremen of the two shifts to his office and asked if they knew what was going on. Both men were extremely evasive with their answers and referred him to the third-shift foreman. When Jim phoned him, he, too, was evasive and said not to worry — that Ralph would explain it to him.

That night Jim decided to make a spot inspection of the mill and test the wastewater. When he arrived at the river, he knew by the smell that something was wrong. Jim immediately went back to the mill and demanded to know what was happening. Chuck, the third-shift foreman, took Jim down to the lowest level of the plant. In one of the many rooms stood four large storage tanks. Chuck explained to Jim that when the pressure gauge reached a certain level, a third-shift worker opened the valve and allowed the waste to mix with everything else. "You see," Chuck told Jim, "the mill was never modernized to meet EPA standards, so we have to divert the bad waste here; twice a week it goes into the river." "Who knows about this?" asked Jim. "Everyone who needs to," answered Chuck. When Jim got home, he told Elaine about the situation. Elaine's reaction was, "Does this mean we're stuck here? Because if we are, I don't know what I'll do!" Jim knew that all the other managers before him must have had the same problem. He also knew that there would be no budget for installing EPA-approved equipment for at least another two years.

The next morning Jim checked the EPA reports and was puzzled to find that the mill had always been in compliance. There should have been warning notices and fines affixed, but he found nothing. That afternoon Ralph Hoad stopped by. Ralph talked about the weather, hunting, fishing, and then he said, "Jim, I realize you're new. I apologize for not coming sooner but I saw no reason to because your predecessor had taken care of me until this month." "What do you mean?" Jim asked. "Ramona will fill you in. There's nothing to worry about. I know no one in town wants to see the mill close down, and I don't want it to either. There are lots of memories in this old place. I'll stop by to see you in another couple of months." With that, Ralph left.

Jim asked Ramona about what Ralph had said. She showed him a miscellaneous expense of $100 a month in the ledgers. "We do this every month," she told him. "How long has this been going on?" asked Jim. "Since the new EPA rules," Ramona replied. She went on to clarify Jim's alternatives. Either he could continue paying Ralph, which didn't amount to much, or he could refuse to, which would mean payment of EPA fines and a potential shutdown of the plant. As Ramona put it, "Headquarters only cares about the bottom line. Now, unless you want to live here the rest of your life, the first alternative is the best for your career. The last manager who bucked the system lost his

job. The rule in this industry is that if you can't manage Cinco's upstate New York plant, you can't manage. That's the way it is."

Questions ■ Exercises

1. Identify the ethical and legal issues of which Jim needs to be aware.
2. Discuss the advantages and disadvantages of each decision Jim could make.
3. Identify the pressures that have brought about the ethical and legal issues.
4. What is Jim's power structure and leadership position at the plant?

This case is strictly hypothetical; any resemblance to real persons, companies, or situations is coincidental.

CHECK YOUR EQ

Check your E.Q., or Ethics Quotient, by completing the following. Assess your performance to evaluate your overall understanding of the chapter material.

1. A compliance program can be deemed effective if it addresses the seven minimum requirements for ethical compliance programs.   Yes   No

2. The accounting and responsibility for appropriate business conduct rest with top management.   Yes   No

3. Ethical compliance can be measured through the observation of employees as well as through investigating and reporting mechanisms.   Yes   No

4. The key goal of ethics training is to help employees identify ethical issues.   Yes   No

5. An ethical compliance audit is designed to determine the effectiveness of ethics initiatives.   Yes   No

ANSWERS 1. No. An effective compliance program has the seven elements of a compliance program in place and goes beyond those minimum requirements to determine what will work in a particular organization. **2. Yes.** Executives in the organization determine the culture and initiatives that would support ethical behavior. **3. Yes.** Sometimes external monitoring is necessary, but internal monitoring and evaluation are the norm. **4. No.** It is much more than that — it involves not only recognition, but also an understanding of the values, culture, and rules in the organization, as well as an understanding of the impact of ethical decisions on the company. **5. Yes.** It helps in establishing the code and in making program improvements.

Business Ethics
in a Global Economy

CHAPTER 9

Chapter Objectives

- To gain an appreciation of culture as a factor in business ethics
- To explore cultural relativism as a framework for global business ethics
- To assess the role of multinational corporations in business ethics
- To examine attempts to establish a universal set of ethics for global business
- To gain awareness of ethical issues around the globe

Chapter Outline

Ethical Perceptions and International Business

Culture as a Factor in Business

Adapting Ethical Systems to a Global Framework: Cultural Relativism

The Multinational Corporation

A Universal Set of Ethics

Ethical Issues Around the Globe
 Sexual and Racial Discrimination
 Human Rights
 Price Discrimination
 Bribery and the Foreign Corrupt Practices Act
 Harmful Products
 Pollution
 Telecommunications Issues

An Ethical Dilemma*

At the Dun and Ready (D&R) Company, Sid was responsible for monitoring the Japanese stock market to determine patterns and identify stocks that could become active. One of ten company representatives in Japan, Sid, who was of Japanese decent and fluent in the language, had been sent to Tokyo. Being relatively new to the firm, he was told to gather information for his boss, Glenna. Glenna had been with D&R for ten years, but because of the cultural barriers, she was not enthusiastic about her Tokyo assignment. Glenna encouraged Sid to get to know the Japanese brokers, traders, and other key people in the business, and thanks to his background, he found that he blended easily into the culture.

In Japan, ceremony and giving favors is a way of life. Sid learned that by observing Japanese customs and perfecting his Japanese he not only became an information resource on the Japanese stock market and its players for his company, but also a resource for the Japanese who wanted to invest in the U.S. market. He found that the locals would talk to him about important investments rather than coming into the office to see Glenna.

Among Sid's duties was taking key customers to bars, restaurants, and vacation spots for entertainment. One day a government official in the group Sid was entertaining hinted that he and the others would like to play golf on some famous U.S. courses. Sid understood what the government official wanted and relayed the request to Glenna, who told him that granting a favor of this kind would normally be against policy, but since such favors seemed to be the custom in Japan, they could do some "creative bookkeeping." "When in Rome, right, Sid?" was Glenna's response to the whole situation. By pulling some strings, Glenna managed to have these officials play at ten of the most exclusive U.S. golf courses. Later several officials passed the word to people in Japan's elite financial circle about Sid's helpfulness.

Six months afterward Glenna was transferred back to the States. Rumor had it that expenses were too high and revenue too low. Her replacement, Ron, didn't like being sent to Japan either. In his very first week on the job, he told the staff that he would shorten his tour in Tokyo by slashing expenses and increasing productivity. Ron was a "by-the-book" person. Unfortunately, company rules had not caught up with the realities of cultural differences. After two months with Ron, seven of the original ten company representatives had quit or been fired.

Sid was barely surviving. Then one of his contacts in the government repaid a favor by suggesting several stocks to buy and several to sell. The information paid off, and Sid gained some breathing room from Ron. Around the same time, some of Sid's Japanese clients lost a considerable amount of money in the U.S. markets and wanted a "discount" — the term used for the practice in some large Japanese brokerage houses of informally paying off part of their best clients' losses. When Glenna was still in Tokyo, she had dipped into the company's assets several times to fund such discounts. Because everything required Ron's approval, Sid and his colleagues believed that this practice would not be tolerated. However, late one afternoon Sid and a few others provided the proper forms, and Ron signed them without realizing what he had done.

Several months passed, and the three survivors had resorted to lowering their expenses by using their own funds. This, in turn, led to Sid churning some of his accounts — that is, he bought and sold stocks for the express purpose of increasing his own revenues. Churning was tolerated in Japan, along with other practices that would be deemed questionable in the United States. Ron was oblivious to what Sid was doing because his focus was on reducing expenses.

In the previous month a group of important D&R clients had given a party for a few of their favorite brokers at one of their local haunts. After the customary toasts and small talk, it was suggested to Sid that a Japanese cartel might be interested in D&R. Sid was cautious, and nothing else was mentioned. Several weeks later at another party, Sid and the two remaining D&R people had been told that a takeover was imminent. But to make the takeover painless, the cartel needed certain sensitive information. Sid's reward for providing it would be a high position in the new, reorganized company and a "wink/nod" agreement that he could go anywhere in the world for his next assignment.

That week Ron had announced that headquarters was pleased with the productivity of the Tokyo group. "It's only a matter of time before I get transferred out, and I want out of Tokyo," he told them. The office knew that if Ron was successful, his next position would be that of vice president. He also informed the group that corporate representatives would be coming to Tokyo the following week. "It seems that they've heard rumors of a possible hostile takeover attempt on D&R from someone in Japan, and they want us to check it out," Ron said, adding with a tight smile, "There will be some changes next week." Sid suspected that this meant even fewer people working harder. It might also mean, however, that someone knew that Sid and the two representatives had been talking to the wrong people, as defined by D&R. Or maybe one of the three had sold out the other two. If Sid was to gather the information sought by the cartel, he would have to act quickly.

Questions ■ Exercises

1. What are the ethical issues?
2. What moral philosophies were Sid, Glenna, and Ron using?
3. What are some control options that D&R could have introduced to create a better ethical climate?
4. Discuss the advantages and disadvantages of each decision Sid could make.
5. Identify the pressures that have caused the ethical issues to develop.
6. Discuss Sid's power structure and leadership position at D&R and what it might be at the new D&R.

This case is strictly hypothetical; any resemblance to real persons, companies, or situations is coincidental.

Advances in communication, technology, and transportation have shrunk the world, resulting in a new global economy. More countries are attempting to industrialize and compete internationally. Because of these trends, more companies are doing business outside their home countries. These activities and all business transactions across national boundaries are defined as global business. Global business brings together people and countries that have different cultures, values, laws, and ethical standards. The international businessperson must not only understand the values, culture, and ethical standards of his or her own country but also be sensitive to those of other countries. In addition, surveys show that whereas about 90 percent of American firms have a written code of ethics, ethical conduct codes are found less frequently outside the United States. For example, 51 percent of German firms, 41 percent of British firms, and 30 percent of French firms surveyed had ethics codes in place.[1]

We often perceive the values of our home country as universal. For example, in the United States we have a strong compliance, or legal, orientation, and when we expand our operations globally, we assume this to be the norm elsewhere. But in other lands and other cultures, some laws are often interpreted situationally or within specific contexts and are either followed or ignored depending on the current economic environment or the rewards offered by business to the community or country.

Given the acceptance of such "situational" considerations in regard to law, regulators tend to be less predatory; consequently, regulators and businesses function in greater harmony. Indeed, in some countries, relationships between regulators and businesses can be more important than contracts or the legal system in dictating behavior. Hence the multinational corporation becomes more complex in the way it must define and handle ethical and legal situations. As organizations merge and grow with global expansion, corporations have a tremendous amount of power. Because of their size and economic power, as well as the diversity of the countries in which they operate, global companies are hard to monitor, influence, and, at times, control.

We first consider the different perceptions of corporate ethics, cultural differences, and cultural relativism. Then we examine multinational corporations and the ethical problems they face. We also discuss a universal, or common, set of ethical principles that is being accepted around the world. Finally, we highlight some of the major global ethical issues. As before, we do not offer absolute answers to the ethical issues. Our goal is to help you understand how international business activities can create ethical conflict and to help you improve your ethical decision making ability.

ETHICAL PERCEPTIONS AND INTERNATIONAL BUSINESS

When businesspeople travel, they sometimes perceive different modes of operation abroad. For example, when doing business in Ukraine, manufacturers and importers must go through inspections and other hurdles to gain access to the market. Before a product is offered for sale, a team of government inspectors must go to the factory where it is made, and the manufacturer must pay the team's travel expenses plus up to $10,000 per visit. Reapproval must be sought every two years. If approval lapses, every single shipment of the product must be quarantined and lab-tested at a cost of $200 to $300 per item.

Current research reveals that there is at least the perception in the United States that American companies are different from "them." Table 9–1 indicates the countries perceived as the most and least corrupt, as seen by businesspeople, risk analysts, and the general public. In business, the perception that "we" differ from "them" is called the **self-reference criterion (SRC).**

The SRC is an unconscious reference to one's own cultural values, experiences, and knowledge. When confronted with a set of facts, we react on the basis of knowledge that has accumulated over a lifetime and is usually grounded in the culture of our origin. Our reactions are based on meanings, values, and symbols that relate to our culture but may not have the same relevance to people of other cultures.

TABLE 9-1   Perceptions of Countries as Least/Most Corrupt

Least	Most
1. Denmark (1)*	1. Cameroon (1)
2. Finland (2)	2. Nigeria (4)
3.** New Zealand (4)	3. Indonesia (6)
3. Sweden (3)	3. Azerbaijan (–)
5. Canada (6)	4. Uzbekistan (–)
5. Iceland (5)	4. Honduras (3)
7. Singapore (7)	5. Tanzania (4)
8. Netherlands (8)	6. Yugoslavia (–)
9. Norway (8)	6. Paraguay (2)
9. Switzerland (10)	6. Kenya (–)

*Numbers in parentheses indicate previous rank. A dash within the parentheses indicates that the country was not in the previous survey ranking.

**The same number ranking indicates a tie (for example New Zealand and Sweden tied for third).

Note: The United States ranked the eighteenth least corrupt country.

Source: "The 1999 Transparency International Corruption Perceptions Index." http://www.transparency.org/documents/cpi/1999/index.html (May 9, 2000). Courtesy of Transparency International.

CULTURE AS A FACTOR IN BUSINESS

To examine the complexities of ethical decision making in the global arena, we must focus on the causes of conflict among people and organizations. One of the most difficult concepts to understand and apply to the business environment is culture. Because customs, values, and ethical standards vary from person to person, company to company, and even society to society, ethical issues that arise from international business activities often differ from those that evolve from domestic business activities. Distinctively international issues are often related to differences in cultures. Thus it is important to define and explore the concept of culture as it relates to the global setting.

Culture is defined as everything in our surroundings made by people, both tangible items and intangible concepts and values. Language, religion, law, politics, technology, education, social organization, general values, and ethical standards are all included in this definition. Each nation has a distinctive culture and, consequently, distinctive beliefs about what business activities are acceptable or unethical. Thus, when conducting international business, individuals encounter values, beliefs, and ideas that may diverge from their own because of cultural differences. You can test your "cultural IQ."

e.ethics 1

Cultural differences include differences in speech. Problems of translation into another language often make it difficult for businesspeople to express exactly what they mean. For example, an advertisement in Mexico for a particular Parker ballpoint pen was supposed to say, "It won't leak in your pocket and embarrass you." Parker assumed that *embaraazar* means "to embarrass" in Spanish, but in actuality it means "to impregnate." So the ad read "It won't leak in your pocket and make you pregnant." Similarly, the slogan for Coors beer "Turn it loose" was translated into Spanish inaccurately and read "Suffer from diarrhea."[2] Although blunders in communication may have their humorous side, they frequently offend or anger others, derail important business transactions, and even damage international business relations.

Cultural differences in body language can also lead to misunderstandings. Body language is nonverbal, usually unconscious, communication through gestures, posture, and facial expressions. Americans, for instance, nod their heads up and down to indicate "yes," but in Albania this means "no," and in Britain it indicates that they hear, not that they agree. A commonplace gesture among Americans, pointing a finger, is considered very rude in Asia and Africa. Personal space — the distance at which one person feels comfortable when talking with another — also varies from culture to culture. American and British businesspeople prefer a larger space than do South American, Greek, and Japanese. This difference can make people from different countries ill at ease with each other in their negotiations.

Perceptions of time may likewise differ from country to country. Americans value promptness, but businesspeople from other lands approach meetings in a more relaxed manner. An American firm lost a contract in Greece after it tried to impose its customs on the local negotiators by setting time limits for meetings. Greeks deem such limits insulting and lacking in finesse.[3] Americans, on the other hand, may view the failure to meet contractual obligations on a timely basis as an ethical issue.

When firms transfer personnel, cultural variations can turn into liabilities. Consequently, large corporations spend thousands of dollars to make sure that the employees they send abroad are culturally prepared. To facilitate employees' overseas assignments, for example, Eastman Chemical Company devised a preparation program that is so effective that 99 percent of participating employees successfully complete their term in a foreign country. Eastman offers cultural orientation for the entire family, not just the employee, that includes language training, a house-hunting trip, and counseling to prepare the family for life in a new culture.[4] In addition, seemingly innocuous customs of one country can be offensive or even dangerous in others. For example, employees of a California construction company presented green baseball caps to top Taiwanese company executives at a meeting. To traditional Taiwanese, however, green caps symbolize adultery. Unwittingly, the Americans had accused their associates of having unfaithful wives.[5] Table 9–2 lists acceptable standards of gift giving in selected areas of the world.

TABLE 9–2   Acceptable Standards of Gift Giving in Selected Countries

Japan

- Consult the staff in better department stores in Japan to find an appropriate gift in a particular situation.
- Always wrap gifts, but never in white, which is associated with funerals.
- Give and receive gifts with both hands and a slight bow.

China

- Present a reasonably priced gift only when negotiations are complete or nearly so.
- Give gifts to everyone involved, with each gift's value based on the recipient's rank.
- Do not give gifts involving amounts of four because the number is associated with death in some areas.
- Wrapping in red symbolizes good luck, but red ink is taboo because it implies the severing of a relationship.
- If Chinese people decline your gift, you should do the same if offered one from them.

Singapore

- Gift giving is not a common practice, and corruption is not tolerated.
- If necessary, give only inexpensive, token gifts, such as pens or other items with a company logo.

India

- Graft is widespread.
- Although illegal, bribes are often solicited at each bureaucratic level.
- Rely on the advice of local associates because some Indian businesspeople may expect expensive gifts while others may be offended.

Source: Tibbett L. Speer, "Avoid Gift Blunders in Asian Locales," April 25, 2000. http://www.usatoday.com/life/travel/business/1999/t0316bt2.htm *(May 8, 2000).*

Divergent religious values can also create ethical issues in international business. For instance, before a British fast-food hamburger chain entered the Indian market, its market research indicated a problem. The ruling class in India is predominately Hindu, and its members abstain from eating beef for religious reasons. Even though other Indian religions permit consumption of beef, the British firm decided to avoid giving offense and not use beef for its hamburgers. However, companies are not always so considerate of other cultures' values and mores.

One of the critical ethical issues linked to cultural differences is the question of whose values and ethical standards take precedence in negotiations and business transactions. When conducting business outside their own country, should businesspeople impose their own values, ethical standards, and even laws on members of other cultures? Or should they adapt to the values, ethical standards, and laws of the country in which they are doing business? As with many ethical issues, there are no easy answers to these questions.

ADAPTING ETHICAL SYSTEMS TO A GLOBAL FRAMEWORK: CULTURAL RELATIVISM

"When in Rome do as the Romans do" or "You must adapt to the cultural practices of the country you are in" are the explanations businesspeople offer for straying from their own ethical values when doing business abroad. By defending the payment of bribes or "greasing the wheels of business" and other questionable practices in this fashion, they are resorting to **cultural relativism:** the concept that morality varies from one culture to another and that business practices are therefore differentially defined as right or wrong by particular cultures. For instance, in Afghanistan the custom has been to discriminate against women. Citing Islamic law that forbids women to work, authorities shut down all bakeries run by widows. The bakeries had been started by the United Nations World Food Program and allowed the women to receive salaries for making bread, which was then sold at a subsidized price to other women. One woman who lost her job was heard yelling, "Give me poison and give my five children poison; then we will die fast instead of a slow death from starving and shame."[6] In Hong Kong, a senior buyer explained that in the Chinese culture monetary gifts of 3 percent of sales are customary in some industries and hence deemed ethical. But when a buyer asked for 6 percent and this information was passed on to the company's president, the buyer was fired — not because he took the money, but because he had asked for more than was culturally acceptable, or ethical.

As with all philosophies, relativists ride a continuum. Some profess **ethical relativism:** the belief that only one culture defines ethical behavior for the whole globe, without exceptions. For the business relativist there may be no ethical standards except for the one in the transaction culture. The advantage of this belief is that those who hold it can always adjust to the ethics of the particular foreign culture. The disadvantage is that they may be in conflict with their own individual moral standards and perhaps with their own culture's values and legal system. As business becomes more global and multinational corporations proliferate, the chances of ethical conflict increase. Figure 9–1 details an International Code of Ethics for Canadian business. Developed with the assistance of Errol Mendes, a professor at the University of Ottawa, the code had thirteen signatories, including ALCAN Aluminum and Canadian Occidental Petroleum.

FIGURE 9-1   International Code of Ethics for Canadian Business

INTERNATIONAL CODE OF ETHICS FOR CANADIAN BUSINESS

PRINCIPLES

A. Concerning Community Participation and Environmental Protection, we will:

- strive within our sphere of influence to ensure a fair share of benefits to stakeholders impacted by our activities.
- ensure meaningful and transparent consultation with all stakeholders and attempt to integrate our corporate activities with local communities as good corporate citizens.
- ensure our activities are consistent with sound environmental management and conservation practices.
- provide meaningful opportunities for technology, training and capacity building within the host nation.

B. Concerning Human Rights, we will:

- support and promote the protection of international human rights within our sphere of influence.
- not be complicit in human rights abuses.

C. Concerning Business Conduct, we will:

- not make illegal and improper payments and bribes and will refrain from participating in any corrupt business practices.
- comply with all application laws and conduct business activities in a transparent fashion.
- ensure contractor's, supplier's and agent's activities are consistent with these principles.

D. Concerning Employees Rights and Health and Safety, we will:

- ensure health and safety of workers is protected.
- strive for social justice and promote freedom of association and expression in the workplace.
- ensure consistency with universally accepted labour standards, including those related to exploitation of child labour.

APPLICATION

The signators of this document are committed to implementation with their individual firms through the development of operational codes and practices that are consistent with the vision, beliefs, values and principles contained herein.

FIGURE 9-1   International Code of Ethics for Canadian Business (*cont'd.*)

INTERNATIONAL CODE OF ETHICS FOR CANADIAN BUSINESS

VISION

Canadian business has a global presence that is recognized by all stakeholders as economically rewarding to all parties, acknowledged as being ethically, socially and environmentally responsible, welcomed by the communities in which we operate, and that facilitates economic, human resource and community development within a stable operating environment.

BELIEFS

We believe that:
- we can make a difference within our sphere of influence (our stakeholders).
- business should take a leadership role through establishment of ethical business principles.
- national governments have the prerogative to conduct their own government and legal affairs in accordance with their sovereign rights.
- all governments should comply with international treaties and other agreements that they have committed to, including the areas of human rights and social justice.
- while reflecting cultural diversity and differences, we should do business throughout the world consistent with the way we do business in Canada.
- the business sector should show ethical leadership.
- we can facilitate the achievement of wealth generation and a fair sharing of economic benefits.
- our principles will assist in improving relations between the Canadian and host governments.
- open, honest and transparent relationships are critical to our success.
- local communities need to be involved in decision-making for issues that affect them.
- multistakeholder processes need to be initiated to seek effective solutions.
- confrontation should be tempered by diplomacy.
- wealth maximazation for all stakeholders will be enhanced by resolution of outstanding human rights and social justice issues.
- doing business with other countries is good for Canada, and vice versa.

VALUES

We value:
- human rights and social justice.
- wealth maximization for all stakeholders.
- operation of a free market economy.
- a business environment which mitigates against bribery and corruption.
- public accountability by governments.
- equality of opportunity.
- a defined code of ethics and business practice.
- protection of environmental quality and sound environmental stewardship.
- community benefits.
- good relationships with all stakeholders.
- stability and continuous improvement within our operating environment.

Source: Errol Mendes, Human Rights Research and Education Center, University of Ottawa. Reprinted by permission.

THE MULTINATIONAL CORPORATION

Multinational corporations (MNCs) are corporate organizations that operate on a global scale without significant ties to any one nation or region. It is not uncommon, for instance, to find a Mexican-based MNC, which operates in Venezuela, Puerto Rico, and the United States, dominating markets with its products. MNCs represent the highest level of international business commitment and are characterized by a global strategy of focusing on opportunites throughout the world. Examples of multinational corporations include Shell Oil Company, Nike, Inc., Monsanto Company, and Cisco Systems, Inc.

Because of their size and financial power, MNCs have been the subject of much ethical criticism, and their impact on the countries in which they do business has been hotly debated. Thus, U.S. labor unions argue that it is unfair for MNCs to transfer jobs overseas, where wage rates are lower. Other critics have charged that MNCs use labor-saving devices that increase unemployment in the countries where they manufacture. MNCs have also been accused of increasing the gap between rich and poor nations and of misusing and misallocating scarce resources. Their size and financial clout enable MNCs to control money supplies, employment, and even the economic existence of less-developed countries. In some instances, MNCs have controlled entire cultures and countries.

Although there are reported abuses by some MNCs, there are also ones that strive to be good global citizens. Several years ago, in an effort to counter negative publicity and improve its citizenship performance, Shell Oil adopted a code of ethical principles, opened its doors to activist groups, and began publishing an environmental section in its annual report. Now, Shell is rated as one of the most ethical oil companies by shareholder activists. Another example is Cisco Systems. The maker of Internet pipelines has donated computer systems to schools, given $50 million to NetAid for Africa, and pushed for Third World debt relief.[7]

Critics believe that the size and power of MNCs create ethical issues related to the exploitation of both natural and human resources. One question is whether MNCs should be able to pay a low price for the right to remove minerals, timber, oil, and other natural resources and then sell products made from those resources for a much higher price. In many instances, only a small fraction of the ultimate sale price of such resources comes back to benefit the country of origin. This complaint led many oil-producing countries to form the Organization of Petroleum Exporting Countries (OPEC) in the 1960s to gain control over the revenues from oil produced in those lands.

Critics also charge that MNCs exploit the labor markets of host countries. Although some MNCs have been accused of paying inadequate wages, the ethical issue of fair wages is complicated. Sometimes MNCs pay higher wages than local employers can afford to match; then local businesses complain that the most productive and skilled workers go to work for multinationals. Measures have been taken to curtail such practices. For example, many MNCs are trying to help organize labor unions and establish minimum-wage laws. In addition, host governments have levied import taxes to increase the price MNCs charge for their products and reduce their profits; they have also imposed export taxes to force MNCs to share more of their profits. Import taxes are meant to favor local industry as sources of supply for an MNC manufacturing in the host country. If such a tax raises the MNC's costs, it might lead the MNC to charge higher prices or accept lower profits, but such effects are not the fundamental goal of the law. Many companies, including Coca-Cola, Du Pont, Hewlett-Packard, Levi Strauss & Co., Texaco, and Wal-Mart, endorse business responsibility abroad. These companies support a globally based resource system called Business for Social Responsibility (BSR). BSR tracks emerging issues and trends, provides information on corporate leadership and best practices, conducts educational workshops and training, and assists in developing practical business ethics tools. BSR has also established formal partnerships with other organizations that focus on corporate responsibility in Brazil, Israel, the United Kingdom, Chile, and Panama.[8]

*e.*ethics 2

The activities of multinational corporations may also raise issues of unfair competition. Because of their diversified nature, MNCs can borrow money, using up all local capital resources so that little is left for local firms. MNCs have also been accused of not carrying an appropriate share of the cost of social development. They frequently apply advanced technologies that local companies cannot afford or cannot implement because of a lack of qualified workers. The MNCs thus become more productive and can afford to pay higher wages to workers. Because of their advanced technology, however, they hire fewer people than would be hired by the local firms that produce the same product. And, given their economies of scale, MNCs can also negotiate lower tax rates; by manipulating transfer payments among affiliates, they may pay little tax anywhere. The overall result is the claim that MNCs compete unfairly. For example, many heavy-equipment companies in the United States try to sell construction equipment to foreign companies that build major roads, dams, and utility complexes. They argue that this equipment will make it possible to complete these projects sooner, to the benefit of the country. Some less-developed countries counter that such equipment purchases remove hard currency from their economies and increase unemployment. Certain nations, such as India, believe that it is better in the long run to hire laborers to do construction work than to buy a piece of heavy equipment. The country keeps its hard currency in its own economy and creates new jobs, which increases the quality of life more than having a project completed sooner.

Although MNCs are not inherently unethical, their size and power often seem threatening to less-developed countries. The ethical problems that MNCs face arise from the conflicting demands made from opposing points of view. Differences in cultural perspectives may be as important as differences in economic interests. Because of their size and power, multinational corporations must take extra care to make ethical decisions that not only achieve their own objectives but also benefit the countries in which they manufacture or market their products. Even premier MNCs sometimes find themselves in ethical conflict — and liable because of it. After investigating the tires in connection with sixty-two accidents and more than forty deaths involving Ford automobiles in Venezuela, authorities there were expected to submit a report to the Venezuelan attorney general that could lead to fines or criminal prosecution against tire maker Bridgestone/Firestone, Inc., and automaker Ford Motor Co. Ford had requested that Bridgestone/Firestone insert an extra nylon layer between the tires' steel belt and tread (cap ply) to accommodate the hotter, more humid, and more demanding driving conditions in Venezuela. Firestone's Venezuelan plant began producing the tires for Ford. According to a Firestone spokesman, the Venezuelan plant "inadvertently began marketing tires without a cap ply as tires that had a cap ply." The spokesman did not say for how long a period the tires were mismarked or how many mismarked tires were delivered to Ford.[9]

A UNIVERSAL SET OF ETHICS

Many theorists have tried to establish a set of global or universal ethical standards. Table 9–3 lists six books and documents that show a pattern of shared values — such as truthfulness, integrity, fairness, and equality — within the world. When applied to global business, these values constitute a universal set of ethics.

e,ethics 3

The Caux Round Table in Switzerland, in collaboration with business leaders in other European countries, Japan, and the United States, has created an international ethics code (see Table 9–4). The shared values assume that we all have basic rights and responsibilities that must be adhered to when doing business. By reviewing many of the laws enacted around the world, it becomes apparent that many of the values described in the Caux Round Table universal set of ethics have been codified. Fraud, for instance, has a universal definition. However, many manufacturing firms have been hurt through fraudulent use of their trademarks by others — that is, through counterfeiting or ambiguous misrepresentation of a product as that of a major name-brand company. The problems involving name brands are as varied as the countries in which they occur. Guatemala City's downtown streets are filled with vendors selling copies of everything from Adidas sneakers to Ferrari jeans. For example, consumers can buy a fake pair of Lee's $40 rivet jeans for just $9. Business leaders and clothing manufacturers urged the Guatemalan president to veto a new law that encourages contraband and counterfeiting. The problem with the law, according to an attorney representing Lee Apparel Company, Inc., Levi Strauss & Co., and Tommy Hilfiger Corp. is that "I can confiscate counterfeit merchandise from a warehouse, but I can't do anything about the people in the street" selling it.[10] Consumer goods companies such as Unilever and Procter & Gamble say they lose millions of dollars annually in India and China to "look-alike" brands that use similar-sounding names and identical packaging. Procter & Gamble estimates its losses in India at more than $370 million annually and in China at about $6.5 million a year. The counterfeiting problem has prompted some companies, including Coca-Cola Ltd. and Colgate-Palmolive Ltd., to form a brand protection committee. The committee's web site (http://www.fake-busters.com) was established to help consumers and officials verify packaging and identify the real brands.[11]

TABLE 9–3   Global Management Ethics

1993 Parliament of the World's Religions *The Declaration of a Global Ethic*	State of California *Handbook on . . . Moral and Civic Education . . .*	Michael Josephson *Character Counts, Ethics: Easier Said Than Done*
Nonviolence (love)	Morality	Trustworthiness
Respect for life	Truth	Honesty
Commitment	Justice	Integrity
Solidarity	Patriotism	Promise keeping
Truthfulness	Self-esteem	Loyalty
Tolerance	Integrity	Respect for others
Equal rights	Empathy	Responsibility
Sexual morality	Exemplary conduct	Fairness
	Reliability	Caring
	Respect for family, property, law	Citizenship
William J. Bennett *The Book of Virtues*	Thomas Donaldson *Fundamental International Rights*	Rushworth W. Kidder *Shared Values for a Troubled World*
Self-discipline	Physical movement	Love
Compassion	Property, ownership	Truthfulness
Responsibility	No torture	Fairness
Friendship	Fair trial	Freedom
Work	Nondiscrimination	Unity
Courage	Physical security	Tolerance
Perseverance	Speech and association	Responsibility
Honesty	Minimal education	Respect for life
Loyalty	Political participation	
Faith	Subsistence	

Source: "Global Management Ethics," from Andrew Sikula, Sr., Applied Management Ethics, 1996, p. 127. Used by permission of the author, Andrew Sikula, Sr.

If there is a universal set of ethics, why then do businesses have problems understanding what is ethical and unethical? The answer lies partially in how these basic rights and responsibilities are operationalized, or put into use. When someone from another culture mentions integrity or democracy, listeners look reassured. However, when these concepts are explained, differences surface. For example, in both Japan and the United States honesty is valued. Part of honesty is operationalized, or made tangible, by trust. In Japan's banking industry, people demonstrated that trust by hiring retired Japanese bureaucrats to become auditors, directors, executives, and presidents. The practice is known as *amakudari,* or "descent from

TABLE 9–4   The Caux Round Table Business Principles of Ethics

Principle 1. The Responsibilities of Businesses: Beyond Shareholders Toward Stakeholders

The value of a business to society is the wealth and employment it creates and the marketable products and services it provides to consumers at a reasonable price commensurate with quality. To create such value, a business must maintain its own economic health and viability, but survival is not a sufficient goal.

Businesses have a role to play in improving the lives of all their customers, employees, and shareholders by sharing with them the wealth they have created. Suppliers and competitors as well should expect businesses to honor their obligations in a spirit of honesty and fairness. As responsible citizens of the local, national, regional, and global communities in which they operate, businesses share a part in shaping the future of those communities.

Principle 2. The Economic and Social Impact of Business: Toward Innovation, Justice, and World Community

Businesses established in foreign countries to develop, produce, or sell should also contribute to the social advancement of those countries by creating productive employment and helping to raise the purchasing power of their citizens. Businesses also should contribute to human rights, education, welfare, and vitalization of the countries in which they operate.

Businesses should contribute to economic and social development not only in the countries in which they operate, but also in the world community at large, through effective and prudent use of resources, free and fair competition, and emphasis upon innovation in technology, production methods, marketing, and communications.

Principle 3. Business Behavior: Beyond the Letter of Law Toward a Spirit of Trust

While accepting the legitimacy of trade secrets, businesses should recognize that sincerity, candor, truthfulness, the keeping of promises, and transparency contribute not only to their own credibility and stability but also to the smoothness and efficiency of business transactions, particularly on the international level.

Principle 4. Respect for Rules

To avoid trade frictions and to promote freer trade, equal conditions for competition, and fair and equitable treatment for all participants, businesses should respect international and domestic rules. In addition, they should recognize that some behavior, although legal, may still have adverse consequences.

Principle 5. Support for Multilateral Trade

Businesses should support the multilateral trade systems of the GATT/World Trade Organization and similar international agreements. They should cooperate in efforts to promote the progressive and judicious liberalization of trade, and to relax those domestic measures that unreasonably hinder global commerce, while giving due respect to national policy objectives.

Principle 6. Respect for the Environment

A business should protect and, where possible, improve the environment, promote sustainable development, and prevent the wasteful use of natural resources.

Principle 7. Avoidance of Illicit Operations

A business should not participate in or condone bribery, money laundering, or other corrupt practices; indeed, it should seek cooperation with others to eliminate them. It should not trade in arms or other materials used for terrorist activities, drug traffic, or other organized crime.

Principle 8. Customers

We believe in treating all customers with dignity, irrespective of whether they purchase our products and services directly from us or otherwise acquire them in the market. We therefore have a responsibility to:

- provide our customers with the highest quality products and services consistent with their requirements;

- treat our customers fairly in all aspects of our business transactions, including a high level of service and remedies for their dissatisfaction;

TABLE 9–4   The Caux Round Table Business Principles of Ethics (*cont'd.*)

- make every effort to ensure that the health and safety of our customers, as well as the quality of their environment, will be sustained or enhanced by our products and services;

- assure respect for human dignity in products offered, marketing, and advertising; and

- respect the integrity of the culture of our customers.

Principle 9. Employees

We believe in the dignity of every employee and in taking employee interests seriously. We therefore have a responsibility to:

- provide jobs and compensation that improve workers' living conditions;

- provide working conditions that respect each employee's health and dignity;

- be honest in communications with employees and open in sharing information, limited only by legal and competitive restraints;

- listen to and, where possible, act on employee suggestions, ideas, requests, and complaints;

- engage in good faith negotiations when conflict arises;

- avoid discriminatory practices and guarantee equal treatment and opportunity in areas such as gender, age, race, and religion;

- promote in the business itself the employment of differently abled people in places of work where they can be genuinely useful;

- protect employees from avoidable injury and illness in the workplace;

- encourage and assist employees in developing relevant and transferable skills and knowledge; and

- be sensitive to serious unemployment problems frequently associated with business decisions, and work with governments, employee groups, other agencies and each other in addressing these dislocations.

Principle 10. Owners/Investors

We believe in honoring the trust our investors place in us. We therefore have a responsibility to:

- apply professional and diligent management in order to secure a fair and competitive return on our owners' investment;

- disclose relevant information to owners/investors subject only to legal requirements and competitive constraints;

- conserve, protect, and increase the owners/investors' assets; and

- respect owners/investors' requests, suggestions, complaints, and formal resolutions.

Principle 11. Suppliers

Our relationship with suppliers and subcontractors must be based on mutual respect. We therefore have a responsibility to:

- seek fairness and truthfulness in all of our activities, including pricing, licensing, and rights to sell;

- ensure that our business activities are free from coercion and unnecessary litigation;

- foster long-term stability in the supplier relationship in return for value, quality, competitiveness, and reliability;

- share information with suppliers and integrate them into our planning processes;

- pay suppliers on time and in accordance with agreed terms of trade; and

- seek, encourage, and prefer suppliers and subcontractors whose employment practices respect human dignity.

Principle 12. Competitors

We believe that fair economic competition is one of the basic requirements for increasing the wealth of nations and, ultimately, for making possible the just distribution of goods and services. We therefore have a responsibility to:

- foster open markets for trade and investment;

- promote competitive behavior that is socially and environmentally beneficial and demonstrates mutual respect among competitors;

- refrain from either seeking or participating in questionable payments of favors to secure competitive advantages;

TABLE 9–4   The Caux Round Table Business Principles of Ethics (*cont'd.*)

- respect both tangible and intellectual property rights; and
- refuse to acquire commercial information by dishonest or unethical means, such as industrial espionage.

Principle 13. Communities

We believe that as global corporate citizens, we can contribute to such forces of reform and human rights as are at work in the communities in which we operate. We therefore have a responsibility in those communities to:

- respect human rights and democratic institutions, and promote them wherever practicable;
- recognize government's legitimate obligation to the society at large and support public policies and practices that promote human development through harmonious

relations between business and other segments of society;

- collaborate with those forces in the community dedicated to raising standards of health, education, workplace safety, and economic well-being;
- promote and stimulate sustainable development and play a leading role in preserving and enhancing the physical environment and conserving the earth's resources;
- support peace, security, diversity, and social integration;
- respect the integrity of local cultures; and
- be a good corporate citizen through charitable donations, educational and cultural contributions, and employee participation in community and civic affairs.

Source: Reprinted with permission from Business Ethics, *P.O. Box 8439, Minneapolis, MN (612) 879-0695.*

heaven." The rationale was that because these men were so trusted, nothing bad or unethical would happen to the banks. The relationship between regulated and regulator became fuzzy because the regulators implicitly trusted their former superiors. In the United States, businesspeople may trust former superiors, but they also understand that there should always be a separation between those who regulate and those who are regulated.[12] Although honesty, charity, virtue, and doing good for others may be qualities that are universally agreed on, the differences in implementing them can cause problems. To address such problems, General Motors Corp., Unocal, Procter & Gamble, the Shell Group, and about thirty other companies agreed to abide by the Global Sullivan Principles (see Table 9–5), which seek to encourage social responsibility around the world. Announced by the United Nations, the principles are designed to encourage companies to support economic, legal, social, and political justice; encourage equal opportunity at all levels; train and advance disadvantaged workers; assist greater tolerance among all people; improve the quality of life for communities; and support human rights.[13] In addition, fifty of the world's largest corporations have signed the UN Global Compact, whose purpose is to support free trade unions, abolish child labor, and protect the environment. The companies are required to post an annual update on their progress in these areas and are expected to cooperate with UN agencies on social projects in the developing countries in which they operate.[14]

A major challenge to businesses operating in global markets is how to accommodate inconsistencies in ethics and regulations and how to be proactive in developing responsible conduct. A review of regulatory efforts in some regions shows

TABLE 9-5   The Global Sullivan Principles

As a company which endorses the Global Sullivan Principles we will respect the law, and as a responsible member of society we will apply these Principles with integrity consistent with the legitimate role of business. We will develop and implement company policies, procedures, training and internal reporting structures to ensure commitment to these principles throughout our organization. We believe the application of these Principles will achieve greater tolerance and better understanding among peoples, and advance the culture of peace.

Accordingly, we will:

- Express our support for universal human rights and, particularly, those of our employees, the communities within which we operate, and parties with whom we do business.

- Promote equal opportunity for our employees at all levels of the company with respect to issues such as color, race, gender, age, ethnicity or religious beliefs, and operate without unacceptable worker treatment such as the exploitation of children, physical punishment, female abuse, involuntary servitude, or other forms of abuse.

- Respect our employees' voluntary freedom of association.

- Compensate our employees to enable them to meet at least their basic needs and provide the opportunity to improve their skill and capability in order to raise their social and economic opportunities.

- Provide a safe and healthy workplace; protect human health and the environment; and promote sustainable development.

- Promote fair competition including respect for intellectual and other property rights, and not offer, pay or accept bribes.

- Work with government and communities in which we do business to improve the quality of life in those communities — their educational, cultural, economic and social well-being — and seek to provide training and opportunities for workers from disadvantaged backgrounds.

- Promote the application of these principles by those with whom we do business.

- We will be transparent in our implementation of these principles and provide information which demonstrates publicly our commitment to them.

Source: Reprinted from Ethikos: Examining Ethical and Compliance Issues in Business (Mamaroneck, NY).

that there is international consensus on approaches to encouraging ethical conduct in business organizations. The concern is not only to develop legal limitations for behavior but also to develop incentives for self-regulation and ethical conduct that are acceptable in a global business environment. The challenge is not only the enforcement of ethical conduct but also the development of organizational value systems that promote an ethical business environment. Identification of ethical issues and implementation of codes of conduct that incorporate both legal and ethical concerns compose the best approach for preventing violations and avoiding civil litigation. Companies and trade associations need to assess how to better develop the programs and determine the management practices that will result in excellent legal and ethical performance. Also important in developing better global ethical and legal performance is determining the relationship between national differences in individual moral philosophies and corporate core values in management systems.[15]

In the next section we turn to some common global ethical issues that arise when companies do business internationally. Our list should not be taken as complete, but only as a sampling of the complexity of ethical decision making in the global arena.

ETHICAL ISSUES AROUND THE GLOBE

Major ethical issues that complicate international business activities include sexual and racial discrimination, human rights concerns, price discrimination, bribery and the Foreign Corrupt Practices Act, harmful products, pollution, and telecommunications.

Sexual and Racial Discrimination

As noted in Chapter 4, various U.S. laws prohibit American businesses from discriminating on the basis of sex, race, religion, or disabilities in their hiring, firing, and promotion decisions. However, the problem of discrimination is certainly not limited to the United States. In the United Kingdom, East Indians have traditionally been relegated to the lowest-paying, least-desired jobs. Australian aborigines have long been the victims of social and economic discrimination. In many Southeast Asian and Far Eastern countries, employees from particular ethnic backgrounds may not be promoted. In Russia, job advertisements frequently specify the age and gender of prospective employees. Female business owners in Russia face endless bureaucracy, problems obtaining credit, and a tangled legal system. One female entrepreneur was jailed and then released ten days later with no charges made, evidence brought, or apologies given.[16]

In many Middle Eastern nations, businesswomen are a rarity. Often Middle Eastern women must wear special clothing and cover their faces; in public, they may be physically separated from men. Since many Middle Eastern countries prescribe only nonbusiness roles for women, companies negotiating with Middle Eastern firms have encountered problems in using women sales representatives. Indeed, a Middle Eastern company may refuse to negotiate with saleswomen or may take an unfavorable view of foreign organizations that employ them. The ethical issue in such cases is whether foreign businesses should respect Middle Eastern values and send only men to negotiate sales transactions, thus denying women employees the opportunity to further their careers and contribute to organizational objectives. The alternative would be to try to maintain their own ideas of social equality, knowing that the women sales representatives will probably be unsuccessful because of cultural norms in those societies.

Racial discrimination has been a much-discussed issue in the United States. Racial discrimination is also apparent in Germany, which will not grant citizenship to Turkish workers, even though some of them are second-generation German residents. It can also be seen in the glass ceiling that exists in Japan for Japanese Koreans in business.

Human Rights

Corporate interest in human rights has emerged in the last decade. News stories depicting opportunistic use of child labor, payment of low wages, and abuses in foreign factories have helped reshape our attitude of what can be considered acceptable behavior for organizations. Eight clothing retailers, including Liz Claiborne and Tommy Hilfiger, settled a lawsuit alleging that they were responsible for abuses against foreign workers in textile factories on the Pacific Island of Saipan. As part of the settlement, the factory workers are getting better working conditions, such as relaxed restrictions on bathroom breaks.[17]

Companies struggling with human rights issues sometimes make short-term decisions to boost company profitability that have long-term negative implications. These include concerns about the treatment of minorities and women, as well as the issues of child labor and employee rights. Multinationals have even greater challenges in this area because of the nature of relationships with manufacturers and subcontractors in varying cultures. The International Labor Organization estimates that 250 million children between the ages of 5 and 14 work in developing countries (61 percent in Asia, 32 percent in Africa, and 7 percent in Latin America). Although only an estimated 5 percent of these child laborers work in export industries, this still represents an ethical issue for multinational corporations.[18]

Although companies appear to be more concerned about human rights issues than they used to be, there is still widespread abuse. Multinational companies should view the law as the floor of acceptable behavior and strive toward greater improvements in workers' quality of life. An understanding of each country's culture will aid MNCs in making improvements that will be valued. At an annual Human Rights Survey meeting, the executive director of Human Rights Watch mentioned three guidelines that managers should consider in advancing human rights. First, an open dialogue needs to be encouraged between workers and management. Second, members of MNCs should be aware of the human rights issues and concerns in each country where they engage in business. Amnesty International can provide such information. Finally, MNCs should adopt the prevailing legal standard but seek to improve and embrace a "best practices" approach and standard; internationally acceptable behavior in any country should be their goal.[19]

Price Discrimination

The pricing of products sold in other countries also creates ethical issues. A frequently debated issue in international business is **price discrimination,** which occurs when a firm charges different prices to different groups of consumers. Price differentials are legal if they do not substantially reduce competition or if they can be justified on the basis of costs — for example, the costs of taxes and import fees associated with bringing products into another country. However, price discrimination may be an ethical issue, or even be illegal, under the following conditions: (1) the practice violates either country's laws, (2) the market cannot be divided into segments, (3) the cost of segmenting the market exceeds the extra revenue from legal price discrimination, or (4) the practice results in extreme customer dissatisfaction.

When a market is artificially divided into segments that are charged different prices, an inequality can emerge that cannot be explained by added costs, thus creating an ethical concern. In some cases, such pricing policies may be judged illegal when courts rule that they substantially decrease competition. In the United States, price discrimination that harms competition is prohibited under the Robinson-Patman Act. In other countries, judgments of illegality result from precedent or fairness rulings.

When companies market their products outside their own countries, the costs of transportation, taxes, tariffs, and other expenses can raise the prices of the products. However, when the price increase exceeds the costs of these additional expenses, an ethical issue emerges. Increasing prices in this way is sometimes referred to as **gouging.** Gouging can also refer to charging unusually high rates over a period of time due to situational shortages — for instance, when lumber suppliers charge premium prices to earthquake victims seeking to rebuild. Sydney hotels were accused of increasing their rates for the 2000 Olympics. Some Olympic officials were quoted a room rate for a three-star hotel during the games at $550 per night plus $45 for breakfast and $75 for lunch and dinner.[20] Most countries have laws forbidding companies to charge exorbitant prices for lifesaving products, which include some pharmaceuticals. However, these laws do not apply to products that are not lifesaving, even if they are in great demand and have no substitutes.

In contrast, when companies charge high prices for products sold in their home markets while selling the same products in foreign markets at low prices that do not cover all the costs of exporting the products, the practice is known as **dumping.** Dumping is unethical if it damages competition or hurts firms and workers in other countries. It becomes illegal under many international laws if it substantially reduces competition. After investigating allegations from U.S. steel producers and two steelworkers' unions, the U.S. Department of Commerce determined that Russia was dumping steel in the United States and should be assessed tariffs as high as 217 percent to reverse the effects of the dumping. It was estimated that the practice had cost ten thousand jobs in the U.S. steel industry. Later, the Department of Commerce announced it was considering settling its case with Russia and suspending the tariffs. The announcement brought protests from attorneys general in four steel-producing states.[21]

Dumping may occur for several reasons. Charging low prices allows a company to enter a market quickly and capture a large market share. Sometimes dumping occurs when the domestic market for a firm's product is too small to support an efficient level of production. In other cases, technologically obsolete products that are no longer salable in the country of origin are dumped overseas. Dumping is difficult to prove, but even the suspicion of dumping can lead to the imposition of import quotas, which can hurt innocent firms.

Price differentials, gouging, and dumping create ethical issues because some groups of consumers have to pay more than a fair price for products. Pricing is certainly a complicated issue in international marketing because of the additional costs imposed by tariffs, taxes, customs fees, and paperwork. Nonetheless, corporations should take care to price their products to recover legitimate expenses and earn a reasonable profit while still competing fairly.

Bribery and the Foreign Corrupt Practices Act

In many cultures, giving bribes — also known as **facilitating payments** — is an acceptable business practice. In Mexico, a bribe is called *la mordida*. South Africans call it *dash*. In the Middle East, India, and Pakistan, *baksheesh*, a tip or gratuity given by a superior, is widely used. The Germans call it *schimengeld*, grease money, and the Italians call it *bustarella*, a little envelope. Companies that do business internationally should be aware that bribes are an ethical issue and that the practice is more prevalent in some countries than in others. Transparency International commissioned a study to determine the degree to which international corporations are engaging in paying bribes in fourteen emerging market economies. The resulting Bribe Payers Index (Table 9–6) reveals that on a scale of 0 to 10, where 10 represents a corruption-free country, companies in China were found to be highly likely to pay bribes to win or retain business.[22] Bribes or payoff requests are frequently associated with large construction projects, turnkey capital projects, and large commodity or equipment contracts.

Since 1977 the U.S. **Foreign Corrupt Practices Act (FCPA)** has prohibited American corporations from offering or providing payments to officials of foreign governments for the purpose of obtaining or retaining business abroad. Violators of the FCPA face corporate fines of up to $2 million, while company executives face a maximum of five years in prison or $10,000 in fines, or both. The FCPA does permit small "grease" payments to foreign ministerial or clerical government employees. Such payments are exempted because of their size and the assumption that they are used to persuade the recipients to perform their normal duties, not to do something critical to the distribution of new goods and services.

Some critics of the FCPA say that although the law was designed to foster fair and equal treatment for all, it places American firms at a disadvantage in the international business arena. The FCPA applies only to American businesses; other nations have not imposed such restraints on their companies doing business abroad. For example, if three companies — from the United States, France, and Korea — were bidding on a dam-building project in Egypt, the French and Korean firms could bribe Egyptian officials in their efforts to acquire the contract, but it would be illegal for the American firm to do so. Thus the issue of bribery sets the values of one culture — the U.S. disapproval of bribery — against those of other cultures.

When the FCPA was enacted, the Securities and Exchange Commission (SEC) established a voluntary disclosure program. The FCPA was developed because an SEC investigation in the mid 1970s revealed that 400 U.S. companies admitted making questionable or illegal payments in excess of $300 million to foreign government officials, politicians, and political parties. In 1988 the **Omnibus Trade and Competitiveness (OTC) Act** reduced FCPA legislation in the following ways:

TABLE 9–6   Bribe Payers Index

Rank	Country	Score*
1	Sweden	8.3
2**	Australia	8.1
2	Canada	8.1
4	Austria	7.8
5	Switzerland	7.7
6	Netherlands	7.4
7	United Kingdom	7.2
8	Belgium	6.8
9	Germany	6.2
9	United States	6.2
11	Singapore	5.7
12	Spain	5.3
13	France	5.2
14	Japan	5.1
15	Malaysia	3.9
16	Italy	3.7
17	Taiwan	3.5
18	South Korea	3.4
19	China	3.1

*10 represents a corruption-free country.

**The same number ranking indicates a tie.

Source: "The 1999 Transparency International Bribe Payers Index." http://www.transparency.org/documents/
cpi/bps.html (May 9, 2000). Courtesy of Transparency International.

lobbying, "reason to know," facilitating payments, affirmative defenses, and the repeal of the Eckhardt Amendment. The Eckhardt Amendment had prevented senior managers from using agents or employees as scapegoats when bribes were given. The new act makes prosecution even more difficult, thus decreasing the power and applicability of the FCPA in global business settings. Subsequent support for the Foreign Corrupt Practices Act has come through a global treaty, the Convention on Combating Bribery of Foreign Public Officials in International Business Transactions, which has been signed by thirty-four nations. Dominated by some of the largest countries in the world, the majority in support of the treaty are members of the Organization of Economic Cooperation and Development (OECD). The treaty requires signatories to make it a criminal offense for any person to "offer, promise or give away undue pecuniary or other advantage . . . to a foreign public official" for the purpose of obtaining "business or other improper advantage in the conduct of international commerce." Punishment is to be swift and effective as a deterrent for future offenses and is determined by the country in which the company operates.[23] However, at the time of the Transparency International Study, only eighteen of the thirty-four treaty-signing countries had deposited all necessary ratification instruments.[24]

Table 9–7 lists the key factors thought to influence bribe-taking. Many business-people view bribes as a necessary cost of conducting business in certain countries. Many MNCs have been fined under the FCPA for bribery. Companies can receive fines up to $2 million or, under the Alternate Fines Act, fines up to twice the value of their gain. General Electric was fined $70 million in Israel under the FCPA, a U.S. law. To win a contract for three C-130 cargo planes, a vice president at Lockheed Martin bribed a member of the Egyptian parliament. This vice president was sentenced to eighteen months in jail, and the total cost to Lockheed Martin was $24 million.[25] Once a company starts paying bribes in one country, other countries will expect the same, regardless of the culture. About one-third of those interviewed for the Transparency International study felt that bribery was increasing.[26]

Harmful Products

In the advanced industrialized nations, governments have banned the sale of certain products that are considered harmful. However, some companies based in advanced nations continue to sell such products in other countries where they are still legal. For example, many recent news stories have focused on the safety of

TABLE 9–7   Key Factors Influencing Bribe-Taking

Factor	Percentage Who Thought Factor Influential
Low public-sector salaries	65%
Immunity of public officials	63%
Secrecy in government	57%
Worsening public procurement practices	51%
The privatization process	37%
Increase in foreign investment and trade	30%
Restrictions on the media	24%
Financial liberalization	19%
Multiparty elections	18%
Other	15%
Not stated	6%

Source: "The 1999 Transparency International Bribe Payers Survey." http://www.transparency.org/documents/cpi/bps.html *(May 9, 2000). Courtesy of Transparency International.*

genetically engineered products. Investors have filed resolutions at American Home Products, Archer Daniels Midland, Dow Chemical, Du Pont, and Monsanto seeking to stop the marketing of genetically engineered products "until long-term safety testing has shown that they are not harmful to humans, animals, and the environment."[27] Similar proposals at the Coca-Cola Co. and General Mills ask for labeling of genetically engineered ingredients until such ingredients are removed from the companies' products. Many countries, including Japan, those in the European Union, Australia, and New Zealand, already require labeling of genetically engineered food products.[28]

Another ethical issue relates to the export of tobacco products to less-developed countries. Cigarette sales in the United States are declining in the face of stricter tobacco regulations and increasing evidence that smoking causes a number of illnesses and other medical problems. In addition, there are signs that cigarette smoking is becoming socially unacceptable in the United States. As U.S. sales decline, tobacco companies have increased their efforts to sell cigarettes and other tobacco products in other countries, particularly less-developed ones. U.S. cigarette exports exceeded $200 billion in the late 1990s, almost tripling the 1982 amount of $73.6 billion.[29] The overseas sales volume of tobacco manufacturers now exceeds their domestic sales volume. The ethical issue becomes whether tobacco marketers should knowingly sell in other countries a product that is considered harmful in their home country.

Many consumers in underdeveloped countries view tobacco as good, both physically and economically. They argue that the tobacco industry provides jobs and stimulates economies and that cigarette consumers enjoy smoking. Many also cite low longevity rates as a reason to discount the health hazards of tobacco. In the long run, however, as industrialization raises the standard of living in less-developed countries, in turn increasing longevity rates, those countries may change their views on tobacco. As people live longer and the health hazards begin to cost both the people and the government more in time and money, ethical issues will increase.

The dumping of waste materials into less-developed countries is also becoming an issue, especially when countries and communities do not know the contents of the trash. Although Africa and Latin America have banned the trade in trash, the People's Republic of China has not. Its companies supposedly purchase the garbage for its residual metals, plastics, and other useful material. By using cheap labor, they are able to make a profit. With cheap labor in Cambodia, Vietnam, and Laos, the global garbage business will continue to inflict long-term harm on other peoples.

At times products that are not harmful in some countries become harmful to consumers in others because of illiteracy, unsanitary conditions, or cultural values. For example, products marketed by the Nestlé Corporation in the mid to late 1970s included infant formulas, which are used in the supplemental feeding of infants and have been tested as safe when used correctly. When the company introduced its product into African countries as an alternative to breast-feeding, local mothers quickly adopted the product. However, as time passed, infant mortality rates rose dramatically. Investigators found that, because of high illiteracy rates, many mothers were not able to follow instructions for using the formula correctly. In addition, the water used for mixing with the powdered formula was often unsafe, and poor mothers also diluted the formula to save money, which reduced the nutritional value of the feeding. Nestlé was further criticized for its aggressive promotion of the infant formula; the company employed so-called milk nurses to discourage mothers from breast-feeding by portraying the practice as primitive and to promote Nestlé's infant formulas instead. Under heated pressure from international agencies and boycotts by consumer groups, Nestlé agreed to stop promoting the infant formula; it also revised its product labeling and educational materials to point out the dangers of using the formula incorrectly and the preferability of breast-feeding.[30] After a period of time, however, the company reverted to its previous practices, and as of 1996 the World Health Organization had renewed the boycott. Thus even traditionally safe and adequately tested products can create ethical issues when a marketer fails to evaluate foreign markets accurately or to maintain adequate responses to health problems associated with its products in certain markets.

Pollution

Whereas there are boundaries on the implications of many legal and ethical violations in the case of environmental abuses, the effects of these abuses are far-reaching. Consequently, a number of companies are working to create standards for environmental responsibility. For example, Delphi Automotive Systems Corporation, a world leader in component and systems technology for transportation, telecommunications, aerospace, and heavy-equipment industries, is committed to protecting human health, natural resources, and the global environment. Delphi's Design for the Environment process requires teams to evaluate the environmental impacts of product designs, materials, and manufacturing processes before the manufacturing begins. A leading producer of products that reduce emissions and improve fuel efficiency, Delphi is working to achieve ISO14001 certification, a global standard that recognizes facilities with systems that proactively manage and reduce environmental impact.[31] Other companies have modified products or stopped production and sale of products that negatively impact the environment. For example, as mentioned earlier, after tests showed that Scotchguard does not decompose in the environment, 3M announced a voluntary end to production of the forty-year-old product that had generated $300 million in sales.[32]

Seeking to defend their air and water quality, some countries are taking legal action against polluting firms. In Mexico, for example, firms that fail to cut back emissions or that deny access to inspectors during smog alerts face legal sanctions.[33] In other situations, outside organizations such as Greenpeace issue warnings about countries that engage in environmental abuses. Greenpeace has accused Israel of defying international convention and dumping toxic waste in the Mediterranean.[34]

In some countries, however, groups have lobbied their governments to increase the level of pollution allowed — for instance, emission standards in Australia. Its per capita emissions from energy consumption and industrial manufacturing will rise from twenty-one metric tons per head to twenty-six tons in 2010, making Australia the largest greenhouse gas polluter in the world. One member of the Australia Institute stated, "If they had been aware of the facts, other nations would not have agreed to Australia's demand for an increase in emission but would have required us to cut our emissions more than other countries."[35]

For organizations to thrive globally, all should form joint agreements, such as the North American Free Trade Agreement between the United States, Canada, and Mexico, and set reasonable standards for emissions for all members to follow. Many pollution-control efforts have relatively short payback periods and have a long-term positive effect on profitability. In contrast, violation of environmental initiatives has both human and financial costs, with the human cost being the health hazards associated with pollution. An example of the financial costs incurred by violating environmental initiatives involves Willamette Industries, which allegedly failed to control the amount of air pollution released from its wood-product factories in four states. The company will spend more than $90 million to settle a lawsuit, including an $11.2 million penalty, an additional $8 million to be spent on environmental projects, and installation of state-of-the-art pollution controls at thirteen facilities.[36]

Telecommunications Issues

With the advent of satellites, e-mail, and the Internet, information can be accessed in a matter of seconds instead of weeks — and businesses can become the victims as well as the perpetrators of unethical actions. Information overload and Internet slowdowns are becoming more common — sometimes intentionally caused. An on-line attack involving mass accessing of certain web sites in early 2000 lasted almost five days, slowed the Internet by 20 percent, and crashed many of the world's most popular e-commerce sites.[37] On-line protests to criticize or disrupt corporate operations are increasing: protesters send mass e-mail messages, use "distributed denial of service" tools to interrupt company web sites, and attempt to deflate stock prices by posting negative comments on on-line message boards.[38] Also, with the ease of information access come ethical issues, which can differ by country, and no geographic or time barriers exist. For example, copyright laws were established to protect originators of products and services. However, as use of the Internet and electronic bulletin boards spread, it has become difficult to enforce country-specific laws. The case of the popular song-swapping web site, Napster, is one example. Napster's downloadable MusicShare software allows computer users worldwide to send and receive digital music files among themselves for free. The Recording Industry Association of America filed suit against Napster, alleging that Napster's service aided in large-scale copyright infringement. A federal judge ruled that Napster had to shut down the trading of copyrighted material by its 60 million users. Napster denied any wrongdoing and filed court documents saying its users are protected by federal law that allows the copying of music for personal use. However, the ruling was upheld by the court of appeals. Napster's $1 billion settlement offer was not accepted by the RIAA. In the midst of its legal troubles, Napster became one of the top fifty most-visited web sites, with 5.4 million visitors in July 2000.[39]

In an effort to address computer crimes ranging from theft of intellectual property to digital vandalism, the U.S. Justice Department designated $300,000 as seed money to develop school curriculums, identify successful educational programs, and otherwise spread the word that children and teenagers need ethical as well as technical education to become responsible citizens in the Internet age. Scholastic, Inc., has developed materials for a curriculum in cyberethics. Not everyone agrees that these types of programs will solve the Internet's security problems. According to a government adviser who is frequently consulted on security issues, "This is an international problem. Are you going to educate the hackers in China and Bulgaria? The winning strategy is to improve the security of our infrastructures."[40]

The speed of global communications has also affected virtually all industries, with the fashion industry being a good case in point. Imitations have always been a problem, with "knockoffs" usually entering the market a few months behind the originals and then by way of a few retailers. The situation has changed dramatically. A photograph can be taken at a fashion show in Milan, scanned, and sent electronically to a Hong Kong factory; the next day a sample garment is sent by overnight delivery to a New York showroom for retail buyers. Stores order these lower-priced "interpretations" for their own private-label collections and sometimes even show the costlier designer versions at the same time. Since competition in the malls is fierce and fashion merchandise is highly perishable, the industry has become very competitive. Some designers are countering these imitations by suing and by bringing out affordable knockoff versions before anyone else can.

Questionable financial activities, such as money laundering, have been made easier by global telecommunications. **Money laundering** means that illegally received funds are transferred or used in a financial transaction so as to conceal their source or ownership or facilitate an "illegal" activity. Money laundering can be legal depending on the countries involved and their interpretations of each other's statutes. A decade ago actual paper currency such as dollars, francs, or British pounds would have had to be converted by smuggling. Now drug traffickers and others move funds through wire transfers and checks that are sent to other countries. Allegations of money laundering have been lodged against officers of Mexican banks. There was general concern that banking controls had not been enforced despite statements by Mexico's president that his country would be a more law-abiding place. Many Mexicans are losing confidence in the efforts of their bankers to conform to ethical norms.[41] As Mexico becomes a major partner in NAFTA (the North American Free Trade Agreement), there is a need to bring its business practices into conformity with ethical standards shared by the United States and Canada.

SUMMARY

Global business involves the development, promotion, pricing, and distribution of goods and services across national boundaries. The global businessperson must not only understand the values, culture, and ethical standards of his or her own country but also be sensitive to those of other countries. Culture is defined as everything in our surroundings made by people — both tangible items and intangible concepts, including language, law, religion, politics, technology, education, social organizations, and general values and ethical standards. Each nation has a different culture and hence different beliefs about what business activities are acceptable or unethical. Cultural differences that create ethical issues in international business include differences in language, body language, time perception, and religion.

According to cultural relativism, morality varies from one culture to another, and business practices are defined as right or wrong by the particular culture. Ethical relativism, on the other hand, assumes that only one culture defines ethical behavior for the whole world.

Multinational corporations (MNCs) are companies that operate on a global scale without significant ties to any one nation or region. Because of their size and financial power, MNCs can have a serious impact on the countries where they do business, which may create ethical issues.

When applied to global business, certain shared values — such as truthfulness, integrity, fairness, and equality — constitute a universal set of ethics. The Caux Round Table has also created an international ethics code.

Major global ethical issues range from sexual and racial discrimination, human rights violations, price discrimination, and bribery (also known as facilitating payments) to harmful products, pollution, and telecommunications issues. Although U.S. laws prohibit American companies from discrimination in employment, discrimination in other countries is often justified on the basis of cultural norms and values. Multinational corporations' interest in proactively addressing issues such as the use of child labor, low wages, and abuses in foreign manufacturing has increased. MNCs should strive to understand the human rights issues of each country in which they conduct business.

Price discrimination creates an ethical issue and may be illegal when the practice violates either country's laws; when the market cannot be segmented or the cost of segmenting exceeds the extra revenue from legal price discrimination; or when the practice results in customer dissatisfaction. When companies market their products outside their own countries, the costs of transportation, supplies, taxes, tariffs, and other expenses can raise the prices of the products. However, when the foreign price of a product exceeds the full costs associated with exporting, the ethical issue of gouging exists. When companies sell products in their home markets at high prices while selling the same products in foreign markets at low prices that do not cover the full costs of exporting, the practice is known as dumping. Price differentials, gouging, and dumping create ethical issues because some groups of consumers have to pay more than a fair price for products.

The U.S. Foreign Corrupt Practices Act (FCPA) prohibits American businesses from offering or providing payments to officials of foreign governments for the purpose of obtaining or retaining business. The Omnibus Trade and Competitiveness (OTC) Act reduced FCPA legislation and has made prosecution and applicability of the FCPA in global business settings nonthreatening.

Globally, companies have begun working together to minimize the negative effects of pollution and support environmental responsibility. Joint agreements and international cooperatives have successfully policed and prosecuted offenders of reasonable emission standards.

Advances in telecommunications have intensified such ethical issues as copyright infringement and unauthorized duplication of fashion designs. They have also made it easier to carry out questionable financial activities — notably, money laundering, which involves transferring illegally received money or using it in financial transactions so as to conceal the source or ownership or to facilitate an illegal activity.

Important Terms for Review	self-reference criterion (SRC) culture cultural relativism ethical relativism multinational corporations (MNCs) price discrimination gouging	dumping facilitating payments Foreign Corrupt Practices Act (FCPA) Omnibus Trade and Competitiveness (OTC) Act money laundering

A Real-Life Situation*

George Wilson, the operations manager of the CornCo plant in Phoenix, Arizona, had a dilemma. He was in charge of buying corn and producing chips marketed by CornCo in the United States and elsewhere. Several months earlier, George's supervisor, CornCo's vice president, Jake Lamont, called to tell him that corn futures were on the rise, which would ultimately increase the overall costs of production. In addition, a new company called Abco Snack Foods had begun marketing corn chips at competitive prices in CornCo's market area. Abco had already shown signs of eroding CornCo's market share. Jake was concerned that George's production costs would not be competitive with Abco's — hence, profitability would decline. Jake had already asked George to find ways to cut costs. If he couldn't, Jake said, then layoffs would begin.

George had scoured the Midwest looking for cheap corn and finally found some. But when the railcars started coming in, one of the company's testers reported the presence of aflatoxin — a naturally occurring carcinogen that induces liver cancer in lab animals. Once corn has been ground into corn meal, however, the aflatoxin is virtually impossible to detect. George knew that by blending the contaminated corn with uncontaminated corn he could reduce the aflatoxin concentrations in the final product, as, he had heard, other managers sometimes did. According to U.S. law, corn contaminated with aflatoxin could not be used for edible products to be sold in the United States, and fines were to be imposed for such use, yet so far no one had been convicted. But no law prohibited shipping the contaminated corn to other countries.

George knew that because of competition, if he didn't use the contaminated corn, production costs would be too high. When he spoke to Jake, Jake's response was, "So how much of the corn coming in is contaminated?" "It's about 10 percent," replied George. "They probably knew that the corn was contaminated. That's why we're getting such good deals on it." Jake thought for a moment and said, "George, call the suspected grain elevators, complain to them, and demand a 50 percent discount. If they agree, buy all they have." "But if we do, the blends will just increase in contamination!" said George. "That's OK. When the blends start getting high, we'll stop shipping into the U.S. market and go foreign," Jake told him. "Remember, there are no fines for contaminated corn in Mexico."

George learned that one other person, Lee Garcia, an operations manager for the breakfast cereals division, had used contaminated wheat once. "Yeah, so what about it? I've got a family to support and house payments. For me there was no alternative. I had to do it or face getting laid off," Lee said.

As George thought about the problem, word had spread about his alternatives. The following notes appeared in the plant suggestion box:

Use the corn or we all get laid off!

Process it and ship it off to Mexico!

It's just wrong to use this corn!

When George balked at Jake's solution, Jake said, "George, I understand your situation. I was there once — just like you. But you've got to look at the bigger picture. Hundreds of workers out of a job. Sure, the FDA [Food and Drug Adsminstration] says that aflatoxin is bad, but we're talking rats eating their weight in this stuff. What if it does get detected — so what? The company gets a fine, the FDA tester gets reprimanded for screwing up, and it's back to business as usual."

"Is that all that will happen?" asked George. "Of course, don't worry," replied Jake. But George's signature, not Jake's, was on the receipts for the contaminated railcars. "So if I do this, at what aflatoxin percentage do I stop, and will you sign off on this?" asked George. "Look," said Jake, "that's up to you. Remember that the more corn chips produced for the U.S. market, the more profit the company gets and the higher your bonus. As for me signing off on this, I'm shocked that you would even suggest something like that. George, you're the operations manager. You're the one who's responsible for what happens at the plant. It just isn't done that way at CornCo. But whatever you do, you had better do it in the next several hours because as I see it the contaminated corn has to blended with something, and the longer you wait, the higher the percentages will get."

Questions ■ Exercises

1. Discuss the corporate issue of providing questionable products to various markets.
2. Discuss the suggestion box in regard to the decision to be made. Should the suggestions have an influence?
3. Identify the pressures that have caused the ethical and legal issues to arise.

This case is strictly hypothetical; any resemblance to real persons, companies, or situations is coincidental.

CHECK YOUR E.Q.

Check your E.Q., or Ethics Quotient, by completing the following. Assess your performance to evaluate your overall understanding of the chapter material.

1. Most countries have a strong compliance or legal orientation.   Yes   No

2. The self-reference criterion is an unconscious reference to one's own cultural values, experience, and knowledge.   Yes   No

3. Cultural differences also relate to differences in body language.   Yes   No

4. Multinational corporations have an identifiable home country but operate globally.   Yes   No

5. Certain facilitating payments are acceptable under the Foreign Corrupt Practices Act.   Yes   No

ANSWERS 1. No. That's an ethnocentric perspective; in other countries laws may be viewed more situationally. 2. Yes. We react based on what we have experienced over our lifetime. 3. Yes. Personal space, habits, and customs influence interaction among people of different cultures. 4. No. Multinational corporations have no significant ties to any nation or region. 5. Yes. A violation of the FCPA occurs when the payments are excessive or are used to persuade the recipients to perform other than normal duties.

Business Ethics and
Organizational Performance

CHAPTER 10

Chapter Objectives

- To provide evidence that corporate ethical value systems support business performance
- To show the relationship between business ethics, customer satisfaction, corporate quality, and employee commitment
- To relate corporate citizenship to financial performance
- To discuss the relationship of social institutions that support trust-building ethical systems and a nation's economic well-being
- To assess the relationship of a firm's reputation and its economic standing

Chapter Outline

Relationship of Business Ethics to Performance
Trust as Part of Business Ethics
Ethics Contributes to Organizational Quality
Ethics Contributes to Customer Satisfaction
Ethics Contributes to Employee Commitment
Ethics Contributes to Profits
The Role of Ethics in the Economic Performance of Nations
The Importance of Reputation in Creating the Value of a Business

An Ethical Dilemma*

Devin Jacobs looked at his mother as she was receiving chemotherapy and wondered what he should do. Devin, single with no siblings, had a high-paying job at Netna. His career had gone fairly well within the management information systems (MIS) departments at four different companies in the Chicago area.

MIS employees have to stay ahead of the learning curve, and that's what Devin had always tried to do. When he began his first job, it had been very easy. Just out of college, he had been on the cutting edge of technology. After two years, though, Devin realized that his skills needed to be updated, and he began working on an MBA in information systems. This gave him the edge he needed to change jobs with a substantial pay increase. His second job was great. He made strides in the managerial field, but, as time passed, his skills again became outdated. He took several information systems classes and landed a better job with a third company.

Things didn't work out for Devin at this company. The company was being mismanaged, and Devin became the fall guy. After receiving several memos alluding to his incompetence, Devin quickly jumped ship and went with Netna, a large insurance company. As the years went by, Devin's technical skills again became outdated. Then his father died, making it necessary for Devin to spend more time with his mother.

About a year later, Devin's mother was diagnosed with cancer just when he had been assigned a very complex and challenging project. The company was demanding that everyone work extra hours, but the project that stared Devin in the face every day had very little hope of success. He began spending even more time taking care of his mother. When Devin approached his superior, Larry Zamber, about the pressures at work and the demands of caring for his sick mother, Larry said, "Devin, I feel for your situation. However, you can't take more than your allotted five personal days to take your mother to chemotherapy. If you do, I'll have to start docking your pay and put a memo in your permanent personnel file." Devin had already used all five of his personal days.

"But this is my mother, and she has no one else," pleaded Devin.

"Sorry. Rules are rules," responded Larry.

As rumors of Devin and Larry's conversation went through the company, one of Devin's friends approached him. "Devin, I understand what you're going through. I had a similar situation, and Netna was heartless. I know of several other people who have had similar experiences here, too. You'd think that an insurance company would understand, but not Netna. To them, we're just statistics — just like their policyholders. Three claims and Netna cancels them regardless of the reason for the claims. That attitude applies to us as well."

"So, what do I do?" asked Devin. "I couldn't live with myself if I had to hire someone to take my mother to chemo."

"What's your mother's prognosis?" asked the friend.

"It's not good," responded Devin. "The doctors give her from several weeks to just a few months. They just don't know. All they say is that it's terminal and that I should try to spend as much quality

---

The importance of business ethics to an organization has been debated from a variety of perspectives. Many business managers view ethics programs in their organization as an expensive activity that provides rewards only to society. The role of ethical concern in business relationships continues to be misunderstood. Both research and examples from the business world show that it does pay for a company to be viewed as ethical by employees, customers,

time with her as I can before the pain medications cause her to deteriorate."

"Well, there is a way to get around the system for a while," said the friend. "First, use whatever vacation time you have coming. Zamber will probably put a memo in your file about how inconsiderate you were to take vacation at this crucial time, but that's really all he can do. Next, start taking sick leave."

"Wait a minute! What if Netna tries to verify that I'm really sick?" asked Devin.

"Well, they'll either dock your pay or put a memo in your file or both. Either way, they'll probably try to find a way to get rid of you."

Questions ■ Exercises

1. What should Devin do to take more time off to assist his mother?
2. What are the organizational performance issues related to the ethical climate at Netna?
3. Should Netna assist Devin as he cares for his mother? Why or why not?

This case is strictly hypothetical; any resemblance to real persons, companies, or situations is coincidental.

and the general public. The rewards for ethics and social responsibility in business decisions include increased efficiency in daily operations, commitment from employees, improvement of product quality, better decision making, customer loyalty, and better financial performance. Organizations that develop a positive corporate culture with a climate of trust and perceived fairness build a valuable resource that facilitates success. The reputation of a company has a major effect on its relationships with customers, employees, suppliers, and investors. In a survey, executives were asked, "Other than base salary and bonuses, what do recent applicants ask about during job interviews today?" According to their responses, corporate culture was second only to benefits.[1]

What is it worth to a company's reputation, employees' pride, or shareholders' confidence to see the company listed in *Fortune* as one of the top ten most admired companies in the world? The companies listed in Table 10–1 found themselves in that enviable position. Organizations that are perceived as ethical often have a strong and loyal customer base, as well as a strong employee base, because of trust and mutual dependence in the relationship.[2] And such loyalty can affect the bottom line. A recent study found that companies with a strong sense of values experienced revenue growth that was four times faster and stock prices that increased twelve times faster than companies without a strong sense of values.[3] Customers tend to prefer buying from high-integrity companies, especially if the price is comparable to that of competitors. When employees perceive their organization as having an ethical climate, they are more likely to be committed to and satisfied with their work. Suppliers usually want long-term partnerships they can trust with the companies they serve so that through cooperation they can eliminate inefficiencies, costs, and risks in order to satisfy customers. Conversely, companies can hold high ethical expectations of their suppliers. The code of conduct at Toys "R" Us, for example, asks its suppliers to submit voluntarily to an audit by an outside party to ensure that they are not engaging in child labor, forced labor, discrimination, or any health, safety, management, or collective-bargaining prac-

TABLE 10–1   World's Most Admired Companies

2000 Rank	Company	Industry
1	General Electric	Electronics, electrical equipment
2	Cisco Systems	Network communications, Internet technology
3	Microsoft	Computer hardware, software
4	Intel	Computer hardware, software
5	Wal-Mart Stores	Retail: general, specialty
6	Sony	Electronics, electrical equipment
7	Dell Computer	Computer hardware, software
8	Nokia	Network communications, Internet technology
9	Home Depot	Retail: general, specialty
10	Toyota Motor	Motor vehicles

Source: "The All-Stars," Fortune, October 2, 2000, p. 184. Reprinted with permission.

ℰ.ethics 1

tice that does not meet the Toys "R" Us standard. The code has a clause that states that Toys "R" Us has the option of terminating the relationship if the supplier does not meet appropriate standards. Toys "R" Us recently indicated that they will be asking suppliers to seek certification to SA 8000, an international code standard that can be applied to all types of companies and whose intent is to improve working conditions globally.[4]

Many investors are concerned about the ethics, social responsibility, and repu- tation of companies in which they invest, and various socially responsible mutual funds and asset management firms can help investors purchase stock in ethical companies. Investors recognize that an ethical climate is the foundation for effi- ciency, productivity, and profits. On the other hand, investors also know that fines or negative publicity can lower stock prices, diminish customer loyalty, and threaten the long-term viability of the company. Legal problems and negative publicity can have a strong adverse effect on the success of any organization. When Bridgestone/Firestone was investigated after its recall of millions of tires in 2000, the company's stock fell 47 percent in just one month. The estimated cost of the recall was $500 million. The negative publicity surrounding the recall and sub- sequent investigation had an enormous impact on the company and consumer confidence in it. In one poll, 67 percent of people responded "extremely to very likely" to the question, "How likely is it that this tire recall would influence your decision to purchase a Firestone product?"[5] Based on a survey conducted on e-businessethics.com, 82 percent of the respondents believe that Firestone inten- tionally hid safety concerns before the tire recall.[6] Moreover, if certain issues are important to the public, activist special-interest groups can influence a business profoundly. The Walt Disney Company had its plans for a theme park in northern Virginia shattered by community opposition to commercial development. Activist groups have prevented Wal-Mart from opening stores in a number of states. Public demand led Home Depot, the world's largest home-improvement retailer, to commit to stop selling wood from environmentally sensitive areas by the end of 2002 and to give preference to wood that is certified as having been responsibly harvested. Other major retailers, including Lowe's, Home Base, Inc., Wickes Lumber, and Menards, soon followed with similar commitments. However, the current supply of responsibly harvested wood is scarce and could result in unmet demand.[7] These examples demonstrate the potential negative outcomes from preceived unethical or questionable business decisions.

In this chapter we provide evidence that resources spent on corporate ethics programs are an investment that has the potential to improve business performance. The concept of business ethics as a desirable and significant contribution to business activities is still controversial. Because of the expense and commitment required, many companies refuse to establish an effective ethics program as described in Chapter 8, for they do not believe that the benefits of an ethics program exceed the costs. We recognize that business ethics has much merit in its application beyond improving organizational performance. We encourage organizational integrity — because of its potential contribution to society as well as its positive influence on employees, customers, and profits. If more businesses learn about the rewards of ethical conduct, then everyone should benefit. Business ethics should be a corporate concern in strategic planning just as other areas of business are, such as production, finance, employee training, and customer relations, and we offer support for this view.

RELATIONSHIP OF BUSINESS ETHICS TO PERFORMANCE

Diverse sources, including both business and academic research, point out the link between good ethics and good business, and there are logical explanations for this link. Figure 10–1 provides an overview of the relationship between business ethics and organizational performance.

Organizations and their stakeholders are being challenged today by a complex and dynamic business environment. Given such a turbulent business environment, building relationships with important stakeholders is crucial to a firm's well-being. Both customers and employees are major concerns for firms that want to develop loyalty and competitive advantages. And employee loyalty is an important factor influencing employee longevity — which benefits the company. According to the Bureau of Labor Statistics, the average tenure of an employee with a company is less than five years. However, longevity is required in order for employees to learn complex tasks and truly master their responsibilities. Studies have shown that employee longevity leads to customer loyalty and higher profits, particularly in the banking, brokering, and auto-service industries. Even in manufacturing industries, where employees rarely meet customers, long-term employees can produce better products, create better value for consumers, and contribute to better customer retention.[8] The challenge for long-run success in business is to

FIGURE 10-1   The Role of Organizational Ethics in Performance

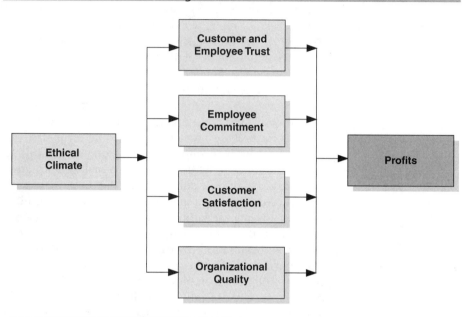

continually increase the customer's dependence on the company to provide products in an environment of mutual respect and perceived fairness. Creating mutually beneficial exchange relationships with customers means that both parties work together to understand needs and develop trust.

In addition, employee relationship building is of great significance to employees, who spend most of their waking hours preparing for work, at work, or commuting to and from work. Creating satisfying relationships with employees means not just providing a job, but also helping employees develop their own goals and take part in a humane and uplifting environment. Such an environment includes acknowledging the value of employees' contribution to the business. A study conducted three different times over the past forty-five years asked one thousand employees to rank work rewards in terms of value. Over the years, the results have barely changed. "Full appreciation of work" has remained at the top of the list."[9] Awareness of the stresses and pressures that employees experience and efforts to adapt the work environment to make it more flexible for employees can strengthen employee loyalty. These efforts might mean offering flextime, telecommuting, job sharing, and so forth, but all such endeavors require trust on both sides.

Leadership plays a key role in creating corporate values and a social network that supports ethical behavior. Leadership that focuses on building strong organizational values among employees creates agreement on norms of conduct and patterns of shared relationships. Leaders in highly visible positions in the organization play a key role in transmitting and diffusing values, norms, and codes of

FIGURE 10–2   Top Management and Supervisors Talking About Ethics at Work

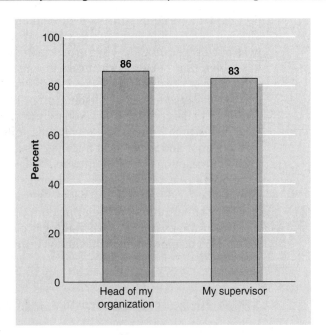

Source: The Ethics Resource Center, 2000 National Business Ethics Survey: How Employees Perceive Ethics at Work, p. 57. Reprinted with permission.

ethics.[10] Figure 10–2 shows that the majority of employees in the National Business Ethics Survey (NBES) agreed that their supervisors and top management in their organizations "talk about ethics and doing the right thing in the work we do."[11] The need for ethical leadership to provide structure to organizational values and to provide deterrents to unethical behavior has been supported in previous research.[12] Leaders can provide this structure by instituting both formal and informal ethics training programs, as well as other guidelines, that will help employees consider ethics in their decision making.

To be successful, relationships with investors must rest on dependability, trust, and commitment. Investors look at the bottom line for profits or the potential for increased stock prices. But investors also look for any potential cracks, or flaws, in the company. Hence many company presidents spend a large amount of their time communicating with investors about the firm's reputation and financial performance and trying to attract them to the company's stock. The issue of drawing and keeping investors is a critical one for CEOs, as roughly 50 percent of investors sell their stock in companies within one year and the average household replaces 80 percent of its common stock portfolio each year.[13] Therefore, gaining investors' trust and confidence is vital for sustaining the financial stability of the firm.

Trust as Part of Business Ethics

In Chapter 3 we define trust as a virtue that creates a predisposition to place confidence in the behavior of others while taking the risk that the expected behavior will not be performed. When trustworthiness becomes part of an individual's character, that person is disposed to engage in trust-building relationships. If your boss or coworkers leave work early, you may be tempted to do so as well. If you see coworkers making personal long-distance phone calls at work and charging them to the company, then you may be more likely to do so, too.

Past research on organizational ethics offers evidence that the "ethical tone" set by senior and lower-level managers is a central factor in shaping employees' overall perceptions of ethics at work.[14] Figure 10–3 shows the NBES findings on employee perceptions of leaders, supervisors, and coworkers who "set a good example of ethical business behavior." As the figure shows, most of the employees saw their organizations as having an ethical climate — a perception that if you are trustworthy, then doing the right thing is part of your character and you will be a role model of appropriate behavior for your coworkers.

FIGURE 10–3   Leaders, Supervisors, and Coworkers Modeling Ethical Behavior

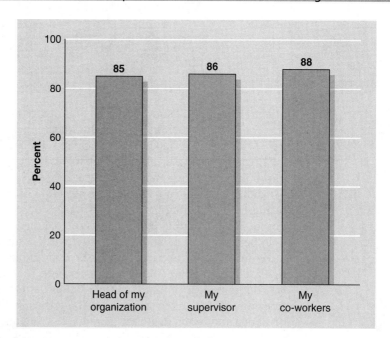

Source: *The Ethics Resource Center,* 2000 National Business Ethics Survey: How Employees Perceive Ethics at Work, *p. 59. Reprinted with permission.*

Employees' perception of their firm as having an ethical climate leads to performance-enhancing outcomes within the organization.[15] Companies perceived by their employees as having a high degree of honesty and integrity had an average three-year total return to shareholders of 101 percent, while companies perceived as having a low degree of honesty and integrity had a three-year total return to shareholders of just 69 percent.[16] For the sake of both productivity and teamwork, it is essential that employees both within various departments and between departments throughout the organization share a common vision of trust. The influence of higher levels of trust is greatest on relationships within departments or work groups, but trust is a significant factor in relationships between departments throughout the organization. Consequently, programs creating a work climate that is trustworthy make individuals more willing to rely and act on the decisions and actions of their coworkers. In such a work environment, employees can reasonably expect to be treated with full respect and consideration by their coworkers and superiors. Trusting relationships within an organization between managers and their subordinates and upper management contribute to greater decision-making efficiencies.

Stephen R. Covey, author of *The 7 Habits of Highly Effective People,* which has sold more than 11 million copies, encourages companies to examine the impact of trust on the bottom line in addition to the impact of profits, earnings per share, and other factors traditionally thought to determine a company's success.[17] Covey indicates that when trust is low, organizations decay and relationships deteriorate, resulting in politics, infighting, and general inefficiency. As ethical conduct decreases, employee commitment to the organization falters, product quality declines, customers leave, and employee turnover skyrockets.[18] In the NBES, more than three-fourths of all employees indicated that their "organization's concern for ethics and doing the right thing" was an important reason for continuing to work there.[19]

Trust is the glue that holds organizations together and allows them to focus on efficiency, productivity, and profits. Without trust, it is very difficult to predict the outcome of human interaction. Compelling trust is the highest form of human motivation. It brings out the very best in people, but it takes time and patience, and it doesn't preclude the necessity to train and develop people so that their competency can rise to that level of trust.[20] The NBES found that when employees see values such as honesty, respect, and trust applied frequently in the workplace, they feel less pressure to compromise ethical standards, observe less misconduct, are more satisfied with their organizations overall, and feel more valued as employees.[21] Figure 10–4 shows employee satisfaction percentages when honesty, respect, and trust are applied.

The public's trust is essential for maintaining a good long-term relationship between a business and consumers. The Millennium Poll of twenty-five thousand citizens in twenty-three countries found that almost 60 percent of people focus on corporate citizenship ahead of brand reputation or financial factors in forming impressions of companies.[22] After the *Exxon Valdez* oil spill, certain groups, as

FIGURE 10–4   Employee Satisfaction by Values Applied in the Workplace

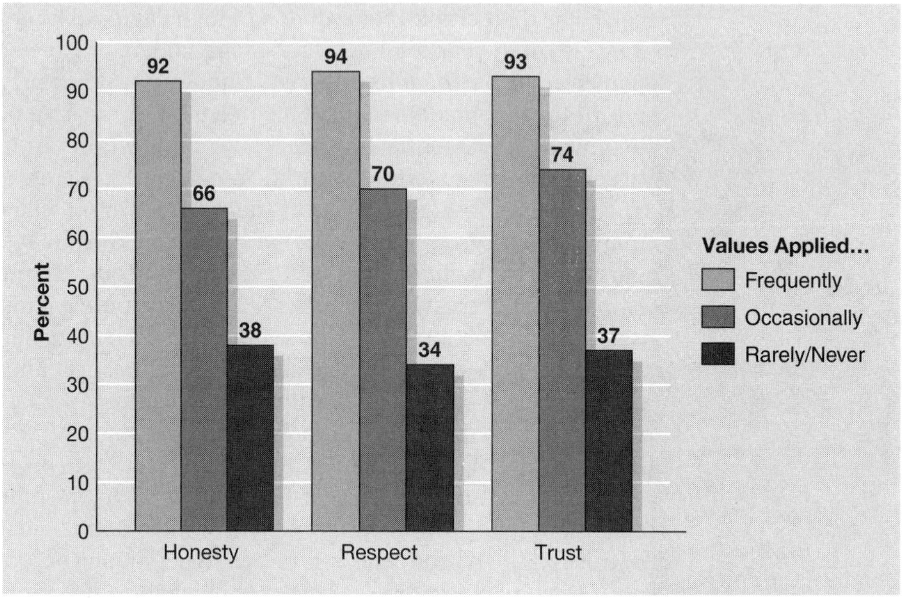

Source: *The Ethics Resource Center,* 2000 National Business Ethics Survey: How Employees Perceive Ethics at Work, *p. 85. Reprinted with permission.*

well as individual citizens, boycotted the company. Before Chicken of the Sea and many of its competitors adopted dolphin-friendly nets in the capture of tuna, many consumers refused to buy tuna. Moreover, consumers may avoid the products of companies that are perceived as not treating their employees fairly.

Companies that subcontract manufacturing operations abroad have had to confront the ethical issues associated with supporting facilities that abuse or underpay their work force. Such facilities have been termed "sweatshops." Gap, Inc., the number-one U.S. clothing chain, and Nike, the world's largest maker of athletic shoes, suspended orders at June Textiles Co. Ltd., a Cambodian garment factory, after learning that the British Broadcasting Corp. planned to air a program alleging use of child labor at the factory.[23] New industry codes of conduct, such as SA 8000, mentioned earlier, have been established to help companies identify and address these ethical issues. When consumers learn about abuses in subcontracting, they may boycott the companies' products.

From an employee's perspective, one way that a company can increase trust is by offering a stock ownership plan (ESOP). Along with stock ownership, giving employees a chance to take part in management planning helps create an environment that many organizations believe increases profits. One example where stock ownership and participation work is Delphi Automotive Systems. Delphi delivered more than 15 million stock options or stock appreciation rights to employees worldwide through its Founder's Grant Program, making it one of the largest such programs in history. In addition, the top one hundred Delphi executives have between 65 and 82 percent of their compensation tied directly to the company's performance.[24] Clearly, these executives understand that the decisions they make impact Delphi as well as themselves, and they also understand the relationship between personal success and organizational success. Other "employee-owned" companies include Cisco Systems, Avis, and Biddeford Textile Company. Maintaining trust is a continuing process of communication and cooperation. Trust between employer and employee helps ensure a company's survival and success over time.

Ethics Contributes to Organizational Quality

When employees perceive an improvement in the ethical climate of their organization, they become more committed to achieving high-quality standards in daily operations. Employees are more willing to discuss ethics issues and to support the quality initiatives of their company if the organization communicates a commitment to ethical conduct. Indeed, those who work in an ethical organizational climate are likely to believe that they must treat all their business partners respectfully, regardless of whether they operate inside or outside the organization. It becomes essential for them to provide the best possible value to all customers and stakeholders.[25]

Since employees' commitment to quality has a positive effect on a firm's competitive position, an ethical work climate should have a positive effect on the financial bottom line. Because the quality of customer service affects customer satisfaction, improvement in the quality of service will have a direct impact on a company's image, as well as on its ability to attract new customers.[26] Companies with high-quality products command high customer loyalty: they include companies such as BMW, Saturn, Waterford Crystal, Sony, and Timberland.

e.ethics 2

Hershey Foods exemplifies a business that seems to draw substantial benefits from its long-lasting commitment to ethical citizenship. Every year all Hershey's employees receive a booklet entitled *Key Corporate Policies*, which describes the values — fairness, integrity, honesty, and respect — at the heart of the company's way of doing business. Employees are asked to signal their acceptance of these moral principles by signing the booklet. They are also made aware of the clear procedures available to report any concern about proper conduct or policies in the workplace. Through such initiatives, employees understand the importance of developing and maintaining respectful relationships with both colleagues and customers. Since the whole organization supports the idea that customers should receive full value for their money, Hershey is committed to delivering the highest quality possible. Employees seem to adapt quickly to the Hershey way of doing business. One employee noted that "as long as you take the 'high road' at Hershey, the company will stand behind you regardless of the outcome, but if you choose to take the 'low road,' you're on your own and will suffer the consequences."[27]

Ethics Contributes to Customer Satisfaction

One of the fundamental responsibilities of a business is for management to exert leadership in promoting the greatest good for its stakeholders, including, of course, its customers. The prevailing business philosophy about customer relationships is that an organization should try to provide products that satisfy customers' needs through a coordinated effort that allows the company to also achieve its goals. It is generally accepted that customer satisfaction is one of the most important factors in successful business strategy. While the company must continue to develop, alter, and adapt products to keep pace with customers' changing desires and preferences, it must also seek to develop long-term relationships with customers. For most legitimate businesses that operate for long-term profitability, repeat purchases, along with an enduring relationship of mutual respect and cooperation between the business and its customers, are absolutely essential for success. By focusing on customer satisfaction, the business continually deepens the customer's dependence on the company, and as the customer's confidence grows, the firm gains a better understanding of how to serve the customer so that the relationship may endure. Successful businesses provide an opportunity for customer feedback, which can engage the customer in cooperative problem solving. As is often pointed out, a happy customer will come back, but a disgruntled customer will tell others about being dissatisfied with a company and discourage friends from dealing with it.

Service customers are especially vulnerable to exploitation or operations that do not respect rights. Service fairness is a customer's perception of the degree of justice in a firm's behavior. Therefore, when information about added service costs is omitted or a guarantee is not honored, the customer reacts negatively to the perceived injustice. The customer's response to the injustice — for instance, complaining or refusing to deal with the business again — may be motivated by the need to punish and the desire to limit a future injustice.[28] Millions of customers are overcharged by retail computer scanners that are not programmed with the correct "sale" price. If the customer is overcharged for an item that has a highly visible sale price displayed, a feeling of injustice likely arises and may provoke an angry verbal response.

There is a reported decline in the level of respect for consumers. Technology is creating a new business model that allows companies to determine exactly what level of service to provide based on the ability to measure service costs on an individual basis and assess return to the business. This permits an adjustment of level of service based on a consumer's potential to produce a certain level of profit for the company. The result could be a new stratification of consumers in society, with those at the highest income levels enjoying an unprecedented level of service and those at the lowest income levels receiving almost no service.[29]

A strong organizational ethical climate usually focuses on the core value of placing customers' interests first.[30] Placing customers' interests first does not mean that the interests of employees, investors, and local communities should be ignored. However, an ethical climate that focuses on customers incorporates the interests of all stakeholders in decisions and actions. Employees working in an ethical climate support and contribute to an understanding of customers' demands and concerns. Ethical conduct toward customers builds a strong competitive position that has been shown to positively affect business performance and product innovation.[31]

In a Cone/Roper national survey of consumer attitudes, 70 percent of consumers said they would be likely to switch to brands associated with a good cause, if price and quality were equal.[32] Results indicated that consumers take it for granted that they can buy high-quality products at low prices; therefore, businesses need to stand out as doing something socially responsible — something that demonstrates their commitment to society. Another way of looking at these results is that perceived unethical behavior could trigger disloyalty and a switch to a competitor's brand, whereas ethical behavior could draw customers to a company's products.

Many companies have developed programs to show overall support for community development and the welfare of their customers. Best Buy, for example, is committed to contributing to the communities in which its employees and customers work and live. In fiscal 2000, the company donated more than $5.5 million in grants and employee volunteer support. The Best Buy Children's Foundation (BBCF) supports organizations and programs committed to making a difference in the lives of school-age children. According to Susan Hoff, president of BBCF, "Best Buy is dedicated to making a meaningful and lasting impact on the quality of life in the communities we serve. That commitment is reflected in our support of nonprofit programs that put young people on the path to become responsible, successful adults."[33] Lowe's Companies, Inc., contributed building materials, the time of more than three hundred employee volunteers, and more than $1 million to the Special Olympics World Games.[34]

Existing research and the experiences of many companies show a strong relationship between ethical behavior and customer satisfaction. Customers are likely to keep buying from companies perceived as having a positive reputation because of their concern for customers and society. Ethical companies that are dedicated to treating customers fairly and that continuously improve product quality, as well as make customer information easily accessible and understandable, are more likely to have a competitive advantage and be profitable. The bottom line is that the cost associated with developing an ethical climate may be balanced by improved customer loyalty.

Ethics Contributes to Employee Commitment

Employee commitment comes from employees who believe their future is tied to that of the organization and their willingness to make personal sacrifices for the organization.[35] The more a company is dedicated to taking care of its employees, the more likely it is that the employees will take care of the organization. Figure 10–5 shows the importance of ethics to employees' commitment to the organization. The issues that may affect the development of an ethical organizational climate for employees include a safe work environment, competitive salaries, and the fulfillment of all contractual obligations toward employees. Social programs that may improve the ethical climate range from work-family programs and stock ownership plans to community service. Home Depot associates, for example, participate in disaster relief efforts after hurricanes and tornadoes by rebuilding roofs, repairing water damage, planting trees, and clearing roads. As part of Home Depot's focus on building affordable housing and assisting at-risk youth, associates are encouraged to participate in the company's partnerships with organizations such as Habitat for Humanity, KaBoom!, and YouthBuild U.S.A.[36] Since employees spend a great deal of their waking time at work, a commitment to goodwill and respect for the employees on the part of the organization usually increases the employees' loyalty to the organization and their support of its objectives.

(e).ethics 3

A global workplace study by Walker Information found that only 34 percent of all employees are truly loyal to their organization. According to a Walker Information vice president, "Our research shows that employers everywhere need to focus on building relationships with their workers so that these employees can feel truly loyal to their organization and believe they are a valued part of the enterprise."

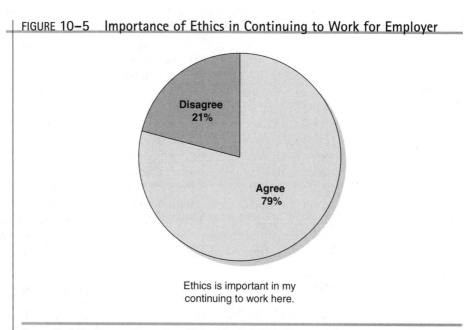

FIGURE 10–5   Importance of Ethics in Continuing to Work for Employer

Disagree
21%

Agree
79%

Ethics is important in my
continuing to work here.

Source: The Ethics Resource Center, 2000 National Business Ethics Survey: How Employees Perceive Ethics at Work, *p. 67.*

Employers need to understand what affects employee loyalty and commitment because employee retention is crucial. The study showed that these six work factors have the greatest influence on employee commitment to an organization:

1. Fairness at work (includes fair pay)
2. Care and concern for employees
3. Satisfaction with day-to-day activities
4. Trust in employees
5. Reputation of the organization
6. Work and job resources.[37]

Almost everyone who has worked in an organization has seen people who do the minimum to get by each day or who have no commitment to what the organization is trying to accomplish because they do not feel they are treated fairly.

Corporate ethical climate seems to matter to employees. According to a recent report on employee loyalty and work practices, companies viewed as highly ethical by their employees were six times more likely to keep their workers.[38] Also, employees who view their company as having a strong community involvement feel more loyal to their employers and feel positive about themselves.

The experience of Starbucks Coffee supports the idea that fair treatment of employees improves productivity and profitability. Starbucks was the first importer of agricultural products to develop a code of conduct protecting workers who harvest coffee beans in countries such as Costa Rica. Recently, Starbucks began selling "Fair Trade" coffee. Fair Trade certification provides a way for small farmers to increase their incomes by helping them organize into cooperatives and linking them directly to coffee importers. Fair Trade farmers are guaranteed a premium over the prevailing rate being paid for coffee on the international market. The premium helps them afford basic health care, education, and housing improvements for their families.[39] A customer buying a cup of coffee at Starbucks can be confident that those who harvested and prepared the coffee were treated fairly by the company. Starbucks recognizes its commitment to employees in its mission statement, which says that "we should provide a great work environment and treat each other with respect and dignity." It is also worth noting that Starbucks gives its employees one pound of free coffee each week. The company has made it clear to shareholders that the employees must be taken care of and that the company must find ways to build value for its employees.

A survey by iSwag.com indicates that as employees gain more confidence in their company, they demonstrate loyalty and are more successful in advancing in the company. For example, 37 percent of workers with a coffee mug bearing a company logo were promoted within the six months prior to the survey, compared to 8 percent who did not have a coffee mug with a company logo.[40] This illustrates a correlation between symbolic employee loyalty and company assessment of employee value.

Ethics Contributes to Profits

As indicated earlier, companies perceived by their employees as having a high degree of honesty and integrity had a much higher average total return to shareholders than did companies perceived as having a low degree of honesty and integrity.[41] A study of the five hundred largest public corporations in the United States found that those who commit to ethical behavior or emphasize compliance with their code of conduct have better financial performance.[42] These results provide strong evidence that corporate concern for ethical conduct is becoming a part of strategic planning in obtaining the outcome of higher profitability. Rather than being just a government-required compliance program, ethics is becoming a management issue in the effort to achieve competitive advantage. Ben and Jerry's was one of the first businesses to widely communicate its ethical values and the role of ethics in its corporate strategy.

Ethical citizenship is positively associated with return on investment, return on assets, and sales growth. It is defined as the extent to which businesses take on the economic, legal, ethical, and discretionary responsibilities placed on them by their various stakeholders.[43] Ethical citizenship is assumed to vary along a continuum ranging from proactive to reactive.[44] A proactive business is aware of, anticipates, and meets the responsibilities imposed by its stakeholders. A firm fulfills its responsibilities by engaging in such activities as ethical training, legal compliance, and communicating and modifying organizational processes to serve stakeholders. These activities are closely associated with economic citizenship. Economic citizenship includes responding to every customer complaint, continually improving the quality of products, and using customer satisfaction as an indicator of business performance. These activities are in line with responsible actions to serve stockholders, employees, customers, and communities concerned about the economic well-being of their citizens.

A company cannot be a good corporate citizen and nurture and develop an ethical organizational climate unless it has achieved adequate financial performance in terms of profits. Businesses with greater resources — regardless of their staff size — have the means to practice corporate citizenship along with serving their customers, valuing their employees, and establishing trust with the public. Many studies have found a positive relationship between corporate citizenship and business performance.[45] Firms convicted of misconduct experience a significantly lower return on assets and return on sales than unconvicted firms. Research indicates that the negative effect on return on sales does not appear until the third year following the conviction, and multiple convictions are more harmful than a single one.[46]

There are many examples of companies that have had significant declines in their financial performance after discovery of their failure to act responsibly toward various stakeholders. Columbia/HCA experienced serious declines in stock prices and earnings after the revelation that it was systematically overcharging the government for Medicare services. Employees and customers also lodged complaints against Columbia/HCA for its failure to take their interests into account on day-to-day operations. Employees were forced to do jobs beyond their abilities, and customers (patients) were charged for services they did not need or were transferred to another hospital if there was a question about their ability to pay. Once Columbia/HCA's misconduct became public knowledge, its reputation was damaged within a few months.[47] Sears suffered because its automotive divisions sold unneeded parts in its repair shops.[48] Texaco lost business as a result of racial insensitivity by some of its employees. Beech-Nut lost customers after selling juice that was labeled as 100 percent pure but actually contained the chemical equivalent of apple juice.[49] Every day business newspapers and magazines provide more examples of the consequences of business misconduct.

The Role of Ethics in the Economic Performance of Nations

An important and often-asked question is whether ethical conduct in business has a bearing on the overall economic performance of a nation. Economists wonder why some market-based economies are productive, providing a high standard of living for their citizens, whereas other market-based economies lack the kinds of social institutions that foster productivity and economic growth.[50] It may be that a society's economic failure can be explained by its lack of business ethics. As one of society's essential virtues that hold relationships together, trust stems from "principles of ethics and morality" and serves as an important "lubricant of the social system."[51] Descriptions of market economies often do not take into account various institutions, such as the family, the educational system, and the social system, in explaining standards of living and economic success. Possibly, some countries do a better job of developing an adequate standard of living and gross domestic product (GDP) than others because of the social structure of economic relationships.

Societal institutions, particularly those that promote trust, are important for the economic well-being of a society.[52] A society becomes economically successful over time "because of the underlying institutional framework persistently reinforcing incentives for organizations to engage in productive activity."[53] In many developing countries, the opportunities for political and economic development are stifled by activities that promote monopolies, graft, and corruption, and by restricted opportunities to advance individual, as well as the collective, well-being. Wealthy nations become wealthy because they are involved in sets of institutions, including business ethics, that encourage productivity. L. E. Harrison points out "four fundamental factors" that promote economic well-being: "(1) the degree of identification with others in a society — the radius of trust, or the sense of community; (2) the rigor of the ethical system; (3) the way authority is exercised within the society; and (4) attitudes about work, innovation, saving, and profit."[54]

Trust is the extent to which individuals identify with, or have a sense of community with, others in society. The smallest radius of trust is in a society in which people trust only themselves. The next level would be societies in which family members and other kin may be trusted. From a societal perspective, economic productivity will fall if day-to-day business activities require maximum use of mechanisms and procedures to control dishonesty. Countries with strong trust-based institutions foster a productivity-enhancing environment because the existence of an ethical system reduces transaction costs, making competitive processes more efficient and effective.[55] In market-based systems where there is high trust — in countries such as the United Kingdom, Canada, the United States, and Sweden — highly successful enterprises can be developed because of a spirit of cooperation and ease in conducting business.[56]

Superior financial performance at the firm level within a society is measured as profits, earnings per share, return on investment, and capital appreciation. Businesses must achieve a certain level of financial performance in order to survive and reinvest in the various institutions in society that provide support. On the other hand, at the institutional or societal level, a key factor distinguishing societies with high standards of living is trust-promoting institutions. The challenge is to explicate the process by which institutions that support business ethics can contribute to firm-level superior financial performance.[57]

A comparison of countries that have a high level of corruption and underdeveloped social institutions with countries that have a low level of corruption reveals differences in the economic well-being of the country's citizens. According to Transparency International's Corruption Perceptions Index, countries such as Malaysia and Taiwan rank high on corruption, whereas countries such as Sweden and Canada rank low on corruption.[58] The differences in these countries' economic well-being and stability provide evidence that ethics plays a vital role in economic development. Conducting business in an ethical and responsible manner generates trust and leads to relationships that promote productivity and innovation.

The Importance of Reputation in Creating the Value of a Business

As you have progressed through this book, you have seen how business misconduct can damage a company's reputation. The wreck of the *Exxon Valdez* creating an environmentally damaging oil spill, Columbia/HCA's overbilling of the Medicare program, as well as the tire recall and subsequent investigations of Firestone illustrate how quickly a reputation can deteriorate. On the other hand, at such companies as Hershey and Procter & Gamble, proactive, culturally based organizational ethics initiatives have provided the infrastructure for strengthening employee commitment, teamwork, and customer loyalty, and for raising economic productivity.

Viewed from a stock growth perspective, a company's reputation enhances its value in the marketplace, as an examination of *Fortune* magazine's annual list of the most admired companies in the world indicates (see Table 10–1 on page 238). Even though some of these companies may have faced accusations of legal and ethical misconduct (Microsoft was convicted but is appealing the charge of attempting to monopolize the market for some of its software), their overall reputation, based on the *Fortune* set of criteria, was superior to all other companies in the *Fortune* list. The specific criteria used in *Fortune*'s evaluation included quality of management; quality of products and services; innovativeness; ability to attract, develop, and retain talent; long-term investment value; financial soundness; community responsibility; use of corporate assets; and global business acumen.[59] Given the *Fortune* criteria, it is probably difficult to rank high without a strong ethical climate and a strong commitment to social responsibility. The Hay Group, the worldwide management consulting firm that produced the list for *Fortune*, found that "the top organizations create performance measures that focus on all the drivers of their businesses — financial performance, shareholder value, employees, and customers."[60]

Thus, there is much evidence that developing effective ethical compliance programs in business not only helps prevent misconduct but also leads to economic advantage. Although ethical conduct in an organization is important from a social and individual perspective, economic prospects are also a factor. One of the problems in gaining support for ethics initiatives in organizations is the assumption that expenditures for ethics programs result only in costs and do not bring any return to the organization. In this chapter we have sought to present evidence that investing in an ethics infrastructure within an organization will help provide a foundation for all of the important business activities required for success. Ethics alone will not generate outstanding financial performance, but it will help shape and sustain a corporate culture that will serve all stakeholders.

SUMMARY

Organizational efforts in regard to ethics affect various organizational stakeholders: customers, employees, suppliers, and investors. Many stockholders want to invest in companies that have strong ethics programs, are socially concerned, and have solid reputations. Employees like working for a company they can trust, and consumers value integrity in business relationships. Stronger organizational ethical climates result in consumer and employee trust, employee commitment, and customer satisfaction, which in turn leads to profitability.

Trust is a key element in holding organizational relationships and stakeholders together. To find favor with the public and consumers, a company must earn their trust. Employees' trust in their firm can be deepened through programs linking the employee more closely with the organization, such as employee stock ownership plans.

Employee commitment to quality has been shown to have a positive effect on the firm's competitive position; hence, companies need to strengthen this commitment. They can do so by fostering an ethical climate. The stronger the employee perception of an ethical climate, the higher is the level of commitment to the organization. A safe work environment, competitive salaries, fulfillment of contractual obligations, work–family programs, stock ownership, and community service all contribute to developing employee commitment to the organization.

Businesses that succeed give consumers the opportunity for feedback. Satisfied customers will return, but dissatisfied ones will continue to damage the firm's reputation. Service fairness — the customer's perception of the degree of justice in a firm's behavior — is a key element in long-term business success.

Corporate citizenship is also positively associated with return on investment, return on assets, and sales growth. Ethics has been found to be particularly important to the development and performance of nations. Societies that promote trust have a more secure economic situation. Indeed, trust-promoting institutions are a key factor distinguishing societies with a high standard of living.

Corporate reputation has an impact on stock price and organizational productivity. Business misconduct can damage a firm's reputation. There is also increasing evidence that developing an effective ethical compliance program not only helps prevent misconduct but also leads to economic productivity.

A Real–Life Situation*

Jacob Franklin, age 25, had graduated with a bachelor of science degree in engineering and had earned his MBA from an Ivy League university. He had taken a job with Richardson Drilling Equipment because of his fiancée, Margurete. Her family had affiliations with the oil industry in Texas and she wanted to be close to her parents. "I was born a Texan and want my children to be Texan as well," she told him when they were dating. Jacob had grown up in Oregon and found the Amarillo, Texas, topography boring.

In his first year with Richardson Drilling, Jacob had been a quick learner. For example, he had learned that at Richardson it was all right to give goods and services to potential clients. When the company was doing business in Mexico, the rule was that 1 percent of the contract would go in an envelope to someone. Jacob had also learned that company policy forbade bribes to government officials. He had learned, too, that since the oil industry was a very competitive place, with many foreign rivals, normal U.S. standards sometimes did not apply. For example, in Brazil, equipment quality varied wildly. In one case, he had inspected some Richardson equipment and discovered that the drilling company had purchased replacement parts from some other supplier, whose parts were substandard. When he warned the drilling foreman, the reply was, "Accidents happen, we pay by the week here."

Six months ago Jacob had taken over the Latin American sales district, which included parts of the United States. He also finally found the time to go through some of the old files that the past sales reps had left. The files revealed that several U.S. clients that had purchased substantial amounts of product years ago had stopped doing so, yet there were no explanatory notes from the old reps. By talking to the clients, Jacob learned about a number of accidents that had occurred almost seven years earlier as the direct result of a failed liner within several Richardson products. "I told the sales rep about this years ago, and the president of your company came to our operations to check it out. There was no explanation offered or assurance that the problem would be fixed," said one company's engineer. "That's why I haven't been buying from you."

When Jacob mentioned his discovery to Hillary, his boss, she said, "Jacob, thank you for letting me know, but my recommendation is that you remain silent until the seven-year statute of limitations has passed. We're in the process of coming out with a new liner that will solve this problem, and in another one to two years all the troublesome liners will be replaced. Besides, the old liner meets federal standards. If this problem should be discovered by outside sources, and it had better not be, we can always discount the rest of our inventory to oil fields abroad — in Venezuela or Brazil — where regulations are less restrictive."

Jacob knew Hillary's reputation of being fair but firm. Several days later Jacob found out that Margurete, now his wife, was pregnant. Jacob was delighted but also nervous. There would be only his income for a while, as well as another person for whom he would be responsible. Around the same time another oil company had called him about a position in its research department. The personnel manager had said, "Jacob, we've heard good things about you. We want you to think about coming over to our company. We know that it would mean leaving Texas for our Seattle facilities, but we're willing to offer you 25 percent more than what you're getting, plus perks."

When Jacob told Margurete about the offer, the plate she was drying slipped from her hand onto the floor. "Are you seriously thinking about the position?" she stammered. "Well, yes, I was," he answered as he scooped up the broken pieces and put them in the trash. "It would be more money at a better company, with possibly better opportunities for advancement."

Margurete slumped into the hard kitchen chair. With tears welling up, she said, "Jacob, you don't understand. I need to be close to my parents. They're getting older. I'm their only child. I hated the Northwest when I was there, and I've been to Seattle with its constant rain. It nauseates me just to think about it. I told you before we were married that Texas was very important to me. You said that

was fine. I didn't lie to you about my feelings, and now you're telling me that you want to move! If you want to move, I'll go to Fort Worth, Abilene, Houston, even College Station, but don't ask me to move to Seattle." With that Margurete's face turned a sickly gray and she rushed to the bathroom.

Later that week Jacob flew down to Mexico City, still pondering the feelings that he had evoked in Margurete. At first he thought that her reaction might be the result of the pregnancy, but the aura of that night's discussion had lingered as the days passed.

In Mexico, Jacob was dealing with ARMCO, which had decided to purchase $50 million worth of equipment. Jacob was the lead person on the deal and after the signing slipped Jose Ortiz several envelopes filled with five hundred crisp $100 bills. As Hillary toasted Ortiz and ARMCO, the celebration started in full force. While the music played, Hillary cornered Jacob and said, "Jacob, you're in the big leagues now. Very few people at Richardson believed that at 25 you could have handled a $50 million deal as complex as this. This contract will give us enough business to expand and hire 15 percent more permanent workers. There'll be the bonus and a probable promotion down the line. We're proud of the work you're doing."

On the flight home Jacob was catching up on the latest business news and read that the previous month Ortiz had taken a position in the Mexican legislature. He reminded himself to send a note of congratulations.

On Monday, when he checked his messages, he found one from the personnel manager of the company recruiting him. When Jacob returned the call, the conversation quickly focused upon a job. "Jacob, congratulations on the ARMCO deal. We've been trying to land that account for years. You certainly have the magic touch, which brings me to why I've called you. We want you to come up and see Seattle for a few days — our treat. No strings attached, just take a look." On a scheduled trip for Richardson to the Northwest, Jacob decided to visit the other firm, and when he arrived, he found it better than he had imagined. He fell in love with the city, the job, and the people with whom he would be associating. One thing surprised him. In his conversations at the Seattle company, the subject of cash payments to customers came up. The personnel manager stated: "Yes, that type of business does happen, especially in other countries. Luckily, most firms are avoiding the problem by a firm policy against such behavior — at least that's our policy. We try to avoid that type of employee." After this conversation, the talk revolved around a client that Jacob was courting, and he inadvertently relayed some sensitive information.

When Jacob returned home, he started talking to Margurete about the "extreme possibility" of Seattle. Not that he was seriously thinking about it, but if something drastic happened at Richardson, this might be a fallback position, was his story. As the months went by, Margurete had somewhat softened to the idea of Seattle. Meanwhile, she had gone in for tests about the pregnancy, and the doctors had found that the baby had a high probability of some genetic disorders. Both Jacob and Margurete were concerned about what this would mean if it were true, but as the doctor explained, "We won't know until the third trimester, which in this case may still be grounds for terminating the pregnancy if you so desire." When Jacob was talking to the insurance carrier, he was told not to worry, that this particular condition would be covered. However, the agent added, "I must caution you that many insurance companies are not covering such conditions if you switch carriers before your baby is born."

On Friday things came to a boil. There had been bad accidents in the United States caused by the old liners. Doing some calculations, Jacob realized that the old liners were becoming increasingly problematic, which meant a higher probability of danger. When he explained the new situation to Hillary, her response was, "Jacob, you're on the fast track here. Why do you want to do something that is going to make waves? In one more year the new liners will be out. We'll give them to our high-risk customers at cost, and the problem will be solved. I believe we've had this conversation once before. Remember, if something goes down on this, it will come out that you knew well in advance." Jacob's next conversation was with the Seattle firm, which had wanted a decision by Monday as to whether he was going to take the offer. "We need you, Jacob, and hopefully you'll bring some of your clients with you." While reviewing the offer, he called the Seattle company's insurance carrier about his unborn child and was told that the potential problem would probably not be covered. Finally, word had spread that AXEON had put out feelers about a takeover bid for Richardson. It was well known that AXEON liked taking a chainsaw to management when it took over.

Questions ■ Exercises

1. Identify the ethical/legal issues for Jacob.
2. What options does Jacob have?
3. Assume you are Jacob and prioritize your decisions.
4. What aspects of Richardson's organizational culture may have a negative influence on long-term performance?

This case is strictly hypothetical; any resemblance to real persons, companies, or situations is coincidental.

CHECK YOUR E.Q.

Check your E.Q., or Ethics Quotient, by completing the following. Assess your performance to evaluate your overall understanding of the chapter material.

1. There is a correlation between perceptions of organizational commitment to ethics and customer loyalty.   Yes   No

2. Legal problems and negative publicity rarely affect the profitability of the organization.   Yes   No

3. An ethical climate leads to profits through investor confidence.   Yes   No

4. Trust between the employer and employee increases the likelihood of survival and success over time.   Yes   No

5. Studies tend to show that financial performance is positively related to ethics and compliance initiatives.   Yes   No

ANSWERS   1. Yes. Also, employee loyalty seems greater in organizations with strong ethical cultures.   2. No. Legal investigations, fines, and negative publicity can decrease the stock price, customer loyalty, and the long-term viability of the company.   3. No. More specifically, an ethical climate leads to profitability through customer and employee trust, employee commitment, and customer satisfaction.   4. Yes. Trust is key in minimizing turnover and increasing employee commitment.   5. Yes. Good ethics is good business.

PART TWO

Cases

Case 1

Hershey Foods' Conflict with R.E.M.

Hershey Foods Corp. is currently the U.S. market leader in chocolate confectionery, with sales last year of $3.9 billion. Hershey manufactures more than fifty-five brands of confectionery products, including such familiar brands as Hershey's milk chocolate bars, Hershey's syrup, Hershey's cocoa, Almond Joy, Mr. Goodbar, Hershey's Kisses, Kit Kat, and Reese's peanut butter cups. Mars and Nestlé are Hershey's major confectionery competitors.

From the beginning, Milton Hershey was concerned about doing what was right. His firm was built with high standards of fairness, integrity, honesty, and respect. These standards influenced his relationship with his community, customers, and employees. An example of Hershey's concern for the community was the founding of an orphanage, the Hershey Industrial School (now called the Milton Hershey School), in 1909. Many of the children who attended the school became Hershey employees, and former Hershey chairman William Dearden (1976–1984) was one of the students. Today the ten-thousand-acre school houses and provides education for nearly eleven hundred socially disadvantaged children. Although Hershey is now a public company, the school is supported by a trust that owns 31 percent of Hershey Foods.

HERSHEY'S VALUES AND ETHICS PROGRAM

The strong value system put in place by Milton Hershey is still the guiding philosophy of Hershey Foods today. His system dictates that all employees conduct their business in an ethical manner. All Hershey employees are made aware of specific policies that provide guidance for handling ethical issues. Specific policies also exist for business relationships both inside and outside the company. The corporate philosophy and policies hinge on behaving with honesty, integrity, fairness, and respect to all employees, shareholders, customers, consumers, suppliers, and society in general. While providing quality products and services at a fair price for

This case was prepared by O. C. Ferrell, John Fraedrich, and Phylis Mansfield for classroom discussion, rather than to illustrate either effective or ineffective handling of an administrative, ethical, or legal decision by management.

an acceptable profit, Hershey also operates within legal and regulatory guidelines and strives to protect the environment.

Each year the company distributes the "Key Corporate Policies" booklet to all employees. The booklet consists of the organization's statement of corporate philosophy and policies regarding the use of corporate funds and resources, conflicts of interest, the antitrust law prohibition on price fixing, trading in Hershey Foods and other related securities, and the personal responsibilities of employees. Employees are asked to review the policies carefully, then sign, date, and return a certification card, which states that the employee has read, agrees with, and "will adhere to Hershey Foods Corp.'s 'Key Corporate Policies.'"

CONCERN FOR CUSTOMERS AND EMPLOYEES

Hershey has always emphasized quality products and good relationships with consumers. Today Hershey's Quality Assurance Division makes certain that customers receive full value for their money. By using the highest-quality ingredients and numerous quality-control checks, the firm even ensures that the right number of almonds go into each Almond Joy.

Ethics and social responsibility are an important part of the corporate culture and the way business is conducted on a daily basis. All managers go through ethics training programs to make sure that they understand how to handle the many complex issues they deal with in operating the company. Employees have a clear idea of the company's ethical values and know they will be supported in following them.

HERSHEY'S ADVERTISING BACKGROUND

Since the 1970s the company has, in part, achieved growth by wisely promoting its products. For example, Hershey directs a significant portion of its promotional expense to sponsorships. It has sponsored the National Collegiate Athletic Association (NCAA) Final Four tournament, marketing with a multibrand promotion linked to the NCAA games. As an NCAA corporate partner, Hershey has promoted special offers on all Hershey loose candy bars and has launched in-store promotions giving customers a shot at a trip to the annual college hoop championship. The Hershey and Reese's lines, along with other Hershey brands such as Kit Kat, Mounds, and Almond Joy, have been flagged in-store with displays. As part of store giveaways, retailers have received basketballs and jackets with the Final Four logos as well as tickets to the Final Four games. Hershey has activated its existing sponsorship of the National Football League (NFL) with a similar retail promotion. Its other sports tie-ins include a National Association for Stock Car Auto Racing (NASCAR) sponsorship and figure-skating and USA gymnastics sponsorships.

Promotional tie-ins are typical in modern advertising. Such tie-ins suggest to consumers an affiliation between the corporate sponsor and the object of the tie-in. The company values consumer perception of an association between sponsor and event or group because it can benefit from the goodwill possessed and generated by the other party.

Recently, sponsorship has turned to rock concert events in order to tap the lucrative high school– and college-age markets. Advertisers use celebrity endorsements to promote their products — realizing that the greater the number of people who recognize the celebrity, the greater the visibility for their products. This onslaught of advertising on the music industry was featured in a front-page story in *Billboard,* entitled "Madison Avenue Eyes Modern Rock, but Acts Remain Wary."

As has been discussed, Hershey is one of the best companies both ethically and financially. Yet as with all large corporations, problems occur on a daily basis. Lawsuits have become an ever-present reality for many, and Hershey is no exception. One such lawsuit involved R.E.M.

R.E.M.: Its Music and Reputation

R.E.M. formed as a group while the four members were students at the University of Georgia in Athens, Georgia, in April 1980. During the past two decades R.E.M. has developed a national and international reputation and has grown into one of the premier musical groups in the world. While other bands of similar talent have gone by the wayside, R.E.M. has prevailed by focusing on what is important to them as individuals and as a collective group. Band member Peter Buck cites their individuality and resolve as a group to do what they feel is right as a contributing factor to their success.

> R.E.M. have insisted on retaining creative control over every aspect of their careers, from concert dates to album-cover designs to videos. . . . It's not like we're asking for the brown M&M's to be taken out of the dish. We want the power of our lives in our own hands. We made a contract with the world that says: "We're going to be the best band in the world; you're going to be proud of us. But we have to do it our way."

R.E.M.'s View on Corporate Sponsorship

Part of doing it their way is avoiding corporate sponsorship and product endorsements, which the band members have managed to do since R.E.M.'s inception. While other bands have provided endorsements for tours, appearances, songs, and albums, R.E.M. has refused to participate in what could be extremely lucrative agreements, the band members citing their personal views that such activities are offensive and inappropriate.

This independence is due partly to R.E.M.'s credibility. Credibility in the music-world sense is the "widespread perception that an artist, band or individual has the respect of the population at large, as well as its peers. In rock and roll, credibility has always been a desirable quality."* It does not end with the musical performance, however. It includes integrity in attitude, integrity in regard to the audience, and fidelity to one's beliefs. One example of R.E.M.'s integrity was its refusal of an offer from Microsoft to use R.E.M.'s song "It's the End of the World as We Know It" in Microsoft's worldwide brand campaign. Instead, Microsoft settled on the Rolling Stones's song "Start Me Up," reportedly for a fee of close to $12 million.

R.E.M. has continued to reject corporate sponsorship for its tours. *Amusement Business* quoted R.E.M.'s booking agent as saying that it is the only band to go to Singapore, Taiwan, and Hong Kong without any sponsor affiliation, including airlines and hotels. In addition, the band has a detailed contractual agreement with the concert promoter, which requires prior written approval for the use of the name, logo, photograph, or likeness of the group in connection with any commercial enterprise. Even the concert tickets have specific language that is subject to prior approval. These limitations, which appear in every R.E.M. agreement, have been enforced since the band's inception. At that time R.E.M. acquired rights to a federal trademark and service mark for its own use for entertainment, services, recordings, and clothing. The public knows that R.E.M. is the source of the goods and services bearing that name and mark and accords the mark additional value because of the band's credibility.

THE PROBLEM: HERSHEY'S KIT KAT PROMOTION AND R.E.M.

Hershey was promoting its Kit Kat candy bar and advertising on rock music stations. In Atlanta, the radio advertisement talked about the chance of winning a trip for two to an R.E.M. concert at Hershey Park Stadium or one of twenty-five copies of R.E.M.'s latest CD. There was even a toll-free number to call and a promise that the first ten thousand callers would be automatically entered in the contest to win the concert trip to Hershey, Pennsylvania.

The radio commercial was aired on stations that played a generic rock music piece that sounded like R.E.M.'s, but no R.E.M. music was used. The generic piece, along with the text of the radio commercial, suggested a link with R.E.M. It may have implied R.E.M.'s involvement and possibly its sponsorship or affiliation with Hershey's Kit Kat contest. The message that callers heard on the 800 number may well have reinforced this impression. It began with "Welcome to the Kit Kat R.E.M.

Gina Arnold, "Cashing in on Cred," San Francisco Chronicle, January 22, 1995.

concert at Hershey Park Stadium sweepstakes line" and continued with the same specifics about the prizes as the radio ad. Hershey's promotional agent for the campaign was Westwood Entertainment.

THE CONFLICT

R.E.M. considered Hershey and Westwood Entertainment's actions an infringement of its trademark and service mark. This alleged dilution of and injury to R.E.M.'s business reputation and the misappropriation of identity under the Lanham Act was of critical importance. Citing that among the major elements of R.E.M.'s success are its credibility with fans and its integrity in conducting its business affairs, R.E.M. reiterated that its name and music were not for sale. It charged Hershey with exploiting the magnetism of the R.E.M. name for commercial purposes and thus tarnishing the name and the band's artistic integrity. According to R.E.M., Hershey did not seek authorization for use of the R.E.M. name because it was aware that such authorization would not be granted for product endorsements. R.E.M. also claimed that, because of its public stance against doing product endorsements, the strong suggestion of a link between Kit Kat and R.E.M. in Hershey's ad would lead the public to believe that the band's members are hypocrites.

R.E.M.'s lawsuit charged that Westwood Entertainment's false and misleading representations created a likelihood of confusion and caused damage to R.E.M.'s business, reputation, and the goodwill extended to it by the public. According to the lawsuit, Westwood's actions violated Section 43(a) of the Lanham Act, U.S. Code 1125. R.E.M. asserted that Hershey also misappropriated the name and likeness of R.E.M. for its own gain. Unlike other causes of action for an invasion of privacy, a corporation may have rights and remedies similar to those of a private individual under misappropriation. R.E.M. asserted that Westwood appropriated the goodwill and reputation, commercial standing, and corporate identity of the R.E.M. name, as well as the personal identity of the band's members, for its own use. According to R.E.M., Westwood's conduct was causing and was likely to continue to cause substantial injury. For that reason, R.E.M. considered itself entitled to injunctive relief and to recover damages, including the fair market value of its services and injury to its goodwill, professional standing, and future publicity value, as well as profits, and reasonable attorneys' fees.

In its suit, R.E.M. asked that Westwood, acting as an agent for Hershey, be restrained from engaging in any of these activities:

1. Using the mark "R.E.M." in commercial advertising

2. Expressly or by implication representing to the public that Hershey is in any way connected or associated with R.E.M., including sponsorship

3. Passing off its goods as endorsed or approved by R.E.M.

4. Distributing any promotional materials bearing the R.E.M. name or mark

5. Diluting the distinctive quality of the R.E.M. name or reputation

6. Engaging in violations of Section 43 of the Lanham Act and state statute against false advertising

7. Otherwise infringing on the R.E.M. mark or unfairly competing in any manner whatsoever

R.E.M. also asked that Hershey be required to deliver for destruction all inventories, literature, brochures, or other materials that bear the R.E.M. name or likeness.

CONFLICT RESOLUTION

The lawsuit did not proceed, however, because all the parties involved decided to settle the matter out of court. The settlement included the following points:

1. R.E.M. and Westwood Entertainment would issue a joint press release announcing that the dispute between them had been amicably resolved.

2. Hershey and its agents, including its advertising agency, agreed not to use the R.E.M. name in connection with any commercial endorsement or promotion without prior written approval.

3. Although the prizes offered in the promotional contest would be awarded, neither Hershey nor its agents would make use of the list of names obtained through the contest 800 number or of any other information obtained in connection with the promotion.

4. Westwood One, the radio affiliate of Westwood Entertainment, would contribute $50,000 for distribution to ten charitable entities designated by R.E.M.*

Hershey has experienced few ethical challenges like the R.E.M. conflict. No matter how good the core values or ethics programs that may exist, there is always the possibility of errors in judgment. Because of its promotion agent, Westwood Entertainment, errors were made, but Hershey was ultimately responsible for the ethical issues.

Questions

1. Should celebrities own their "identities" and be able to protect them from the promotional activities of others?

2. Discuss any ethical concerns about the technique used by Hershey and its agents to gain contest entrants.

The law offices of Kilpatrick Stockton LLP, Atlanta, GA; Washington, DC; and Raleigh, NC.

3. Hershey Foods Corp. has an excellent ethical compliance program and a history of being a model ethical and socially responsible company. What organizational factors and/or relationships with its agents caused this ethical conflict? How can Hershey prevent this type of conflict in the future?

4. Do you think the settlement between Hershey and R.E.M. was fair?

These facts are from Hershey Foods Corp. web site, *http://www.hersheys.com/index.shtml* (accessed January 4, 2001); "Hershey Foods Announces Fourth Quarter Results," *PR Newswire,* January 26, 1996; "'Hershey Boys' Push for Postal Stamp," *Charleston Daily Mail,* October 2, 1995, p. 10A; Karen Riley, "Harmful Pleasures Put You at Risk of Paying More for Health Coverage," *Washington Times,* April 22, 1995, p. C1; "The Business Week 1,000," *Business Week,* Special Bonus Issue, 1992, p. 128; Gary Hoover, Alta Campbell, and Patrick J. Spain, *Hoover's Handbook* (Austin, Tex.: California Publishers Group West, 1991), p. 287; "Hershey Foods Philosophy and Values," Hershey Foods Corporation videotape (1990); "A Tradition of Excellence," Hershey Foods Corporation, August 1990; Steven S. Ross, "Green Groceries," *Mother Jones,* 14 (February–March 1989): 48–49. Debbie Gilbert, "R.E.M.: Why They're Still Around," *Memphis Flyer,* November 2, 1995, p. 13; Gina Arnold, "Cashing in on Cred," *San Francisco Chronicle,* January 22, 1995; Robert Sandall, "Sponsorship's Rocky Road," *Times London* (UK), July 2, 1995, p. 16; *Amusement Business* (November 1994); Linda Corman, "All About Chocolate," *New York Times,* February 21, 1993, sec. 3, p. 10; and *R.E.M./Athens, Ltd., Plaintiff* v. *Hershey Foods Corporation, Defendant,* August 1995, verified complaint (civil action court document obtained through America Online).

SPAM Versus Muppets

Jim Henson Productions, Inc., had created a new Muppet character, Spa'am, to debut in its movie *Muppet Treasure Island*. Spa'am, an exotic wild boar, was meant to be a humorous link with the tame domestic luncheon meat SPAM. But Hormel Foods Corporation, the manufacturer of SPAM, wasn't laughing. It claimed that the association would have a negative effect, causing a drop in the consumption of SPAM. Consequently, Hormel filed a civil lawsuit to determine the legality of Henson Productions' use of the Spa'am character. This is an instance of seeking from the legal system a solution to what is really an ethical dispute over the ownership and use of a brand name.

HORMEL AND SPAM

Hormel has made and marketed its popular SPAM luncheon meat since 1937. Made of pork and pork byproducts, SPAM is a distinctive, well-known brand and trademark. Along with the luncheon meat itself, Hormel produces, markets, and licenses other products bearing the SPAM trademark: clothing items, such as T-shirts, and sports items, such as golf balls. In the mid-1990s the SPAM name became more popular and, to some extent, a fashionable brand name.

The ancillary items, a secondary source of income for Hormel, are also meant to promote the sale of SPAM luncheon meat. It is assumed that those who purchase SPAM T-shirts and golf balls are consumers of the luncheon meat and that they associate these items with the meat product. Hormel also promotes the luncheon meat through its character SPAM-man, a person dressed as a giant can of SPAM. In addition, SPAM is featured in cooking contests seeking the most original use for the luncheon meat, as well as in contests focusing on how many different uses one can find for the product. SPAM has even been featured in a book by Joey Green on secondary uses of household products, *Polish Your Furniture with Panty Hose,* in which Green assures the reader that one can use sliced SPAM (and a polishing rag) to polish wood furniture.

At the same time, SPAM is often the target of jokes and disparaging remarks. In SPAMarama, an annual SPAM cooking contest, one of the entries was "SPAMpers,"

This case was prepared by Phylis Mansfield for classroom discussion, rather than to illustrate either effective or ineffective handling of an administrative, ethical, or legal decision by management.

Source: Case 2, "SPAM Versus Muppets," was prepared by Phylis Mansfield and is reprinted with her permission.

which involved a mother and her baby girl, a diaper pail, and a SPAM pâté. According to SPAMarama's founder, a lot of the judges became ill. SPAM has almost become an icon in itself; a surfing expedition on the Internet uncovered a "Church of SPAM," a "SPAM-page," a "SPAM joke-a-day," and numerous anti-SPAM spoofs.

Jim Henson Productions and the Muppets

In the 1950s Jim Henson created a group of puppets, known as the Muppets. Over the years many new puppets have been added to the original cast, and they have been featured in television programs as well as movies. The Muppets characters are well known as parodies of brand names, fictional characters, or celebrities. Even television programs and trademarks have been lampooned. The Muppets characters are primarily intended as children's entertainment and are part of the very popular television program, *Sesame Street*.

In addition, the Muppets are promoted through various articles of clothing, toys, and other products. Some of the Muppet alliances include Henson's joint venture with Hasbro and the makers of Calgon to produce a bath line of licensed products for children. Henson's company also teamed up with Hasbro toys and General Mills to develop a cross-promotion with the Muppets on 10 million boxes of Cheerios. Another cross-licensing program includes Henson's contract with the National Hockey League (NHL), in which its "Muppets Take the Ice" promotes Minute Maid, the league's "official juice sponsor," and the NHL.

The Muppet Movie: *Muppet Treasure Island*

Jim Henson Productions scheduled a movie, *Muppet Treasure Island*, for release in February 1996. Familiar characters such as Kermit the Frog, Miss Piggy, and Rizzo Rat star alongside some newly created puppets. The story line has Kermit, Miss Piggy, and Rizzo Rat landing on Treasure Island, which is inhabited by a tribe of wild boars. They encounter the leader, Spa'am, High Priest of the Boars, a newly created puppet character. At their initial meeting, Spa'am and his tribe capture Kermit and Rizzo, accusing them of "violating" the island, and Spa'am orders the trio to be tied to stakes. However, by the end of the picture, Spa'am has joined forces with Kermit, Miss Piggy, and Rizzo Rat, and the group barely escapes the clutches of the truly evil Long John Silver.

Henson entered into several promotional agreements in connection with the movie, including contracts with General Mills, McDonald's, Hershey, Baskin-Robbins, and Dole. General Mills used characters from the movie on its boxes of

Cheerios, and McDonald's used movie scenes on its Happy Meals boxes. Hershey added candies shaped like the characters from the movie to its Hershey's Amazin' Fruit line. Besides the food product promotions, Henson had licensing agreements that would put the Muppet characters in a CD-ROM video game, in books, and on clothing, including T-shirts. In all merchandise, the character's likeness, as well as its name, would appear on the product, and the name of the movie, *Muppet Treasure Island,* would be prominently displayed.

Pending the outcome of the lawsuit, the Spa'am character was dropped from the licensing guide, but before that, the guidelines described Spa'am as "the noble . . . leader of the tribe of wild boars that live on Treasure Island . . . proud, yet grotesque . . . what they lack in personal hygiene, they make up for in bravery, and loud, spirited grunting." All pages of the licensing guide state in small print that "character names and likenesses are trademarks of Jim Henson Productions, Inc." A "TM" symbol accompanies the characters' names. Henson Productions asserted that consumers would purchase the movie-related merchandise, including Spa'am merchandise, because they liked the movie and/or the Muppets.

CONFLICT RESOLUTION

Hormel made several accusations against Jim Henson Productions in regard to the Muppet character Spa'am. According to Hormel, the character, seen as wild, untidy, and unattractive, would tarnish consumers' attitudes about its product, SPAM. Hormel suggested that its related products, such as T-shirts and golf balls, would be confused with those sold with Spa'am, reducing Hormel's sales. Furthermore, Hormel charged that Henson's use of the Spa'am character in the movie, as well as on ancillary merchandise, constituted both an infringement on its trademark, SPAM, and false advertising, in violation of the Lanham Act. The firm also raised state claims of unfair competition, deceptive practices, and trademark dilution.

Hormel focused on the damaging effect that the character Spa'am might have because of his unattractive physical appearance and hostile behavior. According to Hormel, consumers would be likely to perceive Spa'am as unhygienic and generally unpleasant. To support its charges, Hormel brought in an expert witness, Dr. Laura Peracchio, who had expertise in consumer behavior. In her statement to the court, she noted that the character Spa'am is "unappealing and will lead to negative associations on the part of consumers because he has small eyes, protruding teeth, warts, a skull on his headdress, is generally untidy, and speaks in a deep voice with poor grammar and diction." She added that Spa'am is threatening in his initial contact with Kermit and the others and that his later camaraderie with the trio is inconsistent behavior and will not dispel the negative impression stemming from the earlier negative conduct.

THE LANHAM ACT AND TRADEMARK INFRINGEMENT

The Lanham Act addresses trademark infringement in part:

> Any person who shall, without the consent of the registrant . . . use in commerce any reproduction, counterfeit, copy or colorable imitation of a registered mark in connection with the sale, offering for sale, distribution or advertising of any goods or services on or in connection with which such use is likely to cause confusion, or to cause mistake, or to deceive . . . shall be liable in a civil action by the registrant for the remedies hereinafter provided.

A critical issue in trademark infringement is whether a considerable number of consumers are likely to be misled or confused about the original source of the goods in question. Some factors that might cause confusion are the strength of the registrant's trademark, similarity of uses of the two products, their proximity, the defendant's good or bad faith in using the mark, the quality of the second product, and the sophistication of the consumer. The primary factor in court decisions is the extent to which consumers might confuse the sources of the two products.

However, the Lanham Act also gives some protection to artistic expression. With regard to parodies, which are a form of artistic expression protected by the First Amendment, a decision on trademark protection would be made by weighing the public interest in free expression against the public interest in avoiding consumer confusion. Therefore, if a parody was very likely to confuse a consumer about the source of a product or service, the First Amendment would not protect it. The definition of a parody is that it must convey two messages simultaneously: that it is both imitating and mocking the original. If something presented as a parody does not sufficiently convey the latter message, it is vulnerable under trademark law. Usually, the more distinctive a trademark, the more likely it is that consumer confusion will occur if imitative products are traded. However, in the case of parody — that is, the successful blending of imitation and mockery — the more well known the original trademark, the easier it is to convey a message that the second item is a spoof. A parody relies upon a difference from the original mark, presumably a humorous difference, in order to produce its desired effect.

THE DEBATE IN COURT

SPAM and Spa'am are similar, a requirement for parody; yet they are also easily distinguishable in written form, as well as when spoken. The word *Spa'am* is pronounced in two distinct syllables in the Muppet movie; additionally, it is always used in context with a Muppet character, whether in the movie or in related merchandise. Because the Muppets are well known for parodying brand names and celebrities, consumers are unlikely to confuse the character Spa'am with the luncheon meat SPAM. They would be more likely to conclude that the spoof came from Jim Henson Productions than to believe that Hormel sponsored the joke. While Henson representatives acknowledged that they did mean to conjure up a joke regarding Hormel's trademark, they denied any intent to confuse consumers about the two entities.

Hormel contended that the character Spa'am was competing directly with its SPAM-man, as well as with its own line of clothing. Yet Hormel's own witnesses testified that purchasers of the SPAM clothing line were generally consumers of the luncheon meat. Since the Spa'am character looked like a Muppet-style puppet and was being marketed in association with the movie *Muppet Treasure Island,* it was highly likely that the customers of its ancillary products would associate it with the Muppets. Therefore, the products of luncheon meat and puppet entertainment were sufficiently far apart to prevent consumer confusion. Hormel's argument was further weakened by evidence submitted by Jim Henson Productions: cartoons, news articles, and television clips suggesting that SPAM should consider itself fortunate to be linked to a Muppet parody of its product rather than some other, more negative version.

THE COURT'S DECISION

Although no one enjoys being the butt of a joke, the requirement for a violation under trademark law is that confusion of the source, sponsorship, or affiliation has occurred or is likely to occur. That is not the same as a trademark having the "right not to be made fun of." Possibly, the humorous depiction of the Spa'am character actually reinforces the distinctiveness of the SPAM trademark by its reliance on SPAM's mark to successfully pull off the joke.

The court decided that Jim Henson Productions and its representatives acted in good faith, without "predatory intent" to capitalize on consumer confusion between the two products or to appropriate for itself any goodwill associated with SPAM. Hormel's claims against Jim Henson Productions were judged not sufficient to warrant a decision in its favor, and all claims against the Spa'am characterization, including trademark infringement, unfair competition, and false advertising, were denied. Kimba M. Wood, U.S. district judge, ruled that the Spa'am likeness and name "may be used on merchandise that clearly identifies Spa'am as a character from a Muppet motion picture, because such uses would be unlikely to cause consumer confusion or dilute Hormel's trademark."

Questions

1. Are there ethical implications when a company profits at the expense of another company's product or name, even if a parody is involved? Is the Lanham Act (as described in this case) sufficient for dealing with this type of situation?

2. Should a portion of the income gained from parodies of other trademarks or celebrities be shared with the targets of the spoofs?

3. Because the court ruled that there were no legal violations or damages in this case, does it mean that there were no ethical issues? Justify your answer.

4. What should an organization do in order not to violate the Lanham Act and to avoid costly court disputes over damages in matters such as trademarks and copyrights?

These facts are from Pam Weisz, "Muppetbath Takes Kids Away," *Brandweek*, April 18, 1994, p. 12; Terry Lefton, "Hasbro Bets Muppets Will Be Cereal Killers," *Brandweek*, February 14, 1994, pp. 1, 6; Terry Lefton, "NHL Strikes Minute Maid Promo Pact," *Brandweek*, December 5, 1994, p. 4; segment on *The Today Show*, NBC, December 4, 1995; *Austin American Statesman*, March 30, 1995, p. 16; and U.S. District Court, Southern District of New York, *Hormel Foods Corporation, Plaintiff* v. *Jim Henson Productions, Inc., Defendant.* 95 Civ. 5473 (KMW) Opinion & Order, September 22, 1995.

Case 3

Firestone's Tire Recall

The relationship between Ford and Firestone began in the early 1900s. Firestone emerged in 1900 in Akron, Ohio, and in 1906, the first transaction between the companies occurred when Henry Ford bought two thousand sets of tires from Harvey Firestone. Since that sale, both companies have become major players in their industries. Ford had record operating earnings of $7.2 billion in 1999, the most for any automotive company ever. The company spends about $7 billion annually on research and development and boasts a global portfolio of more than five thousand patents. Ford Motor Co. consists of Ford, Volvo, Mazda, Lincoln, Mercury, Jaguar, Land Rover, and Aston Martin vehicles.

Firestone, despite growth over the past hundred years, has faced more turbulence than Ford. In 1978, Firestone recalled 14.5 million tires — the largest tire recall in history. Excess application of the adhesive that binds the rubber and steel had caused five hundred tread separations and blowouts. Firestone paid a $500,000 fine for concealing safety problems. This recall weakened the financial position of the company and resulted in the 1988 purchase by Tokyo-based Bridgestone, Inc., for $2.6 million. The parent company, founded in 1931 by Shojiro Ishibashi, developed its name from the English translation of the founder's family name, "stone bridge." Bridgestone successfully eased the struggling company back to profits. Firestone composed 40 percent of the parent company's 1999 consolidated sales.

Many other tire manufacturers also faced recalls in the late twentieth century. On March 12, 1980, Uniroyal recalled almost 2 million tires because of tread separation. B.F. Goodrich recalled a million tires on August 13, 1974, because of improper inflation and installation. Kelly-Springfield faced a recall on January 28, 1976, when three hundred thousand tires were recalled because of tread separation. General Tire recalled one hundred and eighty-seven thousand tires on January 24, 1979, because of exposed belt wire. Cooper Tire & Rubber recalled more than one hundred and fifty-six thousand tires on August 11, 1988, because of bead flaw. More recently, on April 14, 1998, Kelly-Springfield recalled more than five hundred thousand tires because of sidewall cracking. The number of recalls shows that tire failure has been an industrywide problem for the past twenty-five years.

The case was prepared by Dana Schubert and O.C. Ferrell for classroom discussion, rather than to illustrate either effective or ineffective handling of an administrative, ethical, or legal decision by management.

THE TIMELINE FOR THE FIRESTONE RECALL

In July 1998, Sam Boyden, an associate research administrator for State Farm Insurance, received a phone call from a claims handler asking him to determine if other cases of Firestone tread failure existed. He discovered twenty such cases dating back to 1992. Being a car fanatic, Boyden realized this was not a coincidence, but rather a series of related accidents. He sent an e-mail to the National Highway Traffic Safety Administration (NHTSA) alerting them to his findings. They thanked him but basically ignored the message until early 2000.

In January 2000, Anna Werner, a reporter for KHOU-TV in Houston, and two colleagues researched tread separation and accidents in Texas after an attorney mentioned the issue. Based on the results of their investigation, the television station aired a nine-minute segment. Werner also reported her findings to Joan Claybrook, former chief of the NHTSA. In the weeks that followed, many citizens called the television station to relate their own stories of Firestone tire failure on Ford Explorers. Soon, KHOU-TV began directing the flood of local calls to the NHTSA.

Despite the flow of information from Sam Boyden and KHOU-TV, the NHTSA was slow to take action. In early march, the initial two investigators, Steve Beretzky and Rob Wahl, found twenty-two complaints of tread separation that they marked for "initial evaluation." Between March and May, the number of complaints on the national level skyrocketed. On May 2, three senior NHTSA officials increased the status of the inquiry to "preliminary investigation." Within six days, the NHTSA requested that Firestone supply production data and complaint files. Firestone submitted this data to the NHTSA on July 27, and Ford was copied the next day.

Sean Kane also tried to alert the NHTSA of the recurrent problems. Kane, a former employee of the Center for Auto Safety, had started Strategic Safety, a research group interested in product-liability issues. In late July, Kane received an e-mail from a Venezuelan source who disclosed Ford's tire-replacement program there. Ford recalled the tires, without Firestone's backing, because of problems with tread separation and mislabeled products dating back to 1998. Ford discovered defect rates from the Valencia, Venezuela, plant one thousand times higher than from the Decatur, Illinois, plant. On August 1, Strategic Safety and the political action group Public Citizen issued a press release asking Ford for a vehicle recall.

After Ford received the data, it immediately started the analysis process, and within eighteen hours the information was crammed into Cray Supercomputers and results were printed. Of the 2,498 complaints logged on tire failure, 81 percent involved the fifteen-inch P235/75R15 models. When tread separation was considered, 84 percent of some 1,699 complaints involved Ford's Explorer, Bronco, Ranger, or F-150 SUVs and trucks. Ford relayed the results to Firestone, and the two companies met in Dearborn, Michigan, on August 5 to discuss the issue. At that time, the NHTSA was investigating twenty-one deaths that were possibly related. When the number of possibly related deaths jumped to forty-six three days later, Ford, Firestone, and the NHTSA met to discuss a plan of action. The next day, August 9, they issued a recall of 6.5 million tires.

THE RECALL

The recall included 3.8 million P235/75R15 radial ATX and ATXII and 2.7 million Wilderness AT tires from the Decatur, Illinois plant. Firestone's official recall procedure was organized by state. The recall immediately affected Arizona, California, Florida, and Texas, where the greatest percentage of casualties had occurred. Based on NHTSA data, Florida and Texas each represented 22 percent of the complaints, followed by California at 20 percent and Arizona at 5 percent. This first recall portion was expected to be complete by October 2000. The second phase, involving Alabama, Georgia, Louisiana, Mississippi, Nevada, Oklahoma, and Tennessee, was expected to be completed by the end of 2000. Firestone announced that the recall in all remaining states would be complete by the end of 2001. It was 90 percent complete in late December 2000.

Firestone issued letters to all affected customers detailing the procedure for replacement. Customers affected by the recall could take their tires to Firestone retailers, Ford dealerships, or other tire retail outlets and expect a similar Firestone tire or equivalent competitor's model. Ford began testing other brands on the Explorer and determined thirty-four acceptable replacements. In addition to the tire cost, the replacement included mounting and balancing fees. If replacements had been purchased before the official recall, customers who provided a receipt would be issued a reimbursement up to $100 per tire.

Both companies developed advertisements and public information announcements to inform consumers how to determine whether their tires were included in the recall. Consumers could call a toll-free number if they had questions about tire models or eligibility. Despite Firestone's gradual plan, Ford encouraged all concerned motorists included in the recall, regardless of their location, to replace questionable tires immediately and, if necessary, to save the receipts for later reimbursement. Consumers not directly included in the recall could purchase new Firestone tires based on a credit system determined by the age and wear of their current tires.

After continued investigations, the NHTSA encouraged Firestone to expand the recall to other sizes and models of tires, but Firestone declined. On September 1, the NHTSA issued a consumer advisory to warn of potential problems with other Firestone tires. These included ATXP205/75R15 tires on Chevy Blazers and ATX 31X10.50R15LT tires on 1991 through 1994 Nissan pickups, as well as other sizes of ATX, Firehawk ATX, ATX23 Degree, Widetrack Radial Baja, and Wilderness AT tires — mostly those originating from the Decatur factory. Because these tires are not included in the official recall list, replacements are not free. The NHTSA suggested that consumers save receipts in the event that Firestone increased the depth of the recall. Included in this advisory was a list of precautionary measures for consumers to help avoid tire failure.

FIRESTONE'S RESPONSE TO THE CRISIS

- During the recall, Firestone faced a potential strike by the United Steelworkers of America that would have disrupted production at nine of eleven U.S. plants. Firestone successfully negotiated with union officials to avoid that potentially disruptive strike.

- Firestone began receiving tires from the parent company's plant in Japan on August 23 and expected between three hundred and twenty-five thousand and three hundred and fifty thousand to arrive before September 1. Bridgestone planned to send at least one shipment per day until the recall issue is resolved.

- The Firestone U.S. factories doubled the number of tire molds in use and increased production by seven thousand tires per day.

- During Senate hearings, Firestone officials accepted full responsibility and admitted the company had made "bad tires." Masatoshi Ono stepped down as CEO, and former Executive Vice President John Lampe was named to replace Ono. Information surfaced that Firestone had prior knowledge of potential tread separation problems dating back to 1994. The company admitted it had increased production during this time in order to dilute the failure rate. Additionally, internal memos warned of bubbles on the tire shoulder. Company officials stated that further investigation was not warranted because historically failure rates were determined by warranty claims and those had not shown significant patterns.

FORD'S RESPONSE TO THE CRISIS

- Ford increased the staff monitoring its help line from three hundred to eight hundred employees and kept it open twenty-four hours a day.

- Ford closed new car production plants for three weeks so that tires would not be used on new cars but would be available as replacement tires. The six thousand workers from the three closed plants were still paid and spent much of their time assisting in the transport of tires to dispersal outlets.

- Ford created a five-hundred person crisis-management team to devise creative tactics to speed the recall procedure.

- Ford purchased tire molds for Firestone competitors, to enable the entire industry to produce a greater quantity of replacement tires.

- Ford approached other tire manufacturers to request that they increase production of suitable replacement tires.

"THE BLAME GAME," OR WHOSE FAULT WAS IT?

The delay between the discovery of tire failure and the decision to communicate with owners of Ford Explorers is a highly debated issue in this recall. The tire problem is now better understood, with statistical studies pointing to the same conclusions. Firestone made a public announcement accepting full responsibility for the faulty tires. When Ford analyzed Firestone's data, the company noticed ten times more complaints stemming from tires originating in the Decatur factory, specifically tires made in 1994 and 1995. Questions have arisen about the skill of replacement workers who filled in at the Decatur factory during its two-year employee strike known as "The War of '94–'95." Many people suggest that quality inspections were compromised as tires piled up on the factory floor and that when employees returned from the strike, old dried rubber was used in production.

Another factor under consideration is the quality of the Decatur facility. The building was constructed in 1942, used to store telecommunications for the United States Armed Forces for nineteen years, and then purchased by Firestone in 1962. Because the Decatur plant was insufficiently air-conditioned, it had a high humidity level, which decreases the adhesive properties needed to bind rubber to steel. This effect became apparent because tires produced during the low-humidity winters were of higher quality than those produced during the humid summer months. Another contributing factor was the age and condition of the equipment used to mix raw materials and press steel together. In addition, the plant's vulcanization process, which uses heat and pressure to unite the rubber fragments into one product, is suspected of having had temperature-control problems. Poor quality can result when temperatures are too hot or not hot enough.

Although many people feel that Firestone is the culprit, others believe that Ford should share in the blame. The design of the Ford Explorer as well as tire-pressure recommendations have been under scrutiny to determine if these factors contributed to the rate of tire separations and rollover accidents. Ford initially recommended a low tire pressure of 26 psi for two main reasons. First, lower tire pressure compensates for the stiff suspension and thus produces a softer ride. Underinflated tires are problematic, however, because more surface area encountering the road creates more wear and more flexible sidewalls, ultimately leading to overheated tires. Second, the Explorer's design consists of a high center of gravity and short wheelbase. Both of these traits are characteristic of high rollover frequency. Low tire pressure creates sloppy steering, or low responsiveness, which could increase the chance that a driver would roll over because of overcorrecting or making sudden maneuvers. Excess weight is another factor that leads to high friction and high heat. Because Ford Explorers are often overloaded with passengers, luggage, and other items, investigators are trying to determine if this could be a contributing factor.

After learning that tread separation might be an issue, Ford requested that Firestone complete tests to determine if a problem existed in the specific combination of Ford Explorers and Firestone tires. The tests, completed in Arizona in late

February and early March, involved two hundred and forty-three heavily worn tires from sixty-three Explorers. No problems were discovered at that time and both companies dropped the issue.

Regardless of what consumers believe to be the predominant cause of the problem, research is being conducted to develop more concrete evidence. Until that time, both companies and the NHTSA are taking precautions by increasing suggested acceptable tire-pressure requirements to between 26 and 30 psi as well as advising consumers to wear seat belts, travel lighter, reduce speeds, and limit travel in hot areas.

LEGAL AND FINANCIAL IMPLICATIONS FOR FORD AND FIRESTONE

According to current vehicle liability conditions, automobile manufacturers are not responsible for replacing poor-quality tires. While Ford is therefore not directly liable for the recall costs, it is subject to private lawsuits and criminal charges for the fourteen hundred complaints, five hundred twenty-five injuries, and one hundred forty-eight deaths in the United States. The Venezuelan government and its consumer protection agency are pursuing Ford concerning forty-six deaths involving Explorers that occurred in Venezuela.

The financial implications of the recall have been detrimental to the survival of Firestone. Although the company is trying to isolate the problem as one involving only certain tires made in one Illinois plant, it is having a difficult time maintaining an image of overall quality. According to a Harris poll, 67 percent of eight hundred and fourteen people responded "extremely to very likely" to the question, "How likely is it that this tire recall would influence your decision to purchase a Firestone product?" An additional 18 percent responded "somewhat likely." After the recall announcement, Firestone's stock price dropped 47 percent in just one month. The estimated costs to Bridgestone are $500 million. It is yet to be determined whether Firestone will recover from this substantial blow. It is unlikely that another U.S. tire manufacturer will purchase Firestone because the market share of the combined companies would exceed the recommended limits, resulting in suspicions of monopolistic intent.

Ford has suffered a less severe financial setback than Firestone thus far, but its image and stock price are not unaffected. In the same poll mentioned above, the tire recall was "extremely or very likely" to influence 25 percent of the respondents in their decision to purchase a Ford product, while 22 percent said the recall was "somewhat likely" to influence their decision. Ford has tried to focus the problem on Firestone by saying it is a "tire issue" not a "vehicle issue." Ford's stock price dropped 18 percent in the month after the recall announcement, partially as a result of decreased consumer confidence.

THE IMPACT ON OTHER COMPANIES

Many other organizations were influenced by the recall, including tire distributors nationwide. Many large tire retailers took a proactive stance and removed Firestone brands from their sales floors. Leading this movement was Sears, which made that decision before the recall was officially announced. Sears, National Tire and Battery, and other retailers fully refunded money to customers who had purchased recalled tires and included the mounting and balancing costs if replacements were purchased. Many small retail operations that focused strictly on Firestone tires changed their names and expanded or altered their product lines to avoid the possibility of becoming obsolete or going bankrupt.

The recall affected competing tire companies as well. Other manufacturers, such as Goodyear and Michelin, helped ease the recall effort by increasing production to reduce the tire shortage caused by so many consumers seeking replacements. However, many consumers speculate on possible gains made by competitors because of the crisis. Goodyear spent an extra $1 million on television and radio promotions, full-page newspaper ads, and banner ads on Yahoo! and AOL, saying that the increases were "in specific response to the recall, but done with good taste." Michelin decided to continue with normal advertising plans, which happened to coincide with the recall news. Before the crisis, each tire company had a brand image it hoped to promote: Goodyear produced reliable tires; Michelin produced safe tires; and Firestone made high-performance tires. Now those images are being called on to help customers associate desired benefits with the companies that provide them.

THE FUTURE

In addition to the financial and legal implications for Ford and Firestone, the problems and subsequent recall will affect the government, regulatory agencies, and other businesses. Many suggestions have arisen at the organizational, industry, and national levels. These include implementing a nylon layer, or cap, to brace the tire and reduce the risks of separation and creating stricter quality-inspection procedures and requirements within the individual companies. On the industry level, it has been suggested that tires pass more rigorous testing by nonbiased parties. Currently, consumers can research all aspects of car quality except tires. Creating consumer reports on tire durability, traction, strength, and other important traits has been suggested. During the Senate hearings, Ford vowed to voluntarily disclose to the U.S. government any future overseas recalls.

On September 7, 2000 the Senate introduced a bill that would hold executives criminally liable for withholding information on foreign recalls or defective products that result in death. The charge would be second-degree murder with a punishment up to fifteen years in prison for selling unsafe merchandise. The bill passed on October 11, 2000. Additionally, the Tread Act was proposed on September 14, 2000, to improve consumer protection and increase communication between the government, tire manufacturers, and motor vehicle companies.

Questions

1. To what extent do companies need to make a proactive effort to collect and analyze data concerning possible safety issues?

2. What mistakes did Ford, Firestone, and the NHTSA each make in early attempts to handle the crisis?

3. What possible ethical implications are involved in accepting responsibility versus blaming others?

4. Suggest measures that Firestone could take to improve tire quality in the future.

These facts are from Stephen Power and Clare Ansberry, "Bridgestone/Firestone Says It Made 'Bad Tires,'" *Wall Street Journal,* September 13, 2000, pp. A3, A6; Bill Vlasic, "Anatomy of a Crisis," *Fort Collins Coloradoan,* September 4, 2000, pp. C1, C2; Devon Spurgeon, "State Farm Researcher's Sleuthing Helped Prompt Firestone Recall," *Wall Street Journal,* September 1, 2000, pp. B1, B6; Jason Szip, "Firestone's Japanese Parent Hit Again," *Fox Market Wire,* September 1, 2000, *http:// foxmarketwire.com/090100/tirestrike_side2.sml* (accessed September 1, 2000); Melita Marie Garza, Lauren Comander, and Patrick Cole, "Problems at Tire Plant Alleged," *Chicago Tribune,* August, 20, 2000, pp. 1, 10; Lori Grant, "More Retailers Pull 3 Firestone Tires from Stock," *USA Today,* August 7, 2000, p. 1B; Timothy Aeppel, "Firestone Milestone Brings on Dilemma," *Wall Street Journal,* August 18, 2000, p. B8; Lauren Comander, "Firestone Tires Shipped from Japan to Boost Supply," *Chicago Tribune,* August 23, 2000, pp. 1, 2; Claudia H. Deutsch, "Where Rubber Meets the Road; Recall of Firestone Tires Is Aimed at Damage Control," *New York Times on the Web,* August 10, 2000, *http://archives.nytimes.com.../fastweb?getdoc_allyears2-qpass+db365+564511+11+ wAAA+ Firestone%7* (accessed August 21, 2000); Calvin Sims, "A Takeover with Problems for Japanese Tire Maker," *New York Times on the Web,* August 10, 2000, *http://archives.nytimes.com.../ fastweb?getdoc+allyears2qpass+db365+564535+10_wAAA=Firestone%7* (accessed August 21, 2000); David Kiley, "Bridgestone Exec Will Speak to Congress," *Fort Collins Coloradoan,* August 30, 2000, p. D7; James R. Healey, "What You Don't Know About Your Tires," *USA Today,* August 11, 2000, p. B1; Robert L. Simison, "For Ford CEO Nasser, Damage Control Is the New 'Job One,'" *Wall Street Journal,* September 11, 2000, pp. A1, A8; Kathryn Kranhold and Erin White, "The Perils and Potential Rewards of Crisis Management for Firestone," *Wall Street Journal,* September 8, 2000, pp. B1, B4; Robert Guy Matthews, "How the Rubber Meets the Road," *Wall Street Journal,* September 8, 2000, pp. B1, B4; Stephen Power, "Update Needed for Tire Rules, Activists Argue," *Wall Street Journal,* September 8, 20000, pp. B1, B4; "Consumer Advisory: Potentially Dangerous Tires," *Fox Market Wire,* September 1, 2000, *http://www.foxmarketwire.com/090100/tiredeaths_ list.sml* (accessed September 1, 2000).

Sunbeam Corporation and "Chainsaw Al"

W hen John Stewart and Thomas Clark founded the Chicago Flexible Shaft Company in Dundee, Illinois, in 1897 they probably never expected that the company would be facing ethical and financial dilemmas more than a hundred years later. Like many corporations, the firm has changed and faced many crises. It has acquired rival companies, added totally new product lines, changed its name, gone through bankruptcy, gone public, rebounded, re-structured, relocated, and hired and fired many CEOs, including "Chainsaw Al."

A HUNDRED PLUS YEARS OF CHANGE

Sunbeam is a well-known and recognized designer, manufacturer, and marketer of consumer products. Sunbeam products are considered household staple items and are known for their use in cooking, health care, and personal care. During its hundred years of operation, Sunbeam has grown and changed according to soci-etal needs. It operates facilities in Canada, England, Hong Kong, Mexico, the United States, and Venezuela. A few of the most recognized brand names Sun-beam markets today include Coleman, First Alert, Grillmaster, Health-O-Meter, Mixmaster, Mr. Coffee, Oster, Osterizer, Powermate, and Campingaz.

The first products that it manufactured and sold were agricultural tools. In 1910 the company began manufacturing electrical appliances, one of the first be-ing a clothes iron. The 1930s were the time of the Great Depression, yet Sunbeam's electric products sold well. Despite the Depression, housewives throughout the country quickly accepted the Sunbeam Mixmaster, automatic coffeemaker, and pop-up toaster, which were launched in those years.

Although the company name was not officially changed to Sunbeam Corpora-tion until 1946, John Stewart and Thomas Clark adopted the name Sunbeam and started using it in their advertising campaigns in 1910. The fourteen years following

This case was prepared by Carol A. Rustad and Linda E. Rustad for classroom discussion, rather than to illustrate either effective or ineffective handling of an administrative, ethical, or legal deci-sion by management.

Source: "Sunbeam Corporation and 'Chainsaw Al'" was prepared by Carol A. Rustad and Linda E. Rustad and is reprinted with their permission.

the Depression were times of growth and innovation; businesses were booming, and the U.S. economy was stable. The next major development came in 1960 as Sunbeam acquired its rival appliance maker, the John Oster Manufacturing Company. That acquisition helped make Sunbeam the leading manufacturer of electric appliances.

In the 1980s, a time of high inflation and interest rates, the world was recovering from the Vietnam conflict and corporations were going through acquisitions, mergers, closing, and restructuring — doing whatever they could to continue operating profitably. In 1981 Allegheny International, an industry conglomerate, acquired Sunbeam. Allegheny kept the Sunbeam name and added John Zink (air-pollution control devices) and Hanson Scale (bathroom scales) to the Sunbeam product line. In 1988 sales of other divisions of Allegheny International declined, and the company was forced into bankruptcy.

In 1990, the Sunbeam division was bought from Allegheny International's creditors by investors Michael Price, Michael Steinhardt, and Paul Kazarian. They renamed the division the Sunbeam-Oster Company. Just two years after the purchase, Sunbeam-Oster went public. The next year, Kazarian was forced out of his chairman position and out of the company. Sunbeam-Oster relocated to Florida that same year and bought the consumer products unit of DeVilbiss Health Care. In 1994 Sunbeam-Oster bought Rubbermaid's outdoor furniture business. In 1995 the company changed its name back to Sunbeam Corporation.

ALBERT DUNLAP, A.K.A. "CHAINSAW AL"

In June 1996 Sunbeam had more than twelve thousand stock-keeping units (SKUs). SKUs are individual variations of product lines; every different style or color of a product results in an item having a different SKU. Sunbeam also had twelve thousand employees, as well as twenty-six factories worldwide, sixty-one warehouses, and six headquarters. That was the situation when "Chainsaw Al" — Albert Dunlap — came into the picture.

Also known as "Rambo in Pinstripes" or "The Shredder," Dunlap gained his reputation as one of the country's toughest executives because he eliminated thousands of jobs. He was known for his ability to restructure and turn around companies that were failing financially. Sunbeam Corporation needed help. Its earnings had been declining rapidly since December 1994, and by 1996 the stock was down 52 percent and earnings had declined by 83 percent.

Dunlap's reputation and business theory preceded him throughout the world. His operating philosophy was to make extreme cuts in all areas of operations, including extensive layoffs, to streamline business. Dunlap authored a book entitled *Mean Business*. In the preface he stressed that making money for shareholders is the most important goal of any business.

In order to make money for shareholders, Dunlap had created four simple rules of business: (1) get the right management team, (2) cut back to the lowest costs, (3) focus on the core business, and (4) get a real strategy. By following those four rules, Dunlap helped turn around companies in seventeen states and across three continents. According to Al Dunlap in the preface of *Mean Business,* the list of companies he had worked with included Sterling Pulp & Paper (1967–1977), American Can (1977–1982), Lily-Tulip (1983–1986), Diamond International, Canenham Forest Industries, formerly Crown-Zellerback (1986–1989), Australian National Industries (1989), Consolidated Press Holdings (1991), as well as Scott Paper Company (1994–1995).

AL'S FIRST STEP

In July 1996 Michael Price and Michael Steinhardt hired Dunlap as the CEO and chairman of the board for Sunbeam Corporation. Price and Steinhardt were two of the original investors who had bought Sunbeam from bankrupt Allegheny International and together owned 42 percent of the stock. Before hiring Dunlap, they had tried, unsuccessfully, to sell Sunbeam. The failure to sell made them decide to see if Dunlap could save the company.

By hiring Chainsaw Al, Price and Steinhardt knew full well that his reputation and operating theory would mean huge cuts in all areas of the company, as well as extensive layoffs. They believed, however, that he was the one person who could turn the company around and increase stock prices and profits.

The increase in stock prices did occur, almost instantly. On July 19, 1996, the day Dunlap was named chairman and CEO of Sunbeam, the stock jumped 49 percent. The jump increased the share price from $12\frac{1}{2}$ to $18\frac{5}{8}$, adding $500 million to Sunbeam's market value. The stock continued to increase and reached a record high of $52 per share in March 1998.

Dunlap's reputation and his acceptance of the position at Sunbeam caused the initial stock increase. Dunlap realized, however, that his reputation alone would not hold the stock price up and that he needed to start the process of turning Sunbeam around.

The first move he made was to get the right management team. His very first hire was Russ Kersh, a former employee of Dunlap. A contract was written during a weekend so that Kersh could start the same day as Dunlap, as executive vice president of finance and administration. In *Mean Business,* Dunlap called the right management team his "Dream Team for Sunbeam" (p. 281). Only one senior executive was kept from the old Sunbeam management team. The new management team included Kersh and twenty-five people who had previously worked for Dunlap at various companies. Dunlap saw logic in hiring these people because they had all worked with him and had been successful in past turnarounds. Once the first step had been accomplished, Dunlap and the Dream Team for Sunbeam quickly went into action, implementing the second rule: to cut back to the lowest costs.

SECOND STEP: CUT BACK

All the employees at Sunbeam knew of Dunlap's reputation for eliminating jobs. According to Dunlap, "Sunbeam's employees wanted a leader and knew things had to change. Employees want stability. Restructuring actually brings stability, because the future is more clear" (*Mean Business*, p. 283). What people want and need, many could argue, is job security, and knowing his reputation did not make the employees feel secure.

The premise of wanting and needing security relates to psychologist Abraham Maslow's hierarchy of needs, which can be applied to what motivates employees to perform. The theory states that all people have five basic needs, which they strive to satisfy in a hierarchical order: physiological, security, social, esteem, and self-actualization. These needs can be satisfied through various means, but each need must be met before a person will move to the next level in the hierarchy. Security needs, which are posited as being second in the hierarchy of needs, relate to protecting oneself from physical and economic harm. The employees' security needs were being threatened at Sunbeam, and economic harm was about to occur to many of them. On hearing of Dunlap's layoff plans, Labor Secretary Robert Reich remarked: "There is no excuse for treating employees as if they are disposable pieces of equipment" (*Chainsaw*, p. 68).

As expected, and true to Dunlap's reputation, layoffs occurred. After less than four months as the chairman and CEO of Sunbeam, Chainsaw Al announced plans to eliminate half of the twelve thousand worldwide employees. Layoffs affected all levels at Sunbeam. Management and clerical staff positions were cut from 1,529 to 697, and headquarters staff was cut by 60 percent, from 308 to 123 employees. Around the same time the company's share prices rose to the mid-20s, and one of the original investors, Michael Steinhardt, sold his shares and divested himself of his Sunbeam connection altogether.

Another method used by Dunlap to cut back to the lowest costs was to reduce the number of SKUs from twelve thousand to fifteen hundred. When Dunlap took over at Sunbeam, it had thirty-six variations of styles and colors of a clothes iron. Variation, of course, allows differentiation, which is an acceptable strategy in business. But having thirty-six variations of a consumer product such as an iron can be viewed as unnecessary and costly. Eliminating variation and duplication helps eliminate cannibalization. Companies need to differentiate themselves from the competition in areas that are not easily duplicated, or they end up competing on price alone. Dunlap pursued service as the area to differentiate Sunbeam from competitors in the appliance business.

Eliminating ten thousand five hundred SKUs enabled Dunlap to rid the company of factories and warehouses — another cost-saving method. He disposed of eighteen factories worldwide, reducing their number from twenty-six to eight, and brought down the number of warehouses from sixty-one to eighteen. The layoff of thousands of employees, coupled with the reduction of SKUs, factories, and warehouses meant that fewer headquarter locations would be needed. Thus the six headquarters located throughout the country were consolidated into one facility in Delray Beach, Florida — Dunlap's primary residence.

STEPS THREE AND FOUR

Once the cost-cutting strategies had been carried out, Dunlap began to practice his third rule: that is, to focus on Sunbeam's core business, which first needed to be defined. Dunlap and his Dream Team for Sunbeam defined the core business as electric appliances and appliance-related businesses. Five categories surrounding the core business were identified as vital to Sunbeam's success: kitchen appliances, health and home, outdoor cooking, personal care and comfort, and professional products. All products that did not fit into one of the five categories were sold. The criterion Dunlap used to decide whether to keep or sell a product line was simple. Since he believed firmly that consumers recalled the Sunbeam brand name fondly, if the product related to the Sunbeam brand name, it was kept. Identifying Sunbeam's core business and paring down to it was the goal in implementing the third rule.

The final of Dunlap's four rules of business called for a real strategy. Dunlap and his team defined Sunbeam's strategy as driving the growth of the company through core business expansions by further differentiating the products, moving into new geographic areas around the globe, and introducing new products that were linked directly to emerging customer trends as lifestyles evolved around the world. As the first step in implementing the strategy, the electrical appliances were reengineered to 220 volts so that they could be sold and used internationally. Another step was reclaiming the differentiation between the Oster and Sunbeam lines. Each was designed, packaged, and advertised to target different markets. Oster products were positioned as upscale, higher-end brands and sold at completely different retailers than the Sunbeam lines. The Sunbeam line of products was positioned as an affordable, middle-class brand. Early in 1997 Sunbeam opened ten factory outlet stores to increase brand awareness, sales, and ultimately shareholder wealth. Dunlap made all these changes within seven months of taking up the challenge to turn around Sunbeam. The stock rose to more than $48 per share, a 284 percent increase since July 1996.

THE TURNAROUND OF SUNBEAM

In October 1997, just fifteen months after accepting the position as chairman and CEO, Dunlap issued a press release stating that the turnaround was complete and that Morgan Stanley of Stanley Dean Witter & Co. had been hired to find a buyer for Sunbeam. According to John A. Byrne in his book *Chainsaw,* "no one was the least bit interested" (p. 190). He also wrote that Dunlap misled a journalist into reporting that Philips, a Dutch electronics giant, was interested in purchasing Sunbeam for $50+ per share but that Dunlap wanted $70.

On March 2, 1998, Dunlap announced plans to buy three consumer products companies. Sunbeam acquired 82 percent of Coleman (camping gear) from Ronald Perelman for $2.2 billion Perelman received a combination of cash and stock, giving him 14 percent ownership of Sunbeam. The other two purchases were from Thomas Lee for Signature Brands (Mr. Coffee) and First Alert (smoke and gas alarms). Lee was paid $425 million in cash, and Sunbeam obtained 95.7 percent control of First Alert and 98.5 percent control of Signature Brands. Two days after the announcement of purchasing the three companies, Sunbeam's stock closed at a record high of $52 a share. With share prices the highest they had ever been and 1997 net income reported at $109.4 million, Sunbeam truly seemed to be turned around — at least on paper.

Dunlap publicly praised himself and his Dream Team for Sunbeam for turning around the failing corporation within seven months of taking over. He was confident in the success of their mission at Sunbeam and added a complete chapter to his book *Mean Business* titled "Now There's a Bright Idea. Lesson: Everything You've Read So Far About Restructuring Works. This Chapter Proves It — Again." Dunlap stated that Kersh and a dozen other people tried to dissuade him from taking the Sunbeam job because they were convinced that even he could not save the company. Dunlap disagreed with them, pointing out that where others see the impossible, he sees opportunity.

In the chapter, Dunlap stated that the tremendous media attention given to the first edition of his book made it an unofficial handbook for Sunbeam employees and also provided free publicity for the company. He mentioned that he did not need to take the position at Sunbeam or with any other company because of his wealth. A whole section of the chapter recalled how the media arrived in full force to cover the promotional tour and signing of his book. Dunlap also mentioned how strangers, including a Greek Orthodox cleric, praised him and his book, and pointed out that he was at the top of the most admired CEOs list in a survey of business students at U.S. colleges and universities. In the concluding paragraph of the chapter, Dunlap suggested that all CEOs and boards of directors should read his book and use him as a role model in running their companies.

At the time, Dunlap's management philosophy seemed to underlie his success at Sunbeam. He streamlined the company and even attained what he considers the most important goal of any business: he made money for the shareholders. In February 1998 the board of directors expressed satisfaction with Dunlap's leadership and signed a three-year employment contract with him that included 3.75 million shares of stock.

DUNLAP'S ACCOUNTING PRACTICES RAISE QUESTIONS

Dunlap accomplished what he had set out to do at Sunbeam, but the shareholder wealth did not last. Nor did the board's satisfaction. Sunbeam again faced rough times — and not because of excessive costs or lack of a strategy. The three purchases that more than doubled Sunbeam's size and helped push the price per share to $52 are part of what caused the upheaval and restructuring of Sunbeam a second time. Rumors began surfacing that these purchases had been made to disguise losses by write-offs.

Paine Webber, Inc. analyst Andrew Shore had been following Sunbeam since the day Dunlap was hired. Shore's job as an analyst was to make educated guesses about investing clients' money in stocks. Shore had been scrutinizing Sunbeam's financial statements every quarter and considered the reported levels of inventory for certain items to be high for the time of year. He noted massive increases in sales of electric blankets in the third quarter, although they usually sell well in the fourth quarter. He also found that sales of grills were high in the fourth quarter, which is an unusual time of year for grills to be sold, and noted that accounts receivable were high. On April 3, 1998, hours before Sunbeam announced a first-quarter loss of $44.6 million, Shore downgraded the stock. By the end of the day Sunbeam's stock prices had fallen 25 percent.

Shore's findings were indeed cause for concern. Dunlap had been using a "bill-and-hold" strategy with retailers, which boosted Sunbeam's revenue, at least on the balance sheet. The bill-and-hold strategy entails selling products at large discounts to retailers and holding them in third-party warehouses to be delivered at a later date. By booking sales months ahead of the actual shipment or billing, Sunbeam was able to report higher revenues in the form of accounts receivable, which inflated its quarterly earnings. Basically, what the strategy did was to shift sales from future quarters to the current one, and in 1997 the strategy helped Dunlap boost Sunbeam's revenues by 18 percent.

The strategy Dunlap used is not illegal and follows the Generally Accepted Accounting Principles (GAAP) of financial reporting. Nevertheless, Sunbeam shareholders filed lawsuits, alleging that the company had made misleading statements about its finances and deceived them so that they would buy Sunbeam's artificially inflated stock. A class-action lawsuit was filed on April 23, 1998, naming both Sunbeam Corporation and CEO Albert Dunlap as defendants. The lawsuit alleged that Sunbeam and Dunlap had violated the Securities Exchange Act of 1934 by misrepresenting and/or omitting material information concerning the business operations, sales, and sales trends of the company. The lawsuit also alleged that the motivation for artificially inflating the price of the common stock was so that Sunbeam could complete millions of dollars of debt financing so as to complete the mergers with Coleman, First Alert, and Signature Brands. Sunbeam's subsequent reporting of earnings significantly below the original estimate caused a huge drop in the stock. A web site at http://defrauded.com/sunbeam.html provided information about the lawsuit and alleged financial damage to stockholders due to the alleged deception.

Dunlap continued to run Sunbeam and the newly purchased companies as if nothing had happened. On May 11, 1998, Dunlap tried to reassure two hundred major investors and Wall Street analysts that the first-quarter loss would not be repeated and that Sunbeam would post increased earnings in the second quarter. That same day he announced another fifty-one hundred layoffs at Sunbeam and the acquired companies, possibly to gain back confidence and divert attention away from the losses and lawsuits. The tactic did not work. The press continued its reports about the bill-and-hold strategy and the accounting practices Dunlap allegedly used to artificially inflate revenues and profits.

CHAINSAW AL'S REPUTATION BACKFIRES

Dunlap called an impromptu board meeting on June 9, 1998, to address and rebut the reported charges. A partner of Sunbeam's outside auditors, Arthur Andersen LLP (limited liability partnership), assured the board that the company's 1997 numbers were in compliance with accounting standards and firmly stood by the firm's audit of Sunbeam's books. Robert J. Gluck, the controller at Sunbeam, was also present at the board meeting and did not counter the auditor's statement. The meeting seemed to be going well until Dunlap was asked if the company was going to make the projected second-quarter earnings. His response that sales were soft was not what the board expected to hear. Nor was his statement that he had a document in his briefcase outlining a settlement of his contract for his departure from Sunbeam. The document was never reviewed. However, Dunlap's behavior made the board members suspicious, which led to an in-depth review of Dunlap's practices.

The review took place during the next four days in the form of personal phone calls and interviews between the board members and select employees — without Dunlap's knowledge. A personal conversation with Sunbeam's executive vice president, David Fannin, revealed that the 1998 second-quarter sales were considerably below Dunlap's forecast and that the company was in crisis. Dunlap had forecasted a small increase, but the numbers revealed by Fannin showed that Sunbeam could lose as much as $60 million that quarter. Outside the boardroom and away from Dunlap, the controller Robert J. Gluck revealed that the company had tried to do things in accordance with GAAP, but allegedly everything had been pushed to the limit.

These revelations caused the board of directors to call an emergency meeting. On Saturday, June 13, 1998, the board of directors, Fannin, and a pair of lawyers discussed the informal findings. They agreed that they had lost confidence in Dunlap and his ability to turn Sunbeam around. The board of directors unanimously agreed that Dunlap had to go and drafted a letter stating that his immediate departure would be necessary. Chainsaw Al was told that same day, in a one-minute conference call, that he was the next person to be cut at Sunbeam.

SUNBEAM LOOKS FORWARD

Once again, Sunbeam faced the need to revitalize. This time, however, its challenges had a different focus. The company once again was looking for a new CEO. The stock price had dropped as low as $10 per share. Shareholder lawsuits had been filed; legal action regarding Dunlap's firing was under way; the Securities and Exchange Commission was scrutinizing Sunbeam's accounting practices; the audit committee of the board of directors was requiring Sunbeam to restate the audited financial statements of 1997, possibly for 1996, as well as for the first quarter of 1998; and creditors were demanding payment in full. Additionally, on August 24, 1998, Sunbeam announced that it would discontinue a quarterly dividend of $0.01 per share. Shareholder confidence was at an all-time low.

Less than two years after Dunlap was hired, Sunbeam was again announcing a new organizational structure and senior management team. Jerry W. Levin accepted the position of president and CEO. He outlined a new strategy for Sunbeam focusing on growth through increased product quality and customer service. The plan was to decentralize operations while maintaining centralized support and organizing into three operating groups. Four of the eight plants that were scheduled to be closed under Dunlap's management remained open to ensure consistency of supply. In late 1998 Levin outlined his strategy for revitalizing Sunbeam in a press release:

> Although we still have much to do in the short term to stabilize Sunbeam's businesses, our strategic focus is on growth. With some of the most powerful brand names in consumer durables, we will focus on our consumers. We are now conducting consumer research which should have a significant impact on our rate of new product introductions in the second half of 1999.
>
> In contrast to the prior management's approach, we are decentralizing operations while maintaining centralized support. Our goal is to increase accountability at the business unit level, and to give our employees the tools they need to build their businesses. We are shifting Sunbeam's focus to increasing quality in products and customer service.*

On October 21, 1998, Sunbeam announced that it had signed a memorandum of understanding to settle, subject to court approval, the class-action lawsuit brought by public shareholders of Coleman Co., Inc. The court approved, and on January 6, 2000, Sunbeam completed the acquisition of the publicly held shares of Coleman. The terms of the merger allowed all public stockholders of Coleman to receive $6.44 in cash, .5677 of a share of Sunbeam common stock, and .381 of a warrant to purchase one share of Sunbeam common stock for each of their shares of Coleman stock.

There were legal ramifications regarding Dunlap's firing. Dunlap stated in an interview on July 9, 1998, that he intended to challenge Sunbeam's efforts to deny him severance under his contract, although both Dunlap and Sunbeam agreed not to take legal action against each other for a period of six months. Dunlap claimed that his mission was aborted prematurely and that three days after receiving the board of director's support, he was fired without being given a reason. On March 15, 1999, Dunlap filed an arbitration claim against Sunbeam to recover $5.5 million in unpaid salary, $58,000 worth of accrued vacation, and $150,000 in

---

*Sunbeam Corporation, "Sunbeam Outlines New Strategy, Organizational Structure, Senior Management Team," PRNewswire, September 13, 1998, http://www.prnewswire.com.

benefits, as well as to have his stock options repriced at $7 a share. Additionally, he sued the company for dragging its feet in reimbursing him for more than $1.4 million in legal and accounting fees racked up in defending himself in lawsuits that alleged securities fraud. Although the board made it clear that they had no intention of paying Dunlap any more money, a judge ruled in his favor in June 1999.

In a letter to the shareholders at the beginning of 1999, Levin stated that Sunbeam had gone back to basics and intensified its focus on its powerful family of brands. He also wrote that the lending banks had extended covenant relief and waivers of past defaults until April 10, 2000. The $1.7 billion credit agreement was extended until April 14, 2000, at which time Sunbeam hoped to have a definitive agreement extending the covenant relief and waivers for an additional year. Sunbeam was required to restate their audited accounting reports. It took auditors four months to unravel the accounting statements from Dunlap's tenure, which were confirmed to be legal — just inaccurate. The 1997 net income was restated from $109.4 million to $38.3 million.

Sunbeam moved forward. A new company — Thalia Products, Inc. (Thinking and Linking Intelligent Appliances) — was created to produce smart appliances and services and to license HLT (home linking technology) to other manufacturers. At the International Housewares show in January 2000, Sunbeam and Thalia introduced nine new products. These products automatically network when plugged in and "talk" to each other to coordinate tasks. Such tasks include an alarm clock turning on the coffee pot ten minutes before the alarm goes off — no matter what time it is set for — and an alarm that will ring if water has not been added to the coffee pot. Sunbeam announced on March 23, 2000, that its Thalia Products division had an agreement with Microsoft Corp. to join the Universal Plug and Play (UPnP) Forum, which would further the companies' shared objective of establishing industry-leading standards for home appliance networking.

At this point, CEO Levin still had confidence in Sunbeam's ability to recover. A press release on May 10, 2000, stated that the first-quarter results showed that net sales had increased 3 percent to $539 million and that operating results had narrowed to a loss of $3 million. Levin stated:

> These results, though improved, are not indicative of the value we have created, and will continue to create for Sunbeam's shareholders. Looking forward, we expect operating results to further improve as we execute our long-range strategy that focuses on consumer-oriented new products.

On January 25, 2001, Sunbeam announced that it had been notified by the New York Stock Exchange (NYSE) that the company was not in compliance with minimum listing criteria. As a result, the NYSE "de-listed" the company's common stock. This means that the stock is no longer traded at this time.

The bad news continued with the announcement by Sunbeam on February 6, 2001, of its plan to reorganize under Chapter 11 of the U.S. Bankruptcy Code. The company expected no interruption in production or distribution. Senior management committed to remain in place and lead Sunbeam throughout the bankruptcy process and beyond.

Levin stated:

Chapter 11 reorganization provides a legal framework that allows us to keep the business running normally while we put our financial house in order. When we emerge from the proceedings in a matter of months, Sunbeam will be a stronger, more competitive company.

We intend for this restructuring of our financial obligations to free Sunbeam from its debt burden and litigation expenses and put the reorganized Sunbeam on the track for economic viability and successful operations. I look forward to working with our management team and dedicated employees, as well as our suppliers and retailers, to continue to build on Sunbeam's solid foundation of outstanding brands and a global reputation for quality and dependability.*

Questions

1. How did pressures for financial performance contribute to a Sunbeam organizational culture that tried to manipulate quarterly sales and influence investors?

2. What were Al Dunlap's contributions to financial and public relations embarrassment at Sunbeam that caused investors and the public to question Sunbeam's integrity?

3. Identify ethical issues that Al Dunlap's management team may have created by using a short-run focus on financial performance. What lessons could be learned from the outcome?

These facts are from "Sunbeam Corporation," *Hoover's Online, http://www.hoovers.com/premium/ profiles/11414.html* (accessed September 19, 1998); Albert J. Dunlap and Bob Aldeman, "How I Save Bad Companies and Make Good Companies Great," *Mean Business*, rev. ed. (New York: Simon and Schuster, 1997); Matthew Schifrin, "Chainsaw Al to the Rescue," *Forbes*, August 26, 1996, *http://www.forbes.com/forbes/082696/5805042a.htm* (accessed September 9, 1998); Patricia Sellers, "First: Sunbeam's Investors Draw Their Knives — Exit for Chainsaw?" *Fortune*, June 8, 1998, pp. 30–31; Matthew Schifrin, "The Unkindest Cuts," *Forbes*, May 4, 1998, *http://www.forbes. com/forbes/98/0504/6109044a.htm* (accessed September 14, 1998); Matthew Schifrin, "The Sunbeam Soap Opera: Chapter 6," *Forbes*, July 6, 1998, pp. 44–45; John A. Byrne, "How Al Dunlap Self-Destructed," *Business Week*, July 6, 1998, pp. 58–65; Daniel Kadlec, "Chainsaw Al Gets the Chop," *Time.com*, June 29, 1998, *http://cgi.pathfinder.com/time/ham...29/business.chainsaw-al-get15.html* (accessed September 14, 1998); The Alexander Law Firm, *http://defrauded.com/sunbeam.shtml* (accessed September 13, 1998); Martha Brannigan and Ellen Joan Pollock, "Dunlap Offers Tears and a Defense," *Wall Street Journal*, July 9, 1998, p. B1; "Dunlap and Kersh Resign from Sunbeam Board of Directors," *Company News On-Call, http://www.prnewswire.com* (accessed September 13, 1998); "Sunbeam to Restate Financial Results," *Company News On-Call, http://www.prnewswire. com* (accessed September 13, 1998); "Sunbeam Outlines New Strategy, Organizational Structure,

* *Sunbeam Corporation press release, "Sunbeam Corporation Announces Plan to Reorganize under Chapter 11." February 6, 2001.* http://www.sunbeam.com/media_room/soc_reorg.htm *(accessed February 13, 2001).*

Senior Management Team," *Company News On-Call, http:// www.prnewswire.com* (accessed September 13, 1998); John A. Byrne, "The Notorious Career of Al Dunlap in the Era of Profit-at-Any-Price," *Chainsaw* (New York: HarperCollins Publishers, 1999); Douglas Bell, "Take Me To Your Leader," *ROB Magazine,* June 10, 2000, *www.robmagazine.com/archive/2000ROBfebruary/html/idea_log.html* (accessed November 30, 2000); Steve Matthews, "Sunbeam's Ex-CEO Seeks $5.25 Million in Arbitration Claim," *Bloomberg News,* March 15, 1999; "Sunbeam Balks at Dunlap's Demand for $5.5 Million," *Naples Daily News,* March 17, 1999; "Sunbeam Signs Memorandum of Understanding to Settle Coleman Shareholder Litigation," *PR Newswire,* October 21, 1998, *www.prnewswire.com* (accessed October 23, 1998); "Sunbeam Announces Eastpak Sale Complete," *PR Newswire,* May 30, 2000, *www.prnewswire.com* (accessed June 2, 2000); "Sunbeam Credit Waivers Extended to April 14, 2000," April 11, 2000, *www.prnewswire.com* (accessed April 11, 2000); "Letter from CEO Jerry W. Levin," Sunbeam homepage, June 10, 2000, *www.sunbeam.com* (accessed June 12, 2000); "Sunbeam Reports First Quarter 2000 Results," Sunbeam press release, May 10, 2000, *www.sunbeam.com* (accessed May 12, 2000); "Time for Smart Talk Is Over," Sunbeam press release, January 14, 2000, *www.sunbeam.com* (accessed January 16, 2000); "Sunbeam Joins Microsoft in the Universal Plug and Play Forum to Establish a "Universal" Smart Appliance Technology Standard," Sunbeam press release, March 23, 2000, *www.sunbeam.com* (accessed March 24, 2000); "VF To Acquire Eastpak Brand," Sunbeam press release, March 20, 2000, *www.sunbeam.com* (accessed March 24, 2000); and "Sunbeam Completes Acquisition of Coleman Publicly Held Shares," Sunbeam press release, January 6, 2000, *www.sunbeam.com* (accessed January 9, 2000).

Napster: The Debate Over Copyright Infringement

Shawn Fanning, a 17-year-old freshman at Northeastern University, left college to develop a method, utilizing advanced MP3 technology, to trade music over the Internet. MP3s provide almost perfect digital copies of music originally recorded on CDs. Napster, Fanning's company, began operation on June 1, 1999. Its downloadable MusicShare software allows computer users worldwide to send and receive high-quality digital music files among themselves for free. Napster's first round of funding came from Shawn's uncle, John Fanning, and other investors. Its first official CEO, Eileen Richardson, was hired in September 1999. A largely unknown venture capitalist from Boston, Richardson took the job during the most crucial months of Napster's development. Although she was viewed as combative and inexperienced, Napster moved forward with Richardson at the helm.

PROBLEMS BEGIN

Unhappy with what they viewed as copyright infringement, recording industry executives met with Napster management in late 1999 to discuss an acceptable means of distributing music over the Internet. CEO Richardson's abrasive style, however, destroyed any chance of a compromise at the time. Therefore, on December 7, 1999, the Recording Industry Association of America (RIAA) filed suit against Napster for copyright infringement, requesting damages of $100,000 each time a song was copied.

Napster's woes continued. By March 2000, some universities were banning Napster because of the congestion it caused in their computer systems. In addition, on April 13, 2000, the rock band Metallica filed suit against Napster for copyright infringement. The suit requested that all Metallica music be removed from the web site. Claiming they could not physically remove the Metallica songs, Napster attempted to demonstrate concern by booting more than three hundred thousand members from its site for downloading Metallica songs. On May 21,

---

This case was prepared by Robyn Smith, Dana Schubert, Jane Swoboda, and O.C. Ferrell for classroom discussion, rather than to illustrate either effective or ineffective handling of an administrative, ethical, or legal decision by management.

2000, Napster hired a new CEO, Hank Barry. Barry was a member of the venture-capital firm Hummer Winbald, which had invested $15 million in Napster. Soon after Barry was hired, Richardson left the company.

The RIAA continued its fight against Napster, filing a motion on June 13, 2000 for an injunction of blocking all trading of major-label music through Napster. It was time for Napster management to think seriously about its defense. David Boies, the lawyer who had litigated for the Department of Justice in the Microsoft case and for Al Gore in the Florida presidential election challenge, was hired on June 15, 2000. To demonstrate its "good-faith" efforts, Napster announced plans to work with Liquid Audio, a digital-rights technology company, in an attempt to make music downloads safe for copyright holders. This move was not enough to convince U.S. District Judge Marilyn Hall Patel, who basically ordered Napster's demise by ruling that the company must stop allowing copyrighted material to be traded over the Internet. However, on July 28, 2000, only nine hours before Napster would have had to shut down, the Ninth U.S. Circuit Court of Appeals issued a stay, allowing Napster to continue operating. A trial date with the Ninth U.S. Circuit Court of Appeals was set for October 2, 2000. The decision favored the RIAA, thus leaving Napster's fate in the hands of the appellate court.

Parties to the Controversy

In addition to Napster, this controversy affects four other parties — artists, the recording industry, retailers, and consumers. Artists have mixed feelings about Napster. Leading the opposition are Dr. Dre and Metallica, who both sued Napster, as well as several universities, in an attempt to remove their songs from the play list, shut down the service, and receive compensation for copyright infringement. Lars Ulrich, Metallica's drummer, said, "It is sickening to know that our art is being traded like a commodity rather than the art that it is."

Some music artists, however, have come to realize how Napster can benefit them. In 1999, Tom Petty released his song "Free Girl Now" on MP3 before the release date of his new album. The group Offspring released its first single on MP3 on September 29, 2000, and proceeded with other releases on MP3 until the album officially went on sale on November 14, 2000. The lead singer, Dexter Holland, said, "Digital downloading was not hurting our sales. In fact, it may have been helping." The band also showed its support of Napster by giving away $1.83 million as a promotional tool to get people to download music. Other artists, such as Beck and the Beastie Boys, stated that they, too, had seen an increase in album sales after releasing an MP3 file. Still other artists, such as Chuck D, are working with Napster to create deals on such items as concert tickets, T-shirts, posters, and other promotional merchandise. Although some artists may have individual interactions with Napster, their contracts are nonetheless upheld by the RIAA, therefore requiring them to remain subservient to the larger organization's fight.

The second group involved in the Napster controversy is the recording industry, represented by the RIAA, which says it is fighting to protect its investment in promoting artists. The recording studios listen to aspiring artists and determine which ones to support. The recording studios organize the business side, which allows the musicians to concentrate on the creative development of songs. The industry is facing the concern of "dis-intermediation" and is wondering whether the Internet and the changing economy will eliminate its role in the distribution chain. Music companies are trying to compete on-line by opening their own subscription music service provider.

How does Napster affect listeners' purchasing practices and, therefore, the third group — music retailers? The results of investigation are varied. A study by Jupiter Media Metrix showed that people who use Napster are 15 percent more likely to purchase music than are nonusers. Another survey by Digital Media Association and Yankelovich Partners showed that of the "two-thirds of respondents who had downloaded music from an on-line source, 66% said listening to a song on-line had at least once prompted them to later buy a CD or cassette featuring that song." According to a survey by the Wharton School of Business, "70% of Napster members polled reported they have used the service to sample music before buying it." Evidence supporting these statistics varies among those most affected—record stores.

As owner of a nine-store music chain in Maine stated: "We've had absolutely no negative effect from Napster . . . sales are actually up because Napster has brought music to the forefront. Everybody's talking about music . . . if Napster is stealing sales from Eminem; I want it to steal from every new release. Because that was our biggest-selling CD, ever." Another record store owner agreed that "our sales are up 19 percent over last year because of all the publicity . . . you can't open a newspaper or magazine and not see a Napster headline. We've never got so much free advertising. Music is exciting again."

Not all record store owners paint such a rosy picture when discussing the effects of Napster, however. Oliver's Records, Inc., in Syracuse, New York, has virtually been wiped out by the widespread use of Napster. According to owner Charlie Robbins, the store sells approximately $37 a day in walk-in sales, down from $500 a day two years ago.

Conflicting information has surfaced about the fourth group — the Napster audience — and their music-purchasing practices. Many people believe college students are the dominant music downloaders. However, according to a study conducted by Webnoize, Inc., of almost 4,300 New England college students, 19.2 percent used Napster daily, 37.6 percent weekly, and 16 percent monthly, whereas 27.3 percent had never used the service. The same study also determined the number of times the students downloaded and stored music. As Table 1 indicates, college students varied in the quantity of downloads but, overall, stored relatively few music files. In addition, a significant number of students (more than 42 percent) never stored music.

Some universities struggled to accommodate Napster traffic. Napster was prohibited at Indiana University because its use expanded to represent 50 percent of

TABLE 1   College Students' Use of Napster

Number of Music Files	Percentage Who Downloaded	Percentage Who Kept and Stored
1–10	32.2%	45.6%
11–100	26.6%	6.6%
101–250	15.3%	3.1%
250+	10.7%	2.4%
None	15.3%	42.2%

the school's Internet traffic on campus between January and February 2000. Because of student demand, however, the university improved its network's performance in order to reinstate the service and accommodate its use.

Contrary to popular belief, college students are not the only fans of on-line music sites. In fact, Jupiter Media Metrix found that adults over age 50 composed 17 percent of the visitors to music sites in June 2000, an increase of 92 percent over the course of just one year. In October 2000, Napster had 32 million registered users, marking an increase of 2 million in just one week. Many supporters increased their usage in fear of a shutdown.

LEGAL ASPECTS

Although many people are concerned with the outcome of this controversy, the only groups involved in the litigation are Napster and Napster-like music providers and the recording industry. The first two suits were against MP3.com and Napster. Both concern intellectual property and copyright infringement over the Internet.

MP3.com settled out of court in June 2000, agreeing to begin paying 1.5 cents each time a user stores a song and one-third of a cent each time a song is downloaded. Sony Music, Bertelsmann AG's BMG, Warner Music Group, and EMI, four of the five top music labels, agreed to accept payment of nearly $20 million each for past copyright violation. Universal Music decided not to accept the settlement offer and has since filed suit requesting $45,000 for each of ten thousand CDs produced by Universal that were available on-line. This could amount to a fine of $450 million for MP3.com.

In July 2000, Scour, a company based in Beverly Hills, was sued by the RIAA and the Motion Picture Association of America. The duo targeted Scour for its attempt to bring music, movies, and pictures to the Internet public. The suit filed by the RIAA and the Motion Picture Association of America (MPAA) labeled Scour as "a vehicle for global piracy of copyrighted motion pictures and sound recordings." As a result of the pending lawsuit, Scour laid off fifty-two of its sixty-four employees.

Napster's Arguments and the Industry's Rebuttal

Despite lawsuits against other companies, the biggest player in the battle over piracy remains Napster. For its defense in the war with the RIAA, Napster has turned to two statutes (the 1992 Audio Home Recording Act and the 1998 Digital Millenium Copyright Act), as well as the Sony Betamax ruling on copyright infringement.

Napster argues it should have the same protections that saved the Sony Betamax in the early 1980s. In this case, the MPAA filed a lawsuit against Sony, stating that its home videocassette recorder (VCR) unlocked the door for widespread film reproduction. Napster believes the Sony Betamax case supports its claim because Napster is using a technology that has legitimate uses, such as promoting new bands, but as in the Sony case, Napster cannot control what users do with the technology once it has been downloaded. The lower courts found Sony, just like Napster, guilty of copyright infringement. However, in the Sony Betamax case, the Supreme Court overruled the lower court's decision, stating that technology must be "merely capable of substantial non-infringing uses in order to be protected by law." Supporters argue Napster should have the same protection as Sony because its technology has other legitimate uses.

The opposing side states that Napster technology is not unique. Another argument against Napster is that its service would not be banned from the Internet; it would just be prevented from listing unauthorized music. For these reasons, opponents do not feel that the Sony Betamax ruling applies to the Napster case.

The 1992 Audio Home Recording Act (AHRA) may apply to Napster. This act, allowing people to make copies of music for personal use, was passed in response to the development of digital audiotape recorders. This occurred prior to the Internet revolution and therefore did not consider Web transport of music. Napster enthusiasts say that this case is relevant because the music copied is for personal use, not redistribution for profit. Of the music downloaded, users listen to 92 percent on their desktops, 10 percent on portable devices, and 14 percent on home stereos. More than one medium is used by some individuals. Because the AHRA was based on digital audiotapes, not Web music, many people do not agree that it is relevant to the Napster case. The Justice Department, Patent Office, and most of the legal community agree that this act does not support Napster.

The 1998 Digital Millennium Copyright Act (DMCA) addresses the issue of whether or not there is knowledge and blatant disregard of copyrighted material. The DMCA grants immunity to Internet service providers (ISPs), holding that online service providers cannot be held responsible for the actions of their customers. According to Napster, it has broad protection from copyright claims because it functions like a search engine rather than having direct involvement with music swapping. The main argument against Napster based on the DMCA pertains to its "search engine" status. According to the legal community, "Napster does not take the legal steps required of search engines in dealing with copyright violations."

Intellectual Property

Intellectual property losses in the United States total more than $11 billion a year in lost revenue from the illegal copying of computer programs, movies, compact discs, and books. The argument against intellectual-property rights is not that protection is not warranted, but that the protection should not go so far as to destroy competition. According to copyright experts at the University of California at Berkeley, "Intellectual-property owners are not entitled to prohibit or exercise monopoly control over new technologies that incidentally threaten their established business models. . . . Having to change business plans in response to evolving technologies is what competition is all about." Based on this argument, all developers of intellectual property — whether it is music, computer software, or written text — need to develop new methods to market and distribute their products. The other side of the controversy suggests that the creation of intellectual property will be stifled if such property is unprotected and suggests that copyright laws should cover the gamut of possibilities.

DUAL STANDARDS?

Napster claims to support protection of intellectual property and has tried diligently to protect its own creation. In June 2000, the rock band Offspring sold T-shirts displaying the Napster logo. Napster was not pleased with this action and requested that a cease-and-desist order be issued against Offspring. Napster reconsidered this request when postings on Web sites began commenting on the hypocrisy involved. Along these lines, Napster has also attempted to prevent independent software developers from creating Napster-compatible software and web sites. To ensure this, Napster refused to share its software code and has made changes to its own software that prevent other copycat software from running with Napster. It has also blocked outside music sites from accessing its database of songs. Napster, in guarding the method of its own operations, has also demanded that users of its software agree that they will not "decompile, reverse, engineer or dissemble" their program. According to the RIAA, these actions only reinforce the fact that Napster is a euphemism for music piracy on a large scale.

THE FUTURE OF INTERNET SERVICES SUCH AS NAPSTER

Although there are other sites that offer Napster-like services, they have not faced the same legal issues as Napster. Scour, Exchange, iMesh, and CuteMX, for example, can be used to search for audio and video images, as opposed to only the MP3 searching done by Napster. These services allow all file types to be shared. Wrapster is a Napster spinoff that allows any file to be disguised as an MP3 and therefore transmitted via Napster. Finally, Gnutella, an AOL site, does not require a central web site as Napster does. Instead, this site directly connects users to each other to trade desired music files.

Despite the strong arguments for both sides, many people feel that the best solution is to develop a compromise between the recording studios, the artists, and Napster-like music providers. Bertelsmann, parent company of BMG Music, was the first in the recording industry to strike a deal with Napster. Project Thunderball, the code name for the attempt to join the two businesses, was first made public on October 31, 2000. Bertelsmann provided Napster with $50 million to expand and improve its current software with the goal of prohibiting pirated music transfer and counting the number of times a song is downloaded in order to reimburse the artists. Suggestions include using the "MD5 hash," a digital fingerprint, or using software that monitors sound patterns to detect illegal copies. The joint venture is dependent on the development of such a system because Bertelsmann will not withdraw its lawsuit until Napster proves it can protect the artists' music. Napster and BMG will also have to develop a revenue model for future service. The most likely solution is a monthly subscription fee for users who want to download music from Napster. Bertelsmann is hoping to rally rival music producers behind the effort to use Napster-like services in order to expand the industry to include on-line books, films, and magazines. EMI and Sony have expressed interest in similar negotiations with Napster. Universal and Warner, however, have begun work on their own digital distribution projects, therefore decreasing the likelihood of a joint venture between these companies and Napster. With the details of the current Bertelsmann arrangement not yet determined, the agreement with other labels will most likely be delayed until Napster can prove itself.

THE FINAL DECISION

Without a doubt, file sharing will continue to exist in both the media and entertainment industries. However, a ruling by the District Court of Appeals on February 12, 2001 made it clear that the court feels that current copyright laws apply to the Internet. In a unanimous decision by the appeals court, the original ruling by Judge Marilyn Hall Patel that Napster was aware users were swapping copyrighted materials was upheld. The appeals court refuted all of Napster's defense tactics in one form or another and ordered the company to stop allowing its millions of users to swap copyrighted material without a fee.

The appeals document stated that the RIAA adequately verified ownership of the copyrighted material in question. It further stated that approximately eighty-seven percent of the music traded on Napster belongs to the RIAA. Because of a direct violation of rights of reproduction and distribution, Napster was found guilty of direct infringement of the RIAA's musical recordings. Napster insists that its service does not directly infringe copyrights because its users engage in fair use of the material. The uses referred to are 1) sampling, where temporary copies may be heard prior to purchasing; 2) space-shifting, which refers to a user accessing the recording of a CD he or she already owns; and 3) permissive distribution of material by artists.

The court did not agree that those who frequent Napster practice fair use for several reasons. First, the court determined that Napster users engage in commercial use of the copyrighted material because users are able to obtain something they would normally have to pay for, and the recordings are permanent. Second, the fair use claim was refuted because of the creative nature of musical recordings. Third, because Napster users engage in "wholesale copying" of copyrighted material, the use is not fair. According to the court, space-shifting does not apply because the copyrighted material is distributed from the individual who downloads the material to other individuals. Finally, the use of Napster harms the market by reducing CD sales among consumers, especially college students, and raising the barrier of entry into the digital download music market for the RIAA. This decision was supported by several studies conducted on behalf of the RIAA.

One study known as the "Jay Report," conducted by Dr. E. Deborah Jay, randomly sampled college and university students to track the impact Napster had on their buying habits. Evidence proved a loss of sales attributable to use of the service. Another study (known as the "Fine Report") conducted by Michael Fine, CEO of Soundscan, determined that on-line file sharing resulted in a loss of album sales within college markets. Napster tried to refute these studies with one of its own but was unsuccessful as the judge determined the administrator, Dr. Peter S. Fader, did not properly oversee the study or collect enough objective data.

Napster was also labeled as a contributor to copyright infringement by the court. It was determined that Napster knowingly contributed to the infringing conduct of its users by providing the site and service for infringement. Napster could block users who violated infringement laws. The court determined that Napster should be held liable for contributory copyright infringement because it failed to remove copyrighted material from its service.

Vicarious copyright infringement applies to whether or not the system operator has the ability to supervise infringing activity and also whether or not the system operator has direct financial interest in the activity. The court decided that Napster had financial interest in the activity of infringement. It was determined that Napster's future revenue is dependent on the number of users. As more users register, more music would be made available. Napster had shown its ability to police its service because users had been blocked in the past when lawsuits were filed by Metallica and Dr. Dre. Napster has a reservation of rights policy on its web site that specifically states that it has the "right to refuse service and terminate accounts at its discretion, including, but not limited to, if Napster believes that user conduct violates applicable law . . . or for any reason in Napster's sole discretion, with or without cause."* Again, the court of appeals noted that Judge Patel did not fully recognize the ability of Napster to monitor its users. The appeals court suggested that the architecture of the current system limited the extent to which Napster could police the service. In other words, Napster did not have a control

---

*Appeal from the United States District Court for the Northern District of California. Marilyn Hall Patel, Chief District Judge, Presiding, argued and submitted October 2, 2000, San Francisco, CA. Filed February 12, 2001.

system to document all usage of its site. Regardless of the recognition, the court determined that Napster was a vicarious copyright infringer.

The courts also addressed the two statutes and the Sony Betamax case used by Napster in its defense. The court determined the Audio Home Recording Act was "irrelevant" because it does not cover downloading of MP3 files or a digital audio recording device. The court refused the argument on behalf of the Digital Millennium Copyright Act, simply stating that it does not include contributory copyright infringers. Finally, the court refuted Napster's argument that if Sony could not be held liable when consumers used their device to record television programs or movies for personal use, then it should not be liable for its users' behavior. The noticeable difference between the two cases is that people use videotaped movies and programs for use in their own home; they generally do not distribute the material to others as is done with Napster.

Since the court of appeals agreed with Judge Patel on all accounts, Napster was ordered to shut down once Judge Patel revised and condensed her report. Napster requested to pay royalties to the RIAA in place of the injunction but was denied.

In response to the ruling, Hank Barry, CEO of Napster, and Shawn Fanning, Napster's founder, released statements to the public. The two claim they are still working on an industry-supported solution, such as a membership-based service. They acknowledged the negotiations with Bertelsmann and still believe that service will be up and running within a few months. They also agreed that they plan to make payments to the affected artists as needed. Both Barry and Fanning encouraged all users to contact their local congressional representative to let them know how much Napster means to the public.

On February 20, 2001, Napster offered $1 billion to the recording industry to settle the lawsuit. Under the proposal, $150 million would be paid annually for the first five years to Sony, Warner, BMG, EMI, and Universal, with $50 million allotted annually for independent labels. The proposal was not accepted by the record industry representatives who were not willing to settle for anything less than shutting down Napster. To date, Napster has not been shut down because doing so could violate the rights of artists who have given Napster permission to trade their music. However, the company is supposed to block all songs in a list of 5,000 that the RIAA provided. As of early April 2001, however, 84 percent of these titles were still being traded. On April 11, Judge Patel announced that she considered Napster's efforts to date to block the copyrighted material "disgraceful." She ordered technology expert A. J. Nichols to find technology to expedite the process. If Napster continued its slow pace, Judge Patel said she would put an end to the site. Go to www.e-businessethics.com for updates on this case.

Questions

1. Are current court rulings favoring copyright owners? Why or why not?

2. Based on the facts in the Napster case, who do you think should have control over intellectual property — the artists or the agents? What are the arguments for both sides?

3. How do intellectual-property copyrights relate to fair competition? Can Napster's existence be defended based on the idea that other on-line services would take Napster's place if it was shut down?

4. Although there are many legal issues in this case, identify several ethical issues that relate to Napster's activities in serving its users' needs.

These facts are from "Napster Not Trying Hard Enough, Judge Warns," *www.foxnews.com/story/0, 2933, 5497, 00.html*, April 11, 2001 (accessed April 12, 2001); "Napster, Inc., Response to Ninth Circuit Court of Appeals Ruling on the U.S. District Court Injunction in A&M, Inc., v. Napster." February 12, 2001, *http://www.napster.com/pressroom/pr/010212.html* (accessed February 13, 2001); Martin Peers and Ron Harris, "Napster Offers $1 Billion to Settle Copyright Suit," *Commercial Appeal*, January 2, 2001, pp. C1, C6; "Survey Studies Napster's Spread on Campuses," *Wall Street Journal*, May 5, 2000, p. B8; "University to Lift Napster Ban," March 23, 2000, *http://news.cnet.com* (accessed August 30, 2000); Anna Wilde Mathews, "Web Music Isn't Just for Kids," *Wall Street Journal*, September 26, 2000, p. B1; "Study: Napster Boosts CD Sales," *http://www.zdnet.com* (accessed July 21, 2000); "Stats Speak Kindly of Napster," *http://www.thestandard.com* (accessed July 21, 2000); "Napster: Downloading Music for Free Is Legal," *http://news.cnet.com/news* (accessed July 3, 2000); "Napster vs. the Record Stores," *http://www.salon.com/business/feature* (accessed August 7, 2000); Martin Peers and Lee Gomes, "Music CD Sales Suffer in Stores Near 'Wired' Colleges, Study Says," *Wall Street Journal*, June 13, 2000, p. A4; Ron Harris, "Heavy Metal Thunder," *http://www.abcnews.go/com* (accessed September 25, 2000); "Early Birth on Web for Latest Offspring," *http://www.smh.com.au/news* (accessed September 19, 2000); "Napster Grows Up," *http://www.redherring.com/industries* (accessed March 10, 2000); Margarita Lenk, "Our Music: Can We Mutually Support the Artist and the Business?" Colorado State University; Amy Doan, "MP3.com Loses Big in Copyright Case," September 6, 2000, *http://www.forbes.com* (accessed September 7, 2000); Lee Gomes, "Napster Ruling May Be Just the Overture," *Wall Street Journal*, July 28, 2000, pp. B1, B4; "How VCR's May Help Napster's Legal Fight," *http://www.thestandard.com/article* (accessed July 24, 2000); Anna Wilde Mathews, "Sampling Free Music over the Internet Often Leads to Sale," *Wall Street Journal*, June 15, 2000, pp. A3, A12; Lee Gomes, "Napster, Fighting for Survival, to Make Case Before Appeals Panel," *Wall Street Journal*, October 2, 2000, p. B24; "Bigger Battle Brewing: Napster-RIAA Court Case Becoming Goliath vs. Goliath," *http://www.sfgate.com* (accessed September 18, 2000); Lee Gomes, "Think Music Moguls Don't Like Sharing? Try Copying Software," *Wall Street Journal*, August 14, 2000, p. B1; Don Clark and Martin Peers, "Can the Record Industry Beat Free Web Music," *Wall Street Journal*, June 20, 2000, p. B1; Lee Gomes, "When Its Own Assets Are Involved, Napster Is No Fan of Sharing," *Wall Street Journal*, July 26, 2000, pp. A1, A10; "Napster Wins Reprieve; Next Move up to Recording Industry," July 28, 2000, *http://www.cnn.com* (accessed August 30, 2000); and Jack Ewing, "A New Net Powerhouse?," *Business Week*, November 13, 2000, pp. 46–52.

Dow Corning's Breast Implants

Dow Corning Corp., a fifty-fifty joint venture between Dow Chemical Co. and Corning Incorporated, has long been viewed as a pioneer in corporate ethics. Dow recognized the importance of ethical issues early and was among the first to develop an ethics program, described by some as the most elaborate in corporate America. The program performs audits to monitor company compliance with rules and regulations and communicates with its employees about ethics. Despite its emphasis on ethics, Dow Corning came under fire for problems related to its silicone breast-implant product.

THE HISTORY OF SILICONE BREAST IMPLANTS

During the Second World War, Corning Glass and Dow Chemical developed liquid silicone as a substitute for rubber to be used as an insulator in transformers. From that research, a revolutionary idea emerged. During the war, Japanese prostitutes allowed the injection of liquid silicone directly into their breasts to increase their bustline. By the 1960s silicone injections had spread to the United States, but the trend slowed when the long-term results of the silicone injections became known: the silicone liquid migrated to other parts of the body, causing lumpy breasts, scars, and, in extreme cases, death.

After the health risks became apparent, the U.S. Food and Drug Administration (FDA) outlawed silicone injections. Doctors at Dow Corning continued to research the process in an effort to find a safer alternative. In 1962, two doctors at Dow Corning, Frank Gerow and Thomas Cronin, developed a new technique, using a silicone gel wrapped in a thin silicone polymer envelope; the envelope was then implanted into the breast. Dow Corning began marketing the new product in 1963. Initial reactions to breast implants were positive, and the "silicone gel in the sandwich bag" was implanted in more than 2 million American women. About 80 percent of the implants were done for cosmetic reasons, with the remainder being

---

This case was prepared by John Fraedrich, Terry Gable, and Gwyneth Vaughn for classroom discussion, rather than to illustrate either effective or ineffective handling of an administrative, ethical, or legal decision by management.

reconstructive surgery after mastectomies. However, the procedure was not risk-free, and complications soon emerged.

HEALTH HAZARDS?

The health risks associated with breast implants are still being debated and are of concern among women who have them. The dangers include adverse reactions to the silicone gel; rupturing gel sacs, which allow the gel to flow to other parts of the body; and the role implants play in preventing early detection of breast cancer. An estimated 10 percent of women with implants have experienced a condition called capsular contracture, in which the body reacts to the silicone by producing a fibrous tissue around the implant, causing the breast to harden. If the silicone gel migrates to other parts of the body and interacts with internal organs and bodily fluids, it has been alleged that it can affect the body's immune system and connective tissues, causing immune system disorders, arthritis, debilitating fatigue, swollen lymph nodes, or lupus. Some studies have found that silicone used in other medical products — such as tubes, valves, clips that close fallopian tubes in sterilization surgeries, penile prostheses, intraocular lenses, and tubing for blood oxygenators and dialysis machines — also presents health hazards.

The subject of silicone implants was so sensitive and controversial that some doctors were reluctant to do breast surgery to remove the silicone sacs from women who had not experienced any immediate detrimental side effects from their implants. Many women filed lawsuits against Dow Corning because they believed the breast implants were endangering their health.

TESTING ETHICS

While preparing for one of these lawsuits, attorneys Nancy Hersh and Dan Bolton of the firm Hersh & Hersh researched Dow Corning's testing process and found evidence suggesting that Dow knew of the potential health hazards of its silicone gel products. Patient files contained complaints of gel envelopes rupturing and silicone migrating to other parts of the body. The envelope used to contain the gel was permeable and allowed the gel to bleed out, and the migrating silicone often affected the body's immune system.

Bolton claims to have found evidence that Dow Corning knew that the silicone gel implants had an adverse effect on the immune system when the company tested the effects of the implants in dogs. One version presented to the FDA indicated that the implants did not affect the future health of the dogs and that their lives were normal. A second set of scientific reports, which Dow Corning did not present to the FDA, stated that all thirty-eight dogs faced chronic inflammation after receiving the silicone implants.

Internal memos from Dow Corning further suggest concerns about the safety of the silicone gel. A Dow Corning engineer, Thomas D. Talcott, who helped develop the silicone gel used in the implants, warned that the polymer sac could rupture and leak, thereby posing serious health threats. His warnings went unheeded and he resigned in protest. Another employee addressed his concerns in a memo claiming that fifty-two of four hundred implants had resulted in ruptures. There is no evidence that Dow Corning took any corrective actions following these warnings. On the contrary, it has been suggested that Dow Corning conducted few safety studies and that the studies it had conducted were not comprehensive.

One scientist who questioned Dow Corning's testing claimed he had found a direct link between the silicone in breast implants and disorders of the immune system. But Dow Corning rebuffed his efforts to continue researching the alleged link. Studies done by Dr. John Paul Heggers of the University of Texas at Galveston suggested that the human body reacts to the silicone in breast implants by producing antibodies against it and that the antibodies attack not only the silicone but also the body's own tissues associated with the silicone.

Further evidence against silicone implants came from Dr. Steven Weiner of the School of Medicine at the University of California at Los Angeles (UCLA). He has treated women with implants who have experienced immune disorders. Dr. Weiner reported that there is no solid evidence to prove the implants cause any health hazards but that a majority of his patients' conditions improved after their implants were removed. A UCLA colleague, Dr. Nir Kossovsky, claimed that silicone is not the direct cause of the immunal disorders but that the body reacts to the silicone by producing proteins resulting in an autoimmune reaction. That reaction then spills over to the rest of the body, indirectly causing other health problems.

Dow Corning countered by arguing that its own research disagreed with research that found a link between the immune system and silicone. Dow said that medical studies support the safety of the silicone gel, and the company specifically stated that it "disagreed with Dr. Heggers' scientific approach to the problem." As a result of Dr. Heggers's suggestion, a number of studies — some of them funded, in part, by Dow Corning — investigated implants and the risk of breast cancer.

A nationwide Swedish study can serve as an example of this research and its conclusions. It included 3,473 women who had had cosmetic breast implant procedures in the period from 1965 through 1993. Followed for an average of 10.3 years, eighteen women developed breast cancer, compared with twenty-five expected cases.

MORE PROBLEMS FOR DOW CORNING

Dow Corning faced its first breast-implant lawsuit in 1977, which suggests that the company was aware of the potential dangers more than a decade before the public crisis occurred. When Dow Corning was deluged with implant lawsuits in the early 1990s, more than forty insurers balked at paying claims. They argued that

Dow Corning had misrepresented the litigation risks posed by the implants. They also cited previous allegations made against Dow Corning regarding inadequate implant testing procedures and the firm's production and marketing of the product in spite of evidence questioning its safety.

In 1995 Dow Corning announced that it was contributing $2 billion to a lawsuit-settlement fund designed to end massive litigation against it and other implant marketers. However, later that year the company decided to file for bankruptcy court protection, partly on the basis that it could not pay the billions of dollars in outstanding consumer claims against it without the money it felt it was owed by its insurers. As a result of the filing, more than nineteen thousand outstanding lawsuits against the company were put on hold until Dow Corning's problems regarding its financial and legal capabilities and responsibilities could be resolved. The bankruptcy filing also brought into question the status of the $4.25 billion industry lawsuit settlement fund.

Dow Corning eventually sued the insurance companies for their refusal to pay claims related to the lawsuits against it. After a three-month trial in 1996, a Michigan jury returned a verdict in favor of Dow Corning. The jury found neither misrepresentation nor concealment of any significant facts that might have affected Dow Corning's ability to obtain insurance.

According to a Dow Corning spokesperson, the insurance proceeds, estimated at between $700 million and $1 billion, would make more money available to compensate women pursuing liability claims against the company. A Dow Corning attorney pointed out that the verdict bolstered Dow Corning's contention that the implants are safe and that there is no scientific proof of their causing disease. Regarding the latter assertion, lawyers for women with outstanding lawsuits against Dow Corning expressed concern that the verdict could hurt their cases should they come to trial since the jury found that the company did not withhold information on product risks, a key allegation in most of the lawsuits. This concern has not lessened despite an earlier ruling, by a Nevada court, that the Dow Chemical Company was solely liable for health problems caused by the breast implants. In that case, the jury awarded a Nevada woman $14 million in compensatory and punitive damages.

The Nevada verdict raised hopes that other claimants would soon receive damage payments from Dow Corning or its larger joint owner, Dow Chemical, but these hopes proved to be premature. They were further undercut when attorneys for the insurance companies announced that they would appeal the Michigan verdict that made them responsible for paying claimants.

In late 1999, a federal judge approved Dow Corning's plan to emerge from bankruptcy. Approved by 94 percent of the women who voted on the plan, the $4.5 billion offer included $3.2 billion to settle claims by more than one hundred and seventy thousand women alleging that they suffered from a range of health problems after receiving silicone gel breast implants made by Dow Corning. The plan offered from $1,000 to $5,000 for those with ruptured implants and up to $200,000 for more serious problems. In addition, foreign claimants could receive 40 to 60 percent of the settlement awarded to U.S. claimants. The plan also included

$1.3 billion to settle other claims, including those by creditors and health care organizations. Although the bankruptcy court confirmed the plan, it attempted to modify it by including an opinion that would allow anyone who did not vote in favor of it to sue Dow Corning's shareholders and other third parties. In early 2000, Dow asked that the opinion be set aside. Updates to this controversy, including press releases, recent federal court rulings, and related web sites, may be viewed on Dow Corning's Web site (http://www.implantclaims.com/index.html).

At one time Dow Corning was considered a leader in business ethics and took pride in itself as such, but manufacturing and marketing silicone gel implants with possible health risks tarnished its reputation. Some at Dow Corning have termed the legal morass a nuisance that has nothing to do with "right" or "wrong," but merely with lawyers attempting to attack a large corporation for their own gain. Others believe differently, as a letter to former FDA Commissioner David Kessler from Dr. Sidney Wolfe, director of Public Citizen's Health Research Group, makes clear:

> We believe that Dow Corning violated federal law by deliberately withholding safety data on its use of silicone in medical devices, especially breast implants. Because of the potential harm of serious illness facing tens if not hundreds of thousands of women who have received silicone breast implants since the time the false report was filed, we believe that the FDA should seek criminal prosecution of the company and responsible Dow Corning officials.*

In 1999, a report by the Institute of Medicine Committee on the Safety of Silicone Breast Implants concluded that it could find "no definitive evidence linking breast implants to cancer, immunological disease, neurological problems, or other systemic diseases."** Given these findings and despite the legal battle and bad publicity on breast implants, it was projected that the number of procedures performed would not only increase but would exceed past numbers. The projection proved to be true, with nearly two hundred thousand such procedures performed in 1999, at costs ranging from $3,000 to $8,000 per procedure.

Questions

1. What ethical issues arise in regard to a product that can alter the human body? Is it up to women to decide whether the risk outweighs vanity, or is it the manufacturer's duty to be socially responsible toward its clients and therefore either sell a safe product or not sell the product at all?

2. Consumers make the final decision to have surgery for problems that are not life-threatening. Given the risks involved when a foreign substance is put into

---

*Russell Mokhiber, "The 10 Worst Corporations of 1993: Dow Corning. Breast Implants Gone Bad," Multinational Monitors Corporate Rap Sheet, http://www.ratical.com/corporations/mm10worst93. htm#n2 (accessed June 11, 1998).

**Nancy Nelson, "Institute of Medicine Finds No Link Between Breast Implants and Disease," Journal of the National Cancer Institute, July 21, 1999, p. 1191.

the body, who bears the responsibility of potential hazards: the consumer, for making the final decision; the surgeon, for not discouraging the procedure; or the manufacturer, for making the option available? (Assume that all know the risks involved.)

3. Dow Corning was praised for its ethics program before the silicone gel implant controversy. How valid are the reports of the whistle-blowers and internal memos today if they were deemed unimportant in 1976? Why did they fail?

4. Given the recent jury findings, what is the responsibility of the parent company — Dow Chemical — in the future for breast implant products?

These facts are from John Morgan, "Breast Surgery Boom Brings Back Silicone," *USA Today,* April 17, 2000, *http://www.usatoday.com/life/health/doctor/lhdoc131.htm* (accessed January 4, 2001); Kara Sissell, "Dow Corning Increases Breast Implant Settlement Plan to $4.4 Billion," *Chemical Week,* February 25, 1998, *http://www.findarticles.com/m3066/n7_v160/20385608/p1/article.jhtml* (accessed November 14, 2000); Katie LaPlant, "The Dow Corning Crisis: A Benchmark," *Public Relations Quarterly,* 44 (Summer 1999): 32–33; Nancy Nelson, "Institute of Medicine Finds No Link Between Breast Implants and Disease," *Journal of the National Cancer Institute,* July 21, 1999, p. 1191; Gary Strauss, "Payments Detailed in Implant Lawsuit," *USA Today,* November 10, 1998, p. B1; Lucette Lagnado, "Women Find Breast Surgery Attractive Again," *Wall Street Journal,* July 14, 1998, pp. B1, B5; Geoffrey Cowler, "Silicone: Juries vs. Science," *Newsweek,* November 13, 1995, p. 75; "Dow Corning Insurers Must Pay Up, Jury Says," *Los Angeles Times,* February 15, 1996, p. D1; Barnaby J. Feder, "Dow Corning in Bankruptcy over Lawsuits," *New York Times,* May 16, 1995, p. A1; "Financial Digest," *Washington Post,* February 3, 1996, p. H1; Barry Meier, "Implant Jury Finds Dow Chemical Liable," *New York Times,* October 29, 1995, sec. 1, p. 33; Joseph Nocera, "Fatal Litigation," *Fortune,* October 16, 1995, p. 60; John Byrne, "The Best Laid Ethics Programs Couldn't Stop a Nightmare at Dow Corning. What Happened?" *Business Week,* March 9, 1992, pp. 67–69; Alison Frankel, "From Pioneers to Profits: The Splendid Past and Muddled Present of Breast Implant Litigation," *American Lawyer,* June 1992, pp. 82–91; Philip J. Hilts, "FDA Tells Company to Release Implant Data," *New York Times,* January 21, 1992, p. C7; Philip J. Hilts, "Strange History of Silicone Held Many Warnings," *New York Times,* January 18, 1992, pp. 1, 8; Tim Smart, "Breast Implants: What Did the Industry Know, and When?" *Business Week,* June 10, 1992, pp. 94–98; "This Man Sounded the Silicone Alarm — in 1976," *Business Week,* January 27, 1992, p. 34; H. Berkel, D. C. Birdsell, and H. Jenkins, "Breast Augmentation: A Risk Factor for Breast Cancer?" *New England Journal of Medicine,* 326 (1992): 1649–1653; D. C. Birdsell and H. Jenkins, "Breast Cancer Diagnosis and Survival in Women with and without Breast Implants," *Plastic Reconstruction Surgery,* 92 (1993): 795–800; L. A. Brinton, K. E. Malone, R. J. Coates, J. B. Schoenberg, C. A. Swanson, J. R. Daling, and J. L. Stanford, "Breast Enlargement and Reduction: Results from a Breast Cancer Case-Control Study," *Plastic Reconstruction Surgery,* 97 (1996): 269–275; H. Bryant and P. Brasher, "Breast Implant and Breast Cancer — Reanalysis of a Linkage Study," *New England Journal of Medicine,* 332 (1995): 1535–1539; D. M. Deapen, L. Bernstein, and G. S. Brody, "Are Breast Implants Anticarcinogenic? A 14-Year Follow-Up of the Los Angeles Study," *Plastic Reconstruction Surgery,* 99 (1997): 1346–1353; D. M. Deapen and G. S. Brody, "Augmentation Mammaplasty and Breast Cancer: A 5-Year Update of the Los Angeles Study," *Plastic Reconstruction Surgery,* 89 (1992): 660–665; D. M. Deapen, M. C. Pike, J. T. Casagrande, and G. S. Brody, "The Relationship Between Breast Cancer and Augmentation Mammaplasty: An Epidemiologic Study," *Plastic Reconstruction Surgery,* 77 (1986): 361–367; S. Friis, J. K. McLaughlin, L. Mellemkjaer, K. H. Kjoller, W. J. Blot, J. D. Boice, J. F. Fraumeni, and J. H. Olsen, "Breast Implants and Cancer Risk in Denmark," *International Journal of Cancer,* 71 (1997): 956–958; J. W. Glasser, N. C. Lee, and P. A. Wingo, "Does Breast Augmentation Increase the Risk of Breast Cancer?" *The Epidemic Intelligence Service Conference,* April 1989; K. A. Kern, J. T. Flannery, and P. G. Kuehn, "Carcinogenic Potential of

Silicone Breast Implants: A Connecticut Statewide Study," *Plastic Reconstruction Surgery*, 100 (1997): 737–749; K. E. Malone, J. L. Stanford, J. R. Daling, and L. F. Voigt, "Implants and Breast Cancer," *The Lancet*, 339 (1992): 1365; J. K. McLaughlin, O. Nyren, W. J. Blot, L. Yin, S. Josefsson, J. F. Fraumeni, and H. O. Adami, "Cancer Risk Among Women with Cosmetic Breasts Implants: A Population-Based Cohort Study in Sweden," *Journal of the National Cancer Institute*, 90 (1998): 156–158; J. K. McLaughlin, J. F. Fraumeni, O. Nyren, and H. O. Adami, "Silicone Breast Implants and Risk of Cancer?" *Journal of the American Medical Association*, 273 (1995): 116; J. K. McLaughlin, J. F. Fraumeni, J. Olsen, and L. Mellemkjaer, "Re: Breast Implants, Cancer, and Systemic Sclerosis," *Journal of the National Cancer Institute*, 86 (1994): 1414; and J. Y. Petit, M. G. Le, H. Mouriesse, M. Rietjens, P. Gill, G. Contesso, and A. Lehmann, "Can Breast Reconstruction with Gel-Filled Silicone Implants Increase the Risk of Death and Second Primary Cancer in Patients Treated by Mastectomy for Breast Cancer?" *Plastic Reconstruction Surgery*, 94 (1994): 115–119.

Mitsubishi: Sexual Harassment in the Workplace

T he public will never know exactly what happened at the Normal, Illinois, plant. However, in 1998 Mitsubishi Motor Manufacturing of America agreed to pay $34 million to settle sexual harassment claims from five hundred women. In addition to the money, Mitsubishi agreed to the establishment of a panel of three "monitors" to oversee the implementation and review of the company's new sexual harassment policies.

The allegations began in 1990 at a plant located in a town that prides itself on being conservative and family oriented. One complaint was of an employee being sexually harassed by a superior. After the woman's complaint, the supervisor was moved to another area of the plant. The woman then said that a fellow assembly-line worker harassed her. Her first two complaints drew warnings for the worker; however, the company did not acknowledge the third. When she complained again, she was transferred to Final 4, the area in charge of seats and seat belts. When the woman sued the company, she was treated coldly by many of the male employees. Another woman stated that one branch manager would stand close to her and try to sniff her body, smacking his lips. One woman told of an incident in the human resources department that she felt was inappropriate. When department executives held a Christmas party at an employee's home, one executive and his girlfriend wore sumo wrestler costumes and simulated sex. A videotape was made and distributed at the plant. Another woman told of being in the plant's computer room when Mitsubishi's system crashed. She asked the network administrator if he knew what the problem was and, in front of coworkers, the man grabbed her by the shoulders and began shaking her while screaming obscenities.

When the lawsuits started appearing, Mitsubishi's response was to attack the attackers in the news media forum. The company allegedly paid employees to demonstrate outside Chicago offices of the Equal Employment Opportunity Commission (EEOC). At the rally, Mitsubishi also took the names of those who attended so as to know who did not attend. At the same time employees were taking visiting Japanese officials to strip bars, and on occasion women at the plant were asked by male coworkers to bare their breasts. The attitude at the plant seemed to be that anything short of physical contact was acceptable. One woman at the

---

This case was prepared by John Fraedrich for classroom discussion, rather than to illustrate either effective or ineffective handling of an administrative, ethical, or legal decision by management.

plant said, "You see photos of your boss giving oral sex to the strippers, and this is all in your workplace. It made a lot of women uncomfortable." When an in-house investigation was conducted, ten male employees were fired, and the company believed that it had done enough, although it intended to do more in the future. Some outside sources thought that the Japanese executives did not hire the right people. Many of these executives, although having good technical abilities, had limited English proficiency and poor intercultural communication skills. Also, some outside sources believed that the top executives at Mitsubishi's headquarters in Japan did not have a good understanding of the cultural significance of sexual harassment in the United States.

WORKPLACE AWARENESS

Employers are beginning to realize the pervasiveness of sexual harassment. A poll by the National Association for Female Executives revealed that 53 percent of the thirteen hundred members surveyed had been, or knew someone who had been, sexually harassed. Another poll found that half of the men surveyed admitted having done something that a woman might view as harassment. Statistics have shown that 50 to 67 percent of harassment is done by men toward women. However, the number of charges filed with the EEOC by men has increased to more than two hundred per year. Desire for revenge against the boss, disappointing job-performance appraisals, and even the desire for a transfer to another department have been found to be catalysts for sexual harassment complaints.

In 1991 Congress amended Title VII of the Civil Rights Act of 1964 to permit victims of sexual harassment to recover damages, including punitive damages. In 1993 the U.S. Supreme Court broadened the law by making it easier to prove injury. In 1998 the Supreme Court declared that workers need no longer prove that an employer knew or should have known about the sexual harassment and failed to stop it. In addition, victims do not necessarily have to show being passed over for promotion or being fired because they spurned a boss's sexual advances. "It is by now well recognized that . . . sexual harassment by supervisors (and, for that matter, co-employees) is a persistent problem in the workplace," wrote Justice David H. Souter. He added that sexual policing of the work area is now "one of the costs of doing business." "When a person with supervisory authority discriminates . . . , his actions necessarily draw upon his superior position over the people who report to him." Souter added that "an employee generally cannot check a supervisor's abusive conduct the same way that she might deal with abuse from a co-worker. When a fellow employee harasses, the victim can walk away or tell the offender where to go, but it may be difficult to offer such responses to a supervisor. . . . "

More companies are now realizing that the penalties of being accused of sexual harassment can be greater than expected. Here are some examples of recent settlements:

- Ford Motor Co. — $9 million
- Chevron Corporation — $2.2 million
- Microsoft Corp. — $2.2 million
- Astra — $9.85 million

IDENTIFYING THE ISSUE

Sexual discrimination was made illegal by the 1964 Civil Rights Act, but the act contained no specific provisions to deal with sexual harassment. In the mid-1970s a Washington, D.C., woman complained of retaliation after she declined to have an after-hours affair with her boss. A federal judge ruled that the 1964 Civil Rights Act did not apply to her case. As women joined the work force in increasing numbers, especially in professions previously dominated by men, they became targets of harassment. However, it took the EEOC more than a decade after the Civil Rights Act of 1964 to develop specific definitions of and guidelines on sexual harassment. Recognition by the law came when the EEOC initiated the incorporation of sexual harassment into the Civil Rights Act of 1964, making it possible for victims to seek compensatory damages. In general, sexual harassment is not limited to any one profession or to any level of employment. Victims range from secretaries to renowned neurosurgeons.

One of the nation's leading brain surgeons at Stanford University Medical School finally resigned after being subjected to sexual harassment by a male colleague. A machinist at American National Can Company saw that her excellent performance did not compensate for her being a woman. When she filed suit, her boss told her that she had provoked the incidents and had not done enough to stop the treatment. In fact, winning a sexual harassment claim is anything but easy, especially if the woman has allowed the behavior to continue or is viewed as having sent "mixed signals."

DEFINING SEXUAL HARASSMENT

What exactly constitutes sexual harassment? Is it harassment when a man displays photos of nude women or tells off-color jokes in the presence of women colleagues? What about the situation where a woman repeatedly refuses a coworker's request for a date, but he won't give up? What about instances when a man feels harassed by a woman? The issue is complicated by the fact that men and women have different attitudes about what constitutes sexual harassment. According to one study, 67 percent of the men surveyed would be flattered to be propositioned at work, but 63 percent of the women would be offended by such behavior from men. Another survey reported that 23 percent of the men surveyed would be flattered if a woman looked at them suggestively, whereas only 8 percent of the women felt likewise about such a look from a man.

Under Title VII of the Civil Rights Act of 1964 as interpreted by the courts, unwelcome sexual advances, requests for sexual favors, and other verbal or physical conduct of a sexual nature constitute sexual harassment when submission to or rejection of this conduct explicitly or implicitly affects an individual's employment, unreasonably interferes with an individual's work performance, or creates an intimidating, hostile, or offensive work environment.

Sexual harassment can occur in a variety of circumstances, including but not limited to the following:

The victim as well as the harasser may be a woman or a man. The victim does not have to be of the opposite sex.

The harasser can be the victim's supervisor, an agent of the employer, a supervisor in another area, a coworker, or a nonemployee.

The victim does not have to be the person harassed but could be anyone affected by the offensive conduct.

Unlawful sexual harassment may occur without economic injury to or discharge of the victim.

The harasser's conduct must be unwelcome.*

Federal law recognizes two different sets of legal grounds for claiming sexual harassment (see Figure 1). The first is quid pro quo. Under this form of harassment a person in authority would demand sexual favors of a subordinate as a condition of getting or keeping a job benefit. When this happens, the company becomes responsible as well because the manager is an extension (power base) of the corporation. What makes business even more concerned is that the perpetrator does not even have to be an employee but merely an agent for the company.

The second set of legal grounds is a hostile work environment. A hostile work environment arises when a coworker or supervisor, engaging in unwelcome and inappropriate sexually based behavior, renders the workplace atmosphere intimidating, hostile, or offensive. In one early case, *Bundy* v. *Jackson,* the District of Columbia Circuit Court of Appeals characterized hostile-environment cases as presenting a "cruel trilemma." In *Bundy* the victim had three options: (1) to endure the harassment, (2) to attempt to oppose it and likely make the situation worse, or (3) to leave the place of employment. In another case the Supreme Court stated that a hostile work environment constitutes grounds for an action only when the conduct is unwelcome, based on sex, and severe or pervasive enough "to alter the conditions of [the victim's] employment and create an abusive working environment." But what is unwelcome? When is conduct based on sex? Are employees still allowed to

---

The U.S. Equal Employment Opportunity Commission, "Facts About Sexual Harassment," http://www.eeoc.gov/facts/fs-sex.html *(accessed January 15, 1999).*

FIGURE 1   Sexual Harassment

SEXUAL MISCONDUCT
Unwelcome sexual advances, requests for sexual favors,
and other verbal or physical conduct of a sexual nature

Plus

Quid pro Quo	**Hostile Enviroment**
Submission to such conduct	Conduct has the purpose or effect of
1. is made a term or condition of employment or	1. unreasonably interfering with work performance or
2. forms a basis for employment decisions affecting that individual.	2. creating an intimidating, hostile, or offensive environment.
RESULTS IN	**RESULTS IN**
The employer being always liable.	The employer being liable if the employer knew or should have known about the harassment and failed to take appropriate corrective action.

flirt on the job? Can they tell off-color jokes? What happens when someone gets offended? Who decides what is appropriate and what is not? Should employees be required to tolerate some minimal level of offensive sexual behavior within the workplace?

The EEOC itself has stated, "Title VII does not proscribe all conduct of a sexual nature in the workplace." However, such conduct becomes unacceptable when it is unwelcome. As a result of recent cases, courts will likely find an illegal hostile environment present when the workplace includes sexual propositions, pornography, extremely vulgar language, sexual touching, degrading comments, or embarrassing questions or jokes. For example, according to one court case, a construction company hired three women to work at construction sites. One woman developed a skin reaction to the sun, whereupon the men nicknamed her "Herpes." The women were subjected to the men's "mooning" them, showing pornographic pictures, urinating in water bottles and gas tanks, and writing obscenities in the dust on the women's cars.

Finally, even if the victim allows or consents to the harassing conduct, the employer remains liable if the victim's behavior indicated that the conduct was unwelcome. A ruling by the Supreme Court has shed more light on the sexual harassment issue. In *Harris* v. *Forklift Systems Inc.,* Teresa Harris argued that she was working in a hostile environment because she was made to serve coffee at meetings of the other managers although her superior never asked the male managers to do so. Her boss also made comments such as "You're a woman, what do you know" and referred to her as "a dumb --- woman." In addition, he would ask her to retrieve coins from his front pockets and then comment on or make sexual innuendoes about her attire. On one occasion her superior suggested in front of other employees that they go to a motel to negotiate her raise. Harris endured these comments for two years.

Although the concept of a hostile work environment is becoming more defined, it is still imprecise. Courts are now emphasizing that the determination as to whether a work environment is hostile or abusive must be made by looking at all the circumstances. Certain factors that now constitute a hostile work environment include the frequency of the discriminatory conduct, its severity, whether it is physically threatening or humiliating or merely an offensive utterance, whether it unreasonably interferes with an employee's work performance, and whether a reasonable woman may view it as creating a hostile environment.

AVOIDING SEXUAL HARASSMENT COMPLAINTS

Experts advise companies to focus on prevention. They recommend that employers develop and distribute policies that precisely define unacceptable conduct and the punishment for violating the policy. They also advise holding training seminars that sensitize workers to the issue through videos, lectures, and role-playing exercises. Companies are also urged to set up dispute-resolution procedures that permit confidential complaints of harassment and do not require the victim to report the harassment to immediate supervisors, who are often the harassers.

Technological advances have opened a new arena for potential sexual harassment. One survey of four thousand executives found that even though 80 percent of their management-level employees had access to the Internet, one-third of the companies did not have a policy in place on the use of computers, e-mail, and the Internet as related to sexual harassment. Many employees are not aware that sexually explicit jokes sent or received via e-mail or pornography viewed, downloaded, or forwarded to others may constitute sexual harassment. One CEO of an international company settled out of court when it was documented that all his Internet "hits" were porn sites and that he had eighty-one sexually explicit jokes in his personal folders. In another case, six months of sexually harassing e-mail from a CEO to an employee prompted a quick, out-of-court settlement.

Many people are unaware that these types of activities can be traced even after they have been "deleted." Employees at Xerox, the *New York Times,* and First Union Bank were fired for inappropriate Internet use. What triggered the dismissals was workplace behavior and declining work productivity that could be traced to Internet use. Some employees spent too much time on the Internet, while others sent offensive content to other employees. Some engaged in heavy surfing of pornographic sites, and some even sent materials via e-mail that included videos of people engaged in sex.

Chevron Corporation was sued because of an e-mail circulated within the company that listed twenty-five reasons why beer is better than a woman. The company settled out of court for $2.2 million. Microsoft also settled a sexual harassment suit for $2.2 million that involved pornographic messages sent within the company via e-mail. Such cases underscore the necessity of operating with a clear policy that governs the use of the Internet and e-mail by employees when using company equipment on company time.

Companies need to measure the consequences of sexual harassment in more than monetary terms. The costs of lawsuits in the form of compensatory and punitive damages are obvious. Less obvious and longer lasting are the costs associated with increased stress, strained personal relationships for the victims, decreased work effectiveness, absenteeism, higher turnover, lower morale among peers, and an overall loss of image for the company. Sexual harassment will plague the business world for many years because of its complexity and the difficulty in proving and enforcing measures against it. However, some chief executives acknowledge that the Mitsubishi case has heightened their awareness of the problem and will help improve ways in which companies follow up sexual harassment charges.

In the case of Mitsubishi, supervisors were being hired by non-Americans, who were not as culturally sensitive to sexual harassment. Within Japanese society, sexual harassment, as defined in the United States, was tacitly approved of during the time prior to the lawsuits. As time passed and more interaction occurred between Normal, Illinois, and Japan, it appears that supervisors started to adopt more of a "Japanese" perspective toward women, and eventually this attitude resulted in actions that became tolerated workplace behavior. The differences in cultures, the hiring of potentially insensitive supervisors, and time created the environment that caused Mitsubishi's problem in the United States.

Although Japan made progress in the late 1990s, several experts suggest that the Japanese stance on gender equality lags about two decades behind the American perspective. A new government survey in Japan showed that more than two-thirds of female public servants suffer from some form of sexual harassment. Laws introduced in 1998 that prohibit sexual harassment have helped reduce such serious acts as stalking and body touching, but cases involving appearance and sexual jokes still abound. A separate survey showed that sexual harassment complaints increased 35 percent in one year.

HAS MITSUBISHI LEARNED?

The result of the Mitsubishi case was that nineteen employees lost their jobs for engaging in sexual harassment. Others were demoted, transferred, or disciplined. The message that Mitsubishi wanted their employees to hear was: "Violate our values, jeopardize your career." In 1997, the opportunity programs department was staffed and charged with enforcing all equal employment opportunity laws. A process to review all cases and a toll-free hot line for employee reporting of violations were established. Also, more than four thousand employees attended a mandatory eight-hour training seminar on preventing sexual harassment. In 1998, Mitsubishi found that there were still some problems with language on the plant floor and strengthened its program in that area.

In September 2000, Mitsubishi announced the establishment of the Employee Advice Bureau to discuss with, or give advice to, employees who contact the bureau with problems, including the "seeking of advice and grievances or complaints on sexual harassment and other human rights–related issues." Also in 2000, the panel of three sexual harassment consent decree monitors found that sexual harassment was not a significant problem at the Normal, Illinois, plant and that the company had made commendable progress.

The "zero-tolerance" program at Mitsubishi does not mean "zero occurrence," however. Although headlines have faded, apparently many problems have not. A *New York Times* article published in late 2000 said that many current and former Mitsubishi workers still paint a "disturbing portrait" of a factory that remains hostile toward women. Some workers said harassment remains a serious problem. Others declined to discuss the issue, and few were willing to speak on the record. Those who agreed to interviews indicated that the most extreme forms of harassment have ended and that the number of incidents has declined sharply. However, disturbing events still continue, according to some employees. One woman says she was the target of offensive drawings, while another accused a male coworker of tampering with cars on the assembly line just before they reached her. Other employees say the rude language continues. The women say that what is troubling is not that there are still incidents, but that investigations are not kept confidential and that little effort is made to find the source of problems. Some indicated that, after making complaints, they were transferred to other areas of the plant where they had to learn new, sometimes more difficult, jobs. Mitsubishi officials say female workers are moved permanently to other areas only with their consent.

Has the culture changed at Mitsubishi? Only time will tell.

Questions

1. What is your evaluation of the "reasonable woman" clause in sexual harassment cases? Would it be preferable to use a gender-neutral standard? If so, why?

2. What actions should Mitsubishi take to avoid future sexual harassment problems? Japan and the United States have very different cultural backgrounds. Do these cultural differences between Japan and the United States affect how the Japanese executives view and deal with sexual harassment problems?

3. Some argue that sexual harassment is not as severe as it has been made out to be. They suggest that because women have decided to join the work force, they should learn to tough it out. Some also argue that women are overly sensitive and take even a "harmless joke" too personally. Discuss these opinions.

These facts are from Reed Abelson, "Can Respect Be Mandated? Maybe Not Here," *New York Times*, September 10, 2000, p. 3; "Establishment of Employee Advice Bureau," September 1, 2000, *http:// www.mitsubishi-motors.co.jp/inter/NEWS/0004-09/n000901b.htm* (accessed October 22, 2000); "Public Servants and Sexual Harassment," *Yahoo! News*, December 27, 1999, *http://dailynews.yahoo. com/h/nm/20001227/od/harassment_dc_1.html* (accessed January 4, 2001); "Internet Surfing — The Newest Workplace Liability Is on a Screen Near You Today," *Industry Week*, February 7, 2000, pp. 58–64; Alan Deutschman, "Dealing with Sexual Harassment," *Fortune*, November 4, 1991, pp. 145, 148; Michele Galen, Zachary Schiller, and Joan O'C. Hamilton, "Ending Sexual Harassment: Business Is Getting the Message," *Business Week*, March 18, 1991, pp. 98–100; Michele Galen, Joseph Weber, and Alice Z. Cuneo, "Out of the Shadows: The Thomas Hearings Force Businesses to Confront an Ugly Reality," *Business Week*, October 28, 1991, pp. 30–31; Susan B. Garland and Troy Segal, "Thomas vs. Hill: The Lessons for Corporate America," *Business Week*, October 21, 1991, p. 32; Ted Gest, Amy Saltzman, Betsy Carpenter, and Dorian Friedman, "Harassment: Men on Trial," *U.S. News and World Report*, October 21, 1991, pp. 38–40; John Leo, "Getting Reasonable About Feelings," *U.S. News & World Report*, November 18, 1991, p. 30; Sarah J. McCarthy, "Cultural Fascism," *Forbes*, December 9, 1991, p. 116; Gretchen Morgenson, "May I Have the Pleasure . . ." *National Review*, November 18, 1991, pp. 36–41; "Watch That Leer, Stifle That Joke," *Forbes*, May 15, 1989, pp. 69–72; Daniel Niven, "HBR Case Study: The Case of the Hidden Harassment," *Harvard Business Review*, 70 (March–April 1992): 12–14; Eloise Salholz and Douglas Waller, "Tailhook: Scandal Time," *Newsweek*, July 6, 1992, pp. 40–41; Daniel Seligman, "The Milestone Menace," *Fortune*, January 15, 1990, p. 153; Geoffrey Smith, "Consciousness Raising Among Plain Old White Boys," *Business Week*, October 28, 1991, p. 32; Charlene Marmer Solomon, "Sexual Harassment After the Thomas Hearings," *Personnel Journal* 70 (December 1991): 32; Barry S. Roberts and Richard A. Mann, "Sexual Harassment in the Workplace: A Primer, *http://www.uakron.edu/lawrev/ robert1.html;* Kirstin Downy Grimsely, "Community Still Split in Aftermath of Mitsubishi Settlement," *Washington Post*, June 15, 1998, p. A9; Kirstin Downy Grimsely, "Mitsubish Settles for $34 Million," *Washington Post*, June 12, 1998, p. A1; Kathy McKinney, "Judge Oks Settlement on MMMA," *Pantagraph Business Writer*, *http://www.pantagraph.com/mmmsettle.html#million;* Kathy McKinney, "Settlement a Warning to Industry," *Pantagraph Business Writer*, *http:// www.pantagraph.com/mmmsettle.html#million* (accessed June 13, 1998); Kathy McKinney, "$34 Million Deal Is a Record," *Pantagraph Business Writer*, *http://www. pantagraph.com/mmmsettle. html#million* (accessed June 12, 1998); Steve Arney, "I Don't Feel I'm Part of History . . . Today's the Same as Yesterday," *Pantagraph Business Writer*, *http://www.pantagraph.com/mmmsettle. html#million* (accessed June 12, 1998); Kathy McKinney, "EEOC Will Determine Who Gets How Much," *Pantagraph Business Writer*, *http://www.pantagraph.com/mmmsettle.html#million* (accessed June 12, 1998); David Brummer, "Controversy Leaves Twin Cities Unharmed," *Pantagraph Business Writer*, *http://www.pantagraph.com/mmmsettle.html#million* (accessed June 12, 1998); Kathy McKinney, "Mitsubishi Settles Suit," *Pantagraph Business Writer*, *http://www.pantagraph. com/mmmsettle.html#million* (accessed June 11, 1998); and Philip Berkowitz, "Sexual Harassment and Lawyers: Advice for Foreign Law Firms in the U.S., *International Legal Practitioner*, *http://www.ebglaw.com/newsstand/sexual_harassment.html* (accessed September 1997).

Case 8

Tobacco Under Fire: Advertising a Harmful Product

Tobacco's detrimental effects have been well documented. It is one of the primary factors in illnesses such as cancer, heart and circulatory disease, and respiratory disease. Smoking causes nearly 90 percent of all lung cancers, and secondhand smoke has been shown to contribute to the development of lung cancer in nonsmokers. Tobacco-related death estimates are at approximately 4 million per year worldwide, with four hundred and thirty thousand of those deaths in the United States. Given current trends, this statistic is projected to rise to 10 million by 2030.

HISTORY OF CIGARETTE ADVERTISING

Cigarette ads started as early as 1929. One of the first ads, by Lucky Strike, touted the fact that more than twenty thousand physicians had said that its product was less irritating than other cigarettes and that prominent athletes used its product with no harmful effects. In 1939 Philip Morris promoted its cigarettes as having advantages to the nose and throat. A decade later Camel was also extolling the benefits of its product. By the early 1950s consumers had begun to suspect that smoking might be harmful. To counter this perception, Kent ran an ad arguing that if you were one of those "sensitive smokers" who worried about the harmful effects of smoking, Kent provided you with health protection and gave "taste satisfaction."

As a result of growing public concern, the health hazards of cigarette smoking were investigated in the early 1950s. In 1953 a Memorial Sloan-Kettering Cancer Center report linked smoking to cancer in rats. The first attempt to regulate the cigarette industry came in 1955, when the Federal Trade Commission (FTC) prohibited claims of the presence or absence of any positive physical effects of smoking in cigarette advertising or labeling.

In the 1960s and 1970s consumers and the U.S. government began to understand the harmful effects of smoking. In 1964, Surgeon General Luther Terry de-

---

This case was prepared by John Fraedrich and Barbara Gilmer for classroom discussion, rather than to illustrate either effective or ineffective handling of an administrative, ethical, or legal decision by management.

clared cigarettes to be a cause of cancer. The following year trade regulation rules were formulated, mandating a health warning on all cigarette packaging and prohibiting cigarette advertising to people under 25 years of age. In addition, several developed countries started banning television ads. Nevertheless, consumption increased.

Smoking did not decline until soon after the "fairness doctrine" was implemented in 1967. Although developed for political advertising, it was applied to require radio and television broadcasters to give equal time to antismoking advertisements. In 1971 the Cigarette Advertising and Labeling Act banned cigarette advertisements from U.S. television and radio altogether. A 1984 amendment required cigarette manufacturers or importers to display on cigarette packaging and advertising one of four different health warnings, which were rotated every quarter.

But in the 1980s the tobacco industry discovered a new promotional vehicle, which soon became an industry standard — movie endorsements. For example, Sylvester Stallone agreed to smoke B&W cigarettes in four movies — *Rhinestone Cowboy, Rambo, 50/50,* and *Rocky IV* — for $500,000.

The tobacco industry had vehemently opposed all legislation restricting cigarette advertising. In contrast, the medical profession and various consumer groups wanted even more stringent regulation of the industry. Many advocated a complete ban on cigarette advertising. In 1998 cigarette makers agreed that they would not target youths in advertisements. However, according to studies by the Massachusetts Department of Public Health and the American Legacy Foundation, advertising in magazines with large teen readerships actually increased the following year. Cigarette makers spent $119.9 million on advertising in magazines popular among youths, which was a 30 percent increase over the amount spent in the period prior to the settlement. Faced with investigations into whether their advertising violated the 1998 settlements, Philip Morris, the nation's largest tobacco company, announced that it would stop placing ads in forty-two magazines with teen readership greater than 15 percent. A spokesman for *Sports Illustrated* said the readership figures used by Philip Morris were inaccurate, and *Entertainment Weekly*'s publisher said that the move by Philip Morris was "a suspension and not a forever cancellation."

HIGH STAKES

Cigarettes are big business. With approximately 6 trillion cigarettes smoked annually at a cost of $50 billion, the economic stakes are enormous. Twenty-two states grow tobacco, making it the sixth-largest cash crop in the United States. The vast and complex tobacco-supply network extends the chain of economic dependence on tobacco to include manufacturers of farm equipment, advertising agencies, advertising media, and other businesses around the world. Arguably, banning cigarettes and their advertising could have serious repercussions for the economy. Moreover, even many nonsmokers believe cigarette advertising is commercial speech protected under the First Amendment. There are also those who fear that a ban on cigarette advertising would set a dangerous precedent for more government interference in commercial activities.

TRUTH IN ADVERTISING

Opponents of the commercial free-speech argument counter that if commercial speech is to be free, it should not be deceptive and misleading. For example, in 1985 R. J. Reynolds ran an advertisement in the *New York Times* and other newspapers around the United States entitled "Of Cigarettes and Science." The FTC filed a formal complaint against the company, saying that the advertisement was a distortion of an important study demonstrating the relationship between a number of risk factors and heart disease. R. J. Reynolds countered by arguing that "Of Cigarettes and Science" was an expression of opinion on an issue of social and political importance and was therefore protected by the First Amendment. A commercial law judge dismissed the complaint, concluding that "Of Cigarettes and Science" was not commercial speech and therefore not subject to FTC regulation. The court did not consider whether the advertisement was deceptive, false, or misleading.

THE FUTURE

Recent documents, as well as legislation in the United States and a host of suits brought by state prosecutors, have sent the tobacco industry a message of being unwelcome — but not the taxes it brings in. The key in starting this future was Jeffrey Wigand, former research executive of Brown & Williamson Tobacco Corp. When Wigand came forward to testify against the tobacco giants, a five-hundred page dossier attacking him was developed. After careful review of this document, the *Wall Street Journal* asserted that much of it was poorly substantiated, thus giving rise to the argument that a "smear" campaign was being created. National news shows such as *60 Minutes* opened the debate wider as to whether tobacco companies should be legally liable for damages caused by smoking. Billions of dollars were sought from the tobacco companies, as well as a plan to keep the industry going so that it could continue to pay taxes and create jobs. Wigand's decision to blow the whistle on "big Tobacco" and the subsequent results were dramatized in the movie *The Insider*. Wigand now travels the country giving guest lectures to children in grades K–6 about the dangers of tobacco. Wigand says that "the tobacco industry's manipulation continues to capture more than 3,000 kids a day as new addicts" and that the key "is to keep young people from ever taking that first puff."* Government statistics indicate that 80 percent of the 50 million to 60 million Americans habituated to cigarettes began smoking as children.

If there are no dramatic changes in cessation rates and no new interventions and if children start smoking at expected rates, then the current number of smokers in the world, 1.1 billion, is predicted to rise to 1.64 billion by 2025. In developing countries, women will be a particular focus as smoking rates are much lower at present among women than men. The prevalence of smoking among women in developing countries is currently 12 percent, but that figure is likely to triple by 2025. It is in the developing countries that the tobacco companies see their future, as the following statements indicate:

> They have to find a way to feed the monsters they've built. Just about the only way will be to increase sales to the developing world.†

> Tobacco use in the developed nations will trend down slightly through the end of the century, while in the developing countries use could rise by about three percent annually. A bright picture indeed! Not a smoke-free society, but continued growth for the tobacco industry.#

> We should not be depressed simply because the total free world market appears to be declining. Within the total market, there are areas of strong growth, particularly in Asia and Africa; there are new markets opening up for our exports, such as Indo-China and the Comecon countries; and there are great opportunities to increase our market share in areas like Europe. . . . This industry is consistently profitable. And there are opportunities to increase that profitability still further.@

> You know what we want . . . we want Asia.**

In the twenty-first century, tobacco companies in the United States and Europe appear to be rethinking their strategies for developed countries. For example, several companies are trying to create a "safer" cigarette. Star Scientific, Inc., has test-marketed a new cigarette that contains a charcoal filter and cured tobacco in an effort to reduce nitrosamine, a potent carcinogen. R. J. Reynolds' *Eclipse* brand is the result of a technology explored in the 1980s that relies on heating tobacco rather than burning it, thus producing fewer toxic substances. The hope is that the risk of cancer, chronic bronchitis, and possibly emphysema will be reduced. However, *Eclipse*'s filter can release glass fibers into the lungs.

While reducing advertising and trying to develop a safer product, tobacco companies still have litigation to address. More than thirty-six states are attempt-

---

*A.J.S. Rayl, "Tobacco Targets Kids, Threatens Health," USA Today, March 31, 2000, http://www. usatoday.com/life/health/doctor/lhdoc122.htm (accessed January 4, 2001).

†R. Morelli, "Packing It In," Marketing Week, 14(16) (June 28, 1991): 30–34.

#"Growth Through 2000," Tobacco Reporter, February 1989.

@"Tobacco Explained: 7 Emerging Markets," Action on Smoking and Health, U.K. Paper. http:// ash.org.uk/papers/tobexpld7.html (accessed June 16, 1999).

**L. Heise, "Unhealthy Alliance," World Watch, October 1988, p. 20 [c. 7].

ing to settle Medicare and Medicaid claims to recover the $20 billion a year spent on smoking-related illnesses. However, a judge ruled recently that although the government would not be allowed to recover those expenses, it could pursue racketeering charges against the tobacco companies.

Cracks opened up by civil litigation have hurt the tobacco companies in that they are spending more time in courtrooms instead of dealing with the manufacturing and marketing of their products. Tobacco firms will probably settle all state claims, although with some sort of clause eliminating further legal actions against them. The payment of the claims will most likely be structured in such a way that jobs and taxes the companies provide will not be jeopardized.

Although the use of tobacco products is not expected to be banned in the United States, the promotion of such products is restricted. Antismoking campaigns and increased public awareness have helped reduce the number of cigarettes smoked within the last two decades by 42 percent in the United States. Also contributing to this reduction is the fact that the price of cigarettes rose 80 percent in the last two years. The average state tax on a pack of cigarettes is 34 cents.

While tobacco consumption will continue to decrease overall in developed countries, a more aggressive marketing strategy is being pursued in developing countries, where tobacco companies are sponsoring sporting and other events and aiming their advertising toward younger people. The World Health Organization (WHO) anticipates that 70 percent of tobacco-related deaths will be in developing countries by 2030. WHO and the World Bank are trying to convince developing countries to follow the U.S. example of raising cigarette taxes in order to prevent the tobacco companies from gaining new and larger markets in these countries. It is likely that the lessons learned by the tobacco companies in the U.S. court system will be applied to emerging markets so that future litigation can be kept to a minimum.

Questions

1. What are the arguments for and against the issue of tobacco use, tobacco advertising, and free speech?

2. Is selling a potentially harmful or addictive product that is legal a problem for businesspeople? How should a society regulate such products and protect its citizens from them?

3. If the cost of cigarettes becomes prohibitive in the United States, what, if any, are the ethical ramifications of selling cigarettes in other countries?

These facts are from "Judge Limits Tobacco Cases: Health Laws Can't Be Used to Recover Costs of Sick Smokers," *Detroit News,* September 29, 2000, p. 3; "America Smokes, Exports Fewer Cigarettes," *Detroit News,* May 22, 2000, p. 8; "Deaths from Tobacco Will Soar," *Chicago Sun-Times,* August 8, 2000, p. 12; Gordon Fairclough, "Magazines Brace for Cigarette Ad Pullout," *Wall Street Journal,* June 7, 2000, p. B5; "U.S. House Approval of Foreign Sales Corporation Bill Providing $100 Million in Tax Breaks for U.S. Tobacco Companies," *U.S. Newswire,* September 13, 2000, p. 1; "Dying to

Quit," *Advocate*, August 3, 2000, p. 2A; "Memo on Tobacco Trends in 21st Century: Domestic and Global Outlook," *U.S. Newswire*, December 16, 1999, pp. 1–2; "Cigarette Sales on Web Will Resolve Tax Issues," *Portland Press Herald*, August 30, 2000, p. 10A; "Expecting a World Which Is Free from Tobacco," *Jakarta Post*, May 31, 2000, p. 3; "You're Going Too Far, Baby," *The Village Voice*, August 15, 2000, pp. 62–63; A. J. S. Rayl, "Tobacco Targets Kids, Threatens Health," *USA Today*, March 31, 2000, *http://www.usatoday.com/life/health/doctor/lhdoc122.htm* (accessed January 4, 2001); Nancy Shute, "Building a Better Butt," *U.S. News & World Report*, September 18, 2000, p. 66; *American Voices: Prize Winning Essays on Freedom of Speech, Censorship, and Advertising Bans* (New York: Philip Morris USA, 1987); Daniel Seligman, "Camel Rights," *Fortune*, May 18, 1992, p. 120; Kathleen Deveny, "Joe Camel Is Also Pied Piper, Research Finds," *Wall Street Journal*, December 11, 1992, pp. B1, B4; Walecia Konrad, "I'd Toddle a Mile for Camel," *Business Week*, December 23, 1991, p. 34; Gary Levin, "Poll: Camel Ads Effective with Kids: Brand Recognition Highest Among Preteens," *Advertising Age*, April 27, 1992; Joanne Lipman, "Why Activists Fume at Anti-Smoking Ads," *Wall Street Journal*, February 20, 1992, p. B3; Barbara Lippert, "Camel's Old Joe Poses the Question: What Is Sexy?" *AdWeek's Marketing Week*, October 3, 1988, p. 55; "R. J. Reynolds Takes on the AMA, Defending Joe Camel Cartoon Ad," *Wall Street Journal*, February 5, 1992, p. B8; Camille P. Schuster and Christine Pacelli Powell, "Comparison of Cigarette and Alcohol Advertising Controversies," *Journal of Advertising*, 16(2) (1987): 26–33; Fara Warner, "Novello Throws Down the Gauntlet: The Surgeon General's Crusade to Kill Off Joe Cool," *AdWeek's Marketing Week*, March 16, 1992, pp. 4–5; Larry C. White, *Merchants of Death* (New York: Beech Tree Books, 1988); Alan Blum, *New England Journal of Medicine*, 324 (March 28, 1991) : 913–916; Kevin Goldman, "Philip Morris Dresses Up Virginia Slims," *Wall Street Journal*, February 26, 1993; U.S. DHHS, National Center for Chronic Disease Prevention and Health Promotion Study, cited in *Wall Street Journal*, April 2, 1993, p. A1; U.S. DHHS, National Institute on Drug Abuse, press release, 1989 National High School Senior Drug Abuse Survey, "Monitoring the Future Survey," February 13, 1990; Stop Teen Addiction to Tobacco (STAT), "Cigarette Advertising Increases Smoking," *Tobacco Free Youth Reporter*, Fall 1992; A. O. Goldstein, P. M. Fischer, J. W. Richards, and D. Creten, "The Influence of Cigarette Advertising on Adolescent Smoking," Action on Smoking and Health, U.K. Paper, June 25, 1998, *http://www.ash.org.uk/papers/tobexpld7.html* (accessed June 16, 1999); Joe B. Tye, "Lusting After Children: The Tobacco Industry's Investment in a Profitable Future," *Social Science Record*, Fall 1988; "World No-Tobacco Day: Health Versus Smoking," World Health Organization (WHO), press release, May 27, 1993; William Ecenbarger, "America's New Merchants of Death," *Reader's Digest*, April 1993; "Africa: Ashtray of the World," *Sunday Times* (London), May 13, 1990; L. Bird, "Joe Smooth for President," *Adweek's Marketing Week*, May 20, 1991; Paul M. Fischer, Meyer P. Schwartz, John W. Richards, Jr., Adam O. Goldstein, and Tina H. Rojas, "Brand Logo Recognition by Children Aged Three to Six Years," *Journal of the American Medical Association (JAMA)*, December 11, 1991; Joseph R. DiFranza, John W. Richards, Paul M. Paulman, Nancy Wolf-Gillespie, Christopher Fletcher, Robert D. Jaffe, and David Murray, "RJR Nabisco's Cartoon Camel Promotes Camel Cigarettes to Children," *JAMA*, December 11, 1991; Karen Lewis, "Addicting the Young: Tobacco Pushers and Kids," *Multinational Monitor*, January–February 1992; Stop Teenage Addiction to Tobacco (STAT), "RJRNabisco: Targeting Teens for Addiction," *Tobacco Free Youth Reporter*, Fall 1992; "Tobacco Explained:7 Emerging Markets," Action on Smoking and Health, U.K. Paper, *http://ash.org.uk/papers/tobexpld7.html* (accessed June 16, 1999); "Tobacco Trials Research," The Wilmington Institute, 1998, *http://www.tobacco-litigation.com/index.html-ssi* (accessed June 16, 1999); Rekha Balu and Ernest Beck, "Heeding Critics, Sara Lee Corp. Kicks Tobacco," *Wall Street Journal*, April 8, 1998, pp. B1, B4; Sally Beatty, "Tobacco Pact Pays to Combat Teen Smoking," *Wall Street Journal*, April 13, 1998, pp. B1, B12; Ann Davis and Ernest Beck, "U.S. Tactics Stoke Britain's War on Tobacco," *Wall Street Journal*, April 9, 1998, pp. B1, B9; Ann Davis, "Top Ad Agency Defends Tossing Joe Camel Files," *Wall Street Journal*, April 30, 1998, pp. B1, B5; Milo Geyelin, "Airline Staff Objects to Deal in Smoke Case," *Wall Street Journal*, January 7, 1998, p. B5; Milo Geyelin, "Texas, Tobacco Industry Are Close to 14.5 Billion Settlement of Suit," *Wall Street Journal*, January 12, 1998, p. B8; Milo Geyelin, "Lonely Lawyers for Liggett Feel Minnesota Chill," *Wall Street Journal*, February 6, 1998, pp. B1, B18; Milo Geyelin, "An Ex-Official of Philip Morris Invokes Fifth Amendment Rights," *Wall Street Journal*, February 18, 1998, p. B2;

Milo Geyelin and Ann Davis, "Tobacco's Foes Target Role of Lawyers," *Wall Street Journal*, April 23, 1998, pp. B1, B2; Milo Geyelin, "Gallup Big Tobacco of Misusing Poll in Court," *Wall Street Journal*, June 26, 1998, pp. B1, B7; Suein L. Hwang and John Lippman, "Hollywood to Antismoking Activist: Butt Out," *Wall Street Journal*, March 17, 1998, pp. B1, B8; Suein L. Hwang, "A Vast Trove of Tobacco Documents Opens Up," *Wall Street Journal*, April 23, 1998, pp. B1, B12; Suein L. Hwang, "Tobacco Memos Detail Passive-Smoke Attack," *Wall Street Journal*, April 28, 1998, pp. B1, B4; John Harwood and Jeffrey Taylor, "Voter Backlash Could Be Proud for New Tobacco Bill," *Wall Street Journal*, June 19, 1998, pp. B1, B5; Suein L. Hwang, "Tobacco Takes New Stab at a Settlement," *Wall Street Journal*, July 10, 1998, pp. B1, B5; and Jeffrey Taylor, "Lawyers, Once Chary of Big Tobacco, Rush to Line Up Plaintiffs," *Wall Street Journal*, April 1, 1998, pp. A1, A7.

Ben & Jerry's Homemade: Social Responsibility and Growth

B en Cohen and Jerry Greenfield opened their first ice-cream shop in 1978 in a converted gas station in Burlington, Vermont, investing $12,000 in some secondhand equipment. Their business credentials consisted of much enthusiasm and a $5 Pennsylvania State University correspondence course in ice-cream making. Driven by Cohen and Greenfield's 1960s ideals, Ben & Jerry's Homemade, Inc., has become very successful, with brand-name recognition of the company much greater than its size and sales of $237 million in 1999.

From the beginning, Cohen and Greenfield have incorporated into their business a strong sense of social responsibility — to their employees, the community, and the world at large. The company lives by its mission statement: "We're not part of the economic machine that makes profits and oppresses people. We think there should be a spiritual aspect to business. As we help others, we cannot help but help ourselves." Although Ben & Jerry's has experienced some trying times of late, it remains firmly based on its original, socially responsible corporate vision.

THE BEN & JERRY STORY

Cohen and Greenfield's converted gas station served rich, all-natural ice cream, which quickly became popular with local residents. During the winter months, however, the customers turned to warmer treats, so Cohen and Greenfield had to come up with new ideas to survive their first year. Soon they were packaging their ice cream and hauling it around to local restaurants. Gradually, they began to include grocery stores among their customers, soon gaining shelf space in one hundred fifty stores across the state.

Ben & Jerry's has always been a bit unorthodox in its business practices, ranging from Greenfield's executive title of "Big Cheese" to its products. For example, a popular Ben & Jerry's ice cream flavor is Cherry Garcia, named after (now de-

---

This case was prepared by O. C. Ferrell, John Fraedrich, and Terry Gable for classroom discussion, rather than to illustrate either effective or ineffective handling of an administrative, ethical, or legal decision by management.

ceased) guitarist Jerry Garcia of the rock band the Grateful Dead. Another flavor, Wavy Gravy, is named after the master of ceremonies at Woodstock and, naturally, is packaged in a tie-dyed container.

When the company went public in 1984 as Ben & Jerry's Homemade, Inc., Cohen initially limited the sale of the company's stock to Vermont residents. His idea was that if local residents were part owners of the firm, the community would share in the success of the business. In Cohen's words, "What a strange thing we're discovering: As our business supports the community, the community supports us back." A national stock offering did follow two years later, but the company has continued its philosophy of supporting the local community.

CARING CAPITALISM

When Cohen and Greenfield first went into business together, they wrote their own rules. Their corporate mission statement listed not only the goals of making and selling the finest-quality natural ice cream and operating in such a way as to achieve success for both shareholders and employees, but also the requirement that they initiate "innovative ways to improve the quality of life of a broad community — local, national, and international."

In the early 1990s Cohen and Greenfield felt they were losing control of their company — its growth, creativity, organization, and values. Greenfield even dropped out of the business for a while. Cohen considered selling the company until a friend pointed out to him that he could make it into whatever he wanted. He then developed the concept of "caring capitalism," which he applies by donating part of the company's profits to worthy causes as well as by finding creative ways to improve the quality of life of the firm's employees and of the local community. Greenfield rejoined the company soon after.

Shortly after Greenfield rejoined, Cohen set up the Ben & Jerry's Foundation, which is dedicated to encouraging social change through the donation of 7.5 percent of the company's yearly pretax profits. Ben & Jerry's social concern can also be seen in some of its products. One of the firm's ventures was the Peace Pop, an ice-cream bar on a stick, from which 1 percent of the profits were used to build awareness and raise funds for peace. The company purchases rain-forest nuts for its Rainforest Crunch ice cream, thus providing a market for goods from the rain forests that do not require their destruction. Additionally, sales of Rainforest Crunch are funneled back into rain-forest preservation efforts. Ben & Jerry's environmental concern was apparent with the company's switch to the "Eco-Pint," a more environmentally friendly unbleached paperboard container. Standard paper making uses chlorine compounds for bleaching, a process that discharges millions of gallons of organochlorine-laced water daily. Chemicals found in this water are considered hazardous to human health.

Cohen and Greenfield extend their social awareness to their own employees. A salary ratio at the firm limits the salaries of top executives. This helps give all employees a sense of working together as a team. And when it seemed that the company was expanding too quickly (the company went from a hundred and fifty employees to three hundred almost overnight), company executives made a conscious decision to slow growth to ensure that the company's family atmosphere and core values would not be lost. Additional benefits employees receive include three pints of ice cream a week, free health-club memberships, and use of a partially subsidized company child care center.

Another effort to utilize the "caring capitalism" concept was in their advertising techniques. Rather than buy television, radio, or newspaper advertising, Ben & Jerry's promotes things and events of value to the community. The company sponsors peace, music, and art festivals around the country and tries to draw attention to the many social causes it undertakes. One such cause is opposition to the bovine growth hormone (a substance injected into cows to increase milk production). Cohen and Greenfield fear that its use will drive small dairy farmers out of business. A venture targeted directly to Burlington residents is the Giraffe Project, which recognizes people willing to stick their own necks out and stand tall for what they believe. Local residents and customers of Ben & Jerry's scoop shops nominate the recipients of Giraffe Commendations.

LONG-TERM GOALS VERSUS COST EFFICIENCY

Based on his many years of international development and citizen action experience, David Korten, a former Harvard Business School professor, contends that long-term-oriented, socially responsible companies often face hard times in today's fast-paced, often shortsighted, and profit-minded economic system. According to this perspective, the economic system focuses on the current value of company stock, which rewards cost efficiency and punishes those that it sees as inefficient. Firms that are able to externalize or shift their costs to other parties are rewarded, whereas the socially responsible organization is considered inefficient and wasteful. Consequently, the firm's stock price suffers and the company is labeled as "in trouble." According to Korten,

> With financial markets demanding maximum short-term gains and corporate raiders standing by to trash any company that isn't externalizing every possible cost, efforts to fix the problem by raising the social consciousness of managers misdefine the problem. There are plenty of socially conscious managers. The problem is a predatory system that makes it difficult for them to survive. . . . They must either compromise their vision or run a great risk of being expelled by the system. . . . Corporate managers live and work in a system that is virtually feeding on the socially responsible.*

Ben & Jerry's appears to be one socially responsible firm faced with such issues. In April 2000, Ben & Jerry's Homemade, Inc. agreed to join forces with Unilever to create an even more dynamic, socially positive ice-cream business with global reach. The terms of the agreement include an independent board of directors for

Ben & Jerry's, which will focus on providing leadership for the company's social mission and brand integrity. In this transaction, shareholders were rewarded for their investment, Ben & Jerry's employees were protected, the current social mission was to be encouraged and well funded, and an opportunity was presented for Ben & Jerry's to contribute to Unilever's social practices worldwide. Both co-founders of the company were to continue to be involved.

In November 2000, Yves Couette was named the new CEO of Ben & Jerry's. One of Unilever's leading ice-cream professionals, Couette had worked in the United States, Mexico, Indonesia, and the United Kingdom. Vowing to build on what Ben & Jerry's had achieved as a business, he said, "I am determined to deliver on Ben & Jerry's social mission commitment."† Dissatisfied with Unilever's choice of Couette and unhappy that a co-CEO had not been named, Ben Cohen threatened to leave the company in December 2000. Cohen said, "The only way the social mission of Ben & Jerry's and the heart and soul of the company will be maintained is to have a CEO running the company who has a deep understanding of our values-led social business philosophy, who had experience with the company and with how that worked in practice."# Cohen also expressed dissatisfaction that the promised "social audit" of Unilever's operations had not been completed. He was also upset that Unilever would not allow a $5 million fund set up to help new businesses with a social agenda get on their feet to carry the Ben & Jerry's name.

UNILEVER'S RESPONSE

Unilever countered Cohen's claims by saying that Couette had the needed experience. While he was working in Mexico, Unilever had established an ice-cream shop, run by a nonprofit organization, to support disabled children. Couette said, "Working in countries like Mexico and Indonesia, I have seen first hand the glaring social problems people face everyday. This has strengthened my belief that business has an important role to play in achieving social progress."*

Unilever also countered with a list of the company's social objectives for 2001, which included helping to build playgrounds and launching a new flavor tied to that effort; lobbying to extend the life of the Northeast Interstate Dairy Compact, which provides more income for farmers; and developing more environmentally friendly packaging. As for Cohen's concern about the $5 million fund not carrying the Ben & Jerry's name, a Unilever spokesman replied that Unilever wants to protect the Ben & Jerry's brand name and indicated the fund could be called "Ben's

---

*David C. Korten, When Corporations Rule the World *(West Hartford, Conn.: Kumarian Press, 1995), pp. 212–214.*

†Ben & Jerry's press release, "Ben & Jerry's Appoints Yves Couette as Chief Executive Officer," *November 20, 2000,* http://lib.benjerry.com/pressrel/press1120.html *(accessed January 12, 2001).*

#David Gram, "Ben Worried Ben & Jerry's Good Work Is Melting Away After Merger," The Register Citizen, *December 1, 2000,* http://www.zwire.com *(accessed January 12, 2001).*

Venture Capital Fund" but not "Ben & Jerry's Venture Capital Fund." The spokesman said, "We understand that Ben's very concerned. He's a founder of the company. He has a huge emotional stake in the company. Our view is, judge us by our actions."**

Questions

1. Ben & Jerry's donates a percentage of its yearly pretax profits to encourage social change. Is this an appropriate role for a profit-making corporation?

2. Discuss how the corporate culture at Ben & Jerry's, as described in this case, influences the daily implementation of ethical decision making.

3. Do you feel that Ben Cohen's concerns about Unilever's actions and CEO appointment were warranted? Why or why not?

These facts are from "Ben & Jerry's & Unilever to Join Forces," April 12, 2000, *http://lib.benjerry.com/pressrel/join-forces.html* (accessed January 12, 2001); "Ben & Jerry's Appoints Yves Couette as Chief Executive Officer," November 20, 2000, *http://lib.benjerry.com/pressrel/press1120.html* (accessed January 12, 2001); David Gram, "Ben Worried Ben & Jerry's Good Work is Melting Away After Merger," *The Register Citizen*, December 1, 2000, *http://www.zwire.com* (accessed January 12, 2001); Simon Goodley, "Ben & Jerry Frosty over Unilever Choice for Key Job," *Electronic Telegraph*, issue 2019, December 4, 2000, *http://www.telegraph.co.uk/* (accessed January 12, 2001); "Ben & Jerry's Announces Environmentally-Friendly Packaging Innovation," February 22, 1999, *http://lib.benjerry.com/pressrel/unbleached.html* (accessed January 12, 2001); Mark Albright, "At Ben & Jerry's, Social Agenda Churns with Ice Cream," *St. Petersburg Times*, November 11, 1995, p. 1E; Peter Newcomb, "Is Ben & Jerry's BST-free?" *Forbes*, September 25, 1995, p. 98; Hanna Rosin, "The Evil Empire: The Scoop on Ben & Jerry's Crunchy Capitalism," *New Republic*, September 11, 1995, p. 22; Andrew E. Serwer, "Ben & Jerry's Corporate Ogre," *Fortune*, July 10, 1995, p. 30; David C. Korten, *When Corporations Rule the World* (West Hartford, Conn.: Kumarian Press, 1995), pp. 212–214; Erik Larson, "Forever Young," *Inc.* July 1988: pp. 50–62; Maxine Lipner, "Ben & Jerry's: Sweet Ethics Evince Social Awareness," *Compass Readings* July 1991, pp. 22–30; Blair S. Walker, "Good-Humored Activist Back to the Fray," *USA Today*, December 8, 1992, pp. 1B, 213; and Eric J. Wieffering, "Trouble in Camelot," *Business Ethics* 5 (January–February 1991): 16–19.

*Ben & Jerry's press release, November 20, 2000.

**David Gram, December 1, 2000.

The Wreck of the
Exxon Valdez

In 1989, Exxon Corporation and Alyeska Pipeline Service Co., an eight-company consortium that operates the Trans-Alaska pipeline and the shipping terminal in Valdez, Alaska, were severely criticized for their handling of a major oil spill from an Exxon tanker. The *Exxon Valdez* ran aground near Valdez, Alaska, on March 24, 1989, and spilled two hundred and forty thousand barrels — 11 million gallons — of crude oil, which eventually covered twenty-six hundred square miles of Prince William Sound and the Gulf of Alaska. Although the Exxon spill was not the largest ever, it was the worst in terms of environmental damage and disruption of industry, and it jeopardized the future of oil production in environmentally sensitive areas of Alaska. The effects of the spill could still be seen more than ten years after the wreck.

THE WRECK

At 12:04 A.M. on March 24, 1989, the *Exxon Valdez* was under the command of Third Mate Gregory Cousins, who was not licensed to pilot the vessel through the waters of Prince William Sound. The ship's captain, Joseph Hazelwood, apparently was asleep below deck. In an effort to dodge floating ice in the sound, Cousins performed what officials later described as an unusual series of right turns. The ship ran aground on Bligh Reef, spilling much of its cargo through the ruptured hull. The spill spread rapidly during the next few days, killing thousands of sea birds, sea otters, and other wildlife; covering the coastline with oil; and closing the fishing season in the sound for several years.

The Prince William Sound area was home to abundant wildlife. More than two hundred species of birds had been reported there, including one-fifth of the world's trumpeter swans. The fishing industry derived annual sales of $100 million from the sound's herring, salmon, Pacific cod, Alaska pollock, rockfish, halibut, flounder, and sharks, as well as crabs and shrimp. The world's largest concentration of killer whales and about one-fourth of the total U.S. sea otter population had inhabited the sound at the time of the wreck.

This case was prepared by O. C. Ferrell, John Fraedrich, and Gwyneth Vaughn for classroom discussion, rather than to illustrate either effective or ineffective handling of an administrative, ethical, or legal decision by management.

RESPONSE TO THE DISASTER

The events following the March 24 spill reveal what some observers say was a pattern of unpreparedness, mismanagement, and negligence. According to the transcripts of radio conversations between Captain Hazelwood and the Coast Guard immediately after the accident, the captain tried for an hour to rock the tanker free from the reef, an action that Coast Guard officials claim might have sunk the ship and spilled more oil. They say that Hazelwood ignored their warnings that rocking the ship might make the oil spill almost five times as bad.

When Coast Guard officers boarded the tanker at 3:30 A.M., they reported that one hundred and thirty-eight thousand barrels of crude oil had already been spilled. According to a contingency plan filed when the Valdez terminal first began operations, Alyeska crews should have arrived at the ship with containment equipment within a very short period of time; they did not. A frantic Coast Guard officer radioed, "We've got a serious problem. . . . She's leaking and groaning. There's nobody here. . . . Where's Alyeska?"

After being notified of the accident, Alyeska Pipeline Service, in the first line of defense against oil spills, sent an observation tug to the scene and began to assemble its oil-spill containment equipment, much of which was in disarray. It loaded containment boom and lightering equipment (emergency pumps to suction oil from the *Exxon Valdez* onto other vessels) onto a damaged barge. The Coast Guard decided, however, that the barge was too slow and the need for the lightering equipment more urgent, so Alyeska crews had to reload the lightering equipment onto a tugboat, losing still more time.

The first Alyeska containment equipment did not arrive at the scene until 2:30 in the afternoon; the rest of the equipment came the next morning. Neither Alyeska nor Exxon had enough containment booms and chemical dispersants to fight the spill. They were not ready to test the effectiveness of the dispersants until eighteen hours after the spill, and then they conducted the test by tossing buckets of chemicals out the door of a helicopter. The helicopter's rotor dispersed the chemicals, and they missed their target. Moreover, the skimmer boats used to scoop oil out of the sea were old and kept breaking down. The skimmers filled up rapidly and had to be emptied into nearby barges, taking them out of action for long periods of time. Some of the makeshift work crews were assigned to boats with no apparent mission. Cleanup efforts were further hampered by communication breakdowns between coordinators on shore and crews at the scene because of technical problems and limited range. Messages had to be relayed through local fishermen. In addition, although a fleet of private fishing boats was standing by ready to assist with the containment and cleanup, Exxon and Alyeska failed to mobilize their help. Exxon has admitted that the early efforts were chaotic but says that they were no more so than the response to any major disaster.

The *Exxon Valdez* was not fully encircled by containment booms until Saturday afternoon, thirty-six hours after the accident. By then the oil spill covered an area of twelve square miles. Exxon conducted more tests with chemical dispersants Saturday night, but the tests were inconclusive because conditions were too calm. (The chemical dispersants require wave action to be effective.) On Sunday afternoon the Coast Guard gave Exxon permission to use the dispersants on the spill. But that night a storm with winds as high as seventy-three miles an hour drove the oil slick thirty-seven miles into the southwestern section of the sound. All cleanup efforts were halted until the next afternoon because of the weather. Exxon eventually applied fifty-five hundred gallons of chemical dispersants; however, by then, because of the delay caused by the storm, the oil had become too emulsified for dispersants to work properly. By the end of the week, the oil slick had spread to cover twenty-six hundred miles of coastline and sea.

Coast Guard officers tested Captain Hazelwood for alcohol nine hours after the wreck. They apparently did not realize that the ship was equipped with a testing kit. The test showed that Hazelwood had a blood-alcohol content of 0.061. It is a violation of Coast Guard regulations for a person operating a ship to have a blood-alcohol level in excess of 0.04. Four other crewmen, including the third mate, tested negative for alcohol. Exxon officials later admitted that they knew the captain had gone through an alcohol detoxification program, yet they still gave him command of the *Exxon Valdez*, Exxon's largest tanker.

ALYESKA'S CONTAINMENT PLAN

Since the early 1970s, Alaskan officials and fishermen had expressed concern that a major oil spill was inevitable. In response, Alyeska Pipeline Service, its eight oil-company owners, and federal officials promised in 1972 that the tanker fleet operating out of Valdez would incorporate safety features such as double hulls and protective ballast tanks to minimize the possibility of spills. By 1977, however, Alyeska had convinced the Coast Guard that the safety features were not necessary, and only a few ships in the Valdez fleet incorporated them. The *Exxon Valdez* did not.

Alyeska Pipeline Service had filed a comprehensive contingency plan detailing how it would handle spills from the pipeline or the Valdez terminal. In the event of an oil spill from a tanker, emergency crews were to encircle the spill with containment booms within five hours — yet it took them a day and a half to encircle the *Exxon Valdez*. Alyeska's contingency plan further specified that an emergency crew of at least fifteen people would be on hand at all times. However, in 1981 much of the team had been disbanded to cut costs. In 1989 Alyeska maintained a crew of eleven to monitor terminal operations, but because the *Exxon Valdez* spill occurred at the beginning of the Easter holiday weekend, the company had trouble rounding up the team. Furthermore, Exxon's staff of oil-spill experts had been cut back since 1985. At least nine oil-spill managers, including Exxon's chief environmental officer, had left or retired. An Exxon spokesman said that he was not aware that the cutbacks affected Alyeska's initial readiness to combat a spill.

A state audit of Alyeska's equipment demonstrated that the company was un-prepared for the spill. It was supposed to have three tugboats and thirteen oil skimmers available but had only two and seven, respectively. Furthermore, the company had only fourteen thousand feet of boom for containing spills rather than the twenty-one thousand feet specified in the contingency plan, and the barge that carried the booms and stored skimmed oil was out of service because it had been damaged in a prior storm. However, even if it had been available, the required equipment would not have been enough because a tanker like the *Exxon Valdez* is almost one thousand feet long and holds 1.2 million barrels of oil. The booms available could barely encircle the giant ship, much less a sizable slick.

Alyeska violated its own contingency plans when it failed to notify state officials that the barge was out of service. A key piece of equipment in the contingency plan, the barge should have been loaded with seven thousand feet of boom. But the boom had been removed during the repair. A replacement barge had been ordered and was on its way from Texas. On March 24, it was in Seattle.

Although Alyeska conducted regular "spill drills," state monitors said that drills in the previous few years had been bungled and were considered unsuccessful. Among other things, the drills showed that crew members often did not know how to operate their assigned equipment. It was also noted that Alyeska's equipment and the crew's responses were inadequate for a real spill. Reporters Ken Wells and Charles McCoy wrote in the *Wall Street Journal:* "The oil companies' lack of preparedness makes a mockery of a 250-page containment plan, approved by the state, for fighting spills in Prince William Sound." Arlon R. Tussing, a Seattle oil consultant, commented, "The system that was set up early on has disintegrated."

CLEANING UP, 1989–2000

Exxon's chairman, Lawrence Rawl, apologized to the public for the spill in full-page advertisements in many newspapers and in a letter to Exxon stockholders. The company accepted liability for the spill and responsibility for its cleanup. By summer Exxon had ten thousand people, one thousand vessels, thirty-eight oil skimmers (including one sent by Russia to help out for a short time), and seventy-two aircraft working to clean up beaches and wildlife.

Exxon hoped to have completed its cleanup before September 15, 1989, but a 1990 survey showed that much work remained to be done. Shoreline surveys and limited cleanup efforts were made in 1991, 1992, 1993, and 1994. In 1992 crews from Exxon and the state and federal governments reported that an estimated seven miles of the 21.4 miles of shoreline surveyed still showed some surface oiling. The surveys also indicated that subsurface oil remained at many sites that were heavily oiled in 1989. The surveys determined that the potential environmental impact of further cleanup, as well as the cost, was greater than the problems caused by leaving the oil in place. The 1992 cleanup and the 1993 shoreline assessment were concentrated in those areas where oil remained to a greater degree: Prince William Sound and the Kenai Peninsula. In 1994 restoration workers cleaned a dozen important subsistence and recreation beaches in western Prince William Sound.*

Exxon claims that it saved $22 million by not building the *Exxon Valdez* with a second hull. During the period of the oil spill, Exxon spent more than $2.2 billion for cleanup and for reimbursements to the federal, state, and local governments for their expenses in response to the oil spill. In addition, thirty-one lawsuits and thirteen hundred claims had been filed against Exxon within a month of the spill. On August 15, 1989, the state of Alaska also filed a suit against Exxon for mismanaging the response to the oil spill. The suit demanded both compensatory and punitive damages that would exceed $1 billion. Captain Hazelwood, who was fired by Exxon soon after the accident, was found guilty in March 1990 of negligent discharge of oil, a misdemeanor. He was acquitted on three other more serious charges, including drunk driving.

Exxon also faced heated criticism from the public and from state and federal officials, who believed the cleanup efforts were inadequate. A Coast Guard spokesman in Valdez said, "We're running into a problem with the definition of the word 'clean.' The concept of being clean makes you think no oil is there. The oil is still there, but it may be three feet or two feet beneath the surface." Lee Raymond, Exxon's president, said, "Assuming that we can have people working till mid-September, we have a good shot at having all the beaches treated. But not clean like Mr. Clean who shows up in your kitchen. Our objective is to make sure the ecosystems are back in shape." Many Alaskans and environmentalists did not believe Exxon's idea of "clean" was clean enough. In addition, there were disputes as to how much oil had actually been cleaned up. By 1989 six hundred miles of shoreline had been "treated," but another two hundred miles still required treatment. Moreover, incoming tides often brought new oil slicks to cover just-treated beaches, slowing cleanup efforts considerably.

In addition, Exxon came under fire for the way it had managed the crisis. Chairman Lawrence Rawl did not comment on the spill for nearly six days, and then he did so from New York. Although Rawl personally apologized for the spill, crisis-management experts say that it is important for the chief executive to be present at the site of an emergency. Harry Nicolay, a Boston crisis-management consultant, said, "When the most senior person in the company comes forward, it's telling the whole world that we take this as a most serious concern." The crisis-management experts believe that Rawl's delayed response and failure to appear on the scene angered the public despite Exxon's efforts to clean up the spill.

Some of Exxon's statements to the public have also been criticized as bad public relations moves. For example, one Exxon executive told reporters that consumers would pay for the costs of the cleanup in the form of higher gas prices. Although that statement may have been truthful, it did nothing to placate already angry consumers. The public also reacted skeptically to Exxon officials' attempts

---

*American Petroleum Institute, "Oil Spill Prevention and Response: It's in Everyone's Best Interest," http://www.api.org/resources/valdez/ (accessed June 14, 1999).

to blame cleanup delays on the Coast Guard and Alaskan officials. Gerald C. Meyers, a specialist in corporate crisis management, said that Exxon's newspaper apology was "absolutely insincere. They were ill advised to say they sent 'several hundred people' to the scene. This is a company with more than 100,000 employees." Furthermore, Exxon insisted that it would stop all cleanup operations on September 15, 1989, regardless of how much shoreline remained to be cleaned. In a memorandum released in July 1989, that September deadline was said to be "not negotiable." After much public and government protest, however, the company's president promised that Exxon would return in the spring of 1990 if the Coast Guard determined that further cleanup was warranted. "It's our best guess that there will be a lot less oil than people think," he said. "But if the conclusion is reached by the Coast Guard that something needs to be made right and it can be made right, we'll be there. We're not trying to run off." Exxon did return that spring and the next four years for further cleanup efforts.

Exxon's response to the crisis certainly hurt its reputation and credibility with the public. National consumer groups urged the public to boycott all Exxon products, and nearly twenty thousand Exxon credit card holders cut up their cards and returned them to the company to express their dissatisfaction with its cleanup efforts.

THE EFFECTS OF THE *EXXON VALDEZ* DISASTER IN THE TWENTY-FIRST CENTURY

Many changes have been made since the *Exxon Valdez* incident. Because Captain Hazelwood was found to have had a high blood-alcohol content after the spill, three of Alyeska's largest owners (including Exxon) began mandatory random drug and alcohol searches of all ships using the Valdez port. In 1999, Captain Hazelwood began serving a sentence of one thousand hours of community service after he failed in a nine-year appeal of his 1990 conviction of negligent discharge of oil. Alaska's Governor Steve Cowper ordered Alyeska Pipeline to restock the Valdez terminal with all the booms, skimmers, and other equipment that were required by the original contingency plan. Alyeska was also ordered to form an emergency crew to respond immediately to spills. Governor Cowper demanded that Alyeska stock enough additional equipment to allow it to respond within two hours to a 10-million-gallon spill in Prince William Sound. Alyeska is now required to encircle all tankers with containment booms as they are loading and unloading, and it also had to change other procedures. The state of Alaska also eliminated many of the tax exemptions granted to oil companies producing in many Alaskan oil fields. The elimination of the tax breaks was expected to cost the affected oil companies about $2 billion over the next twenty years. In a civil settlement with the state of Alaska and the federal government, Exxon agreed to make ten annual payments — ending in the twenty-first century — totaling $900 million, for injuries to natural resources and services and for the restoration and replacement of natural resources. In addition, $5 billion was awarded in punitive damages, which must be divided evenly among the fourteen thousand commercial fishermen, natives, business owners, landowners, and native corporations that were part of the class-action suit. Exxon appealed this judgment, but in late 2000, the Supreme Court refused to free the company from having to pay the $5 billion in damages.

In a criminal plea agreement, Exxon was fined $150 million, of which $125 million was remitted in recognition of Exxon's cooperation in cleaning up the spill and paying private claims. Of the remaining $25 million, $12 million went to the North American Wetlands Conservation Fund and $13 million to the Victims of Crime Fund. In addition, Exxon agreed to pay restitution of $50 million to the United States and $50 million to the state of Alaska.

The spill has jeopardized further oil exploration and production in other parts of Alaska. Before the spill, a U.S. Senate committee and a House panel passed separate bills to allow drilling in Alaska's environmentally sensitive Arctic National Wildlife Refuge, but neither came up for a final vote. Alaska State Senator Frank Murkowski, who supported further drilling, believed it was "premature" to introduce additional legislation until the oil industry develops stronger contingency plans to deal with spills and accidents.

But the court debate has not ended. Exxon is involved in a highly contested lawsuit with its numerous insurance providers over their refusal to pay Exxon for its spill-cleanup efforts. The insurance companies, led by Lloyd's of London, refused to pay Exxon because (1) the cleanup efforts engaged in were not required by law; (2) the efforts were conducted in substandard fashion; (3) Exxon's level of liability coverage was well below the expenses sought; and (4) the spill itself was a result of "intentional misconduct," thus disqualifying insurance coverage of the accident. In short, the insurance companies contend that Exxon's cleanup activities were little more than "an expensive public relations exercise," designed to make the public think of Exxon as an ethical and socially responsible corporation. Claiming that it had incurred between $3.5 billion and $4 billion in expenses for the cleanup, Exxon in turn filed suit against the two hundred and fifty insurance companies, originally seeking around $3 billion in compensation, even though it was covered for only $850 million. Most of the original amount sought from the insurers, $2.15 billion, was for "bad-faith" conduct related to initial refusals to pay, interest charges, and attorneys' fees. The original figure of $3 billion was later reduced to about $1 billion, and insurers agreed to pay Exxon $300 million as a partial settlement of claims related to cleanup activities.

According to one analyst, "We're still seeing the same number of spills. What has improved is the response to those spills." The one positive consequence of the *Exxon Valdez* oil spill has been better industry response to the spilling of oil into our waters. However, this hardly compensates for the harm inflicted by Exxon's negligent spillage of 11 million gallons of crude oil into the Prince William Sound area. Years later, the area is still trying to recover fully.

Questions

1. In the context of this incident and the circumstances that led up to it, discuss the role of individual moral development, organizational factors, and significant others in decisions.

2. If Exxon had had an ethics program, would this have prevented the wreck of the *Exxon Valdez*?

3. Should Exxon and Alyeska be held responsible for cleaning up the spill, or should taxpayers and consumers pay for it (in the form of higher gasoline prices and taxes)?

4. In future oil-production efforts, which should take precedence: the environment or consumers' desires for low-priced gasoline and heating oil? Why?

These facts are from "Exxon Mobil Must Pay *Valdez* Fine," *USA Today,* October 2, 2000, *http://www. usatoday.com/news/court/nsco1379.htm* (accessed January 4, 2001); American Petroleum Institute, "Oil Spill Prevention and Response: It's in Everyone's Best Interest," *http://www.api.org/resources/ valdez/* (accessed June 14, 1999); Reed Abelson, "Tax Reformers, Take Your Mark," *New York Times,* February 11, 1996, sec. 3, p. 1; Scott Allen, "Oil Spills a Fossil-Fuel Fact of Life," *Boston Globe,* January 27, 1996, p. 13; "Exxon Will Pay $3.5 Million to Settle Claims in Phase Four of *Valdez* Case," *BNA State Environment Daily,* January 19, 1996; Aliza Fan, "Exxon May Still Get More Than $3 Billion in Dispute with Lloyd's," *Oil Daily,* January 22, 1996, p. 3; Tony Freemantle, "Billion-Dollar Battle Looms over Spill Costs: Exxon Corp. Trying to Collect from Its Insurance Companies," *Anchorage Daily News,* September 5, 1995, p. IA; *Institute for Crisis Management Newsletter,* 4 (March 1995): 3; Dave Lenckus, "Exxon Seeks More Spill Cover: Oil Giant Reaches Partial Agreement with Insurers," *Business Insurance,* January 22, 1996, p. 1; Natalie Phillips, "$3.5 Million Settles Exxon Spill Suit," *Anchorage Daily News,* January 18, 1996, p. 113; Wayne Beissert, "In *Valdez's* Wake, Uncertainty," *USA Today,* July 28, 1989, p. 3A; Amanda Bennett, Julie Solomon, and Allanna Sullivan, "Firms Debate Hard Line on Alcoholics," *Wall Street Journal,* April 13, 1989, p. 131; Cable Network News, March 22, 1990; Carrie Dolan, "Exxon to Bolster Oil-Cleanup Effort After Criticism," *Wall Street Journal,* May 11, 1989, p. A10; Carrie Dolan and Charles McCoy, "Military Transports Begin Delivering Equipment to Battle Alaskan Oil Spill," *Wall Street Journal,* April 10, 1989, p. A8; Stuart Elliot, "Public Angry at Slow Action on Oil Spill," *USA Today,* April 21, 1989, pp. B1, 132; William Glasgall and Vicky Cahan, "Questions That Keep Surfacing After the Spill," *Business Week,* April 17, 1989, p. 18; Kathy Barks Hoffman, "Oil Spill's Cleanup Costs Exceed $1.3B," *USA Today,* July 25, 1989, p. B1; "In Ten Years You'll See 'Nothing'" (interview with Exxon chairman, Lawrence Rawl), *Fortune,* May 8, 1989, pp. 50–54; Charles McCoy, "Alaska Drops Criminal Probe of Oil Disaster," *Wall Street Journal,* July 28, 1989, p. A3; Charles McCoy, "Alaskans End Big Tax Breaks for Oil Firms," *Wall Street Journal,* May 10, 1989, p. A6; Charles McCoy, "Heartbreaking Fight Unfolds in Hospital for Valdez Otters," *Wall Street Journal,* April 20, 1989, pp. A1, A4; Charles McCoy and Ken Wells, "Alaska, U.S. Knew of Flaws in Oil-Spill Response Plans," *Wall Street Journal,* April 7, 1989, p. A3; Peter Nulty, "The Future of Big Oil," *Fortune,* May 8, 1989, pp. 46–49; Wayne Owens, "Turn the Valdez Cleanup Over to Mother Nature," editorial, *Wall Street Journal,* July 27, 1989, p. A8; Lawrence G. Rawl, letter to Exxon shareholders, April 14, 1989; "Recordings Reveal Exxon Captain Rocked Tanker to Free It from Reef," [Texas A&M University] *Battalion,* April 26, 1989, p. 1; Michael Satchell, with Steve Lindbeck, "Tug of War over Oil Drilling," *U.S. News & World Report,* April 10, 1989, pp. 47–48; Richard B. Schmitt, "Exxon, Alyeska May Be Exposed on Damages," *Wall Street Journal,* April 10, 1989, p. A8; Stratford P. Sherman, "Smart Way to Handle the Press," *Fortune,* June 19, 1989, pp. 69–75; Caleb Solomon and Allanna Sullivan, "For the Petroleum Industry, Pouring Oil Is in Fact the Cause of Troubled Waters," *Wall Street Journal,* March 31, 1989, p. A4;

Allanna Sullivan, "Agencies Clear Exxon Oil-Cleanup Plan Despite Coast Guard Doubts on Deadline," *Wall Street Journal*, April 19, 1989, p. A2; Allanna Sullivan, "Alaska Sues Exxon Corp., 6 Other Firms," *Wall Street Journal*, August 16, 1989, pp. A3, A4; Allanna Sullivan and Amanda Bennett, "Critics Fault Chief Executive of Exxon on Handling of Recent Alaskan Oil Spill," *Wall Street Journal*, March 31, 1989, p. B1; Ken Wells, "Alaska Begins Criminal Inquiry of Valdez Spill," *Wall Street Journal*, March 30, 1989, p. A4; Ken Wells, "Blood-Alcohol Level of Captain of Exxon Tanker Exceeded Limits," *Wall Street Journal*, March 31, 1989, p. A4; "*Valdez* Captain Serves Sentence,"Associated Press, June 22, 1999; Ken Wells, "For Exxon, Cleanup Costs May Be Just the Beginning," *Wall Street Journal*, April 14, 1989, pp. B1, B2; Ken Wells and Marilyn Chase, "Paradise Lost: Heartbreaking Scenes of Beauty Disfigured Follow Alaska Oil Spill," *Wall Street Journal*, March 31, 1989, pp. A1, A4; Ken Wells and Charles McCoy, "How Unpreparedness Turned the Alaska Spill into Ecological Debacle," *Wall Street Journal*, April 3, 1989, pp. A1, A4; Ken Wells and Allanna Sullivan, "Stuck in Alaska: Exxon's Army Scrubs the Beaches, but They Don't Stay Cleaned," *Wall Street Journal*, July 27, 1989, pp. A1, A5; and Scott Allen, "Oil Spills: A Fossil-Fuel Fact of Life," *Boston Globe*, January 27, 1996, p. 13.

Case 11

Archer Daniels Midland Company: The Costs of Price Fixing

A rcher Daniels Midland Company (ADM), based in Decatur, Illinois, can be traced to 1902, when John Daniels formed the Daniels Linseed Company in Minneapolis, Minnesota. Daniels had been crushing flaxseed to produce linseed oil since 1878. George Archer, also an experienced flaxseed crusher, joined the Daniels firm in 1903. With the purchase of Midland Linseed Products in 1923, the company became known as Archer Daniels Midland.

ADM rapidly expanded in the domestic and international production of linseed oil, as well as in flour milling and soybean processing through the 1930s, 1940s, and 1950s. In 1966 its leadership passed to the former Chairman and Chief Executive Officer, Dwayne O. Andreas. ADM is currently engaged in the business of procuring, transporting, storing, processing, and merchandising agricultural commodities and products. It is one of the world's largest processors of oilseeds, corn, and wheat, with more than twenty-two thousand employees worldwide, three hundred sixty-eight processing plants, and net sales in excess of $12.8 billion. The firm's extensive reach into the products eaten and drunk by consumers around the globe is reflected in its promotional efforts: it proudly calls itself the "supermarket to the world."

Andreas was a key player within ADM and appeared to control the direction of its corporate culture. He made various comments about how ADM would continue to be a profitable company. International business relations were something for which he strove. However, he believed that the free-market enterprise was not a possibility for American agriculture and that it could not compete in foreign markets without help from the U.S. government. He preached that it was time to accept taxes to keep America solid and preserve democracy.

This case was prepared by John Fraedrich, O. C. Ferrell, and Terry Gable for classroom discussion, rather than to illustrate either effective or ineffective handling of an administrative, ethical, or legal decision by management.

THE PROBLEM

Because of the type of industry ADM is in and the strategy of procuring government subsidies for its markets, there was a very close relationship between ADM and politics. In the past several decades ADM had given liberally to both major political parties, depending on which one was in power and who could get the best legislation passed for the company. For example, while 1995 was a banner year for ADM in terms of record sales and profits, it was also a time of turmoil. There was discussion in the media and among competing firms that ADM had gained special access to the political process, resulting in laws, regulations, and loopholes favoring its individual interests. This access was seen as a consequence of Andreas's close personal relationships with then-President Bill Clinton and presidential candidate Bob Dole, as well as with other major political figures, and of the company's history of large political contributions to legislators. Allegations circulated that ADM and several of its larger competitors in the flour-milling industry had grown too large and powerful, thus potentially limiting consumer choice. There were also charges that ADM's board of directors had grown too large, was too well paid, and was excessively dominated by company insiders. Although these issues raised damaging ethical, legal, and performance problems at ADM, the firm's turmoil had another source. It stemmed from widespread allegations that it worked with competitors to set, or "fix," artificially high prices for a biochemical product, lysine. These allegations grew out of a lengthy FBI probe, conducted with the cooperation of ADM bioproducts executive Mark Whitacre.

MARK WHITACRE: RISING STAR AT ADM

After earning bachelor's and master's degrees in animal science from Ohio State University and a Ph.D. in nutritional biochemistry from Cornell University, Mark Whitacre went to work briefly for Ralston Purina in St. Louis and then for Degussa, a German chemical company. While at Degussa, Whitacre negotiated with ADM in hopes of striking a joint venture between the two firms involving lysine production. Lysine is an essential amino acid used to stimulate animal muscle growth and is a component of feed for hogs, poultry, and fish. The alliance between Degussa and ADM was never forged. However, Whitacre was hired by ADM in 1989 to run its newly formed biochemical products division that was to produce lysine. Former Chairman Andreas's son, Michael, himself vice chairman of the firm, was particularly instrumental in Whitacre's hiring. The younger Andreas told Whitacre that success in the new division was a high priority for the company.

When Whitacre was hired, there were no American firms in the lysine industry, which was dominated by two Japanese companies, Kyowa Hakko and Ajinomoto. To establish itself in the market, ADM made an initial investment of $150 million in lysine production, sales, and marketing. According to Whitacre, ADM's first strategy as the new market entrant "was to get customers," as evidenced in market share. Consistent with ADM philosophy and practice, profitability would then follow.

ADM gained market share quickly, and a fierce price war followed, with the per-pound lysine price dropping from about $1.30 to 60 cents. In early 1992, Michael Andreas and Jim Randall, ADM's then-president, informed Whitacre that he would be working more closely with the president of the corn-processing division, Terrance Wilson. Whitacre states that during his first year with ADM he had been told "to beware" of Wilson because of his alleged involvement in price-fixing activities in several of the firm's other divisions. According to Whitacre, Andreas and Randall told him that he would be working with Wilson so that Wilson could "teach me some things about how ADM does business."

Whitacre claims that when he and Wilson met in February 1992, the content of their initial discussion was far different from what he had expected. Rather than asking Whitacre about his sales force or the location of ADM lysine offices and other typical strategic issues, Wilson asked Whitacre if he "knew our competitors." He told him that he wanted to meet with these Japanese firms because ADM was losing several million dollars a month on its lysine operations, despite gaining a 30 percent share of the global lysine market. According to Whitacre, Wilson then stated: "We're not blaming that on you. Obviously, we needed to get market share first, and that's what we did. That was stage one. But now we need to take the business to a different tier."

Whitacre claims that Wilson's initial tactic to overcome the coldness of the Japanese was to suggest that the three firms form a cooperative amino acids association to jointly promote and expand lysine sales. Kyowa Hakko and Ajinomoto representatives were receptive to the idea. Following a meeting at Kyowa's headquarters, additional meetings in Hawaii and Mexico City were planned. According to Whitacre, Wilson summed up ADM's problem at the Mexico City meeting by saying that the company had 20 to 25 percent more production capacity than what usage levels were and the difference amounted to $200 million. This situation was not benefiting ADM, but rather the customer. Then Wilson said something that was a common phrase around ADM: "The competitor is our friend, and the customer is our enemy."

Whitacre was so successful at this task and others that toward the end of 1992 he was promoted to corporate vice president and given responsibility for all of ADM's Asian market development projects. In early 1993 Randall informed Whitacre that he was "the top candidate to be the next president of this company." That promotion never took place.

JAPANESE COMPETITORS SUSPECTED OF SABOTAGE

ADM continued to lose money on its lysine operations. Production costs continued to run at roughly twice the market price due to contamination problems long since mastered by the Japanese producers, both of which had sent representative engineers to inspect ADM facilities in the summer of 1992. During one of his phone conversations with technical personnel at Ajinomoto, Whitacre, frustrated by the lingering contamination problem, jokingly stated: "Hey, you guys don't have a guy out here sabotaging our plant, do you?" The lack of a response made Whitacre wonder if there was in fact competitive sabotage taking place. He contacted Michael Andreas about the issue, and Andreas suggested that the Ajinomoto technician be offered a finder's fee for information regarding the problem. When Whitacre made the offer — a perfectly legal practice — he again received a vague, neutral response, further confirming his suspicion that the Japanese competitor had indeed planted someone inside ADM's lysine production facility.

In further conversations with Michael Andreas, Whitacre claims he was told that maybe it would be more productive to worry less about finding the mole planted by the Japanese and to see instead if the informant would be willing to divulge inside technological information. Such information might not only help end the contamination problem but also improve ADM's competitive position in other ways. Although Whitacre says that he was aware that ADM had gained technological information in this manner in the past, he also admits that the practice was very risky: "They're stealing in-house technology, and you can end up with quite a lawsuit on your hands." Conversations with the technician took place with no deal being struck.

CHAIRMAN ANDREAS CALLS IN THE FBI

On hearing about the potential sabotage problem, then-Chairman Andreas called a personal friend at the FBI, who expressed great interest in the matter. According to Whitacre, Michael Andreas was not pleased with his father's decision: "His father hadn't thought about all the ramifications." Whitacre claims that Michael Andreas then coached him about what to say and not to say to the FBI. Michael Andreas allegedly told Whitacre that he should tell the FBI about the contamination but not about approaching the employee about the technology. Whitacre said that Andreas wanted the FBI to think that the Japanese had approached ADM. Andreas also allegedly wanted Whitacre to lie to the FBI about which of his two home phones he had used concerning the price fixing so that if the agents decided to tap the phone, they would tap the wrong one.

Whitacre, accompanied by ADM's head of security at the time, Mark Cheviron, met with FBI officials at FBI offices located in Decatur. As allegedly instructed, Whitacre lied to the FBI about the attempted technology purchase and the phone line. Whitacre did not feel comfortable about the lie, and when FBI Agent Brian Shepard arrived at his home to install phone taps, Whitacre told him the truth. According to Whitacre, he explained about the phone line and the price fixing. Whitacre contends that he would have told Shepard the truth in their first meeting if it had not been for the presence of Cheviron, who, Whitacre feels, was sent along with him to make sure that he lied as allegedly instructed.

MARK WHITACRE: FBI MOLE

As Whitacre talked to his contacts at Kyowa and Ajinomoto about the proposed ly-sine association, the FBI listened. Highly interested in what it heard, the FBI asked for and received permission from Whitacre to supply him with a small, wired recorder, which was concealed and used to tape ADM meetings on lysine and other products.

Near Christmas 1992, the FBI informed Whitacre that, based on what it had learned from the secretly taped ADM meetings, he had to choose among three al-ternatives: he could (1) stay with the company and engage in price fixing; (2) leave the company having committed no wrongdoing; or (3) work with the FBI to pre-vent price fixing from occurring. Whitacre chose the last alternative.

Whitacre met with FBI agents on the case "on average a couple of nights a week for three years." They discussed meetings recorded both by Whitacre using a tape recorder concealed inside a panel in his briefcase and by the FBI itself, which would wire hotel rooms where meetings were to take place after receiving ad-vance notice from Whitacre as to the location of the meeting. The tapes revealed where agreements on world volume were reached, as well as the prices. The recordings have Terry Wilson saying, "Before we go to this meeting, I'm going to go to Mick [Michael Andreas] and get our marching orders." On one occasion Wilson and Whitacre were on their way to meet with one of the competitors when the general counsel and the assistant counsel were getting into a different taxi and the general counsel said, "Hey, guys, good luck with your price-fixing meeting." As a result of what it had heard, the FBI conducted a raid on ADM corporate head-quarters in search of further evidence regarding alleged price-fixing practices.

ADM'S RESPONSE TO PRICE-FIXING ALLEGATIONS

ADM responded to Whitacre's and the FBI's allegations by stating that it had not engaged in price fixing. Then-Chairman Andreas pointed out that fixing the price of a commodity item such as lysine would be nearly impossible because artifi-cially inflated prices would cause customers to switch to alternative feed-additive products, such as soy meal. Furthermore, Andreas stated that Whitacre, once a rising star in the firm, was telling "fairy tales" to cover up his alleged theft of $9 million from the firm. Whitacre, in hiding because of alleged threats to his family's well-being, furiously denied the embezzlement charges.

An unnamed friend of Whitacre told the courts that a large sum of money, $2.5 million, was transferred from ADM to Whitacre after his firing and that the money was not stolen but rather was an "agreed-upon part" of Whitacre's compensation. This friend further stated that ADM disguised the money as disbursements to out-side suppliers and then funneled it into foreign bank accounts — an executive compensation practice referred to by the individual as common at ADM. The legal director of an advocacy group based in Washington, D.C., commented about ADM charges against Whitacre that "organizations under threat do everything they can to neutralize that threat. If there is one common denominator among whistle-blowers, it is that they face harassment, retaliation, and professional apocalypse."

ADM's response, however, was not limited to denial and countercharges against Whitacre. Angry shareholders and other critics contended that the root of the problem was in the firm's complacent and insider-dominated seventeen-member board of directors. Critics claimed that the alleged price fixing, along with other antitrust and compensation-related activities that were also being investigated, was a clear sign of director oversight. They argued that these problems should have been detected and dealt with long before they were nationally publicized. Specific reasons cited for the corporate board's negligence were its unusually large size, extraordinarily high levels of member compensation, and the fact that ten of the seventeen directors were either retired ADM executives or relatives of senior management.

These issues were addressed at the October 1995 annual meeting of ADM shareholders. At one point in the meeting, then-Chairman Andreas shouted at the shareholders and ordered audience microphones silenced. To one company pension official who questioned ADM's top-management style, Andreas shouted, "This meeting, sir, runs according to my rules." However, it was decided that change in the composition and nature of the board was required. Two board members not related to the Andreas family, O. Glenn Webb and Ray A. Goldberg, were entrusted with overseeing the transformation. However, the fact that both had long-time close personal and business ties with the Andreases and ADM caused some to question whether meaningful change would indeed take place.

When the FBI raided ADM, they warned Whitacre that he would need an attorney not associated with ADM. However, Whitacre did speak to an ADM attorney. The following day someone at ADM called him and said, "Hey, Dwayne told me your attorney just told him that you're the mole. You're the one who caused all this. . . ." Whitacre was threatened by individuals within ADM, but he still sticks to his story, which has been corroborated by the tapes.

Despite being shaken by the consequences of his actions, Whitacre continues to stand firmly behind his allegations that ADM conspired with its major competitors to fix lysine and other product prices. He believes that he did the right thing in exposing these practices.

ADM ATTEMPTS TO SETTLE DISPUTES

ADM settled a number of legal suits for $45 million, but none of the companies involved admitted to any wrongdoing. ADM also filed a lawsuit against Whitacre, arguing that he should return his salary because he had been working for the FBI. In addition, ADM claimed that he broke his confidentiality agreements with the company, as well as embezzled $9 million. Whitacre denied any wrongdoing and claimed that the $9 million was "off-the-books" compensation that was a common practice for top ADM officials.

Whitacre pleaded guilty to thirty-seven counts of wire fraud, money launder-ing, conspiracy to defraud the IRS, filing false income tax returns, and interstate transportation of stolen goods, which all related to his work at ADM.

Prior to sentencing, the distraught Whitacre attempted suicide. His sentence was nine years, some of which was to be spent in a psychiatric hospital.

The Department of Justice pressured ADM to release information not only in the lysine price-fixing case but also in other investigations. For its cooperation, ADM pleaded guilty to only two felony counts for its participation in the lysine and citric acid price fixing, paid $100 million in fines, and received immunity in the $3 billion HFCS (High Fructose Corn Syrup) price-fixing probe. In the HFCS market, ADM would allegedly buy cane sugar and inflate the price so that HFCS would be a lower-cost alternative for beverage companies.

In late 1998 the following ADM executives were convicted on federal price-fixing charges: Michael Andreas, executive vice president; Terrance Wilson, retired head of ADM's corn-processing unit; and Reinhard Richter, former president of ADM's Mexico operations. One comment from one of the trials was that "This is not Business Ethics 101. This is how you deal in the real world. . . . That's how Dwayne Andreas told . . . [his people] to do business." After a lengthy appeals process, Andreas's and Wilson's convictions were upheld in June 2000 by the Sev-enth U.S. Circuit Court of Appeals. The court ruled that the sentences imposed on the two were too light. In September 2000, a federal judge increased Andreas's sentence to three years and Wilson's sentence to two years and nine months. In late November 2000, the Supreme Court turned down appeals by the two former executives.

Questions

1. Was ADM's response to the allegations of price fixing adequate? Do you think that the firm was simply "blaming the messenger" (Mark Whitacre) for reporting what he perceived as a widespread aspect of ADM corporate culture, or did the firm adequately exonerate itself from alleged misconduct?

2. How could ADM have dealt better with the potentially serious ethical and legal dilemmas it faced regarding alleged price-fixing practices? Suggest an ethical compliance program that could have prevented the problem.

3. Comment on Mark Whitacre's expressed opinion that he was doing the right thing by cooperating with the FBI and that he felt that he would eventually stay with and prosper at ADM. Was he "doing the right thing"? Was he naive in thinking that he could stay with the firm? Why or why not?

These facts are from "ADM Executives Lose Appeals in Feed Case," *USA Today,* November 27, 2000, *http://www.usatoday.com/news/court/nsco1431.htm* (accessed January 17, 2001); "Archer Daniels Midland Selects J. D. Edwards' Oneworld Xe . . ." J. D. Edwards & Co. press release, December 5, 2000, *http://biz.yahoo.com/prnews/001205/co_jdedwar.html* (accessed January 17, 2001); Matt Kel-ley, "ADM Top Executives Told of Possible Indictments, Company Admits," *http://www.sddt.com/*

files/librarywire/96wireheadlines/09_96/DN96_09_26/DN96_09_26_fk.html (accessed September 26, 1996); Matt Kelley, "Archer Daniels Midland Sues FBI Mole for $30 Million," *http://www.sddt.com/ files/librarywire/96wireheadlines/09_96/DN96_09_20/DN96_09_20_far.html* (accessed September 20, 1996); "Former ADM Executive Gets Probation," *http://www.grainnet.com/ArticleLibrary/articles. html?ID=1567* (accessed March 1, 1998); "Mentoring: A Double-Edged Sword, Cont.," *Maxima's Inside Fraud Bulletin, http://www.maximag.co.uk/bull0025.html* (accessed February 28, 1999); "Former ADM Official Mark E. Whitacre Indicted on Criminal Charges," press release, January 15, 1997, *http://www.usdoj.gov/opa/pr/1997/January97/index.html* (accessed February 28, 1999); "Dutch Company Charged with Price Fixing on Citric Acid: Agrees to Pay $400,000 Criminal Fine," press release, June 23, 1998, *http://www.usdoj.gov/opa/pr/1998/June/* (accessed October 12, 1998); "Japanese Subsidiary Charged with International Conspiracy to Fix Prices for Graphite Electrodes in U.S.," press release, February 23, 1998 *http://www.usdoj.gov/opa/pr/1998/February/* (accessed October 12, 1998); John Bovard, "Corporate Welfare Fueled by Political Contributions: Archer Daniels Midland's Ethanol Program," *Business and Society Review,* June 22, 1995, p. 22; Greg Burns and Richard A. Melcher, "A Grain of Activism at Archer Daniels Midland," *Business Week,* November 6, 1995, p. 44; Dan Carney, "Dwayne's World: Archer Daniels Midland CEO Dwayne Orville Andreas," *Mother Jones,* July 1995, p. 44; Major Garrett, "The Supermarket to the World Pols: Clinton, Dole Helped Campaign Contributor ADM, Now Probed for Price Fixing," *Washington Times,* September 5, 1995, p. A1; Ronald Henkoff, "So Who Is This Mark Whitacre, and Why Is He Saying These Things About ADM?" *Fortune,* September 4, 1995, pp. 64–68; *Hoover's Handbook* (Austin, Tex.: Reference Press, 1995) (accessed via American Online); David C. Korten, *When Corporations Rule the World* (West Hartford, Conn.: Kumarian Press, 1995), pp. 75, 224; Joann S. Lublin, "Is ADM's Board Too Big, Cozy, and Well-Paid?" *Wall Street Journal,* October 17, 1995, p. B1; Richard A. Melcher and Greg Burns, "Archer Daniels' Cleanup: Don't Stop Now," *Business Week,* January 29, 1996, p. 37; Robyn Meredith, "Archer Daniels Investors Launch Revolt," *Wall Street Journal,* October 20, 1995, pp. B1, B2; "10 Little Piggies: Corporations That Receive Government Benefits," *Mother Jones,* July 1995, p. 48; Mark Whitacre and Ronald Henkoff, "My Life As a Corporate Mole for the FBI," *Fortune,* September 4, 1995, pp. 52–62; Laurie P. Cohen, "Tough Battle Looms as ADM Lawyers Plot Price-Fixing Defenses," *Wall Street Journal,* March 27, 1996, p. A1; and James Bovard, Archer Daniels Midland: A Case Study in Corporate Welfare. Policy Analysis No. 241, *http://livelinks.com/sumeria/politics/adm.html* (accessed September 26, 1995).

Columbia/HCA Healthcare Corporation

In 1997, Columbia/HCA Healthcare Corporation was one of the largest health care services companies in the United States. The company operated three hundred and forty-three hospitals, one hundred and thirty-six outpatient surgery centers, and approximately five hundred and fifty home health locations. It also provided extensive outpatient and ancillary services in thirty-seven states, the United Kingdom, and Switzerland. The comprehensive network included more than two hundred and eighty-five thousand employees and used economies of scale to increase profits. Columbia/HCA was the seventh-largest U.S. employer and had revenues of nearly $20 billion. Its stated mission was "to work with our employees, affiliated physicians and volunteers to provide a continuum of quality healthcare, cost-effectively for the people in the communities we serve." The vision for Columbia/HCA was "to work with employees and physicians, to build a company that is focused on the well-being of people, that is patient-oriented, that offers the most advanced technology and information systems, that is financially sound, and that is synonymous with quality, cost-effective healthcare."

Columbia/HCA's goals included the desire to measure and improve clinical outcome and patient satisfaction, as well as to reduce costs and to provide services with compassion. The company built the nation's largest chain of hospitals, based on cost-effectiveness and financial performance. It competed by taking advantage of its size, thus increasing economies of scale, in the internal control of costs and sales activities. The focus was bottom-line performance and new business acquisitions.

A number of critics charged that at Columbia/HCA, health care services and staffing often took a back seat to the focus on profits. For example, shorter training periods were used compared with training time provided by competitive hospitals. One former administrator indicated that, in a Columbia/HCA hospital, training, which typically should take six months, was sometimes done in as little as two weeks. In addition, the company was accused of patient dumping, which is defined as discharging emergency-room patients or transferring them to other hospitals when they are not in stable condition. In 1997 officials at the Department of Health and Human Services Inspector General's Office indicated that

---

This case was prepared by O. C. Ferrell for classroom discussion, rather than to illustrate either effective or ineffective handling of an administrative, ethical, or legal decision by management.

they were considering imposing fines on Columbia/HCA for an unspecified number of patient-dumping cases.

The corporate watchdog INFACT publicly challenged the company's practices, inducting Columbia/HCA into its Hall of Shame for corporations that manipulate public policy to the detriment of public health.

ETHICAL AND LEGAL PROBLEMS BEGIN

In late July 1997, Fawcett Memorial Hospital in Port Charlotte, Florida, a Columbia/HCA hospital, was named as the focal point of the biggest case of health care fraud in the industry. The government investigation resulted in the indictment of three mid-level Columbia/HCA Healthcare Corporation executives, who were charged with filing false cost reports for Fawcett, resulting in losses of more than $4.4 million from government programs. The government alleged that Columbia/HCA had gained at least part of its profit by overcharging for Medicare and other federal health programs; that is, executives had billed the government for nonreimbursable interest expenses. Other concerns were alleged illegal incentives to physicians and the possible overuse of home health services. Federal investigators claimed that Columbia/HCA had engaged in a "systematic effort to defraud government health care programs." In a seventy-four-page document, federal investigators quote confidential witnesses who stated that Columbia/HCA's former chief executive officer, Richard Scott, and former president, David Vandewater, were briefed routinely on issues relating to Medicare reimbursement claims that the government charged were fraudulent. It was claimed, too, that Samuel Greco, Columbia/HCA's former chief of operations, also knew of the alleged fraud.

One of the issues was whether Columbia/HCA had fraudulently overstated home health care laboratory test expenses and knowingly miscategorized other expenditures to inflate the amounts for which it sought reimbursement. For example, Columbia/HCA's Southwest Florida Regional Medical Center in Fort Myers was found to have claimed $68,000 more in property taxes than it paid. Documents showed that the hospital had set aside money to return to the government in case auditors caught the inflated figure. Technically, expenses claimed on cost reports must be related to patient care and be in the realm of allowable Medicare reimbursements. However, medical billing can be confusing, chaotic, imprecise, and open to wide subjective interpretation. Hence, it is not unusual for hospitals to keep two sets of accounting books. One set is provided to Medicare, and the other set, which contains records for set-aside money, is held on to in case auditors interpret the Medicare cost report differently than the hospital does. It is deemed appropriate by some for a hospital to set aside money to return to the government if the hospital in good faith believes the Medicare cost claims are legitimate. However, if administrators believe strongly or know that certain claims are not allowable yet still file the claims and note them in the second set of books, this is an indication of fraud.

Confidential witnesses said that Columbia/HCA had made an effort to hide from federal regulators internal documents that could have disclosed the alleged fraud. In addition, Columbia/HCA's top executive in charge of internal audits had instructed employees to soften the language used in internal financial audits that were critical of Columbia/HCA's practices. According to FBI agent Joseph Ford, "investigation by the [Federal Bureau of Investigation] and the [Defense Criminal Investigative Service] has uncovered a systematic corporate scheme perpetrated by corporate officers and managers of Columbia/HCA's hospitals, home health agencies, and other facilities in the states of Tennessee, Florida, Georgia, Texas, and elsewhere to defraud Medicare, Medicaid, and the [Civilian Health and Medical Program of the Uniformed Services]." Indicted Columbia/HCA officials pleaded not guilty, and defense lawyers for Columbia/HCA tried to diminish the importance of the allegations contained in the government's affidavits.

DEVELOPING A NEW ETHICAL CLIMATE AT COLUMBIA/HCA

Soon after the investigation was launched, Dr. Thomas Frist Jr. was hired as chairman and chief executive of Columbia/HCA. He had been president of Hospital Corporation of America (HCA) before it merged with Columbia. He vowed to cooperate fully with the government and to develop a one-hundred-day plan to change the corporate culture. Under the Federal Sentencing Guidelines for Organizations (FSGO), companies with effective due diligence compliance programs can obtain reduced organizational fines if convicted of fraud. In order for penalties to be reduced, though, an effective compliance program must be in place before misconduct occurs. Although the FSGO requires that a senior executive be in charge of the due diligence compliance program, Columbia/HCA's general counsel had been designated to take charge of the program.

After a hundred days as chairman and chief executive of Columbia/HCA, Frist outlined changes that would reshape the company. His reforms included a new mission statement, as well as plans to create a new senior executive position, the duties of which would be to oversee ethical compliance and quality issues. Columbia/HCA's new mission statement emphasized a commitment to quality medical care and honesty in business practices. It did not, however, mention financial performance. "We have to take the company in a new direction," Frist said. "The days when Columbia/HCA was seen as an adversarial or in your face, a behind-closed-doors kind of place, is a thing of the past." (It has been claimed that Columbia/HCA's corporate culture had been viewed by some managers as so unethical that they had resigned before the fraud investigation.)

Columbia/HCA hired Alan Yuspeh as the senior executive to oversee ethical compliance and quality issues. Yuspeh, senior vice president of ethics, compliance, and corporate responsibility, was given a staff of twelve at the corporate headquarters and assigned to work with group, division, and facility presidents to create a "corporate culture where Columbia workers feel compelled to do what is right." Yuspeh's first initiatives were to refine monitoring techniques, boost workers' ethics and compliance training, develop a code of conduct for employees, and create an internal mechanism for workers to report any wrongdoing. As a result of these activities, Columbia/HCA dropped its company icon as well as the name "Columbia" in many locations.

Because of the investigation, consumers, doctors, and the general public lost confidence in Columbia/HCA as an institution. Columbia/HCA's stock price dropped more than 50 percent from its all time high. New management was concerned much more about developing the corporation's ethical compliance program than about the corporation's growth and profits. For instance, at a conference in Phoenix, Arizona, twenty Columbia managers were asked to indicate by a show of hands how many of them had escaped taunts about being a crook from friends. No hands went up. The discussion that followed that question did not focus on surgery profit margins. It focused on resolving the investigation and on the importance of the corporation's intangible image and values.

COLUMBIA/HCA LAUNCHES AN ETHICAL COMPLIANCE TRAINING PROGRAM

Columbia/HCA released a press statement indicating that it was taking a critical step in developing a companywide ethics, compliance, and corporate responsibility program. To initiate the program, the company designated more than five hundred employees as facility ethics and compliance officers (ECOs). The new ECOs started with a two-day training session in Nashville, Tennessee. The facility ECOs were to be the key links in ensuring that the company continued to develop a culture of ethical conduct and corporate responsibility. It was felt that local leadership for each facility would bring the overall ethics program for Columbia/HCA to its full implementation.

As part of the program, Yuspeh made a fifteen-minute videotape that was sent to managers throughout the Columbia/HCA system. The tape announced the launching of the compliance training program and the unveiling of a code of ethics that was designed to effectively communicate Columbia/HCA's new emphasis on compliance, integrity, and social responsibility. Frist stated that "we are making a substantial investment in our ethics and compliance program in order to ensure its success" and that "instituting a values-based culture throughout this company is something our employees have told us is critical to forming our future. The ethics and compliance initiative is a key part of that effort."

Training seminars for all employees, which would be implemented locally by each ECO, included introductions to the training, the Columbia/HCA code of conduct, and the Columbia/HCA overall ethics and compliance program. The training seminars also included presentations by members of senior management as well as small-group discussions in which participants discussed the application of the new Columbia/HCA code of conduct in ethics-related scenarios.

It was not believed that the program would change personal values. Although the company wanted individuals to bring their highest sense of personal values to work each day, the purpose of the program was to help employees understand the company's strict definition of ethical behavior. Columbia/HCA's ethical guidelines tackled basic issues, such as whether nurses can accept $100 tips — they cannot — and complicated topics, such as what constitutes Medicare fraud. In addition, the company developed certification tests for employees who determine billing codes.

In 1998 a forty-minute training video was shown to all two hundred and eighty-five thousand employees; it featured three ethical scenarios for employees to examine. Columbia/HCA apparently recognized the importance of ethical conduct and quality service to all of its constituents.

Changes at Columbia/HCA

In 1997–1998 Columbia/HCA Healthcare Corporation settled an Internal Revenue Service (IRS) tax dispute for $71 million over allegations that Columbia/HCA had made excessive compensation and golden parachute payments to some one hundred executives. As a result of the settlement, the IRS, which had sought $276 million in taxes and interest, agreed to drop the charges against Columbia/HCA that the pay generated when the executives exercised stock options following a new public offering of HCA constituted excessive compensation. Frist at the time reportedly earned about $125 million from exercising stock options after the public offering, and seventeen other top executives each made millions on the deals.

The effort to quickly change the corporate culture and become the model corporate citizen in the health care industry was a real challenge for what was Columbia/HCA. This health care provider learned the hard way that maintaining an organizational ethical climate is the responsibility of top management. The name of the health care giant was changed to HCA — The Healthcare Company. Since 1997, the company has closed or consolidated more than one hundred hospitals; it is currently composed of locally managed facilities that include one hundred and ninety-six hospitals and seventy outpatient surgery centers in twenty-four states, England, and Switzerland.

In August 2000, HCA became the first corporation ever to be removed from INFACT's Hall of Shame. The executive director of INFACT indicated that HCA had drastically reduced its political activity and influence. The corporation has no active federal lobbyists and has a registered lobbying presence in only twelve states. According to the executive director, "This response to grassroots pressure constitutes a landmark development in business ethics overall and challenges prevailing practices among for-profit health care corporations."

In December 2000, HCA announced it would pay the federal government more than $840 million in criminal fines and civil penalties in the largest governmental fraud settlement in history. In January 2001, Jack Bovender Jr. (formerly chief operating officer) was named CEO. Frist relinquished the title to focus on other interests but will continue to be involved in corporate strategy as chairman of HCA's board of directors. Of the fraud investigation, Bovender said, "We think the major issues have been settled," although the company still has some "physician relations issues and cost report issues" to resolve in civil actions involving individual hospitals.

Questions

1. What were the organizational ethical leadership problems that resulted in Columbia/HCA's misconduct?

2. How did the marketing techniques affect the level of service quality received by patients and/or customers?

3. Discuss the fundamental differences in perception between for-profit and not-for-profit companies regarding their responsibilities to their publics.

4. What caused Columbia/HCA's corporate culture to encourage unethical behavior?

5. What other suggestions could have been implemented to sensitize Columbia/HCA to ethical issues?

Sources: These facts are from "Corporate Influence Curtailed," *PR Newswire*, August 2, 2000; Duncan Mansfield, "HCA Names Bovender Chief Executive," January 8, 2001, *http://biz.yahoo.com/apf/010108/hca_change_2.html* (accessed January 16, 2001); "Columbia/HCA to Sell Part of Business," *Commercial Appeal*, June 3, 1998, p. B8; Columbia/HCA Healthcare Corporation, *1996 Annual Report to Stockholders;* "INFACT Urges Columbia/HCA to Remove Itself from the Hall of Shame," *PRNewswire, http://www.prnewswire.com* (accessed May 27, 1999); Kurt Eichenwald and N.R. Kleinfield, "At Columbia/HCA, Scandal Hurts," *Commercial Appeal*, December 21, 1997, pp. C1, C3; "Columbia/HCA Launches Ethics and Compliance Training Program," *AOL News*, February 12, 1998, *http://cbs.aol.com* (accessed February 7, 2001); Charles Ornstein, "Columbia/HCA Prescribes Employee Ethics Program," *Tampa Tribune*, February 20, 1998, p. 4; Tom Lowry, "Loss Warning Hits Columbia/HCA Stock," *USA Today*, February 9, 1998, p. 2B; Kurt Eichenwald, "Reshaping the Culture at Columbia/HCA," *New York Times*, November 4, 1997, p. C2; Tom Lowry, "Columbia/HCA Hires Ethics Expert," *USA Today*, October 14, 1997, p. 4B; Lucette Lagnado, "Columbia Taps Lawyer for Ethics Post: Yuspeh Led Defense Initiative of 1980s," *Wall Street Journal*, October 14, 1997, p. B6; Chris Woodyard, "FBI Alleges Systemic Fraud at Columbia," *USA Today*, October 7, 1997, p. 1B; and Eva M. Rodriguez, "Columbia/HCA Probe Turns to Marketing Billing," *Wall Street Journal*, August 21, 1997, p. A2.

Case 13

Microsoft and the U.S. Government

In 1975 William H. (Bill) Gates III and Paul G. Allen started Microsoft; in 1981 Microsoft incorporated. Microsoft's mission has been to create software for the personal computer in the workplace, school, and home. Microsoft's innovative products and marketing have made it the world's leading software provider. Some of its products include operating systems for personal computers, server applications for client–server environments, business and consumer productivity applications, interactive media programs, and Internet platform and development tools. Microsoft also markets on-line services, personal computer books, and input devices, and it researches and develops advanced technology software products. The company's products now extend their capabilities to international communication. Microsoft Office 2000 offers a MultiLanguage Pack, which allows users to deploy a single version of Office all around the world. The user can work with a standard English interface, then switch on-line help to another language. Microsoft's products are compatible with most personal computers (PCs), including Apple computers and those using Intel microprocessors.

Along with its innovative products and marketing, Microsoft contributes substantially to charities. Its community affairs programs rely on both corporate commitment and employee involvement to provide money, software, and volunteer support for nonprofit organizations nationwide. For example, when Microsoft employees donated to the annual giving campaign in 1999, the company matched each employee contribution up to $12,000. Organizations that benefit from such contributions include low-income housing developments, the YMCA, Easter Seals, Boys and Girls Club of America, museums, and schools. Microsoft also donated to eighteen Connected Learning Community grants, totaling $270,000 in cash and $325,000 in software, in 1999. Another Microsoft program is Libraries Online, whereby Microsoft provides computers, cash, and software to help link libraries to the Internet. The goal is to enable people who may not have access to computers to learn about PCs, explore the latest software, and experience the Internet. In addition, in 1999 Microsoft provided nearly $47.4 million in cash and software to eight hundred K–12 schools nationally to support teacher training. The company

This case was prepared by Robyn Smith and John Fraedrich for classroom discussion, rather than to illustrate either effective or ineffective handling of an administrative, ethical, or legal decision by management.

also donated more than $982,000 in cash and $6,234,000 in software to universities and colleges, not including the amount contributed by employees.

Issues Demeaning Microsoft's Reputation

Regardless of Microsoft's reputation for innovation and charity, the company is facing ethical and legal issues. The Federal Trade Commission (FTC) began investigating Microsoft in 1990 for possible violations of the Sherman and Clayton Antitrust Acts, which are designed to stop restraint of trade by businesses, especially monopolists. In August 1993 the FTC was deadlocked on a decision regarding possible Microsoft violations of the Sherman and Clayton Antitrust Acts. However, instead of dropping the case, the FTC handed it to the Department of Justice. At the time, Microsoft agreed to settle the lawsuit without admitting any wrongdoing. Part of the settlement provided the Justice Department with complete access to Microsoft's documents for use in subsequent investigations.

An important part of the settlement was a stipulation that would end Microsoft's practice of selling MS-DOS to original equipment manufacturers at a 60 percent discount. Those manufacturers received the discount if they agreed to pay Microsoft for every computer they sold (this is called a "per processor" agreement) as opposed to paying Microsoft for every computer they sold with MS-DOS preinstalled (which would be termed a "per copy" agreement). If an original equipment manufacturer wished to install a different operating system in some of its computers, the manufacturer would, in effect, be paying for both the Microsoft and the other operating system — that is, paying what is called "double royalties."

The argument goes that such business practices are unfair because consumers, in effect, pay Microsoft when they buy another product. Furthermore, the practices are deemed unfair because they make it uneconomical for an original equipment manufacturer to give up the 60 percent discount in favor of installing a less popular operating system on some of its computers. These issues focus on whether Microsoft has a monopoly in the market.

The Supreme Court has defined monopoly power as the "power to control prices or exclude competition." In other words, a monopolist is a company that can significantly raise the barriers to entry within the relevant market. A monopolist may engage in practices that any company, regardless of size, could legally employ; however, it cannot use its market power in such a way so as to prevent competition. In essence, a company is allowed to be a monopoly, but when a monopolist acts in a way that only a monopolist can, the monopolist has broken the law.

Another battle that Microsoft faced was with Apple Computer. Apple alleged that Microsoft's chief executive officer, Bill Gates, called and threatened to stop making Macintosh products if Apple did not stop the development of a program that was to compete with a similar Microsoft program. Because Microsoft is the largest producer of Macintosh-compatible programs, Apple argued that it was being forced to choose between a bad deal or extinction. Apple also alleged that Microsoft would not send it a copy of Windows 95 until Apple dropped Microsoft's name from a lawsuit. This issue was not as significant for the Justice Department as it started out to be because the two companies formed closer ties and are now hesitant about cooperating with the federal government. In late 1998, Microsoft bought $150 million of nonvoting stock in Apple, as well as paid $100 million for access to Apple's patents.

Microsoft was also under a federal court order to surrender part of its blueprints for Windows 95 to a rival, Caldera, Inc. However, Microsoft showed only the so-called source code for Windows 95 to Caldera lawyers and experts; it is difficult to make commercial products based on the code alone. U.S. Magistrate Ron Boyce refused a request by Microsoft to prevent Caldera's experts from consulting on the design of any operating system software for up to eighteen months. Caldera also sued Microsoft in federal court for designing early Windows software that allegedly was deliberately incompatible with DR-DOS, an operating system that competed directly with Microsoft's own similar product, MS-DOS. Caldera further claimed that Microsoft intentionally misled customers into believing that Windows 95 made it unnecessary for computer users to buy DR-DOS or MS-DOS. Prior versions of Windows ran explicitly as a supplement to the underlying operating system, whether consumers chose Microsoft's or Caldera's operating system. However, Caldera's own witnesses admit there was technical justification for the changes made by Microsoft to its own MS-DOS product to make it run better with Windows. Also, the problems that Caldera mentioned regarding the incompatibility between DR-DOS and Windows have been proven *not* to be a result of Microsoft's improvement to Windows. Under federal antitrust law, a company generally cannot require customers who buy one of its products to also buy another without some benefit to the customers — a practice known as "tying." The appeals court specifically cited the integration of MS-DOS and Windows into Windows 95 as an example of innovation that was beneficial to consumers. Microsoft agreed to a settlement of the lawsuit on January 10, 2000.

There was also a claim regarding Sun Microsystems, Inc.'s trademark and a breach-of-contract case against Microsoft. The case accused Microsoft of deliberately trying to sabotage Sun's Java "write once, run anywhere" promise by making Windows implementations incompatible with those that run on other platforms. Specifically, the suit alleged that Microsoft's Java-compatible products omitted a so-called Java native interface (JNI), as well as a remote method invocation (RMI) — features that help developers write Java code. Sun claimed Microsoft replaced certain parts of the Java code with Windows-specific code in a way that confused programmers into thinking they were using pure Java.

Sun acknowledged that Microsoft fixed some of the earlier glitches, but Sun added two new alleged incompatibilities to its list. One allegation concerns the addition of new keywords that are available to programmers, and the other revolves around new directives in Microsoft's Java compiler that make it dependent on Windows implementations.

In late 1998 Sun added new allegations of exclusionary conduct on the part of Microsoft and Windows 98. Sun requested an injunction that would require Microsoft either to make the Java features in the new operating system compatible with its tests or to include Sun's version of Java with every copy of Windows sold. In January 2000, the Ninth District Court of Appeals ruled that it was software developers and consumers, not Sun, who would decide the value of Microsoft's language extensions. Therefore, Microsoft is allowed to support its development tools with its own Java enhancements. Furthermore, Sun's motion to reinstate the injunction on the basis of copyright infringement was denied. The court ruled that the compatibility test was a contractual issue, not a copyright issue.

Overall, however, the federal government has taken an aggressive stand in that it believes Microsoft is practicing anticompetitive tactics, thus creating a monopolistic environment that has substantially lessened and reduced competition in the industry. In October 1997 the Justice Department asked a federal court to hold Microsoft in civil contempt for violating the terms of a 1995 consent decree. The decree barred Microsoft from imposing anticompetitive licensing terms on manufacturers of personal computers and asked the court to impose a $1 million-per-day fine. Microsoft argued that its Internet Explorer was an integrated, inseparable part of Windows 95 and that it was legal to install the entire program. However, the U.S. District Court judge did not agree with the argument and issued an injunction prohibiting the company from requiring Windows 95 licensees to bundle Internet Explorer with the operating system. Microsoft filed an appeal against the injunction and asked for the petition to be heard on an expedited basis, while it supplied PC makers with an older version of Windows 95 without the Internet Explorer files or with a current version of Windows 95 stripped of all Internet Explorer files. The problem was that this product would not boot up, and Microsoft admitted that it knew about it beforehand. Consequently, the Justice Department asked the district court to hold Microsoft in contempt. At the same time Microsoft's stock began to drop. Possibly fearing larger stock devaluation, Microsoft agreed to provide computer vendors with the most up-to-date version of Windows 95 without the Internet Explorer desktop icon.

MICROSOFT'S REBUTTAL TO THE ALLEGATIONS

Under the 1995 consent decree, Microsoft was unable to require companies such as Dell or Hewlett-Packard to obtain a license for the Windows operating system. In lay terms, Microsoft could not make others include Windows. However, the decree did not restrict Microsoft from integrating other products. Because the Web browser was put into the Windows operating system, users would be buying a product that they might not need or want.

In response to its detractors and the Justice Department, Microsoft denied all of the essential allegations, in that it had planned to integrate its Internet Explorer technologies into the Windows operating system long before rival Netscape even existed. Microsoft also refuted the government's central accusation that the company incorporated its browser technologies into Windows only to disadvantage

Netscape. Microsoft argued that its Internet Explorer was gaining popularity with consumers for the simple reason that it offered superior technology.

In addition, Microsoft rejected government allegations that the company tried to "illegally divide the browser market" with rival Netscape and that it had entered into exclusionary contracts with Internet service providers or Internet content providers. Finally, Microsoft argued that it did not illegally restrict the ability of computer manufacturers to alter the Windows desktop screen that users see when they turn on their computers for the first time.

Like other software products, Windows 95 and Windows 98 are subject to the protections afforded by the Federal Copyright Act of 1976, enacted in accordance with Article 1, Section 8 of the U.S. Constitution. The Copyright Act states that copyright owners have the right to license their products to third parties in an unaltered form. Microsoft asserted a counterclaim against the state attorneys general because Microsoft believed the state attorneys general were inappropriately trying to use state antitrust laws to infringe on Microsoft's federal rights.

MICROSOFT ON TRIAL

The federal government, along with twenty states, charged Microsoft with abusing its monopoly in the computer software business. The three primary issues were (1) bundling the Internet Explorer Web browser with the Windows 98 operating system to damage its competition, particularly Netscape Communications Inc.; (2) using cross-promotional deals with Internet providers to extend its monopoly; and (3) illegally preventing PC makers from customizing the opening screen showing Microsoft. The trial started October 19, 1998, and the government specifically accused Gates of illegal bullying, coercion, and predatory pricing to undermine Netscape because that company's products were becoming more popular than Microsoft's. Gates denied ever being concerned about Netscape's increasing browser market. However, Microsoft memorandums and e-mail messages showed otherwise.

In June 1995 Microsoft and Netscape executives had met to discuss "ways to work together" regarding the browser market and each other's share of that market. Netscape's CEO, James Barksdale, testified that Microsoft's proposal regarding working together involved illegally dividing the market. When Netscape rejected the proposal, Microsoft supposedly used predatory pricing, along with other tactics, to "crush" the company.

The government and economists put two years into negotiations with Microsoft. The intended purpose of the intervention, according to the government, was to help competitors regain some market share. The government and economists are hopeful that this will also decrease prices for computers and software, as well as spark innovation while expanding choice and quality. The purpose of the intervention is to prevent Microsoft from punishing other companies that wish to sell operating and application systems other than Windows, an allegation made by many competitors throughout the legal process.

The Depositions

In August 1998, the deposition of Microsoft management began in Redmond, Washington. Bill Gates was placed under oath and before a camera for thirty hours. During the taping, Gates did not help Microsoft's case, since he refused to answer most questions on his own during the deposition. He also quibbled over the exact meaning of words such as *complete* and *ask* when they were used in questions throughout the deposition. When questioned about the controversial e-mails sent throughout the company regarding treatment of competition, he did not have an effective argument as to their exact meaning. It seemed at this point that Gates was not concerned about the forthcoming trial.

His feelings might have changed, however, in November 1998, when Judge Thomas Penfield Jackson released his findings of facts. The document consisted of four hundred and twelve paragraphs, only four of which were favorable toward Microsoft. Jackson also named Jim Allchin, a computer expert and long-time Microsoft employee, as the mastermind behind the bundling of Internet Explorer and the operating system in an attempt to destroy Netscape. It seemed there was nothing Microsoft could do at this point to eliminate its monopolistic image.

The Trial

By January 1999, the credibility of Microsoft had been severely damaged. During this time, several company witnesses testified regarding the e-mails in question. However, the prosecutor was usually able to rebut his or her version of the story. The most damaging testimony by far came from Jim Allchin, who was often referred to as "Microsoft's lord of Windows." Allchin's testimony was supposed to demonstrate that Explorer could not operate without Windows. However, the videotaped demonstration proved otherwise. Because of the reappearing Explorer icon, it was apparent that the tape had been doctored. This was just one more serious blow to the reputation of Microsoft. This led to an attempt to settle by Microsoft, but the two sides could not agree to the terms of a settlement.

By the end of February 1999, Microsoft had three proposals ready for the Justice Department. The meetings were still unsuccessful, as both sides had opposing ideas for a solution. The government suggested that Microsoft place government-appointed people as active members on the Microsoft board. Microsoft only saw this as a government attempt to take control of the company. In April 2000, the government began talks about splitting Microsoft into two companies.

Judge Jackson appointed Judge Richard Ponser, a well-respected member of the Seventh Circuit Court, to try one more time to make a deal, but the gap was still too wide. Judge Jackson felt Microsoft was "untrustworthy," and some of the states that were also parties in the suit opposed all negotiations. The last meeting took place on June 2, 2000. By this time, all negotiations had reached a stalemate. Both the government and Microsoft had exhausted all efforts. All that was left was the judge's decision.

The Ruling

On June 7, 2000, Judge Jackson ordered Microsoft to split into two independent companies — one company to sell Windows and the other to sell everything else. Jackson provided several grounds for his decision, the first being simply that Microsoft would not admit to any wrongdoing. He also stated that one intention of his decision was to prevent Microsoft from insulting the government by refusing to comply with antitrust laws. Jackson said he found Microsoft to be "untrustworthy" because of past antics, including sending defective Windows software when ordered to unbundle the Internet browser from the operating system. Finally, Jackson said he was also trying to prevent Microsoft from bullying its competitors.

By splitting Microsoft into two independent companies, Jackson was hoping to achieve several objectives. First, the split was intended to respark competition in the industry. Second, dividing Microsoft into two companies possibly could spur some innovation that had been stifled by the size and force of the software giant. Third, the split, it was hoped, would rejuvenate some of the "dead zones" in the industry, such as word processing, spreadsheets, databases, and e-mail. Fourth, and possibly most importantly, lessening Microsoft's power in the industry, it was hoped, would renew creativity among software engineers. Although Judge Jackson had high hopes that these things would happen, Microsoft's opinion of the outcome fell at the opposite end of the spectrum.

According to Microsoft, splitting the company in two would be the equivalent of the government's imposing a "corporate death sentence." Contrary to Jackson's idea of spurring innovation, Microsoft believed the split would do just the opposite — stifle innovation. Also, the split would impose complexity on software development. With two businesses working separately, it would be more difficult to effectively integrate two or more programs. In addition, because of the difficulty in bundling, software would be marketed separately, thus driving the prices higher for consumers. Finally, Microsoft saw the split as causing a delay in product completion and introduction.

The government and Microsoft may be the two entities directly involved in this trial; however, the public will also be affected in the long run, and many have voiced an opinion on the case. Microsoft has long seen itself as the symbol of the American Dream for its customers, and a public opinion poll conducted by Harris Interactive supported that notion. A little more than half of 3,830 people surveyed agreed that Bill Gates was a positive role model. The respondents were randomly selected to participate in a survey regarding the possible split of Microsoft. Of the respondents, nearly half said they disagreed with the government's proposal to split Microsoft into two companies. However, there were negative responses as well. Of those surveyed, 42 percent believed that Microsoft was a monopolist, and only 23 percent felt that Microsoft treated its competitors in an appropriate manner. Another survey showed that 55 percent of 137 respondents felt that Microsoft was guilty of deliberately trying to crush its competitors.

The Appeal

Microsoft's appeal of Judge Jackson's ruling could delay an actual split until at least 2001. The Justice Department would like to have the Supreme Court review the case next, bypassing the D.C. (District of Columbia) Circuit Court of Appeals, which has already backed Microsoft once in a similar case. The Supreme Court has declined the case, however, so it will go first to the Circuit Court of Appeals. Until the appeals process is over, the split has been stayed, or suspended. The government-imposed restrictions should have taken effect by September 2000; however, Microsoft appealed. The request was granted. Therefore, Microsoft will continue to operate as in the past.

The D.C. Circuit Court of Appeals will consist of a three-judge panel selected randomly from the full eleven members by a computer. It is believed that the court will support Bill Gates's claim that courts should not meddle in the high-tech industry, as the court ruled in 1998 when Microsoft was first accused of tying software. Regardless of the speculation, however, in order for an appellate court to overturn a trial judge's factual findings, it must prove that the findings were clearly flawed. If Microsoft is not happy with the ruling of the three-judge panel, it may appeal to the full eleven members.

WHERE DOES MICROSOFT GO FROM HERE?

The only certainty in this case is that a final decision likely will not be announced before 2002, which in reality will likely "kill" the case all together. So what does this mean for Microsoft? First, it means business will go on as usual. With the industry dramatically changing, Microsoft will have to change as well. The company will focus on the bottom line, while developing and promoting .NET, its newest venture for the wireless world. It also means the odds of winning have increased dramatically. Go to www.e-businessethics.com for updates on this case.

Questions

1. Why has there been so much debate about the software industry and Bill Gates?

2. What legal and ethical issues in the Microsoft case relate to U.S. culture, and do these issues extend to other countries that use Microsoft products?

3. Discuss Microsoft's corporate culture in regard to the issues involved and how it has affected the U.S. debate.

4. Identify the types of power associated with each player in this case and discuss how and why each player is using these types of power. What are the potential ramifications of their actions?

These facts are from Richard B. McKenzie, *Trust on Trial: How the Microsoft Case Is Reframing the Rules of Competition* (Cambridge, Mass: Perseus Publishing, 2000); Michael J. Martinez, "Microsoft Buys Time to Retool," *Fort Collins Coloradoan,* September 27, 2000, pp. A1, A2; Robert O'Brien, "Kodak, Lexmark Lead Decline as Profit Warnings Hurt Stocks," *Wall Street Journal,* September 27, 2000, p. C2; Jared Sandberg, "Microsoft's Six Fatal Errors," *Newsweek,* June 19, 2000, pp. 23–27; Paul Davidson, "Microsoft Split Ordered: Appeal Could Go Directly to Supreme Court," *USA Today,* June 8, 2000, p. A1; Jon Swartz, "Microsoft Split Ordered: Will Breakup Help or Hurt Consumers?" *USA Today,* June 8, 2000, pp. A1, A2; Patrick McMahon, "Stoic Staffers Shake Heads, Return to Work," *USA Today,* June 8, 2000, p. B3; Edward Iwata and John Swartz, "Bill Gates Won't Be Dethroned So Easily: Software King — and His Myth — to Survive on Iron Will, Talent," *USA Today,* June 8, 2000, p. B3; Paul Davidson, "Microsoft Awaits a New Hand: Executives Expect Appeals Judges to Be More Amenable," *USA Today,* June 8, 2000, pp. B1, B2; Jared Sandberg, "Bring on the Chopping Block," *Newsweek,* May 8, 2000, pp. 34–35; Rebecca Buckman, "Go Figure: In Valuing a Split Microsoft, Analysts Offer a Wide Range of Numbers," *Wall Street Journal,* May 2, 2000, pp. C1, C3; Rebecca Buckman, "Looking Through Microsoft's Window: On the Firm's Sprawling Campus, It's Almost Business As Usual As Talk of Breakup Brews," *Wall Street Journal,* May 1, 2000, pp. B1, B10; Geri Coleman Tucker and Will Rodger, "Facing Breakup, Gates to Take Case to People; Microsoft Says Don't Punish Success," *USA Today,* May 1, 2000, pp. B1; B2; Don Clark and Ted Bridis, "Creating Two Behemoths? Company Bets Appeals Court Will Overturn Jackson, Making Any Remedy Moot," *Wall Street Journal,* April 28, 2000, pp. B1, B4; Lee Gomes and Rebecca Buckman, "Creating Two Behemoths? Microsoft Split Might Not Be Much Help for Competitors and Could Harm Consumer," *Wall Street Journal,* April 28, 2000, p. B1; Kevin Maney, "Microsoft's Uncertain Future Rattles Investors: Justice Must Make Recommendation: Breakup Possible," *USA Today,* April 25, 2000, p. B1; Bill Gates and Steve Ballmer, "To Our Customers, Partners and Shareholders," *USA Today,* April 5, 2000, p. B7; Paul Davidson, "Expert's View May Influence Ruling," *USA Today,* Feburay 2, 2000, p. B1; Paul Davidson, "Microsoft Responds to Judge's Findings," *USA Today,* January 19, 2000, p. B1; "Survey Results: May 2000 Final Survey Results," *http://e-businessethics.com/view_results.htm* (accessed September 8, 2000); "Java Contract Lawsuit Update," *http://msdn.microsoft.com/visualj/lawsuitruling.asp* (accessed September 8, 2000); "Notice Regarding Java Lawsuit Ruling: Notice to Customers," *http://msdn.microsoft.com/visualj/statement.asp* (accessed September 8, 2000); "New Microsoft Connected Learning Community Program Fact Sheet," *http://www.microsoft.com/PressPass/press/1999/May99/CLCFS.asp* (accessed September 8, 2000); "International Design for Office 2000," *http://www.microsoft.com/Office/ORK/2000Journ/LangPack.htm* (accessed September 8, 2000); "Microsoft Files Summary Judgment Motions in Caldera Lawsuit: Technological 'Tying' and Incompatibility Issues Shown to be Without Merit," *http://www.microsoft.com/PressPass/press/1999/Feb99/Calderapr.asp* (accessed September 8, 2000); Dan Goodin, "New Microsoft Java Flaws Alleged," *http://www.microsoft.com/BillGates/billgates_1/speeches/6-25win98launch.htm#bill* (accessed July 9, 1998); Lisa Picarille, "Microsoft, Sun Postpone Java Hearing," *Computer Reseller News, http://headlines.yahoo.com/Full_Coverage/Tech/Sun_Microsoft_Lawsuit/* (accessed July 7, 1998); Malcolm Maclachlan, "Sun Attacks an Embattled Microsoft," *TechWeb* (May 14, 1998); Malcolm Maclachlan, "New Lawsuit Is Over Java, Sun Says," *TechWeb* (accessed May 12, 1998); Malcolm Maclachlan, "Sun Targets Microsoft: Software Maker Says Windows 98 Must Be Java Compatible," *Tech Web, http://www.techweb.com/news/story/TWB19980512S0012* (accessed May 12, 1998); Dana Gardner, "Java Is an Unleashed Force of Nature, Says JavaOne Panel," *InfoWorld Electric* (posted March 26, 1998); Michael Moeller, "Amended Complaint: Microsoft Wants Access to 'Highly Confidential' Documents," *PC Week Online* (August 4, 1998); "Microsoft Asks Court to Limit Gates Deposition," *http://dailynews.yahoo.com/headlines/politics/story.html/s=z/reuters/980805/politics/stories/microsoft_1.html;* Margaret A. Jacobs, "Injunction Looms As Showdown for Microsoft," *Wall Street Journal,* May 20, 1998, pp. B1, B6; John Harwood and David Bank, "CyberSpectacle: Senate Meets Electronic Elite," *Wall Street Journal,* March 4, 1998, pp. B1, B13; John R. Wilke and David Bank, "Microsoft's Chief Concedes Hardball Tactics," *Wall Street Journal,* March 4, 1998, pp. B1, B13; U.S. Justice Department and State Attorneys General, "Statement by Microsoft Corporation," *http://www.microsoft.*

com/presspass.doj.7-28formalresponse.htm (accessed August 3, 1998); Christopher Barr, "The Justice Department's Lawsuit Against Microsoft," *http://www.cnet.com/content/voices/Barr/012698/ss01.html* (accessed July 13, 1998); "Microsoft Corporate Information. What We Do," *http://www.microsoft. com/ mscorp/* (accessed August 3, 1998); Dan Goodin, "New Microsoft Java Flaws Alleged," *http:// www.news.com/News/Item/Textonly/0,25,24007,00.html?st.ne.ni.pfv* (accessed August 3, 1998); Tim Clark, "Go Away," *http://ne2.news.com/News/Item/0,4,2076,00.html* (accessed August 7, 1996); Nick Wingfield, "Net Assault," *http://ne2.news.com/News/Item/0,4,1940,00.html* (accessed July 25, 1996); Nick Wingfield and Tim Clark, "Dirty," *http://ne2.news.com/News/Item/0,4,2072,00.html* (accessed August 7, 1996); "Feud Heats Up," *http://ne2.news.com/SpecialFeature...d/0,6,2216_2,00.html'st. ne.ni.prev* (accessed July 13, 1998); Dan Check, "The Case Against Microsoft," *http://ourworld. compuserve.com/homepages/spazz/mspaper.htm* (accessed Spring 1996); "Microsoft Antitrust Ruling," *http://www.courttv.com/legaldocs/cyberlaw/mseruling.html* (accessed July 13, 1998); Bob Trott and David Pendery, "Allchin E-Mail Adds to Microsoft's Legal Woes"; Ted Bridis, "More Accusations Hit Microsoft," *Denver Post*, October 23, 1998, sec. B; Aaron Zitner, "Feds Assail Gates," *Denver Post*, October 30, 1998, sec. C; Julie Schmit, "Tech Industry's Direction Hangs in Balance," *USA Today*, October 16, 1998, p. 3B; and Eun-Kyung Kim, "Microsoft Court Gets Lesson on Monopolies," *Fort Collins Coloradoan*, November 20, 1998, p. B2.

The Straying of Astra USA

Astra USA was a wholly owned subsidiary of the international pharmaceutical company Astra AB of Sweden. To understand Astra USA and its former president CEO, Lars Bildman, one needs to understand the parent company. Established in the early 1900s, because of the abolishment of the drug monopolies in Sweden and other countries, Astra began manufacturing its first pharmaceutical drug called Digitotal — a heart medicine. In the next twenty years Astra continued to be aggressive in marketing, research and development, and forming subsidiaries in Finland and Latvia. By the 1950s Astra had subsidiaries in Italy, Canada, West Germany, Colombia, Mexico, Australia, and the United States. The drug that propelled Astra into an elite group of competitors was Xylocaine, a local anesthetic. In the 1960s and 1970s Astra diversified heavily into a wide variety of medical drugs and products. A four-pronged strategy was developed in the following areas: cardiovascular preparations, local anesthetics, anti-asthma agents, and antibiotics. In 1982 Astra signed a long-term agreement in the U.S. market with the conglomerate Merck & Co. During the 1980s Astra shares were introduced onto the London stock exchange. Profit sharing was introduced, and research centers were established in India and England.

HÅKAN MÖGREN

In 1987 Håkan Mögren was appointed president of the company. Before Mögren came to Astra it was a slow-moving, sedate company. When the wealthy Wallenberg family of Sweden who owned Astra chose Mögren, many in the industry thought it was a mistake. After all, Håkan Mögren knew nothing of molecular research or the drug business. He had been the chief executive of a local chocolate and foodstuff company. Soon after being hired, Mögren shook up the sleepy company. He took an unknown anti-ulcer drug, Losec, and marketed it globally. He tripled the international sales staff, built subsidiaries overseas, and bought back licenses in strategically located markets.

Under Mögren, Astra's international marketing intensified. The results included several licensing agreements, which gave the company significant market-

---

This case was prepared by John Fraedrich and Barbara Gilmer for classroom discussion, rather than to illustrate either effective or ineffective handling of an administrative, ethical, or legal decision by management.

ing control in Italy, Spain, Japan, and the United States. Astra shares were finally listed on the New York Stock Exchange in 1996, and in 1998 Astra's market capitalization surpassed $30 billion. The highest sales increase was in the North American market, in which sales rose more than 50 percent, to nearly $1 billion. Astra spent more than 21 percent of its revenues on research and development in 1998. The restructuring relationship of Astra USA with Merck & Co. in early 1998 gave it strategic marketing freedom within the United States, as well as the right to buy out Merck's interest in 2008.

Mögren's appetite for growth seemed to know no bounds. In late 1998, Mögren, who said that he was not interested in rapid growth, decided first to sever and then to buy out the joint venture it had with Merck. It cost Astra approximately $10 billion to acquire control of the Merck joint venture. The move paved the way for Astra, one of Europe's strongest pharmaceutical companies, to pursue a multibillion dollar merger in the consolidating global drugs industry. On April 6, 1999, Astra AB of Sweden and Zeneca Group PLC of the United Kingdom officially merged to form AstraZeneca PLC. The company has become a giant in the industry with forty thousand employees worldwide and sales in 2000 of $18 billion. C. G. Johannsson is the chief executive, and Håkan Mögren serves as deputy chairman.

The style of Håkan Mögren certainly was not traditionally Swedish — conservative, group oriented. Some former employees talk of extravagances in personal indulgence. Allegedly, tax-free "gifts" of expensive wines as well as other items were given to Mögren from suppliers and subordinates because of his known love of such things. Mögren also loved the opera and would fly his family to other countries to attend performances. His lifestyle helps to shed light on the type of culture he established at Astra and what subsequently happened.

LARS BILDMAN AND THE ASTRA WAY

Whether Mögren influenced Lars Bildman's business approach and lifestyle or whether Bildman's business approach and lifestyle were already set before he came to Astra USA is still in question. Bildman started out with the company as a young chemical engineer. He was vice president of the company's German subsidiary and from there went to Astra USA as CEO. A lanky man with piercing eyes, he was a charismatic, if somewhat quirky, employer. For example, Bildman favored suits in purple, coral, or traffic-cone orange. Insiders report that he was also a connoisseur of fine wines, caviar, and Dom Perignon champagne. Many believed these things were acceptable, especially for a man who had taken a company from annual revenues of $30 million to $360 million. People around Bildman described him as a very disciplined, goal-oriented man, who ruled over his fifteen hundred plus "troops" in Westborough, Massachusetts, a Boston suburb.

Bildman's management style was described as autocratic. He established a rigid, militaristic atmosphere at Astra headquarters. For example, most staffers were required to go to lunch at precisely the same time every day and had to get permission to hang anything personal on their cubicle walls. All but the highest-ranking executives had to use one centralized fax number, and Bildman received copies of all messages. Others told about the way that he would exercise power. For example, at one meeting he did not like the suit one of his executives was wearing and told him to change it; the executive did so quickly. Bildman also insisted that everyone wear the Astra pin. Employees who forgot their pin were severely reprimanded. One employee said, "The fear got so out of hand that I recall at least six times that I gave somebody an extra pin and they were literally shaken by the fact that they had lost theirs."

To fuel the growth that was taking place at Astra USA, Bildman began to hire hundreds of young salespeople. For female recruits, appearance seemed very important. This comment illustrates the prevailing attitude: "They told me in no uncertain terms why they wanted her hired — because she was extremely attractive." An Astra executive said about someone else: "We're not hiring her. I can't see me sitting at a bar having a drink with her."

Selling pharmaceuticals is a high-paying, much-sought-after profession; starting salaries are high and include a car and hefty bonuses — with compensation at Astra being better. However, the new hires that Astra recruited were not the norm. Few had prior pharmaceutical experience. All had to attend a rigorous nine-week training course, which included in-depth sales instruction, as well as topics such as anatomy and physiology. Tests, studying, and physical activities were the standards for the nine-week period. The training also immersed the new hires in the Astra culture, known as the "Astra Way." Each class of up to a hundred was lodged for the entire nine weeks at the Westborough Marriott near Astra headquarters. The company paid for just one plane ticket home and discouraged trainees from leaving before the nine weeks were completed or from having visitors during that period. The Astra Way consisted of a set of rigid rules covering everything from sales techniques — presentations had to be memorized and delivered to doctors virtually by rote — to acceptable casual dress. (No jeans. No shorts. Socks required.) Trainees were also taught and expected to use European etiquette. New recruits were marched around buildings in sweats for a day, as managers, dressed in fatigues, barked questions. Those who could not answer quickly enough were made to do pushups. The atmosphere was one of domination.

Socializing also appeared to play a key role in the Astra Way. Recruits were told that to succeed they had to play hard as well as work hard. "Work eight hours, play eight hours, sleep eight hours" was a phrase Bildman and other top managers frequently used. Because entertaining was the Astra Way, open-bar nights were frequent. Managers would take new hires and have drinking parties, which usually went on until the early-morning hours, three or four nights a week. At these open-bar nights, the attractive women drew most of the attention. "Upper management was barely paying attention to the male students, but they were all over the female students," said a 1993 trainee who left Astra a year later. The pressure to go to these events was high, especially when Bildman and other executives were in attendance. With a 15 percent washout rate, trainees realized that making the right impression could mean the difference between being assigned to San Francisco or to Fargo, North Dakota. "You had to go to the bar," said one female rep. Another former employee had this comment: "They would use their power and authority to make you think you didn't have a job if you didn't go along."

It has been claimed that Bildman and other managers would also invite new hires out on the town. For example, it has been claimed that on one occasion Bildman organized a night out with six trainees — four women and two men. After dinner the group retired to a darkly lit piano bar, where Bildman ordered people to dance. One trainee remembered it as a "come-on" bar, "the type of place where you'd meet somebody, have a steamy dance, and go home." As the party moved to another nightclub, it is alleged that sexual improprieties occurred. "I didn't feel I could say no," recalled one trainee, whom Bildman allegedly steered to a bed at one of the private parties. "I kept thinking: He's the president of the company. Is there any way to get out of this discreetly?"

This seemed to be a pattern during Bildman's tenure at Astra USA. In addition, it was also alleged that Bildman and his colleagues chartered yachts with high-priced prostitutes, and took relatives and family on vacations on company funds. Bildman also allegedly renovated his house and Vermont ski lodge with more than $2 million in Astra money. According to prosecutors, Bildman's Boston suburban home was furnished with a sauna, pool, wine cellar, and a martial arts facility for his children — all on company funds.

What is not in question is that Lars Bildman was terminated as president and CEO in June 1996. In January 1998, the trial between U.S. authorities and Bildman was concluded with a plea bargain in which Bildman pleaded guilty to three counts of filing false federal income tax returns. In exchange for the plea, prosecutors dropped fraud and conspiracy charges. Bildman was sentenced to twenty-one months in prison, to be followed by three years' probation, and payment of $281,190 in back-taxes and a $30,000 fine. Bildman was released from the Oakdale, Louisiana, Federal Correctional Institution in December 1999.

After a year-long investigation, the U.S. Equal Employment Opportunity Commission (EEOC) found that Bildman was guilty of extensive sexual harassment. In a settlement with the EEOC, Astra agreed to establish a claim fund of $9.85 million to be apportioned among eligible claimants. Of the one hundred and eighty-one claims, one hundred and twenty-four have been substantiated. To date, litigants have received compensation as follows:

Number of Litigants	Compensation Received
20	$12,000
16	25,000
20	30,000
13	40,000
10	50,000

3	$ 75,000
15	100,000
10	150,000
1	200,000
10	250,000
6	300,000

Astra filed suit against Bildman, demanding damages of $15 million.

THE RESPONSE FROM MÖGREN AND SWEDEN

In contrast to many other companies that have in the past attempted to bury the truth, Astra addressed the problems in a very open way. The following is part of a speech given by Mögren:

> . . . As a result of a preliminary investigation . . . we were able to confirm that a violation had been made of the fundamental principles for working at Astra and of the culture that we have developed. . . .
>
> . . . Concerning the sexual harassment now in question, it should be said that what has occurred is at best a violation of good style and form. At worst, a number of our employees have also been caused inconveniences or suffering. To the extent this may have occurred, we are deeply regretful. We will do everything we can to prevent it from ever happening again.
>
> . . . We have decided to review the adherence to all applicable rules. At first glance our view is that it is not the rules that are at fault. What has happened is that some people have tried to put themselves above the rules, at the same time that they have made great efforts to cover up what has happened.
>
> . . . We have adopted measures aimed at strengthening the staff's position. We have established a telephone hotline in the U.S. with an impartial party, where persons who feel they are exposed to any form of harassment can call under protection of anonymity.
>
> . . . We have also conducted a great deal of self-reflection . . . and asked ourselves what we can improve upon.
>
> . . . I would like to [note] that sexual harassment is not viewed in the same way in all cultures. . . . Since views differ, it is all the more important for a company that is active around the world to work according to a carefully thought-out policy. But there is no doubt about the principal objective: no employee . . . should have to tolerate harassment of any kind. All misuse of power must be condemned.*

The merger of Astra and Zeneca combined the extensive experience and skills of more than forty-seven thousand employees worldwide. Recognizing that diver-

---

Håkan Mögren, "Address to Astra's Annual Meeting, May 13, 1996," Astra AB of Sweden.

sity and creative potential are valuable assets, one of AstraZeneca's main priorities since the merger "has been to develop and widely communicate the new company values and principles, and to build a culture which unites employees in a common purpose." AstraZeneca's code of conducted was published in June 2000, and all employees are required to comply with the letter and spirit of the code.

Questions

1. Discuss the interaction between Bildman and Mögren as well as the Astra corporate culture. Who or what was ultimately responsible, and why?

2. Evaluate the Astra corporate culture during Bildman's tenure and discuss whether or not it has changed.

3. Was Bildman a rogue executive who was not following Astra's corporate culture, or was he its epitome? Discuss both sides of the argument.

These facts are from "Key Facts," *http://www.astrazeneca.com/AboutUs/Key_facts.htm* (accessed January 9, 2001); "Clarification from Astra Concerning Information in the Swedish Newspaper *Dagens Industri,*" March 4, 1998, *http://www.astrazeneca.com/NewSection/newsreleases/2_1_65e.htm* (accessed January 9, 2001); "People, Culture & Values," *www.astrazeneca.com/AboutUs/People_culture_and_values.htm* (accessed January 9, 2001); Bob Kievra, "Former Astra CEO Bildman Released from Federal Prison," *Worcester Telegram & Gazette,* November 9, 1999; Bob Kievra, "Astra Sex-Harassment Payments OK'd. $9.1M Ready to Go to 120 Claimants," *Worcester Telegram & Gazette,* May 27, 1999, p. E1; *http://www.astra.com/astra/news/2_4_5.HTM;www.astra.com/Astra/news/enewsrel/2_1_59e.htm;www.law.emory.edu/1circuit/sept96/96-1751.01a.html; www.astra.com/Astra/news/ENEWSREL/2_1_65e.htm; www.astra.se/om_astra/pressmeddelanden/pm/pm59.htm; www.businessweek.com/1996/21/b347654.html; http://lawlibrary.ucdavis.edu/LAWLIB/March98/0139.html; http://www.wcinet.com/th/News/020698/National/94318.htm; http://www.consult-dtc.com/news.html; http://www.civiljustice.com/astra515.htm; http://www.businessweek.com/; http://www.communityadvocate.com/; http://www.s-t.com/; http://www. uiowa.edu/; http://www.civiljustice.com/astra72.htm;* and *http://www.newsday.com/mainnews/rnmi012a.htm.*

Case 15

Mattel, Inc.: The Serious Business of Toys

Mattel, Inc., with $5.5 billion in annual revenues, is a world leader in the design, manufacture, and marketing of family products. The company's major toy brands include Barbie (with more than one hundred and twenty different Barbie dolls), Fisher-Price, Disney entertainment lines, Hot Wheels and Matchbox cars, Tyco Toys, Cabbage Patch Kids, and board games such as Scrabble. In addition, Mattel promotes international sales by tailoring toys for specific international markets instead of simply modifying favorites in the United States. The company has its headquarters in El Segundo, California, and offices in thirty-six countries. It markets its products in more than one hundred and fifty nations throughout the world.

This top manufacturing company for toys was under the managerial control of CEO Jill Barad from January 1997 to February 2000. The chief executive's management style has been characterized as strict and business- and people-oriented. When Barad was named chief executive in January 1997, Mattel's stock was trading for less than $30 a share. However, by March 1997, it had risen to more than $46. Before being made CEO, Barad had also helped build the sales of Barbie from $200 million in 1982 to $1.9 billion in 1997. Some of her challenges grew more difficult in 1998. Mattel announced in October 1998 that earnings growth for the year would be between 9 and 12 percent, rather than the 18 percent that Wall Street had anticipated. This was due to the declining sales to Toys "R" Us, the retail chain that accounted for 18 percent of Mattel's revenue in 1997. Barad stated in an interview that if performance continued to deteriorate sharply, the generous rewards given to employees would have to be cut back. Problems continued during Barad's three-year tenure. Mattel bought software maker The Learning Co., which immediately began draining $1 million a day in cash from the company. Also during this time, sales of Barbie fell 20 percent, earnings per share dropped to 43 cents, and the stock price plummeted. Barad resigned in early 2000.

This case was prepared by Marisol Paradoa and Debbie Thorne for classroom discussion, rather than to illustrate either effective or ineffective handling of an administrative, ethical, or legal decision by management.

Source: Marisol Paradoa and Debbie Thorne, Southwest Texas State University. Reprinted with permission.

New CEO Robert Eckert sold the money-losing Learning Co. unit, cut three hundred and fifty jobs, and eliminated marginally profitable toy lines. Also in 2000, Mattel was granted the highly sought-after licensing agreement for products related to the literary phenomenon *Harry Potter.* In addition, Nickelodeon and Mattel signed a new, multiyear, worldwide licensing agreement, giving Mattel the master toy license for all Nickelodeon entertainment properties.

MATTEL'S CORE PRODUCTS

Barbie and American Girl

The Barbie doll is one of Mattel's major product lines, and the number-one girls' brand in the world. Approximately 1 billion Barbie dolls have been sold since its introduction in 1959. The average American girl aged 3 to 11 owns ten Barbie dolls, and the doll is currently sold in more than one hundred and fifty countries around the world. Sales in 1999 were more than $1.5 billion. The Barbie line today includes not only dolls and accessories but also Barbie software and a broad assortment of licensed products such as books, apparel, food, home furnishings, and home electronics.

To augment Barbie, in the summer of 1998 the giant toy company announced that it would pay $700 million to Pleasant Co., for its American Girl collection, a well-known line of historical dolls, books, and accessories. Sold exclusively through catalogs, the American Girl dolls, which are made to look like 9-year-olds, have a wholesome and educational image. The American Girl brand is the number-two girls' brand in the world. This purchase by Mattel represented a long-term strategy to reduce reliance on traditional products.

Hot Wheels

Hot Wheels roared into the toy world in 1968. More than thirty years later, the brand is hotter than ever and now includes high-end collectibles, NASCAR (National Association for Stock Car Auto Racing) and Formula One models for adults, and high-performance cars, track sets, and play sets for children of all ages. The brand is involved with almost every racing circuit in the world, including NASCAR, Formula One, NHRA (National Hot Rod Association), CART (Championship Auto Racing Teams), AMA (American Motorcyclist Association), and many others. More than 15 million boys aged 5 to 15 are avid collectors, with the average collector owning more than forty-one Hot Wheel cars. Somewhere in the world, two Hot Wheels cars are sold every second of every day. The brand that started with cars on a track has evolved into a "lifestyle" brand with licensed Hot Wheels shirts, caps, lunch boxes, backpacks, and more. Together, Hot Wheels and Barbie generate 45 percent of Mattel's revenue and 65 percent of its profits.

Cabbage Patch Kids

Since the introduction of Cabbage Patch Kids in 1983, more than 90 million of these dolls have been purchased around the world. The dolls were unique in many respects, including their representation of many races and ethnicities through individualized facial and body features. When Mattel brought out the Cabbage Patch Kids Snacktime Kids in the fall of 1996, it expected the dolls to continue the success of the original product line.

The Snacktime Kids had moving mouths that enabled children to "feed" the doll. However, this unique feature proved dangerous to some children. Reports of children getting their fingers or hair caught in the dolls' mouths surfaced soon after the 1996 holiday season. By January 1997, Mattel had voluntarily pulled all Snacktime Kids from store shelves. In addition, consumers were offered a cash refund of $40 when returning the dolls. The U.S. Consumer Product Safety Commission applauded Mattel's handling of the Snacktime Kids situation. Current "hot" products in the Cabbage Patch Kids line include Preemie Surprise and Butterfly Fairies.

MATTEL'S COMMITMENT TO ETHICS AND SOCIAL RESPONSIBILITY

Mattel's core products and business environment can present ethical issues. For example, since the company's products are primarily designed for children, it must be sensitive to societal concerns about children's rights. In addition, the international environment often complicates business transactions. Different legal systems and cultural expectations about business can create ethical conflict. Finally, the use of technology may present ethical dilemmas, especially with regard to consumer privacy. Mattel has recognized these potential issues and has taken steps to strengthen its commitment to business ethics and social responsibility.

Privacy and Marketing Technology

Advances in technology have created special issues for Mattel's marketing efforts. Mattel has recognized that, because it markets to children, it has the responsibility to communicate with parents about corporate marketing strategy. The company has taken special steps to inform both children and adults about its philosophy regarding Internet-based marketing tools, such as the Hot Wheels web site. For example, the Mattel, Inc., web site for Hot Wheels contains a lengthy on-line privacy policy, some of which is reprinted here:

> Mattel is committed to protecting your on-line privacy when visiting any web sites operated by us or our family of companies, such as The Learning Com-

pany.* We do not collect and keep any personal information from you unless you volunteer it and you are 13 or older. We also do not collect and keep personal information on-line from children under the age of 13 without their parent's consent. Please review the information below to familiarize yourself with our policies on web site privacy, so that you can take full advantage of all the fun stuff available at our sites for you and your family.

A SPECIAL NOTE FOR PARENTS: Mattel adheres to the Children's Online Privacy Protection Act of 1998 and the guidelines of the Children's Advertising Review Unit (CARU) of the Council of Better Business Bureaus, Inc. in each of our web sites for children. Parents, you can help by spending time online with your children and monitoring your children's online use. Please help us protect your child's privacy by instructing them never to provide personal information on this site or any other without your permission.

IF YOU ARE UNDER 18, PLEASE BE SURE TO READ THIS POLICY WITH YOUR PARENTS AND ASK QUESTIONS ABOUT THINGS YOU DO NOT UNDERSTAND. CHILDREN UNDER 13 SHOULD GET YOUR PARENT'S PERMISSION BEFORE GIVING OUT YOUR E-MAIL ADDRESS OR ANY PERSONAL INFORMATION TO MATTEL — OR TO ANYONE ELSE ON THE INTERNET.†

Expectations of Mattel's Business Partners

Beyond concerns about marketing to children, Mattel, Inc., is making a serious commitment to business ethics. In late 1997 the company completed its first full ethics audit of each of its manufacturing sites as well as the facilities of its primary contractors. The audit indicated that the company was not using any child labor or forced labor, a problem that has plagued other overseas consumer products' manufacturers. However, several contractors were found in violation of Mattel's standards and have been forced to change their operations or lose Mattel's significant business. In an effort to continue its strong record on human rights and related ethical standards, Mattel instituted a code of conduct called "Global Manufacturing Principles." One of these principles requires all Mattel-owned and contracted manufacturing facilities to favor business partners who are committed to ethical standards that are comparable with Mattel's. Other principles relate to safety, wages, and adherence to local laws.

Mattel's audits and subsequent code of conduct were not designed as a punitive measure. Rather, the international company is dedicated to creating and encouraging responsible business practices. As one company consultant has noted, "Mattel is committed to improving the skill level of workers . . . [so that they] will experience increased opportunities and productivity." This statement reflects Mattel's concern for relationships with employees and business partners that extend beyond pure profit considerations. While the company will surely benefit from its

---

*The Learning Co. was sold in 2000.

†*Mattel, Inc., Online Privacy Policy,* http://www.hotwheels.com/policy.asp (*accessed January 17, 2001*).

code's principles, Mattel has formally acknowledged its willingness to consider multiple stakeholders' interests and benefits in its business philosophy. The company's code is a signal to potential partners, customers, and other stakeholders that Mattel is making a serious commitment to ethical values and is willing to base business decisions on them.

International Manufacturing Principles

As a U.S.-based multinational company that owns and operates facilities and has contractor relationships around the world, Mattel has had to establish international workplace and business practice standards. These standards must not only reflect its need to conduct all manufacturing responsibly; they must also respect the cultural, ethical, and philosophical differences of the many countries in which Mattel operates. In addition, these manufacturing principles set standards for every facility manufacturing Mattel products in every location where they are made. The principles not only benefit the men and women who manufacture Mattel's products, but also ensure that Mattel's customers can continue to buy its products with the confidence that they have been made in an environment emphasizing both safety and respect for individual rights.

Mattel's Global Manufacturing Principles cover such issues as wages and work hours at Mattel, child labor, forced labor, discrimination, freedom of association, and working conditions. All Mattel factories and vendors set working hours, wages, and overtime pay that are in compliance with governing laws. Workers must be paid at least minimum wage or a wage that meets local industry standards, whichever is greater, and no one under the age of 16 or the local age limit (whichever is higher) may be allowed to work in a facility that produces products for Mattel. Furthermore, under no circumstances will Mattel use forced or prison labor of any kind, nor will it work with any manufacturer or supplier that does. As for discrimination, it is absolutely not tolerated by the company. Mattel firmly believes that individuals should be employed on the basis of their ability to do a job — not on the basis of individual characteristics or beliefs. Its concept of freedom of association is linked to its abidance to all the laws and regulations of every country in which it operates. The company recognizes all employees' rights to choose to affiliate — or not to affiliate — with legally sanctioned organizations or associations without unlawful interference.

In regard to working conditions, all Mattel facilities and those of its business partners must provide a safe working environment for their employees. The requirements include the following:

- Complying with all applicable local laws regarding sanitation and risk protection and meeting Mattel's own stringent standards
- Maintaining proper lighting and keeping aisles and exits accessible at all times
- Properly maintaining and servicing all machinery
- Sensibly storing and responsibly disposing of hazardous material

- Having an appropriate emergency medical and evacuation response plan for employees
- Never using corporal punishment or any other form of physical or psychological coercion on any employee

Legal and Ethical Business Practices

Mattel favors business partners who are committed to ethical standards that are compatible with its own. At a minimum, all the company's business partners must comply with the local and national laws of the countries in which they operate. In addition, all the partners must respect the significance of all patents, trademarks, and copyrights of Mattel's and other products and support Mattel in the protection of these valuable assets. They also have responsibilities in the five areas that fall under legal and ethical practices: product safety and quality, the environment, customs, evaluation and monitoring, and compliance.

First, all of Mattel's business partners must share a commitment to product safety and quality and must adhere to workplace practices that are necessary to meet Mattel's stringent safety and quality standards. Second, Mattel will work only with those manufacturers or suppliers who comply with all applicable laws and regulations and who share its commitment to the environment. Third, because of the global nature of Mattel's business and its history of leadership in this area, the company insists that all its business partners strictly adhere to all local and international customs laws. These partners must also comply with all import and export regulations. When it comes to evaluation and monitoring, Mattel audits manufacturing facilities to ensure compliance with the Global Manufacturing Principles. Mattel also insists that all manufacturing facilities provide it with the following:

- Full access for on-site inspections by Mattel or parties designated by Mattel
- Full access to those records that will enable Mattel to determine compliance with its principles
- An annual statement of compliance with Mattel's Global Manufacturing Principles, signed by an officer of the manufacturer or manufacturing facility

Acceptance of and compliance with the Mattel Global Manufacturing Principles are part of every contract agreement signed with all Mattel's manufacturing business partners.

Supporting Mattel's Global Manufacturing Principles is an independent monitoring system created to provide objective checks and balances to ensure that standards are consistently met. With the creation of the Mattel Independent Monitoring Council (MIMCO), Mattel became the first global consumer products company to apply such a system to facilities and core contractors on a worldwide basis.

Mattel Children's Foundation

The Mattel Children's Foundation promotes the spirit of philanthropy and community involvement among its employees and makes charitable investments aimed at furthering Mattel's goal of bettering the lives of children in need. Foundation staff carefully examine and evaluate its initiatives and grants to ensure that its financial resources are invested in ways that result in maximum impact. Current funding priorities include building the Mattel Children's Hospital at the University of California, Los Angeles (UCLA), sustaining the Mattel Family Learning Program, and continuing to promote the spirit of giving among Mattel employees.

In November 1998, Mattel announced a multiyear, $25 million gift to UCLA Children's Hospital to support the existing hospital and provide for a new state-of-the-art facility, which is currently being built. In honor of Mattel's donation, the hospital was renamed the Mattel Children's Hospital at UCLA. The new facility is expected to be completed by 2004.

The Mattel Family Learning Program establishes computer learning labs as part of the company's commitment to the concept of advancing the basic skills of children worldwide. Now numbering more than eighty throughout the United States, Hong Kong, Canada, and Mexico, the labs offer literacy software and adaptive technology designed specifically to help children with special needs and those with limited English proficiency.

Mattel employees at its California headquarters and other locations are encouraged to participate in a wide range of activities as part of a volunteer program called "Mattel Volunteers: Happy to Help." Employees who serve on the boards of local nonprofit organizations or who help with ongoing programs at such organizations are eligible to apply for Volunteer Grants to support the organization with which they are involved. Mattel employees who contribute to higher education or to nonprofit organizations that serve children in need are eligible to have their personal donations matched dollar for dollar, up to $5,000 per employee per year. And recognizing that many employees require financial assistance in order to send their children through college, Mattel has established a scholarship fund for them.

MATTEL'S FUTURE CHALLENGES

As noted earlier, Mattel's principles are intended to create and encourage responsible manufacturing business practices around the world, not to serve as a guideline for punishment. Moreover, Mattel expects all its business partners to meet these principles on an ongoing basis. But if certain aspects of the principles are not being met, current partners can expect the company to work with them to effect change. Future business partners will not be engaged unless they meet all Mattel's manufacturing principles. If the company determines that any one of its manufacturing facilities or any vendor has violated these principles, it can either terminate its business relationship or require the facility to implement a corrective action plan. If corrective action is advised but not taken, Mattel will immediately terminate current production and suspend placement of future orders. Thus a key challenge for Mattel is the certification of business partners and potential partners with respect to the manufacturing principles.

Since Mattel is actively engaged in business around the world, the company must be sensitive to economic downturns in other parts of the world. Shifts in the economic viability of markets can create pressure on sales targets, business relationships, and the establishment of new business ventures. As economic pressures increase, normal business procedures may be changed, resulting in unethical and sometimes illegal practices. In attempts to cut corners and meet financial goals, managers and employees may purposely or inadvertently ignore the high ground established by regulations and agreements on ethical standards. Yet Mattel relies on overseas manufacturers to uphold key ethical principles, regardless of economic stability.

Overall, Mattel is very committed to both business success and ethical standards, but it recognizes that this commitment is part of a continuous improvement process. The company's position is very clear in this statement: "[At Mattel, Inc.,] management is concerned not only with the safety and quality of the products manufactured, but with the safety and fair treatment of the men and women who manufacture these products as well."*

Questions

1. What role does the chief executive officer have in creating an organizational culture that values ethics and compliance?

2. Do manufacturers of products for children have special obligations to consumers and society? If so, what are these responsibilities? If not, why not?

3. How effective has Mattel been at encouraging ethical and legal conduct by its manufacturers? What changes and additions would you make to the company's Global Manufacturing Principles? What are other companies doing in this area?

These facts are from the Mattel Web site (*http://www.mattel.com*): "About Mattel — Company History," "Responsibility — Executive Summary," "Cabbage Patch Kids Overview," "Barbie Overview," "Hot Wheels Overview," "Mattel Press Releases: 9/29/00," "Responsibility — Independent Monitoring," "Mattel Children's Foundation" (accessed January 17, 2001); Mattel, Inc., Online Privacy Policy from *http://www.hotwheels.com/policy.asp* (accessed January 17, 2001); Rachel Engers, "Mattel Board Members Buy $30 Million in Stock: Insider Focus," *Bloomberg.com*, December 22, 2000; "Mattel, Inc., Launches Global Code of Conduct Intended to Improve Workplace, Workers' Standard of Living," *Canada NewsWire*, November 21, 1997 (for more information on Mattel's code, the company can be contacted at 310 252-3524); Adam Bryant, "Mattel CEO Jill Barad and a Toyshop That Doesn't Forget to Play," *New York Times*, October 11, 1998; Bill Duryea,

*Mattel, Inc., "Global Manufacturing Principles," 1998, p. 1.

"Barbie-holics: They're Devoted to the Doll," *St. Petersburg Times,* August 7, 1998; James Heckman, "Legislation," *Marketing News,* December 7, 1998, pp. 1, 16; Mattel, Inc., Hot Wheels web site, *http://www.hotwheels.com/;* Marla Matzer, "Deals on Hot Wheels," *Los Angeles Times,* July 22, 1998; Patricia Sellers, "The 50 Most Powerful Women in American Business," *Fortune,* October 12, 1998; "Toymaker Mattel Bans Child Labor," *Denver Post,* November 21, 1998; "Mattel and U.S. Consumer Product Safety Commission Announce Voluntary Refund Program for Cabbage Patch Kids Snacktime Kids Dolls," U.S. Consumer Product Safety Commission, Office of Information and Public Affairs, Release No. 97-055, January 6, 1997; and Michael White, "Barbie Will Lose Some Curves When Mattel Modernizes Icon," *Detroit News,* November 18, 1997.

Appendix A

Association and Industry Codes of Ethics

American Association of University Professors: Statement on Professional Ethics*

The statement that follows, a revision of a statement originally adopted in 1966, was approved by Committee B on Professional Ethics, adopted by the Council as Association policy, and endorsed by the Seventy-third Annual Meeting in June 1987.

Introduction

From its inception, the American Association of University Professors has recognized that membership in the academic profession carries with it special responsibilities. The Association has consistently affirmed these responsibilities in major policy statements, providing guidance to professors in such matters as their utterances as citizens, the exercise of their responsibilities to students and colleagues, and their conduct when resigning from an institution or when undertaking sponsored research. The *Statement on Professional Ethics* that follows sets forth those general standards that serve as a reminder of the variety of responsibilities assumed by all members of the profession.

In the enforcement of ethical standards, the academic profession differs from those of law and medicine, whose associations act to assure the integrity of members engaged in private practice. In the academic profession the individual institution of higher learning provides this assurance and so should normally handle questions concerning propriety of con-

*American Association of University Professors. Reprinted by permission.

duct within its own framework by reference to a faculty group. The Association supports such local action and stands ready, through the general secretary and Committee B, to counsel with members of the academic community concerning questions of professional ethics and to inquire into complaints when local consideration is impossible or inappropriate. If the alleged offense is deemed sufficiently serious to raise the possibility of adverse action, the procedures should be in accordance with the 1940 *Statement of Principles on Academic Freedom and Tenure*, the 1958 *Statement on Procedural Standards in Faculty Dismissal Proceedings,* or the applicable provisions of the Association's *Recommended Institutional Regulations on Academic Freedom and Tenure.*

The Statement

I. Professors, guided by a deep conviction of the worth and dignity of the advancement of knowledge, recognize the special responsibilities placed upon them. Their primary responsibility to their subject is to seek and state the truth as they see it. To this end professors devote their energies to developing and improving their scholarly competence. They accept the obligation to exercise critical self-discipline and judgment in using, extending, and transmitting knowledge. They practice intellectual honesty. Although professors may follow subsidiary interests, these interests must never seriously hamper or compromise their freedom of inquiry.

II. As teachers, professors encourage the free pursuit of learning in their students. They hold before them the best scholarly and ethical standards of their discipline. Professors demonstrate respect for students as individuals and adhere to their proper roles as intellectual guides and counselors. Professors make every reasonable effort to foster honest academic conduct and to assure that their evaluations of students reflect each student's true merit. They respect the confidential nature of the relationship between professor and student. They avoid any exploitation, harassment, or discriminatory treatment of students. They acknowledge significant academic or scholarly assistance from them. They protect their academic freedom.

III. As colleagues, professors have obligations that derive from common membership in the community of scholars. Professors do not discriminate against or harass colleagues. They respect and defend the free inquiry of associates. In the exchange of criticism and ideas professors show due respect for the opinions of others. Professors acknowledge academic debt and strive to be objective in their professional judgment of colleagues. Professors accept their share of faculty responsibilities for the governance of their institution.

IV. As members of an academic institution, professors seek above all to be effective teachers and scholars. Although professors observe the stated regulations of the institution, provided the regulations do not contravene academic freedom, they maintain their right to criticize and seek revision. Professors give due regard to their paramount responsibilities within their institution in determining the amount and character of work done outside it. When considering the interruption or termination of their service, professors recognize the effect of their decision upon the program of the institution and give due notice of their intentions.

V. As members of their community, professors have the rights and obligations of other citizens. Professors measure the urgency of these obligations in the light of their responsibilities to their subject, to their students, to their profession, and to their institution. When they speak or act as private persons they avoid creating the impression of speaking or acting for their college or university. As citizens engaged in a profession that depends upon freedom for its health and integrity, professors have a particular obligation to promote conditions of free inquiry and to further public understanding of academic freedom.

U.S. Dept. of Commerce:
Model Business Principles

The following statement of Model Business Principles and subsequent procedures were released by the U.S. Dept. of Commerce and should be viewed as voluntary guidelines for U.S. businesses.

Recognizing the positive role of U.S. business in upholding and promoting adherence to universal standards of human rights, the Administration encourages all businesses to adopt and implement voluntary codes of conduct for doing business around the world that cover at least the following areas:

1. Provision of a safe and healthy workplace.

2. Fair employment practices, including avoidance of child and forced labor and avoidance of discrimination based on race, gender, national origin or religious beliefs, and respect for the right of association and the right to organize and bargain collectively.

3. Responsible environmental protection and environmental practices.

4. Compliance with U.S. and local laws promoting good business practices, including laws prohibiting illicit payments and ensuring fair competition.

5. Maintenance, through leadership at all levels, of a corporate culture that respects free expression consistent with legitimate business concerns, and does not condone political coercion in the workplace; that encourages good corporate citizenship and makes a positive contribution to the communities in which the company operates; and where ethical conduct is recognized, valued and exemplified by all employees.

In adopting voluntary codes of conduct that reflect these principles, U.S. companies should serve as models, encouraging similar behavior by their partners, suppliers, and subcontractors.

Adoption of codes of conduct reflecting these principles is voluntary. Companies are encouraged to develop their own codes of conduct appropriate to their particular circumstances. Many companies already apply statements or codes that incorporate these principles. Companies should find appropriate means to inform their shareholders and the public of actions undertaken in connection with these principles. Nothing in the principles is intended to require a company to act in violation of host country or U.S. law. This statement of principles is not intended for legislation.

Model Business Principles: Procedures

The President's office has made it clear that U.S. business can and does play a positive and important role promoting the openness of societies, respect for individual rights, the promotion of free markets and prosperity, environmental protection, and the setting of high standards for business practices generally.

The Administration today is offering an update on our efforts to follow through on the President's commitment to promote the Model Business Principles and best practices among U.S. companies. The Principles already have gained the support of some U.S. companies. A process is ongoing to elicit additional support for these Principles and to continue to examine issues related to them.

The elements of this process are as follows:

Voluntary Statement of Business Principles

The Administration, in extensive consultations with business and labor leaders and members of the Non-Governmental Organization (NGO) community, developed these model principles, which were reported widely in the press earlier this spring. A copy is attached. This model statement is to be used by companies as a reference point in framing their own codes of conduct. It is based on a wide variety of similar sets of principles U.S. companies and business organizations already have put into global practice. The Administration encourages all businesses everywhere to support the model principles. (Copies of the model statement are available by calling the U.S. Department of Commerce Trade Information Center, 1-800-USA-TRADE.)

Efforts by U.S. Business

As part of the ongoing effort, U.S. businesses will engage in the following activities:

Conferences on Best Practices Issues   In conjunction with Business for Social Responsibility, a non-profit business organization dedicated to promoting laudable corporate practices, and/or other appropriate organizations, the Administration will work to encourage conferences concerning issues relating to the practices contained in the Model Business Principles. Such conferences can provide a forum for information-sharing on new approaches for the evolving global context in which best practices are implemented.

Best Practices Information Clearinghouse and Support Services   One or more non-profits will work with the U.S. business community to develop a clearinghouse of information regarding business practices globally. The clearinghouse will establish a library of codes of conduct adopted by U.S. and international companies and organizations, to be catalogued and made available to companies seeking to develop their own codes. The clearinghouse would be available to provide advice to companies seeking to develop or improve their codes, advice based on the accumulated experience of other companies. Business for Social Responsibility (described above) is highly respected and is one resource that businesses and NGOs alike can turn to for information on best business practices.

Efforts by the U.S. Government

The U.S. Government also will undertake a number of activities to generate support for the Model Business Principles:

Promote Multilateral Adoption of Best Practices   The Administration has begun and will continue its effort to seek multilateral support for the Model Business Principles. Senior U.S. Government officials already have met with U.S. company officials and U.S. organizations operating abroad as well as with foreign corporate officials to seek support for the Principles. For example, the American Chambers of Commerce in the Asia Pacific recently adopted a resolution by which their members agreed to work with their local counterparts in the countries in which they operate to seek development of similar best practices among their members. The United States also will present the Model Business Principles at the Organization for

Economic Cooperation and Development (OECD) and the International Labor Organization (ILO) as part of these organizations' ongoing behavior. Therefore, on an annual basis, the Administration will offer a series of awards to companies for specific activities that reflect best practices in the areas covered by the Model Business Principles. The awards will be granted pursuant to applications by interested companies. NGOs and private citizens will be encouraged to call attention to activities they believe are worthy of consideration. (For further information on the Best Practices Awards Program, contact Melinda Yee, U.S. Department of Commerce, (202) 482-1051.)

Presidential-Business Discussions   The President's Export Council (PEC), a high-level advisory group of Chief Executive Officers, provides a forum for the President to meet regularly with U.S. business leaders to discuss issues relating to U.S. industries' exports and operations abroad. The Administration will put the Model Business Principles on Appropriate PEC meeting agendas.

For further general information about the Model Business Principles, please contact U.S. Commerce Department, (202) 482-5151, or U.S. Department of State, (202) 647-1625.

American Advertising Federation:
The Advertising Principles of American Business*

Truth   Advertising shall tell the truth, and shall reveal significant facts, the omission of which would mislead the public.

Substantiation   Advertising claims shall be substantiated by evidence in possession of the advertiser and advertising agency, prior to making such claims.

Comparisons   Advertising shall refrain from making false, misleading, or unsubstantiated statements or claims about a competitor or his products or services.

Bait Advertising   Advertising shall not offer products or services for sale unless such offer constitutes a bona fide effort to sell the advertised products or services and is not a device to switch consumers to other goods or services, usually higher priced.

Guarantees and Warranties   Advertising of guarantees and warranties shall be explicit, with sufficient information to apprise consumers of their principal terms and limitations or, when space or time restrictions preclude such disclosures, the advertisement should clearly reveal where the full text of the guarantee or warranty can be examined before purchase.

Price Claims   Advertising shall avoid price claims which are false or misleading, or savings claims which do not offer provable savings.

Testimonials   Advertising containing testimonials shall be limited to those of competent witnesses who are reflecting a real and honest opinion or experience.

Taste and Decency   Advertising shall be free of statements, illustrations or implications which are offensive to good taste or public decency.

International Franchise Association: Code of Principles and Standards of Conduct[†]

Section 1: Preamble

Franchising is a business relationship utilized in more than 65 different industries. A wide variety of franchise relationships exist between thousands of franchisors and hundreds of thousands of franchisees. Franchising offers an excellent opportunity for individuals who are seeking to enter into business for themselves, by providing a framework for a mutually beneficial business relationship. In recognition of the increasing role of franchising in the marketplace and the very beneficial and positive contributions of franchising to the American economy, the franchisor and franchisee members of the International Franchise Association ("IFA") believe that franchising must reflect the highest principles and standards of fair business practices. The IFA seeks to promote this ob-

---

*Courtesy of the American Advertising Federation.

[†]International Franchise Association. Reprinted by permission.

jective by means of a strong and effective *Code of Principles and Standards of Conduct (the "Code")* that is applicable to its franchisor and franchisee members. To protect and promote the interests of consumers, franchisees, and franchisors, and to ensure that this unique form of entrepreneurship continues to flourish with a high degree of success and security, we, the members of the IFA, do hereby set forth the following principles and standards of conduct. The policies and practices of members of the IFA shall not be inconsistent with the *Code*.

Section II: Principles

Franchisors and franchisees shall conduct their businesses professionally, with truth, accuracy, fairness, and responsibility.

Franchisors and franchisees shall use fair business practices in dealings with each other and with their customers, suppliers and government agencies.

Franchisors and franchisees shall comply with all applicable laws and regulations in all of their business operations. Franchisors and franchisees shall not engage in any activity that will bring discredit to their business, industry, or their franchised network.

Franchisors and franchisees shall recognize the interdependence of the franchisor and franchisees of a franchised network and the responsibility of the franchisor and each franchisee of the network to every other franchisee in the network.

Franchisors and franchisees shall offer opportunities in franchising to minorities, women and disabled persons on a basis equal to all other persons.

Section III: Applicability and Interpretation

1. **Applicability.** The *Code* shall be applicable to all franchisor and franchisee members of the IFA in their United States operations. These principles and standards of conduct reflect the collective beliefs of the franchisor and franchisee members of the IFA with respect to the manner in which franchise relationships generally should be established, structured, and implemented. Franchise relationships should be established by the delivery of clear and complete disclosure document, as required by law, and by clear and unambiguous franchise agreements. A franchise relationship is governed by the franchise agreement. The principles and standards of conduct contained in the *Code* do not substitute for or supplement the franchise agreements between franchisors and their franchisees or create any rights for either franchisors or their franchisees. Franchise agreements entered into before these principles and standards were adopted may not be in accord with all of these principles and standards. Some franchise relationships, due to their structure, product or service, may not be able to be implemented in complete accord with these principles and standards. Therefore, these principles and standards must be applied with flexibility, taking into consideration the wide range of structures, forms of agreement and reasonable business practices used to document and implement franchise relationships in the past and currently.

2. **Interpretation.** Developing and applying standards to a wide variety of franchised businesses is a challenging undertaking. For this reason, changes to the *Code* and interpretative releases may be issued from time to time. Interpretations of the *Code* will be made by the Board of Directors of the IFA and its interpretations will be final and binding on the franchisor and franchisee members of the IFA. The Board of Directors will consider the interpretations recommended by the Standards Committee of the IFA. With respect to all matters relating to the *Code,* whenever the Board of Directors is not meeting, the Executive Committee of the Board of Directors may act for and on behalf of the Board of Directors. To the extent that applicable law imposes standards of conduct that are different from those contained in the *Code,* franchisor and franchisee members shall comply with both such applicable law and the *Code,* except to the extent that compliance with the *Code* might constitute a violation of such law.

Section IV: Enforcement

The IFA's enforcement philosophy, summarized below, has been shaped by its recognition that in most instances it is not possible for the IFA itself to engage in fact finding in the context of franchisor-franchisee disputes and that negotiation, franchised network dispute settlement procedures, and/or nonbinding mediation are generally preferable to litigation and should be encouraged.

1. **Enforcement Philosophy:** The *Code* enforcement philosophy of the IFA is:

   (a) To educate franchisor and franchisee members of the IFA regarding the *Code* and to assist members to comply with the *Code*.

   (b) To require franchisor members to develop fair and effective dispute resolution procedures, to publicize the existence of these procedures within their respective franchised networks and to make a good faith effort to resolve disputes by use of such procedures and/or third party mediation whenever practicable. Such dispute resolution procedures need not involve any specific format, but they should be designed to be fair and effective in resolving disputes. Examples of dispute resolution procedures include the evaluation and resolution of a dispute by a senior officer of the franchisor member, an ombudsman, a panel composed of franchisor management personnel and franchisees or a neutral person or panel of neutrals. The procedures should afford each party to the dispute an opportunity for a full and fair hearing of its view of the relevant facts. If the franchised network has a franchisee advisory council, such procedures should be supported by such council.

   (c) To rely on third party fact finding, since the IFA does not have investigative resources and, therefore, will generally limit its role to application of the *Code* to facts determined by courts, arbitrators, and administrative agencies. Exceptions may be made when the facts of a dispute are agreed upon by the parties to the dispute, or are readily determinable by the Standards Committee.

   (d) To require members who in isolated cases have violated the *Code* to adopt procedures and policies that will reduce the likelihood of future violations and to reserve suspension or termination of IFA membership for members whose policies and practices reflect systemic disregard of the *Code*.

2. **Enforcement Policies and Procedures**

   (a) A complaint to the IFA alleging facts that may constitute a violation of the *Code* by a franchisor or franchisee member must be in writing. While no form of complaint is prescribed, the facts and the relief sought by the complainant should be clearly stated. The complainant should also indicate the extent to which the internal dispute resolution procedures of the franchised network, negotiation and/or mediation have been utilized, and the results thereof. The complaint should also indicate whether litigation or arbitration relating to the complaint has previously occurred or is currently pending.

   (b) In consideration of the IFA's efforts to facilitate a resolution of a dispute, and in the interest of full and open disclosure and discussion by all parties to the dispute, such parties, on behalf of themselves and their respective shareholders, members, partners, directors, officers, employees, and agents, must agree in writing to waive any and all claims that any such person or entity may have against (1) the other parties to such dispute, and their respective shareholders, members, partners, directors, officers, employees and agents and (2) the IFA, any director, officer, employee, attorney or agent of the IFA, any officer or member of a committee or advisory group of the IFA or any person occupying a similar position, that may arise out of any IFA investigation, discussion or disciplinary action, or statements made incident thereto, including, without limitation, claims for defamation of character and trade libel. The parties to a dispute, on behalf of themselves and their respective shareholders, members, partners, directors, officers, employees and agents, must acknowledge and agree in writing that statements made by any such person in relation to such investigation or disciplinary action shall have an unqualified privilege. Such waivers do not, of course, include any claims that any such party may have against another party that are not related to the IFA investigation or disciplinary action with respect to the complaint.

   (c) The IFA will send the complainant's written complaint to the other parties to the dispute and request that such other parties submit written replies to the IFA responding to the factual allegations contained in the complaint, describing any claims that any such other party has against the complainant and describing any dispute resolution, negotiation and/or third party mediation procedures that such party believes to be applicable to the dispute, their prior use and/or future availability to resolve the dispute and such party's willingness to make a good faith effort to resolve the dispute. The IFA will send such written responses to the complainant.

(d) A relatively small category of disputes between a franchisor and its franchisee involve issues so fundamental to the franchise relationship that such disputes cannot practicably be resolved by negotiation, internal dispute resolution procedures or third party mediation. The great majority of disputes between franchisors and franchisees do not fall within this category and are susceptible to resolution by such techniques. If a complaint, or a party's response to a complaint, indicates the existence of a dispute that may be resolved by such techniques, a franchisor and/or franchisee member are obligated to make a good faith effort to resolve the dispute by means of (1) negotiation, (2) dispute resolution procedures available within the franchised network and/or (3) third party mediation.

(e) If litigation or arbitration involving the principal issues of a dispute is pending, the IFA will, as a general rule, take no further action with respect to the dispute until the conclusion of such litigation or arbitration. If no such litigation or arbitration is pending, and if a member fails to respond to a complaint that complies with these enforcement procedures, and the parties do not resolve the dispute, or the Standards Committee believes that the facts are determinable from the letters and documents in its possession, the Standards Committee will determine whether a violation of the *Code* has occurred and will report its findings to the Board of Directors. Failure of a member, without good cause, to make a good faith effort to resolve a dispute is grounds for disciplinary action against the member or dismissal of the complaint, as appropriate.

(f) If the parties fail to resolve their dispute, and subsequently the dispute is resolved in litigation or arbitration, or by an administrative agency, with findings of fact that are publicly available, the Standards Committee will, at the request of any party to the dispute, evaluate such findings of fact to determine whether a violation of the *Code* has occurred, and will report its findings to the Board of Directors.

(g) The final determination of whether the *Code* has been violated by a member will be made by the Board of Directors. If the Board of Directors determines that the *Code* has been violated, it may (1) issue a warning to the member, (2) suspend the membership of the member for a period of time deemed appropriate by the Board of Directors or (3) terminate the membership of the member. All proceedings shall be private and confidential, except for the final written decision of the Board of Directors. It shall be within the discretion of the Board of Directors to include in or exclude from its written decision the reasons for its decision and disciplinary action, if any.

Section V: Standards of Conduct Applicable To Franchisor and Franchisee Members

1. **Franchise Sales and Disclosure.** The sale of franchises is heavily regulated in the United States under federal and state law and may be subject to regulation in other countries. Franchisors that comply with such regulation disclose an extensive body of information to prospective franchisees regarding the franchisor, the nature and costs of an investment in its franchise and the franchise relationship that it offers. Therefore, in the advertisement and grant of franchises, a franchisor shall comply with all applicable laws and regulations. Disclosure documents shall comply with all applicable legal requirements. A franchisor shall advise prospective franchisees to seek legal or other professional advice prior to the signing of a franchise agreement and to contact existing franchisees to gain a better understanding of the requirements and benefits of the franchise and the business.

All matters material to the granting of a franchise shall be contained in or referred to in one or more written documents, which shall clearly set forth the terms of the relationship and the respective rights and obligations of the parties. (A franchisor may establish and periodically modify system standards and policies and prescribe such standards and policies in a separate document, such as an operations manual.) Disclosure documents shall be provided to a prospective franchisee on a timely basis as required by law. A franchisor that complies with applicable federal and state laws relating to the grant of franchises will be in compliance with this paragraph.

Prior to entering into franchise relationships, franchisees have a responsibility to effectively utilize the information made available to them and to undertake the due diligence necessary to a full understanding of the business segment of the franchisor, the history and status of the franchisor in its business segment, the investment requirements and terms of the franchise and the effort required to operate the franchised business successfully. This responsibility includes a thorough reading of the offering circular, franchise agreements and other documents furnished by the franchisor and consultation with existing franchisees of the franchised network and professional advisors.

2. **Good Faith Dealing.** In the United States, many jurisdictions imply in every contract an obligation of good faith on all parties to the contract. However, the good faith obligation does not supersede, enlarge or diminish the rights and obligations contained in an agreement.

Therefore, franchisors and franchisees shall deal with each other fairly and in good faith, which means dealing honestly, ethically, and with mutual respect, in accordance with the terms of their franchise agreements. A franchisor and a franchisee that act in compliance with the terms of their franchise agreement are dealing with each other fairly and in good faith. Franchisees and franchisors shall conduct their relationships with other franchisees, suppliers and customers fairly and with respect.

3. **Franchisor-Franchisee Cooperation.** Cooperation between a franchisor and its franchisees promotes a healthy, competitive and financially sound franchised network. Effective communication between a franchisor and its franchisee also promotes a healthy franchise relationship. Many franchisors have established advisory councils to which franchisees elect and/or the franchisor appoints franchisees. A number of franchised networks have associations that represent a majority or a minority of their franchisees. Some franchised networks have both an advisory council and an association that represents some of the network's franchisees. Franchisors have increasingly utilized advisory councils and franchisee associations to improve communication between the franchisor and its franchisees and as the mechanism to foster discussion and exchange of ideas that enhances the competitive capability of the network and its ability to deal efficiently and effectively with any problems or disagreements that arise in the franchise relationship. The effective operation of a franchised network and cooperation among the franchisor and the franchisees of the network requires the dissemination of substantial information within the network. Much of this information is confidential and may include trade secrets of the franchisor.

Therefore, the franchisor and franchisees of a franchised network shall foster open dialogue within their network by such means as they determine to be most effective, including one or more franchisee advisory councils, an association of franchisees or other communication mechanisms. A franchisor shall not prohibit a franchisee from forming, joining, or participating in any franchisee association. A franchisor and the franchisee of a franchised network should at all times endeavor to work together cooperatively to advance the interests of the franchisor and each franchisee of the network. Franchisees of a franchised network and their advisory councils and associations shall support and assist other franchisees of the network that experience problems in the operation of their businesses. Franchisees shall comply with the confidentiality requirements of their franchise agreements and maintain the confidentiality of the information circulated within their networks that is indicated to be confidential or subjected to disclosure restrictions.

4. **Termination of Franchise Agreements.** Termination of franchise agreements before their expiration is a rare occurrence. Such terminations are

initiated by both franchisors and franchisees. Terminations by a franchisor are usually the result of the franchisee's failure to pay fees in compliance with the franchise agreement. Terminations by a franchisor also occur when a franchisee has failed to comply with system standards or other obligations set forth in the franchise agreement or collateral documents and has failed to remedy such defaults after notice and an opportunity to do so. Terminations by franchisees are usually the result of the franchisee's belief that the franchisor has failed to comply with its obligations or, occasionally, a desire by the franchisee to avoid paying continuing fees to the franchisor. Termination may be costly to both the franchisor and the franchisee.

The franchisor and the franchisees of a franchised network work together to maintain the competitiveness of the network. A franchisor and its franchisees have a strong interest in diligent enforcement by the franchisor of (1) franchisees' payment obligations, which support a wide range of franchisor activities that maintain and enhance the competitiveness of the franchised network, and (2) system standards, which are the foundation of the goodwill of the network. A franchisee who attempts to unilaterally disaffiliate from its franchised network, in violation of the terms of its franchise agreement, harms the other franchisees of the network as well as the franchisor.

Therefore, franchisors and franchisees shall apply the following standards in connection with the termination of franchise agreements:

(a) Franchisees shall comply with the requirements of their franchise agreements relating to maintaining standards of appearance, product and service quality, health, safety, cleanliness, customer service, advertising and financial reporting and payment to their franchisor. Franchisees shall endeavor in good faith to avoid acts or omissions that constitute noncompliance with their obligations to their franchisor and that may lead to termination of their franchises. Franchisees shall not commit any act or engage in any activity that may cause adverse customer, public, or government reaction with respect to their franchised network.

(b) A franchise agreement may only be terminated for good cause, which includes the failure of a franchisee or franchisor to comply with any lawful requirement of the franchise agreement. Some franchise agreements permit franchisees to terminate the agreement without cause and a termination by a franchisee of a franchise agreement pursuant to such a contractual right shall not violate this *Code*.

(c) A franchisee and a franchisor shall be given notice and a reasonable opportunity to cure breaches of the franchise agreement that are curable under the terms of the franchise agreement. The cure period shall be consistent with the nature of the breach.

(d) A franchise agreement may be terminated immediately, without prior notice or opportunity to cure, in the event of a franchisee's abandonment of the franchised business, repeated breaches of its franchise agreement, material dishonesty, criminal misconduct or endangerment of public health or safety.

(e) A franchise agreement may be terminated pursuant to an express provision in the franchise agreement providing for a reciprocal right to terminate the agreement without cause.

5. **Expiration of Franchise Agreements.** Most franchises are granted for a specific term. Some franchise agreements grant qualified renewal rights to the franchisee and others do not address the issue of a franchisee's post expiration rights to continue to operate as a franchisee. The continuation of a franchise relationship subsequent to the expiration of a franchise is an element of the franchise relationship that each franchisor must determine and express in its franchise agreement. However, expiration of a franchise need not necessarily deprive a franchisee of the value of his or her business (as distinct from the value of the expired franchise). This value can be preserved by giving a franchisee reasonable advance notice that his or her franchise relationship with the franchisor will not continue subsequent to the expiration of the franchise and an opportunity to sell his or her business to a successor franchisee (who will acquire a new franchise from the franchisor).

Alternatively, the franchisee can be granted the right to continue in the same business at the same location or in the same market or otherwise be able to realize the value of his or her business (as distinct from the value of the expired franchise).

Therefore, a franchisor shall apply the following standards in connection with the expiration of franchise agreements that provide for a specific term:

(a) A franchisee shall be given notice, at least 180 days prior to expiration, of a franchisor's intention not to grant a new franchise agreement to the franchisee.
(b) The franchisor may determine not to grant a new franchise agreement:
   (1) for good cause, which includes the failure of the franchisee to comply with any lawful requirement of the franchise agreement; or
   (2) if the franchisor permits the franchisee to:
      (i) during the 180 days prior to the expiration of the franchise, sell the business to a purchaser meeting the then-current qualifications and requirements specified by the franchisor; or
      (ii) continue to operate the business under a different trade identity at the same location or within the same trade area; or
      (iii) if the franchisee is otherwise permitted to realize the value of the business (as distinct from the value of the expired franchise).
(c) The franchisor may determine not to grant a new franchise agreement to a franchisee, without prior notice, in the event of the franchisee's abandonment of the franchise business, repeated breaches of its franchise agreement, material dishonesty or bad faith, criminal misconduct or endangerment of public health or safety.
(d) The franchisor may exercise any right to purchase the franchisee's business as provided in the franchise or other agreement.
(e) The franchisor may determine not to grant a new franchise agreement to a franchisee if the franchisor is withdrawing from the market area.

A franchisee shall comply with the terms of the franchise agreement relating to expiration. Such requirements may include diligent efforts to sell his or her businesses to a successor franchisee or to the franchisor or the deidentification of his or her business.

6. **Transfer of Franchise.** The great majority of franchise agreements grant to the franchisee a qualified right to transfer the franchise in connection with the sale of his or her business. Transfer rights are important to franchisees, because transferability is an important element of the value of the franchise and the franchisee's business. Restrictions on transferability are equally important to the franchisor, which has a compelling interest in the right to determine the persons who operate under its franchise and the terms on which its franchises are acquired.

Therefore, except with respect to franchises that are expressly nontransferable personal service contracts, a franchisor shall not withhold approval of a proposed transfer of a franchise when the following criteria are met:

(a) The transferring franchisee is in compliance with the terms of the franchise agreement;
(b) The proposed transferee meets the then-current qualifications of the franchisor;
(c) The terms of the transfer meet the then-current requirements of the franchisor and the transfer provisions of the franchise agreement;
(d) The franchisor determines not to exercise a right of first refusal in accordance with the franchise or other agreement.

A franchisee shall fully comply with the transfer restrictions of the franchise agreement, including without limitation the required advance notice to the franchisor, cooperation in furnishing information to the franchisor about the proposed transferee and the terms of the transfer, and cooperating with the franchisor if it exercises a right of first refusal to buy the franchisee's business.

7. **System Expansion.** The granting of territorial protection to franchisees varies widely among franchised networks due to differing business and competitive considerations. Accurately predicting the competitive impact of establishing an additional outlet (whether a fixed location or mobile

facility) in a market already served by one or more franchisees may not be possible. Nevertheless, in addition to respecting the legal rights of a franchisee, sound franchising practice requires a franchisor to consider those factors relevant to its business that will determine the impact of an additional outlet on the business of an existing franchisee and to balance the projected impact with the needs of the franchisor's network to expand, gain market share and meet competition.

Therefore, in determining whether to open, or to authorize the opening of, an outlet in close proximity to an existing franchised outlet, that will offer products or services similar to those of the existing outlet, a franchisor shall take into account the factors that are relevant to its business, which may include any or all of the following:

(a) Territorial rights of existing franchisees contained in their franchise agreements.
(b) The similarity of the new outlet and the existing outlet in terms of products and services to be offered and the trademarks to be used.
(c) Whether the new outlet and the existing outlet will sell products or services to the same customers for the same occasion.
(d) The competitive activities in the market.
(e) The characteristics of the market.
(f) The ability of the existing outlet to adequately supply anticipated demand.
(g) The positive or negative effect of the new outlet on the existing outlet.
(h) The quality of operations and physical condition of the existing outlet.
(i) Compliance by the franchisee of the existing outlet with the franchise agreement.
(j) The experience of the franchisor in similar circumstances.
(k) The benefit or detriment to the franchise system as a whole in opening the new outlet.
(l) Relevant information submitted by existing franchisees and the prospective franchisee.

A franchisor and its franchisee should work cooperatively to develop systems and procedures for dealing with potential system expansion conflicts in a manner that is effective in terms of network expansion and fair to both the franchisor and its franchisees. Any program, method or procedure agreed to by a franchisor and its franchisees to re-solve system expansion issues will comply with this *Code.*

8. **Supply Sources.** A franchisor has a compelling interest in maintaining system standards and protecting its trademark. Controlling the sources of operating assets, goods sold and materials and supplies utilized by its franchisee in developing and operating his or her business is an effective method of policing system standards compliance. Such controls can also protect a franchisor's trade secrets and other confidential information and can constitute a valuable service to franchisees by assuring sources of high quality goods and services at competitive prices. Franchisors that derive their principal revenue by selling goods to their franchisees for resale must be able to be assured that their franchisees will not buy such goods from other sources, thereby impairing the franchisor's revenue base. Restrictions on the suppliers from which franchisees may buy goods and services used in the establishment and operation of their business is comprehensively regulated under federal and state antitrust and trade regulation laws.

Therefore, with respect to the formulation and implementation of designated and approved supplier programs and other restrictions on the suppliers from which franchisees are permitted to purchase goods and services, franchisors shall comply in all respects with applicable franchise disclosure laws and antitrust and trade regulation laws. Franchisees shall comply with the restrictions contained in supply programs established by their franchisor that are in compliance with applicable franchise disclosure, antitrust and trade regulation laws.

9. **Disputes.** Litigation between franchisors and franchisees has frequently been costly and antithetical to productive franchise relationships. Franchisors and franchisees should resort to judicial dispute resolution only after other methods have failed to resolve a dispute.

Therefore, whenever practicable, a franchisor and its franchisee shall make a diligent effort to resolve disputes by negotiation, mediation, or internal appeal procedures. A franchisor and its franchisees shall consider the use of additional alternative dispute resolution procedures in appropriate situations to resolve disputes that are not resolved by negotiation, mediation or internal appeal.

10. **Discrimination.** Discrimination is not consistent with fair and sound franchising practices. A franchisor should make its franchises available to the widest possible spectrum of individuals. Many franchisors have adopted programs to assist minority and other disadvantaged persons to become franchisees. Both franchisors and franchisees should make employment opportunities available to the widest possible spectrum of individuals.

   Therefore, a franchisor shall not discriminate in the operations of its franchised network on the basis of race, color, religion, national origin, gender, sexual preference or disability. Franchisors and franchisees shall not discriminate in hiring, other aspects of their employment relationships or otherwise in the operation of their businesses on the basis of race, color, religion, national origin, gender, sexual preference or disability. Franchisors and franchisees may utilize reasonable criteria in determining eligibility for its franchise and employees and may grant franchises to some franchisees and hire some employees on more favorable terms than are granted to other franchisees or employees as part of a program to make franchises and employment opportunities available to persons lacking capital, training, business experience or other qualifications ordinarily required of franchisees and employees. A franchisor and its franchisees may implement other affirmative action programs. ▰

American Marketing Association:
Code of Ethics*

Members of the American Marketing Association (AMA) are committed to ethical professional conduct. They have joined together in subscribing to this Code of Ethics embracing the following topics:

Reprinted by permission of the American Marketing Association.

Responsibilities of the Marketer

Marketers must accept responsibility for the consequences of their activities and make every effort to ensure that their decisions, recommendations, and actions function to identify, serve, and satisfy all relevant publics: consumers, organizations and society. Marketers' professional conduct must be guided by:

1. The basic rule of professional ethics: not knowingly to do harm;

2. The adherence to all applicable laws and regulations;

3. The accurate representation of their education, training and experience; and

4. The active support, practice and promotion of this Code of Ethics.

Honesty and Fairness

Marketers shall uphold and advance the integrity, honor, and dignity of the marketing profession by:

1. Being honest in serving consumers, clients, employees, suppliers, distributors and the public;

2. Not knowingly participating in conflict of interest without prior notice to all parties involved; and

3. Establishing equitable fee schedules including the payment or receipt of usual, customary and/or legal compensation for marketing exchanges.

Rights and Duties of Parties

Participants in the marketing exchange process should be able to expect that:

1. Products and services offered are safe and fit for their intended uses;

2. Communications about offered products and services are not deceptive;

3. All parties intend to discharge their obligations, financial and otherwise, in good faith; and

4. Appropriate internal methods exist for equitable adjustment and/or redress of grievances concerning purchases.

It is understood that the above would include, *but is not limited to*, the following responsibilities of the marketer:

In the Area of Product Development Management:

- Disclosure of all substantial risks associated with product or service usage
- Identification of any product component substitution that might materially change the product or impact on the buyer's purchase decision
- Identification of extra-cost features

In the Area of Promotions:

- Avoidance of false and misleading advertising
- Rejection of high pressure manipulations, or misleading sales tactics
- Avoidance of sales promotions that use deception or manipulation

In the Area of Distribution:

- Not manipulating the availability of a product for purpose of exploitation
- Not using coercion in the marketing channel
- Not exerting undue influence over the resellers' choice to handle a product

In the Area of Pricing:

- Not engaging in price fixing
- Not practicing predatory pricing
- Disclosing the full price associated with any purchase

In the Area of Marketing Research:

- Prohibiting selling or fund raising under the guise of conducting research
- Maintaining research integrity by avoiding misrepresentation and omission of pertinent research data
- Treating outside clients and suppliers fairly

Organizational Relationships

Marketers should be aware of how their behavior may influence or impact on the behavior of others in organizational relationships. They should not encourage or apply coercion to obtain unethical behavior in their relationships with others, such as employees, suppliers or customers.

1. Apply confidentiality and anonymity in professional relationships with regard to privileged information.

2. Meet their obligations and responsibilities in contracts and mutual agreements in a timely manner.

3. Avoid taking the work of others, in whole, or in part, and representing this work as their own or directly benefit from it without compensation or consent of the originator or owner.

4. Avoid manipulation to take advantage of situations to maximize personal welfare in a way that unfairly deprives or damages the organization or others. Any AMA member found to be in violation of any provision of this Code of Ethics may have his or her Association membership suspended or revoked.

Standards of Ethical Conduct for Institute of Management Accountants*

Candidates and CMAs are expected to maintain the highest standards of personal and professional integrity. The Institute of Certified Management Accountants requires compliance with the provisions of the Standards of Ethical Conduct for Management Accountants. The ICMA has established procedures for reviewing alleged behavior inconsistent with these standards.

Management accountants have an obligation to the organizations they serve, their profession, the public, and themselves to maintain the highest standards of ethical conduct. In recognition of this obligation, the Institute of Certified Management Accountants and

---

*Statement of Management Accounting IC, Institute of Management Accountants (formerly National Association of Accountants), Montvale, NJ 07645. Reprinted by permission.

the Institute of Management Accountants have adopted the following standards of ethical conduct for management accountants. Adherence to these standards is integral in achieving the objectives of management accounting. Management accountants may not commit acts contrary to these standards nor shall they condone the commission of such acts by others within their organization.

Competence

Management accountants have a responsibility to:

- Maintain an appropriate level of professional competence by ongoing development of their knowledge and skills.

- Perform their professional duties in accordance with relevant laws, regulations, and technical standards.

- Prepare complete and clear reports and recommendations after appropriate analyses of relevant and reliable information.

Confidentiality

Management accountants have a responsibility to:

- Refrain from disclosing confidential information acquired in the course of their work except when authorized, unless legally obligated to do so.
- Inform subordinates as appropriate regarding the confidentiality of information acquired in the course of their work and monitor their activities to assure the maintenance of that confidentiality.
- Refrain from using or appearing to use confidential information acquired in the course of their work for unethical or illegal advantage either personally or through third parties.

Integrity

Management accountants have a responsibility to:

- Avoid actual or apparent conflicts of interest and advise all appropriate parties of any potential conflict.

- Refrain from engaging in any activity that would prejudice their ability to carry out their duties ethically.

- Refuse any gift, favor, or hospitality that would influence or would appear to influence their actions.

- Refrain from either actively or passively subverting the attainment of the organization's legitimate and ethical objectives.

- Recognize and communicate professional limitations or other constraints that would preclude responsible judgment or successful performance of an activity.

- Communicate unfavorable as well as favorable information and professional judgments or opinions.

- Refrain from engaging in or supporting any activity that would discredit the profession.

Objectivity

Management accountants have a responsibility to:

Communicate information fairly and objectively. Disclose fully all relevant information that could reasonably be expected to influence an intended user's understanding of the reports, comments, and recommendations presented.

Water Quality Improvement Industry:
Code of Ethics* promulgated by the Water Quality Association for the Water Quality Improvement Industry

The Water Quality Association is dedicated to promoting the highest principles of honesty, integrity, fair dealing and professionalism in the water quality improvement industry. It is equally dedicated to preserving the consuming public's right to quality water. This Code of Ethics sets standards of conduct for industry members in their dealings with their customers, among themselves, with members of related industries, and the public at large.

Obligations

Industry Members Shall:

- Conduct themselves as informed, law abiding citizens dedicated to ethical business practices.

*Reprinted with permission from the Water Quality Improvement Industry.

- Be informed of and adhere to all laws, statutes, ordinances, codes, and regulations applicable to the industry including those dealing with restraint of trade, consumer protection, truth in advertising, truth in lending, intellectual property protection, selling, registration, sanitation and effluent disposal.

- Build their business on the merits of their products, services and abilities.

- Accurately represent credentials, training, experience and abilities of all employees and agents.

- Serve their customers competently and honestly.

- Ensure that their products or services are properly applied or installed when they are responsible for such application or installation.

- Respond in a timely manner to customer complaints.

- Provide for the availability of timely and competent installation and service for their products.

- Inform customers of the general maintenance, service requirements and related costs.

- Pursue the advancement of knowledge and skills utilized in the water quality improvement industry.

- Adhere to and promote the Code of Ethics.

Marketing Guidelines

1. The word "product" as used in these Guidelines and Procedures includes publicly and privately supplied water, bottled water, and water quality improvement products and services or systems.

2. Product performance, benefits or other claims, either written or verbal, shall be based on factual data obtained from tests conducted by technically competent personnel utilizing verifiable scientifically valid test procedures. These data must be available in writing at the time such claims are made.

3. Accurately represent the source water supply, the performance of the water improvement process and the benefit of the products or services.

4. Those who develop or disseminate, either in writing or verbally, product marketing claims or materials, including packaging, labeling, and installation, operating or maintenance materials, shall make available reputable, verifiable, factual substantiation for those product marketing claims or materials.

5. Statements, either verbal or written, which are false, misleading, deceptive, fraudulent, or which deceptively disparage publicly or privately supplied water, bottled water, water quality improvement products or systems, or other competitors or competitive products, shall not be used.

6. Pictures, exhibits, graphs, charts or other portrayals used in product marketing shall not be used in a false or misleading manner.

7. Sweeping, absolute statements, either verbal or written, shall not be made if they are false or not applicable in all situations.

8. It shall not be stated or implied that the water to which the word "pure" is applied is "pure," unless the word is clearly defined by the user or by regulation. In addition, words such as purification, purifier, healthy, safe, clean, clear and free of contaminants must be defined.

9. Advertisements or marketing materials and practices, either verbal or written, shall be true and accurate in their entirety. Not only shall each sentence or statement, standing alone and separately considered, be literally true, but the combined overall effect of the materials shall also be accurate and not misleading.

10. Facts shall not be omitted from product advertising or marketing material or practices if the result would be to mislead or to misrepresent.

11. Devices or techniques, used to demonstrate the presence of hardness, chlorine, color, or other water characteristics of the water supply, shall not be used in sales presentations without, at the same time, accurately informing the consumer of their scope.

12. The words "warranty," "guarantee," or equivalent terms shall not be used verbally or in writing in connection with industry products unless such use meets the requirements of the United States Federal Trade Commission's Guides for the Advertising of Warranties and Guarantees, 16 CFR

239.1 et seq., effective May 1, 1985 and corrected May 21, 1985, as they may be amended from time to time.

13. The composition of advertisements or other forms of product promotion materials shall be such as to minimize the possibility of being misleading. Product performance or benefit claims shall not be placed in advertisements or promotional material or used in sales presentations to give the impression that they apply to additional or different merchandise when such is not the fact.

14. An asterisk may be used to direct attention to additional information about a word or term which is not in itself inherently deceptive. The asterisk or other referenced symbols shall not be used as a means of contradicting or substantially changing the meaning of statements or graphic portrayals.

15. Prior to an advertiser's publishing or otherwise using an endorsement or testimonial, the person whose endorsement is being used shall have previously made and approved the contents and given permission for the advertiser's use of the endorsement.

American Marketing Association:
Code of Ethics for Marketing on the Internet*

Preamble

The Internet, including on-line computer communications, has become increasingly important to marketers' activities, as they provide exchanges and access to markets worldwide. The ability to interact with stakeholders has created new marketing opportunities and risks that are not currently specifically addressed in the American Marketing Association Code of Ethics. The American Marketing Association Code of Ethics for Internet Marketing provides additional guidance and direction for ethical responsibility in this dynamic area of marketing. The American Marketing Association is committed to ethical professional conduct and has adopted these principles for

*Reprinted by permission of the American Marketing Association.

using the Internet, including on-line marketing activities utilizing network computers.

General Responsibilities

Internet marketers must assess the risks and take responsibility for the consequences of their activities. Internet marketers' professional conduct must be guided by:

1. Support of professional ethics to avoid harm by protecting the rights of privacy, ownership and access.

2. Adherence to all applicable laws and regulations with no use of Internet marketing that would be illegal, if conducted by mail, telephone, fax or other media.

3. Awareness of changes in regulations related to Internet marketing.

4. Effective communication to organizational members on risks and policies related to Internet marketing, when appropriate.

5. Organizational commitment to ethical Internet practices communicated to employees, customers and relevant stakeholders.

Privacy

Information collected from customers should be confidential and used only for expressed purposes. All data, especially confidential customer data, should be safeguarded against unauthorized access. The expressed wishes of others should be respected with regard to the receipt of unsolicited e-mail messages.

Ownership

Information obtained from the Internet sources should be properly authorized and documented. Information ownership should be safeguarded and respected. Marketers should respect the integrity and ownership of computer and network systems.

Access

Marketers should treat access to accounts, passwords, and other information as confidential, and only examine or disclose content when authorized by a responsible party. The integrity of others' information systems should be respected with regard to placement of information, advertising or messages. ◄

ESOMAR: (European Society for Opinion and Marketing Research) Guideline for Conducting Marketing and Opinion Research Using the Internet*

Basic Principles

Marketing and opinion research is the professional activity of collecting and interpreting consumer, business, and social data so that decision makers can make better and more efficient marketing and social decisions.

All research carried out on the Internet must conform to the rules and spirit of the main ICC/ESOMAR International Code of Marketing and Social Research Practice and also to Data Protection and other relevant legislation (both international and national).[1]

Such marketing and opinion research must always respect the rights of respondents and other Internet users. It must be carried out in ways which are acceptable to them, to the general public and in accordance with national and international self regulation. Researchers must avoid any actions which might bring Internet research into disrepute or reduce confidence in its findings.

Introduction

The rapid growth of the Internet has opened dramatic new opportunities for collecting and disseminating research information worldwide. At the same time it raises a number of ethical and technical issues

---

Copyright © 2000 by ESOMAR/ARF, Amsterdam, The Netherlands. All Rights Reserved. For further information, please refer to the ESOMAR web site http://www.esomar.nl. Please note that this guideline will be revised on a regular basis to take into account the latest legal and technical developments. The most recent text will be available on the ESOMAR web site.

1. ICC/ESOMAR Codes and Guidelines are always subordinate to existing national law. There is currently no international unanimity as to whether country of origin or country of destination applies to research on the Internet.

---

which must be addressed if the medium is to be used effectively and responsibly for marketing and opinion research purposes.

The fact that the Internet is inexpensive to use and difficult to regulate means that it can be open to misuse by less experienced or less scrupulous organisations, often based outside the research industry. Any Internet surveys which fall seriously below the high standards promoted by ESOMAR and other leading professional bodies will make it more difficult to use the medium for research and could seriously damage the credibility of such research, as well as being an abuse of the goodwill of Internet users generally.

ESOMAR has issued this Guideline to protect the interests both of Internet respondents and of the users of Internet research findings. Because information technology and the Internet are evolving and changing so rapidly it is not practicable to discuss in detail all the technical features of Internet research in such a Guideline. This therefore concentrates on the main principles which must be followed in carrying out research on (or about) the Internet and in reporting the findings of such research.

Requirements

Co-operation is voluntary

1. Researchers must avoid intruding unnecessarily on the privacy of Internet respondents. Survey respondents' co-operation must at all times be voluntary. No personal information which is additional to that already available from other sources should be sought from, or about, respondents without their prior knowledge and agreement.

2. In obtaining the necessary agreement from respondents the researcher must not mislead them about the nature of the research or the uses which will be made of the findings. It is however recognised that there are occasions on which in order to prevent biased responses, the purpose of the research cannot be fully disclosed to respondents at the beginning of the interview. In particular, the researcher should avoid deceptive statements that would be harmful or create a nuisance to the respondent — for example, about the likely length of the interview or about the possibilities of being re-interviewed on a later occasion. Respondents should also be alerted when appropriate to any

costs that they may incur (e.g., of on-line time) if they co-operate in the survey. They are entitled at any stage of the interview, or subsequently, to ask that part or all of the record of their interview be destroyed or deleted and the researcher must conform to any such request where reasonable.

The researcher's identity must be disclosed

3. Respondents must be told the identity of the researcher carrying out the project and the address at which they can without difficulty re-contact the latter should they wish to do so.

Respondents' rights to anonymity must be safeguarded

4. The anonymity of respondents must always be preserved unless they have given their informed consent to the contrary. If respondents have given permission for data to be passed on in a form which allows them to be personally identified, the researcher must ensure that the information will be used for research purposes only. No such personally identified information may be used for subsequent non-research purposes such as direct marketing, list-building, credit rating, fund-raising or other marketing activities relating to those individual respondents.

Privacy Policy Statements

5. Researchers are encouraged to post their privacy policy statement on their on-line site. When such privacy policy statements exist, they should be easy to find, easy to use and comprehensible.

Data security

6. Researchers should take adequate precautions to protect the security of sensitive data. Researchers must also reasonably ensure that any confidential information provided to them by clients or others is protected (e.g., by firewall) against unauthorised access.

Reliability and validity

7. Users of research and the general public must not be in any way misled about the reliability and validity of Internet research findings. It is therefore essential that the researcher:

   (a) follows scientifically sound sampling methods consistent with the purpose of the research

   (b) publishes a clear statement of the sample universe definition used in a given survey, the research approach adopted, the response rate achieved and the method of calculating this where possible

   (c) publishes any appropriate reservations about the possible lack of projectability or other limitations of the research findings, for instance, resulting from non-response and other factors.

It is equally important that any research about the Internet (e.g., to measure penetration, usership, etc.) which employs other data collection methods, such as telephone or mail, also clearly refers to any sampling, or other, limitations on the data collected.

Interviewing Children and Young People

8. It is incumbent on the researcher to observe all relevant laws specifically relating to children and young people although it is recognised that the identification of children and young people is not possible with certainty on the Internet at this time. ESOMAR requirements about the precautions to be taken are set out in the ESOMAR Guideline on Interviewing Children and Young People. According to the ESOMAR Guideline, permission of a responsible adult must be obtained before interviewing children aged under 14 and asking questions on topics generally regarded as sensitive should be avoided wherever possible and in any case handled with extreme care. Researchers must use their best endeavours to ensure that they conform to the requirements of the Guideline referred to, for example, by introducing special contacting procedures to secure the permission of a parent before carrying out an interview with children under 14. Where necessary researchers should consult ESOMAR or their national society for advice.

Unsolicited E-mail

9. Researchers should not send unsolicited messages on line to respondents who have indicated that they do not wish to receive such messages relating to a research project or to any follow-up research resulting directly from it. Researchers will reduce any inconvenience or irritation such E-mail might cause to the recipient by clearly stating its purpose in the subject heading and keeping the total message as brief as possible.

Appendix B

Company Codes of Ethics

Lockheed Martin: Code of Ethics and Business Conduct*

This booklet, *Setting the Standard*, has been adopted by the Lockheed Martin Board of Directors as our Company's Code of Ethics and Business Conduct. As we strive to be the world's finest technology and systems enterprise, it summarizes the virtues and principles that are to guide our actions in the global marketplace. We expect our agents, consultants, contractors, representatives, and suppliers to be guided by these standards as well.

At Lockheed Martin, we believe that ethical conduct requires more than compliance with the laws, rules, and regulations that govern our business. We are a company that values teamwork, sets team goals, assumes collective accountability for actions, embraces diversity, and shares leadership. We are an organization that is deeply committed to excellence and pursues superior performance in every activity. Underlying and supporting ethics at Lockheed Martin is the personal integrity of each of our employees and the highest standards in their personal and professional conduct. Our Code deals both with "doing things right" and with "the right thing to do" so as to maintain our personal and institutional integrity.

While maintaining sensitivity to the diverse social and cultural settings in which we conduct our business, Lockheed Martin aims to set the standard for ethical conduct at all of our localities throughout the world. We will achieve this through behavior in accordance with six virtues: Honesty, Integrity, Respect, Trust, Responsibility, and Citizenship.

---

*Courtesy of Lockheed Martin.

Honesty:
to be truthful in all our endeavors; to be honest and forthright with one another and with our customers, communities, suppliers, and shareholders.

Integrity:
to say what we mean, to deliver what we promise, and to stand for what is right.

Respect:
to treat one another with dignity and fairness, appreciating the diversity of our workforce and the uniqueness of each employee.

Trust:
to build confidence through teamwork and open, candid communication.

Responsibility:
to speak up — without fear of retribution — and report concerns in the workplace, including violations of laws, regulations and company policies, and seek clarification and guidance whenever they are in doubt.

Citizenship:
to obey all the laws of the countries in which we do business and to do our part to make the communities in which we live and work better.

There are numerous resources available to assist you in meeting the challenge of performing your duties and responsibilities. If you are faced with a difficult ethical decision, your supervisor is usually the best source of information and guidance. Additionally, Human Resources, Legal, Procurement, Contracts, Information Services, Environmental Safety & Health, Finance, Security and Company or Corporate Ethics Officers are available to assist you whenever necessary. Corporate Policy Statements and local policies and procedures that provide details pertinent to many of the provisions of the Code can be accessed via the Lockheed Martin Information Network (http://pageone.global.lmco.com) or obtained from your supervisor. Although there can be no better course of action for you than to apply common sense and sound judgement to the manner in which you conduct yourself, do not hesitate to use the resources that are available whenever it is necessary to seek clarification.

We are proud of our employees and the leadership role we play in making the world a better place to live. Thank you for doing your part to create and maintain an ethical work environment . . . and for *Setting the Standard.*

VANCE D. COFFMAN
Chief Executive Officer

Treat in an Ethical Manner Those to Whom Lockheed Martin Has an Obligation

For our employees we are committed to honesty, just management, fairness, providing a safe and healthy environment free from the fear of retribution, and respecting the dignity due everyone.

For our customers we are committed to produce reliable products and services, delivered on time, at a fair price.

For the communities in which we live and work we are committed to observe sound environmental business practices and to act as concerned and responsible neighbors, reflecting all aspects of good citizenship.

For our shareholders we are committed to pursuing sound growth and earnings objectives and to exercising prudence in the use of our assets and resources.

For our suppliers and partners we are committed to fair competition and the sense of responsibility required of a good customer and teammate.

We are committed to the ethical treatment of those to whom we have an obligation.

Obey the Law   We will conduct our business in accordance with all applicable laws and regulations.

The laws and regulations related to government contracting are far-reaching and complex, thus placing responsibilities on Lockheed Martin beyond those faced by companies without government customers. Compliance with the law does not comprise our entire ethical responsibility. Rather, it is a minimum, absolutely essential condition for performance of our duties.

We will conduct our business in accordance with all applicable laws and regulations.

Promote a Positive Work Environment   All employees want and deserve a workplace where they feel respected, satisfied, and appreciated. As a global enterprise, we respect cultural diversity and recognize that the various countries in which we do business may have different legal provisions pertaining to the workplace. As such, we will adhere to the limitations specified by law in all of our localities, and further, we will not tolerate harassment or discrimination of any kind — especially involving race, color, religion, gender, age, national origin, disability, and veteran or marital status.

Providing an environment that supports honesty, integrity, respect, trust, responsibility, and citizenship permits us the opportunity to achieve excellence in our workplace. While everyone who works for the Company must contribute to the creation and maintenance of such an environment, our executives and management personnel assume special responsibility for fostering a work environment that is free from the fear of retribution and will bring out the best in all of us. Supervisors must be careful in words and conduct to avoid placing, or seeming to place, pressure on subordinates that could cause them to deviate from acceptable ethical behavior.

Work Safely: Protect Yourself, Your Fellow Employees, and the World We Live In   We are committed to providing a drug-free, safe, and healthy work environment, and to observe environmentally sound business practices throughout the world. We will strive, at a minimum, to do no harm and where possible, to make the communities in which we work a better place to live. Each of us is responsible for compliance with environmental, health, and safety laws and regulations. Observe posted warnings and regulations. Report immediately to the appropriate management any accident or injury sustained on the job, or any environmental or safety concern you may have.

We are committed to providing a drug-free, safe, and healthy work environment.

Keep Accurate and Complete Records   We must maintain accurate and complete Company records. Transactions between the Company and outside individuals and organizations must be promptly and accurately entered in our books in accordance with generally accepted accounting practices and principles. No one should rationalize or even consider misrepresenting facts or falsifying records. It will not be tolerated and will result in disciplinary action.

No one should rationalize or even consider misrepresenting facts or falsifying records.

Record Costs Properly   Employees and their supervisors are responsible for ensuring that labor and material costs are accurately recorded and charged on the Company's records. These costs include, but are not limited to, normal contract work, work related to independent research and development, and bid and proposal activities.

Employees and their supervisors are responsible for . . . the Company's records.

Strictly Adhere to All Antitrust Laws   Antitrust is a blanket term for laws that protect the free enterprise system and promote open and fair competition. Such laws exist in the United States, the European Union, and in many other countries where the Company does business. These laws deal with agreements and practices "in restraint of trade" such as price fixing and boycotting suppliers or customers, for example. They also bar pricing intended to run a competitor out of business; disparaging, misrepresenting, or harassing a competitor; stealing trade secrets; bribery; and kickbacks.

Antitrust laws are vigorously enforced. Violations may result in severe penalties such as forced sales of parts of businesses and significant fines against the Company. There may also be sanctions against individual employees including substantial fines and prison sentences.

Know and Follow the Law When Involved in International Business   Corruption erodes confidence in the marketplace, undermines democracy, distorts economic and social development, and hurts everyone who depends on trust and transparency in the transaction of business. The Company is committed to conduct its activities free from the unfair influence of bribery and to foster anti-corruption awareness among its employees and business relations throughout the world. The Foreign Corrupt Practices Act (FCPA) is a United States law that prohibits corruptly giving, offering or promising anything of value to foreign officials or foreign political parties, officials or candidates, for the purpose of influencing them to misuse their official capacity to obtain, keep, or direct business or to gain any improper advantage. In addition, the FCPA prohibits knowingly falsifying a company's books and records or knowingly circumventing or failing to implement accounting controls. Employees involved in international operations must be familiar with the FCPA and with similar laws that govern our operations in other countries in which we do business.

International transfers of equipment or technology are also subject to laws and regulations — such as the International Traffic in Arms Regulations (ITAR) in the United States — that may contain prior approval, licensing, and reporting requirements.

Additionally, it is illegal to enter into an agreement to refuse to deal with potential or actual customers or suppliers, or otherwise to engage in or support restrictive international trade practices or boycotts.

It is always important that employees conducting international business know and abide by the laws of the countries which are involved in the activities or transactions. These laws govern the conduct of Lockheed Martin employees throughout the world. If you participate in these business activities, you should know, understand, and strictly comply with these laws and regulations. If you are not familiar with these rules, consult with your supervisor and the Legal Department prior to negotiating any foreign transaction.

Follow the Law and Use Common Sense in Political Contributions and Activities   Lockheed Martin encourages its employees to become involved in civic affairs and to participate in the political process. Employees must understand, however, that their involvement and participation must be on an individual basis, on their own time, and at their own expense. In the United States, federal law prohibits corporations from donating corporate funds, goods, or services, directly or indirectly, to candidates for federal offices — this includes employees' work time. Local and state laws also govern political contributions and activities as they apply to their respective jurisdictions, and similar laws exist in other countries.

Carefully Bid, Negotiate, and Perform Contracts

We must comply with the laws and regulations that pertain to the acquisition of goods and services by our customers. We will compete fairly and ethically for all business opportunities. In circumstances where there is reason to believe that the release or receipt of non-public information is unauthorized, do not attempt to obtain and do not accept such information from any source.

Appropriate steps should be taken to recognize and avoid organizational conflicts in which one business unit's activities may preclude the pursuit of a related activity by another Company business unit.

If you are involved in proposals, bid preparations, or contract negotiations, you must be certain that all statements, communications, and representations to prospective customers are accurate and truthful. Once awarded, all contracts must be performed in compliance with specifications, requirements, and clauses.

Avoid Illegal and Questionable Gifts or Favors

The sale of Lockheed Martin products and services should always be free from even the perception that favorable treatment was sought, received, or given in exchange for the furnishing or receipt of business courtesies. Employees will neither give nor accept business courtesies that constitute, or could be reasonably perceived as constituting, unfair business inducements or that would violate law, regulation or policies of the Company or customer, or could cause embarrassment to or reflect negatively on the Company's reputation. Although customs and practices may differ among the many marketplaces in which we conduct our business, our policies in this regard are substantially similar within the United States and elsewhere throughout the world. As a matter of respect for the rich and diverse customs practiced among our business relations internationally, permissive conduct may differ somewhat in accordance with applicable policy or upon guidance from the business unit's Ethics Officer and Legal Department.

Gifts, Gratuities, and Business Courtesies to U.S., State, and Local Government Employees

Federal, state and local government departments and agencies are governed by laws and regulations concerning acceptance by their employees of entertainment, meals, gifts, gratuities, and other things of value from firms and persons with whom those government departments and agencies do business or over whom they have regulatory authority. It is the policy of Lockheed Martin to comply strictly with those laws and regulations.

Federal Executive Branch Employees

Lockheed Martin employees are prohibited from giving anything of value to federal Executive Branch employees, except as follows:

- Lockheed Martin advertising or promotional items of little intrinsic value (generally $10.00 or less) such as a coffee mug, calendar, or similar item displaying the Company logo;

- Modest refreshments such as soft drinks, coffee, and donuts on an occasional basis in connection with business activities; or

- Business-related meals and local transportation having an aggregate value of $20.00 or less per occasion, provided such items do not in aggregate exceed $50.00 in a calendar year. Although it is the responsibility of the government employee to track and monitor these thresholds, no Lockheed Martin employee shall knowingly provide meals and/or transportation exceeding the $20.00 individual or $50.00 annual limit.

- Certain other exceptions regarding widely attended gatherings and business activities outside U.S. borders are detailed in company policy.

Federal Legislative and Judiciary Branches, and State and Local Government Employees

Employees of the federal Legislative and Judiciary Branches and employees of state and local government departments or agencies are subject to a wide variety of different laws and regulations. These laws and regulations and Corporate Policy Statements pertaining to them must be consulted prior to offering such employees anything of value.

Business Courtesies to Non-Government Persons

Meals, Refreshments and Entertainment   It is an acceptable practice for Lockheed Martin employees to provide meals, refreshments, entertainment, and other business courtesies of reasonable value to non-government persons in support of business activities, provided:

■ The practice does not violate any law or regulation or the standards of conduct of the recipient's organization. It is the offeror's responsibility to inquire about prohibitions or limitations of the recipient's organization before offering any business courtesy; and

■ The business courtesy must be consistent with marketplace practices, infrequent in nature, and may not be lavish or extravagant. While it is difficult to define "lavish or extravagant" by means of a specific dollar amount, a common sense determination should be made consistent with reasonable marketplace practices.

Gifts   Lockheed Martin employees are prohibited from offering or giving tangible gifts (including tickets to sporting, recreational, or other events) having a market value of $100.00 or more, to a person or entity with which the Company does or seeks to do business, unless specifically approved by his or her supervisor, and the business unit's Ethics Officer or the Corporate Office of Ethics and Business Conduct.

Business Courtesies to Foreign Government Personnel and Public Officials   The Company may be restricted from giving meals, gifts, gratuities, entertainment, or other things of value to personnel of foreign governments and foreign public officials by the Foreign Corrupt Practices Act and by laws of other countries. Employees must obtain prior Legal Department approval where the hospitality (i.e., meal, gift, gratuity, entertainment or other thing of value) to be given is not clearly permissible under the Hospitality Guidelines and Matrix maintained by the Legal Department.

Employees must discuss such situations with Legal Counsel . . .

Steer Clear of Conflicts of Interest and Know the Rules About Employing Former Government Officials   Playing favorites or having conflicts of interest — in practice or appearance — runs counter to the fair treatment to which we are all entitled. Avoid any relationship, influence, or activity that might impair, or even appear to impair, your ability to make objective and fair decisions when performing your job. There are extensive conflict of interest laws and regulations regarding the employment or use of former military and civilian government personnel. These rules extend to contact or negotiations with current government employees to discuss their potential employment by the Company or their use as consultants or subcontractors. Conflict of interest laws and regulations must be fully and carefully observed. When in doubt, consult corporate and company policies and procedures, and share the facts of the situation with your supervisor, Legal Department, Human Resources, or Ethics Officer.

When in doubt, share the facts of the situation with your supervisor, Legal Department, Human Resources or Ethics Officer

Here are some ways a conflict of interest could arise:

■ Employment by a competitor or potential competitor, regardless of the nature of the employment, while employed by Lockheed Martin.

■ Acceptance of gifts, payment, or services from those seeking to do business with Lockheed Martin.

■ Placement of business with a firm owned or controlled by an employee or his/her family.

■ Ownership of, or substantial interest in, a company which is a competitor or a supplier.

■ Acting as a consultant to a Lockheed Martin customer or supplier.

Maintain the Integrity of Consultants, Agents, and Representatives   Business integrity is a key standard for the selection and retention of those who represent Lockheed Martin. Agents, representatives, or consultants must certify their willingness to comply with the Company's policies and procedures and must never be retained to circumvent our values and principles. Paying bribes or kickbacks, engaging in industrial espionage, obtaining the proprietary data of a third party without authority, or gaining inside information or influence are just a few examples of what could give us an unfair competitive advantage in a government procurement and could result in violations of law.

Protect Proprietary Information   Proprietary Company information may not be disclosed to anyone without proper authorization. Keep proprietary documents protected and secure. In the course of normal business activities, suppliers, customers, and competitors may sometimes divulge to you information that is proprietary to their business. Respect these confidences.

Keep proprietary documents protected and secure.

Obtain and Use Company and Customer Assets Wisely   Proper use of Company and customer property, electronic communication systems, information resources, material, facilities, and equipment is your responsibility. Use and maintain these assets with the utmost care and respect, guarding against waste and abuse, and never borrow or remove them from Company property without management's permission. Be cost-conscious and alert to opportunities for improving performance while reducing costs. While these assets are intended to be used for the conduct of Lockheed Martin's business, it is recognized that occasional personal use by employees may occur without adversely affecting the interests of the Company. Personal use of Company assets must always be in accordance with corporate and company policy — consult your supervisor for appropriate guidance and permission.

All employees are responsible for complying with the requirements of software copyright licenses related to software packages used in fulfilling job requirements.

Do Not Engage in Speculative or Insider Trading   In our role as a multinational corporation and a publicly owned company, we must always be alert to and comply with the security laws and regulations of the United States and other countries.

. . . we must always be alert . . .

It is against the law for employees to buy or sell Company stock based on material, non-public "insider" information about or involving the Company. Play it safe: don't speculate in the securities of Lockheed Martin when you are aware of information affecting the Company's business that has not been publicly released or in situations where trading would call your judgment into question. This includes all varieties of stock trading such as options, puts and calls, straddles, selling short, etc. Two simple rules can help protect you in this area: (1) Don't use non-public information for personal gain. (2) Don't pass along such information to someone else who has no need to know.

This guidance also applies to the securities of other companies (suppliers, vendors, subcontractors, etc.) for which you receive information in the course of your employment at Lockheed Martin.

For More Information:

In order to support a comprehensive Ethics and Business Conduct Program, Lockheed Martin has developed education and communication programs in many subject areas.

These programs have been developed to provide employees with job-specific information to raise their level of awareness and sensitivity to key issues.

Interactive Video Training Modules are available on the following topics:

Antitrust Compliance	Kickbacks & Gratuities
Domestic Consultants	Labor Charging
Drug-Free Workplace	Leveraging Differences (Diversity)
Environment, Health and Safety	Material Costs
Ethics Organizational	Conflicts of Interest
Ex-Government Employees	Procurement
Export Control	Procurement Integrity
Foreign Corrupt Practices Act	Product Substitution
Government Property	Record Retention

Harassment in
the Workplace

Insider Trading

International
Consultants

International Military
Sales

Security

Software License
Compliance

Truth in Negotiations Act

The current list of Interactive Video Compliance Training Modules and Corporate Policy Statements relating to the above topics and others can be accessed via the Lockheed Martin Information Network at http://pageone.global.lmco.com/ or obtained from your supervisor.

Warning Signs — You're On Thin Ethical Ice When You Hear . . .

"Well, maybe just this once . . ."

"No one will ever know . . ."

"It doesn't matter how it gets done as long as it gets done."

"It sounds too good to be true."

"Everyone does it."

"Shred that document."

"We can hide it."

"No one will get hurt."

"What's in it for me?"

"This will destroy the competition."

"We didn't have this conversation."

You can probably think of many more phrases that raise warning flags. If you find yourself using any of these expressions, take the Quick Quiz on the following page and make sure you are on solid ethical ground.

Quick Quiz — When In Doubt, Ask Yourself . . .

Are my actions legal?

Am I being fair and honest?

Will my action stand the test of time?

How will I feel about myself afterwards?

How will it look in the newspaper?

Will I sleep soundly tonight?

What would I tell my child to do?

How would I feel if my family, friends, and neighbors knew what I was doing?

If you are still not sure what to do, ask . . . and keep asking until you are certain you are doing the right thing.

Our Goal: An Ethical Work Environment

We have established the Office of Vice President — Ethics and Business Conduct to underscore our commitment to ethical conduct throughout our company.

This office reports directly to the Office of the Chairman and the Audit and Ethics Committee of the Board of Directors, and oversees a vigorous corporatewide effort to promote a positive, ethical work environment for all employees.

Our Ethics Officers operate confidential Ethics HelpLines at each operating company, as well as at the corporate level. You are urged to use these resources whenever you have a question or concern that cannot be readily addressed within your work group or through your supervisor.

Contact the Ethics Office

In addition, if you need information on how to contact your local Ethics Officer — or wish to discuss a matter of concern with the Corporate Office of Ethics and Business Conduct — you are encouraged to use one of the following confidential means of communication:

Call: 800-LM ETHICS
         Domestic: 800-563-8442

         International: 800-5638-4427

         For the Hearing or Speech Impaired: 800-441-7457

Write: Office of Ethics and Business
         Conduct

Write: Lockheed Martin Corporation

                      P.O. Box 34143

                      Bethesda, MD 20827-0143

Fax: 301-897-6442

Internet E-Mail: corporate.ethics@lmco.com

When you contact your Company Ethics Officer or the Corporate Office of Ethics and Business Conduct:

- You will be treated with dignity and respect.

- Your communication will be protected to the greatest extent possible.

- Your concerns will be seriously addressed and, if not resolved at the time you call, you will be informed of the outcome.

- You need not identify yourself.

- Remember, there's never a penalty for using the Ethics HelpLine. People in a position of authority can't stop you; if they try, they're subject to disciplinary action up to and including dismissal.

HCA – The Healthcare Company:
Code of Conduct*

Mission and Values Statement

Above all else, we are committed to the care and improvement of human life. In recognition of this commitment, we will strive to deliver high quality, cost-effective healthcare in the communities we serve.

In pursuit of our mission, we believe the following value statements are essential and timeless:

- We recognize and affirm the unique and intrinsic worth of each individual.

- We treat all those we serve with compassion and kindness.

Courtesy of HCA — The Healthcare Company. http://hcahealthcare.com.

(Note: All references to "HCA" or the "organization" in this Code of Conduct refer to HCA — The Healthcare Company and/or its affiliates, as applicable.)

- We act with absolute honesty, integrity and fairness in the way we conduct our business and the way we live our lives.

- We trust our colleagues as valuable members of our healthcare team and pledge to treat one another with loyalty, respect, and dignity.

Purpose of Our Code of Conduct

Our Code of Conduct provides guidance to all HCA colleagues and assists us in carrying out our daily activities within appropriate ethical and legal standards. These obligations apply to our relationships with patients, affiliated physicians, third-party payers, subcontractors, independent contractors, vendors, consultants, and one another.

The Code is a critical component of our overall Ethics and Compliance Program. We have developed the Code to ensure we meet our ethical standards and comply with applicable laws and regulations.

The Code is intended to be comprehensive and easily understood. In some instances, the Code deals fully with the subject covered. In many cases, however, the subject discussed has so much complexity that additional guidance is necessary for those directly involved with the particular area to have sufficient direction. To provide additional guidance, we have developed a comprehensive set of compliance policies and procedures which may be accessed on the Ethics and Compliance site of our Intranet, as well as our external web site at www.hcahealthcare.com. Those policies expand upon or supplement many of the principles articulated in this Code of Conduct.

Though we promote the concept of management autonomy at local facilities in order to meet local needs, the policies set forth in the Code are mandatory and must be followed.

Leadership Responsibilities

While all HCA colleagues are obligated to follow our Code, we expect our leaders to set the example, to be in every respect a model. They must ensure that those on their team have sufficient information to comply with laws, regulations, and policies; as well as the resources to resolve ethical dilemmas. They must help to create a culture within HCA which promotes the highest standards of ethics and compliance. This culture must encourage everyone in the organization to share concerns when they arise. We must never sacrifice ethical and compliant behavior in the pursuit of business objectives.

Our Fundamental Commitment to Stakeholders*

We affirm the following commitments to HCA stakeholders:

To our patients: We are committed to providing quality care that is sensitive, compassionate, promptly delivered, and cost-effective.

To our HCA colleagues: We are committed to a work setting which treats all colleagues with fairness, dignity, and respect, and affords them an opportunity to grow, to develop professionally, and to work in a team environment in which all ideas are considered.

To our affiliated physicians: We are committed to providing a work environment which has excellent facilities, modern equipment, and outstanding professional support.

To our third-party payers: We are committed to dealing with our third-party payers in a way that demonstrates our commitment to contractual obligations and reflects our shared concern for quality healthcare and bringing efficiency and cost effectiveness to healthcare. We encourage our private third-party payers to adopt their own set of comparable ethical principles to explicitly recognize their obligations to patients as well as the need for fairness in dealing with providers.

To our regulators: We are committed to an environment in which compliance with rules, regulations, and sound business practices is woven into the corporate culture. We accept the responsibility to aggressively self-govern and monitor adherence to the requirements of law and to our Code of Conduct.

To our joint venture partners: We are committed to fully performing our responsibilities to manage

_____

The term "stakeholder" refers to those groups of individuals to whom an institution sees itself as having obligations.

our jointly owned facilities in a manner that reflects the mission and values of each of our organizations.

To the communities we serve: We are committed to understanding the particular needs of the communities we serve and providing these communities quality, cost-effective healthcare. We realize as an organization that we have a responsibility to help those in need. We proudly support charitable contributions and events in the communities we serve in an effort to promote good will and further good causes.

To our suppliers: We are committed to fair competition among prospective suppliers and the sense of responsibility required of a good customer. We encourage our suppliers to adopt their own set of comparable ethical principles.

To our volunteers: The concept of voluntary assistance to the needs of patients and their families is an integral part of the fabric of healthcare. We are committed to ensuring that our volunteers feel a sense of meaningfulness from their volunteer work and receive recognition for their volunteer efforts.

To our shareholders: We are committed to the highest standards of professional management, which we are certain can create unique efficiencies and innovative healthcare approaches and thus ensure favorable returns on our shareholders' investments over the long term.

Relationships with Our Healthcare Partners

Patients

Patient Care and Rights   Our mission is to provide high quality, cost effective healthcare to all of our patients. We treat all patients with warmth, respect and dignity and provide care that is both necessary and appropriate. We make no distinction in the admission, transfer or discharge of patients or in the care we provide based on age, gender, disability, race, color, religion, or national origin. Clinical care is based on identified patient healthcare needs, not on patient or organization economics.

Upon admission, each patient is provided with a written statement of patient rights. This statement includes the rights of the patient to make decisions regarding medical care and conforms to all applicable state and Federal laws.

We seek to involve patients in all aspects of their care and obtain informed consent for treatment. As applicable, each patient or patient representative is provided with a clear explanation of care including, but not limited to, diagnosis, treatment plan, right to refuse or accept care, care decision dilemmas, advance directive options, estimates of treatment costs, organ donation and procurement, and an explanation of the risks and benefits associated with available treatment options. Patients have the right to request transfers to other facilities. In such cases, the patient will be given an explanation of the benefits, risks, and alternatives.

Patients are informed of their right to make advance directives. Patient advance directives will be honored within the limits of the law and our organization's mission, philosophy, and capabilities.

In the promotion and protection of each patient's rights, each patient and his or her representatives will be accorded appropriate confidentiality, privacy, security and protective services, opportunity for resolution of complaints, and pastoral care or spiritual care.

Patients are treated in a manner that preserves their dignity, autonomy, self-esteem, civil rights, and involvement in their own care. HCA facilities maintain processes to support patient rights in a collaborative manner which involves the facility leaders and others. These structures are based on policies and procedures, which make up the framework addressing both patient care and organizational ethics issues. These structures shall include informing each patient, or when appropriate the patient's representative of the patient's rights, in advance of furnishing or discontinuing care. Additionally, the facilities have established processes for prompt resolution of patient grievances which include informing patients of whom to contact regarding grievances and informing patients regarding the grievance resolution. HCA colleagues will receive training about patient rights in order to clearly understand their role in supporting them.

Compassion and care are part of our commitment to the communities we serve. We strive to provide health education, health promotion, and illness-prevention programs as part of our efforts to improve the quality of life of our patients and our communities.

Emergency Treatment　　We follow the Emergency Medical Treatment and Active Labor Act ("EMTALA") in providing emergency medical treatment to all patients, regardless of ability to pay. Provided we have the capacity and capability, anyone with an emergency medical condition is treated and admitted based on medical necessity. In an emergency situation or if the patient is in labor, financial and demographic information will be obtained only after an appropriate medical screening examination and necessary stabilizing treatment (including treatment for an unborn child). We do not admit, discharge or transfer patients simply on their ability or inability to pay.

Patients will only be transferred to another facility at the patient's request or if the patient's medical needs cannot be met at the HCA facility (*e.g.,* we do not have the capacity or capability) and appropriate care is knowingly available at another facility. Patients may only be transferred in strict compliance with the EMTALA guidelines.

Patient Information　　We collect information about the patient's medical condition, history, medication, and family illnesses to provide quality care. We realize the sensitive nature of this information and are committed to maintaining its confidentiality. We do not release or discuss patient-specific information with others unless it is necessary to serve the patient or required by law.

HCA colleagues must never disclose confidential information that violates the privacy rights of our patients. No HCA colleague, affiliated physician, or other healthcare partner has a right to any patient information other than that necessary to perform his or her job.

Subject only to emergency exceptions, patients can expect their privacy will be protected and patient specific information will be released only to persons authorized by law or by the patient's written consent.

Affiliated Physicians　　Any business arrangement with a physician must be structured to ensure precise compliance with legal requirements. Such arrangements must be in writing and approved by the Corporate Legal Department.

In order to ethically and legally meet all standards regarding referrals and admissions, we will adhere strictly to two primary rules:

1. We do not pay for referrals. We accept patient referrals and admissions based solely on the patient's clinical needs and our ability to render the needed services. We do not pay or offer to pay anyone — colleagues, physicians, or other persons — for referral of patients. Violation of this policy may have grave consequences for the organization and the individuals involved, including civil and criminal penalties, and possible exclusion from participation in federally funded healthcare programs.

2. We do not accept payments for referrals we make. No HCA colleague or any other person acting on behalf of the organization is permitted to solicit or receive anything of value, directly or indirectly, in exchange for the referral of patients. Similarly, when making patient referrals to another healthcare provider, we do not take into account the volume or value of referrals that the provider has made (or may make) to us.

Third-Party Payers

Coding and Billing for Services   We will take great care to assure all billings to government payers, commercial insurance payers and patients are true and accurate and conform to all pertinent Federal and state laws and regulations. We prohibit any colleague or agent of HCA from knowingly presenting or causing to be presented claims for payment or approval which are false, fictitious, or fraudulent.

We will operate oversight systems designed to verify claims are submitted only for services actually provided and services are billed as provided. These systems will emphasize the critical nature of complete and accurate documentation of services provided. As part of our documentation effort, we will maintain current and accurate medical records.

Any subcontractors engaged to perform billing or coding services must have the necessary skills, quality control processes, systems, and appropriate procedures to ensure all billings for government and commercial insurance programs are accurate and complete. HCA prefers to contract with such entities that have adopted their own ethics and compliance programs. Third-party billing entities, contractors, and preferred vendors under contract consideration must be approved consistent with the corporate policy on this subject.

For coding questions in a hospital or ambulatory surgery center contact the Coding Helpline at 1-800-537-1666. For questions regarding Health Information Management Services (HIMS) Policies and Procedures, contact the HIMS P & P Helpline at 1-800-690-0919 or e-mail at: HIMS P&P Helpline. For billing questions in a hospital or ambulatory surgery center, contact the Billing Helpline at 1-888-735-3669. For billing or coding questions in HCA Physician Services, call 1-800-373-5620, ext. 320.

Cost Reports   We are required to submit certain reports of our costs of operation. We will comply with all applicable Federal and state laws relating to all cost reports. These laws and regulations define what costs are allowable and outline the appropriate methodologies to claim reimbursement for the cost of services provided to program beneficiaries. Given their complexity, all issues related to the completion and settlement of cost reports must be communicated through or coordinated with our Reimbursement Department.

Legal and Regulatory Compliance

HCA provides varied healthcare services in many states. These services may be provided only pursuant to appropriate Federal, state, and local laws, regulations and conditions of participation. Such laws, regulations and conditions of participation may include subjects such as certificates of need, licenses, permits, accreditation, access to treatment, consent to treatment, medical record-keeping, access to medical records and confidentiality, patients' rights, terminal care decision making, medical staff membership and clinical privileges, corporate practice of medicine restrictions, and Medicare and Medicaid program requirements. The organization is subject to numerous other laws in addition to these healthcare regulations and conditions of participation.

We will comply with all applicable laws and regulations. All colleagues, medical staff members, privileged practitioners, and contract service providers must be knowledgeable about and ensure compliance with all laws, regulations and conditions of participation; and should immediately report violations or suspected violations to a supervisor or member of management, the Facility Ethics and Compliance Officer, the Ethics Line, or the Corporate Ethics and Compliance Officer.

HCA will be forthright in dealing with any billing inquiries. Requests for information will be answered with complete, factual, and accurate information. We will cooperate with and be courteous to all inspectors and surveyors and provide them with the information to which they are entitled during an inspection or survey.

During a survey or inspection, you must never conceal, destroy, or alter any documents; lie; or make misleading statements to the agency representative. You should not attempt to cause another colleague to fail to provide accurate information or obstruct, mislead, or delay the communication of information or records relating to a possible violation of law.

In order to ensure we fully meet all regulatory obligations, HCA colleagues must be informed about stated areas of potential compliance concern. The Department of Health and Human Services, and particularly its Inspector General, have routinely notified healthcare providers of areas in which these government representatives believe insufficient attention is being accorded government regulations. We should be diligent in the face of such guidance about reviewing these elements of our system to ensure their correctness.

HCA will provide its colleagues with the information and education they need to comply fully with all applicable laws, regulations and conditions of participation.

Dealing with Accrediting Bodies

HCA will deal with all accrediting bodies in a direct, open and honest manner. No action should ever be taken in relationships with accrediting bodies that would mislead the accreditor or its survey teams, either directly or indirectly.

The scope of matters related to accreditation of various bodies is extremely significant and broader than the scope of this Code of Conduct. The purpose of our Code of Conduct is to provide general guidance on subjects of wide interest within the organization. Accrediting bodies may be focused on issues both of wide and somewhat more focused interest. In any case, where HCA determines to seek any form of

accreditation, obviously all standards of the accrediting group are important and must be followed.

Business Information and Information Systems

Accuracy, Retention, and Disposal of Documents and Records   Each HCA colleague is responsible for the integrity and accuracy of our organization's documents and records, not only to comply with regulatory and legal requirements but also to ensure records are available to support our business practices and actions. No one may alter or falsify information on any record or document.

Medical and business documents and records are retained in accordance with the law and our record retention policy. Medical and business documents include paper documents such as letters and memos, computer-based information such as e-mail or computer files on disk or tape, and any other medium that contains information about the organization or its business activities. It is important to retain and destroy records only according to our policy. You must not tamper with records, nor remove or destroy them prior to the specified date.

Information Security and Confidentiality   Confidential information about our organization's strategies and operations is a valuable asset. Although you may use confidential information to perform your job, it must not be shared with others unless the individuals have a legitimate need to know this information and have agreed to maintain the confidentiality of the information. Confidential information includes personnel data maintained by the organization; patient lists and clinical information; patient financial information; passwords; pricing and cost data; information pertaining to acquisitions, divestitures, affiliations and mergers; financial data; details regarding federal, state and local tax examinations of the organization or its joint venture partners; research data; strategic plans; marketing strategies and techniques; supplier and subcontractor information; and proprietary computer software. If your relationship with HCA ends for any reason, you are still bound to maintain the confidentiality of information viewed during your employment. This provision does not restrict the right of a colleague to disclose, if he or she wishes, information about his or her own compensation, benefits, or terms and conditions of employment.

Our clinical and business processes rely on timely access to accurate information from our computer systems. Your passwords act as individual keys to our network and to critical patient care and business applications, and they must be kept confidential. It is part of your job to learn about and practice the many ways you can help protect the confidentiality, integrity and availability of electronic information assets.

Electronic Media   All communications systems, including electronic mail, intranet (Koala), Internet access, and voice mail, are the property of the organization and are to be primarily used for business purposes. Highly limited reasonable personal use of HCA communications systems is permitted; however, you should assume these communications are not private. Patient or confidential information should not be sent through Koala or the Internet until such time that its confidentiality can be assured.

HCA reserves the right to periodically access, monitor, and disclose the contents of Koala, e-mail, and voice mail messages. Access or disclosure of individual employee messages may only be done with the approval of the Corporate Legal Department.

Colleagues may not use internal communication channels or access to the Internet at work to post, store, transmit, download, or distribute any threatening materials; knowingly, recklessly, or maliciously false materials; or obscene materials including anything constituting or encouraging a criminal offense, giving rise to civil liability, or otherwise violating any laws. Additionally, these channels of communication may not be used to send chain letters, personal broadcast messages, or copyrighted documents that are not authorized for reproduction; nor are they to be used to conduct an external job search or open mis-addressed mail.

Colleagues who abuse our communications systems or use them excessively for non-business purposes may lose these privileges and be subject to disciplinary action.

Financial Reporting and Records   We have established and maintain a high standard of accuracy and completeness in the documentation and reporting of all financial records. These records serve as a basis for managing our business and are important in meeting our obligations to patients, colleagues, shareholders, suppliers, and others. They are also necessary for compliance with tax and financial reporting requirements.

All financial information must reflect actual transactions and conform to generally accepted accounting principles. No undisclosed or unrecorded funds or assets may be established. HCA maintains a system of internal controls to provide reasonable assurances that all transactions are executed in accordance with management's authorization and are recorded in a proper manner so as to maintain accountability of the organization's assets.

Workplace Conduct and Employment Practices

Conflict of Interest   A conflict of interest may occur if your outside activities or personal interests influence or appear to influence your ability to make objective decisions in the course of your job responsibilities. A conflict of interest may also exist if the demands of any outside activities hinder or distract you from the performance of your job or cause you to use HCA resources for other than HCA purposes. It is your obligation to ensure you remain free of conflicts of interest in the performance of your responsibilities at HCA. If you have any question about whether an outside activity might constitute a conflict of interest, you must obtain the approval of your supervisor before pursuing the activity.

Controlled Substances   Some of our colleagues routinely have access to prescription drugs, controlled substances, and other medical supplies. Many of these substances are governed and monitored by specific regulatory organizations and must be administered by physician order only. It is extremely important these items be handled properly and only by authorized individuals to minimize risks to us and to patients. If you become aware of the diversion of drugs from the organization, you should report the incident immediately.

Copyrights   HCA colleagues may only use copyrighted materials pursuant to the organization's policy on such matters.

Diversity and Equal Employment Opportunity   Our colleagues provide us with a wide complement of talents which contribute greatly to our success. We are committed to providing an equal opportunity work environment where everyone is treated with fairness, dignity, and respect. We will comply with all laws, regulations, and policies related to non-discrimination in all of our personnel actions. Such actions include hiring, staff reductions, transfers, terminations, evaluations, recruiting, compensation, corrective action, discipline, and promotions.

No one shall discriminate against any individual with a disability with respect to any offer, or term or condition, of employment. We will make reasonable accommodations to the known physical and mental limitations of otherwise qualified individuals with disabilities.

Harassment and Workplace Violence Each HCA colleague has the right to work in an environment free of harassment and disruptive behavior. We will not tolerate harassment by anyone based on the diverse characteristics or cultural backgrounds of those who work with us. Degrading or humiliating jokes, slurs, intimidation, or other harassing conduct is not acceptable in our workplace.

Any form of sexual harassment is strictly prohibited. This prohibition includes unwelcome sexual advances or requests for sexual favors in conjunction with employment decisions. Moreover, verbal or physical conduct of a sexual nature that interferes with an individual's work performance or creates an intimidating, hostile, or offensive work environment has no place at HCA.

Harassment also includes incidents of workplace violence. Workplace violence includes robbery and other commercial crimes, stalking cases, violence directed at the employer, terrorism, and hate crimes committed by current or former colleagues. As part of our commitment to a safe workplace for our colleagues, we prohibit colleagues from possessing firearms, other weapons, explosive devices, or other dangerous materials on HCA premises. Colleagues who observe or experience any form of harassment or violence should report the incident to their supervisor, the Human Resources Department, a member of management, the Facility Ethics and Compliance Officer, or the Ethics Line.

Health and Safety All HCA facilities must comply with all government regulations and rules, HCA poli-

cies, and required facility practices that promote the protection of workplace health and safety. Our policies have been developed to protect you from potential workplace hazards. You should become familiar with and understand how these policies apply to your specific job responsibilities and seek advice from your supervisor or the Safety Officer whenever you have a question or concern. It is important for you to advise your supervisor or the Safety Officer of any serious workplace injury or any situation presenting a danger of injury so timely corrective action may be taken to resolve the issue.

Hiring of Former and Current Government and Fiscal Intermediary Employees The recruitment and employment of former or current U.S. government employees may be impacted by regulations concerning conflicts of interest. Hiring employees directly from a fiscal intermediary requires certain regulatory notifications. Colleagues should consult with the Corporate Human Resources Department or the Corporate Legal Department related to such recruitment and hiring.

Insider Information and Securities Trading In the course of your employment, you may become aware of non-public information about HCA material to an investor's decision to buy or sell the organization's securities. Non-public, material information may include plans for mergers, marketing strategy, financial results, or other business dealings. You may not discuss this type of information with anyone outside of the organization. Within the organization, you should discuss this information on a strictly "need to know" basis only with other colleagues who require this information to perform their jobs.

Securities law and HCA policy prohibit individuals from trading in the marketable securities of a publicly held organization or influencing others to trade in such securities on the basis of non-public, material information. These restrictions are meant to ensure the general public has complete and timely information on which to base investment decisions.

If you obtain access to non-public, material information about the organization or any other company while performing your job, you may not use that information to buy, sell, or retain securities of HCA or that other company. Even if you do not buy or sell securities based on what you know, discussing the information with others, such as family members, friends, vendors, suppliers, and other outside acquaintances, is prohibited until the information is considered to be public. Information is considered to be public two days after a general release of the information to the media.

International Business   In today's global economy, it is important to understand fully the laws and regulations governing our interactions within other countries. All HCA colleagues, agents, and representatives are expected to abide by the laws of the United States and the laws of any other countries in which we do business. Colleagues outside the United States are responsible for knowing and complying with the laws of the countries in which they do business. Where differences exist between US law and the laws of the country in which we do business, please consult the Legal Department for guidance.

License and Certification Renewals   Colleagues and individuals retained as independent contractors in positions which require professional licenses, certifications, or other credentials are responsible for maintaining the current status of their credentials and shall comply at all times with Federal and state requirements applicable to their respective disciplines. To assure compliance, HCA may require evidence of the individual having a current license or credential status.

HCA will not allow any colleague or independent contractor to work without valid, current licenses or credentials.

Personal Use of HCA Resources   It is the responsibility of each HCA colleague to preserve our organization's assets including time, materials, supplies, equipment, and information. Organization assets are to be maintained for business related purposes. As a general rule, the personal use of any HCA asset without the prior approval of your supervisor is prohibited. The occasional use of items, such as copying facilities or telephones, where the cost to HCA is insignificant, is permissible. Any community or charitable use of organization resources must be approved in advance by your supervisor. Any use of organization resources for personal financial gain unrelated to the organization's business is prohibited.

Relationships Among HCA Colleagues   In the normal day-to-day functions of an organization like HCA, there are issues that arise which relate to how people in the organization deal with one another. It is impossible to foresee all of these, and many do not require explicit treatment in a document like this. A few routinely arise, however. One involves gift giving among colleagues for certain occasions. While we wish to avoid any strict rules, no one should ever feel compelled to give a gift to anyone, and any gifts offered or received should be appropriate to the circumstances. A lavish gift to anyone in a supervisory role would clearly violate organization policy. Another situation, which routinely arises, is a fund-raising or similar effort, in which no one should ever be made to feel compelled to participate.

Relationships with Subcontractors, Suppliers, and Educational Institutions   We must manage our subcontractor and supplier relationships in a fair and reasonable manner, consistent with all applicable laws and good business practices. We promote competitive procurement to the maximum extent practicable. Our selection of subcontractors, suppliers, and vendors will be made on the basis of objective criteria including quality, technical excellence, price, delivery, adherence to schedules, service, and maintenance of adequate sources of supply. Our purchasing decisions will be made on the supplier's ability to meet our needs, and not on personal relationships and friendships. We will always employ the highest ethical standards in business practices in source selection, negotiation, determination of contract awards, and the administration of all purchasing activities. We will not communicate to a third-party confidential information given to us by our suppliers unless directed in writing to do so by the supplier. We will not disclose contract pricing and information to any outside parties. (The subject of Business Courtesies, which might be offered by or to subcontractors or suppliers, is discussed on pages 15 to 17 of this Code. [See "Business courtesies" below.])

Any hospital having a relationship with an educational institution must have a written agreement which defines both parties' roles and the hospital's retention of the responsibility for the quality of patient care.

Research   We follow high ethical standards in any research conducted by our physicians and professional staff. We do not tolerate intentional research misconduct. Research misconduct includes making up or changing results or copying results from other studies without performing the research.

All patients asked to participate in a research project are given a full explanation of alternative services that might prove beneficial to them. They are also fully informed of potential discomforts and are given a full explanation of the risks, expected benefits, and alternatives. The patients are fully informed of the procedures to be followed, especially those that are experimental in nature. Refusal of a patient to participate in a research study will not compromise his or her access to services.

All personnel applying for or performing research of any type are responsible for maintaining the highest ethical standards in any written or oral communications regarding their research projects as well as following appropriate research guidelines. As in all accounting and financial record-keeping, our policy is to submit only true, accurate, and complete costs related to research grants.

Sanctioned Individuals   The organization has policies and procedures in place to ensure we do not contract with, employ or bill for services rendered by an individual or entity that is excluded, suspended, debarred, or ineligible to participate in Federal health care programs; or has been convicted of a criminal offense related to the provision of health care items or services and has not been reinstated in a Federal health care program after a period of exclusion, suspension, debarment, or ineligibility, provided that we are aware of such criminal offense. We routinely search the Office of Inspector General and General Services Administration's lists of such excluded and ineligible persons.

Substance Abuse and Mental Acuity   To protect the interests of our colleagues and patients, we are committed to an alcohol and drug-free work environment. All colleagues must report for work free of the influence of alcohol and illegal drugs. Reporting to work under the influence of any illegal drug or alcohol; having an illegal drug in your system; or using, possessing, or selling illegal drugs while on HCA work time or property may result in immediate termination. We may use drug testing as a means of enforcing this policy.

It is also recognized individuals may be taking prescription or over-the-counter drugs, which could impair judgment or other skills required in job per-

formance. If you have questions about the effect of such medication on your performance, or you observe an individual who appears to be impaired in the performance of his or her job, consult your supervisor.

Marketing Practices

Antitrust   Antitrust laws are designed to create a level playing field in the marketplace and to promote fair competition. These laws could be violated by discussing HCA business with a competitor, such as how our prices are set, disclosing the terms of supplier relationships, allocating markets among competitors, or agreeing with a competitor to refuse to deal with a supplier. Our competitors are other health systems and facilities in markets where we operate.

At trade association meetings, be alert to potential situations where it may not be appropriate for you to participate in discussions regarding prohibited subjects with our competitors. Prohibited subjects include any aspect of pricing, our services in the market, key costs such as labor costs, and marketing plans. If a competitor raises a prohibited subject, end the conversation immediately. Document your refusal to participate in the conversation by requesting your objection be reflected in the meeting minutes and notify the Corporate Legal Department of the incident.

In general, avoid discussing sensitive topics with competitors or suppliers, unless you are proceeding with the advice of the Corporate Legal Department. You must also not provide any information in response to an oral or written inquiry concerning an antitrust matter without first consulting the Corporate Legal Department.

Gathering Information about Competitors   It is not unusual to obtain public information about other organizations, including our competitors, through legal and ethical means such as public documents, public presentations, journal and magazine articles, and other published and spoken information. However, you should avoid seeking or receiving information about a competitor throughout other non-public means if you know or have reason to believe the information is proprietary or confidential. For example, you should not seek proprietary or confidential information when doing so would require anyone to violate a contractual agreement, such as a confidentiality agreement with a prior employer.

Marketing and Advertising   We may use marketing and advertising activities to educate the public, provide information to the community, increase awareness of our services, and to recruit colleagues. We will present only truthful, fully informative, and non-deceptive information in these materials and announcements. All marketing materials will reflect services available and the level of licensure and certification.

Environmental Compliance

It is our policy to comply with all environmental laws and regulations as they relate to our organization's operations. We will act to preserve our natural resources to the full extent reasonably possible. We will comply with all environmental laws and operate each of our facilities with the necessary permits, approvals, and controls. We will diligently employ the proper procedures with respect to handling and disposal of hazardous and biohazardous waste, including but not limited to medical waste.

In helping HCA comply with these laws and regulations, we must understand how job duties may impact the environment, adhere to all requirements for the proper handling of hazardous materials, and immediately alert our supervisors to any situation regarding the discharge of a hazardous substance, improper disposal of medical waste, or any situation which may be potentially damaging to the environment.

Business Courtesies

General   This part of the Code of Conduct should not be considered in any way as an encouragement to make, solicit, or receive any type of entertainment or gift. For clarity purposes, please note that these limitations govern activities with those outside of HCA. This section does not pertain to actions between HCA and its colleagues or actions among HCA colleagues themselves. (See "Relationships Among HCA Colleagues" [above].)

Receiving Business Courtesies   We recognize there will be times when a current or potential business associate may extend an invitation to attend a social event in order to further develop your business relationship. You may accept such invitations, provided: (1) the cost associated with such an event is reasonable and appropriate, which, as a general rule, means the cost will not exceed $100.00 per person; (2) no expense is incurred for any travel costs (other than in a vehicle owned privately or by the host company) or overnight lodging; and (3) such events are infrequent. The limitations of this section do not apply to business meetings at which food (including meals) may be provided. Sometimes a business associate will extend training and educational opportunities that include travel and overnight accommodations to you at no cost to you or HCA. Similarly, there are some circumstances where you are invited to an event at a vendor's expense to receive information about new products or services. Prior to accepting any such invitation, you must receive approval to do so consistent with the corporate policy on this subject.

As an HCA colleague, you may accept gifts with a total value of $50.00 or less in any one year from any individual or organization who has a business relationship with HCA. For purposes of this paragraph, physicians practicing in HCA facilities are considered to have such a relationship. Perishable or consumable gifts given to a department or group are not subject to any specific limitation. You may accept gift certificates, but you may never accept cash or financial instruments (*e.g.*, checks, stocks). Finally, under no circumstances may you solicit a gift.

This section does not limit HCA facilities from accepting gifts, provided they are used and accounted for appropriately.

Extending Business Courtesies to Non–Referral Sources
No portion of this section, "Extending Business Courtesies to Non-referral Sources," applies to any individual who makes, or is in a position to make, referrals to an HCA facility.

There may be times when you wish to extend to a current or potential business associate (other than someone who may be in a position to make a patient referral) an invitation to attend a social event (*e.g.*, reception, meal, sporting event or theatrical event) to further or develop your business relationship. The purpose of the entertainment must never be to induce any favorable business action. During these events, topics of a business nature must be discussed and the host must be present. These events must not include expenses paid for any travel costs (other than in a vehicle owned privately or by the host entity) or overnight lodging. The cost associated with such an event must be reasonable and appropriate. As a general rule, this means the cost will not exceed $100.00 per person. Moreover, such business entertainment with respect to any particular individual must be infrequent, which, as a general rule, means not more than four times per year. With regard to the $100.00 guideline, if circumstances arise where an entertainment event was contemplated prior to the event to meet the guideline but unforeseeably exceeded it, a report to that effect with the relevant details must be filed consistent with the corporate policy on this subject. If you anticipate an event will exceed the $100.00 guideline, you must obtain advance approval as required by corporate policy. That policy requires establishing the business necessity and appropriateness of the proposed entertainment. The organization will under no circumstances sanction participation in any business entertainment that might be considered lavish. Departures from the $100.00 guideline are highly discouraged.

Also, HCA facilities may routinely sponsor events with a legitimate business purpose (*e.g.,* hospital board meetings or retreats). Provided that such events are for business purposes, reasonable and appropriate meals and entertainment may be offered. In addition, transportation and lodging can be paid for. However, all elements of such events, including these courtesy elements, must be consistent with the corporate policy on such events.

It is critical to avoid the appearance of impropriety when giving gifts to individuals who do business or are seeking to do business with HCA. We will never use gifts or other incentives to improperly influence relationships or business outcomes. Gifts to business associates who are not government employees must not exceed $50.00 per year per recipient. You may accept gift certificates, but you may never accept cash or financial instruments (*e.g.,* checks, stocks). The corporate policy on business courtesies may from time to time provide modest flexibility in order to permit appropriate recognition of the efforts of those who have spent meaningful amounts of volunteer time on behalf of HCA.

U.S. Federal and state governments have strict rules and laws regarding gifts, meals, and other business courtesies for their employees. HCA's policy is to not provide any gifts, entertainment, meals, or anything else of value to any employee of the Executive Branch of the Federal government, except for minor refreshments in connection with business discussions or promotional items with the HCA or facility logo valued at no more than $10.00. With regard to gifts, meals, and other business courtesies involving any other category of government official or employee, you must determine the particular rules applying to any such person and carefully follow them.

Extending Business Courtesies to Possible Referral Sources   Any entertainment or gift involving physicians or other persons who are in a position to refer patients to our healthcare facilities must be undertaken in accordance with corporate policies. We will comply with all Federal laws, regulations, and rules regarding these practices.

Government Relations and Political Activities

The organization and its representatives will comply with all Federal, state and local laws governing participation in government relations and political activities. Additionally, HCA funds or resources will not be contributed directly to individual political campaigns, political parties or other organizations which intend to use the funds primarily for political campaign objectives. Organization resources include financial and non-financial donations such as using work time and telephones to solicit for a political cause or candidate or the loaning of HCA property for use in the political campaign. The conduct of any political action committee is to be consistent with relevant laws and regulations. In addition, political action committees associated with the organization will select candidates to support based on the overall ability of the candidate to render meaningful public service. The organization will not select candidates to support as a reflection of expected support of the candidate on any specific issue.

The organization will engage in public policy debate only in a limited number of instances where it has special expertise that can inform the public policy formulation process. When the organization is directly impacted by public policy decisions, it may provide relevant, factual information about the impact of such decisions on the private sector. In articulating positions, the organization will only take positions that it believes can be shown to be in the larger public interest. The organization will encourage trade associations with which it is associated to do the same.

It is important to separate personal and corporate political activities in order to comply with the appropriate rules and regulations relating to lobbying or attempting to influence government officials. No use of corporate resources, including e-mail, is appropriate for personally engaging in political activity. You may, of course, participate in the political process on your own time and at your own expense. While you are doing so, it is important not to give the impression you are speaking on behalf of or representing HCA in these activities. You cannot seek to be reimbursed by HCA for any personal contributions for such purposes.

At times, HCA may ask colleagues to make personal contact with government officials or to write letters to present our position on specific issues. In addition, it is a part of the role of some HCA management to interface on a regular basis with government officials. If you are making these communications on behalf of the organization, be certain that you are familiar with any regulatory constraints and observe them. Guidance is always available from the Corporate Government Relations and Legal Departments as necessary.

The Corporate Ethics and Compliance Program

Program Structure   The Corporate Ethics and Compliance Program is intended to demonstrate in the clearest possible terms the absolute commitment of the organization to the highest standards of ethics and compliance. The elements of the program include setting standards (the Code and Policies and Procedures), communicating the standards, providing a mechanism for reporting potential exceptions, monitoring and auditing, and maintaining an organizational structure that supports the furtherance of the program.

These elements are supported at all levels of the organization. There is an oversight committee of the Board of the Directors; a Senior Vice President for Ethics, Compliance and Corporate Responsibility, who serves as the Corporate Ethics and Compliance Officer; a Corporate Ethics and Compliance Steering Committee consisting of senior management; a Corporate Ethics and Compliance Policy Committee consisting of senior management and three facility CEOs; and Responsible Executives. Collectively, these groups and individuals are responsible for the development of the Ethics and Compliance Program, including the creation and distribution of ethics and compliance standards; the development and delivery of ethics and compliance training; auditing and monitoring compliance with laws, regulations, conditions of participation and policies; and providing a mechanism for reporting exceptions.

At the facility level, there are Facility Ethics and Compliance Officers and Facility Ethics and Compliance Committees. These are responsible for implementation of the Ethics and Compliance Program in each of our facilities.

All of these individuals or groups are prepared to support you in meeting the standards set forth in this Code. Membership lists for each of the Corporate entities and the Facility ECOs can be found at the Ethics and Compliance site on the organization's Intranet and external web site.

Resources for Guidance and Reporting Violations
To obtain guidance on an ethics or compliance issue or to report a suspected violation, you may choose from several options. We encourage the resolution of issues, including human resources-related issues (*e.g.,* payroll, fair treatment and disciplinary issues), at a local level whenever possible. You may want to use the human resources-related problem solving procedure at your facility to resolve such issues. It is an expected good practice, when you are comfortable with it and think it appropriate under the circumstances, to raise concerns first with your supervisor. If this is uncomfortable or inappropriate, another option is to discuss the situation with your Facility ECO or another member of management at your facility or in your organization. You are always free to contact the Ethics Line at 1-800-455-1996.

HCA will make every effort to maintain, within the limits of the law, the confidentiality of the identity of any individual who reports possible misconduct. There will be no retribution or discipline for anyone who reports a possible violation in good faith. Any colleague who deliberately makes a false accusation with the purpose of harming or retaliating against another colleague will be subject to discipline.

Personal Obligation to Report We are committed to ethical and legal conduct that is compliant with all relevant laws and regulations and to correcting wrongdoing wherever it may occur in the organization. Each colleague has an individual responsibility for reporting any activity by any colleague, physician, subcontractor, or vendor that appears to violate applicable laws, rules, regulations, or this Code.

Internal Investigations of Reports We are committed to investigating all reported concerns promptly and confidentially to the extent possible. The Corporate Ethics and Compliance Officer will coordinate any findings from the investigations and immediately recommend corrective action or changes that need to be made. We expect all colleagues to cooperate with investigation efforts.

Corrective Action Where an internal investigation substantiates a reported violation, it is the policy of the organization to initiate corrective action, including, as appropriate, making prompt restitution of any overpayment amounts, notifying the appropriate governmental agency, instituting whatever disciplinary action is necessary, and implementing systemic changes to prevent a similar violation from recurring in the future at any HCA facility.

Discipline All violators of the Code will be subject to disciplinary action. The precise discipline utilized will depend on the nature, severity, and frequency of the violation and may result in any or all of the following disciplinary actions:

- Oral warning;
- Written warning;
- Written reprimand;
- Suspension;
- Termination;
- Restitution.

Internal Auditing and Other Monitoring HCA is committed to monitoring compliance with its policies. Much of this monitoring effort is provided by the Internal Audit & Consulting Services Department, which routinely conducts internal audits of issues that have regulatory or compliance implications. The organization also routinely seeks other means of ensuring and demonstrating compliance with laws, regulations, and HCA policies. Additionally, facilities regularly conduct self-audits pursuant to compliance policies and procedures, and Responsible Executives routinely undertake monitoring efforts in support of those policies and compliance in general.

Acknowledgment Process HCA requires all colleagues to sign an acknowledgment confirming they have received the Code, understand it represents mandatory policies of HCA and agree to abide by it. New colleagues will be required to sign this acknowledgment as a condition of employment. Each HCA colleague is also required to participate in annual Code of Conduct training, and records of such training must be retained by each facility.

Adherence to and support of HCA's Code of Conduct and participation in related activities and training will be considered in decisions regarding hiring, promotion, and compensation for all candidates and colleagues. New colleagues must receive Code of Conduct training within 30 days of employment.

AstraZeneca Code of Conduct*

Policy

The Group requires its companies, and their employees, to observe high standards of integrity and honesty and act with due skill, care, diligence and fairness in the conduct of business.

To this end all Group companies, and their employees, are required to comply with the laws of all countries in which they operate and with the high ethical standards detailed by the Group in support of this policy.

Compliance

It is the responsibility of management to ensure that the Group Code of Conduct and standards are com-

---

Copyright © 1999–2000 AstraZeneca. Reprinted with permission.

municated, understood and acted upon. They must positively promote them by personal example and are not entitled to permit exceptions to the required behaviour.

All employees should familiarise themselves with the Code of Conduct and must comply with it. Failure to act in compliance with the Code is likely to result in disciplinary action against both the employee committing the breach and others who condone it.

The Standards set out in the code are general and do not address each and every situation that may confront employees in markets around the world. Guidance on the application of the Code to particular situations should be sought from management. In addition, Legal Department and Group Internal Audit are available on a confidential basis as independent sources of advice. Where confidential phone lines are available, these should be used to raise issues of concern. So long as this is done in good faith, the Group assures individual employees who raise issues that they will be protected from any adverse impact on their employment as a result.

Standards of Conduct

Business Practices   *Group Companies, and their employees, should comply with the laws of all countries in which they operate, with appropriate international and national industry codes of practice and with the high ethical standards specified by the Group.*

It is the responsibility of all employees to ensure, by taking advice where appropriate, that they are fully aware of all relevant laws, practices and codes of practice. While this standard applies without exception, particular areas where compliance must be ensured are laws concerned with competition, employment, new product research and development, manufacturing, marketing and selling and safety, health and the environment.

Employees should ensure that, within their sphere of business activity, Group Companies carry out their contractual obligations in a proper and timely manner and are not in breach of contract.

Business practice, and what amounts to improper conduct, varies from country to country and from industry to industry. All employees will comply with (a) the high ethical standards specified by the Group (b) any overall AstraZeneca Code published relating to business practices and (c) any international and national codes of practice applicable to the conduct of business in each environment.

Gifts, entertainment and personal favours may only be offered to a third party if they are consistent with customary business practice and not in contravention of any applicable law or code of practice.

No employee should seek or accept a gift, entertainment or personal favour which might reasonably be believed to have a significant influence on business transactions. An offer of entertainment must not be accepted unless the offer is within the bounds of accepted business hospitality. Gifts which do not meet the above criteria should be reported to management who shall determine how they shall be dealt with.

Group funds should not be used in payments, direct or indirect, to government officials, people participating in government bodies, employees of state organisations or representatives of political parties, for unlawful or improper purposes.

Equal Opportunities   *All employees should be treated with equal respect and dignity and should be provided with equality of opportunity to develop themselves and their careers.*

AstraZeneca values the individuality, diversity and creative potential that every employee brings to its business and supports the continuous development of their skills and abilities.

Judgments about people for the purpose of recruitment, development or promotion should be made solely on the basis of a person's ability and potential in relation to the needs of the job and should take no account of any matter not relevant to the performance of that job. Overall, success and advancement within the Group should depend solely on personal ability and work performance.

In some countries these principles may be modified by national legal requirements for positive discrimination.

Personal Harassment   *Conduct involving the harassment of any employee of the Group, its suppliers or customers is unacceptable. In particular, sexual harassment will not be tolerated.*

Any person who believes they have been personally harassed should report the incident and circumstances to their immediate manager or personal manager or other senior manager who will arrange for it to be investigated impartially and confidentially.

AstraZeneca is fully supportive of the principles set forth in the UN Declaration of Human Rights. These include freedom from torture and arbitrary arrest, the right to a fair trial and equality before the law.

Political Contributions   *Any political contributions by Group companies must be lawful and approved under procedures laid down by the board or governing body of the company concerned.*

Approval should not be given to any political contributions which, by their scale or affiliation, might embarrass the Group. The Group's accounting procedures require any political contributions to be reported to Group headquarters as part of the annual consolidation of results.

Conflicts of Interest   *Employees dealing with the Group's business must act in the best interests of the Group and must disregard any personal preference or advantage.*

Employees should avoid entering into situations in which their personal, family or financial interests may conflict with those of the AstraZeneca Group. Where any potential conflict of interest may arise, the employee should declare that interest and seek advice from senior management.

Examples of conflict that must be declared and resolved include:

- having a family interest in a transaction with AstraZeneca or one of its subsidiaries (the Company) or any supplier or customer;

- hiring of a family member in any capacity;

- having an interest in a competitor, supplier or customer of the Company;

- having an interest in an organisation that has, or seeks to do business with the Company;

- acquiring an interest in property (such as real estate, patent rights or securities) where the Company has, or might have, an interest.

These examples do not extend to normal financial investments in publicly quoted companies.

Insider Information   *Employees must not use confidential information obtained through their employment for personal gain.*

It is AstraZeneca policy, and in certain countries a legal requirement carrying criminal sanctions, that employees in possession of confidential 'price sensitive' information (in relation to securities) must not make use of such information to deal in securities of AstraZeneca or provide such information to third parties for that purpose. The same considerations apply in relation to confidential 'price sensitive' information relating to other companies and dealing in their securities.

Group Property and Resources   *Group resources should be kept securely and should only be applied for the proper advancement of its business and not for personal gain.*

Individuals expending Group resources should recognise that they owe a duty of care to the shareholders of the Group, who are its ultimate owners. Commitments and expenditure should only be such as could be justified to shareholders if the facts were known.

Group resources include not only tangible assets such as materials, equipment and cash, but also intangible assets such as computer systems, trade secrets and confidential information. Employees must observe Group and local guidelines concerning the classifying and handling of documents and electronic data. The storage of personal data in an electronic medium may be governed by laws with which relevant employees should familiarise themselves.

Information generated within the Group, including research and development and manufacturing data, costs, prices, sales, profits, markets, customers and methods of doing business, is the property of the Group and should not, unless legally required, be disclosed outside the Group without proper authority.

Group Policies, Delegated Authorities and Reserved Powers   *Group employees are expected to make themselves aware of and comply with the letter and spirit of all Group policies and with the reserved powers and delegated authorities established by the Board from time to time. Copies of these are available on the Company's intranet site.*

The freedoms which individuals have to carry out their jobs should be exercised within both the letter and spirit of Group policies and procedures, reserved powers and delegated authorities. These are designed to empower people to carry out their responsibilities within a necessary framework of corporate control and legal responsibility but are not so voluminous as to prescribe appropriate action in every circumstance. In the exercise of their authorities, individuals must bear Group and legal entity requirements in mind and must surface problems, and consult on issues, which have significant Group implications. When considering whether an issue does require reference to another authority, the overall substance of the issue must be considered and when sharing an issue with another authority all facts relevant to a decision must be fully and fairly presented.

Endnotes

Chapter 1

1. Paul W. Taylor, *Principles of Ethics: An Introduction to Ethics,* 2nd ed. (Encino, Calif.: Dickenson, 1975), p. 1.
2. Copyright © 1996 by Houghton Mifflin Company. Adapted and reproduced from *The American Heritage Dictionary of the English Language,* Third Edition.
3. Wroe Alderson, *Dynamic Marketing Behavior* (Homewood, Ill.: Irwin, 1965), p. 320.
4. Geoffrey Colvin, "America's Most Admired Companies," *Fortune,* February 21, 2000, p. 110.
5. Archie B. Carroll, *Business and Society: Ethics and Stakeholder Management* (Cincinnati, Ohio: South-Western, 1989), pp. 30–33.
6. Joseph T. Hallinan, "High Rollers," *Wall Street Journal,* October 23, 2000, p. Al.
7. "Judge Allows Passengers' Claims to Proceed Against APA for Illegal Sickout," *PR Newswire,* November 17, 1999.
8. Jennifer Rewick, "Connecticut Attorney General Launches Probe of Priceline.com After Complaints," *Wall Street Journal,* October 2, 2000, p. B16.
9. *In the News,* August 2000. http://www.bsr.org/resourcecenter/news/news_output.asp?newsDT=2000-08&hTID=266 (accessed September 18, 2000).
10. Carroll, *Business and Society,* pp. 225–227.
11. Alan R. Yuspeh, "Development of Corporate Compliance Programs: Lessons Learned from the DII Experience," in *Corporate Crime in America: Strengthening the "Good Citizenship" Corporation* (Washington, D.C.: U.S. Sentencing Commission, 1995), pp. 71–79.
12. *1999 Annual Report,* http://www.dii.org (accessed October 19, 2000).
13. Eleanor Hill, "Coordinating Enforcement Under the Department of Defense Voluntary Disclosure Program," in *Corporate Crime in America: Strengthening the "Good Citizenship" Corporation* (Washington, D.C.: U.S. Sentencing Commission, 1995), pp. 287–294.
14. "Huffing and Puffing in Washington: Can Clinton's Plan Curb Teen Smoking?" *Consumer Reports,* 60 (October 1995): 637.
15. Richard P. Conaboy, "Corporate Crime in America: Strengthening the Good Citizen Corporation," in *Corporate Crime in America: Strengthening the "Good Citizenship" Corporation* (Washington, D.C.: U.S. Sentencing Commission, 1995), pp. 1–2.
16. *United States Code Service* (Lawyers Edition), 18 U.S.C.S. Appendix, Sentencing Guidelines for the United States Courts (Rochester, N.Y.: Lawyers Cooperative Publishing, 1995), § 8A.1.
17. Terry W. Loe and O. C. Ferrell, "Ethical Climate's Relationship to Trust, Market Orientation and Commitment to Quality: A Single Firm Study," paper presented at the Academy of Marketing Science annual conference, May 1997.
18. Gary R. Weaver and Linda K. Trevino, "Compliance and Values Oriented Ethics Programs: Influence on Employees' Attitudes and Behavior," *Business Ethics Quarterly,* 9(2) (1999): 315.
19. Ethics Resource Center, *2000 National Business Ethics Survey, How Employees Perceive Ethics at Work,* pp. 4, 28, 29.
20. "Today's Briefing," *Commercial Appeal,* March 2, 2000, p. C1.
21. "Time, Inc., Agrees to Pay $4.9 Million to Settle Sweepstakes Complaint," *Wall Street Journal,* August 25, 2000, p. C20.
22. "Employee Stole Secrets, Wal-Mart Suit Alleges," *Commercial Appeal,* July 30, 2000, p. B8.
23. Penelope Patsuris, "Bid for Surgery Can't Cut It," *Forbes.com.* http://www.forbes.com/2000/03/10/feat.html (accessed October 13, 2000).
24. "U.S. Equal Employment Opportunity Commission: An Overview." *http://www.eeoc.gov/overview.html,* November 3, 1997 (accessed October 12, 2000).
25. Peter Brimelow, "Is Sexual Harassment Getting Worse?" *Forbes,* April 19, 1999.
26. Ellen Pierce, Carol A. Smolinski, and Benson Rosen, "Why Sexual Harassment Complaints Fall on Deaf Ears," *The Academy of Management Executive,* 12 (August 1998): 41.

27. Michelle Kessler, "Harassment Decreases in Mitsubishi Plant," *USA Today,* September 7, 2000, p. B1.

28. Michael Schroeder, Ruth Simon, and Aaron Elstein, "Teenage Trade Runs Afoul of the SEC as Stock Touting Draws Charges of Fraud," *Wall Street Journal,* September 21, 2000, pp. C1, C17.

29. Scott Kilman and Devon Spurgeon, "Safeway Recalls Its Taco-Shell Brand On Charge It Contains Unapproved Corn," *Wall Street Journal,* October 12, 2000, p. A8.

Chapter 2

1. Ellen E. Schultz, "Retirees Found Varity Untruthful," *Wall Street Journal,* November 6, 2000, p. C1.

2. The Ethics Resource Center, *2000 National Business Ethics Survey: How Employees Perceive Ethics at Work,* p. 34.

3. Ibid., p. 41.

4. Michael Schroeder, "SEC Probes Andersen for Conflict of Interest," *Wall Street Journal,* August 25, 2000, p. C1.

5. Jenny Summerour, "Bribery Game," *Progressive Grocer,* January 2000, p. 43.

6. "Fuji Heavy Chairman Questioned in Bribery Case," *Kyodo News Service,* November 27, 1998.

7. Gregory Zuckerman, "Insurer Cites Bond-Trade Kickbacks," *Wall Street Journal,* May 30, 2000, pp. C1, C2.

8. Ernest Beck, "Stores Told to Lift Prices in Germany," *Wall Street Journal,* September 11, 2000, p. A27.

9. Vernon R. Loucks, Jr., "A CEO Looks at Ethics," *Business Horizons,* 30 (March–April 1987): 4.

10. Shailagh Murray and Lucette Lagnado, "Drug Companies Face Assault on Prices," *Wall Street Journal,* May 11, 2000, p. B1.

11. Eric H. Beversluis, "Is There No Such Thing as Business Ethics?" *Journal of Business Ethics,* 6 (February 1987): 81–88. Reprinted by permission of Kluwer Academic Publishers, Dordrecht, Holland.

12. Ibid., p. 82.

13. The Ethics Resource Center, *2000 National Business Ethics Survey,* p. 45.

14. Lindsey Tanner, "Doctors Admit They Have Lied to Insurers," *Fort Collins Coloradoan,* April 12, 2000, p. B1.

15. James Heckman, "Puffery Claims No Longer So Easy to Make," *Marketing News,* February 14, 2000, p. 6.

16. Sara Nathan, "Phony Jobs," *USA Today,* March 7, 2000, p. B1.

17. Russell Mokhiber, "Warning Signs," *Business Ethics,* May/June 1999, p. 8.

18. "Mott's Will Rewrite Some Labels Blamed for Misleading People," *Wall Street Journal,* August 2, 2000, p. B7.

19. "AT&T Settles Lawsuit Against Reseller Accused of Slamming," *Business Wire,* May 26, 1998 (from America Online newswire search).

20. Archie B. Carroll, *Business and Society: Ethics and Stakeholder Management* (Cincinnati, Ohio: South-Western, 1989), pp. 228–230.

21. Privacy (Employee). *http://www.bsr.org/resource center/topic_output.asp?topicID=574,* p. 3 (accessed September 18, 2000).

22. Quoted in John Galvin, "The New Business Ethics," *SmartBusinessMag.com,* June 2000, p. 86.

23. Ibid, p. 97.

24. "Privacy (Employee),"p. 2.

25. Julene Snyder, "Should Overworked Employees Be Allowed to Surf the Web on the Job?" *CNN.com* (accessed May 11, 2000).

26. Galvin, "The New Business Ethics," p. 97.

27. "Ethical Issues in the Employer–Employee Relationship," Society of Financial Service Professionals. *http://www.financialpro.org/sfsp/Press/ ethics/ es2000/Ethics_Survey_2000_Report_FINAL .html,* p. 6 (accessed October 11, 2000).

28. "Sprint Phone-Tracking Chip Raises Privacy Issues, WSJ Reports," *Bloomberg News,* November 10, 2000.

29. Eve M. Caudill and Patrick E. Murphy, "Consumer Online Privacy: Legal and Ethical Issues," *Journal of Public Policy & Marketing,* 19 (1) (Spring 2000): 7.

30. Ibid., p. 18.

31. Galvin, "The New Business Ethics," p. 98.

32. Margaret Littman, "How Marketers Track Underage Consumers," *Marketing News,* May 8, 2000. pp. 4, 7.

33. Galvin, "The New Business Ethics," pp. 89, 97.

34. Anna Wilde Mathews, "Copyrights on Web Content Are Backed," *Wall Street Journal,* October 27, 2000, p. B10.

35. "Today's Briefing," *Commercial Appeal,* November 15, 2000, p. C1.

36. "Weyerhaeuser Achievement in Pollution Prevention Recognized," *Business Wire,* May 21, 1998 (from America Online newswire search); and Robert Weller, "Louisiana-Pacific Fined $37 Million," May 28, 1998 (from America Online newswire search).

37. Bruce Meyerson, "'Send,' Not 'Hello,' Starts Meter on Cell-Phone Call," *Fort Collins Coloradoan,* July 7, 1999, p. A1.

38. Elizabeth Douglas, "PUC Head Contests PacBell Ruling," *Los Angeles Times,* January 28, 2000, p. C2.

39. Jayne O'Donnell and Paul Davidson, "Charges Ready for 10 More Vitamin Makers," *USA Today,* June 17, 1999, p. B1.

40. Kalpana Srinivasan, "Supplier of Shoes Settles Antitrust Lawsuit," *Commercial Appeal,* March 7, 2000, p. B12.

41. Schroeder, "SEC Probes Andersen," p. C1.

42. Michael Hirsh and Kenneth Klee, "Ubiquity and Its Burdens," *Newsweek International.* http://newsweek.com/nw-srv/printed/int/sr/a54645-2000jan24.htm (accessed June 6, 2000).

43. Philip Johanson, "25 Sizzling SRI Funds That Beat a Tough Market," *Business Ethics,* July/August 2000, p. 18.

44. Steve Stecklow, "False Profit: How New Era's Boss Led Rich and Gullible into a Web of Deceit," *Wall Street Journal,* May 19, 1995, pp. A1, A4.

45. Barbara Carton, "Unlikely Hero: A Persistent Accountant Brought New Era's Problems to Light," *Wall Street Journal,* May 19, 1995, pp. B1, B6.

46. Robert Allen and Marshall B. Romney, "Lessons from New Era," *Internal Auditor,* October 1998, p. 40.

47. Galvin, "The New Business Ethics," p. 90.

48. Calmetta, Coleman, "Sticky Fingers," *Wall Street Journal,* September 8, 2000 Al, A6.

49. Ibid.

50. "Merrill Lynch Settles Gender Discrimination Lawsuit," *PR Newswire,* May 4, 1998 (from America Online newswire search).

51. Jef Feeley, "Shareholder Suing to Fight Swallowing Hilton Poison Pill," *Commercial Appeal,* March 1, 2000, p. C6.

52. "More Online and Offline Surveillance in the Workplace," Business for Social Responsibility Global Business Responsibility Resource Center. *In the News.* http://www.bsr.org/resourcecenter/news/news_output.asp?newsDT=2000-08&hTID=266 (accessed September 18, 2000).

53. Ibid.

54. "PlanetRx.com Endorses the Highest Standards of Online Conduct," *PRNewswire.* http://www.prnewswire.com (accessed May 8, 2000).

55. "Protecting What Is Precious: Privacy," *Business Ethics,* March/April 2000, p. 10.

56. "Mitsubishi Electric Reveals TV Dangers After 8-Year Silence," *Wall Street Journal,* September 13, 2000, p. A21.

57. Quoted in "Cut Down: Timber Town Is Bitter over Efforts to Save the Rare Spotted Owl," *Wall Street Journal,* January 6, 1992, pp. A1, A8.

58. Betsy McKay, "Coke Begins Talks with Mexico to Avoid Legal Fight over Its Marketing Practices," *Wall Street Journal,* August 28, 2000, p. A4.

59. Murray and Lagnado, "Drug Companies Face Assault."

60. Rhonda L. Rundle, "SEC Files Securities Fraud Suits; Executives Also Face Indictments," *Wall Street Journal,* September 28, 2000, p. B18.

Chapter 3

1. James R. Rest, *Moral Development Advances in Research and Theory* (New York: Praeger, 1986), p. 1.

2. Abhijit Biswas, Jane W. Licata, Daryl McKee, Chris Pullig, and Christopher Daughtridge, "The Recycling Cycle: An Empirical Examination of Consumer Waste Recycling and Recycling Shopping Behaviors," *Journal of Public Policy & Marketing,* 19(1) (Spring 2000): 93.

3. John Fraedrich and O. C. Ferrell, "Cognitive Consistency of Marketing Managers in Ethical Situations," *Journal of the Academy of Marketing Science,* 20 (Summer 1992): 245–252.

4. Manuel Velasquez, Claire Andre, Thomas Shanks, S.J., and Michael J. Meyer, "Thinking Ethically: A Framework for Moral Decision Making," *Issues in Ethics* (Winter 1996): 2–5.

5. Leslie Cauley "AT&T to Offer Hard-Core Adult Movies in Drive for Digital-Cable Subscribers," *Wall Street Journal,* May 31, 2000, p. B16.

6. Erin White, "Study on Teen Readership of Magazines May Step Up Pressure on Tobacco Firms," *Wall Street Journal,* October 31, 2000, p. A8.

7. "Court Says Businesses Liable for Harassing on the Job," *Commercial Appeal,* June 27, 1998, p. A-1.

8. Ibid.

9. Richard Brandt, *Ethical Theory* (Englewood Cliffs, N.J.: Prentice-Hall, 1959), pp. 253–254.

10. J. J. C. Smart and B. Williams, *Utilitarianism: For and Against* (Cambridge, England: Cambridge University Press, 1973), p. 4.

11. C. E. Harris, Jr., *Applying Moral Theories* (Belmont, Calif.: Wadsworth, 1986), pp. 127–128.

12. Immanuel Kant, "Fundamental Principles of the Metaphysics of Morals," in *Problems of Moral Philosophy: An Introduction*, 2nd ed., ed. Paul W. Taylor (Encino, Calif.: Dickenson, 1972), p. 229.

13. Example adapted from Harris, *Applying Moral Theories*, pp. 128–129.

14. Gerald F. Cavanaugh, Dennis J. Moberg, and Manuel Velasquez, "The Ethics of Organizational Politics," *Academy of Management Review*, 6 (July 1981): 363–374.

15. Kant, "Fundamental Principles," p. 229.

16. Thomas E. Weber, "To Opt In or Opt Out: That Is the Question When Mulling Privacy," *Wall Street Journal*, October 23, 2000, p. B1.

17. Manuel G. Velasquez, *Business Ethics Concepts and Cases*, 4th ed. (Upper Saddle River, N.J.: Prentice-Hall, 1998), pp. 132–133.

18. Ibid.

19. Ian Maitland, "Virtuous Markets: The Market as School of the Virtues," *Business Ethics Quarterly*, January 1997, p. 97.

20. Surendra Arjoon, "Virtue Theory as a Dynamic Theory of Business," *Journal of Business Ethics*, 28 (May 2000): 159.

21. Maitland,"Virtuous Markets," p. 97.

22. Stefanie E. Naumann and Nathan Bennett, "A Case for Procedural Justice Climate: Development and Test of A Multilevel Model," *Academy of Management Journal*, 43(5) (October 2000): 881–889.

23. Company News, *Business Ethics* (November–December 1998): 5.

24. Naumann and Bennett, "A Case for Procedural Justice Climate."

25. Company News, p. 5.

26. "Wainwright Bank and Trust Company Award for Social Justice Inside and Out," *Business Ethics* (November–December 1998): 11.

27. "Company News," p. 5.

Chapter 4

1. Archie B. Carroll, "The Pyramid of Corporate Social Responsibility: Toward the Moral Management of Organizational Stakeholders," *Business Horizons* (July–August 1991): 42.

2. Isabelle Maignan, O.C. Ferrell, and G. Tomas M. Hult, "Corporate Citizenship: Cultural Antecedents and Business Benefits," *Journal of the Academy of Marketing Science*, 27(4) (Fall 1999): 457.

3. Joann Muller, "Ford: The High Cost of Harassment," *Business Week*, November 15, 1999, pp. 94–96.

4. John Greenwald, "Lloyd's of London Falling Down," *Time*, February 28, 2000, pp. 54–60.

5. "A Child Shall Lead the Way: Marketing to Youths," *Credit Union Executive* (May–June 1993): 6–8.

6. "Federal Web Sites Ignore Children's Privacy Law," *Commercial Appeal*, October 7, 2000, p. A7.

7. Otto Krusius, "From Out of the Mouses of Babes," *Kiplinger's*, November 2000, p. 32.

8. "Federal Web Sites."

9. "Bristol-Myers Squibb Tops List of Eco-Friendly Companies," *PRNewswire*. http://www.prnewswire.com (accessed August 18, 2000).

10. From the General Motors' Corporation web site. *http://www.gmev.com* (accessed November 21, 2000).

11. CNN News, "Not in My Backyard," CNN Special Report, December 19, 1988.

12. Dave Bryan, "Royal Caribbean Guards Against Pollution." *http://www.usatoday.com/life/travel/lt092.htm* (accessed October 13, 2000).

13. John Yaukey, "Discarded Computers Create Waste Problem." *http://www.usatoday.com/news/ndsmonl4.htm* (accessed October 13, 2000).

14. Matthew Barakat, "Women Closing Up Pay Gap, Most Still Lag Men, *Commerical Appeal*, July 5, 2000, p. C1.

15. Win Swenson, "The Organizational Guidelines' 'Carrot and Stick' Philosophy, and Their Focus on 'Effective' Compliance," in *Corporate Crime in America: Strengthening the "Good Citizenship" Corporation* (Washington, D.C.: U.S. Sentencing Commission, 1995), pp. 17–26.

16. *United States Code Service* (Lawyers Edition), 18 U.S.C.S. Appendix, Sentencing Guidelines for the United States Courts (Rochester, N.Y.: Lawyers Cooperative Publishing, 1995), § 8A.1.

17. Lynn Sharp Paine, "Managing for Organizational Integrity," *Harvard Business Review* (March–April 1994): 111.

18. Tom Klusmann, "The 100 Best Corporate Citizens," *Business Ethics,* March/April 2000, p. 13.

19. G. A. Steiner and J. F. Steiner, *Business, Government, and Society* (New York: Random House, 1988).

20. Milton Friedman, "Social Responsibility of Business Is to Increase Its Profits," *New York Times Magazine,* September 13, 1970, pp. 122–126.

21. 1997 Cone/Roper Cause-Related Marketing Trends in "Does It Pay to Be Ethical?" *Business Ethics* (March–April 1997): 15.

22. Isabelle Maignan, "Antecedents and Benefits of Corporate Citizenship: A Comparison of U.S. and French Businesses," unpublished Ph.D. dissertation, University of Memphis, 1997.

23. Ibid.

24. Excerpted from R. Edward Freeman and Daniel R. Gilbert, Jr., *Corporate Strategy and the Search for Ethics* (Englewood Cliffs, N.J.: Prentice-Hall, 1988), pp. 7, 90, 105. Reprinted by permission.

25. Ibid. Reprinted by permission.

26. Ibid., p. 7. Reprinted by permission.

27. Ibid., p. 7. Reprinted by permission.

28. Michael Arndt, Wendy Zellner, and Peter Coy, "Too Much Corporate Power," *Business Week,* September 11, 2000, p. 148.

29. Ibid.

30. Ibid., p. 150.

31. Stephen R. Covey, *The 7 Habits of Highly Effective People* (New York: Simon and Schuster, 1990).

32. Arndt, Zellner, and Peter Coy, "Too Much Corporate Power," *Business Week,* September 11, 2000, p. 149.

33. Ibid.

34. Ibid., p. 154.

35. Graef Crystal, "Conseco Pays Dearly to Rid Itself of Failing Chief," *Commercial Appeal,* May 16, 2000, p. B6.

36. Gregory T. Gundlach, "Price Predation: Legal Limits and Antitrust Considerations," *Journal of Public Policy & Marketing,* 14 (Fall 1995): 278.

37. Quoted in "Software Publishers Association Applauds Department of Justice Antitrust Competition Action; Department Acts in Support of Software Industry Competition Principles," *PR Newswire,* May 18, 1998.

38. "Store Files Antitrust Lawsuit Against Microsoft," *PR Newswire,* May 18, 1998.

39. This section is adapted from Ingrid Murro Botero, "Charitable Giving Has 4 Big Benefits," *The Business Journal of Phoenix,* January 1, 1999. http://www.bizjournals.com/phoenix/stories/1999/01/04/smallb3.html (accessed November 1, 2000).

40. "Cisco Systems to Provide Technology Assistance for Non-Profit Community Organizations in Massachusetts, New Hampshire," Cisco press release. *http://www.cisco.com/warp/public/146/pressroom/2000/oct00/corp_100400.htm* (accessed November 1, 2000).

41. "Career Opportunities in Finance: Corporate Citizenship." *http://www.merck.com/careers/finance/citizenship.html* (accessed November 1, 2000).

42. "Corporate Community Relations." http://www.ibm.com/ibm/ibmgives/ (accessed November 1, 2000).

43. Adapted from O. C. Ferrell and Geoffrey Hirt, *Business: A Changing World* (Homewood, Ill.: Richard D. Irwin, Inc., in a joint venture with Austen Press, 1993), pp. 45–46. Reprinted with permission of The McGraw-Hill Companies, Inc.

44. "Business Bulletin," *Wall Street Journal,* May 25, 2000, p. Al.

45. Klusmann, "The 100 Best Corporate Citizens."

46. Ibid.

47. Ibid.

48. "Sara Lee Corp. Donates Its Art Collection to Various Museums," *Bloomberg Newswire,* June 3, 1998.

49. "Worth Magazine Ranks America's Most Generous Companies," *Fund Raising Management,* January 2000, p. 18.

50. From the Hewlett-Packard web site. *http://www.corp.hp.com/grants/* (accessed January 24, 2000).

51. "McDonald's Employees Honor Ray Kroc's Birthday by Giving Back to Communities Natiowide," *PR Newswire,* http://www.prnewswire.com/cgi-bin/stories.pl?ACCT=104&story=/www/story/10-03-2000/0001328811&EDATE= (accessed October 13, 2000).

Chapter 5

1. Thomas M. Jones, "Ethical Decision Making by Individuals in Organizations: An Issue-Contingent Model," *Academy of Management Review,* 16 (February 1991): 366–395; O. C. Ferrell and Larry G. Gresham, "A Contingency Framework for Understanding Ethical Decision Making in Marketing," *Journal of Marketing,* 49 (Summer 1985):

87–96; O. C. Ferrell, Larry G. Gresham, and John Fraedrich, "A Synthesis of Ethical Decision Models for Marketing," *Journal of Macromarketing,* 9 (Fall 1989): 55–64; Shelby D. Hunt and Scott Vitell, "A General Theory of Marketing Ethics," *Journal of Macromarketing,* 6 (Spring 1986): 5–16; William A. Kahn, "Toward an Agenda for Business Ethics Research," *Academy of Management Review,* 15 (April 1990): 311–328; Linda K. Trevino, "Ethical Decision Making in Organizations: A Person-Situation Interactionist Model," *Academy of Management Review,* 11 (March 1986): 601–617.

2. Jones, "Ethical Decision Making," pp. 367, 372.

3. Donald P. Robin, R. Eric Reidenbach, and P. J. Forrest, "The Perceived Importance of an Ethical Issue as an Influence on the Ethical Decision-Making of Ad Managers," *Journal of Business Research,* 35 (January 1996): 17.

4. Anusorn Singhapakdi, Scott J. Vitell, and George R. Franke, "Antecedents, Consequences, and Mediating Effects of Perceived Moral Intensity and Personal Moral Philosophies," *Journal of the Academy of Marketing Science,* 27(1) (winter, 1999): 19.

5. Robin, Reidenbach, and Forrest, "The Perceived Importance."

6. Singhapakdi, Vitell, and Franke, "Antecedents."

7. Robin, Reidenbach, and Forrest, "The Perceived Importance."

8. Cora Daniels, "How to Love a Bad Report Card," *Fortune,* July 10, 2000, p. 189.

9. "When Racial Discrimination Takes Hidden Forms," *Business Ethics,* July/August 2000, p. 7.

10. Robin, Reidenbach, and Forrest, "The Perceived Importance," p. 17.

11. Lawrence Kohlberg, "Stage and Sequence: The Cognitive Developmental Approach to Socialization," in *Handbook of Socialization Theory and Research,* ed. D. A. Goslin (Chicago: Rand McNally, 1969), pp. 347–480.

12. Ibid.

13. Glenn R. Simpson, "Raytheon Offers Office Software for Snooping," *Wall Street Journal,* June 14, 2000, pp. B1, B4.

14. Kohlberg, "Stage and Sequence."

15. Harvey S. James, Jr., "Reinforcing Ethical Decision Making Through Organizational Structure," *Journal of Business Ethics,* 28 (November 2000): 45.

16. The Ethics Resource Center, *2000 National Business Ethics Survey: How Employees Perceive Ethics at Work,* p. 18.

17. Ibid., p. 19.

18. Ibid., p. 20.

19. George Izzo, "Compulsory Ethics Education and the Cognitive Moral Development of Salespeople: A Quasi-Experimental Assessment," *Journal of Business Ethics,* 28 (December 2000): 223.

20. John Fraedrich and O. C. Ferrell, "Cognitive Consistency of Marketing Managers in Ethical Situations," *Journal of the Academy of Marketing Science,* 20 (Summer 1992), 245–252.

21. John Fraedrich, Debbie M. Thorne, and O. C. Ferrell, "Assessing the Application of Cognitive Moral Development Theory to Business Ethics," *Journal of Business Ethics,* 13 (1994): 829–838.

22. Ibid.

23. James, "Reinforcing Ethical Decision Making."

24. Ann Harrington, "Prevention Is the Best Defense," *Fortune,* July 10, 2000, p. 188.

25. "Coca-Cola Announces Plan to Put $1 Billion in Diversity Programs," *Wall Street Journal,* May 17, 2000, p. B10.

26. Richard T. De George, *Business Ethics,* 3rd ed. (New York: Macmillan, 1990), pp. 14, 26–27, 40, 63, 79–80, 83–85, 105–108, 160–178.

27. Margaret H. Cunningham and O. C. Ferrell, "Ethical Decision-Making Behavior in Marketing Research Organizations," working paper, School of Business, Queen's University, Kingston, Ontario, 1999.

28. Ferrell and Gresham, "A Contingency Framework," pp. 87–96.

29. The Ethics Resource Center, *2000 National Business Ethics Survey,* p. 33.

30. Ibid.

31. Deborah M. Clubb, "DuPont Must Pay in Sexual Harassment Suit from '98," *Commercial Appeal,* May 27, 2000, p. B1.

32. Cunningham and Ferrell, "Ethical Decision-Making Behavior."

33. "How Employees Make Workers Happy," *USA Today Snapshot,* June 14, 2000.

34. Marilyn Adams, "Some Airlines Stretch Truth in Advertising," *USA Today,* April 5, 2000, p. B1.

35. "Reeve's Ad Touches a Nerve," *Commercial Appeal,* February 2, 2000, p. A6.

36. Nick Wingfield, "DoubleClick Moves to Appoint Panel for Privacy Issues," *Wall Street Journal,* May 17, 2000, p. B10.

Chapter 6

1. Louis P. White and Long W. Lam, "A Proposed In-frastructural Model for the Establishment of Organizational Ethical Systems," *Journal of Business Ethics,* 28 (November 1, 2000): 35–42.

2. Michael Hirsh and Kenneth Klee, "Ubiquity and Its Burdens." *http://newsweek.com/nw-srv/printed/int/sr/a54645-2000jan24.htm* (accessed June 6, 2000).

3. Gary Edmondson, Kate Carlisle, Inka Resch, Karen Anhalt, and Heidi Dawley, "Human Bondage," *Business Week,* November 27, 2000, pp. 147–160.

4. Peter D. Bennett, ed., *Dictionary of Marketing Terms* (Chicago: American Marketing Association, 1988), p. 45. Reprinted by permission.

5. Richard L. Daft, *Organizational Theory and Design* (St. Paul, Minn.: West Publishing, 1983), p. 482.

6. Stanley M. Davis, quoted in Alyse Lynn Booth, "Who Are We?" *Public Relations Journal* (July 1985): 13–18.

7. T. E. Deal and A. A. Kennedy, *Corporate Culture: Rites and Rituals of Corporate Life* (Reading, Mass.: Addison Wesley, 1982), p. 4.

8. G. Hofstede, "Culture's Consequences: International Differences," in *Work-Related Values* (Beverly Hills, Calif.: Sage Publications, 1980), p. 25.

9. N. M. Tichy, "Managing Change Strategically: The Technical, Political and Cultural Keys," *Organizational Dynamics* (Autumn 1982): 59–80.

10. J. W. Lorsch, "Managing Culture: The Invisible Barrier to Strategic Change," *California Management Review,* 28 (Winter 1986): 95–109.

11. Mutual of Omaha Web site. *http://www.careerlink.org/emp/mut/corp.htm* (accessed October 11, 2000).

12. Ford Motor Company, 1999 Annual Report, pp. 2–3.

13. "Today's Briefing," *Commercial Appeal,* September 5, 2000, p. B4.

14. Chip Cummins, "Workers Wear Feelings on Their Hard Hats and Show True Colors," *Wall Street Journal,* November 7, 2000, p. A1.

15. R. Eric Reidenbach and Donald P. Robin, *Ethics and Profits* (Englewood Cliffs, N.J.: Prentice-Hall, 1989), p. 92.

16. Greg Farrell and Lorrie Grant, "Employee Theft Grows for Retailers," *USA Today,* November 10, 2000, p. B2.

17. "Employers Should Focus on Worker Loyalty to Improve Job Performance, Bottom Line," *BNA Daily Labor Report,* June 1, 2000. http://www.shrm.org/hrnews/articles/bna06016.htm (accessed June 6, 2000).

18. Reidenbach and Robin, *Ethics and Profits,* p. 92.

19. N. K. Sethia and M. A. Von Glinow, "Arriving at Four Cultures by Managing the Reward System," in *Gaining Control of the Corporate Culture* (San Francisco: Jossey-Bass, 1985), p. 409.

20. Marjorie Kelly and Tom Klusmann, "Is IBM Still Socially Responsible?" *Business Ethics,* July/August 2000, pp. 4–5.

21. From Southwest Airlines web site. *http://www.southwest.com/about_swa/press/factsheet.html#Leadership* (accessed October 11, 2000).

22. Barbara Whitaker, "UPS Program Softens Managers' Hearts," *Commercial Appeal,* July 30, 2000, p. E2.

23. Elyse Tanouye, "J&J to Admit to Shredding Retin-A Papers," *Wall Street Journal,* January 11, 1995, pp. B1, B4.

24. Kevin Drawbough, "Columbia/HCA Fires 2 Tenn. Executives in Alleged Scam," *Reuters Newswire,* June 18, 1998 (from America Online newswire service).

25. "Small Virtues: Entrepreneurs Are More Ethical." *http://www.businessweek.com/smallbiz/0003/ib3670029.htm?scriptFramed* (accessed May 8, 2000).

26. John Byrne, "How Al Dunlap Self-Destructed," *Business Week,* July 6, 1998, pp. 44–45.

27. Quoted in Andrew Kupfor, "Mike Armstrong's AT&T: Will the Prices Come Together," *Fortune,* April 26, 1999, p. 89.

28. Daniel Goleman, "Leadership That Gets Results," *Harvard Business Review,* March–April 2000, pp. 78–90.

29. Lyman W. Porter, "Job Attitudes in Management: II. Perceived Importance of Needs as a Foundation of Job Level," *Journal of Applied Psychology,* 47 (April 1963): 141–148.

30. Clayton Alderfer, *Existence, Relatedness, and Growth* (New York: Free Press, 1972), pp. 42–44.

31. John R. P. French and Bertram Ravin, "The Bases of Social Power," in *Group Dynamics: Research and Theory,* ed. Dorwin Cartwright (Evanston, Ill.: Row, Peterson, 1962), pp. 607–623.

32. Gael McDonald, "Business Ethics: Practical Proposals for Organizations," *Journal of Business Ethics,* 25, 2000, p. 179.

33. Margaret Cunningham, "Walking the Thin White Line: A Role Conflict Model of Ethical Decision Making Behavior in the Marketing Research Process," Ph.D. dissertation, Texas A&M University, 1991.

34. Ibid.

35. The Ethics Resource Center, *2000 National Business Ethics Survey: How Employees Perceive Ethics at Work*, p. 25.

36. O. C. Ferrell, Larry Gresham, and John Fraedrich, "A Synthesis of Ethical Decision Making Models for Marketing," *Journal of MacroMarketing* (Fall 1989): 58–59.

37. Michael Connor, "Philip Morris: More Spent on Health Ads," *Yahoo! News*, May 23, 2000. http://dailynews.yahoo.com/h/nm/2000523/bs/tobacco_engle_1.html (accessed May 24, 2000).

38. Richard B. Schmitt, "Maker of Ritalin, Psychiatric Group Sued," *Wall Street Journal*, September 14, 2000, p. B19.

Chapter 7

1. Merck & Co., Inc. web site, "The Merck Corporate Philosophy." *http://www.merck.com/overview/philosophy.html* (accessed December 4, 2000).

2. Rogene A. Buchholz and Sandra B. Rosenthal, *Business Ethics* (Upper Saddle River, N.J.: Prentice-Hall, 1998), p. 171.

3. Ibid.

4. John Fraedrich and O. C. Ferrell, "Cognitive Consistency of Marketing Managers in Ethical Situations," *Journal of the Academy of Marketing Science*, 20 (Summer 1992): 243–252.

5. Karl Perez, "Today's Lesson: Do Your Homework," *Crain's International* (Fall 1995): 1–11.

6. Society of Financial Service Professionals, "Ethical Issues in the Employer–Employee Relationship." *http:///www.financialpro.org/sfsp/Press/ethics/es2000/Ethics_Survey_2000_Report_FINAL.html*, p. 3 (accessed October 11, 2000).

7. Margaret Cunningham, "Walking the Thin White Line: A Role Conflict Model of Ethical Decision Making Behavior in the Marketing Research Process," unpublished Ph.D. dissertation, Texas A&M University, 1991, p. 323.

8. Mary Zey-Ferrell and O. C. Ferrell, "Role-Set Configuration and Opportunity as Predictors of Unethical Behavior in Organizations," *Human Relations*, 35, (7) (1982): 587–604.

9. O. C. Ferrell and K. Mark Weaver, "Ethical Beliefs of Marketing Managers," *Journal of Marketing* (July 1978): 69–73.

10. The Ethics Resource Center, *2000 National Business Ethics Survey: How Employees Perceive Ethics at Work*, p. 55.

11. Terry W. Loe and O. C. Ferrell, "Ethical Climate's Relationship to Trust, Market Orientation and Commitment to Quality: A Single Firm Study," *Academy of Marketing Science Proceedings*, May 1997, pp. 211–215.

12. Stephen R. Covey, "Is Your Company's Bottom Line Taking a Hit?" *PR Newswire*, May 29, 1998.

13. Vikki Kratz, "Don't Be Shy," *Business Ethics* (January–February 1996): 15.

14. E. Sutherland and D. R. Cressey, *Principles of Criminology*, 8th ed. (Chicago: Lippincott, 1970), p. 114.

15. O. C. Ferrell and Larry G. Gresham, "A Contingency Framework for Understanding Ethical Decision Making in Marketing," *Journal of Marketing*, 49 (Summer 1985): 90–91.

16. Mary Zey-Ferrell, K. Mark Weaver, and O. C. Ferrell, "Predicting Unethical Behavior Among Marketing Practitioners," *Human Relations*, 32 (1979): 557–569.

17. James S. Bowman, "Managerial Ethics in Business and Government," *Business Horizons*, 19 (October 1976): 48–54; William C. Frederick and James Weber, "The Value of Corporate Managers and Their Critics: An Empirical Description and Normative Implications," in *Research in Corporate Social Performance and Social Responsibility*, ed. William C. Frederick and Lee E. Preston (Greenwich, Conn.: JAI Press, 1987), pp. 149–150; Linda K. Trevino and Stuart Youngblood, "Bad Apples in Bad Barrels: A Causal Analysis of Ethical Decision Making Behavior," *Journal of Applied Psychology*, 75 (August 1990): 38.

18. "Reporter Wins Whistleblower Case." *http://www.wired.com/news/business/0,1367,38493,00.html* (accessed September 7, 2000).

19. "Today's Briefing," *Commercial Appeal*, March 2, 2000, p. C1.

20. The Ethics Resource Center, *2000 National Business Ethics Survey*, p. 42.

21. Ibid., p. 43.

22. Ibid., p. 51.

23. Ibid., p. 46.

24. Ibid., p. 45.

25. Maynard M. and Carolyn C. Dolecheck, "Ethics: Take It from the Top," *Business* (January–March 1989): 12–18.
26. "Wal-Mart Sweatshops in Honduras." *http://www. nlcnet.org/walmart/honwal.htm* (accessed September 7, 2000).
27. The Ethics Resource Center, *2000 National Business Ethics Survey*, p. 30.
28. Nicole Harris, "Spam That You Might Not Delete," *Business Week*, June 15, 1998, p. 116.
29. The Ethics Resource Center, *2000 National Business Ethics Survey*, p. 30.
30. Ibid.
31. Vince Horiuchi, " 'Boy Crazy' Stacks the Deck with Dreamy Mugs, But Is It Demeaning?" *Commercial Appeal*, March 2, 2000, pp. F1, F3.
32. "FTC Says Violent Products Aimed at Children," *Commercial Appeal*, September 12, 2000, pp. A1, A2.
33. Ibid.
34. Ibid.
35. Kalpa Srinivasan, "FTC: Show Industry Marketed Violence," *Yahoo! News*, September 10, 2000. http://dailynews.yahoo.com/h/ap/2000910/pl/ entertainment_violence_3.html (accessed September 14, 2000).
36. Mary K. Feeney, "Benetton Death Row Ads Anger Sears, But Campaign Lives On," *Commercial Appeal*, January 25, 2000, C6.
37. Frederick and Weber, "The Value of Corporate Managers," pp. 149–150.
38. Gene R. Laczniak and Patrick E. Murphy, *Ethical Marketing Decisions: The Higher Road* (Boston: Allyn & Bacon, 1993), p. 14.

Chapter 8

1. "Fast Fact," *Fast Company*, September, 2000, p. 96.
2. Merck & Co., Inc., 1999 Annual Report, p. 29.
3. "Fast Fact."
4. Jim Carlton and Pui-Wing Tam, "Online Auctioneers Face Growing Fraud Problem," *Wall Street Journal*, May 12, 2000, p. B2.
5. U.S. Sentencing Commission, *Federal Sentencing Guidelines Manual* (St. Paul, Minn.: West Publishing, 1994).
6. "TI Recognized as an Ethics Benchmark." *http:// www.ti.com/corp/docs/company/citizen/ethics/ benchmark.shtml* (accessed September 26, 2000). Courtesy Texas Instruments, Inc.
7. "Ethics Is the Cornerstone of TI." *http://www. ti.com/corp/docs/company/citizen/ethics/brochure /index.shtml* (accessed September 26, 2000). Courtesy Texas Instruments, Inc.
8. "The TI Ethics Quick Test." *http://www.ti.com/ corp/docs/company/citizen/ethics/quicktest. shhtml* (accessed September 26, 2000). Courtesy Texas Instruments, Inc.
9. "Starbucks Executives Promoted: Shelley Lanza Assumes Expanded Role," *Yahoo! Finance*, May 23, 2000. http://biz.yahoo.com/bw/000523/wa_ starbuc.html (accessed May 24, 2000).
10. Meredith Alexander, "Do You Need an Ethics Officer?" *The Industry Standard*, July 10–17, 2000, p. 236.
11. SHRM/Ethics Resource Center, "Business Ethics Survey Report," 1998, p. 8.
12. Richard P. Conaboy, "Corporate Crime in America: Strengthening the 'Good Citizen' Corporation," in *Corporate Crime in America: Strengthening the "Good Citizen" Corporation* (Washington, D.C.: U.S. Sentencing Commission, 1995), pp. 1–2.
13. Susan J. Harrington, "What Corporate America Is Teaching About Ethics," *Academy of Management Executive*, 5 (February 1991): 21–30.
14. "Boeing: Ethics and Business Conduct Program." *http://www.boeing.com/companyoffices/aboutus/ ethics/index.htm* (accessed June 6, 2000). Courtesy of Boeing Business Services Company.
15. O. C. Ferrell and Larry Gresham, "A Contingency Framework for Understanding Ethical Decision Making in Marketing," *Journal of Marketing*, 49 (Summer 1985): 87–96.
16. Diane E. Kirrane, "Managing Values: A Systematic Approach to Business Ethics," *Training and Development Journal*, 1 (November 1990): 53–60.
17. Marjorie Kelly, "Anatomy of an Ethics Officer," *Business Ethics*, Millennium-End Double Issue, 1999, p. 14.
18. "Boeing: Ethics and Business Conduct Program." *http://www.boeing/com/companyoffices/aboutus/ ethics/index.htm* (accessed June 6, 2000). Courtesy of Boeing Business Services Company.
19. Edward Iwata, "More Firms Falsify Revenue to Boost Stocks," *USA Today*, March 29, 2000, p. B1.
20. The Ethics Resource Center, *2000 National Business Ethics Survey: How Employees Perceive Ethics at Work*, p. 7.

21. Curt S. Jordan, "Lessons in Organizational Compliance: A Survey of Government-Imposed Compliance Programs," *Preventive Law Reporter* (Winter 1994): 7.

22. Robert Howard, "Values Make the Company: An Interview with Robert Haas," *Harvard Business Review*, 68 (September–October 1990): 134.

23. William C. Frederick and James Weber, "The Value of Corporate Managers and Their Critics: An Empirical Description and Normative Implications," in *Research in Corporate Social Performance and Social Responsibility*, ed. William C. Frederick and Lee E. Preston (Greenwich, Conn.: JAI, 1987), pp. 149–150.

24. Linda K. Trevino and Stuart Youngblood, "Bad Apples in Bad Barrels: Causal Analysis of Ethical Decision Making Behavior," *Journal of Applied Psychology*, 75 (August 1990): 390.

25. Ibid., p. 400.

26. Kevin J. Sobnosky, "The Value-Added Benefits of Environmental Auditing," *Environmental Quality Management* 9 (Winter 1999): 25–32.

27. John Pearce, *Measuring Social Wealth* (London: New Economics Foundation, 1996) as reported in Warren Dow and Roy Crowe, *What Social Auditing Can Do for Voluntary Organizations* (Vancouver: Volunteer Vancouver, July 1999), p. 8.

Chapter 9

1. Alan K. Reichert, Marion S. Webb, and Edward G. Thomas, "Corporate Support for Ethical and Environmental Policies: A Financial Management Perspective," *Journal of Business Ethics*, 25 (May, 2000): p. 54.

2. O.C. Ferrell and Geoffrey Hirt, *Business: A Changing World* (Burr Ridge, Ill.: Irwin/McGraw-Hill, 2000), pp. 89–90.

3. David A. Ricks, *Big Business Blunders: Mistakes in Multinational Marketing* (Homewood, Ill.: Dow-Jones Irwin, 1983), pp. 83–84.

4. Ferrell and Hirt, *Business*, p. 257.

5. Tibbett L. Speer, "Avoid Gift Blunders in Asian Locales," *USA Today*, April 25, 2000. http://www.usatoday.com/life/travel/business/1999/t0316bt2.htm (accessed May 8, 2000).

6. Amir Shah, "Talebian Shuts Widows' Bakeries," *Yahoo! News*, August 16, 2000. http://dailynews.yahoo.com/h.ap/20000816/21/afghanistan_bakeries_2.html (accessed August 17, 2000).

7. Michael Hirsh and Kenneth Klee, "Ubiquity and Its Burdens," *Newsweek International*, January 31, 2000. http://newsweek.com/nw-srv/printed/int/sr/a54645-2000jan24.htm (accessed June 6, 2000).

8. Business for Social Responsibility. *http://www.bsr.org* (accessed October 10, 2000).

9. Tom Sharp, "Tiremaker Admits Mislabels," *Commerical Appeal*, August 29, 2000, pp. B5, B10.

10. Greg Brosman, "Guatemalan Counterfeit Law Fuels Illegal Industry," *Yahoo! Finance*, July 28, 2000. http://biz.yahoo.com/rf/000728/n28384015.html (accessed August 17, 2000).

11. Mrinalini Datta, "Unilever, Others Lose Millions in India to Copycats," *Bloomberg.com*, September 7, 2000. http://...fgcgi.cgi?ptitle=All%20Columns&touch=1&s1-blk&tp=ad_topright_bbco&T-markets=fgcgi_ (accessed September 7, 2000).

12. Michael Williams, "Many Japanese Banks Ran Amok While Led by Former Regulators," *Wall Street Journal*, January 19, 1996, pp. A1, A9.

13. Andrew Singer, "General Motors: Ethics Increasingly Means Social Responsibility Too," *Ethikos*, May/June 2000, pp. 9, 11–13.

14. Edward Alden, "Multinationals in Labour Pledge . . . ," *Financial Times*, July 28, 2000. http://www.globalarchive.ft.com/search-components/index.jsp (accessed September 7, 2000).

15. O.C. Ferrell, Thomas N. Ingram, and Raymond W. LaForge, "Initiating Structure for Legal and Ethical Decisions in a Global Sales Organization," *Industrial Marketing Management*, November 2000, pp. 1–10.

16. Rebecca Santana, "Women Entrepreneurs Take on Russia," *MSNBC*, September 4, 1999. http://www.msnbc.com/news/420132.asp (accessed September 7, 2000).

17. "Bottom-Line Ethics," *Christian Science Monitor*, April 3, 2000, p. 8. http://www.csmonitor.com/durable/2000/04/03/p8sl.htm (accessed August 22, 2000).

18. Human Rights Watch 1999 World Report, "Children's Rights." *http://www.hrw.org/wr2k/Crd.htm* (accessed August 17, 2000).

19. Matthew L. Kish, "Human Rights and Business: Profiting from Observing Human Rights," *Ethics in Economics*, nos. 1 and 2 (1998).

20. "Sydney Hotels Deny Price Gouging," *Associated Press Newswire*, June 4, 1998.

21. *http://www.prnewswire.com/cgi-bin/stories.pl? ACCT=104&STORY=/.../0000889557&EDATE* (accessed May 8, 2000).

22. "The 1999 Transparency International Bribe Payers Survey." *http://www.transparency.org/documents/ cip/bps.html* (accessed May 9, 2000).

23. Skip Kaltenhauser, "Bribery Is Being Outlawed Worldwide," *Business Ethics*, May–June 1998, p. 11.

24. "The Transparency International Bribe Payers Survey."

25. Skip Kaltenhauser, "Avoiding Ethical Minefields in Global Business," *Business Ethics*, May–June 1997, p. 9.

26. "The Transparency International Bribe Payers Survey."

27. "Genetic Engineering Hot New Topic in Shareholder Resolutions," *Business Ethics*, March/April 2000, p. 22.

28. Francesca Lyman, "Should Gene Foods Be Labeled?" *MSNBC*, September 15, 1999. http://www.msnbc .com/news/312001.asp (accessed July 18, 2000).

29. "U.S. Cigarette Exports," *USA Today*, Snapshots. http://www.usatoday.com/snapshot/money/ msnap078.htm (accessed May 8, 2000).

30. "Nestlé Infant Formula: The Consequences of Spurning the Public Image," in *Marketing Mistakes*, 3rd ed., ed. Robert F. Hartley (Columbus, Ohio: Grid Publishing, 1986), pp. 47–61; "Nestlé and the Role of Infant Formula in Developing Countries: The Resolution of a Conflict," a series of reports, articles, and press releases provided by Nestlé Coordination Center for Nutrition, Inc., 1984.

31. Delphi Automotive Systems Corporation 1999 Annual Report, p. 17.

32. Aaron Bernstein, Michael Arndt, Wendy Zellner, and Peter Coy, "Too Much Corporate Power," *Business Week*, September 11, 2000, p. 150.

33. "Mexico City Takes Action Against Polluters," *Reuters Newswire*, May 31, 1998 (from America Online newswire service).

34. "Greenpeace Warns Israel to Stop Sea Dumping," *Reuters Newswire*, June 5, 1998 (from America Online newswire service).

35. "Australia May Be Worst Air Polluter," *Associated Press Newswire*, June 1, 1998.

36. "Willamette Industries to Spend More Than $90 Million to Settle Clean Air Act Case," *PRNewswire*, July 20, 2000. http://www.prnewswire.com (accessed August 18, 2000).

37. M.J. Zuckerman and Will Rodger, "Linking Online Kids with Real-World Ethics," *USA Today*, March 16, 2000. http://www.usatoday.com/life/cyber/ tech/cth562.htm (accessed May 8, 2000).

38. "In the News — April 2000." *http://www.bsr.org/ resourcecenter/news/news_output.asp?newsDT= 2000-04&hTID=266* (accessed August 22, 2000).

39. Jefferson Graham, "Napster Ordered to Shut Down," *USA Today*, July 2, 2000. http://www.usa today.com/life/music/music208.htm (accessed August 24, 2000); "Napster Brief Denies Wrongdoing," *USA Today*, July 27, 2000 http://www. usatoday.com/life/cyber/tech/review/crh283. htm (accessed August 24, 2000); "Napster Wins Respite from Shutdown Order, *USA Today*, July 29, 2000 http://www.usatoday.com/life/cyber/ tech/review/crh356.htm (accessed August 24, 2000); "Napster Among Top 50 Web Sites," *USA Today*, August 23, 2000. http://www.usatoday. com/life/cyber/tech/review/crh438.htm (accessed August 24, 2000).

40. Quoted in Zuckerman and Rodger, "Linking Online Kids."

41. Geri Smith, "Mexico: Zedillo Has to Sweep the Banks Clean," *Business Week* online (international edition), June 1, 1998.

Chapter 10

1. "The Role of Longevity Award Programs in a Comprehensive Recognition Strategy." *http:// www.jostens.com/recognition/why/studies/ roleoflongevity* (accessed September 7, 2000).

2. Terry W. Loe, "The Role of Ethical Climate in Developing Trust, Market Orientation and Commitment to Quality," unpublished Ph.D. dissertation, University of Memphis, 1996.

3. John Galvin, "The New Business Ethics," *SmartBusinessMag.com*, June 2000, p. 97.

4. Andrew W. Singer, "When It Comes to Child Labor, Toys 'R' Us Isn't Playing Around," *Ethikos*, May/June 2000, pp. 4–4, 14.

5. Stephen Power and Clare Angberry, "Bridge-

stone/Firestone Says It Made 'Bad Tires.'" *Wall Street Journal,* September 13, 2000, p. A3.

6. "Firestone Survey Results," *http://e-businessethics .com/surveys.htm* (accessed February 2, 2001).

7. "Growing Pains for Responsibly Harvested Wood," *Business Ethics,* March/April 2000, p. 5.

8. "The Role of Longevity."

9. Ibid.

10. Daniel J. Brass, Kenneth D. Butterfield, and Bruce Skaggs, "Relationships and Unethical Behavior: A Social Network Perspective," *Academy of Management Review,* 23 (1998): 14–31.

11. The Ethics Resource Center, *2000 National Business Ethics Survey: How Employees Perceive Ethics at Work,* p. 57.

12. Brass, Butterfield, and Skaggs, "Relationships and Unethical Behavior."

13. David Rynecki, "Here Are 8 Easy Ways to Lose Your Shirt in Stocks," *USA Today,* June 26, 1998, p. 3B.

14. L. K. Trevino, G. R. Weaver, D. G. Gibson, and B. L. Toffler, "Managing Ethics and Legal Compliance: What Works and What Hurts," *California Management Review,* 41(2): 141–142.

15. Loe, "The Role of Ethical Climate."

16. Galvin, "The New Business Ethics," p. 94.

17. Stephen R. Covey, "Is Your Company's Bottom Line Taking a Hit?" America Online, *http://www. prnewswire.com* (accessed June 4, 1998).

18. Ibid.

19. The Ethics Resource Center, *2000 National Business Ethics Survey,* p. 67.

20. Covey, "Is Your Company's Bottom Line Taking a Hit?"

21. The Ethics Resource Center, *2000 National Business Ethics Survey,* p. 5.

22. "Trend Watch," *Business Ethics,* March/April 2000, p. 8.

23. "Today's Briefing," *Commercial Appeal,* October 12, 2000, p. C1.

24. Delphi Automotive Systems 1999 Annual Report, p. 16.

25. O. C. Ferrell, Isabelle Maignan, and Terry W. Loe, "Corporate Ethics + Citizenship = Competitive Advantage," Florida State University, 1998 working paper.

26. Michael D. Hartline and O. C. Ferrell, "The Management of Customer-Contact Service Employees: An Empirical Investigation," *Journal of Marketing,* 60 (October 1996): 52–70.

27. "Hershey Foods Philosophy and Values," Hershey Foods Corporation videotape (1990).

28. Kathleen Seiders and Leonard Barry, "Service Fairness: What It Is and Why It Matters," *Academy of Management Executive,* 12 (9) (May 1998): 9.

29. Diane Brady, "Why Service Stinks," *Business Week,* October 23, 2000, pp. 120–121.

30. Loe, "The Role of Ethical Climate."

31. Ferrell, Maignan, and Loe, "Corporate Ethics."

32. The 1997 Cone/Roper Cause-Related Marketing Trends Report, a National Survey of Consumer Attitudes, reported in *Business Ethics,* March–April 1997, pp. 14–16.

33. Quoted in Best Buy Co., Inc., Fiscal 2000 Annual Report, p. 15.

34. Lowe's Companies, Inc., 1999 Annual Report, p. 9.

35. Bernard J. Jaworski and Ajay K. Kohli, "Market Orientation: Antecedents and Consequences," *Journal of Marketing,* July 1993, pp. 53–70.

36. The Home Depot 1999 Annual Report, p. 14.

37. "1999 Employee Relationship Report Benchmark." *http://www.walkerinfo.com* (accessed October 11, 2000).

38. "The New Business Ethics," p. 99.

39. *http://www.starbucks.com/product_detail .asp?pfid=562&sid=GT6GBOPRWNB18PPUTO HEKOKH91B7EG3* (accessed October 11, 2000).

40. Michael Isikoff, Susannah Meadows, Devin Gordon, and Bret Begun, "Logos," *Newsweek,* May 1, 2000, p. 8.

41. Galvin, "The New Business Ethics."

42. Curtis C. Verschoor, "A Study of the Link Between a Corporation's Financial Performance and Its Commitment to Ethics," *JBE,* October 1998, p. 1509.

43. Isabelle Maignan, "Antecedents and Benefits of Corporate Citizenship: A Comparison of U.S. and French Businesses," unpublished Ph.D. dissertation, University of Memphis, 1997.

44. Archie B. Carroll, "A Three-Dimensional Conceptual Model of Corporate Performance," *Academy of Management Review,* 4 (1979): 497–505; Max Clarkson, "A Stakeholder Framework for Analyzing and Evaluating Corporate Social Performance," *Academy of Management Review,* 20 (1995): 92–117.

45. S. B. Graves and S. A. Waddock, "Institutional Owners and Corporate Social Performance: Maybe

Not So Myopic After All," *Proceedings of the International Association for Business and Society,* San Diego, 1993; and S. Waddock and S. Graves, "The Corporate Social Performance–Financial Performance Link," *Strategic Management Journal,* 18 (1997): 303–319.

46. Melissa A. Baucus and David A. Baucus, "Paying the Payer: An Empirical Examination of Longer Term Financial Consequences of Illegal Corporate Behavior," *Academy of Management Journal* (1997): 129–151.

47. Kurt Eichenwald and N. R. Kleinfeld, "At Columbia/HCA, Scandal Hurts," *Commercial Appeal,* December 21, 1997, pp. C1, C3.

48. Julia Flynn, "Did Sears Take Other Customers for a Ride?" *Business Week,* August 3, 1992, pp. 24–25; Harriet Johnson Brackey, "Auto Repair Rip-Offs Bane of Consumer," *USA Today,* July 15, 1992.

49. Chris Welles, "What Led Beech-Nut Down the Road to Disgrace?" *Business Week,* February 22, 1988, pp. 124–128.

50. D. C. North, *Institutions: Institutional Change, and Economic Performance* (Cambridge: Cambridge University Press, 1990).

51. K. J. Arrow, *The Limits of Organization* (New York: W. W. Norton, 1974), pp. 23, 26.

52. Shelby D. Hunt, "Resource-Advantage Theory and the Wealth of Nations: Developing the Socio-Economic Research Tradition," *Journal of Socio-Economics,* 26 (1997).

53. North, *Institutions,* p. 9.

54. L. E. Harrison, *Who Prospers? How Cultural Values Shape Economic and Political Success* (New York: Basic Books, 1992), p. 16.

55. Hunt, "Resource-Advantage Theory," p. 353.

56. Ibid.

57. Ibid., pp. 351–352.

58. "The 1999 Transparency International Bribe Payers Survey." *http://www.transparency.org/documents/cpi/bps.html* (accessed May 9, 2000).

59. Nicholas Stein, "The World's Most Admired Companies," *Fortune,* October 2, 2000, p. 183.

60. Ibid., p. 186.

Index